England in the
Later Middle Ages

England in the Later Middle Ages

A POLITICAL HISTORY

M. H. KEEN
Fellow of Balliol College, Oxford

METHUEN & CO LTD
11 NEW FETTER LANE LONDON EC4

First published 1973
by Methuen & Co Ltd
11 New Fetter Lane, London EC4
© *1973 M. H. Keen*
Printed in Great Britain by
Butler & Tanner Ltd,
Frome and London

SBN 416 75990 4

Distributed in the USA by
HARPER & ROW PUBLISHERS INC.
BARNES & NOBLE IMPORT DIVISION

In memoriam
ERNEST JACOB

Contents

Preface

This book is concerned with the period of English medieval history that has always been for me the most interesting. I am attracted by it for a reason that may perhaps seem old-fashioned: because its story is full of martial events, of the adventures in wars in England and beyond the sea of men of fame and ancestry, like the Black Prince and that Earl of Shrewsbury whom the French in fear and respect christened *le roi Talbot*. I have no doubt that my predilections colour my view of the period. Perhaps this book would have been better written by someone with a deep knowledge of the legal and administrative records of late Plantagenet England (a knowledge to which I can lay no claim), for these are the sources that are currently shedding most new light on the history of the age. But I believe that there may still be this to be said for looking at it in a rather traditional way; that if they could be consulted, the men of the period would probably have hoped that their times would be remembered most for their great victories, Falkirk and Crecy and Poitiers and Agincourt.

Writing a textbook is not altogether an agreeable task; it teaches one too much about one's own ignorance. Faced with topics with which one's own acquaintance is entirely superficial – in my own case, notably, the problems of late medieval economic history and ecclesiastical history – what can one do but reproduce, as best one may, the views of others who are better informed? I am conscious of a very great debt to the books of those scholars who have made this period of English history their special field. I am also conscious that the period is one in which the results of extensive and important research, undertaken over the last twenty years, are beginning to multiply in print, and that at the present moment it is one where almost all views are interim views. Statements made now are likely to date quickly. I have tried nevertheless to be definite in presenting my points of view; a textbook can, in my experience, be occasionally useful simply because the student can find in it unsound opinions to attack.

I have received much generous help in writing this book. My principal debts are to Mr G. L. Harriss of Magdalen College,

Oxford, who read through the whole text in typescript and made many valuable suggestions and criticisms, and to Mr C. R. J. Currie, a research student of my own college, who went through substantial parts of it in an effort to root out as many as he could of the errors of fact – of proper names, precise dates and relationships – that he knew had always marred my work. Where he read he found much to correct, but I am afraid there will be many more mistakes of mine that will appear uncorrected. I must also thank a number of scholars and friends who have looked at parts of the book and have assisted me with criticism and advice: Miss Barbara Harvey, Dr Michael Prestwich, Dr Christopher Allmand, and Dr Seymour Philips. Dr Prestwich and Dr J. R. Maddicott both most kindly allowed me to read their doctoral theses, both of which were at the time unpublished; without their help I am not sure what I could have made of the early part of the period, the years with which I am least familiar. Mr K. J. Leyser very kindly allowed me to look at a copy of the late Mr K. B. McFarlane's Ford Lectures on the English nobility in the later Middle Ages, perhaps the most influential and seminal set of lectures ever given on this period of English history. I must finally thank Mrs Glynis Donovan, Mrs Mary Clapinson and Mr David Vaisey for their help with the proofs; and Miss Pat Lloyd, Mrs Mary Budge and, above all, my wife, for assistance at various stages of writing and typing, and with the index.

There is a special debt that I have tried to record in the dedication of this book, to the late Dr E. F. Jacob. I at least have never met a scholar who has been more generous in sharing with others his insights, based on a profound knowledge and understanding. How much he showed me, or suggested, I shall never be able to record, because so much was given, so unobtrusively, in the course, almost entirely, of casual conversations. The most pleasurable of all to remember were talks near the banks of rivers, where he was as full of wisdom on the ways of fish as on the ways of the past, and always had much to say about both.

Maurice Keen
Balliol College
Oxford

Abbreviations

A.H.R.	*American Historical Review*
A.P.S.	*Acts of the Parliament of Scotland*
B.E.C.	*Bibliothèque de l'École des Chartes*
B.I.H.R.	*Bulletin of the Institute of Historical Research*
B.J.R.L.	*Bulletin of the John Rylands Library*
C.C.R.	*Calendar of the Close Rolls*
C.H.J.	*Cambridge Historical Journal*
C.P.R.	*Calendar of the Patent Rolls*
C.S.P.	*Calendar of State Papers*
Econ.H.R.	*Economic History Review*
E.E.T.S.	Early English Text Society
E.H.R.	*English Historical Review*
Foed.	*Foedera Conventiones Literae et cujuscunque generis Acta Publica*, ed. T. Rymer (London, 1704–32)
H.J.	*Historical Journal*
K. de L.	*Oeuvres de Froissart*, ed. Kervyn de Lettenhove (Brussels, 1870–7)
L. and P.	*Letters and Papers Illustrative of the Wars of the English in France*, ed. J. Stevenson (Rolls Series, 1861–4)
L.Q.R.	*Law Quarterly Review*
P.B.A.	*Proceedings of the British Academy*
P.L.	*The Paston Letters*, ed. J. Gairdner (London, 1872–5: the references throughout are to the numbers of the letters in this edition)
P.P.C.	*Proceeding and Ordinances of the Privy Council*, ed. H. Nicholas (London, 1834–7)
P.W.	*Parliamentary Writs*, ed. F. Palgrave (London, 1827–34)
R.P.	*Rotuli Parliamentorum*

R.S.	Rolls Series
S.H.R.	*Scottish Historical Review*
Storey, *H. of L.*	R. L. Storey, *The End of the House of Lancaster* (London, 1966)
Tout, *Chapters*	T. F. Tout, *Chapters in the Administrative History of Medieval England* (Manchester, 1920–33)
T.R.H.S.	*Transactions of the Royal Historical Society*
V.C.H.	*Victoria History of the Counties of England*

I

Introduction

The structure of government and politics

The year 1290 may seem a strange date at which to commence a political history of the late Middle Ages in England. It marks neither the beginning nor the end of a reign: in fact it was the twenty-eighth year of King Edward I, who had another seventeen years of authority ahead of him. All the same, it is an important date. It was in this year that the death of the Maid of Norway, titular queen of Scotland, started a chain of events which were to lead in 1296 to the outbreak of a great war of the English against the Scots. Two years before that, in 1294, another major war had commenced, with France; this is why the 'auld alliance', of France and Scotland against England, came into being at this point in the 1290s. From then onwards, with only short intervals, England was to remain at war with Scotland, or France, or both, until the end of the medieval period. These prolonged hostilities exposed her government and its resources to unprecedented strains. The consequences, both of the wars directly and of the strains and pressures that they engendered, were only beginning to work themselves out when the first Tudor, Henry VII, came to the throne in 1485.

The course of the great wars of the late Middle Ages shaped England's gradual achievement of self-conscious, insular identity as a nation-state. The period from 1290 to 1485 is therefore a very important one in her political history. It is also a confused and troubled period (though not more troubled, probably, than that which preceded it). As Shakespeare's plays remind us, this was a violent age, in the course of which no less than five kings lost their thrones in civil wars; in whose course also a long and sorry list of noblemen lost their lives in the field or at the block.

This aspect of the late Middle Ages in England is what made their history unpalatable to the scholars of the nineteenth century, with their confidence in constitutional principles and progress. The trouble was not, however, as Stubbs and his generation believed, that the great men of the late Middle Ages were the moral and intellectual inferiors of their ancestors and their descendants. The troubles of the period arose rather because the system of royal government which had been developed earlier, in the twelfth and thirteenth centuries, whose achievements Stubbs and his contemporaries so admired, would not stand up to the strains to which it was exposed by the wars of the fourteenth and fifteenth centuries. These laid bare its essential weaknesses, and in particular two: the financial inadequacy of the crown's resources, and the fact that the king's greater subjects were too powerful for him to manage on the basis of authority alone.

Since so much of the history with which this book will be concerned revolves about these two matters, and about the wars which made them crucial factors in political development, it will be prudent to take a closer look at both at the outset. But before we do that we must first say something very briefly about the structure of royal government at the beginning of the period – about the system that could not bear the strains that war imposed.

Royal government in England, at the end of the thirteenth century, was neither all powerful, nor legally omnicompetent. Its scope was limited by its objectives: it was not designed to foster the public welfare by providing direction and essential services, as in a modern state, but to uphold the dignity of the king as a great hereditary lord, and to protect his legal rights and those of his subjects. The law which the king's courts enforced was not based in royal command; it was the common inheritance of the people, founded in the custom of time past. The king might, with the assent and advice of his council, amend the law in detail, as Edward I did in the early part of his reign through a series of famous statutes, but it was not his law.[1] Moreover, the common law of the king's courts was not the only law that ran in England, nor his the only authority that enforced it. The church, an international community, had its own law, and its own courts enforced its rules on all men in spiritual matters (which included

[1] On Edward I's statutes (the most important of which belong to the period 1275-90, and are, therefore, outside the scope of this book) see T. F. T. Plucknett, *The Legislation of Edward I* (Oxford, 1949).

all matrimonial and testamentary causes). There were great franchises, such as that of the Bishop of Durham, within whose limits their lords exercised the rights that pertained to the king elsewhere. A host of lords of lesser franchises and the citizens of chartered boroughs enjoyed privileges which entitled them to enforce law and local custom with varying degrees of independence, and which gave them, as it were, a private share in the business of governing. At the fringes of the realm, the king's government shaded off into remote control. In the marches of Wales and the principality royal authority was dependent on the cooperation of the marcher lords and the Welsh squirearchy, in the far north on that of the border barons. The king's duchy of Aquitaine and his lordship of Ireland were administered separately from England, and his authority there was exercised over societies whose customs and outlook were foreign, pure southern French in the one case, and in the other deeply affected by the clan life of the native Irish.

For all these limitations on its range, competence and initiative, the English royal administrative system was, at the end of the thirteenth century, precociously developed by contemporary European standards, especially in its central bureaucracy.[2] This bureaucracy was organized around a series of departments, each equipped with one of the royal seals which, as formal authenticating instruments, made it possible to coordinate the private decisions of the king and his trusted advisers into public action, executive, legal, or administrative. The king's household, which travelled about with him, was his personal business headquarters, and included a staff of trained clerks. These clerks were able and experienced men, well capable in emergencies of turning the expertise that they had acquired in supervising the king's everyday expenses in the chamber and wardrobe to tackle such formidable tasks as the victualling and payment of an

[2] An exhaustive list of works dealing with late medieval government would be too long to force into the scope of a bibliographical footnote. For a general survey see J. F. Willard and W. A. Morris (ed.), *The English Government at Work*, 3 vols (Cambridge, Mass., 1940–50). On the household, the rise of the chancery, and the importance of the royal seals, see T. F. Tout's incomparable *Chapters in the Administrative History of Medieval England*, 6 vols (Manchester, 1920–33). On the later medieval chancery see also B. Wilkinson, *The Chancery under Edward III* (Manchester, 1929). On the exchequer, A. Steel, *The Receipt of the Exchequer* (Cambridge, 1954), is essential, in spite of some shortcomings. On the council see J. F. Baldwin, *The King's Council* (Oxford, 1913).

armed host, and of managing, at a pinch, the whole of his correspondence, official and private. In his household the king kept his privy seal, to authenticate the letters that he sent out from his itinerant court – diplomatic correspondence, summonses to appear before him, instructions to the chancellor to draw up official documents in accordance with his council's decisions. Quite early in the fourteenth century the business passing under this privy seal – especially diplomatic and conciliar business – became so considerable that it developed into a separate office, and its keeper became the third officer of state, after the chancellor and the treasurer. When this happened, the signet seal kept by the king's secretary became the seal used to authenticate his private letters, and warrants under the signet were from time to time accepted as authority by the chancery for the issues of letters under the great seal of England.

The great seal, kept by the chancellor, was the most important of the king's seals. The use of the great seal for all purposes except routine business required to be warranted (usually by a letter under the privy seal). It was used to give authority to all important acts of state, to public treaties, statutes, and letters patent appointing men to official posts or commissioning them to discharge essential administrative and judicial duties. There were also many regular writs instituting proceedings in the courts, which had to be sued from the chancery and sealed there. In short, the chancery was the lynchpin of general administration, and the chancellor, who was usually a bishop, was in consequence always a man of influence. He was automatically a member of the royal council, and was often the chief spokesman who laid the king's needs before parliaments. He had a substantial staff of clerks to help him in his business, clerics who could expect a benefice (or perhaps more than one benefice) to provide them with a stipend, and for whom, if they made their mark, there were rosy prospects of ecclesiastical promotion.

The third office of state, beside the privy seal office and the chancery, was also the oldest and the most professional, the exchequer. It had acquired early a seal of its own, the seal of the exchequer. Responsible for supervising the collection, audit and expenditure of the king's revenue in accordance with its own strict rules of procedure, it was also a court dealing with cases in which the king's fiscal rights were involved. The treasurer (like the chancellor, usually a bishop) presided over it, aided by the barons of the exchequer, men learned in the law and in the exchequer's own complicated processes. Every item of the king's

revenue, and every payment made at his order, was entered on
its massive rolls. The accounts, both of local officials (as the
sheriff) and of the royal household, were audited by it. Its task
was more formidable than that of either of the other departments,
and in many ways even more vital. The exchequer alone, through
the treasurer, could give the king and his councillors any idea of
how far his resources really would stretch. Needless to say, it did
not manage to keep the kings of England solvent; it needed more
than clerical efficiency to achieve that, as we shall soon see.

The normal home of the exchequer and the chancery was at
Westminster: it was there too that the king's central courts held
their sessions.[3] The King's Bench was the highest court in the
land, aside from the king's own council and parliament, and was
so called because of its concern with all matters that affected the
crown. The court of common pleas (often called the 'bench'
simply) dealt with cases between parties and corrected the errors
of lower courts. The judges of these courts, appointed by the
crown, were men of great influence, often called to council, who
gave important assistance in the drafting of royal statutes. Most
of them were, at the end of the thirteenth century, recruited from
among the serjeants (senior barristers) who had a monopoly of
pleading in the central courts, and whose legal learning helped to
make pleading almost an arcane science. Given the multiplication
of statutes (a notable feature of the late thirteenth century) and
the number and variety of writs which instituted proceedings in
civil cases, the law had become a highly professional occupation.
In spite of its long delays and the expense incidental to litigation,
the common law was highly prized by the king's subjects, and the
law courts were always busy.

The great offices of state and the central courts were the
essential links between the king's council, the heart and centre of
government where executive decisions were taken and legal
remedies framed, and the local administration. The most important figure in local government at the end of the thirteenth
century was still, as it had long been, the king's sheriff.[4] It was he

[3] On the law and the courts generally, see W. S. Holdsworth, *History
of English Law*, vols 1–3 (London, 1923). On the court of common
pleas, M. Hastings, *The Court of Common Pleas in Fifteenth Century
England*, is valuable.

[4] On the sheriff see W. A. Morris, *The Medieval English Sheriff to 1300*
(Manchester, 1927), which unfortunately only covers as far as the
beginning of our period; and Morris's chapter in vol. II of *The English
Government at Work*.

who, in the county court that met once a month, published royal statutes; he who supervised (in this same county court) the election of representatives when these were summoned to parliaments. He was responsible for the pursuit and custody of criminals, for empanelling juries to try cases, and in general for having all things ready when the king's justices visited his shire. Most judicial work was carried out by justices appointed from time to time to take the assizes, deliver the gaols, or to hear and determine cases between parties: more rarely the counties were visited by justices in eyre, appointed in the exchequer, with power to hear all pleas and to undertake a general review of the administration of the king's rights (these eyres were unpopular, and lapsed in the course of the fourteenth century).[5] It was the sheriff's task to see that the decisions of these judges were implemented, and to levy the fines that they imposed. In his fiscal capacity the sheriff was responsible to the exchequer. Twice a year he had to appear there and account for all the moneys that he had received, the farm of his county, fines (or amercements as they should properly be called), and any other dues that he had collected – less what he had spent in the county at the king's orders, in wages, for victualling the king's castles and repairing his buildings, and so on.

The sheriff was the maid of all work in the county, but by the 1290s he was no longer by any means the omnicompetent royal servant that he had once been, and the late Middle Ages were to witness the further decline of his office. A series of other officials, most of them like the sheriff recruited from among the substantial county gentry, discharged specialized duties in the localities. There was the coroner, who kept the record of the pleas of the crown, and held inquests into matters in which the king had a customary legal interest, such as murders and wrecks. There were the escheators who looked after the king's rights as a feudal landlord, to wardships, marriages, and reliefs. There were the keepers appointed to look after estates which for one reason or another were in the king's hand, as for instance those of a bishopric during a vacancy, the collectors of customs at the ports, the keepers of the royal forests. In all financial matters the exchequer supervised the activities of this host of officials. The process of keeping up with their work was so confusing that in 1323 Bishop Stapledon, the treasurer, ordered that only dues for which the sheriff solely was responsible should henceforward be

[5] On the eyres see W. C. Bolland, *The General Eyre* (Cambridge, 1922), an outstanding work.

entered on the Pipe Rolls, and that others should be accounted for separately (the Cowick Ordinance). This was a necessary reform to simplify the records: the task involved in keeping track of the king's rights remained dauntingly massive.

The system of administration that we have been describing in outline was sufficient only to its foremost intended task, the enforcement of the king's hereditary rights. Those rights were not wide enough, and above all were not productive enough financially to enable him to cope with such an emergency as a major war without further assistance. From his private and prerogative resources the king drew an income in the region of £20,000. Besides this he had the regular revenue brought in by the customs, the levy on wool (6s. 8d. a sack) and certain other exports, payable at the ports, and originally granted to Edward I in the parliament of 1275.[6] In his day this brought in something like £12,000 a year. The income from these combined sources was just about enough to meet the king's regular expenditure on his household, his works, his administration, and the keeping of his castles. There was nothing left over for emergencies, let alone for such a costly emergency as a campaign.

We shall have to look in later chapters at the detailed problems of raising hosts for campaigning and paying for them. It was a very expensive business. There was no standing army. Though there was a general obligation on all men between the ages of sixteen and sixty to serve in defence of the realm, troops who served in a host expected to be paid wages.[7] The cavalry of armoured knights carried expensive equipment, a costly coat of mail with plate at the joints, and they were mounted on great warhorses which could be worth as much as £40 or even £80 (the cavalry soldier supplied his own equipment, but the king paid for horses lost in his service). A man had to be wealthy to support the estate of knighthood, and the knights were a military aristocracy; in 1301 Edward I was able to summon about 900 from all over his kingdom to serve in the Caerlaverock campaign. To every knight in the host there might be ten or even twenty footmen, mostly archers, an increasing proportion of them

[6] On the customs see N. S. B. Gras, *The Early English Customs System* (Cambridge, Mass., 1918).

[7] On military service and the legal and constitutional problems of liability for it see M. R. Powicke, *Military Obligation in Medieval England* (Oxford, 1962); and for the beginning of our period J. E. Morris, *The Welsh Wars of Edward I* (Oxford, 1901), an outstanding study.

usually being mounted for purposes of mobility. In the fourteenth century archers became more important than before with the development of the longbow, the great English six-foot bow of oak or yew which could penetrate armour up to a range of nearly 400 yards and had a rapid rate of fire. The service of archers was cheap compared with that of cavalrymen (in Edward III's time a knight bachelor was paid two shillings a day, a foot archer two pence), but they had to be paid, fed, and increasingly often mounted as well. Over and above these forces, the king needed for a major campaign to recruit expert miners and engineers, to build siege engines, and, if he intended to cross the sea, to hire and impound ships. Here already is an onerous tale of the outlay necessary for a single expedition. As long as hostilities were active a king needed three or four times his ordinary annual revenue if he was to pay his way.

The expense of campaigning meant that, if war broke out, the king had inevitably to look to his subjects for grants of taxation. There was no real question of their refusing to aid him: it was an acknowledged principle that subjects were bound to aid their ruler when necessity and the common interest demanded. But because the king had no automatic right to a stipulated contribution by way of tax, he had to bargain with his taxpayers as to what they should pay, and in order to do so he needed to assemble them, or their accredited representatives (usually in a parliament). This gave them the opportunity to hedge their resulting grants of extraordinary taxation with conditions which might not be to the royal liking. In the late thirteenth century it was not yet clear what constituted a representative parliament; it was the king's recurrent need for taxation and the bargains that his subjects made with him in return for their aid that gave it definition, in the course of the first half of the fourteenth century.[8]

The grants that the king's subjects made to him were normally of two kinds. One was an extra levy on exports, in particular on wool (such were the *maltoltes* that Edward I and Edward III negotiated with assemblies of merchants, and the subsidies on wool which later monarchs were granted by parliaments). The other was a 'lay subsidy', the payment by the king's secular subjects of a given fraction of their movable property and their income, by way of a tax. Early in Edward III's reign the fraction became stereotyped at a fifteenth in the shires and a tenth in the boroughs; and in 1334 the assessments for such subsidies were standardized for future purposes in all localities – so that hence-

[8] On parliament at the beginning of our period see Chapter 4.

forward a lay subsidy could always be reckoned to bring in about
£36,000.[9] The clergy, who in the late thirteenth century were
occasionally assessed for parliamentary taxes, in the fourteenth
established their right to make their own grants of tenths in their
convocations (of York and Canterbury; their standard assessment
was that reached for the tax of a tenth imposed by Pope Nicholas
IV in 1291). The yield of subsidies, both lay and clerical, could
be cut or increased after the assessments had become standardized,
by the grant of fractions or multiples of a subsidy (a double
subsidy, a subsidy and a half or a third).

For the purpose of financing the king's wars grants of assented
taxation had serious shortcomings. They were occasional,
granted for a specific campaign or in a specific military emergency; the idea that a king needed regular grants of taxation was
never accepted in medieval England. The conditions on which
they were granted were often offensive to the king. Besides, they
always took a long time to collect (whereas his needs were usually
immediate), and they were often insufficient – indeed, if hostilities lasted beyond a year or so they almost always were. These
shortcomings regularly drove the kings of England to seek to
raise extra revenue by other means beside assented taxation.
The two most obvious methods of doing so were by borrowing,
and by the more rigorous exploitation of the king's customary
and prerogative rights.

Tyranny – which is what the effort to make the king's rights
yield more than they ordinarily did looked like in the eyes of his
subjects – was in the long run self-defeating. The king had many
rights that he could exploit; to tallage (tax) his demesne boroughs
and manors at his will; to take scutage (the ancient tax in lieu of
feudal military service) from his tenants in chief; to purchase
compulsorily and at his own price ('purvey') goods for his
household. He could send out justices in eyre to delve into the
bottomless history of his subjects' petty crimes and misdemeanours, and make them pay for them, and he could seek
to enforce the forest laws protecting his woods and venison more
effectively. The return on measures such as these was, however,
unrewarding in proportion to the effort involved, nothing like
enough to relieve the king of the need for further assented
taxation. Then, when the king did assemble men to ask them to
grant him subsidies, he would inevitably find himself faced with
demands for the relaxation or abandonment of the rights that he

[9] See further J. F. Willard, *Parliamentary Taxes on Personal Property
1290 to 1334* (Cambridge, Mass., 1934).

had been seeking to enforce, and in his need he seldom had much option but to agree to this. It was in just this way that, in the course of the fourteenth century, popular pressure succeeded in putting an end to the general eyres, which had once been the central government's most effective means of maintaining a tight control over the activities of the local administration.

The dangers of borrowing were less straightforward. Loans to the crown were inseparable from war taxation in the late Middle Ages.[10] Subsidies took time to collect, and it was normal to ask for loans in anticipation of their payment, through commissioners appointed to negotiate personally with potential lenders in the counties. It was to the wealthy, bishops, abbots and knights, and to communities such as boroughs that the commissioners naturally addressed their requests. The subject had not much real option of refusing them; it was much less inconvenient, probably, to lend than to serve the king in person, which at a pinch he might be obliged to do, and anyway he was being offered good security for his loan – repayment out of the subsidy when it came in. If he did try to refuse, he ran a serious risk of being summoned before the king's council to explain why he had done so, a most uncomfortable prospect. English society in the late Middle Ages, and especially its prosperous sector, was small enough for the king's ill will to matter a great deal to quite ordinary people.

Small sums, contributed by individuals and communities who lent voluntarily because they knew that they could be compelled to do so, only dented the king's necessities in wartime. He needed to raise much larger loans as well. In the late thirteenth and early fourteenth century he usually applied to Italian bankers, later more often to the native merchant community. On such loans the crown might have to pay interest, perhaps at a high rate (interest was not paid on its semi-compulsory loans from subjects). The normal method of repayment of both kinds of loan was by 'assignment'; the exchequer gave the lender tallies, notched sticks recording the sum lent, which were assigned for repayment at a future date from a particular revenue – say the subsidy for Oxfordshire, or the customs of Southampton. The creditor then collected the cash from the king's officials himself. All too often it happened, however, that when he came to cash his tally he found that there was no money available – some

[10] For what follows, I have relied heavily on G. L. Harriss, 'Aids, loans, and benevolences', *H.J.* 6 (1963), pp. 1–19, an article of unusual importance.

other creditor had been before him, maybe. In this case he might with luck get his tally renewed, and payment deferred to a later date; but the same thing might happen again. As time went on, if hostilities endured, the exchequer's revenues became weighed down with assignments, and a backlog of bad debt began to accumulate. The customs might have to be pledged to major creditors; and fresh loans might have to be raised, not now in anticipation of subsidies but to repay old debts. Confusion then began to mar the system of accounting. The longer a war continued, the more desperate the exchequer's losing battle against mounting insolvency was likely to become.

Impoverishment and insolvency were directly damaging to the royal reputation, and so to kingly authority. Sir John Fortescue, who served long and faithfully the most indigent of all England's monarchs in the later Middle Ages, Henry VI, summed up their consequences neatly:

> The greatest harm that cometh of a king's poverty is, that he shall by necessity be forced to find exquisite means of getting goods, as to put in default some of his subjects that be innocent, and upon the rich men more than the poor, because they may the better pay: and to show rigour there as favour ought to be showed, and favour there as rigour should be showed: to the perversion of justice and perturbation of the peace and quiet of the realm. For as the philosopher saith in his Ethics, *impossibile est indigentem operari bona*.[11]

Fortescue had another pertinent remark to make at the same time about the dangers of royal poverty, too: 'his subjects will rather go with a lord that is rich, and may pay their wages and expenses, than with a king that hath nought in his purse'.[12] Insolvency not only weakened royal authority: it encouraged aristocratic unruliness. War, we said earlier, exposed two principal weaknesses of the late medieval administration in England; the inadequacy of the crown's finances, and the fact that the king's greater subjects were too powerful for him to manage on the basis of authority alone. As Fortescue makes clear, these two weaknesses were interrelated.

Amongst the king's greater subjects, with whose affairs the rest of this chapter will be principally concerned, we must distinguish at the start two groups: the great lay barons and their ecclesiastical colleagues. The bishops and the great abbots whom the

[11] J. Fortescue, *The Governance of England*, ed. C. Plummer (Oxford, 1885), p. 119.
[12] ibid.

king summoned to parliaments by individual writs were quite
as rich as the lay magnates. They were no less determined to
maintain the integrity of their wide estates, of which they considered themselves custodians for the saints to whom their
churches were dedicated. But their wealth was not hereditary,
and their office and experience set them apart; they were not
involved in the competition for dynastic advantage that preoccupied the lay baronage, and the background of their education
was religious, not martial. Nearly all of them were royal nominees
to their dignities; and many among the bishops had risen through
the administrative service of the crown. This did not always
make them committed royalists in politics, but they usually
looked on political issues with a bias that favoured the monarchy.
Late in the fourteenth century and in the fifteenth, when cadets
of noble houses were more numerous among the episcopate than
they had been, leading churchmen tended, it is true, to become
more easily entangled in the feuds of their fellow peers. Even
then, however, theirs was a moderating influence in politics, in
favour of stable government and backed by a less martial concept
of the common interest than that of the lay lords.

It was the lay lords who presented the real problem of management for the crown. There is a story that, when Edward I
instituted the *Quo Warranto* inquiries and summoned all those
lords who held franchises to prove their title to them in his
courts, appeared the Earl of Warenne before the royal judges
brandishing an 'ancient and rusty sword'. 'Behold, my lords,' he
cried, 'this is my warrant. My ancestors came with William the
Bastard and conquered their lands by the sword; and by the
sword I will defend them against any who may wish to take
them. For the king did not by himself conquer and subject the
land, but our ancestors were his partners and companions in the
business.'[13] These words are full of significance. The great lay
lords did regard themselves as a class apart, companions of the
king with a special political rights and responsibilities. In war they
did act as his partners: contingents recruited and captained by
them always, in the fourteenth and fifteenth centuries, formed a
substantial proportion of the royal hosts, and often the major one.
In Wales and Scotland they often served without pay, and for
service in France they showed themselves willing to wait, sometimes for years, for wages of war for themselves and their men.
But they also expected to give the king counsel about the govern-

[13] *The Chronicle of Walter of Guisborough*, ed. H. Rothwell (Camden
Soc., 1957), p. 216, note d.

ment of his realm, and that he should heed it. If he and his officials threatened them in their rights, or played fast and loose with the laws that were the common inheritance of the people, they regarded it as their right, indeed their duty as his 'born counsellors',[14] to restrain him, and by force if no other way could be found. Men who had such an exalted view of their station as this, and who were respected by others as the king's 'partners' or 'companions', needed to be handled very delicately by their monarch.

The lay magnates could not have claimed the status that they did, or have assumed such high responsibilities, but for their immense wealth which, as Fortescue saw clearly, was what made them difficult to manage. The foundation of this wealth was the individual magnate's inheritance, the network of estates and jurisdictional rights that descended to him by hereditary right (primogeniture was the rule among males; equal division between co-heiresses). From this inheritance, the territorial accumulation that was the fruit of the careful dynastic forethought of his ancestors, the magnate drew his income, partly from rents, partly from farming, partly from the profits of justice – from fines and dues levied in the courts that his reeves and bailiffs presided over on his manors.

The inheritance of a great lay magnate was likely to be scattered through many shires, and its administration demanded the services of an extensive staff of officials. It was usually divided into a series of receiverships – one for each area in which there was a concentration of estates. In each receivership the lord would appoint a steward to supervise the running of his estates, and a receiver to collect his rents and dues; these would be paid into a central treasury, probably called the 'wardrobe', at one of his castles. The work of these officials was controlled and coordinated by the magnate's council, which would naturally include experts in estate management and men learned in the law. On a miniature scale the administration of the inheritance was thus a replica of the royal administration, and a magnate's councillors were quite as conscious of their duty to enforce all his rights and as ingenious in their pursuit of this object as the king's judges and the officials of the exchequer were on the crown's behalf.

All the great magnates held at least a part of their inheritances in chief from the crown by feudal tenure, and many of them the

[14] See Fortescue, *The Governance of England*, p. 147.

major part. As a system of reciprocal services (usually military) connecting lord and tenant feudalism was, before the late thirteenth century, obsolete, but it remained the basis of English common law concerning land tenure. This meant that the king retained his right to his feudal 'incidents': to the wardship of the heir of a dead tenant in chief if he was under age, and to dispose in marriage of his heiresses; and that tenants in chief might not alienate lands held of the king without a royal licence. Still more important, the estates of a tenant in chief who died without heirs reverted ('escheated') to the crown. It was therefore only with the crown's connivance that a magnate could hope to augment his territories by marriage or by collateral inheritance. Direct royal patronage could, of course, enrich him even more splendidly. There were always inheritances which looked like falling in for lack of heirs, the reversion of which was in the king's gift, and rich wardships, not to mention grants that were to be had from time to time from lands forfeited to the crown by the treason of those who had previously held them. Besides this there were many offices of dignity and profit at the crown's disposal, Lord Chamberlain, Warden of the Cinque Ports, Keeper of the King's Forest, chief justice of north or south Wales – to mention a few among the most dignified and profitable.

It was the natural policy of every magnate to seek to augment his inheritance; ambition aside, it was his duty to his kindred to do so. This made individual magnate families the natural rivals of one another, and their competition could become dangerously keen. It also made their relations with the crown peculiarly delicate, because they were so heavily dependent on royal favour for the furtherance of territorial and dynastic ambitions. Of course everyone expected to see loyal service rewarded, and no one grumbled much at the advancement of, say, William Montagu in Edward III's reign to be Earl of Salisbury, or of Henry de Grosmont to be the first Duke of Lancaster. Both men had earned their recompense by service in war, diplomacy and domestic politics. It was quite another thing to witness the rise of one such as Piers Gaveston, Edward II's favourite whom he made Earl of Cornwall, which was the result of favour alone. It was not difficult for jealous rivals to denounce a *parvenu* to the peerage like Gaveston as an evil councillor who was using his influence to plunder his king's resources and make himself rich. Such an evil councillor exercised the sort of influence that it might be the duty of the magnates in the common interest to restrain – by force if there were no other way of doing so. It was the easier to convince others besides magnates that this course might be necessary and justified if, as was the case at the time when Edward II was showering title and riches upon Gaveston, the king's wars were going badly. The charge that the king's patrimony had been depleted by overlavish patronage of the undeserving was one often on the lips of the discontented, coupled always with the demand that unjustified grants be resumed, so as to lighten the burden of his overtaxed subjects.

When the lords denounced evil councillors, or demanded that this or that be changed or amended for the common profit, it was very dangerous for the king to ignore them. Their voice was not theirs only, but that also of their followers, the retainers and dependants who had taken fees from them and were pledged to their service. The system of relations which bound these followers to their magnate leaders is what historians have called 'bastard feudalism'. The name is a little misleading: it denotes not a late and degenerate form of feudalism, only a system that in certain superficial respects resembled tenurial feudalism. We need to be clear about what bastard feudalism should mean, because most of the political ills of late medieval England have been attributed to it, often with rather less than justice.[15]

A great magnate family, with its wide hereditary estates, stood at the centre of a multi-class social group that drew its cohesion from attachment to a particular lord. For this society, the focal centres were the private castles and manors of the lord in question. Wherever he went, he would be accompanied by his permanent household staff: a list of the household people of John de Bek, Lord d'Eresby in the late thirteenth century, includes his steward (a knight), the wardrober (the clerk who supervised his accounts), a chaplain, two friars and a boy clerk, the marshal, and a substantial group of lesser men, ushers, butlers, porters, farriers. This was John de Bek's permanent staff only; there would always be more people with a lord's household – sons of

[15] The most important study of 'bastard feudalism' is K. B. Mc-Farlane, 'Bastard feudalism', *B.I.H.R.* 20 (1943–5), pp. 161–80, a seminal article; also important is N. B. Lewis, 'The organisation of indentured retinues in fourteenth century England', *T.R.H.S.* 4th ser., 27 (1945), pp. 29–39. Some very interesting points are put forward by W. H. Dunham in his *Lord Hastings's Indentured Retainers* (Newhaven, Conn., 1955), especially in his 'argument' and in chapters IV and V. His arguments concerning the 'feudality' of retaining are questionable.

important tenants, knights and esquires who had taken the lord's
fees, messengers, and at each of his residences he would find a
great staff of grooms, huntsmen, and menial servants waiting
for him. John Smyth's description of the household of Thomas
Lord Berkeley, famous as the gaoler of Edward II, gives a fine
picture of the kind of society thus gathered together:

> The knights that had wages by the day and their double liveries of
> gowns furred were usually twelve, each of them with two servants
> and a *garçon* or page, and allowance for the like number of horses;
> the esquires that also had wages by the day, each of them [with]
> one man and a page and allowance for their horses, were twenty
> four . . . from whence it may be conjectured what the number of
> inferior degrees might in probability be. I am confident that the
> number of his standing house, each day fed, were three hundred at
> the least.[16]

Communal living and the lord's liberality gave this society a
coherence that was prized by men at large, for all ate and most
slept together in the lord's great hall. 'Command the officers to
admit your acknowledged men, familiar friends, and strangers
too, with merry cheer', so runs the advice to a lord in a late
medieval tract on the management of a household, 'and always,
as much as you may, eat in the hall before your household, for
that shall be to your profit and worship.'[17]

As this advice reminds us, it was expected of a lord that he
should gather men around him – his following was the outward
and visible sign of his status. It was also expected of him that he
should be generous, showing his people 'merry cheer', that he
should feed and maintain them and reward them for their
service with fees and gifts. And it was not only in his household
that he needed to surround himself with his own people: it was
even more necessary that he should make a good showing,
attended by men clothed in livery with his arms or device, when
he came to parliament, or appeared at a tournament, or answered
the king's summons to serve him in his host. For all these
reasons, the maintenance of his household and retinue made
heavy calls upon his resources. This was a factor that often
accentuated the natural rivalry of magnates, especially their
competition for royal favour, whose rewards could enable them

[16] J. Smyth, *The Lives of the Berkeleys*, ed. Sir J. Maclean (Gloucester,
1883), vol. I, p. 304.
[17] Household statutes, attributed to Robert Grosseteste, printed in
Manners and Meals in Olden Time, ed. F. J. Furnivall (E.E.T.S., 1868),
pp. 328–31.

to take on more men, and to cut a more impressive figure among
their fellows – an attainment gratifying to the self-esteem not
only of a lord himself but also of his followers.

At the centre of every magnate retinue were those men of
substance, knights and esquires, whom the lord had retained for
life by indenture. The indenture was a sealed contract recording
the terms of their mutual relationship. The earliest such document that has survived bears the date 1287; there are quite a
few that belong to the early fourteenth century, and by its later
years a standard form had developed. A good example, somewhat
late in date but on the usual pattern, is the indenture sealed on
26 May 1461 between Richard Neville Earl of Warwick (the
'kingmaker') and Sir John Trafford. For the sum of 20 marks per
annum, assigned on the issues of the earl's lordship of
Middleham, Trafford was retained for life by the earl, in peace
and war, to be 'ready at the desire or commandment of the earl
to come unto him at all such times and in such places as the earl
shall call upon him . . . horsed, harnessed, arrayed and accompanied as the case shall require'.[18] He was to have wages of the
earl when on his service – and no doubt he would also be fed and
maintained when he was in his household. In war he and his
men would get wages, and he was to hand over a third of his
winnings of war (plunder and ransoms) to his lord. 'In witness
whereof', the indenture concludes, 'the parties interchangeably
to the presents have put their seals.' John Trafford in 1461 was
establishing his position in a large retinue led by the most
powerful peer in England. In many retinues the number of
formally indentured retainers was probably not very great: they
were a small, central group in the society that gathered about a
lord and his household. But they were always there in such a
society, and always significant.

Reading between the lines of Trafford's contract, we can see
why indentured retainers were so important to their lords. They
were drawn from among the county gentry, and were not permanently resident in his household. As substantial local men,
they could keep an eye for him on his affairs in their neighbourhood. Theirs was the class that dominated local government,
from whose ranks the sheriff, the under-sheriff and the justices
of the peace in a county would be chosen, and who would
represent the community of the shire in parliaments. The
loyalty of his retainers could entrench their lord's influence

[18] This indenture is printed by A. R. Myers in *English Historical
Documents 1327–1485* (London, 1969), p. 1126.

solidly in a locality. As men of wealth and standing with tenants, kin and neighbours, they made their lord's formal retinue the centre of a web of looser connexions radiating outwards.

The indentured retainers also formed a nucleus round which a fighting company of knights, esquires and archers could be rapidly enlisted for war or in a domestic emergency. Since in the late Middle Ages the main body of a royal host consisted of contingents recruited individually by captains, many of whom were usually magnates, the system of retaining by indenture was valuable to the crown and the realm at large as well as to the magnates themselves. 'Trust it true,' the chronicler John Hardyng wrote of the Percy Earl of Northumberland, 'there is no lord in England that may defend your realm against Scotland so well as he, for they (the Percies) have the hearts of the people by the north, and ever had.' Hardyng spoke from personal know-ledge: 'I, the maker of this book, was brought up from twelve years of age in Sir Henry Percy's house, to the battle of Shrews-bury where I was with him armed, as I had been before at Homildon, Cocklaw, and at divers roads (skirmishes) and fields with him.'[19] It was not on the northern border only that retinues proved their fighting value to the kingdom. Anyone who turns the pages of the Black Prince's *Register* may check for himself the connexion between the service of an extravagantly generous lord of the blood royal who happened also to be the most notable military commander of his age, and a national, martial achievement in the field in France. John Chandos, James Audley, Thomas Felton, Walter Manny, the names familiar from Froissart's chronicles of chivalry are all there, together with notes of the rewards with which their leader saw fit to honour them; fees assigned on his landed revenues; warhorses with memorable names; captured armour, plate and jewels. The wars indeed gave a positive impetus to retaining; many men probably first made contact with the lords with whom they would one day be indentured, when they took service under them temporarily for campaigns in France.

The practice of retaining was regulated, in the late Middle Ages, by a number of statutes (not, it must be admitted, very effectively). The most important of these was Richard II's statute of 1390. This forbade all except peers (that is, men whose substance was not sufficient to guarantee their social responsibility) to retain men who were not their household servants by grants of fees and

[19] J. Hardyng, *Chronicle*, ed. H. Ellis (London, 1812), p. 351.

liveries. It also forbade peers to retain men of low estate, 'valets' and yeomen archers who were not permanently employed in the household, by grants of liveries. But it specifically permitted peers (and no others) to retain for life persons of substance, knights and esquires, who were not household men. Nobody wished to forbid this kind of retaining, because it was the best way that the king or anyone else knew of recruiting responsible men to perform essential services, and was the key to the mobilization of armies in time of war.

What inspired the inhibitions of the statute was the undoubted social fact that, if unrestrained, retaining could be so abused as to enable peers to maintain what were effectively private armies, and gentry to gather about themselves bands of thugs, to the perturbation of the peace of the realm. Every genteel family had its own dynastic aspirations, just as a magnate family had, which involved it in the same sort of rivalries with neighbours, culminating in law suits, and all too often in violence. Nobody, in the late Middle Ages, expected the law to right all wrongs on its own. The story of James Lord Berkeley, heir male of Lord Thomas IV in the fifteenth century, and of his great suit with the heirs general (especially Margaret Countess of Shrewsbury and her husband) reflects a typical situation. He and his sons barricaded themselves into Berkeley castle and conducted a petty war against his rivals, while his wife Isabel went to London, to sue out writs against these rivals in chancery, and to solicit men of influence in her husband's favour. Force and favour were, in fact, necessary adjuncts to a man's right at law, and the expectation that his master's 'good lordship' would help him towards them was one principal reason why county gentry were anxious to enrol in the retinues of great magnates. Maintenance, the offence committed by the powerful when they upheld their followers' legal causes and quarrels by extra-legal means, was in consequence a besetting social problem. Once again the history of the Berkeley family illustrates the difficulty well. 'I will conclude', wrote John Smyth of Lord Thomas III (ob. 1361, but he is referring to the year 1330), 'with the petition of Sir John . . . of Dursley, who therein complaineth against him, that the sheriff, and other officers and ministers of justice in the county of Gloucester, were this lord's household servants, of his standing wages and livery, and therefore he could have no justice against him.'[20] Retaining could all too easily become a means to the systematic perversion of justice.

[20] Smyth, *The Lives of the Berkeleys* vol. I, p. 307.

Maintenance might be more or less subtle: a corrupt sheriff might see to it that no jury was empanelled that would convict his lord's clients (who could then help themselves to their 'rights'), or a band of armed men in a lord's livery might convince a justice that it would not be worth his while to decide a case in a way that they did not like. The result was the same either way 'that true subjects . . . dare not for fear and doubt of their lives complain to your highness (the king) or sue for remedy after your laws'.[21] Those who were not as easily frightened as this, meanwhile, took the only other course open to them, to set the law at defiance and maintain themselves by force until the times should change (this is what the story of outlaws like Robin Hood and Gamelyn, wronged men who have defied their oppressors and taken to the woods until at last they obtain the king's pardon, is largely about).[22] The disorder and disturbance consequent upon maintenance were thus cumulative. Where two magnate families and their followers were competing for influence (as the Nevilles and Percies in the north, for instance) the consequence of their quarrelling and that of their retinues might fall not far short of a local civil war.

A significant fact about maintenance is that, alarmingly frequently, it was the disorderly conduct of the king's own retainers of which men complained. 'Thus liveries overlook your lieges each one', wrote the indignant author of *Mum and the Sothsegger*, addressing Richard II with the king's White Hart retainers in mind.[23] The king's household and retinue were really no different from those of a magnate, except in scale and in the status of the king's greatest followers (a good many peers always had retaining fees from him). Tout's brilliant exposition of the administrative role of the household has probably encouraged historians to concentrate too much on that side of its activity, to forget that its chief officer was the steward, a knight usually with a military background, and that (through most of

[21] *R.P.* vol. V, p. 367.

[22] On these stories and their appeal see J. C. Holt, 'The origins and audience of the Ballads of Robin Hood', *Past and Present* 18 (1960), pp. 89–110. This seems to be as good a place as any to make it clear that I now regard Professor Holt's views about the *milieu* that produced the outlaw legends as far more convincing than those I have aired myself in *The Outlaws of Medieval Legend* (London, 1961) and in *Past and Present* 19 (1961), pp. 7–15.

[23] *Mum and the Sothsegger*, ed. M. Day and R. Steele (E.E.T.S., 1936), Passus II, l. 35.

our period, at least) the knights and esquires of the chamber or of
the body did more to uphold the king's authority in his kingdom
than the household clerks ever did. The king, no less than a
magnate, needed the committed loyalty and service of men
recruited from among the substantial gentlefolk of the counties
to maintain his dignity, look after his interests, and follow him
to war.

We shall deceive ourselves if we think of late medieval England
in modern terms, with political coherence dependent on the
smooth operation of relations between local and central government, and social tensions centring round the competing interests
of classes divided horizontally from one another. Horizontal
divisions, in this period, were less significant than the vertical
ones which separated multi-class groups of men attached to
different and competitive interests, and which were led by the
king and by individual magnates. Good government depended
far less on the work of the central bureaucracy than it did on the
ability of the king and these magnates to cooperate reasonably
among themselves. The king's retinue was only one among
many, whose composition ebbed and flowed with the tides of
political and social competition, since most retainers were ready
to desert the fortunes of a master whose star seemed to have
passed the ascendant for one whose service promised more
effective protection and greater rewards. These were the political
realities behind the statement made much earlier in this chapter,
that the king's greater subjects were too powerful for him to
manage on the basis of authority alone.

'Bastard feudalism' was a version of the system of patronage and
clientage which has been so important throughout English
history, appropriate to the needs of an age in which influential
protection was a prime social necessity, and in which the government could not afford to maintain standing forces against
military emergency. Its social significance and the requirements
of military service are inseparable; indeed the whole ethos in
which the late medieval notions of good lordship and loyal
service was founded had military overtones. The culture, education and ideals of the aristocratic and genteel society which
focused around the great halls and castles of the king and his
magnates were military – or perhaps we should rather use their
own word, chivalrous. The natural training for youths of good
birth was in a noble household, the chief subjects of their
education horsemanship and the exercise of arms; 'as using

jousts, learning to run with a spear and handle an axe, sword and dagger, wrestling ... leaping, running, to make them hardy, free and well bred; so that when the realm in time of need had their service in deeds and enterprises of arms, they might be the more apt to do honourable service'.[24] The history that such youths learned and were taught to value was the story of the martial prowess of their ancestors, and of Christian champions such as Arthur and Charlemagne – and of the loyal followers of these heroes. The insignia (arms and other devices), which were the outward marks of the dignity and ancestry of lords and knights, were military. Livery, the granting of a heraldic badge to a follower, was a way of associating him with his lord in a relationship whose social traditions and ethic were soldierly.

This was why the fortunes of war were so crucial to the relations of king and magnates in the 'bastard feudal' age. Stable government depended on the capacity of kings to restrain the natural competition of their magnates sufficiently for all to cooperate together: to this end a degree of mutual trust and respect was necessary. This respect and confidence a king could obtain by proven martial ability more readily than in any other way. Edward III and Henry V, who won their battles, did not have much difficulty in canalizing the wealth and influence of their magnates and the manpower of their retinues to the service of their own military enterprises. There were material as well as psychological reasons for their success in doing so. Victory brought riches as well as glory to those who shared in it, loot and ransoms; and military service besides opened endless prospects of official advancement. By comparison with the fruits of office and domestic service these prizes were glamorous: Sir John Fastolf told his servant William Worcester that on the day of the battle of Verneuil in 1424 alone he won by the fortune of war 20,000 marks.[25] In the pursuit of such fortune, many were ready to lay aside, for the time being, their jockeying for favour and position at home. Edward III's reign, which witnessed the victories of Crecy and Poitiers and Najera, also witnessed the longest interlude untroubled by civil strife or aristocratic sedition in the whole of the late Middle Ages, and it was no accident.

A king who did not win victories could not obtain the con-

[24] *The Boke of Noblesse*, ed. J. G. Nichols (Roxburghe Club, 1860), p. 76.
[25] See K. B. McFarlane, 'The investment of Sir John Fastolf's profits of war', *T.R.H.S.* 5th ser., 7 (1957), p. 95.

fidence and respect of his powerful subjects with the same ease as one who could. He was likely to find it very difficult to restrain the rivalry of the magnates from finding expression in violence and seditious intrigue. The ambitions of the men who were dependent on them egged on their rivalry, and spread confusion at the local level. This confusion led to the widespread perversion of public justice, and to popular clamour about 'lack of governance'. Worst of all was the fate of the king who fought a losing war. Defeat undermined respect for him and for his advisers; his borrowing and his taxes alienated his subjects at large; and, in the halls of the great, men began to murmur that it was time that someone took a hand to relieve the king of councillors who were serving him ill. Thus popular discontent and disaffection mounted towards the flashpoint of rebellion.

The conclusions of this chapter can be summarized very briefly. As long as the magnates' claim to be the 'companions' or partners of the king in government and his born counsellors was not rejected as factious by men at large; as long as the power of magnates with their retinues made it feasible for them to use force to make a king amend what they regarded as misrule or to dismiss his chosen councillors; as long as the inadequacy of royal revenues drove kings to oppress their subjects in order to meet the extraordinary expenses that were incidental to warfare – so long, under the medieval order, instability was an in-built feature of English national politics. It remained so, more or less inevitably, as long as the wars endured: for England, that is to say, throughout the greater part of the late Middle Ages. In consequence, they were a period of political strain and uncertainty, in which the most significant developments were not those initiated by government, from above, but those evoked from below, by the response of the governed to events. This we shall see, as we begin to examine the story of how the interplay of the factors discussed in this chapter worked out on the stage of history.

Edward I and Edward II
1290–1330

Outward war and troubles at home
1290–1314

On 26 September in the year 1290 Margaret, the seven-year-old queen of Scotland who was called the 'Maid of Norway', died in the Orkneys. She was the granddaughter and heiress of Alexander III, King of Scots, who had died in 1286; and for the last four years her kingdom had been governed by six 'guardians'. In 1290 she was at last on her way home from Scandinavia, where she had been born, and an agreement had that summer been reached for her marriage to the eldest surviving son of Edward I of England, the six-year-old Edward of Caernarvon. The Treaty of Birgham, which settled the terms of the match, had stipulated that Scotland should remain a kingdom separate from England, with her own laws and courts and parliament: but the young Edward and Margaret, and their heirs after them, would naturally inherit both crowns. Edward I of England was already lord of Ireland, and he had earlier in his reign brought the principality of Wales under his direct dominion. The treaty therefore promised in due course (if the children survived) to round off an *imperium* for the English royal house over the whole of the British Isles. It also offered a simple and peaceful solution to the problem of Anglo-Scottish relations, for the Scottish kings in the past had always contested the ill-specified superiority which the English kings claimed over their land. The death of the Maid of Norway was therefore a blow to Edward I, upsetting carefully prepared plans.

Margaret was the only surviving descendant of Alexander III, and when she died it was not clear who had the best claim to her vacant throne. The strongest competitors were John de Balliol, Lord of Galloway (and a substantial landowner besides in northern England), and Robert Bruce, Lord of Annandale. Both were descended in the female line from David, the brother of

King William the Lion (1165–1214): Balliol was the grandson of his eldest daughter Margaret, Bruce the son of his second daughter Isobel. There were other important claimants also, notably the English nobleman John Hastings, who was descended from David's third daughter; and Florence Count of Holland, who was descended from Ada, the sister of William the Lion and David. The situation was confused, and as the news of the child queen's death spread, the supporters of Balliol and Bruce began to prepare for a possible war of succession. To cooler heads there seemed only one way out of the impasse, to refer the whole matter of the arbitrament of the succession to Scotland's powerful and hitherto friendly neighbour, King Edward. The king of England was entirely willing to intervene, but on his own terms. The appeal to his judgement gave him a clear opportunity to gain, if not all that the Treaty of Birgham had promised for the future, at least some essential advantages. He could certainly clear up the old question of the superior right of the English crown over Scotland. It was in this spirit that he approached the question of arbitration, in May 1291, when he went north to meet the representatives of the Scottish kingdom at Norham on the Tweed.

By the end of June 1291 Edward had persuaded the Scots, pending a decision, to put the chief castles of Scotland into his hands, and the competitors had agreed to stand by his judgement. He had not managed to persuade the Scots to admit his feudal overlordship over their kingdom, but the agreement of the individual competitors to do homage to him, if they succeeded, secured the point in a way which was only a little less satisfactory to him. The great case proceeded slowly, and was considered with deliberation and impartiality. It was judged by the king of England's council, assisted by eighty Scots assessors, forty nominated by Balliol and forty by Bruce. Balliol argued that his right was best because he was descended from the royal house by the eldest line; Bruce in that he was a generation nearer in blood to a king than Balliol was. Florence of Holland claimed that David, William the Lion's brother, had resigned his right to the throne to William, who then assigned it to their sister Ada, Florence's ancestress; but he could produce no evidence for this assertion. Hastings claimed a third share in the kingdom on the ground that it was a fief of the English crown, and that therefore, as was the custom in England, co-heiresses (or their descendants) should divide the inheritance. This argument was rejected by King Edward and his advisers; the kingdom of Scotland, as a community entire in itself, could not be divided, they ruled. Proceeding on the principle of seniority in blood they finally, on 17 November 1292, awarded the kingdom, with all its appurtenances included, to Balliol. He was duly installed, and did homage to King Edward as he had promised.[1]

Homage was the recognition of a formal feudal tenurial relationship, and it could be argued that the act implied acceptance by the vassal of the obligations towards his lord normally incidental to feudal tenure; that he must serve his lord in war and with counsel, and that his tenants had a right to appeal from his court to that of his superior. It was soon clear that Edward was quite determined to assert and establish his right to these incidents of feudal superiority with regard to Scotland, and that he would not regard himself as bound by assurances that he had given in the interregnum about the limits of his future demands. Only a week after Balliol's enthronement, he and his council heard at Berwick a case on appeal from the court of the kingdom of Scotland. Over the next year a series of further appeals from the Scottish king's court were heard by the king of England, and King John was forced to appear in King's Bench to defend his judgements. When, in the case of an appeal by MacDuff of Fife, Balliol questioned whether he was obliged to answer, he was declared to be in contempt of court, and condemned to lose three castles until he made amends. Edward clearly meant business, and not to allow the Scots to dodge what he considered to be their legal obligations. The attitude was typical of the man. In earlier years he had forced the Welsh by arms to acknowledge his jurisdiction. In England the *Quo Warranto* inquiries had firmly established the principle that no baron could exercise judicial rights except by the grant of the king, his superior lord and judge. A supremely successful ruler so far throughout his reign, Edward was confident that, when he was asserting legal rights, firmness would pay.

In this instance his judgement was questionable. In his confidence he was insensitive to the offence which his attitude gave, not just to Balliol, but to the lords and people of Scotland.

[1] On the 'great cause' see B. C. Keeney, 'The medieval idea of the state: the great cause 1291–2', *University of Toronto Law Journal* 8 (1949), pp. 48–71; and G. W. S. Barrow, *Robert Bruce* (London, 1965). For all that concerns Scotland in this period, I have relied heavily on this outstanding biography. See also on Scottish affairs from 1295 onward E. M. Barron, *The Scottish War of Independence* (Inverness, 1914).

John's Scottish councillors encouraged him to resist Edward, and finally took over resistance on his behalf. In June 1294 Balliol was summoned, as Edward's feudal subject, to perform military service in the war which had broken out between England and France, in company with the leading men of his kingdom. John agreed in principle, but delayed and made excuses, and to stiffen him into refusal his subjects in July 1295 imposed upon him a council of twelve peers, without whose agreement nothing affecting the realm was to be done. This meant that the summons would not be answered, if the twelve could help it. Edward's firmness thus failed to establish without cavil his feudal superiority over the Scots king. Instead it lost him, in the long run, all that he had hoped to gain in 1290 and 1292, and involved his realm in a war that outlasted his lifetime. The strains of that war taxed his resources to the limit and beyond, and undermined his authority over his own English subjects. It was to shake to its foundations the whole edifice of Plantagenet monarchy, which Edward had built to new strength in the first twenty years of his reign.

In fairness to Edward, it must be made clear that the problem of Scotland did not stand alone. If that had been the case, he might have had his way in the northern kingdom. But in 1294 he was faced with war on two other fronts, in Wales and in Gascony. This was why, in that year, he summoned Balliol to serve him in arms, and it was also why Balliol's subjects thought they had some chance of success if they resisted English demands.

The rebellion which broke out all over Wales at the end of September 1294 was a very serious affair. It kept Edward and his chief barons busy through the winter; and though its back was broken when the Earl of Warwick defeated the most important Welsh leader, Madog ap Llewellyn, in the spring of 1295, Edward had to remain in the principality until well past mid-summer, reestablishing order and English authority.[2] The trouble in his duchy of Gascony was still more serious, and this was what really gave the Scots their chance. In Gascony the English kings had stood in the same position *vis-à-vis* the kings of France as Balliol stood *vis-à-vis* Edward, ever since 1259 (when Henry III as Duke of Gascony had formally recognized

---

[2] On the Welsh rebellion see J. E. Morris, *The Welsh Wars of Edward I* (Oxford, 1901), pp. 242ff.; and J. G. Edwards, 'The battle of Maes Madog and the Welsh campaign of 1294-5', *E.H.R.* 39 (1924), pp. 1-12.

the feudal overlordship of the king of France).[3] Appeals from the ducal court had since then become so frequent that Edward had taken to maintaining permanent attornies to defend his causes before the French king's *Parlement* at Paris. In May 1293 an Anglo-Gascon fleet defeated a superior French Norman fleet off Cape St Mahé in Brittany, and afterwards sacked La Rochelle. Trouble of this sort was constant in the Channel and off the Biscayan coast, but King Philip IV of France took the particular incident seriously, demanding the delivery of the Gascon offenders to his courts, and full reparation for the damage done to his subjects. To back his demands, he summoned Edward to appear in person [before the *Parlement*. Edward, who had no wish for war, reacted diplomatically, and despatched his brother Edmund to Paris to negotiate.

In Paris, Edmund was tricked. He was led to believe that a settlement could be reached – if Edward would permit the temporary surrender of Bordeaux and a number of other southern towns to Philip, for the sake of appearances. On the understanding that the cession would be temporary, and that the proceedings in the *Parlement* would be dropped, the towns were handed over. Notwithstanding this, on 21 April 1294 Edward was again summoned before the court, and on 19 May he was condemned for non-appearance and his duchy declared confiscate. Like Edward in Scotland, Philip had decided that firmness would pay when the right of an overlord had to be upheld. His decision led to the outbreak of a full-scale war.

King Edward's response to the sentence of confiscation was sharp. Orders were sent out immediately to array men for service in Gascony, and summonses were sent to the great men of the kingdom, John de Balliol among them, to be ready to serve with their followers. Abroad English agents went busily to work to recruit allies in the Low Countries and the Empire with the offer of pensions. The dukes of Bar and Brabant, both sons-in-law of Edward, were ready to help, and soon Count Florence of Holland and, much more important, the emperor elect, Adolf of Nassau, were drawn into the alliance. To raise funds for these and other war measures Edward took drastic steps. A threat to seize all wools and woolfells to his use forced the merchants to agree to a new and heavy customs duty at the ports (the *maltolte*). He demanded and, once again by means of threats, obtained a

[3] On these arrangements see P. Chaplais, 'Le Traité de Paris de 1259 et l'inféodation de la Gascogne allodiale', *Moyen Age* 61 (1955), pp. 121–37.

grant of one half of all clerical revenues from the clergy in convocation in September 1294. His commissioners seized to his use the proceeds of the crusading tenths, which had been imposed earlier by Nicholas IV and deposited in English churches and monasteries. In spite of all this frenetic effort, the king was however unable to send such forces to Gascony in 1294 as he had hoped. The rising in Wales intervened; men and money had to be diverted and the king himself was kept busy until the summer of 1295. Then the Scots took their opportunity to stiffen their resistance against English interference. They were in contact with Philip IV early in 1295, and on 23 October entered into a firm offensive and defensive alliance with him. Finally, in March 1296 John de Balliol sent his defiance to the king of England and renounced his homage. In the brief space of eighteen months Edward was thus faced with war on three fronts.

1295 saw the end of the war in Wales. In January next year Edward was able at last to reinforce John of Brittany, who had been sent to Gascony in 1294, with a respectable force under Edmund of Lancaster. In March 1296 the king was mustering a powerful army at Newcastle for the invasion of Scotland. At the end of the month Berwick was taken, and on 27 April the advance guard, under the Earl of Warenne, met and defeated the feudal host of Scotland at Dunbar. The earls of Ross, Atholl and Menteith were taken prisoner; and the English mainguard was now able to take Roxburgh, Edinburgh and Stirling without much trouble. Without an army, Balliol saw no alternative to capitulation. At Brechin castle, on 10 July, he resigned his crown and kingdom into Edward's hands, and was sent into England in custody, after being solemnly stripped of his dignities as king. Edward continued north, as far as Elgin, touring rather than conquering the country, and by the end of August he was back at Berwick. Thither he formally summoned the parliament of Scotland, and the great men of the kingdom did homage to him. The lands of those who had opposed him he restored; there were no great punitive measures. The government of the kingdom, however, was placed in English hands. The Earl of Warenne was left behind as 'keeper' of Scotland, and Hugh Cressingham as treasurer. Edward himself returned into his own kingdom.

Having now dealt with Wales and Scotland, Edward's plan for the next year, 1297, was to turn upon his third and most powerful enemy, the king of France. He would attack him on two fronts. One force, under the Constable (Bohun of Hereford) and the

Marshal (Bigod of Norfolk), would go to Gascony; he himself would cross to Flanders, whose Count Guy had joined the English alliance, so as to make contact with his other allies in the Low Countries, and invade France from the north-east.

This plan was too ambitious: it overstretched Edward's resources which were already strained when it was formulated. In response to the complaints of the clergy both in England and France, that they were being plundered by the secular authorities in order to pay for the war, Pope Boniface VIII in 1296 issued his bull *Clericis Laicos*, forbidding clergy to contribute to taxation for secular purposes. On the strength of this bull, Archbishop Winchelsey for the English clergy refused the king's demand for a fifth in the parliament at Bury in November 1296. The king riposted by placing the clergy outside the law (30 January 1297), which action brought many to heel; and by the summer he had managed to achieve a reconciliation with Winchelsey and his bishops.[4] By then, however, Edward was heavily embroiled with a secular opposition to his military plans. In March, at Salisbury, Bigod the Marshal had flatly refused to serve in Gascony, unless in the personal company of the king. He and the Constable reiterated this refusal in London in July. By this time the scope of their opposition had widened: they challenged now the legality of the *maltolte* and of the summons that Edward had sent in May to all who held £20 worth of land to be ready to go with him to Flanders. Later, the two of them appeared armed in the exchequer, to protest against the levy of an eighth, which had been granted to the king by certain nobles and knights assembled in his chamber (probably at some time in July). Although Edward did sail for Flanders, on 22 August, he went too late, with too small a force and inadequate funds at his disposal; and he left his kingdom on the verge of civil war.

Edward achieved nothing in Flanders, and he was glad enough, in October 1297, to make a truce with Philip IV. He was not able to return at once, since he had first to pay off some of the large debts that he had contracted with his allies. His presence was urgently needed in England, however, for events there were getting ahead of him. On 10 October the regent and his council came to terms with the opposition leaders, and agreed to confirm the Great Charter and the Charter of the Forest, with specific additional concessions which met contemporary complaints; the collection of the eighth was also stopped. What had forced the hand of the council was the rebellion against the new English

4 On Edward's difficulties with the clergy see Chapter 9.

government in Scotland. The success of the 1296 campaign had
been too swift to be effective. Opposition gathered force all
through the summer of 1297: William Wallace and Sir Andrew
Murray emerged as leaders of the patriot party, with the backing of influential churchmen such as Robert Wishart, Bishop
of Glasgow, and the connivance of some of the nobility. On
11 September at Stirling Bridge Wallace and Murray inflicted a
bloody defeat on Warenne, the justiciar who Edward had left in
Scotland. Though the English garrisons held out at Edinburgh
and Stirling, the whole country was in revolt thereafter; and in
October Wallace and his men were raiding over the English
border. In this situation the regent had no real alternative but to
seek a reconciliation with the leaders of domestic opposition.

1297 saw the climax of Edward I's difficulties. After his return
to England in March 1298, he never again had to cope with war
on so many fronts, or with such determined opposition to his
policies at home as he had done in that year. The truce that he had
made with Philip IV proved to be the end of active hostilities in
the war over Gascony. In 1298 the two kings agreed to refer
their quarrel to the arbitration of Pope Boniface, in his private
capacity as Benedetto Caetani; and though he did not succeed in
resolving their differences, he managed to cement the truce by the
arrangement of two important marriages, between Edward and
Philip's sister Margaret, and between Edward's son and heir,
Edward of Caernarvon, and Philip's daughter Isabella (the
latter were not in fact married until 1308). After this Edward had
to wait, for Philip would not brook any of his arguments that
Gascony was not truly a feudal fief, nor would he restore the
lands and towns that he had seized there.[5] The king of France
remained adamant until 1303, when, shaken by his recent defeat
at Courtrai at the hands of the Flemings, he agreed to a final
peace. Edward was restored to his duchy, and agreed to do homage
for it; and Philip agreed at last to abandon his alliance with the
Scots. Up to this point he had continued to recognize John
Balliol as lawful king of Scotland, and had refused to make any
peace in which the independent Scots were not included.

After 1297 the Scots were the one active enemy with whom
Edward had to deal. As regards Scotland, his position was com-

[5] On the question of Gascony see H. Rothwell, 'Edward I's case
against Philip the Fair', *E.H.R.* 42 (1927), pp. 572–82; and P. Chaplais,
'English arguments concerning the feudal status of Gascony', *B.I.H.R.*
21 (1948), pp. 203–13.

plicated by other factors besides purely military ones. Philip's support for his enemies placed one major obstacle in his way. In 1299 the Scots found another powerful diplomatic ally in Pope Boniface VIII. They had provided him with a well-prepared case to show that Edward had no right of superiority in Scotland, but that, in fact, the kingdom was in the special protection of the Holy See. In response to their appeal Boniface in 1299 by his bull *Scimus Fili* ordered Edward to desist from molesting them. The bull was presented to Edward in 1300 by Archbishop Winchelsey, and though he did not interrupt his military operations, he felt bound to make a long and carefully documented answer, while all the greater barons of his realm were persuaded to put their seals to another letter to the pope, in the same sense.[6] Boniface's attitude changed in Edward's favour a little later, when in 1302 his relations with Philip IV began to deteriorate very seriously. It was at this same point that Philip also, shaken by his defeat in Flanders, began to waver in his support for Scotland.

No diplomatic setback would persuade the Scots to submit. The initial success of Wallace and Murray in 1297 had solidified the spirit of resistance to the English among the ordinary free men of the kingdom, and most of the leading clergy pledged themselves firmly to the national cause. Though the secular aristocracy, who stood to lose most in the event of defeat, were not quite so united, a number of them helped to lead the resistance, and others failed to oppose it. Notable among the former were John Comyn of Badenoch and, until 1302, Robert Bruce Earl of Carrick, the grandson of the competitor of 1292 and the future King of Scots. In the absence of John Balliol, a caretaker government of guardians, acting in his name and that of the community of Scotland, was organized. The impressive number of documents which went out in the name of this government between 1297 and 1304 bears witness to its administrative effectiveness.[7] Edward I thus found that nothing short of total military victory could make the northern kingdom his.

His strategy in Scotland seems to have been to overpower opposition by the sheer weight of superior force. This strategy

---

[6] For documentation see E. L. G. Stones, *Anglo-Scottish Relations* (London 1965), pp. 81ff., 96ff.; and *P.W.* vol. I, pp. 103–4. Edward's letter to Boniface is remarkable for its long excursus into the mythological early history of Anglo-Scottish relations.

[7] See Barrow, *Robert Bruce*, pp. 148ff., 168–70.

had two major drawbacks. In the first place, after the ugly domestic confrontations in England in 1297, he never again felt able to put quite the same pressure on his people that he had before, to make them contribute towards the cost of the war in men and money. Secondly, there was the difficulty of the terrain in Scotland. With his superior army Edward might gain control of the principal castles, but there were not enough of these to hold down the country systematically, and he could not afford the money to build more (as he had done in Wales). Hills and forests provided his enemies with an easy refuge; even in southern Scotland their area was too wide to patrol, and he could never hope to control the land north of the Forth. All the same Edward's efforts in time seemed to be telling, because they were sustained. The English control of the sea, complete during the campaigning seasons at least, also worked in the English king's favour, and enabled him to keep his forts and forces victualled, admittedly at great cost.

Edward mounted a whole series of major campaigns in Scotland. When he returned to England in 1298, he moved the exchequer and the judicial bench north to York, so as better to concentrate the whole administrative force of his kingdom on the reconquest. In the summer of 1298 he invaded Scotland with an army which included some 2400 horse, and which may have numbered 30,000 altogether. On 22 July his cavalry overwhelmed Wallace's pikemen at Falkirk, half way between Edinburgh and Stirling, after the archers and infantry had broken the ranks of the wedge-shaped 'scheltrons' of the Scots. But though he later took the castle of Lochmaben, Edward was not able to follow up this victory effectively. In 1299 he was too busy with other affairs to assemble a host, and so it was not until 1300 that he returned. Though the English army was perhaps as large as that of 1298, nothing was achieved beyond the capture of Caerlaverock, a castle which was not of great importance. The campaign of 1301 was not a success either, and though the king wintered in Scotland, early in January he agreed to a truce, to last until November. In 1303, however, it looked as if he would finish the job. At the head of another great host he swept north as far as Kinloss, beyond Elgin; and at the beginning of winter he took up his quarters at Dunfermline. John Comyn, the sole remaining guardian (Bruce had made his peace with Edward in 1302), could not field an army against him, and on 9 February 1304 he surrendered at Strathord in Perthshire. In March Edward was able to hold a parliament at St Andrews, to which virtually all

the prominent men of Scotland came as his lieges.[8] Scotland
seemed once more, as in 1296, to have bowed beneath the
English yoke.

In the peace that he now gave them, Edward treated the
defeated leaders of the Scots leniently. Lands which they had
forfeited for rebellion were to be redeemed, at the cost usually
of two or three years' value. The ancient customs and liberties of
the kingdom were guaranteed. From the peace, only the garrison
of Stirling (which held out till May) and William Wallace were
excluded. Wallace was in fact taken in the next year: he was sent
to London where he was tried by a special commission and
executed as a war criminal and a traitor. If Edward's claim that
he was the rightful overlord of Scotland was just, a traitor is
what Wallace technically was; but in the eyes of his countrymen
he has always, and deservedly, been regarded as a martyr in their
cause.

The pacification of 1304 was followed up, in September 1305,
by a long ordinance which set out the manner of the future
government of Scotland. It was approved by the English parliament, and was framed with the advice and help of ten Scottish
representatives, who had been chosen for this purpose by the
community of Scotland. A lieutenant was appointed, to govern
the land on behalf of the English king; he was to be aided by a
council mainly composed of Scotsmen and would preside over
the Scottish parliaments. Four pairs of justices were assigned to
four administrative districts: Lothian, Galloway, the land
between the Forth and the Mounth, and the land north of that.
Most of the sheriffs appointed in the ordinance to administer the
counties were Scots; only the key castles were left in the hands of
Englishmen.[9] A wealth of experience of the problems of government in strange lands, culled in Ireland and Wales, lay behind the
provisions of this impressive and conciliatory document, which,
while safeguarding the ultimate lordship of the English king,
guaranteed to Scotsmen the major share in the administration of
their country. But though it was designed as a lasting settlement,
and does credit to its architects, it had no significance in the
history of Scotland, or of England for that matter. It was a dead
letter within a few months of its publication, long before its
terms had come to mean anything in practice.

[8] See Barrow, *Robert Bruce*, p. 183; and H. G. Richardson and G. O.
Sayles, 'Scottish parliaments of Edward I', *S.H.R.* 25 (1927–8), p. 311.
  [9] For the ordinance see Stones, *Anglo-Scottish Relations*, pp. 120ff.

On 10 February, in 1306, Robert Bruce met John Comyn of Badenoch in the church of Dumfries, and slew him there. The immediate motive for the killing is not clear, but it seems almost certain that Bruce had gone to the church with plans for a revolt in his mind. On 25 March he was crowned at Scone, in the presence of bishops Wishart of Glasgow and Lamberton of St Andrews, and of the earls of Atholl, Lennox and Menteith. A new chapter had opened in the history of Scotland.

The fury of the king of England knew no bounds when he heard that the work that he thought was done must be begun anew for a second time. On 5 April he appointed Aymer de Valence his personal lieutenant in Scotland, and gave him orders to hang and burn. When in June Valence defeated Bruce at Methven, the prisoners that he took received short shrift. David Earl of Atholl and Simon Fraser were sent to London and there executed as traitors; Christopher Seton was executed at Dumfries. Bishops Wishart and Lamberton, who failed to make their escape from the country, were sent to England and imprisoned there. As many of Bruce's family as the English could find were rounded up; three of his brothers were executed and his sisters imprisoned. This terrible ferocity served little purpose, however. For a few months after Methven Bruce had to wander as a fugitive, but in the spring of 1307 he was back in the field, and was strong enough to defeat Valence at Loudon Hill in May. Edward, irascible, old, and at last weakening physically, was by this time on his way north, but he was without an army comparable to the hosts of 1300 or 1303. On 7 July, after he had been carried with his soldiers for a few miles beyond Carlisle in a litter, he died. With him died the determination that had sustained the continuous English offensive in Scotland: the new chapter in Anglo-Scottish history had begun in earnest.

'I hear that Bruce never had the good will of his own followers or of the people generally so much with him as now. It appears that God is with him, for he has destroyed King Edward's power both among the English and the Scots.'[10] These words were written by a Scottish nobleman a few days after Loudon Hill; they may not have been quite true then, but they soon would be. Edward II had no option, when his father died at Burgh-on-Sands, but to turn his face south: he had a government to take over, a formal coronation to arrange, and other business of his own too. The trouble was that he did not return, as his father

[10] Quoted by Barrow, *Robert Bruce*, p. 245, who conjectures that the writer was Alexander Abernethy.

would certainly have done. Within a year of his accession, he was deeply embroiled in domestic confrontation with his leading magnates. So Bruce was able, in 1308, to consolidate himself against his Scottish rivals, the followers of the Comyns and of Balliol. In 1309 he held his first parliament at St Andrews, and reopened relations with Philip of France. By 1311 he was able to lead raids across the English border, and in 1312 he surprised Durham and ravaged Hexham. No effective effort was made to oppose him. In the autumn of 1310 Edward did, it is true, lead an army into Scotland, but his campaign was devoid of achievement, and it was suspected that his chief motive in going north had been to make things difficult for the commission of magnates who had been appointed in the spring to reform the realm and the royal household—the 'Ordainers'. One by one the great castles which had been in English hands since 1304 or earlier fell to the Scots. In 1313 and the early months of 1314 Perth, Edinburgh and Roxburgh were all taken.

It was in order to relieve the last major English stronghold in Scotland, Stirling, that Edward II at last put himself at the head of a royal host to campaign in earnest, six years too late. On 24 June, at Bannockburn on the way to Stirling, Robert King of Scots met this English army and inflicted on it a crushing defeat. The Earl of Gloucester was killed, and after the battle the Constable, Humphrey Bohun of Hereford, was taken prisoner, along with the Earl of Angus, Thomas Lord Berkeley, and many others of less note. Edward II saved himself by flight. The battle did not end the war, which was to last through the rest of Edward's reign,[11] but it finally dashed any remaining hopes that the English might shake Bruce's hold on Scotland. After twenty years of fighting, they were thus further than ever from establishing that lordship in Scotland which Edward I had originally sought. This failure was a heavy blow to English pride and to the reputation of the Plantagenet monarchy. Bannockburn capped all: no English host had been so humiliated by a foreign enemy since time out of mind.

Because the war had gone on so long, the consequences of Bannockburn were not merely in the military sphere. The full significance of the reverse can only be understood when it is viewed also in the context of the strains to which the long war had exposed the English community. It is to this aspect of events that we must now turn.

[11] From 1323 there was a truce, but no formal peace until after Edward II's deposition.

England was at war, more or less without a break, from 1294 to 1314 (and beyond, indeed). The armies which were set on foot in the period were very large: the force which invaded Scotland in 1298 numbered probably nearly 30,000 men, and the hosts of 1300, 1303 and 1314 were, if smaller, of comparable size. Between 1294 and 1297 Edward I also had to raise and pay large forces for service in Gascony, and in 1297 he sought to gather yet another army for the Flanders campaign. At the same time, his attempts to build up a system of continental alliances against Philip IV placed a heavy additional burden on his resources.[12] He had besides to organize substantial fleets in connexion with both the Scottish and the Gascon wars (his reign saw the first official appointment of an 'Admiral of the Sea of the King of England'). These very considerable efforts posed collectively a threefold problem: of recruitment, of finance, and of war administration.[13]

The department which had to bear the brunt of the exceptional administrative problems posed by the wars was the royal household, and in particular the wardrobe. The king took his privy seal (which was kept in the wardrobe) with him wherever he went, and its controller served as his military and diplomatic secretary. The household clerks played an important role on diplomatic embassies (though the negotiations over Gascony became so complicated that a special officer had to be appointed to look after its documentation, called the Keeper of the Processes).[14] Whenever the king assembled a host, a large proportion of the forces that he raised were taken onto the payroll of the household, and the wardrobe staff had to act in effect as paymasters to the forces. Large sums were allocated to the wardrobe's use at the exchequer, but there was never enough to meet all its commitments, and the keeper, John Droxford, had to supplement his ad-

[12] See B. D. Lyon, *From Fief to Indenture* (Cambridge, Mass., 1957), pp. 211-12.

[13] For what follows, and throughout the rest of this chapter, I am deeply indebted to Mr M. C. Prestwich. His thesis on *Edward I's Wars and Their Financing 1294-1307* (Oxford D.Phil. thesis, 1968) is a work which has for me illumined the whole period. The findings of the thesis will be discussed in his forthcoming book, *War, Politics and Finance under Edward I* (London, in press). I am also in Mr Prestwich's debt for much invaluable advice and guidance, both on the administrative history and on political problems of the period.

[14] See G. P. Cuttino, *English Diplomatic Administration 1259-1339* (Oxford, 1940).

vances with loans – which he had to negotiate himself, as there
was no one else to do it. The creditors were paid with deben-
tures on the wardrobe, cashable at the exchequer (captains of
soldiers were often also paid with these, when ready cash was not
to hand). The wardrobe also had large responsibilities for victualling the army and castle garrisons. The strains of war thus swelled
the king's itinerant household of normal times into a ministry of
war, with national responsibilities for the duration of the emergency. Droxford and his clerks were overworked men, and it is
not surprising that, in spite of their impressive ability in administration, by the end of Edward I's reign their accounts were
getting out of hand. Attempts were still being made to settle
them at the exchequer (to which the Wardrobe had to account)
in the early years of Edward III's reign.[15]

The recruitment of Edward I's armies posed legal and constitutional problems as well as administrative ones. The infantry
was raised by commissions of array (in effect by impressment),
which operated in each county. This system of compulsory
service could be justified in terms of the ancient obligation on all
able bodied men to serve at need in 'defence of the realm'; but it
was not clear just how far this obligation could be made to
extend. The foot soldiers were usually paid, in fact, from the
point when they left their counties, which gives some hint as to
where, strictly, their absolute obligation was thought to end.[16]
Edward also raised substantial forces of paid infantry in Wales
and Ireland. The key arm, however, was the cavalry: it was the
mounted knights who won the day at Falkirk and Methven and
who lost it at Stirling Bridge and Bannockburn. They were also a
very expensive force, requiring costly armour and a warhorse
(the king normally paid for horses lost on campaign). They were
recruited by a number of means, which require a little scrutiny.

The feudal obligation on tenants in chief to serve the king in
war with a following of knights did not provide an adequate
cavalry force in the days of Edward I, if it ever had done. This
system of recruitment was obsolete, and the thirteenth century
writs of watch and ward imposed the obligation to keep the arms
of a knight ready for service not on those who held a knight's fee,
but on those who held land to a certain annual value, £100, or

[15] On the wardrobe and its work in war time see Tout, *Chapters* vol. 2,
especially pp. 125–6, 131ff.
[16] For detailed discussion of military obligations and their legal and
constitutional significance, see M. R. Powicke, *Military Obligation in
Medieval England* (Oxford, 1962).

£50, or £40 a year[17] (£40 was the usual figure; the demand of 1297 that twenty librate landholders should serve as cavalrymen probably asked them to do more than they could afford). When Edward assembled his great hosts, a large number of these men, from the counties, were always taken into the pay of the household. This corps could be supplemented by further paid forces raised on the basis of a contract made between the king and a captain, who would subcontract with other knights to form a troop on a voluntary basis. The greater barons normally served the king in person (as was their traditional feudal duty), and they brought with them to his service their retinues, knights of their own households and other men recruited for the occasion. These retinues were usually considerably larger than the followings which feudal custom obliged the barons to bring, and the barons themselves usually served without pay, in Scotland at least. This was a considerable subvention for the king's forces, and suggests too that military service was not unpopular among the upper classes in Edward I's time. Unpaid service, however, could never be more than a subvention, whether it was voluntary or compulsory. The main body of the cavalry, those knights serving with the household and under contract, all had to be paid, as did the infantry also, and the expense was very high.

Pay apart, the king had to spend money on victuals, ships, siege engines, and on the replacement of mounts for his knights. Between 1294 and 1298 Edward spent something of the order of £730,000 on the war.[18] This was the period of greatest strain, and Gascony proved easily the most expensive theatre of war. But expenditure remained high afterwards, though it is not so easy to calculate, because of the confusion of the accounts. Finance remained throughout the knottiest of the problems that war posed for the first two Edwards.

The ordinary revenue of the crown (from demesne lands, the profits of justice, the forest, and so on) was in Edward I's time about £19,000 per annum. The customs, before 1294, were bringing in between £10,000 and £12,000 annually. These revenues combined were clearly quite inadequate to meet the king's needs in a period of military emergency, and he had perforce in consequence to demand taxes from his people. In each year from 1294 to 1297 the king obtained lay subsidies from

[17] See further M. R. Powicke, 'Distraint of knighthood and military obligation under Henry III', *Speculum* 25 (1950), pp. 457–70.

[18] This figure is based on Prestwich's calculations, in his thesis, *Edward I's Wars*, pp. 275–7.

his subjects with their assent, and he did so again in 1301 and 1306. These usually raised between £30,000 and £40,000 (though the tenth and sixth of 1294 raised much more): perhaps nearly enough, that is to say, to pay for one host for a year in Scotland. In the same years 1294–7 Edward also obtained substantial grants from the clergy, but there was resistance to these levies, and the tenth granted by the clergy in 1297 was the last tax to which they gave assent in the reign.[19] Edward raised more cash through extra levies on exports, over and above the customs. In the period of the *maltolte* on wool, again 1294 to 1297, the extra levy just about trebled the ordinary yield of the customs. The *maltolte* was abolished in 1297, but in 1303 Edward obtained the agreement of the alien merchants to an extra levy on their exports (half as much again on the customs) in return for the promise in his *Carta Mercatoria* of royal protection, freedom of movement in the kingdom, and immunity from the royal right of *prise*.[20] This added some £5000 to the royal revenue annually, and Edward would have liked to extend the levy to the exports of native merchants also, but they would not hear of it. It was only a very inadequate substitute for the *maltolte*.

All these sources of revenue, over and above the customs and the issues of the demesne, depended in some degree on assent for their levy. Even the *maltolte* had had this in the first instance (though it was only under pressure, when threatened with the seizure of their wool, that the merchants had agreed to it). Edward I found other means of raising money which did not need assent at all from those who had to pay. Boniface VIII in 1301 and Clement V later allowed him to keep the greater part of the tenths which they imposed, for three and seven years respectively, on the spiritual revenues of the English clergy.[21] The king also made use of his prerogative to raise revenue. In 1304, for example, he imposed a tallage on the royal boroughs and the estates of his

[19] For further discussion of these revenues see Prestwich, *Edward I's Wars*; J. H. Ramsay, *A History of the Revenues of the Kings of England* (Oxford, 1925); J. F. Willard, 'The taxes upon moveables of the reign of Edward I', *E.H.R.* 28 (1913), pp. 517–21; and M. Mills, 'Exchequer agenda and estimates of revenue: Easter term 1284', *E.H.R.* 40 (1925), pp. 229f. (this last gives a lower figure for the customs, which seem to have risen in value by the 1290s).

[20] See N. S. B. Gras, *The Early English Customs System* (Cambridge, Mass., 1918), pp. 259–64.

[21] See W. E. Lunt, *Financial Relations of the Papacy with England* vol. 1 (Cambridge, Mass., 1937), pp. 366ff., 382ff.

demesne. The most important of his prerogative rights, from a fiscal point of view, was his right to *prise* or 'purveyance', to purchase compulsorily supplies for his household. This was not a very onerous burden on the subject in ordinary times, but when in war the king's household in arms expanded to comprise half and more of his host, it could become in effect a very important and burdensome tax. The officers of the household in these circumstances could not cope with the whole task of raising purveyance: the national administration had to help them. Writs were addressed to groups of counties, through their sheriffs, to supply goods to a quota fixed arbitrarily in advance. The price was also fixed in advance and payment was often made not in cash, but in tallies cashable at the exchequer. Purveyance was the secret of the success of the king and his household agents in organizing the supply of his great armies. It bore very hardly on the people, however, and though some effort was made late in the reign to spread the burden equitably, so that the poor should not be stripped of all they had to live on, it is not clear that this had much effect. Certainly it did not cool the general resentment at the king's extension of his ancient right to supply for his household into what amounted to a general tax.[22]

With all the resources at his disposal, Edward I still never had enough to meet current expenses on his wars. In consequence he often had to borrow, and he raised some very substantial loans from the merchants of Florence and of south-western France, especially those of Bordeaux and Cahors. The Ricardi of Florence virtually bankrupted themselves in his service. Later the Frescobaldi became his chief agents, and virtually the whole of the customs revenue was pledged toward the repayment of their loans by the end of the reign.[23] This meant that the exchequer saw little of this important revenue, for the Frescobaldi collected it themselves directly, at the ports. By this time the crown was also falling a long way behind on the repayment of other debts, to native lenders, to soldiers for their wages, to men whose goods had been compulsorily purchased (or purveyed) for the

[22] This discussion of purveyance owes much to Prestwich, *Edward I's Wars*, pp. 201–5, who examines the subject very thoroughly. See also J. G. Edwards, 'The baronial grievances of 1297', *E.H.R.* 58 (1943), p. 159.

[23] On Edward's loans see W. E. Rhodes, 'The Italian bankers and their loans to Edward I and Edward II', *Historical Essays by Members of Owen's College* (Manchester, 1902), pp. 137–68; and Prestwich, *Edward I's Wars*, pp. 379–405.

forces. This indebtedness may seem surprising, when we recall that the end of hostilities in the Gascon war and the breakdown of Edward's system of continental alliances had greatly reduced expenditure after 1297. Revenue, however, dropped even further than expenditure. Edward I obtained only two lay subsidies after 1297; and he also had to abandon the *maltolte*, which had brought in far more than the new custom granted with the *Carta Mercatoria* ever did. Above all, the king was constricted in all his fiscal expedients in his later years by his ardent desire never again to face an opposition as determined as that which his earlier measures had aroused in 1297.

Edward I never found more than *ad hoc* means of getting round the fiscal and administrative problems which his wars posed. Discontent, in consequence, was never allayed, and when Edward II, who had none of his father's talents, ultimately succeeded, he was faced with a situation with which he was not able to cope.

The troubles really began in 1297. In that year there was opposition to taxation (and to other royal demands too) from both the laity and the clergy. With the latter's special problems we shall deal elsewhere;[24] in any case, as regards the clergy Edward partly got round his difficulties by means of the share that he obtained in taxation imposed by the popes after 1301. The secular opposition was much more serious, and brought the country to the brink of civil war. It was led, as we have seen, by the Constable and the Marshal, the Earls of Hereford (Humphrey de Bohun) and of Norfolk (Roger Bigod).

1297 was the year when the strains that the wars imposed reached their peak. The country had been taxed heavily each year since 1294; the enormously expensive campaign of 1296 in Scotland was just completed and now the king was planning to send one army to Gascony, and to lead another himself to Flanders to cooperate with his continental allies. To make up the requisite forces, all who held twenty librates of land and upwards were summoned to do the king service overseas. The first sign of trouble came at the spring parliament at Salisbury, when Bigod flatly refused to serve in Gascony, unless he was in the personal company of the king. Before they next came to the king, he and Bohun had held a great meeting with knights of their followings in the forest of Wyre on the Welsh march. In London in July they refused to muster the host for Flanders, whose numbers

[24] See Chapter 9.

were in any case pitiably below the expectation of the king when he sent out his summonses. About this time the king's opponents summarized their grievances formally in a celebrated document, the *Monstraunces*, which was drawn up not in the name of the two leading earls only, but of the whole community of the land.[25] Its opening protest was against the summons to those who held twenty librates or more of land to serve in Flanders. This summons had no customary precedent, and there was no promise that the service would be paid; besides, twenty librates of land was not enough to support a knight. It probably did more than anything else to solidify popular feeling on the side of the earls. The *Monstraunces* also protested against the burden of taxation, tallages, aids, and *prises* as a result of which 'many have no sustenance and cannot till the land'; and especially against the *maltolte* on wool, which struck at the chief source of personal wealth in the land. Magna Carta and the Charter of the Forest had been infringed, the *Monstraunces* claimed, and the ancient liberties of the subject 'arbitrarily put aside'. This long and varied list of grievances makes it clear that the earls were justified in claiming that the matters of which they complained affected not just themselves, but the whole community. The movement that they headed was broadly based: this was what made it both important and dangerous.

By the time that the king sailed for Flanders the earls had added another grievance to their list, the order for the levy of an eighth, which had been granted to the king 'in his chamber' by the loyal barons and household men who had assembled for service in Flanders. On 22 August the earls appeared in the exchequer and refused to pay the tax. Civil war seemed imminent, but in September, before things had come to that pass, the news of Wallace's victory at Stirling Bridge was known, and the government, in the king's absence, gave way. The charters were confirmed; the *maltolte* was abolished; and a promise was made on the king's behalf that he would never, in future, take any *maltolte*, or any unaccustomed aids, *mises*, or *prises* in his kingdom without the common assent of the whole kingdom. These undertakings, set out in the document known as the *Confirmatio Cartarum*, met the main points of the opposition. It did not, it is true, go anything like as far as the document called the *De Tallagio non Concedendo*, which seems to be a final draft of what the opposition hoped that the government would concede. This document is much more specific in its restriction of purveyance

[25] The text is given by Edwards, 'The baronial grievances', pp. 170–1.

than the *Confirmatio*, and makes specific reference to the question of the service of twenty librate landholders. Constitutionally, the concessions of the *Confirmatio* were nevertheless very important. The clauses concerning taxation amounted to a formal agreement that the king would only levy extraordinary taxes with the consent of a body representing the community and summoned for that purpose (in effect, if not in name yet, a parliament). Or perhaps it would be more correct to say that this should have been the effect, if Edward had stuck to the promises made in the *Confirmatio* on his behalf, and which he explicitly confirmed himself on his return from Flanders in March 1298.[26]

In 1298 Edward made some further concessions. He ordered a perambulation of the forests, to re-establish their ancient boundaries, and an inquiry into abuses of purveyance. But he had always been determined to be as little trammelled in his prerogative as he might be, and he soon showed that he did not mean to carry conciliation further than was convenient. When he confirmed the Forest Charter in 1299 the first five articles, which were crucial as regards boundaries, were omitted. The war in Scotland continued, and he was soon taking *prises* again on the old scale, without assent. The new customs levy of the *Carta Mercatoria* had the assent of the alien merchants, but not of the community of the realm, as it should have done if the *Confirmatio* had been observed properly. Because of the king's shifty attitude, thus evidenced, opposition was not allayed by the concessions of 1297 and 1298. It was never so fierce again, but strain continued to dog the relations of the king with his subjects over the ensuing years.

The years 1299 to 1301 were the period of greatest difficulty. Bigod protested sharply about the king's evasiveness in the matter of the Forest Charter in the spring parliament of 1299. In 1300 the charters had once more to be solemnly confirmed in parliament, and a number of further articles – the *Articuli super Cartas* – were established at the community's request, though with the exception to all its twenty clauses 'saving the right and prerogative of the crown'. In each county three knights were to be

---

[26] The fullest discussions of the crisis of 1297 are those of Edwards, 'The baronial grievances', pp. 147ff., 273ff.; and of H. Rothwell, 'The confirmation of the charters and baronial grievances in 1297', *E.H.R.* 60 (1945), pp. 16ff., 177ff., 300ff. The special problems raised by the *De Tallagio* are discussed by Edwards, pp. 273ff., and by Rothwell, pp. 300ff.

appointed to hear and deal summarily with allegations of infringement of the charters. *Prises* were to be taken in future only by the customarily authorized purveyors and for the use of the king's *personal* household. Writs under the privy seal were not to be used to initiate cases at common law, and the Court of the Household (the Marshalsea) must not try common law cases of debt or freehold, but only trespasses committed within the verge of the household. Each county should elect its own sheriff. The *Articuli* form an impressive document, and demonstrate the ability of the opposition to draft a statute dealing constructively not only with major fiscal grievances, but also with details of the everyday administration of the land.[27]

A year later, at the Lincoln parliament of 1301, the opposition was still alert and active. A long bill was presented by Henry of Keighley, knight of the shire for Lancashire, in the name of the prelates and magnates. Its clauses returned to the attack on the questions of purveyance, of the keeping of the charters, and the perambulation of the forest; and the lords made the grant of a fifteenth conditional on the perambulation being finished by Michaelmas and on the acceptance of the boundaries it established.[28] The king would not assent to a demand that the prelates should not consent to taxation of the clergy without the pope's leave. This was a significant demand, suggesting that Archbishop Winchelsey had by this time associated himself with the earls in the leadership of the opposition to the crown. Edward certainly later regarded him as his most important opponent; and there is a story that in 1302 there was even a plan to put him at the head of a council which would be imposed on the king.[29]

In fact, after 1301, the opposition to Edward I seems to have slackened. It had won its point for the moment on the question of the forest, and Edward had the full support of his barons at the Lincoln parliament in his rejection of Pope Boniface's claim that Scotland was subject to the Holy See. The magnates had never opposed the war in Scotland, and in 1303 and 1304 their attention and energy, like Edward's, were concentrated on the final conquest of that kingdom. The remainder of the reign was comparatively untroubled domestically, and in 1305 Edward obtained from the new pope, Clement V, a release from all the

[27] For text see *Statutes of the Realm* vol. I, pp. 136–41.

[28] *P.W.* vol. I, p. 104.

[29] See Prestwich, *Edward I's Wars*, p. 58. This story, from an MS chronicle, has not been noted by any previous historian.

undertakings which, under the stress of circumstances, he had made in 1297 and afterwards, except for his obligation to observe the charters (which were part of the ancient law of the land, established long before the recent troubles). His influence with Clement also secured the summons of Archbishop Winchelsey to Rome, to answer charges which the king had preferred against him. Edward seized the temporalities of Canterbury when he went, but, significantly, he did not make much use of the papal absolution from his oaths, except to annul the disafforestations of 1301. Edward, armed as he was with the pope's bull, knew that he must still move warily; the slackening of opposition did not mean that discontent was dead. The old grievances flared up again as soon as Edward himself passed from the world.

There was no real break in the history of the English king's domestic difficulties with his subjects at the accession of Edward II. Edward I bequeathed to his son a massive confusion in his accounts, a heavy burden of debt, and the war with Scotland. He bequeathed to him also a still more dangerous legacy, of widespread dissatisfaction with the manner of royal government. Bohun and Bigod were both dead before 1307, but others who had been prominent in opposition to the old king outlived him, notably Winchelsey, who was then still abroad in virtual exile. Edward II had no desire to keep alive private feuds of the past, and the archbishop was soon back in England at his invitation, but he and his like were as determined as they had ever been to curb what they regarded as misgovernment. In January 1308 a group of powerful men, who were on embassy to France in connexion with the new king's marriage and whose leader seems to have been Anthony Bek, Bishop of Durham, took an oath to stand together to 'redress and amend the oppressions which have been done, and still are being done from day to day, to the king's people'.[30] Bek had not long before seen his palatinate franchise, which had been seized into the king's hand at the orders of Edward I, restored by Edward II. He was to remain, until his death in 1311, on notably better terms with the young king than most of the magnates. What he and his companions at Boulogne had in mind were clearly the long standing grievances generated in the last reign, not the new distrust of royal capacity that was to build up rapidly in the course of 1308.

The continuity between the troubles of Edward I and Edward

[30] See N. Denholm Young, *History and Heraldry* (Oxford, 1965), p. 130.

II is not always adequately stressed, but the evidences of it are clear enough. When Edward II was crowned, a new clause was added to the coronation oath, that the king should observe 'the just laws and customs that the community of the realm shall have chosen'. Though there has been much debate as to its meaning, the object of this addition seems clearly to have been to make sure that the new king should not, as his father had done, go back on enactments made with the assent of the community.[31] In July 1309, at Stamford, Edward II was forced to reissue the main clauses of the *Articuli* of 1300 (in particular that concerning purveyance) in a statute. In the next year, when opposition was mounting to a new climax and the magnates appeared armed in parliament, the king was forced to agree to the appointment of twenty-one 'Ordainers', with powers to draw up ordinances for the reform of the kingdom and the household. Their *Ordinances* are the most important constitutional document that emerged from the troubles of the years before Bannockburn. They are also the most telling testimony that the unrest of the early years of Edward II had its roots in the troubles that Edward's father had experienced in the last ten years of his reign.

The theme of the observance of the charters, so strongly stressed in the earlier period, runs right through the *Ordinances*, which form a long document with forty odd clauses.[32] The question of purveyance, the bone of contention that loomed so large in the *Monstraunces*, the *Confirmatio* and the *Articuli*, was taken up again, and dealt with sternly: those who took *prises* which were not lawful (i.e. were not for the king's own household) were now to be treated as common thieves. The *Carta Mercatoria* of Edward I was quashed on the accurate ground that it had not received the assent of the baronage (as the *Confirmatio* had ruled such levies should). The hold of the Frescobaldi on the customs, which dated from well back into

[31] On the coronation oath, and the discussion that surrounds it, see Chapter 4.

[32] For text see *Statutes of the Realm* vol. I, pp. 157ff. The *Ordinances* are discussed in detail by T. F. Tout, *The Place of Edward II in English History* (Manchester, 1914), and by J. Conway Davies, *The Baronial Opposition to Edward II* (Cambridge, 1918). Both writers, especially Davies, overstress magnate opposition to the administrative activities of the household; see B. Wilkinson, 'The ordinances of 1311' in his *Studies in the Constitutional History of the Thirteenth and Fourteenth Centuries* (Manchester, 1937), pp. 227–46. On more general points see M. McKisack, *The Fourteenth Century* (Oxford, 1959), ch. I.

Edward I's reign, was broken, and their proceeds rerouted to the exchequer. And though Edward II's campaign in the north in late 1310 was no doubt what the Ordainers had most prominently in mind, it is hard to believe that there was no connexion between the striking clause which forbade the king to go to war or to leave the land without the assent of his barons, and Edward I's departure for Flanders in 1297, which the earls who then opposed him had roundly and eloquently condemned in the last paragraph of their *Monstraunces*.[33]

The insistence in the *Ordinances* on annual parliaments has sometimes been taken as one sign of a marked change of attitude since the days of Edward I. It is not clear that this view is justified. Parliaments had in fact been summoned more or less annually, and sometimes more often, since early in the 1290s. The insistence on regular parliaments seems not to reflect a grievance at their irregularity so much as a desire to have clear rules about the meetings of an assembly whose agency seemed necessary to implement a number of important reforms. The *Ordinances* laid down that the chief officers of state should be chosen with the assent of the barons in parliament (in this connexion it should be remembered that at the parliament of Lincoln in 1301 there had been an attempt to force Edward I to dismiss his treasurer, Walter Langton, which had not succeeded). It was in parliament that a commission (of one bishop, two earls and two barons) was to hear complaints against the king's ministers if they contravened the *Ordinances* (which seems to echo the demand of 1300, that the king should punish ministers whose actions contravened the charters, which Edward I refused to consider). Parliament, it should be added here, does not seem in the minds of the Ordainers to have in any sense necessarily included representatives of the commons. This does not mean that their attitude was a narrow, baronially exclusive one. It reminds us rather that what the Ordainers valued chiefly about parliament was its authority as a court which could set right what had been done ill, and could exercise a general supervision over the king's government. This was a natural attitude for men who could remember how, in the previous reign, efforts to limit administrative abuse and to restrain royal officials had been

[33] This connexion is suggested by Prestwich, *Edward I's Wars*, p. 432. His final chapter analyses the links between the political crises of 1297–1301 and the *Ordinances* in a very illuminating manner, and I am much in debt to his suggestions.

repeatedly thwarted by the unwillingness of the cunning and unscrupulous old king to cooperate.[34]

There was, of course, much in the *Ordinances* which had nothing at all to do with events of Edward I's reign. This, however, is not so much a sign of discontinuity between the two periods, as a reflection of the differences of character between the two Edwards, which inevitably in an age of personal government affected their relations with their magnates. Edward I, in his later years, had a long and highly successful career of kingship behind him. He was a great warrior, who had served with distinction in the Holy Land, had conquered Wales and very nearly conquered Scotland. He was also a famous patron of the chivalrous sports and ceremonies which men of the magnate class enjoyed, a veteran of the tournament, an enthusiast for the cult of King Arthur who had been host to jousts of the Round Table at which knights from all over Europe had been present. He had outlived most of the companions of his earlier years, and the majority of the barons who attended his court and his parliaments were younger than he. Some of their fathers had learned by bitter experience how hard he could be when asserting his own right against others, and how terrible his anger was. To the young men who knew him in his late years he must have appeared both venerable and frightening. It is not surprising therefore that at the end of his reign resistance to his will slackened: it was plain common sense to postpone complaint until the formidable old king was dead, as he was soon bound to be.

The younger magnates, many of whom had been brought up with Edward II, must have known that he was of a very different calibre. Strong and tall, he was nevertheless no soldier, and did not care for such martial exercises as the tourney. He enjoyed swimming, and country life, and the company of minstrels, but these were not preferences to earn him respect. He also had two vices from which his father did not suffer: extravagance, and inordinate affection for his favourites. They seem indeed to have supplied the only really firm direction to his weak will. He was not wise in his choice of intimates, particularly in the case of his first and most famous favourite, the handsome Gascon knight Piers Gaveston, with whom his relations were probably homosexual. Gaveston was anathema to the English magnates, who regarded him as an upstart; he retaliated by inventing scurrilous nicknames for them. To make things worse, he could beat them at the tourney. Worst of all was the way in which the grants of lands

[34] On parliament see further Chapter 4.

and offices, which his standing in the king's favour won for him,
disrupted the normal flow of patronage between the monarchy
and the magnates. But no one feared either him or his master, as
they had feared Edward I, and it was this that made the great
difference between the political circumstances of the two reigns,
not a change in the constitutional ideas of the crown's opponents.

The *Ordinances* had a great deal to say, both about Gaveston and
about Edward II's over-lavish expenditure. The two subjects
were related in the eyes of the Ordainers. As soon as he came to
the throne Edward recalled Gaveston from the exile to which his
father had condemned him, and made him Earl of Cornwall. In
the coronation procession the new earl bore the sword of St
Edward before the king, 'so decked out that he more resembled
the God Mars than an ordinary mortal'. The lavish rewards
that were showered on the favourite seemed to the other magnates
unwarrantable, at a time when the crown was heavily in debt,
when creditors were pressing for repayment of loans overdue
years earlier, and when the whole land was complaining bitterly
about arbitrary *prises* taken for the use of the king's household
and soldiers, which were too often never paid for. The magnates
besides could not but resent Gaveston's personal hold over the
king. Without his private advice and assent nothing was done and
nothing was granted. It was on the double charge, that he had
impoverished the crown and alienated the king from his magnates, that the earls, led by Henry of Lincoln, demanded in the
spring parliament of 1308 that he be banished anew.

In 1308 Edward bowed to necessity, and Gaveston left for the
lieutenancy of Ireland. But he was no sooner gone than the king
began to work for his recall, mollifying key opponents with
grants of office and honour, and when he came back he was no
less unbearable than he had been before. So, when the Ordainers
were appointed to draw up reforms in 1310, with Henry of
Lincoln prominent among them, the twin objectives of 1308, the
removal of Gaveston and the curtailing of royal expenditure,
retained high priority. As was to be expected, the *Ordinances*
contained a long and formidable indictment of the favourite,
who was said to have usurped royal power to himself, to have
forced the king to part with lands to the impoverishment of his
estate, and to have estranged the king's heart from his people.
He was sentenced to banishment as an 'enemy of the king and
the people' and forbidden to return. The *Ordinances* also

imposed stringent limits on royal expenditure. No grants of lands, rents, escheats, wardship or office were to be made henceforward, without the assent of the baronage. In order to make sure that household expenditure was kept under control, the Ordainers insisted that the appointments of the steward of the household, the keeper of the wardrobe and the keeper of the privy seal should be vetted in parliament by the barons, as well as the appointments of such officers of state as the chancellor, the treasurer and the judges. It is unimaginable that Edward I would have tolerated for an instant limits such as these on his freedom of action as a monarch. But Edward II did; indeed he offered to accept any ordinances 'howsoever this may redound to my private disadvantage, as long as you shall stop persecuting my brother Piers, and allow him to have the Earldom of Cornwall'.[35] This is a measure of the differences between him and his father, and sufficient commentary on what differentiated opposition to the one and to the other.

Edward I in 1301, when he was faced with uncompromising opposition at Lincoln, conceded more than he wished to, but succeeded in uniting his barons in protest against the pope's demand that he should abandon the Scottish war. He then led them north against the enemy. Edward II could probably have done the same in 1311, but he would not abandon Gaveston. He went north and took the great seal with him, but this was so as not to be divided from his favourite, who had never left the country, and so as to rescind the *Ordinances* from a safe distance. The barons united, but against the king, not the Scots. On 19 May 1312, Gaveston surrendered to the earls of Pembroke and Warenne, on the promise that his life would be safe. He was being taken south by Pembroke, when he was taken from Pembroke at Deddington in Oxfordshire by the Earl of Warwick, who like Pembroke had been an Ordainer. Nine days later he was put to death, in the presence of Lancaster, another Ordainer, in direct breech of the promise of surety that Warenne and Pembroke had made. Pembroke felt that his word of honour had been impugned and never forgave Lancaster and Warwick. Nor did King Edward.

In consequence of Gaveston's death an undying feud was born between Edward and his cousin, Thomas of Lancaster, who since the death in 1311 of his father-in-law Henry of Lincoln, had controlled no less than five earldoms – Lancaster, Leicester,

[35] *Vita Edwardi II*, ed. N. Denholm Young (London, 1957), pp. 17–18.

Lincoln, Derby and Salisbury – and so enjoyed almost viceregal wealth and influence. Lancaster and Warwick claimed that, in putting Gaveston to death, they had merely been enforcing the *Ordinances*. Not all their colleagues, however, saw it that way, and their action broke the unity of the magnates. Aymer de Valence of Pembroke, who had always been close to the court, rallied to the king, and so did Warenne and Gloucester. Humphrey de Bohun of Hereford stood uncertain between the two groups, between whom relations for a time completely broke down. In October 1313 the efforts of Gloucester and of the pope's representatives, Cardinal Arnold and the Bishop of Poitiers, effected a formal reconciliation, but there was no heart in it. The 'cold war' situation that Gaveston's death occasioned had not really ended when Edward in 1314 assembled his host to march against the Scots. Lancaster and Warwick both failed to join him, on the ground that he had not, as the *Ordinances* decreed, consulted with the barons before levying war and marching out of the kingdom.

When Edward was humiliatingly defeated at Bannockburn, his disaster became simply his opponents' opportunity. The king had no option but to accept the counsels of Lancaster, the man who had killed Gaveston, and to reinforce the *Ordinances* at his request. But Lancaster came to power, now, not as the leader of a united baronage, but only of a party among them which, though territorially powerful, was not numerically impressive. The divisions among the great, which the circumstances of Gaveston's death (or murder) had engendered, had hardened to a point where they could not be easily allayed. A new period was beginning in political history, in which the dominant theme was no longer the strains between the king and his greater subjects, but rivalries among the magnates themselves.

The quarter of a century from 1290 to 1314 was a crucial period in the political history of medieval England. Up to 1290, Edward I had ruled with unqualified success. Careful propaganda, to which the writs of summons to his great parliamentary assemblies are witness, had fostered a spirit of cooperation between crown and subject. This had enabled the king, in the earlier part of his reign, to take the initiative in reforming legislation and to control its direction. The great statutes of the years before 1290 cleared up a host of problems of land law and local government which had been fruitful causes of complaint among the king's subjects for three quarters of a century. In these circumstances the king

was able to insist confidently on his rights. The great statute of
Quo Warranto and the inquiries that preceded it firmly established
the principle that all franchises in the land were dependent on
the grant of the crown. The imprisonment of the earls of
Hereford and Gloucester in 1291, for levying unauthorized war
on the march, was a supreme demonstration of the king's power
over even the highest. The royal authority had never seemed so
clear of challenge as it did at that moment.

The strains of the long wars that followed called all this
achievement into question. After 1297 the crown lost its control
of the initiative in reform. The king's use of his prerogative
rights was challenged, and his subjects demonstrated, notably in
1297 and again in 1301, that they could force him to make
concessions by refusing financial supply. Accumulating debts
limited the king's freedom of action, and increased his dependence on the cooperation of his subjects at a time when it was
given less willingly than before. Order began to deteriorate, not
only in the royal accounts but physically and socially in the
counties. In 1305 Edward had to commission special judges of
trailbaston, with exceptional powers, to deal with rising disorder
at the local level; but their severity made them at least as unpopular as the abuses that they were supposed to put down.[36]
Heavy taxation, together with purveyance and the various other
methods by which Edward sought to avoid having to negotiate
with his subjects for assented taxes, were all bitterly resented.
As events showed when Edward I died, men were at the end
only waiting for him to be gone before making new efforts to
throw off their burdens.

Edward II's ineptitude, in particular his refusal to abandon
Gaveston, ensured that, from the monarchy's point of view, the
situation must deteriorate further. Dislike of Gaveston gave a
new sharp edge to the baronial sense of grievance, and united the
magnates in opposition. Edward II's failure, in his early years, to
prosecute the war in Scotland, though it was not altogether his
fault, also undermined confidence in royal leadership. The war
with Scotland had never been unpopular, with the magnates or
with the people more generally. Edward I had repeatedly proved
able to rally support to the crown by the call to arms, very
notably in 1298 and in 1301. In the eyes of the leading men of the
kingdom victory in the field could compensate for a good deal
of domestic tyranny. If the war could have been ended success-

[36] On these commissions see G. O. Sayles, *Select Cases in the Court of
King's Bench* vol. IV (Selden Soc., 1955), pp. liii–lvi.

fully, perhaps even Edward II might have found a way out of his trouble. But after Bannockburn it was clear that the kingdom could not be free either of the Scottish war, or of domestic tensions for a long time.

3

The reign of Edward II
and its aftermath

The period from 1314 to 1330 is a gloomy one in English history. Between 1314 and 1322 the threat of civil war was never remote. It broke out at last in 1322, but the military triumph of the king in that year solved nothing. By 1326 a powerful opposition had been reconstituted, and in 1327 the king was deposed. He had by then been humiliated in external wars with both the Scots and the French, as well as by domestic enemies. The years from 1327 to 1330 form a depressing epilogue to this story. The young Edward III was kept in tutelage by his mother and her paramour Roger Mortimer, who governed England with no more success than Edward II.

The history of the middle years of Edward II's reign, from 1314 to 1322, is confused and anarchic. For convenience it may be divided into three periods. The first runs from the aftermath of Bannockburn to the middle of 1316. After his great defeat at the hands of the Scots, Edward was in no position to resist the demands of his powerful domestic opponents, and in this period the influence of Earl Thomas of Lancaster was a decisive force in government. Partly on account of his own lethargy and incompetence, and partly because of misfortunes which it was beyond the earl's power to avoid, his influence was on the wane well before the end of 1316. By that time a new group of influential men was gathering at the king's court, who were opposed to the earl personally and to his policy of enforcing the *Ordinances* of 1311. The question during our second period, which extends from 1316 to 1320, was whether this hostility would degenerate into an open breach, or whether some *modus vivendi* could be established between the king's new friends at court and the king's greatest subject, Lancaster. Such a reconciliation was the object striven after by a group of moderate men, who included a number of bishops, the Earl of Pembroke, and perhaps the Earl of Hereford (though both these men had close associations with the court too). In 1320, the rapid rise to royal favour and influence of the two Despensers, father and son, upset the balance anew, and here our third period begins. The year 1321 saw a head-on confrontation between the king and the Despensers on the one hand, and a combination of Lancaster with the powerful barons of the Welsh march on the other. The defeat and subsequent execution of the king's chief opponents, including the earls of Lancaster and Hereford, at Boroughbridge in 1322, marks the end of this third period and a turning point in the reign.[1]

We must begin, then, in 1314, at the beginning of the first of these periods. 'After this (the battle of Bannockburn) the king on the advice of his friends left a garrison at Berwick, and retreated to York; and there he took counsel with the earl of Lancaster and the other magnates': so says the *Vita Edwardi II*.[2] The measures of this York parliament of September 1314 set the tone for the next two years. Lancaster had always stood for the enforcement of the *Ordinances* to the letter, and this was given first priority. There were besides some important changes among the officials. John Sandale became chancellor, Walter Norwich treasurer; Ingelard de Warley lost his place as keeper of the wardrobe and was replaced by William Melton; and over the next months nearly all the sheriffs were removed and replaced. The next parliament, which met at Westminster in January 1315, took up the work of the York parliament and pressed ahead further with the enforcement of the *Ordinances*. A perambulation of the forests was promised, and a practical beginning was made in the business of reducing the expense of the king's household; Langton and Despenser were at the same time removed from the king's council. Still more striking, the business of the resumption of grants made by the king since March 1310 (the date given by the *Ordinances*) was taken in hand, and lists of lands to be resumed were despatched to the escheators north and south of Trent. This

[1] The two standard works on Edward II's reign have for long been T. F. Tout, *The Place of Edward II in English History* (Manchester, 1914), and J. Conway Davies, *The Baronial Opposition to Edward II* (Cambridge, 1918). To these must now be added J. R. Maddicott, *Thomas of Lancaster 1307–22* (Oxford, 1970), an outstanding study, to which I am much indebted.

[2] *Vita Edwardi II*, ed. N. Denholm Young (London, 1957), p. 57.

was a delicate affair: as Roger Mortimer of Chirk pointed out, his lands 'had not been given him to do damage to the king, but for the service that he had done for him'.[3] Lancaster consistently attached great importance to this matter of resumption: Mortimer's remark is a useful reminder that the justification or otherwise of the *Ordinances* in the matter of resumption and of economy generally could appear questionable. Lancaster was rich: Mortimer was not in the same street as a territorial magnate, and it seemed to him unjust that he should lose rewards that he prized highly, and that had been given for genuine service.

The Lincoln parliament of 1316 did not carry things much further than its two predecessors had.[4] The most memorable event which it witnessed was the formal invitation to Lancaster to be the 'chief councillor' of the king. Lancaster in fact only agreed to be of the council on conditions: no matter was to be undertaken without the advice of the earls and prelates; any councillor who proffered advice which was not to the king's profit must be removed in the next parliament; and if his, Lancaster's, advice were not accepted, he reserved a right to withdraw from the council. What this last condition really meant was that the earl was to keep a freedom to dissociate himself from the government's actions if he did not approve of them, which was hardly a very responsible attitude for a chief councillor. He had not in fact had much to do with the day-to-day business of government over the last eighteen months. His influence had been a paramount one, but it was most often exercised from a distance. Decisions on important matters were constantly referred to him by letter, and he wrote back to the king and council with his comments from wherever he was staying on his estates. His new appointment did not change his practice. Persistent efforts to enforce the *Ordinances* suggest his continuing influence well into the summer of 1316, but he was not much at court after the spring parliament, and after April was no longer in active communication with the council. Lancaster's unwillingness to take a hand himself at the centre of affairs was one of the reasons why his dominance did not endure much longer after that.

There were other reasons too for his gradual displacement. A chief one was that, apart from formal efforts to implement the *Ordinances*, the period of his preeminence had singularly little to

[3] *R.P.* vol. I, p. 305.

[4] On this parliament see Conway Davies, *The Baronial Opposition*, pp. 408ff.

show in the way of achievement. This was by no means altogether Lancaster's fault, or anybody's; these were years of natural disaster. The heavy rains of the summer of 1314 ruined the harvests; and the famine that followed lasted for two years, for the summer of 1315 was no better. Prices of food soared; murrains broke out among cattle and sheep; exports of English wool fell steeply, and so royal revenue from the customs fell also.[5] In these conditions governmental control at the local level, never very effective, inevitably deteriorated. Some of the outbreaks of local disorder reached serious proportions. In the autumn of 1315 a dangerous revolt broke out on Lancaster's northern estates, led by Adam Banaster, who sacked Manchester and Preston before he was brought to book and executed. In the early months of 1316 one Llewelyn Bren attacked Caerphilly castle, and it looked for a moment as if his movement might develop into a Welsh national rising. This was why many of the great lords of the marches were absent from the parliament of Lincoln that spring. In the summer of 1316 the townsmen of Bristol rose in open revolt against the constable of the castle.

These conditions and these disorders go a long way to explain why, in these years, so little attention was paid to what should have been the chief preoccupation of the government, the defence of the north. In 1315 the Scots had raided in County Durham, and besieged Carlisle, and in 1316 they penetrated further, into Yorkshire. Meanwhile another Scots force, under Edward Bruce, had invaded Ireland. Both in 1315 and 1316 English royal armies were summoned for a Scottish expedition; subsidies were raised to pay the troops, and supplies and transports were purveyed as usual; but in 1315 the host failed to assemble and in 1316 it disbanded without entering on any campaign. In prevailing conditions, the failure of the English to organize defence or reprisal against the Scots is not surprising. It is not surprising either that Lancaster's hold over affairs became more tenuous, in consequence of these failures and of his long absences from the centre of power.

In many respects, the conditions of 1317 were not very different from those of the preceding years. Dearth continued, prices remained high, and local lawlessness was unabated. Politically, however, the complexion of affairs was changing. A new group was gathering at court. From the autumn of 1316 on we find

[5] On the famine see H. S. Lucas, 'The great European famine of 1315, 1316 and 1317', *Speculum* 5 (1930), pp. 343–7.

Edward II sealing a number of indentures with leading men, including the Earl of Hereford, Bartholomew Badlesmere, John Giffard and John Cromwell (and, later, Pembroke), retaining them for life in his personal service, in return for substantial fees. Also very prominent at court at this time, and especially for the rich rewards that favour earned them, were William Montagu, and the three men who had married the co-heiresses of the last Earl of Gloucester (Gilbert of Clare, killed at Bannockburn): Roger Damory, Hugh Audley and Hugh Despenser the younger. This new grouping, in which we find moderates like Badlesmere and Pembroke combining with favourites, was probably the result of the determination of all but Lancaster to see something done to defend the north against Scottish inroads. The emergence of a more united front among the magnates brought into perspective Lancaster's growing isolation. The king had never forgotten, nor forgiven except in name, Earl Thomas's part in the murder of Gaveston. His role in that business had divided him also from Pembroke and Warenne. Guy of Warwick, his erstwhile accomplice, had died in 1315. Because of Lancaster's wealth, his wide estates, and the political and military influence which his vast retinue constituted, he was still a power to be reckoned with; but by the end of 1316 he could no longer dictate policy from his castles by letter to the council.

Lancaster's obdurate stand on the *Ordinances*, in particular his insistence on the resumption of past grants and an embargo on new ones, set him and the courtiers totally at loggerheads. Through the year 1317, their mutual hostility drifted towards the verge of civil war. The courtiers did all that they could to make things difficult for Lancaster, and he responded in kind. On 9 May Lancaster's wife was abducted from Canford in Dorset by John Earl of Warenne, 'not in the way of adultery but for sheer spite of the earl' says the Meaux chronicle.[6] When in the summer the king ordered a muster at York against the Scots, Lancaster's retainers from Pontefract barred the way to the assembling forces. The earl, they declared, was Steward of England, 'whose business it was to look to the advantage of the kingdom', and 'if the king wished to take arms against anyone he ought first to notify the Steward'.[7] Before the end of the summer civil war had come so near that Lancaster made contact with the Scots, in order to secure his position. He and they appear to have connived together at the capture of Louis de Beaumont, Bishop of Durham and

[6] *Chron. de Melsa* (R.S.) vol. II, p. 335.
[7] *Vita Edwardi II*, p. 81.

brother of the courtier Henry, by Sir Gilbert Middleton near Durham in September. In October Lancaster's retainer Lilburn seized Damory's castle at Knaresborough, and when the sheriff of Yorkshire came to besiege him, a Scots force appeared to the relief.[8] At the same time Lancaster's forces were attacking Warenne's castles at Conisborough and Sandal and wasting his lands in Yorkshire.

Thus by the end of 1317 the need for some measure of concilia- tion was becoming urgent. The king's most important subject had gone to the length of seeking an understanding with the king's chief enemy in order to secure himself against the court. The events of the spring of 1318 made conciliation still more necessary. In April Berwick fell to the Scots, and soon after they took the castles of Harbottle and Wark; all northern England was threatened. The task of mediation fell naturally to those moderates who were not committed entirely either to the court or to Lan- caster. Prominent among these was Aymer de Valence, Earl of Pembroke, who had returned from abroad in July 1317, about the same time that the cardinals Anselm of St Marcellin and St Peter and Luke of St Maria arrived from Avignon, with a com- mission from John XXII to mediate both between the king and his magnates, and between the English and the Scots. Alongside Pembroke we must place his fellow the Earl of Hereford, who had been like him an Ordainer but never an extremist in opposi- tion, and among the barons Bartholomew Badlesmere, who in 1318 became steward of the household, replacing William Mon- tagu. These lay magnates all had close associations with the court, moderates though they were, so the guiding influence behind mediation had to be that of the cardinals and of a number of leading ecclesiastics: Reynolds the Archbishop of Canterbury, the Archbishop of Dublin, and the bishops of Norwich, Ely and Chichester were all prominent in negotiations.[9] This whole group has been dubbed by historians, not very appositely, the 'Middle Party'. Conway Davies and other writers have associated with them some other lay barons, Damory, Audley, even the Des- pensers, but, as Dr Maddicott has recently shown, these men were courtier favourites, not moderates.[10] Indeed, its position at court

[8] *Scalacronica*, ed. J. Stevenson (Maitland Club 1836), p. 148.

[9] On the activity of the bishops see further K. Edwards, 'The political importance of the English bishops during the reign of Edward II', *E.H.R.* 59 (1944), pp. 327ff.

[10] See Maddicott, *Thomas of Lancaster*, ch. 6, esp. pp. 195ff. Conway Davies, *The Baronial Opposition*, p. 433, described Audley, Damory

was one of the chief difficulties facing the 'Middle Party'. The enforcement of the *Ordinances* was for Lancaster still the *sine qua non* of any settlement to which he should be a party. This would mean the resumption of grants made to the courtiers, whose new-found favour stamped them in Lancaster's eyes as 'evil councillors' of the kind that the *Ordinances* had condemned: but they, very naturally, were not eager to disgorge.[11]

Negotiations towards a settlement occupied much time and attention late in 1317 and in 1318. The moderates' first success seems to have been with Damory, the courtier who stood highest of all in the king's favour at the time. On 24 November 1317, Pembroke and Badlesmere sealed a bond with him, whereby Damory promised to induce the king to follow the counsels agreed between him and the other two, and specifically to seek to prevent the king from making any grant of more than £20 worth of land without their consent.[12] This was certainly a move in a direction acceptable to Lancaster, and very much in the spirit of the *Ordinances*. The first agreement of the mediators with Lancaster, reached at Leicester in April 1318 (when the disasters in the north must have made agreement seem abnormally urgent) went further, however, than one can imagine Damory ever approving. The *Ordinances* were to be enforced, all evil councillors dismissed, and all lands granted contrary to the *Ordinances* were to be resumed. Lancaster was to be admitted fully to the king's peace, but significantly Warenne was not to be admitted to the peace of the earl: he must make his own terms with Thomas. Not surprisingly, these draconian conditions did not prove acceptable to the courtiers, though they were now prepared to meet concession with concession in the interests of conciliation. At a meeting in June at the exchequer, at which Pembroke, the archbishops of Canterbury and Dublin, and the courtiers Despenser, Damory and Audley were all present, Edward II's friends were willing to guarantee Lancaster safe conduct to come to the king, but pointed out that his refusal to cooperate had contributed in large part to the realm's misfortunes at the hands

---

and the Despensers as 'the raw material from which Pembroke had to build his middle party', which, as Maddicott shows, is misleading.

[11] Maddicott, *Thomas of Lancaster*, is as far as I know the only writer to have brought out clearly the importance of Lancaster's stand on the question of resumption; my views have been strongly influenced by what he has written on this subject.

[12] *P.W.* vol. II, Appendix, p. 120.

of the Scots. The *Ordinances* should be enforced, yes: but he must be prepared to work with others 'without accroaching sovereignty to himself'.[13] It took two more months of hard bargaining, and big concessions from Lancaster, before a settlement was reached in the famous Treaty of Leake in August.

The observance of the *Ordinances* was the formal basis of this settlement: this had to be, if Lancaster was to be a party to it.[14] There were, however, important modifications to the manner of their observance. The issue of evil councillors was solved by the appointment of a formal council: four earls were among its members, Pembroke, Richmond, Hereford and Arundel, but not Lancaster, whose interest was to be represented by a banneret whom he should name. Two bishops, one earl, one baron and this banneret were to be always with the king, and to authorize with him all that could be authorized (according to the *Ordinances*) without a parliament. This arrangement was a concession by Lancaster, modifying his earlier position over evil councillors. In the crucial matter of resumptions the treaty was vague; in fact, grants were considered individually in the subsequent parliament, and on their merits were either cancelled or allowed to stand. Damory, Audley, the Despensers and Montagu all managed to retain some valuable assets. It was a major concession on Lancaster's part that he made no protest over this arrangement.

The Treaty of Leake was ratified in the parliament that was held at York in October 1318, in which the business of resumptions was initiated, and a committee was set up, once again, to consider reform of the king's household. The tenuous unity of king and magnates which the treaty established lasted nearly two years, and enabled Edward to mount a major campaign in the north in 1319, to which Lancaster led a large contingent. Signs of strains which could upset the settlement were, however, early apparent. Lancaster made a good thing out of his concessions at Leake, and in particular was able to maintain his insistence that

[13] E. Salisbury, 'A political agreement of June 1318', *E.H.R.* 33 (1918), p. 82.
[14] On the Treaty of Leake see Maddicott, *Thomas of Lancaster*, ch. 6, pts ii and iii; also J. G. Edwards, 'The negotiating of the Treaty of Leake, 1318', *Essays in History Presented to R. L. Poole*, ed. H. W. C. Davis (Oxford, 1927); and B. Wilkinson, 'The negotiations preceding the "Treaty" of Leake', *Studies in Medieval History Presented to F. M. Powicke*, ed. R. W. Hunt, W. A. Pantin and R. W. Southern (Oxford, 1948). Maddicott's is the clearest and fullest account, and modifies earlier views in some important respects.

Warenne should make his own peace with him. The price that Warenne had to pay for this was the release to Earl Thomas of all his lands in Yorkshire, and of certain estates also in East Anglia and Wales. It would seem that certain of the courtiers had besides to acknowledge large debts to the earl, as the price of conciliation with him.[15] Thomas was still not fully content, even then: in October 1318 he demanded an investigation into his rights as Steward of England, and in May 1319 was claiming the right to appoint the steward of the household. This embroiled him in bitter controversy with the man who actually held the office, Bartholomew Badlesmere.[16]

The courtiers were not satisfied either. In September 1319, when the royal host was before Berwick, Edward's promise that they should be richly rewarded, from the spoil that would be taken there, led to a renewed clash with Earl Thomas, who finally withdrew his forces. In consequence the siege had to be broken up. When, at the end of the year, a two-year truce was taken with the Scots, which seemed humiliating to the English, the courtiers blamed Lancaster (and vice versa). The earl refused to attend the January parliament of 1320. He seems to have been now retreating towards the position of isolated opposition that he had maintained in 1317. The king and the courtiers were beginning to think, as they also had in 1317, in terms of obtaining from the pope release from their oaths to observe the *Ordinances*. Nevertheless, when parliament met in October 1320 the *Ordinances* were still in force. Compromise endured, but it was wearing thin.

By the end of 1320 we are entering on our third period, of renewed confrontation. What destroyed the compromise finally was the rise in favour and influence at court of Hugh Despenser the younger, who by this time had eclipsed all others in the royal graces, as also in the rapacity of his territorial ambitions. His marriage to Eleanor, the eldest of the three daughters of the last Earl of Gloucester, made him co-heir in the great Clare inheritance with Audley and Damory. His desire seems to have been to concentrate all the Welsh territories of the Clares in his own hands, and to obtain in his own favour the revival of the Earldom

[15] See Maddicott, *Thomas of Lancaster*, pp. 233–7; and F. Royston Fairbank, 'The last earl of Warenne and Surrey', *Yorkshire Archaeological Journal* 19 (1907), pp. 212–13.

[16] The clearest explanation of the importance of the question of the stewardship is Maddicott, *Thomas of Lancaster*, pp. 241–3.

of Gloucester. Glamorgan was his share from the start; by a combination of force and persuasion he obtained the county of Gwynllwyg from Audley; to this he soon added Cantrefmawr and Dryslwyn in Carmarthen, and he began to cast envious eyes at William de Braose's barony of Gower, which marched with Glamorgan. De Braose's circumstances were straitened, and Despenser had all along been interested in the purchase of his inheritance; but when he died in 1320 John Mowbray, his son-in-law, entered on his lands on the strength of a grant executed by de Braose in favour of him and his heirs, with remainder to Hereford. Despenser now persuaded the king to order the seizure of Gower as an escheat, on the ground that this grant was unlawful, since land held in chief of the king could not be alienated except by royal licence. This rule had never been accepted as customary in Wales and the march, and the seizure thus constituted a direct challenge to marcher law. It was not only the privileges of the marchers that was in question, moreover: the territorial interests of some of the most powerful among them – Hereford, Mowbray, the Mortimers, Audley and Damory – were also involved. These men were soon the leaders of a confederacy sworn to uphold one another against the overbearing favourite of the king. It was unfortunate that, at this crucial point, Pembroke, who was more loyal, more moderate, and more experienced than most of his colleagues, was out of the country. In January 1321 Despenser was putting his castles in a state of defence, while the marchers were putting out feelers towards Lancaster: by April fighting had broken out in the marches.[17]

The confrontation of the summer of 1321 was complicated by an absence of unanimity both among those who remained loyal to the king, and in the ranks of the opposition. Among the former Pembroke, perhaps Arundel, and the majority of the prelates had no desire to protect the interest of the Despensers, and were anxious to avoid civil war. On the other side, Lancaster's long standing ill will towards Damory and Audley made cooperation between him and these marchers difficult, and he was not prepared to have any dealings at all with Badlesmere, who had thrown in his lot with them. As a result, Edward felt strong enough to refuse to take the immediate action against the Despensers that the marchers demanded; but he was not strong enough to ignore the charges against his favourites altogether. Their consideration was postponed merely, to the coming parlia-

[17] See further J. Conway Davies, 'The Despenser war in Glamorgan', *T.R.H.S.* 3rd ser., 9 (1915), pp. 21–64.

ment. In the meantime the marchers tried to consolidate with Lancaster a united opposition, while he sought to broaden its base with non-marcher elements, and so to strengthen the independence of his position.

On 24 May at Pontefract Lancaster brought together an assembly of the chief magnates of the north, who bound themselves to act together to preserve peace and to defend the realm; but they were not prepared to go further without the advice of the northern prelates, and there was no mention of the Despensers in their agreement.[18] So there had to be a second meeting at Sherburn-in-Elmet, at which, besides the northern magnates and prelates and a large number of Earl Thomas's retainers, some of the important marchers were present. A schedule of grievances for discussion was read at this assembly by Lancaster's retainer, John de Bek, which included complaints about the Despensers but ranged more widely too, mentioning besides the new judicial eyres which the king had instituted, abuses of the staple regulations, and the need for united effort against the Scots. This attempt by Lancaster to unite opposition and broaden its base was not wholly successful. By indentures sealed at Sherburn, Lancaster and the leading marchers swore to act together against the Despensers, but the northerners who were present did not seal these agreements; and the clergy of the northern province, while ready to cooperate in any necessary action against the Scots, requested that the other matters be referred to the next parliament.[19] The situation was thus still full of political ambiguity when parliament began to assemble at Westminster on 15 July.

As they marched towards London, says the St Paul's annalist, the opposition magnates, 'having taken counsel about what they could lawfully do, to displace and destroy the king's evil councillors, put together in writing a certain tract based on ancient custom, against the forthcoming parliament'.[20] This would seem to have been the famous tract which claims for the Steward of England the right 'to supervise and regulate, under and immediately after the king, the whole realm of England and all the officers of the law within the realm, in times of peace and war'.[21]

[18] *Bridlington* (R.S.), pp. 61-2.

[19] On the Sherburn meeting see Maddicott, *Thomas of Lancaster*, pp. 269-79; this revises in important respects B. Wilkinson's previous account 'The Sherburn Indenture and the attack on the Despensers', *E.H.R.* 63 (1948), pp. 1-28.

[20] *Annales Paulini* (R.S.), p. 293.

[21] The tract is printed in full by L. W. Vernon Harcourt, *His Grace*

Lancaster as Steward had made a claim not unlike this in 1317, but the tract went further: it was the Steward's duty also, with the Constable, to guard against evil councillors, and if the king would not act against them, to seize them as 'public enemies' and hold them for judgement in the next parliament. As far as is known, these claims to almost viceregal powers were never formally urged in the subsequent parliament, but they throw revealing light on the manner in which Lancaster's long experience of isolated opposition had developed his political thinking. In fact, when the parliament met, it was not he and his associates, but Pembroke who persuaded Edward to agree to the dismissal of his favourites, telling him that 'it was not worth his while for any living soul to lose his kingdom'.[22] On 19 August judgement was formally passed in parliament on both the Despensers: they were sentenced to total forfeiture and banishment as 'evil and false councillors, seducers and conspirators, and disinheritors of the crown, and as enemies of the king and the kingdom'.[23]

The judgement on the Despensers proved only to be a breathing space, at the brink of civil war. After the parliament, Edward's opponents returned to their estates, and Hugh Despenser the elder went into exile. But Hugh his son did not go further than the Channel, where he remained aboard ship, hovering off the English coast. His chance for *révanche*, and Edward's, came within a few months, when Queen Isabella was refused admittance to Leeds castle in Kent by Bartholomew Badlesmere. Edward made this the pretext for raising an army at once to besiege the castle, and Pembroke, Arundel, Warenne and Richmond were ready to support him, as were also his two young half-brothers, Edmund of Kent and Thomas of Norfolk. Badlesmere's sworn allies of the summer, the marchers, began quickly to mobilize their forces to aid him, but Lancaster felt his grudge too deeply against the man whom he had sought unsuccessfully to displace from the stewardship of the household, and held his hand at the crucial period. He took certain steps to protect his own position, but he made no move outside his own estates while Leeds castle fell, and the king with his new army turned against the marchers.

Resistance to the king began to crumble. The Mortimers of

---

the Steward and Trial of Peers (London, 1907), pp. 164–7 (English translation, pp. 148–51). Its claims for the steward are discussed further in Chapter 4.

[22] *Vita Edwardi II*, p. 113.
[23] ibid. p. 114.

Chirk and Wigmore surrendered into the king's mercy. Lancaster was at Pontefract when Hereford and the other dissidents of the Welsh march, who had retreated before the king's superior force, joined him. Thence they advanced to Burton-on-Trent, but then fell back north together, probably to seek refuge with the Scots, for Lancaster had been in close contact with Bruce and seems to have trusted in him more than in the English barons. At Borough-bridge in Yorkshire, on 16 March 1322, Lancaster and Hereford found their way barred by Andrew Harclay, the sheriff of Cumberland, with the levies of the northern counties. Hereford fell fighting at the bridge itself; Lancaster, Mowbray, Clifford and others surrendered to Sir Andrew, who turned them over to King Edward. On 22 March, after a summary trial, Lancaster was executed at Pontefract. Mowbray, Clifford and a number of other men, including Damory, were also condemned to death and forfeited their estates.[24] The more prominent of their followers were proscribed as traitors and lost their lands. This was the first occasion on which summary sentences of death and forfeiture for high treason were passed on peers of the realm in England. It was an ominous precedent.

In so far as Thomas of Lancaster had had any consistent political programme, he had stood out for the enforcement of the *Ordinances*. His death settled the long dispute on this matter. 'Remember the following: first the statute about the repeal of the *Ordinances*: second, to embody the good points in them in a statute':[25] these are the first items of agenda which the king referred to the council before parliament met at York on 2 May 1322. In the parliament a large number of detailed points taken from the *Ordinances* and which were not offensive to royal dignity were embodied in a statute. The *Ordinances* themselves were condemned, and together with them the manner of their making.

Henceforth, all manner of ordinances and provisions, made under any authority or commission whatever by the subjects of our lord the king or his heirs . . . shall be null and of no validity or force.

---

[24] Damory had in fact been sentenced on 13 March, before Borough-bridge. On these treason trials see J. G. Bellamy, *The Law of Treason in England in the Later Middle Ages* (Cambridge, 1970), pp. 49–51; also M. H. Keen, 'Treason trials under the law of arms', *T.R.H.S.* 5th ser., 12 (1962), pp. 85–103.
[25] Conway Davies, *The Baronial Opposition*, Appendix, No. 93, p. 583.

But the things which are to be established for the estate of the king and of his heirs and for the estate of the realm and people shall be treated, granted, and established in parliament, by our lord the king with the assent of the prelates, earls, and barons and of the commonalty of the realm, as has been accustomed.[26]

The Statute of York here drew a clear distinction between re-forms agreed and authorized in properly summoned parliaments with the king's assent, and reforms forced on the king by any committee or group of subjects outside parliament, whether the king had given them powers (as he had to the original Ordainers) or not (as in the case of the confederates of Sherburn-in-Elmet). The statute thus set a very difficult legal obstacle in the way of any who might seek to revive the *Ordinances*, or to impose restraints on the crown in the same way that the Ordainers and Lancaster had done. Their constitutional methods were, as a point of fact, from this time on a thing of the past.

But the statute did not, of course, do anything about the mat-ters which had driven the Ordainers, Lancaster, and his marcher allies of 1321–2 into opposition: over-lavish expenditure by the crown and too ample patronage of royal favourites. This was why opposition was not slow to re-form, or to strike new constitu-tional attitudes.

When the York parliament of 1322 dispersed the *Ordinances* stood revoked. Figures who had occupied the centre of the political stage for ten years were dead, or discredited. Lancaster, Hereford, Badlesmere and Damory had all been condemned as traitors after Boroughbridge. Audley and the two Mortimers of Chirk and Wigmore were out of the way, prisoners of the triumphant king. Pembroke never recovered the influence that he had previously enjoyed, and died in 1324. Warenne, Richmond and Arundel were still there, and profited by the royal victory, but they were men who had never shown the same independence in politics as Lancaster or Hereford or Pembroke. A number of new men emerged to prominence in consequence, notably Henry, the brother and apparent heir of Earl Thomas, who in 1324 was allowed to enter into the earldom of Leicester (but not to succeed to his brother's other estates and titles); and the king's two half-brothers, Edmund Earl of Kent and Thomas Earl of Norfolk. Very naturally the king's triumph brought back the Despensers, who for the time being were unshakeable in influence.

[26] *Statutes of the Realm* vol. I, p. 189. The constitutional importance of the Statute of York is discussed further in Chapter 4.

The Despensers had not learned very much from the experience of 1321. Their territorial rapacity and their monopoly of the
king's favour soon made them as hated as before. The parliament
of York in 1322 saw Hugh the elder created Earl of Winchester;
Hugh the younger got his reward in vast grants from the forfeited
estates of the late rebels, especially in Wales, where he secured
Gower at last, and the lordship of Usk as well. He was able in
consequence to put aside substantial sums which were deposited
with Italian bankers;[27] and his revenues were swelled from other
sources besides the issues of his estates. Men complained that it
was difficult to approach the king unless one first bribed his
chamberlain, Hugh Despenser. It would seem that, as much as
anything, it was the absence of any opposition leader of real standing that protected the Despensers, father and son, from concerted
attack.

To do the Despensers justice, the period of their dominance,
from 1322 to 1326, did witness attempts to institute some much
needed administrative reforms. As chamberlain, Despenser the
younger extended the system of reserving the issues of certain
royal estates to the chamber and exempting them from exchequer
jurisdiction. This helped towards providing funds for the expense
of the royal household, and generally to give the crown greater
freedom of action in financial affairs. Bishop Stapledon of Exeter,
who was treasurer from 1322 to 1325, strengthened the staff of
the exchequer, and improved its system of accounting. The
number of escheators was also increased, from two to nine. The
functions of the wardrobe were defined more clearly in new
instructions, and the office of keeper of the privy seal was permanently separated from the keepership of the wardrobe.[28]
We should be careful of exaggerating the significance of these
measures, however, important as they may seem to the administrative historian. Better methods of accounting in departments are
not the same thing as better government. Ten years of perpetual
civil insecurity had strained control at the local level to the point
of breakdown. Lawlessness was rife in the 1320s; bands of armed
men roamed at large and made a business of robbery. In 1326 a
gang led by one Eustace de Folville ambushed the chief baron of

[27] See further the illuminating article by E. B. Fryde, 'The deposits
of Hugh Despenser the Younger with Italian bankers', *Econ.H.R.*
2nd ser., 3 (1951), pp. 344-62.

[28] On the household measures of this period, see Tout, *Chapters*
vol. 2, pp. 260f., 304, 338f. On Stapledon's reforms see T. F. Tout,
The Place of Edward II, pp. 193ff.

the exchequer, Robert Bellers, near Melton Mowbray, and killed him.[29] This is a useful commentary on Stapledon's exchequer reforms: given conditions in which the chief baron might be surprised and murdered by bandits, the fact that the exchequer continued to function smoothly, even through the crisis of 1326–1327, loses much of its significance.

The story of England's external relations in the period 1322–6 is even more depressing than her domestic history. The truce which had been agreed with Bruce in December 1319 expired in the summer of 1322, and the Scots crossed the border again to raid as far as Preston and into Yorkshire. King Edward's effort at retaliation by leading an army into Lothian was a dismal failure; Bruce followed his retreat and came near to capturing the English king in a skirmish at Byland. Once again, the men of the north had to make terms for themselves with the Scots. To Andrew Harclay, the victor of Boroughbridge and now Earl of Carlisle, the situation after Byland seemed so desperate that he sought out Bruce himself, concluding, says the chronicle of Lanercost, that Edward II could not rule, 'and that it would be better for the communities of both kingdoms that each king should possess his kingdom freely and peacefully [i.e. without a feudal relation of superiority on the English side], rather than that every year there should be so much slaughter, burning and depredation'.[30] Together, the earl and Bruce entered on a treaty, which, according to a version that the English court heard about, included a plan to bind the king and lords of England to abide by the counsel of twelve arbiters, chosen six from among the English and six from among the Scots, who would settle all issues between the two realms.[31] Fortunately for Edward II, his friends got wind of Harclay's plan before anything could be done to implement it. The earl was arrested and brought to London where he was condemned and executed as a traitor. Though nothing came of it, the incident is significant. Within a year of Boroughbridge the loyalist Harclay had been driven by events to pin his hopes on plans for the constraint of King Edward and his council all too

---

[29] On the Folvilles and their activities see E. L. G. Stones, 'The Folvilles of Ashby Folville, Leicestershire, and their associates in crime, 1326–41', *T.R.H.S.* 5th ser., 7 (1957), pp. 117–36.

[30] *Chron. de Lanercost*, ed. J. Stevenson (Maitland Club, 1839), p. 248.

[31] See further J. Mason, 'Sir Andrew de Harcla, Earl of Carlisle', *Transactions of the Cumberland and Westmorland Antiquarian and Archaeological Society* new series, 29 (1929), pp. 122ff.

similar to those of Thomas of Lancaster, and was planning, like
the dead earl, to use alliance with the Scots to force the king's
hand.

The summer of 1323 saw a kind of settlement, it is true, in the
north. On 30 May at Bishopthorpe a truce for thirteen years was
agreed between the English and the Scots. But no sooner was the
north quiet than troubles began to brew in Gascony. Up to this
date, Edward II had been fortunate in that other preoccupations
had inclined the kings of France toward conciliation in the south-
west. But in 1323 tensions beween the French king's officials and
the English seneschal of Gascony led to the burning of the *bastide*
which Charles IV was building at St Sardos, and war threatened.[32]
In 1324 Charles declared the duchy confiscated, and prepared to
enforce his judgement by arms. There was no serious fighting;
and in 1325 Queen Isabella, who had crossed to France to negotiate with Charles (who was her brother), obtained a truce on
conditions: that Prince Edward be invested with the duchy and
do homage to the French king, and that damages to the rights of
the French crown and to French subjects in the course of the
quarrel should be compensated. The agreement also saddled the
English with responsibility for paying a relief of £60,000 for the
duchy, and left the French in control of the Agenais, for the time
being. Edward later formally went back on these terms. However,
the only effort he made to restore the situation in Gascony itself
was to summon a host in 1325, which never embarked. The infantry were not paid, and devastated the countryside around
Portsmouth to make up for their wages. Thus the story of his
failure in Gascony repeats the pattern of earlier failures in Scotland; and the result was that at the end of the reign the duchy
was effectively in French hands.

Against this background of failures and disasters, it was natural
that opposition to Edward and his ministers the Despensers soon
began to consolidate once again. In 1323 the most troublesome
men seemed to be bishops Orleton of Hereford and Burghersh of
Lincoln (both of whom had been connected with the rebels of
1322). It was with Orleton's aid that in this year Roger Mortimer
of Wigmore escaped from the Tower and fled to France. According to Le Baker's chronicle, it was the same bishop who was
foremost in exciting Queen Isabella against the royal favourites,
playing on her resentment ·at the sequestration of her estates

[32] See further P. Chaplais, *The War of St Sardos* (Camden Soc. 3rd
ser., 87, 1954), esp. pp. x–xiii.

(ordered in September 1324 with the assent of the Despensers, on the pretext of a threat of invasion from France).[33] Whether this is so or not, Isabella was soon to put herself at the head of the opposition. In 1325, as we have seen, she crossed to France to seek peace in the matter of Gascony: once safe at her brother's court she refused point blank to return unless the king got rid of the Despensers.

From this point the opposition began to crystallize as a party. The group which gathered round the queen in Paris was a powerful one. It included bishops Stratford of Winchester and Airmyn of Norwich; Roger Mortimer, whose mistress Isabella soon became; Edmund of Kent, who had been in charge of negotiations until her arrival, joined these, and so did the Earl of Richmond and Henry Beaumont. By September 1326 they were ready to take the initiative. Isabella, Mortimer and the young Prince Edward embarked with a force of Hainaulters at Dordrecht on 23 September; on 25 September they landed at Orwell in Suffolk. Thomas Earl of Norfolk and Henry of Leicester declared for them along with several of the bishops; in London there were riots in their support, in the course of which Bishop Stapledon was assassinated. The queen and her army headed west, in pursuit of the Despensers and the king, who had retreated from the capital and were making for Bristol. There a rising of the townsmen put the city into her hands, and the elder Despenser was taken. He was tried summarily before a tribunal of peers selected at random in the host, and executed (27 October). A few weeks later the king, the younger Despenser, the Earl of Arundel, and the chancellor, Robert Baldock, were captured at Neath Abbey in Wales. Arundel and Despenser were executed as traitors, while Earl Henry of Leicester, Thomas of Lancaster's brother, led King Edward away a prisoner to the castle of Kenilworth.

On 26 October 1326 the magnates who were at Bristol with Isabella had proclaimed her son Edward keeper of the realm. The writs which summoned parliament to Westminster in December went out, however, in Edward II's name. This was no sign of wavering intention: after all that had passed, there could be no question for his opponents of allowing Edward to rule any longer. The problem was how to be rid of him. There were no precedents for a deposition, and no one knew who could judge a monarch or whether anyone could. In so drastic a matter, it was essential to avoid as far as possible anything that might suggest that force was taking the place of law. Unless whatever was done

[33] *Chron. G. Le Baker*, ed. E. M. Thompson (Oxford, 1889), p. 18.

achieved general assent the confusion which would result might be worse than anything which had gone before.

The first week after the parliament met (in January, as a result of a postponement) was in consequence devoted to consolidating a united front, not strictly in parliament, but among the king's lieges who were about the capital for its meeting. The first task for Isabella and Mortimer was to win over certain of the bishops, who were known to be hesitant: the excitement of the Londoners, who were solid in support of the queen, was probably instrumental in persuading them to bury their doubts about a deposition.[34] On 13 January it was clear that a consensus had been reached, when a number of bishops and magnates, together with representatives of the clergy and the boroughs, took an oath at the Guildhall to maintain the queen's cause, 'to uphold all that has been ordained or shall be ordained for the common profit'.[35] Two days later the Archbishop of Canterbury, in a sermon preached in Westminster Hall before all who had come to the parliament (and probably others too) announced that the king was deposed by the unanimous consent of the magnates, clergy and people. His text was *vox populi, vox dei*. It is probable that it was on this occasion that the formal articles of deposition, which had been drafted by Bishop Stratford of Winchester, were read.[36] Next day a deputation set out for Kenilworth in which all the estates of the realm were represented. There were two earls, Warenne and Henry of Leicester, three bishops, four barons, a number of persons representing London, the Cinque Ports and other great towns, and representatives both of the clergy and the shire knights.[37] They reached Kenilworth on 20 January. There Edward II agreed that he would abdicate, if his son were allowed to succeed him. William Trussell, speaking for the delegation,

---

[34] See *Lichfield Chronicle*, quoted by M. V. Clarke, *Medieval Representation and Consent* (London, 1936), p. 181, note 1. Clarke's book contains the most detailed study of the circumstances of Edward II's deposition, and the most illuminating; it has sometimes been underrated on account of the author's concern to link the deposition with the doctrines of the *Modus Tenendi Parliamentum*, which is not entirely convincing.

[35] *Annales Paulini*, p. 323.

[36] *Chron de Lanercost*, p. 258. The formal articles of deposition are given by Twysden, *Historiae Anglicanae Scriptores X* (1652), col. 2765.

[37] M. V. Clarke, *Medieval Representation*, pp. 186ff., analyses the various accounts of the composition of the deputation.

renounced homage and allegiance to Edward 'on behalf of the whole kingdom'.[38]

There was thus no judgement on Edward II, and the fine point as to whether he was deposed by parliament or by some less official assembly of the whole people remains unclear. Though he was declared deposed before he abdicated, his agreement to do so rendered it unnecessary to clarify the situation further. Isabella and Mortimer had got what they wanted. They had forced him to withdraw from kingship, and had associated with themselves in the business not just a party, or the magnates only, but the people of the kingdom as a whole. They had achieved an appearance of communal unanimity in their action, and that was enough. There was no need to stir the dust of past controversy by the resurrection of the *Ordinances*, or by repealing the Statute of York, neither of which had much to do with their real object and that of their associates. That object was much more simple: to pay off the personal scores that had been left outstanding by the events of 1322.

The deposition of Edward II ended a reign, but it did not end the conditions that had characterized it. In spite of all the attempts to create the appearance of consensus, the revolution of 1326-7 was of course a partisan triumph. The first acts of Edward III's first parliament make this clear: they were the reversal of the judgement of 1322 on Thomas of Lancaster (whose title and estates were therefore restored to his brother), and the reaffirmation of the judgement of parliament in 1321 against the Despensers. Mortimer, in power, proved to be as rapacious and overbearing as any of the late king's favourites. He acquired vast estates from the forfeitures of the Despensers and Arundel, and more was added by the queen and by grants of crown land. In the parliament of October 1328 he was created Earl of March, a new title which was to have a long history. By this time he was becoming as much hated as the Despensers had ever been.

The queen and Mortimer were not more successful in their dealing with the Scots than Edward II had been. The truce of 1323 had still a long while to run, but the new government in England wanted to show its strength, with disastrous consequences. Mortimer's campaign in the north in 1327 was expensive and ineffective; the English retreated before the Scots rather than offer battle, and afterwards there seemed no alternative to accepting terms virtually dictated by the Bruce. The Treaty of Northampton of 1328 formally recognized Robert Bruce as ruler

[38] *Chron. G. Le Baker*, p. 28.

of an independent kingdom, with no feudal ties with England. In England this was regarded as the shameful surrender of a just and traditional claim, a bitter and humiliating commencement to a new reign.[39]

Domestic conditions in England remained unstable while Mortimer and Isabella were at the helm. The ex-king, as long as he lived, was an obvious focus of conspiracy, and there were two attempts to rescue him from prison in 1327. The rumour that a third attempt was planned precipitated his murder in Berkeley castle, on Mortimer's orders.[40] His death did not change things any more than his deposition had. Mortimer's failures and his territorial greed had broken up the magnate coalition of 1326. Henry of Lancaster had so far broken with him that he refused to attend the October parliament of 1328 (where Mortimer was created Earl of March). They were reconciled, it is true, in 1329, but only after Mortimer had entered on Henry's Leicester lands with an armed force. In the spring of the next year, 1330, Edmund of Kent was detected in conspiracy against the government and executed. The chronic insecurity and the aristocratic feuding that had marked the whole reign of Edward II did not end until his son decided to take power into his own hands. Mortimer was arrested at Nottingham castle in October 1330; and the king's subsequent declaration that he intended 'to govern our people according to right and reason, as is fitting our royal dignity'[41] marks a break, at last, with these conditions.

England, during the reign of Edward II and its epilogue in the rule of Mortimer and Isabella, suffered twenty years of misgovernment, of chronic internal insecurity and repeated humiliation at the hands of external enemies. Why, we may ask, did these terrible conditions endure so long? Clearly, the magnates of the period must bear a heavy share of responsibility. They showed themselves incapable of sustained cooperation, even in face of the Scottish threat to northern England. None of those who enjoyed the royal favour showed an adequate sense of moderation. Mortimer displayed the same fault as a triumphant opposition leader. Thomas of Lancaster may deserve some credit for his

[39] For the Scottish war 1327-8 see R. Nicholson, *Edward III and the Scots* (Oxford, 1965), ch. 2-4.

[40] See further T. F. Tout, 'The captivity and death of Edward of Caernarvon', in his *Collected Papers* (Manchester, 1934) vol. III, pp. 145-90.

[41] *Foed.* vol. IV, p. 452.

stand on the *Ordinances* and his efforts to enforce them in detail; though it was not a very original or far-sighted policy, it earned him some popularity, both in his lifetime and posthumously. He never understood the need to cooperate with others, however; and the rancour with which he pursued personal grudges against men like Warenne and Badlesmere was ruinous to the cause that he espoused. Pembroke deserves more credit than most, but though he showed himself moderate, well meaning, and above all loyal to the king, he never succeeded in creating an effective political following, probably because he lacked the ability and force of character to do so.

The central and first cause of the troubles was, however, without any doubt, the utter incapacity of Edward II as a monarch. Stratford's indictment of his rule in 1327 summed the situation up aptly: 'the king is incompetent to govern in person. Throughout his reign he has been controlled and governed by others who have given him evil counsel, to his own dishonour and the destruction of Holy Church and all his people, without his being willing to see what is good or evil or to make amendment . . . or to allow amendment to be made.'[42] He was not charged with tyranny: the general complaint was not that he had sought to do too much but that he had not himself done very much at all. Chroniclers talked of his 'wonted fatuity', his unkingly personal habits, his inability to rise in the morning. He allowed himself to be completely controlled by his intimates, and it was their behaviour, not his, that really roused opposition.

In an age when the exercise of patronage was inseparable from the conduct of government, royal favour was always a potential source of friction between a king and his subjects. Edward II's personal attachments were something out of the ordinary, however. The magnates could not be expected to tolerate the degree of control which his favourites exercised over him, which made the sovereign into the subject of other men's whims and ambitions. Unfortunately the only political art of which Edward had a rudimentary understanding was that of patronage, and he was ready to exercise it liberally in order to serve the only political object for which he seems consistently to have striven, the retention of his favourites. The result was that, short of deposition, there was no very obvious remedy to a situation in which the leading men of the kingdom felt that they could not trust the king, and equally that they could not trust one another not to take advantage of him. Edward II, by his stubborn, piteous

[42] Twysden, *Historiae Anglicanae Scriptores* X, col. 2765.

determination to keep his friends about him and to honour them
as he chose, made it impossible to achieve that degree of cooperation between king and magnates, or at least among the magnates
themselves, without which the proper conduct of government
was impossible. The leading men of the kingdom hesitated for
years before they decided to inflict on the monarchy the terrible
humiliation of a deposition, but in the end it is hard to see that
they had much alternative.

The final humiliation, like most of the other catastrophes of
Edward II's reign, is most readily explicable in personal terms,
but this does not mean that the consequences of these catastrophes should be looked at in personal terms only. This is nowhere clearer than in the north, where the mismanagement of the
long drawn out Anglo-Scottish war left scars which it took
centuries, not just generations to heal. In the comparative peace
of the late thirteenth century the border counties had been an
area of advancing prosperity, both in town and countryside; by
1330 only the signs of vanished prosperity remained, in burned
houses and deserted countryside, and in the new power of Robert
Bruce who had enriched himself with the plunder and tribute of
the lands over which he had so constantly raided. Loss of livestock, and the burning of crops and homesteads had ruined
agricultural prosperity, and there was a substantial exodus of
poor folk who could no longer make a safe living from the
country. Many landowners had been reduced to dire straits.
Durham Priory's revenues, which in 1308 stood at £4500, had
dwindled to a mere £1750 in 1335. Setbacks such as this were not
a temporary phenomenon, moreover; the impoverishment was
permanent.[43]

These economic consequences of the Anglo-Scottish war had
important political effects. In Edward's weakness, the lords of the
north were left to organize defence themselves, or to make their
own terms with Bruce. Behind the private treaties that they made
with him in order to secure their own possessions, as too behind
the reluctance of the northerners to throw in their lot with
Lancaster in 1321, we can see developing an independent,
northern attitude in politics, governed by considerations local

[43] See E. Miller, *War in the North* (Hull, 1960), p. 8. In this and
following paragraphs I am heavily indebted to this very illuminating
lecture, to which my attention was drawn by Mr G. L. Harriss. On the
devastation of the north see also J. Scammell, 'Robert I and the north
of England', *E.H.R.* 73 (1958), pp. 385–403.

to the Scottish border. In Harclay's conspiracy of 1323 we see the first effort of a border lord, with a military reputation and following, to direct the English political situation with purely northern ends in view. He was to have some formidable imitators later on, as we shall see, notably among the members of the house of Percy.

The Scottish wars did not end with Edward II, and the outbreak in 1337 of the great Hundred Years War between England and France meant that the lords of the north had to be left to fend for themselves, as they had done under him, more or less permanently. In consequence, the lines of development of the early fourteenth century set firmly. After Edward II's reign the border did not ever, in the Middle Ages, recover its prosperity. It became a land of herdsmen and cattle-thieves, of powerful but intensely local loyalties, where gentry like the Charltons and the Armstrongs lived in fortified dwellings, half as squires, half as bandits, and where men knew 'no prince save a Percy or a Neville'. To a southerner, it was almost a foreign country; it still seemed so to Camden in the sixteenth century when he visited it: 'over all the waste you would think you see the ancient nomads . . . a martial sort of people that from April to August lie in little huts . . . among their several flocks'.[44] The north acquired its own ways of thought and feeling, and its own literature, a balladry that turned its sorrows and violence into high poetry. Most important of all for the political historian, its conditions made the great lords of the border the most formidable, militarily, among the English magnates. This was why, in the later Middle Ages, their private feuds and rivalries were so often a threat to the stability not of the north only, but of the whole kingdom, and why their allegiances proved often to be the deciding factor in domestic politics.

Edward II's reign thus left a lasting mark on the political geography of England. Before his time the lords who had most often proved dangerous to the monarch had been the Welsh marchers, and in 1321 in the war against the Despensers they showed that their fangs were not yet drawn. It was the last occasion, however, on which their intervention, as an identifiable group, was decisive. In the later fourteenth century and afterwards the stormy petrels of English politics were not the men of the west, but the men of the north, above all the Percies – who had come into the north in the host of Edward I in the hope of gain and new lands, and who made it their homeland thenceforward, until in the end their unruliness brought final ruin upon the house.

[44] Quoted by E. Miller, *War in the North*, p. 10.

4

Politics and the constitution
1290–1330

The personal antipathies and rival interests of great men dictated the course of events through most of the long, sad reign of Edward II. Nevertheless, issues of general importance to the people at large were all the time involved. As we have seen, Edward II's difficulties had their origins in the later years of his father's reign, when the king and his magnates were divided on issues that were far from being merely personal. Two crucial problems were directly raised by the troubles of that time, the limit of the king's prerogative power, and the means of redress available to the subject against oppressive acts of the king and his officials. The second of these problems was bound to raise sooner or later a third issue, the question of the subject's right, in extreme circumstances, to resist the king's government. The events of the early years of Edward II brought this third issue squarely into the foreground. The period from 1290 to 1330 was in consequence a most important one in constitutional as well as political history.

The question of the subject's right to sue for lawful redress against the king was one which was raised early, and remained important throughout the period. In the 1290s it provided the central theme of the curious tract known as the *Mirror of Justices*, which provides an interesting illustration of the manner of argument on questions of political principle in the age. To the author of the *Mirror* it seemed quite wrong that the king should be above and beyond the law, as he effectively was, given the practice of the courts at the time.[1] The king's courts, he thought, ought to provide remedies even against the king himself. In the good old days of the first Anglo-Saxon kings they used to do so,

[1] *The Mirror of Justices*, ed. W. J. Whittaker (Selden Soc., 1893), p. 155.

he claimed. When the English first came to the land the earls, who were the king's companions, were each given a district to hold and defend, and it was agreed as law that these earls should hear and determine in parliament all writs and complaints concerning wrongs done by the king, by his family, and by his officials.[2] But now this custom is no longer observed, the *Mirror* laments, and the subject has no redress available against the king at law.

The point which the author of the *Mirror*, with his irresponsible invective and his entirely spurious history, was getting at had also troubled the *doyen* of English thirteenth-century lawyers, Bracton. Bracton stated quite clearly that the king was not beyond the law, but bound by it.[3] Royal authority came from God, and was an authority only to do that which was right and lawful, not to commit injury. But Bracton was much less clear when it came to the question of how the king may be constrained to obey the law. The king according to Bracton has no equal in his kingdom, still less any superior. His writ will not run against him and those who seek redress against the crown can only proceed by petitioning for grace, not by legal action. 'If he [the king] will not correct what is complained of, he must be left to the judgement of God.'[4] This was Bracton's own conclusion, but there were those, he admitted, who did not agree. In a passage where he is explaining that the assize of *novel disseisin* cannot be used against the crown he remarks thus: 'There are however those who say that the *universitas* of the kingdom and the baronage can make him correct his act, and that in the court of the king himself.'[5] This sounds reminiscent of the *Mirror*'s story of the right of the earls to hear complaints against the king in parliament. The reminiscence is much stronger in a passage which seems to have been interpolated into Bracton's text at an early date: 'The king has his court, that is his earls and barons, and earls are so called because they are the king's companions: he who has a companion has a master: if therefore the king is unbridled, that is if he act without the law, they [i.e. the earls] should put a bridle upon him.'[6] This is probably where the author of the *Mirror* got his ideas, though it need not have been: the subject was clearly one which was attracting a

[2] ibid. pp. 6–7.

[3] Bracton, *De legibus et consuetudinibus Angliae*, ed. G. E. Woodbine (Yale, 1922), vol. II, p. 33.

[4] ibid.

[5] ibid. vol. III, p. 43.

[6] ibid. vol. II, p. 110.

good deal of attention. Edward I's extension of such prerogative rights as purveyance to finance his wars gave it direct relevance to political issues of the day.

Another version of the same sort of idea is to be found in the tract called the *Modus Tenendi Parliamentum*, which was written, probably by a chancery clerk, about the year 1320.[7] The *Modus* purports to record the custom of the days of Edmund Ironside, before the Norman Conquest; like the *Mirror* it is a record not of what parliaments ever did, but of what one writer thought they ought to do (though it should be stressed that the author of the *Modus* knew a good deal about parliaments, and was generally much more perceptive about contemporary politics than the author of the *Mirror*). One important chapter of this tract is devoted to what are called 'difficult cases and judgements' in parliament – cases of the sort that may provoke discord between the king and his magnates. They should be referred, says the *Modus*, to a committee of twenty-five persons, to be chosen not by the king but by the Steward, the Constable and the Marshal (hereditary offices, all held by earls). These twenty-five shall choose twelve arbiters in the matter, the twelve six, the six three, and if necessary the three shall choose one (with the king's leave) and his judgement shall be final.[8]

As one might expect, there were attempts to achieve in practice something like what the author of the *Modus* and others suggested. The chronicler Langtoft has a story about the appointment, in the Lincoln parliament of 1301, of a committee of twenty-six discreet men, who should decide whether the king ought or ought not to yield to the petitions of his magnates.[9] A year before this, in the parliament of 1300, the magnates had asked the king to promise that he would punish 'according to the law'

[7] This date for the *Modus* seems to be clearly established by V. H. Galbraith, 'The *Modus Tenendi Parliamentum*', *Journal of the Courtauld and Warburg Institutes* 16 (1953), pp. 81–99. The problems raised by this curious tract have given rise to much discussion; see M. V. Clarke, *Medieval Representation and Consent* (London, 1936); W. A. Morris, 'The date of the *Modus Tenendi Parliamentum*', *E.H.R.* 49 (1934), pp. 407ff.; G. P. Cuttino, 'A reconsideration of the *Modus Tenendi Parliamentum*' in *The Forward Movement of the Fourteenth Century*, ed. F. L. Utley (Ohio, 1961), pp. 31–60 (this includes an English translation of the text); and J. S. Roskell, 'Certain aspects and problems of the English *Modus Tenendi Parliamentum*', *B.J.R.L.* 50 (1967–8), pp. 411–42.

[8] *Modus*, ch. xvii.

[9] *Chron P. de Langtoft* (R.S.) vol. II, p. 330.

officials of his who had contravened the charters. The *Ordinances* of 1311 actually instituted a committee, of one bishop, two earls and two barons, to be appointed in every parliament 'to hear and determine all plaints of those wishing to complain of the king's ministers, whichever they may be, who have contravened the *Ordinances*'. It looks, moreover, as though there was a genuine attempt to implement this clause in 1315, when, after Bannockburn, the *Ordinances* had been re-enforced.[10]

Efforts such as these, to introduce the kind of legal procedures for obtaining redress against the crown that the authors of the *Mirror* and the *Modus* and the interpolator of Bracton wished to see, had little long-term chance of success unless the crown was prepared to acquiesce in them. Edward I was determined never to do this, and Edward II only approved the *Ordinances* under duress. A promise given by a king under duress was a bad guarantee. It seemed to give the *Ordinances* the force of law according to Bracton's authoritative definition: 'that is law which has been justly determined and approved, with the counsel and assent of the great men, the approval of the whole commonwealth, and the authority of the king'. Such laws could not be changed, in Bracton's view, except with the common consent of those who made them.[11] Edward I, however, had drawn a sharp distinction between laws that were made with the common assent and on the crown's initiative (as the charters which his father had freely granted in 1225, and the statutes of his own reign), and those which were made on the initiative of others, as the new laws which he promised to observe in the period 1297-1302. These promises, he told Pope Clement V in 1305, had been wrung from him unwillingly by men who had taken unfair advantage of him in a difficult time. Edward I, who even at the height of his difficulties had never allowed any hint of question about the Bractonian principle, that the king's writ does not run against the king, was determined not to be trammelled by the activities of parliament, which was his own court. As we know, Pope Clement released him from his promises, so setting a precedent that was obviously prejudicial to any future attempt to limit the king's action by the methods that the opposition had adopted in 1297 and afterwards. And Edward II did in fact attempt to follow his father's example, and to obtain from the pope an absolution from his promise to observe the *Ordinances*.

[10] *Ordinances*, cl. 40; and see J. Conway Davies *The Baronial Opposition to Edward II* (Cambridge, 1918), p. 401.
[11] Bracton, *De legibus* vol. II, pp. 19, 21.

It looks as if the fourth clause of Edward II's coronation oath
was drawn up with, among other things, a view to getting round
the difficulty which the absolution of 1305 had posed. 'Sire, do
you grant to be held and observed the just laws and customs that
the community of your realm shall have chosen, and will you, so
far as in you lies, defend and strengthen them to the honour of
God?' – 'I grant and promise them.'[12] This was the text of the
new clause. The magnates seem to have made use of it in 1308 to
secure Gaveston's exile, claiming that since his banishment had
been decreed by the people, for the good of the realm, the king
was bound to enforce it.[13] The doctrine of the fourth clause, if
thus interpreted, was not a comfortable one. Read in this way, it
would seem to imply a transference of sovereignty from the king
to the people too drastic to gain more than temporary acceptance.
For this reason, many historians have doubted whether this was
what the fourth clause really was intended to mean.[14] We will
only say this, that the magnates cannot have hoped that they
could solve their problem for ever by binding the king for the
future to accept rules propounded by the community. In an age
in which it was widely accepted that the king had no superior in
his kingdom and could not be sued, it was very unlikely that he
would accept unwelcome dictates of the community, except
under duress. Sooner or later the question had to be faced,
whether and in what circumstances it could be lawful to use force
against the king, in order to compel him to govern justly.

In connexion with this question of the use of force against the
king, a very important declaration was made by the magnates,

[12] *Statutes of the Realm* vol. I, p. 168.

[13] *Bridlington* (R.S.), p. 34.

[14] Discussion has centred chiefly round the implication of the tense of
the words 'shall have chosen', and on the political circumstances in
which the new form of the oath was drawn up (was opposition to
Edward II already beginning to crystallize?). See B. Wilkinson, 'The
coronation oath of Edward II' in *Historical Essays in Honour of James
Tait*, ed. J. G. Edwards, V. H. Galbraith and E. F. Jacob (Manchester,
1933), pp. 405–16; 'The coronation oath of Edward II and the statute of
York', *Speculum* 19 (1944), pp. 445–69; and in his *Constitutional History
of England* vol. II (London, 1952), pp. 85–111. H. G. Richardson, 'The
English coronation oath', *T.R.H.S.* 4th ser., 23 (1941), pp. 129–58;
and 'The English coronation oath', *Speculum* 24 (1949), pp. 44–75.
R. S. Hoyt, 'The English coronation oath of 1308', *E.H.R.* 71 (1956),
pp. 353–83. And, more generally, P. E. Schramm, *A History of the
English Coronation* (Oxford, 1937).

according to the Canon of Bridlington in the year 1308. It is worth quoting in full:

> Homage and the oath of allegiance are stronger and bind more by reason of the crown than by reason of the person of the king, and this appears in that before the estate of the crown has descended to a person, no allegiance belongs to the person or is owed ... Wherefore if the king by chance be not guided by reason, in relation to the estate of the crown, his liege subjects are bound by their oath made to the crown to guide the king back again by reason and amend the estate of the crown: otherwise the oath would not be kept. Then it is to be asked how they ought to guide the king in such a case, whether by form of law or by violence? He [the king] cannot be directed by course of law, for there are no judges except the king's. In which case, if the king's will be not according to reason, he will only have error maintained and confirmed. Wherefore it behoves in order to save the oath, that when the king will not redress a matter and remove that which is damaging to the crown and hurtful to the people, it is adjudged that the error be removed by violence: for he the king is bound by his oath to govern the people, and his liege subjects are bound to protect the people according to the law.[15]

Two points in this declaration are of particular interest. One is the clear distinction drawn between the crown (kingship as representing lawful authority), and the king in his personal, human capacity. The ability to draw this distinction has often been claimed to be a sign of precocious political thinking on the part of Edward II's opponents. There is nothing precocious about the other important point, however, the assertion that force is a legitimate means of seeking redress where the ordinary course of law cannot prevail.

In this last respect the declaration of 1308 had a sort of precedent in the sanctions clause of the Great Charter of 1215. That clause set up a committee of twenty-five barons, to whom complainants might resort if they believed their rights under the charter had been infringed; and who had the right and duty, if the king and his ministers would not amend the injury in question, to raise men and use every kind of force to distrain them to do so. The ideas of 1215 seem to have struck root, for they appear in another document of Edward II's reign besides the *Declaration*. This is the tract on the *Office of the Steward*, written by someone in the entourage of Thomas of Lancaster and probably

[15] *Bridlington*, pp. 33-4.

in the year 1321.[16] According to this tract it was the Steward's duty to receive the complaints of those who had failed to obtain justice from the king or his courts, and to see that they were remedied in parliament. It also said that it was his duty, if the king followed evil counsel, to proceed together with the Constable and the Marshal against the king's evil counsellors 'with banner raised in the name of the king and the realm, and to take such a counsellor as the public enemy of the king and the kingdom'.[17] The reference to the raising of banners, a sign of open war, is striking. It reminds us of the connexion between the claims of the baronage and of such officers as the Steward in our period to a right to use force against the king, and the old feudal right of a vassal to make war on his overlord, if the overlord outstepped the customary and lawful limits of their contractual relationship.

In the political and legal literature of the late thirteenth and early fourteenth centuries, we have constantly found the same idea cropping up: that there are or should be persons with whom there lies a right to review the conduct of the king and his officials, and to amend it, if necessary by force. This is a very interesting notion, suggesting strongly that men of the period were more concerned by the threat of too much government than its opposite (and it is besides a view which ought to obtain some sympathetic appreciation in this age of protest of the mid-twentieth century). The persons with whom this right and duty to restrain the king was thought to lie were aristocrats, the earls according to some, the baronage or a committee of barons according to others, or the great hereditary officers of state, the Steward, the Constable and the Marshal (who were all earls, and who in fact played leading roles in opposition between 1297 and 1322). Their duty, however, was not viewed in a narrow, sectional way: it was to protect the entire community, not just the baronage, from governmental oppression. The opponents of the crown went out of their way to make it clear that their concern was for the community as a whole, through such propaganda documents as the *Monstraunces* of 1297 and the manifestos of the Lancastrian counter-parliaments of 1321.[18]

There were some seeds of responsible good sense in this approach to the problem of controlling and restraining at need the

[16] The text is given by L. W. Vernon Harcourt, *His Grace the Steward and Trial of Peers* (London, 1907), pp. 164–7 (English translation, pp. 148–51).

[17] ibid. p. 150.

[18] See above, pp. 46, 68.

activities of a busy royal administration that was often oppressive and often corruptly directed. It was an approach that had no real future, however. By the time of Edward II it was already beginning to look antique in conception and unworkable in practice, too aristocratic and too redolent of the feudal past to afford a useful protection to the rights of the community of the king's subjects. This was in large part the result of two other developments of the period, the growth of a new legal concept of the crime of high treason, and the growth of the institution called parliament.

The ancient English idea of treason was an act of disloyalty to an individual lord. In the time of Edward I and Edward II ideas culled from Roman law, with which almost all common lawyers had at least a nodding acquaintance, were introducing into English custom the concept of high treason as a crime against the state, an injury to the majesty of public authority. Edward I and his judges, in proceeding against the leaders of the defeated Welsh and Scots, would not consider their actions in terms of the nobleman's feudal right to resist his overlord if the latter overstepped his rights. They judged armed rebellion to be high treason; and as traitors David of Wales in 1283, and later Rhys ap Mareddud, William Wallace, the Earl of Atholl and Sir Christopher Seton were judged and executed. In Edward II's reign this interpretation of armed resistance to the crown, as an affront to majesty and so high treason, was applied in the cases of Earl Thomas of Lancaster, the Earl of Hereford, Roger Damory, and a number of other rebels in 1322. The penalties of treason included forfeiture of all lands held in fee simple. It thus became very dangerous for a magnate to involve himself in actions which might be construed as treason, and specifically it became obviously dangerous to proceed against counsellors of the king, bad characters though they might be, 'with banners raised', in manner of war.[19]

It should be stressed here that this idea of treason was not just a view of royalist judges: it was an interpretation of the law that was gaining wide acceptance. The opponents of Edward II proceeded against his favourites as traitors and public enemies. Gaveston, the Despensers and the Earl of Arundel were all charged with high treason. The particular treason that they were

[19] J. G. Bellamy provides a useful introduction to the history of the development of the concept of treason in English law, and commentary on the treason trials of Edward I and II's reigns, in *The Law of Treason in England in the Later Middle Ages* (Cambridge, 1970), ch. 1 and 2.

most often held to have committed was the offence of 'accroaching royal power': that is to say, of obtaining a hold over the king which enabled them to make illegitimate and abusive use of royal power, and so to injure its majesty and the public weal. There was an obvious and close connexion between this idea of treason and the view of the Roman lawyers that any exercise of imperial prerogatives by a subject was *lèse majesté*, high treason.[20]

On the basis of the distinction drawn in the 1308 *Declaration* the opponents of Edward II's favourites could claim that their actions did not constitute armed resistance to the crown. They were only using force to make the king exercise the authority of the crown in a lawful manner, and to rescue him from those who were accroaching his power. This distinction was, however, too fine to be comfortably drawn in practice. The charge of 'accroachment' widened the scope of treason to the point where intimacy with the king might in itself be grounds of an accusation. Such extension of the meaning of treason endangered the stability of the realm, because the penalties of treason, death and forfeiture gave the heirs of a dead traitor a vested interest in the reversal of the political *status quo*.

Aside from the danger of facing a charge of treason, there was another reason to make magnates hesitate to implement the claims, put forward on behalf of the nobility, to a right to review the actions of the crown and if necessary to resist them. People in general were not sufficiently satisfied about the nature of this right. This was partly, no doubt, because people distrusted some of the men who claimed to exercise it, such as Thomas of Lancaster. It was also because its basis in custom was flimsy and unclear: no two authors ever described the right in quite the same way. The reaction to the counter-parliaments of 1321 is significant here. Lancaster and his allies went out of their way to make it clear that they were acting in the interests of the community as a whole. It was to provide 'suitable remedy' for the ills of the kingdom 'by common counsel and unanimous consent' that the meeting at Sherburn had been called, John de Bek told those who were assembled there.[21] But at Sherburn the northern

[20] Bellamy, *The Law of Treason*, pp. 64–72, draws a distinction in law between 'accroaching royal power' and actual treason. This distinction may be rather a fine one where the crimes in question were of a political nature.

[21] *Bridlington*, pp. 62ff.; and compare G. L. Haskins, 'The Doncaster petition, 1321', *E.H.R.* 53 (1938), pp. 483–5.

magnates and prelates would not seal indentures to enter into confederacy with Lancaster and his marcher allies. The prelates, and probably the magnates too, wished to see the matters that had been raised dealt with not in an assembly of barons and their retainers, but authoritatively in a parliament summoned by the king in the customary manner.

The anxiety to see great matters dealt with in parliament is in fact a consistent theme of the years of trouble. The opponents of Edward I in 1297 insisted that taxes should only be lawful if granted by a representative assembly called for the purpose. The Ordainers built their scheme for reform round the authority of parliament. Lancaster, true to the principles of the *Ordinances*, told Edward II in 1317 that 'you ought not to wish to enact or treat outside parliament about anything which ought to be determined in parliament'.[22] Bishop Stapledon, a curialist on good terms with the Despensers, was insistent with the king late in 1321 that since the sentence which had been passed on them had been given in parliament, it ought not to be revoked elsewhere.[23] The York parliament of 1322 finally gave this view authority as constitutionally sound doctrine: 'matters which are to be determined for the estate of the king and his heirs, and for the estate of the kingdom and of the people, shall be treated, granted, and established *in parliament* by our lord the king with the consent of the prelates, earls, barons and of the commonalty of the kingdom as has been accustomed in time past'.[24]

Since a lawful parliament could only be assembled by the royal summons, this insistence on parliamentary authority was favourable to the crown. The Statute of York made it clear that counter-parliaments assembled by the Steward or the Constable or any one else had no standing, and that it was unlawful for any assembly but parliament to seek to decide matters affecting the state of the realm.[25] The York parliament of 1322 also quashed

[22] *Bridlington*, p. 52.

[23] *Reg. Stapledon* No. 409, quoted by M. V. Clarke, *Medieval Representation*, p. 169.

[24] *Statutes of the Realm* vol. I, p. 189.

[25] On the Statute of York see further G. Lapsley, 'The interpretation of the Statute of York, 1322', *E.H.R.* 56 (1941), pp. 22–51, 411–46; and J. R. Strayer, 'The Statute of York and the community of the realm', *A.H.R.* 47 (1941), pp. 1–22. Some of the major conclusions of G. L. Haskins, *The Statute of York and the Interest of the Commons* (Cambridge, Mass., 1935), are highly questionable, though it is the fullest treatment of the subject.

the *Ordinances*, and so the machinery that they had set up for the review of royal and official actions by a committee in parliament went by the board, and nothing took its place. This did not of course solve all problems for the king. The implications of the Statute of York were the very opposite of absolutist. The king might still find himself compelled by force of circumstance or duress to summon a parliament which he did not want to meet, and might there find himself compelled to agree to things which he did not like. The statute did not provide the king with any way out of this situation, and it could not stifle the belief that the great men of the realm had a right, even a duty, to rescue the crown from evil counsel, by force if need be (we shall find this notion looming large much later, in Yorkist propaganda in Henry VI's reign). But it did deliver the king, and finally, from the bogy of 'companions' among his subjects who could be his law-ful masters, entitled to review official acts independently of any initiative on his part. Whatever might happen in parliament, in the courts at large the Bractonian principles that the king had no superior and that his writ would not run against himself were firmly retrenched.

In the last few paragraphs a great deal has been said about parlia-ment, but we have not said anything about what the word parlia-ment meant to men in the reigns of Edward I and Edward II. This is a subject which has given rise to a good deal of controversy among historians in the past, and will probably continue to do so in the future. It is a subject, however, on which something has to be said, particularly given that the meaning of the word was shifting importantly within the period in question.[26]

[26] The early history of parliament is a controversial topic. It is not possible to give a full list of the important secondary works. The starting point for most modern study is F. W. Maitland's brilliant introduction to the *Memoranda de Parliamento* (R.S. 1893); E. Miller, *The Origins of Parliament* (Historical Association pamphlet, 1960), is an excellent introduction to all the subsequent debate. Some important articles are cited below, notes 29, 30 and 39; besides these should be mentioned C. H. McIlwain, *The High Court of Parliament* (Yale, 1910); F. M. Powicke, *The Thirteenth Century* (Oxford, 1962), ch. VIII and XI; B. Wilkinson, *Constitutional History of Medieval England* vol. III (London, 1957), ch. V–VII; T. F. T. Plucknett, 'Parliament' in *The English Government at Work 1327–1336*, ed. J. F. Willard and W. A. Morris (Cambridge, Mass., 1940), vol. I, pp. 82–128; H. M. Cam, 'From witness of the shire to full parliament', *T.R.H.S.* 4th ser., 26 (1944), and 'Representation in Medieval England', *History* 38 (1953),

Parliament has been described in the earliest stage of its development as 'rather an act than a body of persons'.[27] This is a useful phrase. Certainly the composition of parliament was unfixed in the late thirteenth and the early fourteenth centuries. Edward I summoned fifty-two parliaments; representatives of the shires and boroughs attended thirteen of them only. On occasion, as for instance in 1295 and the spring parliament of 1305, he summoned to parliament also the representatives of the lower clergy, who later would have attended not parliament but convocations. The number of those who received individual summonses, the bishops, abbots, earls and barons, fluctuated very considerably moreover. Ninety-eight lay lords were summoned in 1300, but four years earlier, in 1296, only forty-three had been. Twenty important men, magnates, bishops, judges and clerks, were all that Edward I summoned to the autumn parliament of 1305, which drew up the ordinance for the government of Scotland with the aid of ten representatives of that kingdom. No knights were called from the English shires, no burgesses from the towns, and only a handful of magnates, though the business that was in hand was of the highest importance.

For this early stage, a definition of the occasions on which parliament might meet is easier to find than a definition of its personnel. 'A session of the king's council is the core and essence of every *parliamentum*,' Maitland wrote,[28] and it is one of the few statements about the early history of parliament that stands virtually unchallenged. The king's council was, of course, a body not more easily defined in terms of personnel than a parliament. There were some efforts to define the membership of the council in Edward II's time, in 1316 and notably in 1318 in the Treaty of Leake; but they were not very successful and things soon reverted to the usual situation in which the king took advice from those whom he chose to consult. There was, however, a difference between a parliamentary session of the council and a routine meeting of the royal familiars in the king's chamber. When parliament met the courts were always in full session, and its session

---

pp. 11–26. H. G. Richardson and G. O. Sayles have summarized a number of their arguments in *Parliaments and Great Councils in Medieval England* (London, 1961); also important among their contributions is 'The king's ministers in parliament', *E.H.R.* 46 (1931), pp. 529–50, and 47 (1932), pp. 194–203, 377–97. Two classic articles by J. G. Edwards are cited below, notes 29 and 39.

[27] F. W. Maitland, intro. to *Memoranda de Parliamento*, p. lxvii.
[28] ibid. p. lxxxviii.

ELMA—D*

brought together in a wider body of great men the heads of the departments of state, the chancellor and treasurer, the judges, and the leading officials of the household. A parliamentary session of the council thus realized the royal authority at its fullest and most formal, and also at the peak of its activity. It was a meeting in consequence which enjoyed a general competence to deal with all the affairs of the realm (except that it might be questioned whether it could grant a general aid, unless the shire and borough representatives were present, or at least a substantial showing of great magnates, lay and ecclesiastical).

The fact that parliaments met in the law terms and involved a plenary session of the king's courts may suggest that the chief function of parliaments at this stage was to deal with judicial business.[29] Certainly pleas and petitions dominate the early records (or 'rolls') of parliament. Strictly speaking, of course, petitions, which normally came from individuals or corporations such as towns, request a remedy of the royal grace, not as of right. But it is reasonable to describe the parliamentary scrutiny of petitions as judicial business, since it concerned primarily the working of the law and of the courts. The usual process was that the council examined a petition handed in at parliament time, and then sent the petitioner on to the relevant court – the King's Bench, or the exchequer, as it might be – to seek a suitable remedy there. His petition was endorsed to this effect by the councillors who had examined it, and was recorded by a clerk of parliament before it was sent on to the lower court.[30] Pleas of parliament were, in contrast, tried and terminated by the council in parliament. They were usually cases of first instance, that for one reason or another it was thought best to hear in parliament. A good example was the trial of Nicholas Segrave for treason in

[29] The importance of judicial business in early parliaments is strongly stressed by H. G. Richardson and G. O. Sayles, 'The early records of the English parliaments', *B.I.H.R.* 5 (1928), pp. 129–54; 6 (1929), pp. 71–88, 129–55. For a different view, see the masterly article by J. G. Edwards, 'Justice in early English parliaments', *B.I.H.R.* 27 (1954), pp. 35–53.

[30] On petitions see G. L. Haskins, 'The petitions of representatives in the parliaments of Edward I', *E.H.R.* 53 (1938), pp. 1–20; and D. Rayner, 'The forms and machinery of the "Commune Petition" in the fourteenth century', *E.H.R.* 56 (1941), pp. 198–233, 549–70. Haskins effectively demolishes the view of D. Pasquet, *Essay on the Origins of the House of Commons* (Cambridge, 1925), that it was a chief business of representatives to present petitions from their communities.

1305. He was a baron of standing who had deserted the king's army in Scotland without the royal licence, and both his status and the gravity of his offence made it imperative that he should be judged in the most formal and authoritative forum available. There was apparently a good deal of discussion of his sentence, with the angry king bent on making an example and the worried magnates urging clemency. In the end Nicholas was released, on condition of finding seven good warrantors that he would hold himself ready at the king's will to surrender his person into prison and his estates into the king's hand.[31]

Parliament was also a convenient forum for the announcement of new legal remedies. Most of Edward I's statutes were authorized in parliament, though this was sometimes done, curiously, after the main body of those summoned had gone home.[32] This is a reminder that statutes did not need the assent of parliament; they were announced there because the king thought it a useful opportunity to give publicity to new legal remedies that he and his judges had devised. It was a time at which men did not yet draw a very sharp distinction between legislation and the judgement of pleas, as the author of the tract on the Steward's office makes clear: 'if it be found that the law is doubtful in an *individual* case', it says, the matter should be referred to a committee 'who shall there ordain, found, and establish remedy of law in all such cases for ever afterward to endure'.[33] Once again we find that parliamentary business is in the broad sense judicial.

The functions of parliament so far reviewed fit well with the famous definition of the law book, *Fleta*: 'the king has his court in his council in his parliaments, where judicial doubts are determined, and new remedies are established for new wrongs, and justice is done to everyone according to his deserts'.[34] They are functions, too, which received sharp emphasis in the *Ordinances* of 1311: 'in parliaments, pleas which are delayed . . . and pleas wherein the justices are of different opinions, shall be recorded and settled; and likewise those bills [i.e. petitions] which are brought to parliament shall be settled as heretofore in accordance

[31] *Memoranda de Parliamento*, pp. 255-62, and intro., pp. lxxvi-lxxvii; and see F. M. Powicke, *The Thirteenth Century*, p. 333.
[32] On statutes and parliament see T. F. T. Plucknett, *The Legislation of Edward I* (Oxford, 1949); and H. G. Richardson and G. O. Sayles, 'The early statutes', *L.Q.R.* 50 (1934).
[33] Vernon Harcourt, *His Grace the Steward*, p. 149.
[34] *Fleta*, ed. H. G. Richardson and G. O. Sayles (Selden Soc., 1953), vol. II, p. 109.

with law and right'.[35] They are also, thirdly, the functions to which the early rolls of parliament give greatest prominence. They probably occupied more of the time of the counsellors and judges whose sessions were at the 'core' of parliament than anything else. That does not mean, however, that they were the only functions of parliaments, or the most essential, or the most important.

Edward I was in fact impatient at the amount of time that had to be spent on petitions. As early as 1279 he was complaining of the number of these, and the time that it took to consider them: henceforth, he ordered, only those which could not be answered without the king should be referred to him, 'so that the king and his council can attend to the great business of the realm'. It was to treat of the great business of the realm that men were summoned from far afield to attend parliaments, not to hear or for that matter to present petitions. The wording of the writs of summons to Edward I's parliaments makes this abundantly clear. This is how the king wrote to Edmund Earl of Cornwall in 1295:

> Because we wish to have colloquy and to treat with you and with the rest of the principal men of our kingdom, to provide for remedies against the dangers which in these days are threatening our whole kingdom, we command you, strictly enjoining you in the fidelity and love in which you are bound to us, that on the Sunday next after the feast of St Martin you be present in person to treat, ordain and act, together with us and with the prelates, and the rest of the principal men and the other inhabitants of our kingdom, as may be necessary to meet dangers of this kind.[36]

The evidence of the writs of summons throws the emphasis on different activities and functions of parliament to those highlighted in the rolls, with their records of pleas and petitions. To judge by the writs, the discussion of great matters of state was the prime purpose of holding parliaments.

Those whom the king summoned from a distance to treat and consult about the affairs of the realm by no means always stayed the whole length of a parliament. In 1305, for instance, the representatives of the shires and boroughs were sent home on 21 March, but the council continued to deal with business in parliament, some of it very important, until Easter (18 April). In fact, there was no special reason why the English kings should have summoned great men to treat on the affairs of the realm and

---

[35] *Ordinances*, cl. 29.
[36] Wilkinson, *Constitutional History* vol. III, p. 178.

representatives of the community to hear and witness what was done, at the same time that they and their counsellors were dealing with petitions and important judicial pleas. It was, however, highly convenient for them to do so, and lent added authority to both the political and the legislative decisions that were reached in great parliamentary assemblies. Had Edward I tried to keep such assemblies separate from the judicial sessions of the council, the English parliament might have developed into a professional judicial body like the *Parlement* of the French kings, and the representative assemblies into something like their *States General*. But he did not do so, and the result was that the political and legislative function of the court called parliament assumed in course of time far greater importance than its judicial authority.

The growing concern of parliaments with matters of more general import than purely judicial business helped to define its composition more clearly. Lack of confidence in Edward II and his intimate counsellors was here an important factor. The general preoccupation in the first part of his reign with correcting what the king and his ministers had done amiss shifted the emphasis of ideas about the authority of parliament. That authority was now to be esteemed, not because the king and all his judges and councillors were present at parliament time, but because other people were as well. The *Ordinances* labour, over and again, the need for matters of general import to be decided 'with the assent of the barons', not just of the council, in parliament. Thomas of Lancaster refused to recognize as 'parliamentary' assemblies to which the whole baronage was not summoned.[37] What precisely he thought this meant must remain in doubt, for it was not yet clear what entitled a magnate to an individual summons to parliament: the number of lords, lay and ecclesiastical, who received one fluctuated throughout the fourteenth century. Nevertheless, by the end of Edward II's reign it was clearly established that a council meeting could not be a parliament, unless a substantial body of peers had been summoned. A meeting such as that of the autumn of 1305, when a score of trusted councillors appeared to advise the king, would no longer have been reckoned a parliament.

In the Statute of York of 1322 parliament was clearly recognized as a body representing the whole community of the realm. That was why all matters affecting the 'estate of the realm and of the people' had to be dealt with in parliament. Earlier, in 1297, the *Confirmatio* had stressed the need for the assent of the

[37] *Bridlington*, pp. 51-2; compare *Vita Edwardi II*, p. 104.

community of the realm to all grants of extraordinary taxation. It is not clear from either document, however, who precisely had to be present in parliament for the whole people to be represented there. Evidence from Henry III's reign shows that, after the middle of the thirteenth century, the baronage alone or a part of it could be understood to represent the community. Parliament, according to the Provisions of Oxford of 1258, should be a meeting of the council with twelve barons chosen by their fellows to represent the community. The aristocratic political tracts of the 1290s and the earlier part of Edward II's reign still assumed that the barons, or in some cases the earls alone, were the lawful guardians of the community's interest. The *Ordinances* again treated parliament as essentially a baronial assembly. This evidence makes it unfortunately impossible to associate the stress of the Statute of York on the representation of the 'commonalty' with the role of the commons in parliament, though the commons were present at York in 1322, as they had been in 1297 when the *Confirmatio* was granted.

If, however, the commons had not yet fully established their position in parliament in 1322, they had certainly come very near to it. After 1290 they were summoned to one in three of the parliaments of Edward I's later years. By the end of Edward II's reign a parliament to which they were not summoned was the exception. Time, the unsettled conditions of the period, and their increasingly regular appearance at parliaments, had made both king and barons aware of their usefulness as 'agents of propaganda and vehicles of public opinion' (to use Professor McKisack's phrase), and they had begun to find a part of their own to play in the redress of popular grievances. By the beginning of the next reign, in the early 1330s, we begin to find that commons' petitions (petitions, that is, which the commons as a whole had agreed to sponsor) were making a mark on the legislation that emerged from parliaments.[38]

There is no doubt that the original reason for the growth of the influence of the commons in parliament was the part that they played in granting taxation. Even in the reign of Henry III doubts had been expressed as to whether the magnates alone, in a great council, could bind others who had not been present in that council to pay a tax that they granted. In this respect, the clause in the summonses to parliament of shire and borough representatives which insisted that they should come with full power

[38] See H. L. Gray, *The Influence of the Commons on Early Leglislation* (Cambridge, Mass., 1932), pp. 207–27.

to bind their communities (*cum plena potestate pro se et comitatu suo* in the case of the shire knights), and which became a regular feature of all writs of summons to them in the late years of Edward I, is clearly important.[39] With the exception of the eighth of 1297, whose collection was abandoned because of opposition, Edward I never sought to collect a subsidy which had not received the assent of representatives armed with full powers to bind their communities. His writs ordering the collection of subsidies granted in parliaments normally referred to the assent which they had received. The principle that the assent of representatives was necessary to give lawful authority to a grant of taxation thus gained ground through regular practical application. In the *Modus* we find the lesson of practice translated into constitutional doctrine. 'Two knights who come to the parliament for the shire have a greater voice in parliament in granting and denying [an aid] than a greater earl of England' because, its author says, the knights of the shire with the burgesses and the proctors of the clergy 'represent the whole community of England', whereas a magnate comes to parliament 'for his own person, and for no other'.[40] The *Modus* is not of course a safe authority: but its author's opinion on this point is supported by the collective evidence of writs of summons to the commons, of writs authorizing the collection of aids, and of the asides of chroniclers.

The idea of representation that is so clearly expressed in the *Modus* had its origins in Roman law and canonical practice, which taught that a community of individuals, such as the chapter of a collegiate church (or a town corporation, for that matter) could act for legal purposes as a body through its proctors, appointed by the members of the community and with power to bind them all. The Roman and canon laws provided a full and elaborate theory of legal representation. Edward I in his summons to representatives of the lower clergy in 1295 actually quoted the canonical tag 'what affects all should be approved by all'. He was then thinking in terms of taxation, but the principle was one

---

[39] On this subject see the masterly article by J. G. Edwards, 'The *Plena Potestas* of English parliamentary representatives' in *Oxford Essays in Medieval History Presented to H. E. Salter*, pp. 141–54 (he stresses in particular the writ of 1294, whose wording became traditional); and, for a rather different approach, G. Post, '*Plena Potestas* and consent in medieval assemblies', *Traditio* i (1943), pp. 355–408.

[40] *Modus*, ch. xxiii; and see further the articles by G. P. Cuttino and G. Post, cited above in notes 7 and 39.

clearly capable of much wider application. At the end of Edward II's reign the procedures adopted at his deposition afforded a very startling demonstration of how far its application might be extended.

The deputation, which was appointed to go to Kenilworth to renounce homage and allegiance to Edward II in January 1327 was carefully constructed so as to represent the whole realm, as that realm was represented in parliament. It included two earls, three bishops, four barons, certain abbots and priors, two barons of the Cinque Ports, four burgesses of London, and some selected representatives of other boroughs and shire knights. At Kenilworth William Trussel, a knight, renounced homage and allegiance 'on behalf of the whole kingdom' (one authority adds 'and of parliament').[41] Though it cannot be proved conclusively that this deputation was appointed in or by parliament, there is no doubt about its representative capacity. The idea of a deputation seems to have originated when discussion was going on as to how King Edward could be forced to attend the January parliament, in which Archbishop Reynolds was much involved. He consulted his old and experienced friend, prior Henry Eastry of Christ Church, Canterbury, who advised 'that the king should be required to attend by an embassy of two earls, two barons, four citizens and four knights of the shire *elected to represent* the whole community of the realm'.[42] From the very beginning, the procedures followed at the time of the deposition assumed that what was to be done must be done with the authority of the whole realm. They also assumed that in order for this authority to be exercised all the estates, not just the magnates and the higher clergy, must be involved through representatives.

The procedures adopted at the deposition of Edward II are testimony to a great shift in the balance of political authority in

---

[41] *Chron G. Le Baker*, ed. E. M. Thompson (Oxford, 1889), p. 28: and MS chronicle quoted by M. V. Clarke, *Medieval Representation*, p. 185, note 4. Miss Clarke discusses (pp. 186ff.) the composition of the deputation (which is reported with slight differences by the various authorities).

[42] Clarke, *Medieval Representation*, pp. 177–8. It should be noted, though, that the deputation which in the event went to Kenilworth to announce the deposition seems to have been designed to represent 'estates' of the realm (earls, barons, prelates, clergy, burgesses and knights), whereas the commons in parliament represented communities (shires and boroughs).

the English kingdom. They involved a tacit abandonment of the claim that had often been put forward in the past on behalf of the magnates, that they, on their own, could be regarded as in a special sense the guardians of the community and its rights. Even more important was the clear demonstration that, in the long run, the authority of the king was grounded in the assent of the community. It was shown that the customary laws, and the rights of the community, had an existence independent of the authority of the king, though not, perhaps, of the crown. The assertion of the representative authority of the people in 1327 turned the flank of the royal prerogative. A constitutional means had been found to deal with a king who would not observe the customary limitations on his right or heed his subjects' demands for redress of legitimate grievances. He could be removed by an act of state sponsored by the whole people and in which all, high and low, assented through their representatives.

The lesson of the humiliation of the monarchy in 1327 could never afterwards be forgotten. Edward I, in his day, had ridden his subjects on a tight rein, magnates and others alike. No king after 1327 could act as he had done with quite the same confidence. This moral is written clear in the subsequent history of the relations of English medieval kings with their subjects. Earlier, in the twelfth and thirteenth centuries most of the great changes in English government had come about as a result of royal initiative. After 1327 until at least the 1470s – as once again after the middle of the sixteenth century – the greatest changes came about not in consequence of the king's wishes, but in response to pressures from the politically conscious elements of the population.

The age of Edward III
1330–1360

5

The early years of Edward III
1330–1338

On the night of 19 October 1330, King Edward III, a young man of eighteen, entered Nottingham castle by a subterranean passage in the company of a group of youthful noblemen, the chief of whom was Sir William Montagu. In the castle he seized Roger Mortimer, the paramour of his mother Queen Isabella, who for the last four years had lorded it in England 'as if he were king over all'.[1] Mortimer was taken bound to London, where he was tried before his peers as a traitor: he was hanged at Tyburn on 29 November.[2] The young king's *coup* had been carefully planned in advance, and the pope had had secret information about the sort of thing that was afoot. It had been a risky business, but the gamble paid off, and Edward in consequence at last began to rule the country of which he had hitherto been king in name only.

Few kings of England ever set out on their reigns with more intractable problems facing them than Edward III did. His father had reigned for twenty years, and for those twenty years nothing had been stable in English politics. In the long struggle between the king and the various groups of magnates that opposed him, order had declined steeply in the counties. In the countryside, marauding gangs wandered armed and unhindered.[3] The final deposition of the king had utterly humiliated the monarchy. The reign had been marked by disasters abroad as

---

[1] See *Chron A. Murimuth* (R.S.), p. 62; and *R. Avesbury* (R.S.), pp. 284, 285.

[2] On Mortimer's trial see T. F. T. Plucknett, 'The origin of impeachment', *T.R.H.S.* 4th ser., 24 (1942), pp. 58ff.

[3] See on this subject E. L. G. Stones, 'The Folvilles of Ashby Folville', *T.R.H.S.* 5th ser., 7 (1957), pp. 117ff; and J. G. Bellamy, 'The Coterel gang: an anatomy of a band of fourteenth century criminals', *E.H.R.* 79 (1964), pp. 698ff.

well as at home. After Bannockburn, the English had never succeeded in organizing any effective resistance to Robert Bruce of
Scotland. There had been a moment when it looked as if his
brother Edward would overrun the English lordship of Ireland.
The end of hostilities in the war of St Sardos had left the French
in occupation of the Agenais, and the English saddled with the
settlement of a long series of claims for indemnity for war
damage from French subjects. The four years of Mortimer's
dominance had done nothing to restore stability at home or failing English fortunes in the Scots war. Edward III, if he was to
make his new won authority respected, had somehow to recreate
a confidence in royal leadership that had been totally lost in the
long years of trouble and misfortune. In order to do so, he had
got to succeed in whatever he took up: he inherited a situation in
which Plantagenet kingship could not afford further failure and
humiliation.

That the attention of the young king should have focused
early on Scotland is not surprising. Bannockburn was the most
signal disgrace that English arms had suffered since the Norman
Conquest; and every subsequent effort to restore English fortunes had failed. Bruce's raids across the border had devastated
northern England, and in the beginning of Edward III's own
reign, when Mortimer and Isabella were in control, the English
had fought two costly campaigns in the north. Both were unsuccessful, and in 1328 the English had little option but to ratify
Bruce's terms for peace: his recognition as king of an independent realm with no ties to England, whose frontiers gave the
English not a foot of the territory that they had fought to conquer
and hold ever since 1296. This peace (the Treaty of Northampton)
was a bitter pill to the English. 'Accursed be the time when this
parliament was ordained at Northampton,' the Brut chronicler
declared, 'for the king by false counsel was fraudulently disinherited'.[4] Many believed, probably rightly, that Edward himself
had been in no way responsible for what had been granted but
that 'the Queen and Mortimer had arranged the whole thing'.[5]
It was obviously to Edward's advantage, in 1330 and after, to
give colour to this suggestion, and the best way to do so was by
taking a more belligerent attitude to the Scots.

There was another powerful motive that may have encouraged
the king in the same direction. In the reign of Edward II the
coincidence of civil confusion with the Anglo-Scottish war had

[4] *Brut Chronicle*, ed. F. W. D. Brie (E.E.T.S., 1906), vol. 1, p. 256.
[5] *Scalacronica*, ed. J. Stevenson (Maitland Club, 1836), p. 156.

demonstrated the danger that might arise from English magnates being drawn into the orbit of a technically foreign power when they found themselves in opposition in domestic politics. Thomas of Lancaster, and later Andrew Harclay, had both become treasonably involved with Bruce. This danger had persisted into the first years of Edward III's reign. The confessions extorted when the Earl of Kent's conspiracy was nipped in the bud in March 1330 revealed that his *coup* should have been assisted by an incursion in force from Scotland. Edward III can have had no wish to live with the possibility that great subjects of his might become involved with an alien and potentially hostile power; and the best way to ensure that they did not was to unite them in action against the power in question.

Robert Bruce had died in 1329, and he left as his heir his son David, a boy of five. David's minority gave Edward the chance to test the prospects of intervention in Scotland without committing himself further than was safe and convenient. Bruce, it will be remembered, was at the beginning of his reign only one of a number of possible claimants to the Scottish throne. In the years before Bannockburn he had been busy eliminating possible rivals and their followers. For the heirs of the families who had opposed him, and for the English lords who had once held estates in Scotland, his victories meant exile and the loss of their lands. So his death seemed a golden opportunity to the little group whom men called 'the disinherited'. The figure round whom they gathered was Edward Balliol, the son of that John Balliol whose claim to the Scottish crown was in 1292 preferred to that of Bruce's grandfather. In 1331 Edward Balliol was brought to England by two leaders of the disinherited, Henry Beaumont and David of Atholl. Using the Beaumont manor of Sandal in Yorkshire as their headquarters, they began to gather a little army. In formal loyalty to the terms of the Treaty of Northampton, the English king's sheriff was instructed to forbid the assembly of men for the expedition and to arrest the leaders. It is virtually certain that he was told in fact not to act on these orders; indeed, Edward III actually connived in the sale of English estates, by means of which the conspirators raised funds for their venture.[6] They sailed from Ravenspur near Hull on

[6] See R. Nicholson, *Edward III and the Scots* (Oxford, 1965), pp. 75–78. This excellent monograph has brought out the importance of Edward III's relations with Scotland in his early years more clearly than any previous work; and I am deeply in its debt for what is said on this subject in the present chapter.

31 July 1332, and on 11 August won an unexpected but conclusive victory over the army of the guardian of Scotland, Donald Earl of Mar, at Dupplin Moor, not far from Perth. In the weeks following many Scottish nobles and churchmen flocked to seek Edward Balliol's peace, and on 24 September he was enthroned at Scone as King of Scotland.

In the autumn of 1332 Edward III travelled north to York, so as to keep a closer eye on events in Scotland. It was well for him that he did so. When the parliament that he had summoned there was fully assembled in January, Balliol was a fugitive suppliant for his aid. He had been surprised at Annan on 17 December by the Earl of Moray and Sir Archibald Douglas, who were faithful to David Bruce, and had to flee for his life. A firm decision on English policy was thus forced on Edward, and it had to be taken quickly.

Edward's reaction was unhesitant. In parliament, a council was appointed to attend and advise him on Scottish affairs, and the commons were then sent home. Three days after they had gone writs went out for the raising of troops. Within the week the Abbot of St Mary's York, acting as treasurer for the king, had made substantial advances to magnates who had agreed to serve in a forthcoming campaign, as well as to Edward Balliol and his followers. Orders were given for the exchequer and the Court of Common Pleas to be transferred from Westminster to York, where they were to remain for the next five years. In May Edward appeared at the head of his army before Berwick, and began to blockade the town. On 19 July, the Scottish army which had marched to its relief was crushingly defeated at Halidon Hill.

Halidon Hill was the first battle which fully demonstrated the potential of the English longbow. Among the Scots, who had charged uphill in the face of the archers' fire, the carnage was terrible. The deaths of five earls, of Sir Archibald Douglas, and of a host of other notable men made the victory seem complete, politically as well as militarily. Edward III left Scotland confidently on 29 July, while Edward Balliol marched forward to reduce the land and the fortresses of his surviving enemies. By midsummer of the next year, 1334, it looked as if Scotland was definitively his. David Bruce had left the country to seek refuge in France; and Balliol was able to leave his kingdom to come to Newcastle, where on 19 June he did homage to Edward III. The disinherited, and the Englishmen who had helped them, had meanwhile been richly rewarded by both king Edwards. John de Warenne was pardoned all his debts to the English crown and made Earl of Strathearn in Scotland; William Montagu was granted the lordship of the Isle of Man; Henry Percy was given custody of the castle of Berwick, and the lordship of Lochmaben and Annandale; David of Atholl received the grant of all the lands of Bruce's still living supporter, Robert Stewart. Edward III, of course, did best of all, by the terms of a treaty with Balliol which must be examined shortly. Bannockburn had been signally avenged.

The settlement of 1334 proved to be as short lived as all the previous attempts at an arrangement between the English and Scots kings. Before the summer was out Robert Stewart and the Earl of Moray, the leaders of the Bruce faction in Scotland, had turned the tables a second time on the new king. It was with difficulty that Balliol, deserted by his followers, managed to reach safety at Berwick. Two months had served to undo all the achievement of Halidon Hill and the year that had followed it.

Edward III's reaction to Scottish national resistance was the same as his grandfather's had been. Like Edward I, he put his trust in numbers. In the summer of 1335 he gathered the largest English royal host that had assembled for many years. Eight earls and twenty-three bannerets brought retinues to serve in his company. The Count of Juliers joined the king with a powerful troop from abroad; and a large contingent was brought over from Ireland. Edward also mobilized a substantial fleet, to guard the coasts and to help revictual his forces from the sea after they had entered Scotland. At the head of this great army Edward crossed the border, heading for Perth. There was no major battle; the appearance of the English awed those who could not avoid contact with them into submission. 'In the face of his might, none but children in their games would answer openly that they were the men of King David.'[7] The formal and temporary submission of the leaders of Scottish resistance was all that Edward gained, however. He could not keep his army in being for ever: even if he had been able to pay the men beyond September, few would have been willing to serve. When his back was turned, the risings began again. On 30 November David of Atholl, the most important of Balliol's Scottish followers, was defeated and killed. Edward in 1336 had to lead another English host into Scotland. Like his grandfather before him, he found that though he might

[7] A. Wyntoun, *Orygynale Cronykil of Scotland* (Edinburgh, 1872) vol. 2, p. 413.

keep his garrisons in the great lowland towns and castles, he could not conquer the countryside. He was back again in Scotland in the summer of 1337, though this time with a smaller force – and he could not stay so long. His relations with the king of France, which had been deteriorating for three years, were reaching breaking point, and the Hundred Years War was about to begin. Edward did not return to the north for five years, and by that time David Bruce was back in Scotland and secure on his throne.

Much the most illuminating document that has survived concerning Edward III's early adventure in Scotland is the treaty which, in 1334, he made with Edward Balliol. An understanding about the outline of its terms seems to have been reached some time earlier, indeed before the massive English intervention of 1333 – a fact which makes it quite clear that Edward III was in it with Balliol from the beginning. The treaty of 1334 was accordingly very generous to the English.[8] Balliol ceded to his friend and patron virtually the whole of the Scottish lowlands, including Roxburgh, Jedburgh, Selkirk, Linlithgow, and Edinburgh itself. What was ceded here was demesne lordship, with no right reserved on the Scots king's behalf. For what was left of Scotland after this, Balliol recognized Edward III as his feudal suzerain, and to mark this dependence he swore to do him homage and to serve him in his wars with a stipulated following. In return, Edward recognized Balliol as king of Scotland, and agreed to abandon any claim to jurisdiction in Scotland, and not to entertain before his court appeals from the court of the King of Scots. Edward I's claim to hear appeals from the court of the Scots king had been the origin of the quarrel between him and Edward Balliol's father John. It is a sign of Edward III's originality that he did not think it worth his while to argue about this traditional right of a feudal overlord, if substantial territories were ceded to him in demesne lordship. He seems clearly to have preferred to be without the problem of overlapping jurisdictions in his relation with Balliol. Very significantly, his attitude in this matter with regard to the Scots anticipated the line which he and his advisers were to take up later in their dealings with the French kings over Gascony.

The treaty of 1334 was still-born: Balliol was a fugitive long before Edward III got possession of the land that it promised him. The English never reachieved the position of *arbitrage* that

[8] *Foed.* vol. IV, p. 614; for commentary see Nicholson, *Edward III and the Scots*, pp. 155, 159ff.

they seemed to have won for a brief moment in that year. It is in consequence tempting to write off Edward III's intervention in Scotland in the 1330s as an ambitious and expensive failure. It may not be right to do so. It is true that the expeditions of 1333 and of 1335 and 1336 were immensely costly; that this cost drove Edward to borrow heavily from Italian merchants; and that in consequence his financial position was already strained when the war with France broke out. It is true also that the English parliament complained a good deal about the way in which men were raised for his armies, and in which money was extorted to pay them, just as they had complained before in Edward I's time. Nevertheless Edward probably gained as much or more than he lost by his policy. The victory of Halidon Hill wiped out the memory of Bannockburn and the tale of reverses that had followed afterwards. To his English magnates, Edward had revealed himself as a capable military leader, and, in the aftermath of victory, a generous one. It is as well to remember here that it was a long time before it became clear that the cause of Balliol was hopeless; it certainly cannot have seemed so even in 1337. The English did not lose Edinburgh until 1341, and by then Edward had won another great battle, over the French in the Channel at Sluys, to which more attention was paid. The intervention in Scotland was not successful in the long run, but was sufficiently successful initially to set a new tone for the new reign.

It was a new tone to which Edward himself sought to give conscious expression, through the scenes and symbolism that chivalrous ritual afforded. There was a great ceremonial creation of knights when his host entered Scotland in 1333. The return from Halidon was celebrated by a great royal tournament at Dunstable; and heralds painted rolls of the arms of those who were present there, as they did of the Scots knights who came with Balliol to do homage to Edward at Newcastle next summer.[9] This event was the occasion for much feasting and minstrelsy. Edward III was clearly aware, very early, of the importance of making the most of success on the instant, in ways that would fix its memory gratefully in men's minds.

The history of Edward's relations with Scotland in the 1330s is perhaps most interesting for the way in which it fits into the pattern of his political apprenticeship in the early and formative years of his authority. It is worth briefly running over the outline of the experience to which this young king had at this stage been

[9] See N. Denholm Young, *The Country Gentry in the Fourteenth Century* (Oxford, 1969), p. 97.

exposed. In 1326 he had been brought over from France in company with his mother and Mortimer and their mercenary bands, and had been a probably unwilling witness of their triumph, which toppled his father. In 1330 he himself had seized power by a daring and dangerous *coup*. He had then watched Edward Balliol and the disinherited gather a little army in secret, and all but win a kingdom. In the situation that their success created, the only sane course for him had seemed to be to ignore whatever legal and diplomatic obstruction the Treaty of Northampton put in the way of intervention in Scotland. In the aftermath of Halidon, he emerged as a victor and a hero in England, and was able to clinch a hard bargain with Balliol. This was a pattern that suggested that, where the advantages were sufficiently great, the niceties of legal and traditional relations were only one factor to be considered; that it was worth taking large risks; and that the manner of an action often mattered more, as far as men's responses were concerned, than its motive. It will be well to bear this pattern of experience in mind, when we have to consider other ventures on which Edward III embarked, in which the risks seem to have been greater than those he ran in the Scots war, and his objectives, viewed from a distance of time, more remote from the sphere of political reality.

The Scottish war can be regarded as a kind of prelude to the much more important war with France, which began in 1337. It was also directly connected with the chain of events which led to the outbreak of that war.[10]

Anglo-Scottish and Anglo-French relations in fact presented from the very beginning problems which could not be separated. The Treaty of Corbeil (1327) had resealed the 'auld alliance' of France and Scotland more firmly than ever. It had even stipulated that, if a new war were to break out between the English and the French, the Scots would be bound to intervene on the French side, notwithstanding any treaty that they might make with the

[10] On the events leading up to the outbreak of the French war see further E. Déprez, *Les Préliminaires de la Guerre de Cent Ans* (Paris, 1902); E. Perroy, *The Hundred Years War* (English translation, London, 1951); H. S. Lucas, *The Low Countries and the Hundred Years War* (Ann Arbor, 1929); G. Templeman, 'Edward III and the beginnings of the Hundred Years War', *T.R.H.S.* 5th ser., 2 (1952), pp. 69ff.; J. Le Patourel, 'Edward III and the kingdom of France', *History* 43 (1958), pp. 173ff.; J. Campbell, 'England, Scotland, and the Hundred Years War' in *Europe in the Late Middle Ages*, ed. B. Smalley, J. R. Hale and J. R. Highfield (London, 1965), pp. 184–216.

English.[11] The king of England was also Duke of Aquitaine, and as such a vassal of France; the French king clearly realized that the Scots could be very useful if he ever wanted to put pressure on him. One of the advantages that Edward stood to gain, if his client Balliol succeeded in making himself king of Scotland, was that it would render this part of the Corbeil treaty void and meaningless. A king of Scotland who had done homage to Edward and promised to serve him in his wars could not be party to the terms that Corbeil had arranged between the French and Scots.

These matters must have been very much in Edward's mind when he was considering whether to support Balliol. If he did so, he would inevitably give the French formal ground to come to the aid of their ally, David Bruce, probably by attacking Gascony. But in the crucial years 1332 and 1333 relations between France and England were good, and Edward had some sound reasons for hoping that they would remain so, whatever he did. King Philip of France was planning a crusade, and looked as if he would soon leave his kingdom; if he did, he would surely be anxious not to leave behind uncertain relations with the Duke of Aquitaine, who was his most formidable vassal. There was also another reason why Philip should have been anxious to remain on good terms with Edward; Edward was a possible claimant to his, Philip's, throne.

In 1328, the last Capetian king of France, Charles IV, had died without a male heir. The two men with the best claims to succeed him were Philip, Count of Valois, and the young Edward III. Edward was nearer in blood to the throne: his mother was the daughter of Philip IV, whereas the Valois claim came through count Philip's father, Charles, who was the younger brother of Philip IV. What stood between Edward and the French throne was the fact that his claim came through the female line, and precedent in 1316 and 1321 (when Louis X and Philip V had died leaving only daughters) had clearly established a rule that the crown of France could not pass to a woman. Edward could of course argue that though a woman could not succeed she might transmit her right to a male, and a claim was formally lodged on his behalf in 1328. But in the aftermath of Edward II's deposition he was not in much of a position to press his right, and it was Philip who was crowned at Rheims.[12]

[11] *A.P.S.* vol. XII, p. 5.
[12] On the French succession crisis of 1328 and the legal principles involved see P. Viollet, 'Comment les femmes ont été exclues en France

Following this, the advisers of Philip VI of Valois were naturally anxious that Edward should recognize and define his relation with the new monarch by doing homage for Aquitaine. Edward was as naturally anxious to avoid so doing, but in the unstable condition of England at the time he was in a poor position to refuse. In 1329 he crossed to France, and did homage to Philip VI at Amiens. Even with this the French were not quite content, and they pressed for a clear recognition that it was liege homage that Edward had promised. The performance of liege homage would imply a clear jurisdictional subjection to the king of France, and the obligation to serve him in time of war. In the fear once again that refusal might be met with force, Edward III gave in 1331 a written recognition that it was liege homage that he had sworn. Shortly after this he once more crossed to France, disguised as a merchant, and met Philip in secret at Pont St Maxence, where they agreed the outline of terms which should serve as the basis for a lasting peace between them.

Edward's recognition that he was the liegeman of Philip relieved, or seemed to relieve, the atmosphere of tension and suspicion that had prevailed between the English and French courts since 1328. In return for it he obtained the prospect of peace, and agreement that the issues outstanding from the recent war of St Sardos (including the question of the boundaries between his duchy and the land that was to be left directly subject to the king of France) should be settled by a 'process' – that is, by a tribunal of legal experts on which both sides had equal representation.[13] The parity of the experts, implying a kind of independence in the relations between the parties, was a concession to Edward, calculated to take the sting out of the indignity of his recent recognition that he was Philip's liegeman. This concession, and the promise of a peace, Edward seems to have taken as an indication that the French were anxious for conciliation and that he could probably intervene in Scotland in support of Balliol with impunity.

---

de la succession à la couronne', *Mémoires de l'Institut: Académie des Inscriptions et Belles Lettres* vol. 34 (1895), ii, pp. 125ff.; J. Viard, 'Philippe VI de Valois – la succession au trone', *Moyen Age* 32, pp. 218ff.; and J. M. Potter 'The development and significance of the Salic Law of the French', *E.H.R.* 52 (1937), pp. 235ff.

[13] See G. P. Cuttino, 'The Process of Agen', *Speculum* 19 (1944), pp. 161ff. On the earlier processes of Montreuil (1305–6) and Perigueux (1311) see G. P. Cuttino, *English Diplomatic Administration 1259–1339*.

Edward III knew that the French were pressing ahead with preparations for the crusade. Philip was anxious to make his mark as a crusader, partly because, like Edward III, he was a new king, untried – and one also with a questionable hereditary title. Ever since the days of St Louis, his Capetian predecessors had felt that they had a special part to play in crusading, and a special place among European rulers on account of it. There was no better way in which Philip VI could impress himself on his subjects as the true heir to the line of St Louis than by leading an expedition to the East. Edward could well appreciate his position, because it was in many ways like his own; indeed, he himself considered taking part in the crusade. In March 1332 at Nottingham he formally announced in parliament his intention of doing so; but the idea was abandoned, for the moment anyway, when more inviting opportunities opened in Scotland as a result of Balliol's victory at Dupplin Moor. When he decided to seize his chance in the north he had to assume that Philip would be too busy to want to make trouble about the matter. It was a good gamble, and he took the precaution in 1333 to give careful instructions to his officers in the Channel ports that nothing was to be done which could offend the French while he was campaigning in Scotland. Unfortunately his assumption, reasonable as it was, proved incorrect.

Relations between France and England remained smooth through 1333, the year which saw Halidon Hill and the conquest of virtually all of Scotland by Balliol. The process of Agen had by now set to work and was making progress. In the spring of 1334 an English embassy crossed to Paris, and after an audience with King Philip they believed that a final peace was about to be settled. They were suddenly called back into his presence and were told by Philip himself 'that his purpose was, that King David of Scotland, and all the Scots, must be included in the peace'.[14] It was soon clear that the French king was in earnest in this unexpected and alarming demand. In May David Bruce landed with a small following in Normandy, where he was received by Philip 'very courteously' and lodged at Château Gaillard. From this point on, every English embassy to France was overlooked by the exiled court of England's open enemy, whom everyone knew that King Philip was sustaining.

The reasons behind the French attitude are easy to understand. The English kings had always been the most intractable vassals

[14] *Les Grandes Chroniques de la France*, ed. P. Paris (Paris, 1837), vol. V, p. 357.

of the crown of France, and the Scottish alliance looked worth
preserving for the hold that it gave the French over the English
king. Philip was anxious to go on crusade, and he wanted to be
sure that Edward would make no trouble in Gascony while he was
away, and he therefore did not want to see Edward free of
anxiety about his northern border. If he did not take action, it
looked, in the spring of 1334, as if Edward would be free of
anxiety there, with his friend Balliol on the Scottish throne.
Philip moreover may not have realized quite what the reaction
to his support for David Bruce would be. Certainly, if those
authorities are right who say that he tried to insist on the acceptance of his own arbitration between the English and the Scots,
he must have misread the situation.

Pope Benedict XII viewed the situation with a clearer eye than
the French king did. From the moment that the king of France
allowed himself to become directly involved, the Scottish
succession war ceased to be a matter affecting the British Isles
only: it assumed importance within the broad framework of
European diplomacy, in the midst of which the papacy was working to make a crusade viable. Benedict saw that the English
could not possibly accept French arbitration. He saw too that if
Philip set out on crusade still nominally allied with Edward's
enemies, and with Edward still nursing a grievance over the
French retention of the Agenais, the prospects of the crusade,
and perhaps for the peace of European Christendom, would be
in jeopardy. Edward had important connexions in the Low
Countries, on the borders of the French kingdom: his wife
Philippa was the daughter of the Count of Hainault. If in Philip's
absence Edward were to make a bid to regain lost land in south-
western France, he would find allies among these connexions,
and also, no doubt, in France itself among those who, for whatever reasons, resented the new-made Valois monarchy. In a letter
sent to Philip in the summer of 1335 Pope Benedict alluded
pointedly to this danger, and warned the king to remember how
powerful some of his enemies in his own realm were.[15]
    Benedict in fact foresaw the future with remarkable clarity.
His difficulty was this, that though he could make sure that
Philip's departure on crusade was delayed, by using his papal
authority, it was very much harder for him to persuade Philip to
moderate the position he had taken up as the committed ally of
David Bruce, which he believed to be essential before he could

[15] E. Deprez, Les Préliminaires, pp. 114-15.

allow the crusade to go forward. Finally, in March 1336, he decided to postpone the crusade *sine die*. Philip still stuck by the exiled king of Scotland. His reaction to the pope's decision was not to moderate his position, but to order the great crusading fleet that he was assembling on the Mediterranean coast to sail round to the ports of the English Channel. Edward III concluded that an invasion of his kingdom was projected.

Edward had suspected that an invasion might be attempted, ever since the day in March 1334 when Philip had declared that there could be no final accommodation over Gascony unless David Bruce's rights were protected in the same peace. This ultimatum was given at the moment when Balliol, Edward's client, was at the height of his fortunes, and David Bruce was a fugitive in hiding: the natural conclusion was that the French must mean to intervene in Bruce's support. This was why Edward III in 1335, though he was straining his resources to raise an outsize army for the invasion of Scotland, felt it necessary to incur extra expense to put the Channel ports and the southern counties into a state of defence. He had good reason to be worried at this moment. In a sermon preached at the French court in July 1335 the Archbishop of Rouen declared that Philip intended to send 6000 men to help the Scots. The draft of a scheme to send a French force to Scotland, which almost certainly belongs to this year or to 1336, actually survives.[16] There was fighting in the Channel in 1336. When Philip's great crusading armada appeared in the narrow seas, Edward was wholly justified in concluding that an invasion would be attempted.

Edward's reaction was swift and far more decisive than Philip's manœuvres had been. In the summonses that were despatched for the parliamentary meeting at Nottingham at Michaelmas he made it clear that measures to resist the French menace would be the first item on the agenda. This parliament granted a tenth and a fifteenth; and the next one, which met at Westminster in March 1337 granted a tenth and a fifteenth for three years. This put the king's finances on a war footing. At the same time that parliament was summoned to Nottingham orders were sent to the seneschal of Gascony to put his fortresses in a state of defence, and to Bayonne requesting the townsmen to supply ships for service in the Channel. Still more significant was the embargo that was imposed on the export of wool from England by a royal

[16] See Campbell, 'England, Scotland, and the Hundred Years War', p. 190, note 10.

ordinance of August 1336. This embargo cut off the weavers of the great Flemish industrial cities from their chief supply of raw wool. Edward's hope was that this would force Louis Count of Flanders into an alliance with England, in order to avoid the social confusion which the embargo would inevitably cause in his territories. Edward did not quite succeed in doing this, for Louis proved obstinately loyal to Philip, who had helped to put down his rebellious subjects eight years before; he did succeed ultimately, however, in forcing the Flemings to abandon their count and join his side (in 1339).

The embargo on wool export was a first step toward carrying the war into the enemy's camp, and was followed up with a vengeance. On 6 December 1336 Edward gave Count William of Holland power to contract military alliances on his behalf in the Low Countries, and to offer fees to those who would promise service. In May 1337 his personal representatives, the Bishop of Lincoln and the earls of Salisbury and Huntingdon, appeared at Valenciennes, and set to work to build up, on the basis of the promise of pensions, a great coalition against France among the princes of the Rhineland and the Low Countries. They were prepared to pay almost any price to secure their master's interests. The counts of Gueldres, Limburg and Juliers, and the Archbishop of Cologne soon came to terms. John Duke of Brabant was less easily won, but he was brought in, hesitating to the end, at the enormous price of £60,000, and by the promise of commercial advantages in the wool trade for his territories. But the biggest prize of all (in spite of the fact that he was an excommunicated heretic) was the Emperor Louis IV of Bavaria, and his price was commensurate with his status, 300,000 florins. Thus Edward's counter-measures to the threat from France began to broaden his quarrel with Philip and the Scots into a European confrontation.[17]

In August 1337 Edward III issued a proclamation which was to be read in all the county courts of the kingdom. Notwithstanding many offers of reasonable terms, it declared, 'the king of France, hardened in his malice, would assent to no peace or treaty, but called together his strong host to take into his hand

[17] On these negotiations see H. S. Lucas, *The Low Countries and the Hundred Years War*, pp. 210–16; J. de Sturler, *Les Relations politiques et les échanges commerciaux entre le duché de Brabant et l'Angleterre au moyen âge* (Paris, 1936), pp. 332–3; B. D. Lyon, *From Fief to Indenture*, p. 216; and H. S. Offler, 'England and Germany at the beginning of the Hundred Years War', *E.H.R.* 54 (1939), pp. 608ff.

the duchy of Aquitaine, declaring against all truth that it was forfeit to him'.[18] Philip had, in fact, declared the duchy confiscate on 24 May, and his Constable, at the head of an army, had entered the duchy to enforce the sentence. Edward's manœuvres had convinced him that war was inevitable, and that he had better have the advantage of the opening move. The formal ground of his sentence was not aggression or misdemeanour on the part of Edward's officials in Gascony. It was that Edward, being a vassal of Philip's, had granted asylum at his court to Count Robert of Artois, whom Philip had stripped of all his honours and lands and had exiled from his kingdom. This was not a real ground for embarking on a war, so much as an excuse to bring matters to a head.

Even after the confiscation of Gascony, there was a moment when it looked as if war might be avoided, but the appearance was deceptive. In a desperate effort to prevent a head-on confrontation between two Christian kings which would be fatal to all crusading schemes, Pope Benedict despatched his *nuncios* to Paris and Westminster to try to reconcile the parties. Edward heard that they would be coming in the late summer of 1337, and wrote to the officials who were arraying men in Wales for a royal host that the muster scheduled for Michaelmas must be postponed. Just before Christmas, after difficult negotiations with the cardinals whom Benedict had sent to speak with him, Edward agreed to suspend hostilities until March; and later, in February, he extended this truce to midsummer. Edward acted, he said, out of reverence for the Holy See; probably his real reason for agreeing to delays was the difficulty of collecting the wool which parliament had granted him to help pay for a campaign in France. He was not really in earnest in seeking peace.

This is clear from a document that he sealed on 7 October 1337, the same day that he granted powers to the Bishop of Lincoln and others to confer on his behalf with the cardinals. It was of much more serious import. In it, he described himself as king of France and England, and appointed Duke John of Brabant his representative, to prosecute his right to the French throne in any way that he might see fit, and to accept on his behalf the homage of his French subjects.[19] Thus his riposte to Philip's confiscation of Gascony was to claim that he, not Philip, was the rightful king of France, and should have been ever since 1328. This deliberate

[18] *Foed.* vol. IV, p. 805.
[19] ibid. vol. IV, p. 818.

reopening of the question of the French succession made it quite
clear that Edward did not intend to compromise in any way on
the issues of Aquitaine or Scotland. If he were pressed to do so,
he would raise this larger and more dangerous issue.

The implications of Edward's new claim are very important,
and it is not easy to be sure precisely what he intended it, in 1337,
to mean. Many have doubted whether he can seriously have
believed that he might be able to wrest their throne from the
Valois, and have believed that his instruction to John of Brabant
can be interpreted simply as a move in the diplomatic game,
whose object was to make it difficult for the papal mediators to
insist on concessions unwelcome to the English.[20] It seems
probable that Edward's move was more serious than this. A
sentence which, a year after 1337, appears in an agreement between Edward and the Emperor Louis IV is here instructive.
The agreement includes the grant to Edward of the powers of an
imperial vicar: these are to last, it is said, 'until such time as he
has conquered a substantial part of the kingdom of France'.[21] If
Louis thought that Edward might make large conquests, why
should not Edward himself have hoped so? Robert of Artois must
certainly have encouraged him to think that way, and many
at the time believed that his influence was decisive. Robert's only
hope of regaining the influence that he had once exercised in
France was through the triumph of Philip's enemies, since
Philip was quite implacable towards him, so he may have been
inclined to exaggerate internal dissatisfaction in Philip's realm.
Wishful thinking may also have affected the attitude of some of
Edward's allies in the Low Countries and the Rhineland, since
recent attempts by the French to claim sovereignty beyond
France's eastern border had roused ill-feeling. But even to impartial observers the condition of the new Valois monarchy did
not look healthy. Benedict XII had warned Philip in 1335 that
he should remember how powerful his domestic enemies were.
Edward III probably had good reason to think he might make
substantial conquests in France, and may even, as early as 1337,
have thought that he really might win her crown.

There is another way of approaching the problem of Edward's

[20] This was the view of Déprez, and of Perroy (see *The Hundred Years
War*, p. 69). J. Le Patourel puts a very different opinion in 'Edward III
and the Kingdom of France', *History* 43 (1958), pp. 173ff. (perhaps the
most important recent contribution to discussion of Edward III's war
aims).

[21] See Offler, 'England and Germany', p. 611, note 17.

deliberate reopening of the succession issue, which also helps to make it understandable. What he did in October 1337 is of a piece with the whole pattern of his direction of affairs in the early years of his reign. He had served a political apprenticeship which taught that fearless seizure of the initiative was the way to win in the game of power. The very boldness of questioning Philip's right to his throne was part of the advantage of doing so. There were obstacles in the way of pressing his own claim, it is true, the most serious being the fact that he had undoubtedly done homage to Philip in 1329, and had confirmed later that it was liege homage that he had done. By 1337, however, he had repudiated at convenience one agreement made in the first years of his reign, the Treaty of Northampton with the Scots – why not these others too? His dealings with the Scots foreshadow his French diplomacy in another way as well, and an important one. The terms of Edward's treaty with Balliol of 1334 suggest that he had then already grasped that, between kings, a feudal juris-dictional relationship could only be fruitful as a source of friction. His claim to the French throne cut the issues between him and Philip of Valois adrift from the old question of overlapping feudal rights in Gascony, which had caused so much trouble in the past. Henceforward, any territory that the English king could win or withhold from Philip in France he could call his own, because he could claim that he was king and sovereign there in his own right.

The issue of the French succession promised to introduce a new element of inflexibility into the Anglo-French confrontation. It would take much more than stalemate in war to persuade the Valois to resign sovereignty in lands where they had once exer-cised it. It would also become very difficult for Edward to retreat from his claim to the French throne, if he once pressed it seriously. This probably explains why, in 1337, he took no more steps to publicize his position than those we have mentioned, and did not, as yet, adopt the style King of France in his ordinary correspondence. He wanted to leave himself as much room for manœuvre as he could for the present. Nevertheless, it had begun to be clear that a war would be fought between France and England on issues more far-reaching than those of feudal right.

6

Edward III and the Hundred Years War
1337-1360

Edward III, at the request of the Pope's *nuncios*, agreed at
Christmas 1337 to suspend hostilities against the French until
March, and this truce was later extended to midsummer. In the
meantime, however, fighting continued in Gascony, and in the
spring of 1338 a French fleet appeared in the Channel, which
attacked Portsmouth and ravaged the Isle of Wight. On 6 May
Edward announced that he regarded the truce as no longer
binding. The war which then began in earnest was to last more
than one hundred years. Hostilities, of course, were nothing like
continuous throughout that period, and this makes it possible to
study the course of the war in phases. A first phase may be said
to have ended when in 1360, at Brétigny near Chartres, a treaty
was agreed between the French and English which came subsequently to be known as the 'great peace'.

This first phase of the war, from 1338 to 1360, may be further
subdivided into three periods. The first of these witnessed, in the
years 1337 to 1341, the attempt of Edward III to bring together
a great coalition against the Valois, and its failure. The second
saw new fronts opened up on French soil, in Brittany and Normandy, and ended with the capture by the English of the port of
Calais in Picardy in 1348. The third period saw the great English
victory at Poitiers, where King John of France was taken prisoner,
and the campaigning which drew to a close when the peace was
agreed at Brétigny.

In 1338 Edward's diplomats had already been at work for two
years, building a network of alliances for England in the Low
Countries. They had succeeded in making agreements with the
Duke of Brabant, the Count of Hainault and Holland, and the
Count of Gueldres, and most important of all, with the Emperor

Louis IV. When Edward sailed with a host from Orwell in July 1338 he was able, therefore, to set up his headquarters immediately on landing at Antwerp, in the duchy of Brabant.

When Edward left England, the position in Flanders had already shifted in his favour. The disruption of industrial life which the embargo on the export of English wool, imposed in 1336, had caused in the great weaving centres of Ghent, Bruges and Ypres, meant that Count Louis's subjects could no longer afford to follow his example, and remain faithful to the French. At a great meeting in the monastery at Biloke their representatives agreed to adopt a scheme of armed neutrality put forward by Jacques van Artevelde of Ghent. In June 1338 they made terms with Edward's representatives, which won their merchants security in English ports and the towns of Holland and Brabant, and in return promised security to English ships in the ports of Flanders (provided they did not put soldiers ashore). Two years later, the exigencies of their commercial situation were to bring the confederation of Flemish towns, and Artevelde who was their 'captain general', into full alliance with Edward.

From Antwerp, Edward set out to meet his fellow ruler, the Emperor Louis, at Coblenz. A few days after their meeting on 15 September, Louis at Frankfurt formally appointed Edward his imperial vicar, with authority to exercise sovereign rights in the empire and in any imperial land reconquered from the French, on Louis's behalf. This office also put Edward into an advantageous relationship with those of his other allies who were imperial subjects. As the emperor's representative he was their sovereign and, if they failed to fulfil the terms of their alliances, he could put them under the ban of empire, as traitors. Edward I in the 1290s had had difficulty in activating the support that he had been promised by the Rhenish princes, whom he had brought into a coalition essentially similar to that of 1338; Edward III could hope that he would not have to face quite the same problem.[1]

Edward's relations with his allies, the emperor included, really depended, of course, on his promises to pay them pensions. If he could not pay them, all the agreements between them, the vicariate and everything else, would be null and void. Financial

[1] On Anglo-Flemish relations at this stage of the war see H. S. Lucas, *The Low Countries and the Hundred Years War* (Ann Arbor, 1929), esp. pp. 257–79, 358–67; on Anglo-Imperial relations see H. S. Offler, 'England and Germany at the beginning of the Hundred Years War', *E.H.R.* 54 (1939), pp. 608ff.

calculations were crucial to the whole scheme on which, at this stage, English hopes centred. In consequence, finance had far more to do with the course of the war in this phase than the largely abortive military operations that were undertaken. This means that in order to understand what happened to Edward and his coalition, we must start by examining the calculations on which his war finances were based.

The ordinary revenue of the crown at the beginning of the Hundred Years War was about £30,000 per annum, of which some £13,000 came from the customs. A lay subsidy would bring in about another £38,000, a clerical grant perhaps £19,000. These figures indicate a revenue position very comparable with that of Edward I, in the time of his wars.[2] Like Edward I, Edward III initially found his subjects ready to be generous. At Nottingham in 1336 and at Westminster in the spring of 1337 he obtained ample subsidies; and the merchants granted him an extra subsidy (or *maltolte*) of 40s. on the sack of wool exported, over and above the customs. Edward III was, nonetheless, rather less well placed in 1337 than his grandfather had been in 1294. The Scottish campaigns had already faced him with very heavy expenses, and he had had to raise substantial loans. The biggest advances had come from the Bardi and the Peruzzi, bankers of Florence, and their loans were secured by assignments on the customs. Edward thus started at a disadvantage, and by September 1337 he was already pledged to pay pensions to allies, totalling over £124,000, by the end of the year. This expenditure, when added to the cost of maintaining the war in Scotland, equipping a fleet and forces for service on the continent, and ordinarily recurrent items of expense, far outran the king's resources, even with the subsidies taken into account.

Edward's confidence in his ability to meet expenditure on a quite unprecedented scale was based on an ambitious and ingenious scheme to create and manipulate a royal monopoly in the export of wool. In the course of 1337 he struck a bargain with a syndicate representing the major English wool merchants, headed by William de la Pole and Reginald Conduit of London. This syndicate was granted a monopoly of export of wool, and powers of compulsory purchase from the producers (to whom a minimum price was guaranteed, but who were expected to allow the syndicate credit for payment until the wool was sold abroad). The embargo on the export of wool imposed in 1336 had stimu-

[2] For these figures and for what follows generally see E. B. Fryde, 'Edward III's wool monopoly of 1337', *History* 37 (1952), pp. 8–24.

lated demand in the continental markets, so that the syndicate was well placed to dictate the price as soon as the ban was lifted in their favour. A very handsome profit was to be expected, which the merchants agreed to share with the king. The wool was to be shipped to Dordrecht in Brabant, thus advantaging one of Edward's most valued continental allies, the Duke of Brabant. In order to make sure that the commercial *coup* envisaged was properly coordinated with the king's military diplomacy, a further agreement with the syndicate gave Edward's envoys in the Low Countries control over the disposal of the wool, and the right, if necessary, to buy it in from the merchants on the king's behalf. It was expected that this scheme would raise some £200,000 in cash for the king's war effort.

When the syndicate's first shipment of wool reached Dordrecht in November 1337, the king's envoys had already realized that he would not be able to pay the pensions due at the end of the year in full, and were negotiating postponements. The embargo on export was at this point just beginning to show signs of telling on the Flemings, so that it seemed desirable to maintain it. The merchants, on the other hand, naturally wished to sell their wool. After long and tricky negotiations, the king's envoys in the end exercised their right, and bought in the wool, paying the merchants a good price – but in notes of acknowledgement, to be 'cashed' by remission of duty on future exports. Most of these 'Dordrecht bonds' were in the end sold by their holders at a disastrous discount.[3] The wool itself was sold by the king's representatives and raised a disappointing price. The merchants now refused to go forward any further with the scheme, which from their point of view had completely broken down. The king's envoys, having failed to realize enough cash, found themselves in a very ugly position, with clients whom they had no hope of satisfying seeking pay.

All this took place in the early months of 1338, before Edward set sail for the continent. In the spring parliament he obtained a grant of 20,000 sacks of wool, and on the strength of this raised new loans with the Bardi and Peruzzi. This cash, together with the proceeds of the sale of wool tided him over the crisis temporarily, and made it possible for him to go forward with his plans unchanged for the immediate future. But once he set foot on continental soil, his financial difficulties began to multiply again. The proceeds of the wool subsidy came in very slowly, and new

[3] On the Dordrecht bonds see Fryde, 'Edward III's wool monopoly', and G. O. Sayles, 'The English company of 1343', *Speculum* 6 (1931), pp. 185–6.

ELMA—E*

loans had to be raised. In February 1339 Edward had to pledge the crown of England to the Archbishop of Trier. In May the Archbishop of Canterbury, the bishops of Durham and Lincoln, and the earls of Derby, Northampton, Suffolk and Salisbury made themselves personal sureties for a loan of 140,000 florins from the Bartolomei of Lucca. At about the same time Edward sent orders to the council in England to stop payment of all fees and pensions there, unless the recipients had no other source of income. So far, though Edward was having to pay his allies and his own forces, there had been no campaigning. In the late summer of 1339 they at last advanced, after much argument, into the Cambrésis, but the French would not meet the English and their allies in the field. In September the Count of Hainault abandoned both the army and his alliance. In the end Edward had to tell his allies to take their men home, and himself retired to Brussels, about £300,000 further into debt for a campaign, so called, that had achieved nothing.

Two events in 1340 did something to lighten the gloom of the deteriorating English position. Early in the new year, the towns of Flanders finally entered into alliance with England. This meant breaking faith with their sovereign, King Philip, and it was partly to regularize their position that Edward at Ghent, on 26 January, solemnly assumed the arms and title of King of France. Then in June, when he was returning from a brief visit to England to try to raise funds, he fell in with a great fleet of French and Genoese at Sluys. Though Edward's flotilla was heavily outnumbered, he decided to attack when the wind and tide turned in his favour. The English archers, firing into an enemy whose ships were crowded together, did terrible execution and the French fleet was virtually destroyed. The victory gave the English almost complete control of the Channel for years to come, and was long remembered by them as a notable judgement of God in their favour, in the quarrel with France. The subsequent operations of Edward and his Flemish allies on land were a disappointment, however. An attempt to besiege Tournai failed to take the city, and English, Brabançons and Flemings alike were all clamouring for pay. In September Edward found he had no option but to agree to a truce with Philip of France for a year, which was arranged at Esplechin through the mediation of Jeanne de Valois, the Dowager Duchess of Hainault.

While Edward was abroad, the council that he had left to govern England in his absence was getting into more and more serious difficulties. Before he left, Edward had issued at Walton a series of ordinances concerning the administration of the realm. Their object was to reaffirm the royal prerogative, and to maintain the king's initiative in government in the military emergency while he was abroad, by subjecting the chancery and the exchequer to the stringent control of the privy seal; and also to ensure economy at the exchequer by careful audit and by disallowing exemptions from taxation and respites of debts to the crown.[4] When Edward went abroad, taking the privy seal with him, the result was the opposite of that intended; the ordinances curtailed the initiative of the king's councillors in England, and their reactions were the less decisive in response to his needs because of them. The consequences of the economies that they imposed at the exchequer were besides highly unpopular, as was Edward's order to the exchequer in 1339 to stop payments of fees and pensions. Archbishop Stratford, who was sent home that year to explain the king's difficulties to the autumn parliament and to take over as chief of the council, found the estates ready to help the king, but insistent that his measures be modified, and that the *maltolte* on wool, which had been granted in 1336 without the commons' assent, should cease. On these conditions they would grant the king the tenth sheep and fleece and lamb in the land, provided a subsequent parliament would confirm the grant. In the spring of 1340 Edward himself was present in parliament, having obtained leave to be away from Brussels from the creditors to whom he was pledged (but he had to be back by midsummer). He was able to persuade parliament to increase its grant to a ninth for the years 1340 and 1341, and to continue the *maltolte* for fourteen months. But there were stringent conditions attached: that many debts and fines be pardoned; that purveyance be strictly controlled; that no aids should be taken in the kingdom without the assent of the commons in parliament. As Edward's debts mounted, the means to secure extra revenue from England were thus being steadily eroded. Even more galling, he had to consent to the appointment of a council, of which Stratford and the earls of Lancaster, Warenne and Huntingdon were to be members, with power to exercise the full royal authority in his absence. The Walton ordinances, one of whose prime objectives had been to maintain in the king's hands a tight royal control over the home government, thus became a dead letter; and Edward was probably not happy to see Stratford promoted to be virtually a chief

[4] On the Walton Ordinances see Tout, *Chapters*, vol. III, pp. 69-80 (for text, pp. 143-50).

councillor. The archbishop had already been encouraging his diocesans to resist royal demands for purveyance. But the commons were not prepared to make their grant unless the king met their conditions, and the appointment of this council was one of them; he had no option but to give way.[5]

By the time that the truce of Esplechin was agreed, Edward III was bankrupt. He did not now dare to ask his creditors for permission to return again to England. As he could not stay on the continent as their virtual prisoner without serious damage to his prestige, he decided to slip away without consulting them. He arrived in England, unheralded, on 30 November 1340. He and those who had been with him in the Low Countries had put down their failures to lack of financial aid from England, and they put this down in turn to the ineffective reaction of the government at home. Edward in his anger was ready to lash out against all and any whom he believed responsible. The chancellor and the treasurer were removed immediately from their offices. Pole, Conduit and a number of other merchants were arrested; so were four judges of the common bench, and a general investigation into the conduct of lesser officials was ordered. Special commissions of *trailbaston* were appointed to make inquiries into all manner of misdemeanours and in particular to make sure that the ninth sheep, fleece and lamb granted by the spring parliament had been paid in full. Archbishop Stratford, who had been at the head of the council and against whom Edward and his intimates seem to have been specially incensed, was ordered to return to Brabant as a hostage for the king's debts.

Edward may well have had some justification for thinking that his servants in England had shown less energy than they ought to have done. But he made too little allowance for the difficulties against which they had to labour, and seriously misjudged the mood of his native kingdom. In the months before his return there had been something approaching a general refusal to pay further taxes. In Essex the sheriff had met armed resistance to the collection of the ninth. The council had feared revolt, writing

[5] On 1340 see G. L. Harriss, 'The commons' petitions of 1340', *E.H.R.* 78 (1963), pp. 625-54. On the king's difficulties in this period generally, see D. Hughes, *Constitutional Tendencies in the Early Years of Edward III* (London, 1915); Tout, *Chapters* vol. III, pp. 69-142; and E. B. Fryde, 'Parliament and the French war 1336-40' in *Essays in Medieval History Presented to B. Wilkinson*, ed. T. A. Sandquist and M. R. Powicke (Toronto, 1969), pp. 249-69.

to the king that 'the people would rise against them rather than contribute more'.[6] In these conditions, Edward's measures on his return only served to exacerbate bitterness, and to rouse popular sympathy for the victims of his purge. In London the inquiries of the justices of *trailbaston* were resisted with violence. The situation seemed to herald a return to the bad old days of Edward II.

Archbishop Stratford, the man against whom the king's rage was most bitter, had taken the measure of things far better than his master. He resolutely refused all summonses to appear before the king and his counsellors: he would answer charges against him before his peers in parliament, he said, not elsewhere. He replied to the broadsheet denunciation of his mismanagement as chief councillor which the king's men put out (the *Libellus Famosus*) in a series of letters which were aimed to broaden the issues between them, and which succeeded in putting across Stratford himself as the champion of all sectors of discontent.[7] He protested against infringements of Magna Carta by the king's judges of *trailbaston*. He insisted on the right of peers and ministers to have their offences examined in parliament. He stressed the privilege of the clergy of being taxed separately from the laity. These protests, which are full of echoes of the constitutional propaganda of Edward II's day, struck the chords of popular sympathy much more surely than the counter claims of the king and the little circle of advisers who had been abroad with him. Stratford succeeded in his object of broadening the issues involved in the crisis to the point where there was no alternative to summoning the parliament that he demanded.

What happened in this spring parliament of 1341 underlined the strength of Stratford's position and the weakness of the king's. Edward's intimates, William Kilsby the keeper of the privy seal, Sir John Darcy the steward of the household, and Bishop Orleton of Winchester were unable to swing the focus away from the issues of principle that the archbishop had raised. Edward wisely bowed before there was a storm. The commissions of *trailbaston* were withdrawn, and the king promised that infringements of the charters should be redressed by the peers in parliament. He promised too that peers should not be judged except in parliament, and that the officers of state should be appointed

---

[6] *The French Chronicle of London*, ed. G. J. Aungier (Camden Soc., 1844), p. 83; for the troubles in Essex see *C.C.R. 1339-41*, p. 536.

[7] See *Foed.* vol. V, p. 225 (*Libellus*), and Birchington in *Anglia Sacra*, ed. H. Wharton (London, 1691), vol. I, pp. 27-36.

and sworn there. The statutes of the parliament of 1340 were confirmed and upheld, and the ninth was commuted to a grant of 30,000 sacks of wool. Finally, the charges against Stratford were sent for consideration to a commission of peers, including the earls of Arundel and Warenne who had spoken out on his behalf early in the parliament. Afterwards they were quietly shelved. The king and the archbishop were formally reconciled, and the other officials who had suffered in the recent purge were forgiven. The king withdrew on all the matters which had given rise to complaint, and the crisis was at an end.[8]

The crisis of 1341, and the failure of the king's ambitious attempt to bring together a great confederation of continental pensioners against the Valois, must be viewed together. If the confederation was to mean anything in military terms it had got to be financed out of monies raised in England, from subsidies in wool or ready cash, and by means of the monopoly of the export of wool. It was in order to maintain strict control of these resources that Edward imposed such severe limits on the discretion of the exchequer in his Walton ordinances. When he found himself deserted by most of his allies and hopelessly in debt, and was forced to agree to the truce of Esplechin, Edward's angry reaction was to assume that his councillors in England had failed him. That this was not the real trouble was shown by the crisis that followed his return. What was really wrong was that Edward and his advisers had grossly miscalculated both the profitability of the monopoly of wool export, and the rate of taxation that his English subjects would tolerate. In consequence of these miscalculations he lost his allies; ruined his bankers, the Bardi and Peruzzi, on whose loans he defaulted; and very nearly provoked serious civil confrontations in his own kingdom.

Nevertheless, Edward weathered the storm very well. He did not worry overmuch about the fate of his bankers. The crisis at home passed over, and by October 1341 he felt so strong again that he repealed the statutes of the spring parliament on his own authority, on the ground that they had been made against his will and at a moment when he had no true freedom of action.[9]

[8] For the history of the crisis of 1341, I have relied largely on G. Lapsley, 'Archbishop Stratford and the parliamentary crisis of 1341', *E.H.R.* 30 (1915), pp. 6–18, 193–215; see also B. Wilkinson, 'The protest of the earls of Arundel and Surrey in the crisis of 1341', *E.H.R.* 46 (1931), pp. 177–93.

[9] *Foed.* vol. V, p. 281; and see H. G. Richardson and G. O. Sayles, 'The early statutes', *L.Q.R.* 50 (1934), pp. 550–2.

This was the same ground on which Edward I had sought absolution from his promise to observe unwelcome rules; Edward III, significantly, did not bother to refer to the pope as his grandfather had done but acted on his own authority. Nevertheless, he showed that he had learnt his lesson. He bore no malice against Stratford, who was readmitted to his intimacy and served the king loyally for the rest of his life. Edward never again sought to raise money in his kingdom on quite the scale that he had in the years 1336 to 1340, and he did not try to rebuild the continental confederacy of which he had hoped so much. He did not, of course, withdraw from his quarrel with the Valois, but prepared to prosecute it in a different way.

'In these days the king became very friendly with the men of Flanders, and he took to himself the title of King of France and England, and changed his seal, quartering thereon the arms of France with those of England. And the communes of Flanders made obedience to him as King of France, for they dared not do otherwise, because the pope had laid an interdict on all Flanders, to take effect if they should rebel against the King of France.'[10] This is how the chronicler Murimuth described Edward's formal assumption of the title of King of France, at Ghent in January 1340. He was not the only historian who explained Edward's action as motivated by the need to give some colour of legality to the alliance that the Flemings were making with him. Edward himself, however, seems to have seen more to it than this.

On 8 February at Ghent he issued a proclamation, addressed to the bishops, peers, counts, barons and all the people of France. This proclamation was subtly worded, and contained the seed of a new diplomatic strategy for the struggle against the Valois.[11]

Edward's proclamation was to the people of France at large, and told them that he had now resolved to take up 'the burden of government' of that kingdom, as the heir of 'Charles of famous memory, the last King of France'.[12] Referring to the usurpation of his right by Philip of Valois, who had taken unlawful advantage of his youth in 1328, he was now ready, he declared, to receive into his homage all those who would follow the example 'of our beloved and faithful men of Flanders', and forget their past

[10] *Chron A. Murimuth* (R.S.), p. 103.

[11] For what follows, I am much indebted to the masterly article by J. Le Patourel, 'Edward III and the kingdom of France', *History* 43 (1958), pp. 173ff.

[12] *Foed.* vol. V, pp. 158, 163.

obedience to the intruder. As king, he promised, he would govern according to 'the good laws and customs which were observed in the time of our ancestor St Louis'. This, and other more specific promises, to strengthen the coinage, to limit the burden of taxa-tion, to seek the advice of the nobles of the realm over its govern-ment, were the subtle parts of Edward's message. For this part of his proclamation echoes directly the demands for the mainten-ance of ancient rights and privileges, which the provincial leagues had made of King Philip IV in 1314, and of Philip V in 1317. To anyone in France, who, for whatever reason, was unsatisfied with the rule of the Valois, Edward offered here a justification, not just in terms of convenience but of principle, for changing allegiance.

Edward had good reason to believe that there would be those who would be willing to give ear to his promises. Robert of Artois, lately one of Philip's most influential subjects, was now his pensioner. In Flanders he had brought a whole province over to his side. Before the truce of Esplechin expired, he found another very important French ally besides these. In April 1341 John Duke of Brittany died, and his succession was contested between Charles of Blois, who had married a daughter of one of Duke John's brothers, and John de Montfort, the duke's younger brother. Both laid their claims before Philip's *Parlement*. De Montfort was in a difficult position, however; he knew that the custom of the duchy would favour his claim, but he knew also that the king had arranged the marriage of Charles of Blois, who was Philip's nephew, with a view to securing the inheritance for him. This situation was precisely of the kind that Edward must have had in mind when he issued his Ghent proclamation. Before Philip's judgement in favour of Charles had been formally given, de Montfort had recognized Edward as King of France, and Edward had recognized him as Duke of Brittany.

John de Montfort himself had the misfortune to fall into the hands of his enemies at Nantes in November 1341, but his duchess Margaret rallied his supporters against the troops of Charles of Blois. By March of the next year a small force of English soldiers, led by Sir Walter Manny, was in Brittany. In the autumn Edward himself appeared there, with a host. Although the English did not achieve much in the field, Philip and Charles, with a superior army, failed to dislodge them from the duchy. They still held their foothold there in the spring of 1343, when a new truce for three years was agreed at Malestroit. The English were in consequence in a much happier position

than they had been when the truce of Esplechin was sealed in
1340. In the three year interim now afforded them, both sides
undertook to seek a final peace through the pope's mediation.

Edward had reasons to be glad of a truce in 1343. In England
memories of the crisis of 1341 were still green, and he knew that
many people had no relish for more costly campaigns. Domestic
pressures demanded that he make at least the motions of seeking
peace. The attitude of the papacy was also worrying; the new
pope, Clement VI, was bent on a pacification, and some of the
king's advisers feared that if Edward was not cooperative he
might be excommunicated. This would be a diplomatic disaster,
since it would give the French cause the standing almost of a
crusade. Besides, it seemed a good moment to embark on serious
negotiations. The situation for the English was more favourable
than it had been in 1340, and they could set their price for peace
high.

The confidence of the English was well demonstrated at the
formal peace conferences which were held at Avignon in 1344,
under the presidency of Pope Clement.[13] So also were the diplomatic advantages which Edward's formal claim to the French
crown had secured. The English negotiators had clearly been
instructed to see, if possible, what the French would offer in the
way of terms, and it took the pope a long time to draw them into
making any suggestion of their own. In the end they agreed to do
so, and stated that the surrender to the king of England of full
sovereignty in Gascony might be a good start towards a peace.
To the objection that this would mean that Philip must divest
himself of an integral part of his royal inheritance, they replied
that the French ought to be ready to consent to 'such a bisection,
. . . seeing that the quarrel between the kings was about their
right to the whole kingdom of France'.[14] They made it quite
clear that, if their king were to compromise at all over his claim
to the crown, it must be in return for sovereign rights in part of
France at least. From this position the English only wavered to
the extent of agreeing to send home for further instructions. This

[13] On these conferences see E. Déprez, 'La Conférence d'Avignon
(1344)' in *Essays in Medieval History Presented to T. F. Tout*, ed. A. G.
Little and F. M. Powicke (Manchester, 1925), pp. 301-20.
[14] K. de L. vol. XVIII, p. 243; see also pp. 242, 245-6. Le Patourel
appears to me to underestimate the importance of Gascony in these
negotiations in his article, 'Edward III and the kingdom of France',
note 11.

was at the end of November 1344, and by then the war was well on its way to reopening in earnest.

Much had happened to alter the diplomatic and military outlook since the truce of Malestroit had been agreed, and most of the changes played in Edward's favour. In 1343 Oliver de Clisson, of a famous and powerful Breton family, had been arrested in Paris and executed at Philip VI's orders. A group of Breton nobles who were captured later in the year suffered the same fate. Among them were two members of the important family of Malestroit. The effect of these executions was to reaffirm the spirit of provincial independence among the Breton nobility, not to crush it. Philip's victims had besides relatives and connexions outside Brittany, and disaffection from the Valois began to spread beyond the duchy. Godfrey, Count of Harcourt in Normandy, threw over his sovereign and came to Brittany to do homage to Edward's representatives. He was only one of a number of leading Normans who were suspected of being involved with the English at the time. It began to look as if the loyalty of a third French province, besides Flanders and Brittany, might be undermined.[15]

In England too Edward felt more in control of the situation. The repeal of the statutes of the 1341 parliament had caused no repercussions. The mood of the people, and especially of the noblemen who were close to him, was not pacific. At the parliament held in June 1344 Edward was able to present the execution of the Breton *seigneurs* as a sure sign that the French did not mean to keep the truce. They were determined, he said, to destroy every ally of England. This propaganda had its effect, and the estates approved generous grants against the probable reopening of the war.

It had become clear by the end of 1344 that the peace conference at Avignon would not achieve a settlement. In the summer of 1345 Edward declared that he regarded himself as no longer bound by the truce, because the proceedings against his Breton allies had rendered it void. In the new conditions, which his efforts to detach leading Frenchmen from the Valois allegiance had created, he found himself able to operate against his enemy on exterior lines. Three English noblemen, Henry de Grosmont Earl of Derby, William de Bohun Earl of Northampton and Hugh Hastings, were appointed royal lieutenants in Gascony,

[15] On Philip VI's difficulties in 1343 see R. Cazelles, *La Société Politique et la crise de la Royauté sous Philippe VI de Valois* (Paris, 1958), especially pp. 152-5.

Brittany and Flanders respectively. The armies they commanded were raised partly in England (largely by means of voluntary contracts, or indentures, and by the leaders themselves), and partly among the natives of the provinces in question. Henry of Derby's campaign in Gascony opened with notable successes; Bergerac, La Réole and finally Angoulême all fell into his hands.[16]

These successes offset the effects of the deaths of two of Edward's allies in 1345: Jacques van Artevelde, who was murdered in Ghent in July, and John de Montfort, who died in September leaving an infant son heir to his claims in Brittany. In 1346 Edward determined to lead a host to France himself. Most of the greatest noblemen who were not already in France were with him when he sailed from Porchester in July. The destination of the expedition was not known until the last moment, and many assumed it would be Gascony; but it was in Normandy, at St Waast la Hogue, that the king landed.

'The people of Normandy have not been used to war; you shall find great towns that have not been walled, whereby your men shall have such gain that they shall be the better twenty years after.'[17] These are the words with which, according to Froissart, Godfrey de Harcourt urged the king to make a descent on the northern French coast. The form that the campaign took was a *chevauchée*, a great raid across enemy territory, which did not pause to besiege towns but went burning and looting through the land. The tactics of the *chevauchée* were calculated to cause maximum dismay to the enemy's subjects and to dislocate government; they also opened alluring prospects of plundering for the individual soldier. They exposed the army to the minimum of hardship, since it was expected to live off the land, and, with luck, the expedition might even pay for itself with loot. There was only one major risk, that the army might find itself cut off, deep into hostile territory, by a superior enemy force.

This risk in fact materialized. Near Rouen Edward found that Philip was waiting with a large force, and was turned south along the Seine. He managed to cross the river at Poissy, and made for the Somme; but when he reached it, Philip was so close on his heels that he could not avoid an engagement. At Crecy, on 26 August, the French made the fatal error of attacking archers in a strong defensive position. Under a hail of arrows, the successive waves of their attack became entangled with one another.

[16] On Derby's campaign see K. Fowler, *The King's Lieutenant, Henry of Grosmont* (London, 1969), ch. IV.

[17] K. de L. vol. IV, p. 381.

Their casualties were terrible; they included John, the blind king of Bohemia, the Duke of Lorraine, the counts of Blois and Flanders and Nevers; no one bothered to count the host of lesser men slain, says the chronicler Geoffrey Le Baker.[18] Philip himself escaped from the fatal field as darkness fell, and Edward was left in possession as victor, free to march on whither he would.

On 4 September Edward and his army appeared before Calais, and settled down to a siege that was to last nearly a year. It was easy here for the English to bring over reinforcements, and also to make contact with the Flemings, who held markets in the host twice a week and virtually supplied it. Philip made one effort to relieve the town, but retreated after reconnoitring the English position. On 4 August 1347 the town was surrendered unconditionally. Virtually all the inhabitants were evacuated, and Calais became, in a few years, an English military and mercantile colony. It remained so for nearly two hundred years.[19]

While the king was busy about his campaign in the north of France, his lieutenants elsewhere were winning other notable successes in his cause. Henry de Grosmont was for a time in 1346 besieged in Aiguillon, but he was able to recoup his losses later and to take the important town of St Jean d'Angely. In the autumn of the same year, the Scots, true to their Valois alliance, attacked northern England, and were met at Neville's Cross near Durham by the Archbishop of York and the barons of the north. Their army was destroyed in the battle, and David Bruce their king was taken prisoner. Finally, in June 1347, Sir Thomas Dagworth, who had succeeded the Earl of Northampton as Edward's lieutenant in Brittany, defeated Charles of Blois at La Roche Derrien, and took him prisoner. When, in September at Calais, a new truce was agreed between the French and the English and all their allies, the English were triumphant in every sphere of the war.

By the autumn of 1347 the English had made just about as much effort as, for the time being, they were capable of doing. Edward, when he came home, had to face complaints of misgovernment in his absence, and against the means that he had used to raise men and money, just as he had done in 1340. But in the aftermath of so many English triumphs these troubles

---

[18] *Chron G. Le Baker*, ed. E. M. Thompson (Oxford, 1889), p. 85; and on Crecy see A. H. Burne, *The Crecy War* (London, 1955), ch. VI and VII.

[19] See further J. Viard, 'Le Siège de Calais', *Moyen Age* 39 (1929), pp. 129–89; and D. Greaves, 'Calais under Edward III' in G. Unwin, *Finance and Trade under Edward III* (Manchester, 1918), pp. 313–50.

could not be as serious as they had then been. They had been triumphs of sufficient stature to alter the whole shape of the Anglo-French struggle. Crecy was an epic victory. Before the battle the French leaders had been so confident 'that each asked for particular Englishmen to be allotted them as prisoners',[20] says Le Baker; after it, the pride of French chivalry was broken and ruined. At Calais Edward took one of the strongest and richest of the French Channel ports, after everyone had seen that the French king would not dare to try to break up his siege. The noise of these things went abroad through Europe. It is no accident that a year after the fall of Calais a party among the princes of Germany was trying to persuade Edward to interest himself in the imperial crown (which he wisely declined to do). The victories of 1346 and 1347 made Edward's name as a conqueror and a leader of chivalry: after them, there could be no more hopes – such as Pope Clement VI had entertained in 1344 – of reordering relations between the kings of France and England as they had been in the time of the last Capetian king.

The terms which in 1354 at Guines were proposed as the basis for a final peace and were accepted as such by Pope Innocent VI's mediator, the Cardinal of Boulogne, give a measure of the English achievement of the late 1340s. Seven years of desultory and occasional fighting had by then made no great alteration to the military situation of 1347. What was proposed was that Edward should renounce his claim to the throne of France; in return he should receive, in full sovereignty, Aquitaine and Poitou, Anjou, Maine, Touraine, and the march of Calais. Secret instructions that were given to Henry de Grosmont, now Duke of Lancaster, and the Earl of Arundel, as Edward's personal representatives to the pope, make it clear that Edward regarded the cession of these lands to him with full sovereignty in the light of compensation for resigning the title of King of France. The compensation was certainly commensurate with the magnificence of the title he was to lose; it would make him a king in France, if not of France. It entailed the virtual dismemberment of the Valois kingdom. That the pope and his cardinals, and even the advisers of John, who had succeeded his father Philip on the French throne, could contemplate the possibility of such a settlement is an index of how mightily Edward had advanced his cause since the early days of the war.[21]

[20] *Chron G. Le Baker*, p. 82.
[21] On the abortive treaty of Guines and the negotiations surrounding it see F. Bock, 'Some new documents illustrating the early years of the

The treaty of Guines was in fact never ratified. It is not entirely clear what went wrong, but it seems that the English at Avignon became suspicious of the pope's good faith and thought that the French would not, in fact, renounce sovereignty in the lands they were to cede. In consequence, Henry of Lancaster refused on Edward's behalf to renounce the title of King of France. Instead of peace being made, the war reopened in earnest.

This was probably not unwelcome from the English point of view. People were already beginning to learn that they might make themselves fortunes out of the spoils of war, and young men were growing up, like Edward the Black Prince, who were anxious to make a name for themselves martially. New opportunities of exploiting domestic discord in France seemed also to be opening for the English. King John was repeating the mistakes of his father Philip. He had become involved in a complicated quarrel with Charles, King of Navarre, who was also Count of Evreux in Normandy and had great estates there and in Picardy. He and Lancaster had met at Avignon, and discussed plans which would virtually give the English control of Normandy.[22] Nothing came of these discussions, and Charles and his sovereign were temporarily reconciled. Then on 5 April 1356, King John broke into the chamber where Charles was dining with the dauphin at Rouen, and took him prisoner. The Count of Harcourt and three or four others of Charles's intimates were executed on the spot. Though Charles remained a prisoner, his brother Philip immediately went over to the English and did homage to King Edward, who despatched forces to Normandy to his aid and that of the Harcourts.

The decisive action of the year 1356 was not in Normandy, but south and west. A year before, the Black Prince, now his father's lieutenant in Aquitaine, had led a great *chevauchée* into Languedoc, in which more spoil was won than in any previous campaign of the war. This summer he set out on another raid, north towards the Loire, probably hoping to effect a junction with Henry of Lancaster who was now commanding for the English in Brittany and lower Normandy. The appearance of King John at the head of a large army forced Lancaster to retreat, however. The Prince,

---

Hundred Years War', *B.J.R.L.* 15 (1931), pp. 60-99, esp. 94-6; and Fowler, *The King's Lieutenant*, ch. XI.

[22] See Fowler, *The King's Lieutenant*; and R. Delachenal, 'Premiers négociations de Charles le Mauvais avec les Anglais', *B.E.C.* 61 (1900), pp. 253-71.

falling back towards Gascony, found that John had turned to attend to him, and having outmarched him, was barring his way at Maupertuis near Poitiers. On Sunday 18 September Cardinal Talleyrand of Perigord failed to mediate terms between the two commanders, and on Monday a great battle took place. The Prince's archers were skilfully disposed in a strong defensive position, and as at Crecy, repulsed a cavalry charge with loss; the French then advanced against them on foot, with still more fatal results. They were overwhelmed completely. In the closing stages of the battle, 'when all around men were running and securing prisoners', King John himself was discovered in a throng of English and Gascons who were quarrelling for the greatest prize of all. He, and a host of other well-born prisoners, all worth great ransoms, were carried with the vast spoils of the expedition to Bordeaux. There a truce was agreed for two years, and the Prince and his royal prisoner sailed for London.[23]

After Poitiers, it must have looked as if Edward would take all. His chief adversary was a captive in his hands. In kingless France government began to disintegrate. The royal council was bitterly attacked by the Estates General; the Parisians took arms and virtually held the dauphin a prisoner. They also released Charles of Navarre from John's prison, and the capital became the centre of a dangerous struggle for power between him and the dauphin. The truce of Bordeaux hardly gave a genuine respite from war. English soldiers in Normandy simply exchanged the banner and war cry of St George for those of Navarre and went on fighting. They found they could live well enough without pay by plundering, putting men to ransom, and levying tribute in the countryside round the castles that they held. 'Free companies' of soldiers in Brittany and in central France acted in a like manner. In these circumstances Edward came to the legitimate conclusion that he might, by a final effort at a crucial moment, be able to win the whole kingdom. A first attempt at settlement between him and John had broken down because the French could not even collect the first instalment of a ransom for their ruler. A second draft treaty was in such preposterous terms that it was probably meant to be refused by the French, and so furnish better excuse for taking to arms again.[24] The English royal host assembled at

[23] On the Poitiers campaign see H. J. Hewitt, *The Black Prince's Expedition of 1355-7* (Manchester, 1958); and Burne, *The Crecy War*, pp. 261-321.

[24] On these treaties see R. Delachenal, *Histoire de Charles V* vol. II (Paris, 1909), pp. 59-88; and J. Le Patourel, 'The Treaty of Brétigny'

Calais in the late summer of 1359, and was swelled with adventurers from Germany and the Low Countries who were anxious to be in at the death. Edward's objective was Rheims, and a gold crown, for use at his coronation there, was with his baggage.

Edward was baulked of his ultimate ambition. He reached Rheims, but failed to force an entry into the city and fell back in the spring towards Calais, harassed by French companies as he marched. Sickness also thinned the ranks of what had been a host twice the size of that which the Prince had commanded at Poitiers, and he must have known that another campaign on the same grand scale would be out of the question for the present. So, when the dauphin's agents proposed negotiations, he was ready to talk of peace in earnest. Within a week the envoys who met at Brétigny near Chartres had agreed the draft of a treaty between the two kingdoms.[25]

This treaty was ratified by the two kings, John and Edward, at Calais in October. John's ransom had been fixed at Brétigny at 3,000,000 crowns and the first instalment of 600,000 was paid before the ratification. Edward promised to renounce his claim to the throne of France. In return he obtained full sovereign rights in a new and broader Gascony, swelled by the addition to the ancient duchy of Poitou, Quercy, Limousin and the Agenais, and also in the march of Calais and in the counties of Ponthieu, Montreuil and Guines in the north. This was far from all that Edward had sometimes hoped for, and much less than he had been offered in 1358. It did not give him any right in Normandy, or the suzerainty over Brittany, both of which he had his eye on. But it made him sovereign in very large parts of what had once been France.

Edward was undoubtedly wise to accept the terms agreed at Brétigny as a settlement. He might have been tempted by the disarray of his enemies to press on in spite of difficulties, but he had learned now not to strain his resources too far. He had never, after the crisis of 1341, tried to raise taxation on the scale that he had in early years; and militarily, as the war went on, he had depended more and more for success on the support of allies in France, and on the free companies who wrought havoc in his enemies' lands without costing him anything. This strategy of

_T.R.H.S._ 5th ser., 10 (1960), esp. pp. 22–31. (I confess to unease about Le Patourel's concept of a 'ransom treaty'.)

[25] _Foed._ vol. VI, pp. 178–96.

waging war on the cheap enabled him to steer clear of dangerous domestic confrontations with his parliaments over issues of taxation and recruitment. But it also made Edward perforce an opportunist, who had to trim the horizon of his ambitions to the circumstances of the moment and the opportunities that they afforded. At Brétigny, he did just that.

There is one curious feature about the Treaty of Brétigny which, when one is considering what Edward had achieved in 1360, must not be overlooked. When the two kings met at Calais in October to ratify the Brétigny agreements, the clauses concerning the renunciations which they were to make, respectively of the title of King of France and of the sovereignty of the lands ceded to the English, were removed from the main treaty and dealt with in a separate document. This postponed the fulfilment of these clauses until November 1361.[26] This was a sensible step, as Edward naturally wished to be in actual possession of the lands in question before he formally renounced his title, and their transfer was bound to take time. When November 1361 came round, however, the renunciations were not made; indeed they were never formally exchanged. Technically therefore, Edward never renounced the title of King of France, and John never renounced sovereignty over Gascony. It was the English, apparently deliberately, who were responsible for delaying the exchange of renunciations. This has led some historians to suggest that Edward was not in earnest at Brétigny or Calais. He had done badly in the campaign of 1359-60 and knew he could no longer get what he had been offered a year before. But he had not given up hope, it is suggested, of pursuing his wider claim again one day under better auspices, and was therefore anxious not to renounce his French title. By delaying this issue, he managed, not very honestly, to keep his options open.[27]

That Edward was pleased to leave himself some loophole which would allow him to resuscitate his claims some day is likely enough. The point, however, should not be stressed too far. Edward in fact ceased to use the title King of France after 1360, and did not employ it again for eight years, until the war began again. Through this period, he appeared quite content with the settlement he had achieved. It was the French king in the end

[26] ibid. pp. 237-46.
[27] See further P. Chaplais, 'Some documents regarding the fulfilment of the Treaty of Brétigny', *Camden Miscellany* vol. XIX (1952), esp. intro. pp. 6-8; and J. Le Patourel, 'The Treaty of Brétigny', pp. 19-39.

who, by receiving in his court the appeals of Edward's Gascon subjects, the counts of Armagnac and Albret, took advantage of the non-fulfilment of the renunciations treaty. It was only when the French made it quite clear that they still claimed sovereignty that Edward revived his claim to the throne.

Privately, Edward in 1360 may have been disappointed that he had not won more from his adversary. Nevertheless, he had won what all contemporaries agreed was a signal triumph. 'When the noble Edward gained England in his youth', wrote Jean le Bel, 'nobody thought much of the English. . . . Now they are the finest and most daring warriors known to man.'[28] Edward had challenged the proudest kingdom in Europe and humbled her rulers in war. He had made himself sovereign lord in the lands in France where his father and his grandfather had been vassals, and in lands where they had never been lords at all. He had won control of the seas between England and France where Bretons and Picards had long preyed on English shipping. He had held the king of Scots his prisoner, and afterwards the king of France, and forced them (at Brétigny) to abandon their old alliance. He had achieved with all this the glamour of martial success in battles that had become famous wherever chivalry was honoured, Sluys, Crecy, Poitiers. If he modelled his court on that of Arthur, the British conqueror of long ago, it could seem only just and fitting for him to do so.

In Edward's time, the English chronicler wrote, 'to live was as if to reign: and his fame sprang so far that it came into heathendom and Barbary, showing and telling that in no land under heaven has been brought forth so noble a king.'[29] The commons in parliament were of the same opinion. 'Sire, the commons thank their liege lord as far as they know how . . . [and] from their hearts entirely thank God who has given them such a lord and governor, who has delivered them from servitude to other lands and delivered them from the charges suffered by them in time past.'[30] Looking back beyond his victories over the French and Scots to the disasters of the war of St Sardos and the years after Bannockburn, they might well speak thus. If Edward had died in 1360, he would be remembered as one of England's most successful medieval rulers – even though he had not won the French crown.

[28] Jean le Bel, *Chronique*, ed. J. Viard and E. Déprez (Paris, 1904), vol. I, pp. 155–6.
[29] *The Brut*, ed. F. W. D. Brie (E.E.T.S., 1908) p. 334.
[30] *R.P.* vol. II, p. 276.

7

England under Edward III
1330–1360

Twenty years of war had very important consequences for
Edward III's subjects in England. The whole framework of
their lives, their prosperity, the opportunities which could open
for them, and their outlook, were all affected by the experience.
Other factors too helped to make the period important in
domestic history. The peers were acquiring new privileges, the
commons in parliament a greater independence as a result of the
part that they played in granting taxes. And in 1348 the Black
Death struck England, with consequences which affected the
lives of people at every social level. Its effects were in fact so far
reaching that they will have to be dealt with in a separate
chapter.

Edward deliberately sought to associate his people with his war
policies, and his propaganda was both imaginative and effective.
His war was given maximum publicity. Whenever parliament
met, proceedings were opened with a speech from one of his
officials, usually the chancellor or the treasurer, which was taken
as an opportunity to remind the estates of the justice of the
king's cause, and the need to support his exertions. On occasion
veterans of the campaigns who were also intimates of the king
were brought in to address them; thus Bartholomew Burghersh
came into parliament in 1343 to talk about the campaign in
Brittany, and in 1355 Walter Manny appeared to explain how the
negotiations at Avignon had broken down because of the deceit
of the French, and the king had had to go to war again. When the
king was abroad, he kept in constant touch with his councillors,
and sent home from time to time reports of his doings, which were
to be read out in fairs and markets and other public places. In
response to requests from the king, the archbishops and bishops

were constantly instructing the clergy of their dioceses to offer prayers for the safety and success of the king's armies, or to thank God for his victories.[1] In 1346 Edward wrote to the Prior Provincial of the Dominicans, explaining to him and to his order the justice of his claim to the French throne, so that they might preach of the matter at large.[2] Sermons and the prayers and intercessions that people heard in church kept the fortunes of the war constantly before their minds, and taught them to associate the king's victories with God's favour to the English.

The subject matter of the proclamations and speeches, through which the king and his advisers appealed for popular support, repays attention. The justice of his quarrel and his faith in God's favour were always to the fore: 'So we hope, by the aid of Jesus Christ our Lord, that we shall do battle shortly in the field, in this our just quarrel, to our honour and that of all our realm, and therefore we beg that you will pray for us devoutly.' Thus Edward wrote to his subjects from Calais in 1347.[3] In other documents one will find a good deal of careful explanation of the legal basis of the king's claims in France. There was much talk of the deceit of the French and their refusal to offer or accept terms reasonable and honourable to the English. One item in propaganda intended for domestic consumption is particularly striking – the labouring of the aggressive intentions of the French. In his letter of 1346 to the Dominican Prior Provincial, Edward described Philip VI as determined 'to root out the English tongue' from the face of the world. A genuine plan for the invasion of England, which was found at Caen by the king's host in that same year but which was undoubtedly drawn up at a much earlier date, was put to endless use. It was read aloud to the next parliament, and represented as a plan of that very year.[4] Of course the French did consider plans for invading England, more than once, but none of them came to very much. Edward and his advisers clearly appreciated the value of the advice that Hobbes later gave to rulers who wished to create solidarity of feeling among their subjects, to 'bring distant terrors near'.

The manner in which Edward sought to associate with his own cause the aspirations of the knights and nobles who were his

[1] See H. J. Hewitt, *The Organisation of War under Edward III* (Manchester, 1966), pp. 161-3.

[2] *Foed.* vol. V, p. 496.

[3] K. de L. vol. XVIII, p. 302.

[4] *R.P.* vol. II, pp. 158-9.

captains shows his handling of public relations at its most positive, and also at its most imaginative. These were men who understood the same language as the king himself. Edward was careful to make sure that glory won in the field was for them as well as him. In the parliament of 1337, when it was known that war was imminent, six new earls were created, all men who were to be prominent among the king's military lieutenants. Henry de Grosmont became Earl of Derby; William Montagu, Earl of Salisbury; Hugh Audley, Earl of Gloucester; William Clinton, Earl of Huntingdon; William Bohun, Earl of Northampton; Robert Ufford, Earl of Suffolk. In 1346, when Edward landed at La Hogue, his first act was to make his son Edward a knight, and with him he knighted the lords Roger Mortimer, William Montagu the younger and William Roos. The prospect of winning fame in the field in France had a natural allure to an aristocracy brought up from youth to martial pursuits. Froissart tells a story that illuminates a typical attitude, of forty young knights of England at Valenciennes in 1339, who all wore a silk patch over one eye, because they had vowed among the ladies of England to see with one eye only until each had performed some deed of arms in France.[5] The making of knights in the field, the chivalrous ceremonial of the royal court, the great tournaments and feasts that Edward held, and such pageants as the torchlight procession of knights at Bristol in 1358, all served to encourage a martial and adventurous enthusiasm which could be channelled into war service.

It was after the great tournament at Windsor in 1344 that Edward laid the foundations for what was to become his Order of the Garter. It was to be a fellowship of knights, bound together as companions by their oaths to aid and support one another and the sovereign of the order, and was modelled on the fellowship of knights of Arthur's round table. The formal institution of the order dates from 1348, following the famous scene at a ball held at Calais when the Countess of Salisbury dropped her garter, and the king, who was in love with her, picked it up and bound it on his knee, afterwards adopting it as the badge of his order. The Black Prince, the earls of Salisbury, March and Warwick, Sir John Chandos, and the Gascon Captal de Buch were all founder members; other famous captains, as Walter Manny and Sir Thomas Felton soon joined them. The code of chivalry of the Arthurian fellowship of romance, which was the ideal model for Edward's order, taught that the first duties of a

[5] K. de L. vol. II, p. 376.

knight were to serve his lord loyally and to uphold the cause of right. The legendary heroes won their fame not by patriotic self-sacrifice, but rather in the vendettas of those who had been injured in their rights. This was the way in which Edward and his captains spoke and thought about their war too; it was his 'just quarrel', which he had 'undertaken', to recover his 'rights and heritage', in which he hoped with God's aid to do battle and to have a good issue of it. Much that would otherwise be puzzling about Edward's war and his aims in it becomes understandable if we remember that he and his companions thought in terms of chivalrous and honourable enterprise, rather than of modern national ambition.

Besides glory and adventure, the war held out prospects of more solid and material advantage to those who served actively in the hosts. There was the hope, for the leaders at any rate, of winning heritages for themselves overseas. Henry de Grosmont added to his estates the lordship of Bergerac in Gascony; John Chandos obtained fiefs in the Cotentin; Robert Knowles made himself a great *seigneur* in Brittany. For all, high and low alike, there was the prospect of loot, and plunder was always at least a subsidiary objective of even the great royal expeditions. 'In Normandy', Godfrey de Harcourt is said to have told Edward III, 'you shall find great towns that have not been walled, whereby your men shall find such gain that they shall be the better twenty years after.'[6] The gains which some men won lasted even longer: William Berkeley told John Leland in the sixteenth century that his house at Beverstone was built out of the ransoms that his great grandfather won at Poitiers.[7]

Ransoms provided the most startling profits which individual soldiers won in the war. Thomas Dagworth, who took Charles of Blois prisoner, got £4900 for him; Sir John Wingfield sold the Sire d'Aubigny, taken at Poitiers, to the king for 2500 marks; and Sir Thomas Holland got 20,000 for the Count of Eu, whom he took at Caen. It was not only the great captains who made fortunes in this way, but the ordinary men at arms too. 'The first time that I bore armour was under the Captal de Buch at Poitiers', a mercenary soldier told Froissart, 'and as it was my hap I had that day three prisoners . . . of whom I had one with another three thousand francs.' Even the very humble saw a share in the winnings of war: in 1358 we find the Black Prince ordering

[6] K. de L. vol. IV, p. 381.

[7] J. Leland, *Itinerary*, ed. L. Toulmin-Smith (London, 1909), vol. IV, p. 133.

his treasurer to pay £8 12s. 6d. to a group of Cheshire archers, for their part in a silver ship, the property of the king of France, which also was taken at Poitiers.[8]

The wealth won in the war was sufficiently considerable to have a noticeable impact on social history. Gains of war made it possible for a good many noblemen to maintain a level of expenditure and to live in a style which would otherwise have impoverished them. The spoils that he made in 1355 and 1356 relieved the Black Prince of a heavy load of debt. Spoils also helped men of more humble origins to acquire solid fortunes which gave them and their descendants status outside the world of the camp and the battlefield. Many of Edward's most famous captains were not of the old nobility. John Chandos began his career as a poor knight of meagre estate. Robert Knowles's origins were even humbler, but he made an immense fortune, and we find him in his old age advancing substantial loans to the king. Ralph Salle, who became a considerable landowner in East Anglia, was said to be the son of a serf. These men of course were among the fortunate few, who outdid all the rest. But there were many county families for whose fortunes lesser gains of war provided a valuable subvention, and others who would have remained utterly obscure but for the chances that adventure abroad created. The doors of opportunity stood open to all. Even for the humblest in the army, the archers, the wage of 2d. a day was attractive by itself, in an age when a ploughman might hope to earn 12s. or 13s. in a twelvemonth.

Rates of pay and rules for the division of spoil in the king's armies were carefully detailed in the sealed contracts which the king made with his captains, and they with their subordinates, which are known as indentures of war. From soon after the beginning of the Hundred Years War these documents begin to survive in large numbers, and the conditions that they lay down become stereotyped. The daily rates of pay in Edward III's time were, for a duke, one mark (13s. 4d.); for an earl 8s.; for a banneret (a baron or knight of wealth and experience) 4s.; for a knight bachelor 2s.; mounted archers were usually paid 6d. a day and foot archers 2d. A captain promised to pay the king a third of all his ransoms and other gains of war, and took a

[8] K. de L. vol. XI, pp. 108–9; and *The Black Prince's Register* part IV, p. 254. On spoils of war see further H. J. Hewitt, *The Black Prince's Expedition of 1355–7* (Manchester, 1958), ch. VII, to which I am much indebted; and D. Hay, 'The division of the spoils of war in fourteenth century England', *T.R.H.S.* 5th ser., 4 (1954), pp. 91–109.

third in turn from the men of his company. Indentures specified also the number of soldiers with whom the contracting captain had to serve, and the period of their service (normally six months or a year). These contracts were voluntary. The survival of war indentures in increasing numbers is thus an indication that service in the king's wars was becoming popular. Though commissioners of array were appointed to impress men more or less compulsorily for all the major expeditions, as those of 1339, 1346, and 1359, the proportion of men serving in the hosts of their own will was growing steadily. With their careful specification of terms of service and rules for the division of spoil the indentures reveal the business of fighting developing into a kind of joint stock enterprise of the king and his subjects.

The indentures are also evidence of a quiet revolution in the administration of war which the reign of Edward III witnessed. The captains who contracted with the king took on the responsibility of themselves recruiting and mustering their companies. They also, most significantly, took upon themselves the direct responsibility for paying the men who contracted to serve under them. The paymasters who accompanied the hosts led by such magnates as the Black Prince and Henry de Grosmont were not clerks of the wardrobe but officials of the magnates' own households. They recovered the wages of their men directly from the exchequer; a first instalment was usually paid in advance but often they had to wait a long time for the rest of the money. In the meantime captains tided things over by paying soldiers from their own personal resources, and by crediting spoil to the account for wages. The fact that they were often prepared to leave their accounts at the exchequer outstanding for long periods is an indication of how profitable war was becoming.[9]

In the old days the basis of a royal host had been the king's

[9] There is a substantial literature on indentures and the organization of war in this period. The most important works include A. E. Prince, 'The indenture system under Edward III' in *Historical Essays in Honour of James Tait*, ed. J. G. Edwards, V. H. Galbraith and E. F. Jacob (Manchester, 1933), pp. 283–97; and 'The payment of army wages in Edward III's reign', *Speculum* 19 (1944), pp. 137–60; J. W. Sherborne, 'Indentured retinues and English expeditions to France 1369–80', *E.H.R.* 79 (1964), pp. 718–46; N. B. Lewis, 'The recruitment and organisation of a contract army, 1337', *B.I.H.R.* 37 (1964), pp. 1–19. More generally, see M. R. Powicke, *Military Obligation in Medieval England* (Oxford, 1962), ch. IX and X; and H. J. Hewitt, *The Organisation of War under Edward III*, an outstandingly useful book to which I owe much.

household in arms, and the wardrobe had looked after pay, commissariat and equipment. Those days were passing, and command in the armies, in consequence, became looser at the top. Commanders such as the Black Prince, Henry de Grosmont of Lancaster, and Sir Thomas Dagworth led their own troops and made their own plans of campaign. The scale of the war that Edward III was fighting made it necessary to give men such as these a wide discretion in their commands, and to rely on the administration of military finance through the exchequer, instead of the household. The readiness with which the king and his administrators adapted to the exigencies of new circumstances is striking, however, and fits, as we shall presently see, into a wider pattern.

One will find the names of almost all the great noble families of England among those who contracted to serve Edward III abroad. This is testimony to the success of his efforts to associate the aspirations and pride of the English nobility with his martial enterprises. This was not the only way in which he sought to fortify the loyalty of the peers to the monarchy, which his father's reign had shaken.

The king was generous to his noblemen. William Montagu, the intimate of his youth, was granted the earldom of Salisbury, the reversion of all the lands that the Earl of Warenne had held for life, and the reversion of the Montalt inheritance. Henry de Grosmont was created Duke of Lancaster, the first to hold the title of duke who was not a king's son, and was granted palatine rights for life in his duchy. William Bohun, another great captain in the wars and brother of the Earl of Hereford, was made Earl of Northampton and granted extensive estates in Oxfordshire and Berkshire. Especially striking are the pains that Edward took, over the years, to restore the fortunes of families that had suffered in his father's time and in his own early years. He looked after Joan, the daughter of his uncle Edmund of Kent, who had been executed in 1330, and when she married Thomas Holland he made him Earl of Kent. He allowed Arundel, whose father had been executed in 1326, to succeed in due course to most of the hereditary estates of his uncle Warenne, and the judgement on his father was solemnly reversed in the parliament of 1354. Also reversed in the same parliament was the judgement on Roger Mortimer, whose son was restored to his father's title of Earl of March. Edward took more pains to restore Mortimer than any other, perhaps because he himself had been the author of the father's undoing. To achieve his end he had to override the rights of the Montagus, the Berkeleys, the Beauchamps, and of others who had profited by the elder Mortimer's fall, but he did not hesitate to do so. These families had, after all, been rewarded well enough in other ways. None of them protested much, and March served Edward well, in his council, in his wars, and as a knight of the Garter.[10]

In the later part of his reign Edward III did not raise many new families to the peerage. His most important new creations were in favour of his own children. The Black Prince was granted the earldoms of Chester and Cornwall (erected into a duchy in 1337), and later the principality of Wales. Lionel, born at Antwerp in 1338, was married to Elizabeth de Burgh, who brought him the honour of Clare, as well as wide lands in Ulster and Connaught. John of Gaunt, the next son, was married to Blanche, the heiress of Henry of Lancaster, and through her right became Duke of Lancaster, and Earl of Leicester, Lincoln and Derby. Edmund of Langley was created Earl of Cambridge in 1362. Thomas of Woodstock, the king's youngest son, married the elder of the co-heiresses of Humphrey de Bohun, Earl of Hereford. The magnificent inheritances which Edward's children acquired by marriage and paternal patronage set them apart among the English aristocracy. They had the wealth and status to aspire to play independent parts not only in English politics but in Europe. The Black Prince, after 1362, was Lord of Aquitaine. Lionel, after his first wife's death, sought a Visconti for his next bride; Edmund was betrothed to the heiress of Flanders (but did not marry her, because the pope at the French king's instance refused a dispensation). John of Gaunt, after Blanche's death, married Constanza, daughter of the deposed King Pedro of Castile, and so acquired a claim to a Spanish throne. Such a galaxy of princes, with ambitions in England and overseas which could easily become competitive, was a new feature of the English political scene. They added lustre to the ranks of the peerage, but lustre that was in the end to prove dangerous; the heads of the half-regal houses who fought one another in the Wars of the Roses were all descended from Edward III.

Families and individuals apart, the peers as a body gained advantages in this reign. As was shown by Edward's concession in 1341, that henceforward no peer should be arraigned or

[10] On these promotions and restorations see G. A. Holmes, *The Estates of the Higher Nobility in Fourteenth Century England* (Cambridge, 1957), ch. I.

judged for any crime, except before his peers in parliament,[11] the magnates were beginning to establish themselves as a class apart with special privileges. Even more important than legal privilege was the new freedom with regard to the administration and disposition of their estates which the nobility acquired through Edward's pliant generosity. The most significant development here was the growth of the device of 'enfeoffment to use' which before this time had been employed from time to time by feudal subtenants, but seldom by magnates (largely in consequence of the crown's determination to maintain a surveillance over the disposition of the lands of tenants in chief). This was the practice whereby a landowner alienated a part or parts of his estates to a group of his relatives or retainers (his 'feoffees'). At common law these 'feoffees' became the owners; the 'feoffor' retained the 'use' of the estates, and drew the profits during his lifetime. After his death his feoffees would proceed according to the instructions that he had left, which would usually be drawn up in a 'last will', a document originally separate from the testament. The owner was thus enabled to secure the integrity of his estates beyond his lifetime, to make arrangements for the settlement of his debts, and to make sure that there was provision after his death for his family and his followers. These for instance are the principal purposes for which, according to his will, Hugh Earl of Stafford made an enfeoffment of a large part of his property: that all his servants and retainers might be sure of enjoying the fees and rents he had promised them for the term of their lives; to provide a dowry for his daughter; and to provide an annuity for life of £100 for each of his younger sons. When all these beneficiaries were dead, the reversion of their interest was secured to the earl's heir.[12]

Magnates who were going to the wars secured considerable benefits for their families through 'uses', in the event of their death abroad in the king's service. Uses also enabled men of the noble class to maintain a greater continuity in the administration of their estates and in their relations with their retainers, which in the past would have been broken when, at death, the crown

[11] See L. W. Vernon Harcourt, *His Grace the Steward and Trial of Peers* (London, 1907), pp. 342–4.

[12] On uses and their development in this period see J. M. W. Bean, *The Decline of English Feudalism* (Manchester, 1968), the most careful study of the topic to date, especially chapters III and IV; also Holmes, *The Estates of the Higher Nobility*, pp. 49ff. (who discusses Stafford's enfeoffment in detail, p. 53).

entered on their estates (where crown officials might remain in charge for a long time if the heir was under age). The feoffees were now the owners at law, and so the enfeoffed estates remained in their hands when the feoffor died. Since few magnates enfeoffed all their estates to use, the crown retained wardship of the body of the heir, and of his lands held in fee simple, and the right to arrange his marriage, but the financial loss to the crown, which was consequent upon large parts of his estate escaping from wardship, was considerable. The magnate who enfeoffed land to use ran a certain risk, of course, that his feoffees would disobey his instructions, and try to make the most of their position at common law as owners, but the advantages of the system greatly outweighed this relatively negligible hazard.[13] In due course a jurisdiction over uses, outside the common law, developed with the chancellor, who judged cases brought by feoffors to use against defaulting or disloyal feoffees by equity, 'according to conscience upon the intent of . . . a feoffment'.[14] This jurisdiction, of which the origins only can be traced back to the fourteenth century, was to be important in the history of the development of the court of chancery.

A royal licence was required before land held in chief of the king was enfeoffed to use. Edward III was, however, generous with his grants of such licences (and of course magnates could anyway enfeoff without licence parts of their estate which were not held in chief).[15] Edward was also generous in granting licences to noblemen to entail their estates. This meant that although a number of great families failed during his reign to produce direct heirs (the earls of Warenne and Oxford are good examples), their lands did not, for the most part, revert to the crown. Since an estate 'in tail' was a life tenancy only for the holder, and inalienable, entail helped to protect the integrity of magnate inheritances. 'Tail male' – the entailing of an estate on the male heirs to the exclusion of all females – had the same effect; for it meant that if a landowner left daughters only, his estate reverted to the next male heir, instead of being divided, as was the rule of common law with regard to estates held in fee

[13] On the foregoing see further Bean, *The Decline of English Feudalism*, pp. 144–5, 152, 232–3.

[14] *Statutes*, I Ric. III, c.1; and see Bean, *The Decline of English Feudalism*, pp. 176–7.

[15] See Bean, *The Decline of English Feudalism*, pp. 116–25, and Appendix II, which tabulates the rapid rise of enfeoffments to use as recorded in Inquisitions *post mortem*.

simple, between the daughters as co-heiresses. 'Tail male' (though only in due course, and after Edward III's time) came to affect the descent of titles, and so to give definition to the concept of a hereditary peerage.[16] The effect of Edward's policy of meeting his magnates' wishes as far as was possible in such matters as 'uses' and entails has been described as 'a revolution in the law of real property'. The tight royal control which Edward I had preserved over the movement of the lands of his tenants in chief was undermined, together with the old simple relation between the crown and its feudal tenants. The crown lost valuable financial perquisites, to the advantage of the magnates; and the magnate families gained a greater degree of control over both the administration and the disposition of their inheritances. The pattern we here observe, of the decline of royal control over noble inheritances, echoes the pattern we observed previously, of the growing independence of the nobility with regard to the recruitment and terms of service of military contingents under their command. Edward III could still, of course, refuse licences to entail or to enfeoff to use, as he could still also summon his military tenants to serve him and array men for war in the counties. But once a new way of doing things has become normal practice, it ceases to be easy to make a break with it. By the end of Edward III's reign a return to the conditions and practices of Edward I's time had become impossible and unthinkable. A new balance had been created in the relations of the king and his magnates. Edward III gained by the loyalty which his generous policies fostered; he did not ever have to face the kind of difficulties in his relations with his magnates that his father and grandfather had.

The great Statute of Treason of 1352 was significant of the changed relations between the king and his magnates. In the reign of Edward II many peers, Gaveston, the Despensers and Lancaster among them, had been summarily convicted of treason on counts which included the wide and vague charge of 'accroaching' or usurping royal power. The new statute secured their successors against the threat of this charge, and of the terrible penalties that followed conviction, by defining high treason in the narrowest possible terms. It must be an 'open act', aimed to compass the death of the king, his chancellor, or his

[16] See K. B. McFarlane, 'The English nobility in the later Middle Ages', *XIIme congrès international des sciences historiques* (1965), vol. I, pp. 337–45.

judges; or the violation of his wife or eldest daughter; or else an act of war done against the king in his kingdom. The statute specifically added that armed robbery, slaughter, and kidnapping were not high treason, but felonies or trespass. This last point was also important for the magnates. The goods of a convicted felon were forfeit to his lord, those of a convicted traitor were forfeit to the king, as were his estates if he possessed any. Robbery and kidnapping – crimes that were common enough – had on a number of occasions been construed by the judges as treason; the statute guaranteed that lords should not lose their forfeitures on a technicality of judicial interpretation.

Interestingly and in a way surprisingly, it was not the pressure of the lords, but of the commons that seems to have been behind the promulgation of the 1352 statute. It was they who asked for a clearer definition of both treason and 'accroachment', and they seem neither to have been responding to magnate promptings nor seeking any specific material advantage to the class that they represented. More simply, they disliked the construction, by which the judges in the 1340s treated highway robbery and riot as usurpations of royal power, because they suspected that the common law was thereby being pressed into the service of a prerogative absolutism whose legal limits were too vague. The fact that local disorder, in the period when the king was often abroad, had become a problem of alarming proportions did not seem to them as important as that men should know where they stood in law and be well protected against the oppression of ill-fettered royal power. This was typical of their whole attitude to royal government.[17]

The commons were able, in Edward III's reign, to make their attitudes towards the king's government felt in an important way, because of the part that they played in granting taxation. Regular subsidies were the only resource adequate to meet the expenses that the French war involved. This put parliament in a commanding position, and the commons were clearly aware both of the advantage to them of formal association in all grants of taxation (a privilege not fully established at the beginning of the reign), and of the potential bargaining power which could stem therefrom.

This was made very plain by the events of the years from 1336

[17] On the Statute of Treason see J. G. Bellamy, *The Law of Treason in England in the Later Middle Ages* (Cambridge, 1970), ch. 4, and the works there cited, pp. 59–60.

to 1341, when the king's financial demands were at their most strenuous. His obligations to allies, to whom he had promised pensions, and to the Italian bankers who had advanced him loans, were getting him steadily into greater difficulties, and Edward and his ministers had no option but to bargain with parliament for what they could get. In 1339 the grant of a tenth sheep and fleece and lamb was made conditional on redress of grievances: exemption from prises and old debts; the grant of a new pardon for past offences; and the abolition of the *maltolte* on wool granted to the king by the merchants outside parliament in 1336. In the spring parliament of 1340 the grant of 1339 was increased to a ninth, but with new conditions, in laying down which it was the commons that took the initiative. Some of these conditions were very important. The king had to agree to confirm the charters; to cease taking any taxes to which parliament and the commons had not assented; and, most striking of all, to appoint a council which would have full and independent authority in domestic government while the king was overseas. It was the commons who wrung these concessions from the king (though prompted, probably, by Stratford). This was the first occasion ever on which they insisted on the appointment of named councillors.[18] They were learning rapidly that their newly established role in granting subsidies could enable them to make demands of a kind that in the past had never been made by any but magnates.

The parliament of 1341, which witnessed the famous clash between the king and Archbishop Stratford, saw still further concessions. The king's ministers and justices must be sworn in parliament to observe Magna Carta, the Charter of the Forest, and all the statutes of the land; and they must be prepared in each subsequent parliament to answer any complaint alleged against them. These radical articles, reminiscent of the *Ordinances* of 1311, did not endure as statutes; later in the year Edward, after consulting with his judges and magnates, declared that his consent to them had been unwilling, and repealed them on his own authority.[19] Significantly, the commons in the next parliament (1343) entered a vigorous (though unsuccessful) protest against this action, on their own account and quite independently of the lords.

[18] See G. L. Harriss, 'The commons' petitions of 1340', *E.H.R.* 78 (1963), pp. 625–54.
[19] See H. G. Richardson and G. O. Sayles, 'The early statutes', *L.Q.R.* 50 (1934), pp. 550–2.

Other actions of the commons in this period have a distinct tone of self conscious independence. In 1339 they refused assent for their part to the grant of the tenth which the lords had proposed, insisting that they must first be given time to go back to their counties and consult with the communities that they represented. When the next parliament met, they retired to debate among themselves and to settle the conditions which they would attach to the grant that they would make. From 1341 onward the evidence that the commons were normally debating apart among themselves in parliament begins to be clear. They had established for themselves an independent role in the shaping of the 'common counsel of the realm'.

After 1341 the king's needs were still pressing, and he had to go through the process of bargaining for assistance many times. The commons did not grant taxes willingly; the cost of the great military efforts of 1346-7 and of 1359-60 caused serious discontent, and the conditions on which they agreed to assist the king were not easy. This was how the commons addressed him in 1348: 'Now we hear, that because of the new turn of events, the king is demanding a charge on his poor commons which is too great: may it therefore please his lordship to hear the burden of the charges and mischief which the said commons already endure.'[20] If they were to make a grant, they said, all judicial eyres must cease; there must be no separate grant made to the king by merchants; the king must undertake not to release the King of Scots or the other prisoners of Neville's Cross without consulting them; and all these conditions must be formally recorded on the parliament roll. A statement like this provides clear testimony to the commons' awareness of the strength of their bargaining position. Some of the demands, too, are very striking; the request for consultation before the King of Scots was released really asked for a right of review of the king's diplomatic negotiations.

The commons did not gain all they asked from the king in 1348, or on any other occasion. Even when the king did assent to their conditions, he did not always abide by them. Nevertheless, if one compares the rolls of the statutes of Edward III's reign with the listed petitions of the commons, one cannot but be made aware of the impressive influence of the commons on contemporary legislation.[21] A very marked change has taken place since the

[20] *R.P.* vol. II, p. 200.
[21] On this see further H. L. Gray, *The Influence of the Commons on Early Legislation* (Harvard, 1932), ch. VIII, especially pp. 215-29.

days of Edward I. Edward I's statutes, it is true, were often framed with an eye to meeting public demand, but the initiative lay always with the king and his advisers; it was he and his judges who framed the statutes. The statutes of Edward III's reign do not reflect simply a response to public opinion; a great many of them stem directly from specific requests expressed in the commons' petitions. This is true of some very important statutes, those of 1340, for instance. Others, like the Statute of Treason and the first Statute of Provisors, were drafted by the judges, but in response to prompting from the commons.

One of the areas in which royal concession to general opinion was most important in its consequences was that of the administration of justice. In the past, the visits to the counties of the justices in eyre, appointed in the exchequer and carefully instructed there in the manner in which they were to investigate all crimes and overhaul the activities of officials at local level, had been the chief means whereby the king and the council maintained a close surveillance over local administration. The eyres were never popular; the commons petitioned regularly against their institution, and by the end of Edward III's reign they had fallen into desuetude. Part of the work that they had once done was now performed by justices of assize, empowered to hear various kinds of cases in the county courts, under commissions of *nisi prius*, *oyer et terminer*, and of gaol delivery. Where violence or particularly flagrant disobedience had been involved, special commissions of *oyer et terminer* or of *trailbaston* might be empowered to deal with a specific case or a special kind of offence. But more and more business, in the course of Edward III's reign, came to be dealt with by the justices of the peace. Originally keepers of the peace empowered only to pursue and arrest criminals, they steadily acquired more powers to hear and determine cases as justices. The commissions of the peace of Edward III's day were named by the king; they usually included at least one great magnate, plus one or two professional lawyers, backed up by gentlemen resident in the counties. The idea of the *quorum* (which means that at least one justice learned in the law must be present to hear important cases) first appears in a statute of 1344. The commons, as their petitions witness, vastly preferred the justice of the commissions of the peace to that of special commissions and eyres. The jurisdiction of the justices of the peace was defined by statute in 1368; it included the enforcement of labour laws; of regulations about prices, weights, and measures; and most important of all, the maintenance of the peace and the determination of felonies and trespass.[22]

One of the objects of the great judicial eyres of the thirteenth century had been to ensure that the king's officials had enforced his royal rights fully and to his advantage. With their passing, pressure from the commons began to effect the reverse of this objective, for what they wanted to ensure was that royal rights were not pressed too far. The statute of 1340 placed new limits on the king's right of purveyance, and later petitions demanded its re-enactment, and strict control of the activities of buyers for the king's household. Similar petitions demanded the restraint of forest officials, and that the bounds of the forest be surveyed, and kept as they were in Edward I's time. The whole question of the forest, of its boundaries and the administration of the forest law, which had been one of the liveliest sources of friction between the king and his subjects at the beginning of the century, ceased to be a bone of contention in the course of Edward III's reign. The forest law itself began to be relaxed.

In the two related fields of the administration of justice and the supervision of the king's prerogative rights the contrast between the reigns of Edward I and Edward III is very sharp. The basis of most of the complaints against Edward I was over-government. His officials seemed to be prying everywhere; he exercised his right to purveyance and to take tallage with the widest freedom; and he made sure by vigorous judicial inquiries that the misdemeanours both of his subjects and of his officials redounded to his pecuniary advantage. Edward III, in the late 1330s, made an effort to follow the example of his grandfather as a ruler and to restore a measure of absolutism; but he found resistance too strong, and changed his course. Thereafter the pattern of his reign was of concession. He needed money and soldiers and was prepared in return for them to relax royal control, to the point where ancient royal rights ceased to be enforceable and justice was administered in the ways that his subjects, and not he, preferred. This did not mean that the country was better or more fairly governed. The justices of the peace, for instance, were not

[22] On the justices of the peace see B. H. Putnam, 'Keepers and justices of the peace', *T.R.H.S.* 4th ser., 12 (1929), pp. 19–48; and *Proceedings before the Justices of the Peace, Edward III to Richard III* (Ames Foundation, 1938), intro. See also C. A. Beard, *The Office of Justice of the Peace in England* (New York, 1904). Putnam discusses the jurisdiction of the J.P.s over labour legislation in her book, *The Enforcement of the Statute of Labourers* (Columbia, 1908).

so easily held to account as the justices in eyre had been at the exchequer, and they were much more easily browbeaten by local magnates. It is clear, however, that men on the whole preferred the new ways. In return for the king's concessions they were prepared to make the financial sacrifices that he requested, and they were proud and grateful for the victories thus purchased.

One final matter that gave rise to long wrangles between the king and the commons in the reign of Edward III demands attention. This is the history of the efforts of the commons to obtain full control over all sorts of grants of taxation, which was essential to them if they were to be able to make the king keep his bargains with them.

There were two very important sectors of the community which in Edward III's reign, as previously, often made grants to the king outside parliament. One of these, the clergy, succeeded until after the medieval period in maintaining their independent right to tax themselves, by means of grants voted in the convocations.[23] The other group in question was the merchants. Since the time of Edward I, English kings had periodically summoned representative assemblies of merchants, in which taxes which usually took the form of a 'subsidy' or *maltolte*, an extra charge on the export of wool over and above the customs, were negotiated. The advantage which merchants gained by their grants was a degree of monopoly in the export trade, usually organized through a 'staple'. A staple was a town or towns through which alone wool might be exported, and in which this monopoly of export was controlled by the merchants whom the assembly which made the grant represented (the 'King's merchants', or the 'Company of the Staple').

There was room in this system for serious conflict of interest. The agreed staple might be situated abroad; in 1338 it was at Dordrecht, in 1343 at Bruges, and after 1363 most often it was at Calais, which at the end of the fourteenth century was to become the permanent headquarters of the Company of the Staple. If the staple was abroad, the company operating it had of necessity to be a relatively small one: in 1343 for instance there were thirty-three members in the syndicate. This increased the potential for profit of the monopoly (these thirty-three members promised to pay the king, over and above the farm of the customs at the staple which they were granted, 10,000 marks a year), but excluded all except the favoured few from the advantages

[23] See Chapter 9.

of the system. A series of staples, located in English towns, was preferable from the point of view of a larger body of merchants, but not so useful from the point of view of the king, who (especially after the failure of his Italian bankers, the Bardi and the Peruzzi, in 1345) relied heavily on the ability of the great English merchants to advance loans to him. Between the staple merchants and the producers (strongly represented among the shire knights of the commons) there was a still more serious clash of interest. The producers always suspected that the effect of *maltoltes* granted by the merchants was offset in the price that they offered for the wool. The producer thus would get no share in the profit, which a staple system ensured to the merchants by enabling them to control the price of wool on the foreign market.

In consequence, Edward and his ministers had to face a series of demands from the commons that *maltoltes* on wool should not be levied without their assent; that the staples abroad should be disbanded; and that the trade in wool and other 'staple' commodities (as hides, lead, and tin) should be entirely free. Thus in 1344, as a result of pressure from the commons, the Bruges staple was abandoned, and free trade permitted in England. The statute of 1353-4, which established a series of home staples and which the commons had a considerable hand in framing, went even further, prohibiting native merchants from exporting wool (the aim being to guarantee a competitive price to the producer, by making sure that alien exporters bought in the native market). The most bitter struggle of all was over the legality of *maltoltes* granted by assemblies of merchants. The view of the commons, clearly and strongly expressed, was identical with that of the magnates who had opposed Edward I's *maltolte* in 1297: *maltoltes* should not be legal, because their effect was felt largely by the 'people', not by the merchants who voted them. In 1339 and 1340, in 1343, in 1347 and in 1350, the commons petitioned for the abolition of *maltoltes* which had not received their assent. Edward gave way, abandoned the offending taxes (on condition, on occasion, that they be continued with common assent); but equally regularly he summoned assemblies of merchants again, with whom he negotiated new *maltoltes* and new staple arrangements.[24]

[24] On the struggles over the *maltoltes* and the staples see further G. Unwin, 'The estate of the merchants' in *Finance and Trade under Edward III*, ed. G. Unwin (Manchester, 1918), pp. 179-255; E. Power, *The Wool Trade in English Medieval History* (Oxford, 1941), ch. 5, on

By 1353, when plans for a system of home staples were being mooted, it was clear that the continued pressure of the commons was beginning to tell, on the merchants if not on the king. A system of home staples was planned and discussed in a great council in 1353, in which the mercantile element was dominant: there were present one knight only from each shire, and eighty-two burgesses from forty-three towns which had special interests in the wool trade. These representatives prepared an 'Ordinance of the Staple'. But they also requested that what they had agreed should be referred to the next parliament for confirmation, and that what was done in the great council should not be 'of record, as if it were done by common assent in parliament'.[25] The eighty-two burgesses clearly had no desire to get their arrangements into difficulties with the commons unnecessarily. Nine years later, in 1362, the position was finally regularized and defined: 'no subsidy or other charge shall be granted on wool by merchants or any others without the consent of parliament'.[26] The commons thus finally won full and effective control of lay taxation.

The statute of 1362 made sure that parliament would not share its fiscal role with another representative body. The implication of the request of the great council of 1353, that what was not done in parliament should not be 'of record' is perhaps even more significant. It was a sign of a recognition that parliament had a formal legislative role, and that its assent was needful to give authority to new laws of general importance. Here we see how the bargains which the commons struck with King Edward when meeting his requests for financial aid helped to define for parliament, and for the commons in particular, an essential place in the constitution.

The stresses of the war taught Edward III to take both the peers and the commons into partnership with the monarchy. After 1341, his plans for campaigns never again outran the limit of his subjects' willingness to serve him and to pay him in the way that they had done in the first four years of hostilities. He was always pressed, however, for ready cash, and had constantly to raise

---

the Staple; B. Wilkinson, 'The beginnings of parliamentary control over the custom on wool' in his *Studies in the Constitutional History of the Thirteenth and Fourteenth Centuries* (Manchester, 1937), pp. 55–81; and M. McKisack, *The Fourteenth Century* (Oxford, 1959), pp. 350–6.

[25] *R.P.* vol. II, p. 253.

[26] *Statutes,* 36 E. III, I, c. 11.

loans in anticipation of revenue. After the collapse of the Bardi and Peruzzi he had to look very largely to native merchants for advances. Of this situation another form of partnership, with another section of his subjects, was born.

The fate of the Bardi (whom he effectively bankrupted) was a reminder of the risks involved in lending to an ambitious king, and native merchants too had had ugly experiences in the early years. When in 1338 Edward's agents compulsorily purchased the wool which English merchants had shipped to Dordrecht, they paid in bonds which enabled the vendors to recover their money by relief from the customs. This was a very slow means of recovering debt, and most of the bonds were sold at a shattering discount. The merchants had also to contend with difficulties which the king's pliancy toward the commons created for them. The new merchant syndicate which was formed in 1343 was ruined because the commons in the next year forced the abandonment of the Flanders staple, from operating which the syndicate had expected to draw its profits.[27] Nevertheless, for the really big merchants there were always attractions in lending to the king. The crown did not always default on its debts, and it seems clear that, to merchants at least, it was often prepared to pay interest on large loans.[28] The crown could also offer a certain protection from the jealousy of fellow merchants and the commons, for instance by granting licences to export in the period when native merchants were excluded by the statute of 1354 from the export trade. William de la Pole of Hull, who was always prominent among the capitalists who lent to the king and suffered many adverse turns of fortune in consequence, nevertheless made an immense fortune. He and others like him understood finance so much better than the commons that they were always able to suggest ways of getting round inconvenient regulations or offsetting them.

The merchants who collectively did most for the king were those of London, which was easily the largest merchant city of England and was beginning to be a 'centre of national credit'.

[27] See further E. B. Fryde, 'Edward III's wool monopoly of 1337', *History* 37 (1952), pp. 8–24; and G. O. Sayles, 'The English company of 1343', *Speculum* 6 (1931), pp. 177–205.

[28] See K. B. McFarlane, 'Loans to the Lancastrian kings: the problem of inducement', *C.H.J.* 9 (1947), pp. 51–68, esp. p. 63ff.; and G. L. Harriss, 'Aids, loans and benevolences', *H.J.* 6 (1963), pp. 1–19, esp. pp. 18–19. Harriss modifies McFarlane's conclusions concerning interest in important respects.

Acting together, the London merchants brought pressure to bear which persuaded the king to abandon the embargo of 1354 on natives exporting wool, and they were probably influential in bringing about the restoration of a foreign staple, at Calais, in 1363. Another way in which the greater London merchants secured rewarding benefits from the crown for their loyal financial assistance was by means of charters which were granted to a number of city companies. These secured to the companies virtual control within the city of the wholesale and retail trade in the products in which their 'misteries' specialized. The drapers in 1364 obtained the virtual monopoly of the city's trade in cloth, and were able to inhibit weavers, fullers and dyers from selling to any but themselves. The vintners' charter gave them control of the wholesale trade in England (except to the nobility), and in consequence over the activities of taverners who sold wine retail. The fishmongers acquired total control of their wholesale trade in the city. The great capitalists who obtained the maximum advantage from these charters were good friends to the king. The value of their friendship was appreciated, and though their privileges were often attacked, royal favour maintained their dominance in London through a long future.[29]

Most of the great London merchants, besides plying their own trade, exported wool. They thus had a direct interest in the king's diplomatic policies, and, because the crown was heavily dependent on them for loans, could bring influence to bear in this quarter. This was to be very clearly demonstrated in 1382, when the preference, which the London merchants made a condition of lending, decided the council to abandon plans for an expedition to Portugal in favour of one to Flanders. The partnership of the crown and the city, whose foundations were laid in Edward III's reign, had an influence with a long future ahead of it; it tutored the monarchy towards the formulation of national commercial policies.

Edward's governmental policy, pliant at home in order to permit adventure abroad, was well calculated to succeed as long as fortune smiled. His successes abroad down to 1360 concealed dangers implicit in the concessions that he made. In particular the growing influence of the commons in parliament made public opinion more formidable to government than it had been. The

[29] See further Unwin, *Finance and Trade under Edward III*, pp. 238ff., esp. pp. 250–3.

control that the commons achieved over the granting of subsidies gave them a weapon that could be used to force the hand of the king and his councillors. This did not matter very much in the 1350s and 1360s when the commons, on the whole, approved the king's major enterprises. But if the king's policies did not justify themselves by prompt success, as they did in the age of Crecy and Poitiers, a more difficult situation might arise. The commons had acquired sufficient power, if they were not satisfied with the king's government or his policies, to obstruct them, to the point at which councillors might no longer be able to choose their own solutions to the problems facing them, let alone stick to them.

Other consequences of Edward III's pliancy also had dangerous potential. The new freedom which magnates acquired in the disposition of their landed wealth enabled them to give a greater degree of cohesion and permanence to the organization of their retinues of followers. The king was now less able than before to get the maximum advantage, in his relations with the magnates, out of his position as their feudal overlord. At the same time, the crown had largely abandoned the effort to enforce order at the local level by direct surveillance through justices in eyre instructed at the exchequer. This made it much easier for the magnates, through retainers recruited in the counties where they had substantial estates, to influence the course of local justice and administration. Justices of the peace, who were local gentlemen, could be intimidated by force which would not deter a justice in eyre, and were often men who had taken the fee of a noble patron. The magnates were in a position to make their position in the localities more formidable, and their local influence was less susceptible of control than in the past. Once again the dangers implicit in developments were not immediately apparent. The magnates put their services at Edward's disposal in the war, willingly and sometimes enthusiastically, and he gained from their ability to raise men from among their tenants and retainers to serve in his armies. The danger would become apparent only if, in a future situation, relations between the king and individual noblemen came under strain.

To sum up, Edward III succeeded impressively in restoring among his subjects respect for the English monarchy which the disasters of Edward II's reign had lowered perilously. But he did so at the cost of royal power and prerogative, not by reasserting them. His policy made successful kingship more dependent than ever on prestige, on the glamour of martial victory and

courtly ceremonial, and on satisfactory personal relations between the king and leading men of the realm. If the partnerships
that he forged with various groups among his subjects broke
down, the resulting confusions and divisions were likely to be
harder to control than they had ever been.

SECTION III

The changing world of the later Middle Ages

8

Plague and the changing economy

In June 1348 the Black Death, the great pandemic of bubonic plague which had originated in Asia, reached England. Ships' rats were what brought it, and the first outbreak was at the port of Melcombe Regis in Dorset. From there it spread through the western and southern counties; in the winter of 1348 London was affected. The plague reached its peak in the early summer of 1349, when it struck the populous eastern counties. Before it subsided, a third of the population may have perished. 'So great a pestilence before this time had never been seen, or heard of, or written of . . . so great a multitude was not swept away, it was believed, even by the flood that happened in the days of Noah.'[1] So wrote the chronicler at Louth Park abbey in Lincolnshire. Still more poignant, because more personal, comes the testimony of the Irish friar, John of Clyn, who watched the impact of the plague on prosperous Kilkenny:

> In scarcely any house did only one die, but all together, man and wife with their children and household, traversed the same road, the road of death. . . . And lest these notable events should perish with time and fade from the memory of future generations, . . . while waiting among the dead for the coming of death I have set them down in writing . . . and lest the writing should perish with the writer and the work with the workman, I leave the parchment for the work to be continued in case in the future any human survivor should remain, or someone of the race of Adam should be able to escape this plague and continue what I have begun.[2]

In 1361–2 there was a second visitation of the plague which, like that of 1348–9, lasted through the winter. There was a third major outbreak in 1369; and others followed, in 1390, in 1407, in 1464 and 1479. Plague had become endemic, an inescapable

[1] *Chron. Abbatie de Parco Lude*, ed. E. Venables (Lincolnshire Record Soc., 1891), p. 38.
[2] *Annals of Ireland*, ed. P. Butler (1849), p. 35.

factor of late medieval existence. The later plagues were much
less severe, however, than the outbreaks of 1348 and 1361. In the
fifteenth century plague was for the most part urban. Men remained plague conscious; treatises on the plague, like that of
John of Bordeaux, were popular and so were patent cures; but
plague mortality no longer had the terrible demographic impact
that it had in the mid-fourteenth century.[3]

We have said that the plague of 1348-9 may have killed a third
of the population. The attempt to assess its mortality with any
precision is beset with problems. It is clear, from manorial
records, that in the countryside this was uneven. In some places
it was very high, as for instance on some Crowland manors, and at
Tilgarsley in Oxfordshire where the village was deserted after
the plague; on some St Albans manors we find, however, that it
was comparatively slight.[4] Statistics have been compiled for
various English dioceses of the institutions in the plague year to
parish churches, which were vacant in consequence, arguably, of
the plague. These produce some impressive figures: what looks
like a 40 per cent mortality in Lincoln and York dioceses, and
over 50 per cent in some others.[5] Unfortunately these are not
absolutely safe figures; episcopal registers do not usually distinguish between death from plague and from other causes,
or state whether the incumbent was or was not resident when he
died, and they sometimes do not even indicate whether a living
was vacant through death or for some other reason. The percen-
tages may err, perhaps heavily, on the high side.

[3] The most useful introduction to the study of the plagues and their
effects remains J. M. W. Bean, 'Plague, population and economic
decline in England in the later Middle Ages' *Econ.H.R.* 2nd ser., 15
(1962-3), pp. 423-37. Also very valuable is P. Ziegler, *The Black Death*
(London, 1969).

[4] See F. M. Page, *The Estates of Crowland Abbey* (Cambridge, 1934),
pp. 121-2; M. Beresford, *The Lost Villages of Medieval England*
(London, 1954), p. 160 (for Tilgarsley); A. E. Levett, *Studies in Manorial
History* (Oxford, 1938), p. 253 and table facing p. 284 (for St Albans).
Levett's study of *The Black Death on the Estates of the See of Winchester*
(Oxford, 1916), though some of its conclusions are questionable in a
general context, remains among the most important local studies of the
effect of the plague.

[5] See articles by A. Hamilton Thompson in the *Archaeological
Journal*, 68 (1911), pp. 301-60 (Lincoln), and 71 (1914), pp. 97-150
(York). Further evidence based on episcopal registers is reviewed at
length by J. F. D. Shrewsbury, *A History of Bubonic Plague in the British
Isles* (Cambridge, 1970), ch. 4.

If it is hard to be dogmatic about the effect of the first plague, it is harder still to generalize about the cumulative demographic impact of the plagues of 1348-9, 1361-2 and 1369. Professor Russell has calculated, on the basis of the poll tax returns of 1377, that the total population was then about 2,250,000: he believes that in 1348, before the plague, it was about 3,700,000. Professor Postan and others who believe that Russell's population figures are too low throughout, think it may have been nearer 3,000,000 in 1377, and about 6,000,000 in 1348. All are agreed that before the plague, at least until the first decades of the fourteenth century, the population was increasing. Postan believes that the population was declining from about 1315; Russell that it continued to increase, after the famines of 1315-17, but more slowly than before. Thus according to the one view, Postan's, there was a reduction of the population by 50 per cent or more between 1300 and 1377; according to the other, Russell's, a reduction of 40 per cent or thereabouts between 1348 and 1377.[6] Even this second estimate according to other authorities may err on the high side. The central, incontrovertible fact remains,

[6] See J. C. Russell, *British Medieval Population* (Albuquerque, 1948), esp. ch. VI and X. M. M. Postan has put his views in a series of papers, notable in *IXme congrès international des sciences historiques* (*1950*): *Rapports*, pp. 225-41, esp. pp. 235ff.; 'Some economic evidence of declining population in the later Middle Ages', *Econ.H.R.* 2nd ser., 2 (1950) pp. 221-46; and *Cambridge Economic History of Europe* vol. I (2nd ed. 1966), pp. 560-70. It should be noted that in the controversy between Russell and Postan two separable questions are involved: (i) the size of the population in *c.* 1300 and in 1377 (which is bedevilled by the absence, for the earlier date, of statistical evidence comparable with the poll tax returns of 1377); (ii) the question whether the population was declining between 1300 and 1348, and if so, at what rate? Both questions are related to a third: (iii) was the country suffering from over-population *c.* 1300? B. F. Harvey in 'The population trend in England between 1300 and 1348', *T.R.H.S.* 5th ser., 16 (1966), pp. 23-42, is concerned chiefly with (ii) and (iii); she argues from economic evidence that overpopulation *c.* 1300 was not such as to generate Malthusian pressures. Her arguments have been criticized by J. Z. Titow, *English Rural Society 1200-1350* (London, 1969), who reviews all three questions at length, pp. 64-96. To myself as a complete amateur in this field, Harvey's arguments remain convincing. It does look, however, as if Postan and Titow must be right in regarding Russell's index figure of 3·5 to the household (essential to his calculations of the population in 1086, 1300 and 1348) as too low, especially in the light of H. E. Hallam's work – in particular his 'Some thirteenth century censuses', *Econ.H.R.* 2nd ser., 10 (1957-8), pp. 340-61.

CHANGING WORLD OF LATER MIDDLE AGES

however, that there was a dramatic contraction of the population as a result of the plagues of the middle of the fourteenth century.

What makes it particularly difficult to accept very high estimates of the mortality is the medical evidence. Bubonic plague is not in the ordinary sense a very infectious disease. It is caused by the invasion of the human body by a bacterium, *pasteurella pestis*, which is carried by a rat flea, *xenopsylla cheopis*. The flea does not leave the host animal until it dies, and will only attack man where there is no alternative rat host, or when its hunger has been accentuated by the multiplication of the bacterium in the flea's stomach. The disease can therefore only be carried and spread by rats, and a plague in the human population is always preceded and accompanied by a plague among rats. This is why its incidence is always uneven, and much less severe in the country than it is in towns, where there is a relatively high density of human population in rat-infested dwellings (this is particularly true if the carrier is the black rat, the only rat known in England in 1348; this infests houses, and does not thrive in the open or migrate widely, as does the brown rat). In addition to all this, *xenopsylla cheopis* does not multiply in cold temperatures, and hibernates in a climate such as England's; autumn therefore puts a period to the spread of bubonic plague. As Professor Shrewsbury, with all the authority of an eminent bacteriologist, emphasizes, it is medically incredible that a bubonic plague simply could have killed 50 per cent of the English fourteenth-century population; he thinks that it might just have killed a twentieth.[7] It seems likely, it is true, that in 1348-9 and 1361-2 there were outbreaks of pneumonic plague (which seems to be generated by a human with a respiratory infection contacting bubonic plague). Pneumonic plague is spread among men by direct contact; it has a higher mortality rate than bubonic plague,

[7] Shrewsbury, *A History of Bubonic Plague*, p. 123. Shrewsbury is deeply sceptical of almost all historians' estimates of plague mortality and believes that other diseases (e.g. typhus, influenza) had a higher mortality than they usually allow for; he also doubts whether the plague of 1361 was bubonic at all. His interests are concentrated on plague carried by rats, and he curiously makes almost no reference to pneumonic plague (see below, note 8). It is impossible for a mere historian to question his medical evidence; but the historical sources suggest very strongly that he has underestimated the mortality of 1348-9 (he is remarkably cavalier in his treatment of economic evidence of population decline).

and is not arrested by the onset of winter; and it seems usually to be virulent only in the early stages of a pandemic.[8] All this tallies with what we know of the plagues of 1348–9 and 1361–2, which affected the countryside severely and lasted through the winter. If we assume that there were severe pneumonic outbreaks in these years, we shall be able to raise the estimate of mortality far above the twentieth that, according to Shrewsbury, a bubonic plague might kill; but a 40 per cent estimate will look a very high one, and even 30 per cent may be a strain on credulity.

The percentage by which the plague reduced the population will probably always remain an open question, but there can be no doubt about its impact on economic life. 'By the winter', Henry Knighton wrote of 1349, 'there was such a dearth of servants and labourers that men were quite bewildered as to what they should do about it.'[9] This scarcity of labour and the sharp consequent rise of wages led directly to the first major attempt of an English government to freeze prices and wages, the famous Ordinance of Labourers of 1349 which, enlarged and amended, became a statute in 1351. The most important clauses of the statute pinned wages at the level of 1346, binding labourers to accept the rate of that year and confirming to their personal lords the first claim on their services. In order to control competition for labour, labourers were forbidden to leave their masters, and other masters were forbidden to receive them before their contracts of work were fulfilled. Prices of manufactured goods were fixed at their pre-plague level; those of foodstuffs were to be 'reasonable'. The statute was enforced from 1352 to 1359 by special commissions of justices in each county, who held their sessions four times a year and received a salary. After this period the statute was enforced by the justices of the peace. The vast majority of those presented before the justices were labourers prosecuted for receipt of excessive wages, and until 1359, at least, the statute was not ineffective in restraining the rise of wages.[10] In the long run it was doomed to failure. Labourers simply would not accept the statutory wages, and the landlord and the employer found in the end that its limits constricted them in the competition for labour. By the last decade of the

[8] See J. M. W. Bean, 'Plague, population and economic decline'; and Wu Lien Teh, *A Treatise on Pneumonic Plague* (Geneva, 1926), esp. pp. 3–4, and ch. III on the epidemiology of pneumonic plague.

[9] *Chron. H. Knighton* (R.S.) vol. II, p. 62.

[10] The foregoing is based on the authoritative study of B. H. Putnam, *The Enforcement of the Statute of Labourers* (Columbia, 1908).

fourteenth century wages stood at an average level which, in terms of purchasing power, was nearly double that of 1346.[11]

Scarcity of labour was a constant of economic conditions in the period after the plagues. It was the chief reason for another constant of the period, almost equally important, the mobility among labourers. In the new situation it ceased to be possible for landlords, or anyone else, to restrain dissatisfied men from leaving home in quest of better things. In time, the reduction of the population consequent on the plagues affected all aspects of economic life: trade, the distribution of urban prosperity, the social and economic structure of the rural world. The progress of change was not fast, and other factors besides plague were involved, notably economic pressures generated by the great war with France. In order to understand the developments we need to examine affairs in detail, and over a much longer period than the decades either side of the years 1348 and 1361, in fact over the whole period from 1290 to 1485.

The middle of the fourteenth century was a very important moment in the history of English commerce and industry, a turning point. Curiously enough, this seems to have had little connexion, at least directly, with the onset of the plague; the war, and the means that Edward III used to raise money for it, had much more to do with it.

At the beginning of our period, at the end of the thirteenth century, England was important in the commercial life of western Europe chiefly as an exporter of raw materials. Most of her export trade was handled by alien merchants, above all by the Italians, though the German merchants of the Hanseatic towns had already established themselves in London as a community with special privileges, possessing a quarter and a quay of their own on the north bank of the Thames, the Steelyard. The most important items of export were wool, hides and coal, and from the west country lead and tin; quite substantial quantities of grain were also exported. In exchange the merchants of Italy

---

[11] For an analysis of the rise of wages, see Sir W. Beveridge, 'Wages in the Winchester manors', *Econ.H.R.* 1st ser., 7 (1936–7), pp. 22–43; for further tables, partly based on Beveridge's work, and for invaluable comment, see M. M. Postan, 'Some evidence of declining population'. For the study of wages and prices the two great pioneering works of J. E. Thorold Rogers, *A History of Agriculture and Prices in England*, 4 vols (Oxford, 1866–82), and *Six Centuries of Work and Wages* (1909) remain essential.

imported cloth which they bought in the markets of the Low Countries, and silks, sweet wines and spices from the Mediterranean and beyond. From the Baltic the Germans brought pitch, potash and furs; from Scandinavia came softwoods and above all fish, fresh and salt, which was a staple item in the diet of the medieval Englishman. From Bordeaux came wine, in huge quantities. Later on, salt from the Bay of Bourgneuf and materials required for cloth manufacture, as alum and dyes (blue woad from Picardy and scarlet from Spain), assumed importance among England's imports. London, at the end of the thirteenth century, was well established as the most important English commercial port and city; but other ports too – Newcastle, Boston, Hull, Southampton and Bristol – were busy with a vigorous commerce.

Wool was easily the most important item of export from the country. England's wool, so the protesting magnates claimed in 1297, amounted 'almost to the value of half the whole land'.[12] At the end of the thirteenth century the trade already had a long history; the wool of the English Cistercians had made a big contribution towards the ransom of Richard I, and great magnates had been keeping flocks running into many thousands on their estates for more than a century.[13] About 1300 Crowland abbey and Peterborough had between them 16,300 sheep in the fenlands; the priory of St Swithun's, Winchester, had a flock of 20,000 and the bishop had even more; Henry Lacy, Earl of Lincoln, had over 13,000 sheep in Lincolnshire and Yorkshire. It was not only the great magnates who grew wool for the market. Knights, gentlemen and small farmers also had their flocks, as did the ordinary customary tenants of many a manor. At Alvediston in Wiltshire the tenants owned between them a flock of over 900 sheep; at Berwick St Johns they had nearly 800 (the greater number, in both cases, owned by a few rich villagers).[14] The finest English wool came from the borders of Wales, from Shropshire and Hereford; the wool of the Cotswolds, Lincoln and Yorkshire was also of high quality. The midlands produced (suitably) a middle grade of wool valued between these fine

---

[12] See J. G. Edwards, 'Confirmatio Cartarum and baronial grievances in 1297', E.H.R. 58 (1943), pp. 171–2.

[13] The essential work on the wool trade is E. Power, The Wool Trade in English Medieval History (Oxford, 1941), on which most of what is said here is based.

[14] See M. M. Postan, 'Village livestock in the thirteenth century', Econ.H.R. 2nd ser., 15 (1962–3), p. 244.

wools and the coarse wools from the chalk downs of the south and south-east.

The commerce in wool was efficiently organized. Most of the English wool was carried to the Low Countries and sold in the markets of Bruges, the financial and commercial headquarters of northern Europe; it was woven into cloth in the great industrial cities of Flanders, Bruges, Ghent and Ypres. But already in 1300 some was going direct to Italy where Florence was famous as a centre of cloth manufacture. The Italians, who handled the lion's share of export both to Flanders and Italy, bought much of their wool direct from the grower. Francesco Peglotti, the agent in England of the Bardi of Florence from 1318 to 1321, compiled a careful list of the major wool-growing abbeys, grading their products from the fine Tintern wool that would fetch 28 marks per sack down to coarse wools only worth 7 marks. But naturally it was only from the big growers that a foreign merchant bought direct, and this opened the way for the English middleman who travelled the countryside collecting his wool from small men and sold to the exporter at great seasonal fairs such as those of Boston and Lincoln. Most of the middlemen of the early period were burgesses of towns like Lincoln and Ludlow, in wool-growing areas. Later the 'woolmen' of the Cotswolds were the most famous and prosperous; men like John Thame whose brass one may see in Fairford church and who ordered the magnificent glass for its windows.

From dealing in wool to exporting was a short step, and the most important development of the first part of the fourteenth century was the capture, by native merchants, of the bulk of the export business. The additional levy which, from 1303, aliens had to pay on all their exports, gave Englishmen an advantage; the location abroad of staples with a monopoly of the sale of wool was decisive in excluding the foreigner from the domestic market. The crown's need for money for war expenses, first in 1294, then in Edward II's reign and later at the outbreak of the Hundred Years War, was the inspiration behind the earliest experiments in grants of a monopoly of wool export to merchant syndicates. Until the capture of Calais the staple, when abroad, was located in the Low Countries, in Brabant or at Bruges. But Calais, once in English hands, was the obvious choice; the staple was first formally established there in 1363, and after some temporary migrations, settled there permanently from 1392. There was some friction, as we have seen in an earlier chapter, about locating the staple abroad. Producers rightly suspected that this enabled the merchants to fix the price of wool to the growers' disadvantage, and that they limited the quantity exported in order to keep the price high in the foreign market. The staplers, however, proved so useful to the crown as a source of loans that they were not to be dispensed with. The control over the sale of all English wool that was ultimately achieved for the Calais staple ensured that the company operating it would always have money to advance; the risk of lending was distributed among the members; and, as exporters, they were easily repaid by assignments on the customs. Finally in 1466 Edward IV handed over to the Company of the Staple the collection of all the custom and subsidy on wools (with the exception of those exported direct to Italy via the Straits of Gibraltar), in return for which the company undertook to meet the expenses of the garrison of Calais, the convoy of the wool fleets thither, and the fees of the customers of the port of London. They also agreed to pay any surplus of their new revenue over £15,000 into the exchequer. They became in effect a nationalized company with responsibility for a particularly significant item of public expenditure.[15]

An elaborate system of credit dealing had by this time established itself round the market in wool. The individual stapler seldom took cash for more than a proportion of his sale of wools; for the rest he accepted bills from the foreign buyer for payment by instalments. These he would probably pass on to a 'merchant adventurer' who was travelling to Flanders to purchase foreign goods; the adventurer would credit the stapler in London, and collect the stapler's payments in Flanders to lay out on his own purchases. With the money that he could draw in London, the stapler could pay the woolman from whom he had bought on credit, and the woolman the producer, from whom he had bought on credit likewise. The smooth running of this system was not infrequently disturbed by the rivalries of staplers and adventurers, who always suspected each other of getting the advantage of the exchange rates, and by the clumsy attempts of crown and commons to use the staple to enforce bullionist policy. This could be achieved by ordinances to ensure that merchants took a fixed proportion of their payments in cash and brought bullion to the mint, in London or Calais. This meant that the stapler found it harder to sell his wool; that the purchaser found that he could only obtain credit by paying a higher price for what he bought;

[15] On the staplers and the crown see E. Power, 'The wool trade in the fifteenth century' in *Studies in English Trade in the Fifteenth Century,* ed. E. Power and M. M. Postan (London, 1933), esp. pp. 72-9.

and that the adventurer found this purchaser, turned vendor, seeking to offset the price of his wool in the exchange rate. Like all government attempts to meddle in economic matters in this period, bullionist regulations proved in the long run ineffective; and their tendency was to reduce, not to encourage, the volume of trade.[16] The heavy custom levied on wool and the monopoly granted to the staple had the same effect.

In the long run, the entanglement of the wool trade with Plantagenet war finance ruined its prosperity. Significantly it is from just about the period of Edward III's rash experiments with a royal wool monopoly at the outbreak of the French war that we begin to see a downward turn in the trade. In the period from 1290 to 1340 some 30,000 sacks of wool were exported from England in most years, and sometimes more (though the average was down between 1315 and 1330, years of difficulty both politically and economically). Between 1350 and 1400 the average was only 23,000 sacks: it sank much lower between 1400 and 1500, the average totalling out at about 10,000 sacks a year.[17] The period from 1430 to 1440, when fortunes in the French war were turning against the English and when relations with Burgundian Flanders broke down for a time, was a particularly depressed one; so were the years of civil disorder in England between 1455 and 1465.

The decline in the export trade is only a chapter in the history of the wool trade in later medieval England. The difficulties in this sector opened up opportunities in another. At the beginning of our period, fine cloths were being imported into England from Flanders, but a considerable quantity of wool had undoubtedly always been woven into cloth at home for domestic consumption. The thirteenth century witnessed a considerable development in the English cloth industry. An important factor in this development was the mechanization of fulling, the process by which the carded and combed wool, woven into a cloth on a handloom, was beaten underfoot in water to shrink it, giving it durability, and to purify it with detergents (as fuller's earth) mixed in the water trough. It is in the late twelfth century that we first hear of fulling mills in England. A revolving drum was axled to the water wheel of a mill, which alternately raised and dropped two

[16] On bullionist regulations see ibid. pp. 79–90.

[17] See A. R. Bridbury, *Economic Growth: England in the Later Middle Ages* (London, 1962), p. 27. This book is one of the most important recent contributions to the economic history of later medieval England.

wooden hammers on the cloth in a trough, thus discharging mechanically the beating process which had previously been performed by men treading the cloth underfoot. All that was needed to make a success of a fulling mill was a steady supply of fast running water and reasonable proximity to supplies of wool. From the time of Edward I references to fulling mills in English records begin to multiply impressively. Soon a nascent industry was attracting an additional population of craftsmen and a new kind of trader into the rural areas where it throve: the West Riding of Yorkshire, the Lake District, the Cotswolds, and Somerset and Devon. Before the end of the thirteenth century the older, urban centres of industry, like Lincoln, Oxford, Northampton and Winchester, where fulling had long been carried out underfoot by the traditional method, were beginning to feel a chill wind of competition.[18]

The mechanization of fulling was only one factor that encouraged the development of the cloth industry in the countryside, it should be noted. Other forces had been at work, rather earlier.[19] In a number of towns where cloth manufacture had a long history behind it, the thirteenth century witnessed serious clashes of interest between the craft gilds of the weavers and fullers on the one hand, and the merchant *entrepreneurs*, firmly entrenched in the civic oligarchies, who controlled the sale of cloth and were in effect their employers on the other. The efforts of the gilds to maintain the level of wages and to limit hours of work encouraged merchants to take their weaving into the countryside, where textile skills were traditional and where there was a plentiful and cheap supply of labour. Another factor was the competition of imported Flemish cloths. In Flanders industrialization on a scale unknown in England had reduced production costs, especially of fine cloths in which the English urban industry had specialized; rural production, catering with coarser fabrics for a more local market, was less affected by this foreign challenge, and so there was more room for development. When, in the early fourteenth century, the Flemish industry was seriously disrupted by social and political unrest, English production in new centres in the countryside was ready to come

[18] On the rise of the fulling mill see E. M. Carus-Wilson, 'An industrial revolution of the thirteenth century' in her *Medieval Merchant Venturers* (London, 1954), pp. 183–238.

[19] For what follows, I have relied on E. Miller's important article 'The fortunes of the English textile industry in the thirteenth century', *Econ.H.R.* 2nd ser., 18 (1965), pp. 64–82.

into its own: and there was a recovery, too, in some towns where the industry had earlier been in difficulties. Mechanized fulling thus began to have an impact at a time when the difficulties incidental to a geographical redistribution of production were passed, and when new opportunities were opening for the English cloth trade.

The rise of the fulling mill was one of the early symptoms of the new significance of an industry whose product, finished cloth, came to rival wool as England's premier export by the end of the fourteenth century, and before the end of the fifteenth outstripped it. The heavy custom on wool and the limitation placed on its export by the staple monopoly gave the export trade in cloth invaluable protection at a crucial period of its growth. From 1347 onwards, when a custom was for the first time imposed on native exports, we can trace its rise systematically. From the mid 1350s, with an interval in the 1370s, exports rose steadily to reach a peak in the last decade of the fourteenth century. Exports maintained a high level in the first half of the fifteenth century, and increased healthily in the 1440s; but they were badly hit after 1450 by the loss of the English provinces in France (Gascony was an important market) and by the civil disorder of the Wars of the Roses. After 1470 exports rose again steadily, and the growth continued far beyond our period; when the sixteenth century dawned, cloth was the chief wealth of England's trade.[20]

By the mid-fifteenth century changes in the commercial geography of England registered even more clearly than had the earlier shift towards rural production. York yielded her place as second city of the realm to Bristol, the chief port for cloth exports to Gascony, Spain and Ireland. Bristol was also now the centre of a shipping industry. William Cannings of Bristol abandoned the cloth trade in which his father had flourished, for the role of shipowner; he had 800 men employed in his ships, and 100 carpenters, masons and other workmen in his pay. York's declining prosperity was in large part, at least, owing to the rise of the cloth towns of the West Riding, Leeds, Wakefield, Bradford. In Wiltshire, Devizes, Wilton and Mere, once villages, were producing so much cloth as to be listed separately from Salisbury and the county in the ulnage accounts (the ulnage was a

[20] For detailed figures of cloth exports see the tables in E. M. Carus-Wilson and O. Coleman, *England's Export Trade 1275–1547* (Oxford, 1963), in particular the graphs on pp. 138–9 which illustrate the fluctuations of the trade.

domestic tax on all cloths exhibited for sale, from which only the coarsest products were exempt).[21] The rise to prosperity of another Wiltshire centre, Castle Combe, can be traced in detail. The manor here, which had possessed a fulling mill in the time of Edward III, came into the hands of John Fastolf in 1409. From 1415 to the end of his long military career in the 1440s, Fastolf clothed the soldiers of his company in red and white cloth of Castle Combe, 'purchasing yearly more than £100 of his tenants there'. Thus the manor began to prosper on a new scale: artisans, who paid 2d. a year *chevage* to live in its boundaries, arrived in numbers; soon the reputation of the town's fine reds led cloth-men from elsewhere, like Roger Robins of Cirencester, to send their cloths to be dyed there. By 1457 'Castle Combs' was a trade name known in London for fine reds. Fastolf's manor court was finding itself meanwhile faced with unfamiliar problems: of the common pasture being overcrowded with sheep; of poaching on an unprecedented scale; of fixing hours for the taverns of the town. It was well worth facing them, for the profits of the lordship were soaring. The really big profits, from production, went of course to the cloth manufacturers themselves, some of them by this time men of considerable substance and property.[22]

The cloths of Castle Combe were sold, as we see, far afield, in London and elsewhere, often directly to the exporter. The chief areas to which English cloth was exported were the Low Countries, Scandinavia and the Baltic; and in the west, Gascony, Spain and Portugal. There was no staple with a monopoly of cloth export, and in consequence a substantial share of the trade was always in the hands of aliens, especially of the Hansards. But native exporters were in the business from the first, and gained over the years at the expense of their rivals. The English 'merchant adventurers' trading to Prussia secured from Richard II in 1391 the right to govern their own colony, which had secured trading privileges from the local authorities; those in the Low Countries (a still more important group) obtained the same privilege in 1407. The English side of the adventurers' organiza-

[21] On the foregoing see further E. M. Carus-Wilson, 'The overseas trade of Bristol' in *Medieval Merchant Venturers*, pp. 1–97; E. Miller in *V.C.H. Yorkshire* (York City volume), p. 90; H. Heaton, *The Yorkshire Woollen and Worsted Industries* (Oxford, 1920); and Bridbury, *Economic Growth*, p. 47 (for Devizes and Wiltshire).

[22] On Castle Combe see E. M. Carus-Wilson, 'Evidences of industrial growth on some fifteenth century manors', *Econ.H.R.* 2nd ser., 12 (1959–60), pp. 190–205, and in *V.C.H. Wiltshire* vol. IV, pp. 129–33.

tion only emerges with clarity in the middle of the fifteenth century. In London the acts of the court of adventurers, which we first hear of in 1465, are recorded with the acts of the mercers' company, with which company all the city adventurers long remained closely associated. The York merchant adventurers, however, had their own charter from 1430, and those of Newcastle, too, were an independent body. Sound organization was necessary to the adventurers, if they were to secure from the crown the diplomatic protection that they often needed in their trading overseas. There was much trouble with the Hanse towns in particular: Danzig and Lubeck wished to exclude the English from the Baltic trade, and the Germans (with some justice) often accused the English of making a double business of export and piracy. The English replied with demands for reciprocal privileges to those that the Germans of the Steelyard enjoyed (they were exempt from some important dues, in particular poundage), or for withdrawal of the Steelyard's privileges. Reprisals and counter-reprisals did much damage both to English and Hanseatic trade in the course of the century. A final agreement was not reached until 1473, when the principle of reciprocity of rights, for the Hanse and for the English in Prussia, was established by the Treaty of Utrecht.[23]

It was no accident that the Treaty of Utrecht was sealed less than three years after Edward IV had returned from the Low Countries to England in ships of the Hanse. Politics, the crown's manœuvres in order to raise loans and taxes from merchants, and England's varying fortunes in the Anglo-French war, had more to do with the changes and fluctuations of English trade in the late Middle Ages than plague did. But plague did, of course, have an effect on English trade. The total quantity of goods exported from the country in the second half of the fourteenth century was lower than it was in the first. If one adds the raw wool exported from England to the cloth in terms of raw wool (reckoning $4\frac{1}{3}$ sacks to the broadcloth) the level of export was still appreciably lower in 1400 than it was in 1300, and it remained so in the fifteenth century. If, however, one thinks not in terms of gross totals, but of production per unit of population,

---

[23] On the adventurers see E. M. Carus-Wilson, 'The origin and early development of the merchant adventurers' organization in London' in *Medieval Merchant Venturers*, pp. 143–82. On relations between England and the Hanse see M. M. Postan, 'The economic and political relations of England and the Hanse 1400–1475' in *Studies in English Trade in the Fifteenth Century*, ed. Power and Postan, pp. 91–153.

then the level did not decline; if anything it increased a little. One must remember too the great differences between the wool trade and the cloth trade, that one was a raw material, the other a finished product. Cloth manufacture involved more people than ever before in the crafts and businesses connected with wool, and the wealth that the trade earned was more widely distributed than that earned by growers. This was because artisans' wages, as a result of the labour shortage that followed the plagues, were considerably higher in the late fourteenth and fifteenth centuries than they had been in 1300. Plague, which was not directly relevant to changes in the pattern of commerce and industry, was directly relevant to the social consequences of such changes.

The later Middle Ages were an important period in the history of English towns. As with commerce, the key period of changes was the second half of the fourteenth century. In this period the impact of the plague upon urban societies was clear; so was the impact of the changing pattern of production and of the export trade.

The thirteenth century and the beginning of the fourteenth was a period of urban growth and prosperity. Town populations were swelled steadily by immigration from the countryside. London had established by 1300 a clear lead over all rivals as the first commercial city of the realm, and with a population of some 30,000 was the only centre that could compare with the great industrial cities of the continent, like Bruges and Ghent.[24] Other towns, as Lincoln, Norwich and York, flourished on local industry, especially on cloth manufacture before difficulties between employers and the weavers' gilds and the advent of the fulling mill took production into the countryside. The thirteenth century was an important period also for the foundation of new towns: Leeds, Liverpool, Harwich and Kingston-on-Hull are familiar names that were among them. Still more numerous were the small towns that grew around a local market, often villages promoted to borough status by a royal or seignorial landlord. The grant of a market helped to make a town a centre for the distribution of finished goods and the sale of produce from the surrounding countryside; it was a royal prerogative to grant the licence for a market, and over 3000 were issued in the thirteenth century. Most boroughs enjoyed a degree at least of self-govern-

[24] On London's growth in the thirteenth and early fourteenth centuries see Gwyn A. Williams, *Medieval London: from Commune to Capital* (London, 1963), esp. pp. 15–20.

ment, paying a farm to the lord for the right to collect tolls and rents, and regulating the everyday lives and commercial dealings of the inhabitants through the borough court.[25]

Because of the nature of the bubonic plague, the towns were particularly hard hit by the Black Death in terms of sheer mortality. It also had serious economic repercussions in many of them. Shortage of labour posed a problem that could be very pressing for the small urban manufacturer or craftsman, the hatter, the weaver, the mason. The burden of the farm of the borough fell more heavily on those that survived the plague, because there were fewer of them. Some towns suffered a further loss of population as a result of migration in the post-plague period; citizens, whose living was too near the margin to meet their heavier share of the fiscal burdens of the borough, simply quit. Their vacant dwellings, falling into disrepair, bore gloomy witness to vanishing prosperity. Small towns, whose prosperity was heavily dependent on a market with a local catchment area, probably felt the cold of changed conditions most of all. At the same time that the effects of the plague were manifesting themselves, moreover, a good many towns began also to feel the pinch of competition from the countryside's rising cloth industry. Lincoln, which had once housed many weavers, was in a bad way in the late 1360s. York's prosperity held up well in the fourteenth century, but afterwards the decline was steep: 'trade goeth these days into the country', her fullers complained in the reign of Edward IV.[26] The effects were visible in decayed rents, the devaluation of property, and derelict houses. In the late fourteenth and fifteenth centuries we hear of a good many towns petitioning for reduction of their farms, claiming that with the decline of their populations they could no longer pay at the old level. What is even more significant is that some towns did get relief from fiscal burdens: Lincoln, for example, was on the ground of poverty totally exempted from payment of the subsidies of 1441, 1445 and 1449.[27]

There is of course another side to this gloomy picture. Reduction of population could spell diminished prosperity, but it did not necessarily do so. Southampton did not have many citizens,

[25] On the growth of towns and new towns see M. Beresford, *New Towns of the Middle Ages* (London, 1967); also E. M. Carus-Wilson, 'Towns and Trade' in *Medieval England*, ed. A. L. Poole (new ed. Oxford, 1958), vol. I, pp. 209–63, esp. pp. 236–47.

[26] Quoted by E. Miller in *V.C.H. Yorks (York City)*, p. 89.

[27] See J. W. F. Hill, *Medieval Lincoln* (Cambridge, 1948), pp. 253, 272.

but it was in the second half of the fourteenth century that she established herself as the chief centre of Genoese shipping in England, and the principal port from which wool and cloths were carried direct to Italy via the Straits of Gibraltar. Bristol, with her magnificent natural harbour and her strategic commercial position, in easy reach of the wool of the Cotswolds, the cloth manufactures of the west country, and of the trade that passed along the Severn, throve to new peaks of prosperity (it was Bristol merchants who, in the last years of the fifteenth century, financed the first English voyage of discovery, that of the Cabots). The development of the cloth industry which affected old centres like Lincoln and York adversely brought new prosperity to others, among them places like Castle Combe which lacked formal burghal status but were becoming urban in all but the strict legal sense. Above all, London continued to thrive. She was the commercial and the administrative capital of the kingdom. Her merchants dominated the Company of the Staple and the fellow-ships of merchant adventurers overseas. Many of them throve to be substantial landowners, like Sir Geoffrey Boleyn who left manors in Kent, Sussex and Norfolk; the 1436 land tax showed London men holding property in most of the counties of England. Parliament met at Westminster more often than anywhere else, and the king's central courts and the exchequer were there; most great magnates had their London houses. This brought prosperity to the city's markets. In the fifteenth century gentry like the Pastons were sending to London for the goods they could not purchase at home. A steady stream of men still came to London to seek their fortunes, among them the historical Richard Whittington.[28]

The merchant aristocracy of London was firmly entrenched in the greater crafts, those with important privileges and charters and among whom admission to the 'livery' of the company was limited to senior gildsmen. As the returns to a government inquiry of 1389 show, there were in most towns a number of craft gilds;[29] and it is clear that the difficulties of the post-plague

---

[28] On the foregoing see A. Ruddock, *Italian Merchants and Shipping in Southampton 1270–1600* (Southampton Records Series, 1951), esp. ch. II; E. M. Carus-Wilson, *Medieval Merchant Venturers*, pp. 1–97 (on Bristol); and S. L. Thrupp, *The Merchant Class of Medieval London* (Chicago, 1948).

[29] T. and L. T. Smith, *The English Gilds* (E.E.T.S., 1870); the returns to the 1389 inquiries form part I of the volume. On the London companies see G. Unwin, *The Guilds and Companies of London* (London,

era had much to do with their multiplication in the late four-teenth century and their enhanced importance. Their nature varied considerably: some were connected with a church or parish; some were associations of small craftsmen and traders, bakers, cobblers, weavers or masons; some, like the great City companies, were essentially mercantile groups, as drapers, grocers or vintners. Membership of a gild was the commonest mode of admission to the freedom of a city or borough and to the privileges of citizenship, and gild regulations were usually subject to approval by the civic authorities. The basic object of these regulations was to secure to the gild the monopoly of production or trade in a given commodity or commodities. This enabled gilds to fix prices and wages, to make sure that the supply of labour in the craft was evenly spread, and in general to resist pressures which, if unfettered, would have driven men out of business in a period of labour shortage and of depressed demand. The gilds also supervised training in their crafts, through their rules of apprenticeship; ensured that the quality of their mem-bers' products was up to standard; and used their funds to look after members and their dependants in poverty, sickness and old age. The activities of the gilds were less socially divisive than their monopolistic and conservative objectives might lead one to expect. One reason for this was that, in many crafts, the unit of production was very small, often just a master, his wife, an apprentice and a single journeyman labourer. Outside London journeymen were seldom sufficiently numerous to organize themselves against the gilds. Another reason was that in this age of shrunken population city authorities and the gilds were often glad to see more people admitted to the freedom via gild member-ship, rather than to exclude them. Men who would help to pay the borough farm were welcome, and in many towns the propor-tion of freemen to unenfranchised inhabitants rose in the period after the Black Death.[30]

In town government, as opposed to gild organization, there was a strong tendency towards narrow oligarchy in the late Middle Ages. The 'more powerful and discreet' among the citizens had always had the decisive voice in the election of aldermen, who often held office for life and from among whom

---

1908); on craft gilds generally see also C. Gross, *The Gild Merchant* vol. I (Oxford, 1890), ch. VII; and E. F. Jacob, *The Fifteenth Century* (Oxford, 1961), pp. 394–405.

[30] See Bridbury, *Economic Growth*, pp. 61–9.

the mayor was usually chosen. The development in the fifteenth century of close corporations took things a stage further. Usually this involved adding a second town council, often a larger one, to an older aldermanic group, but one whose membership was nominated by the mayor and aldermen. Thus at Colchester in 1462 a new council was added to the aldermen and bailiffs and their old council; the new council was named by the former one, which was nominated in turn by the aldermen and bailiffs. All the powers of the community were thus vested in a tight, self-selecting body of forty-two persons in all.[31] A very large number of boroughs acquired constitutions similar to this one by charter or by act of parliament. Once again we have to be careful about interpreting this development in terms of economic and social exclusiveness. The conscious motive behind it seems more usually to have been anxiety to preserve order, to which the rivalries of gilds and factions posed a threat where civic office was elective. The danger was a real one, as we are reminded by the riots at London's mayoral elections in the 1380s, when John of Northampton and his followers, drawn mainly from the middle ranks of the privileged gildsmen, sought to challenge the dominance of the capitalist oligarchy of aldermen. Very similar in some ways were the disturbances at Southampton in the period 1458–1463, where the competition of merchants with Mediterranean and London connexions respectively led to rioting at the mayoral elections. In both cases the crown had in the end to intervene.[32] It is not surprising that in general both the crown and parliament preferred stable oligarchy to the dangers inherent in even a selective democracy of freemen.

It is always particularly difficult to generalize about rural conditions. Soil and the contours impose different modes of agriculture in different places; different landlords have different priorities; and in the Middle Ages the tenurial relations between lord and tenant varied bewilderingly from area to area, often even from manor to manor. Nevertheless there were changes in the age following the Black Death that were very general. Some took a long time to work out, but underlying all of them were factors which resulted from the plague: the reduction of population, the

[31] See J. Tait, *The Medieval English Borough* (Manchester, 1936), pp. 322–3.
[32] On the London troubles in the 1380s see R. Bird, *The Turbulent London of Richard II*, esp. ch. V; on those in Southampton, Ruddock, *Italian Merchants and Shipping in Southampton*, pp. 169–80.

end of land hunger, the shortage of labour and its increased mobility.

Before the plagues, about the end of the thirteenth century, conditions in agriculture were booming. This boom had probably passed its peak well before the Black Death, but there was not much noticeable decline. Evidence can be found of marginal lands that had been taken into cultivation in the thirteenth century being abandoned early in the fourteenth; but it has to be set beside other evidence of more new lands being reclaimed from wastes, in the Yorkshire forests, for instance, and in the fens. Rents and entry fines seem to have remained generally stable until after the plague. There were bad harvests and famines between 1315 and 1317 but recovery afterwards seems to have been fairly rapid, and in the third and fourth decades of the fourteenth century things were going on in the countryside much as they had done time out of mind. The pestilence marks the watershed.[33]

The earlier period was a good time for the landlord, especially for the great landlord who farmed his demesnes for profit. Markets in the thirteenth century were expanding; the price of cereals was high in relation to agricultural wages. In a heavily populated countryside land for cultivation was in demand; there was much clearing of waste which brought in new rents to the landlord, and there was no shortage of tenants for settled land. Especially favoured by these conditions were the great manorial lords who had estates in fertile country where the open field system of arable cultivation predominated. This was the system under which the holdings of the lord and of individual villagers were scattered in strips through two or three great fields cropped in rotation (under a two field system one lay fallow each year; under a three field system two were cropped while one lay fallow). The size of tenant holdings varied enormously, both on individual manors and from area to area. The more considerable

[33] Controversy surrounds the conditions of agriculture in the first half of the fourteenth century. I have followed the views of B. F. Harvey in 'The population trend in England 1300–1348', which seem to me convincing (but as she herself has pointed out to me, the material for analysing the problem is so inexact that it is difficult to tell what trends had set in, say, between 1330 and 1348 – after the period of the famines and before the plague). For a critique of her views see Titow, *English Rural Society*, intro. On the famines of 1315–17 see H. S. Lucas, 'The great European famine of 1315, 1316 and 1317', *Speculum* 5 (1930), pp. 343–77.

among the villagers were those (usually villeins) who held a virgate (perhaps 25 or 30 acres) or a half virgate. Their tenures carried heavy obligations, to perform weekly works on the lord's demesne, and other services such as carting, boon works for the lord at ploughing and harvest, and to pay to the lord various renders in kind. Besides these more prosperous villeins every village had its population of cottagers with tiny holdings of five acres or less, together with some rights of pasture on the waste of the manor; their obligatory services were lighter than those of virgaters, and they provided a reserve of labour that the lord and their neighbours could hire. Land was in demand; there was much clearing of new plots from waste (usually free tenures for which rent was paid); and there was much buying and selling even among peasants of parcels of land that were often very small. Almost all the conditions of this agricultural situation were to the landlord's advantage: the availability of cheap labour; the demand for land; and the relatively high level of rent that was consequent on it.[34]

The great landlord drew his profit not just from his own farming activity, but also from his manorial lordship. Villein tenures were not protected at common law in the thirteenth century, but only by the custom of the manor (except where the estate had been part of the demesne of the crown at the time of the Domesday survey). Those who were villeins by blood, as most virgaters and half-virgaters and many cottagers were, were bound to the soil of the manor and could not leave it without the lord's licence. They must pay the lord *merchet*, a fine when their daughters married, and *leyrwite*, if one of them was got with child outside wedlock. From his manorial (or 'customary') tenants, the lord would take a *heriot*, the best beast, when the tenant died, and the heir must pay a fine to enter his inheritance. The profits of the manorial court were the lord's. The mill was

[34] On agriculture and rural society in the thirteenth century see, among other works, C. S. and C. S. Orwin, *The Open Fields* (3rd ed. Oxford, 1967); E. A. Kosminsky, *Studies in English Agrarian History in the Thirteenth Century* (Oxford, 1956); G. C. Homans, *English Villagers of the Thirteenth Century* (Cambridge, Mass., 1942); and Titow, *English Rural Society*. The open fields have recently been the subject of controversy; see J. Thirsk, 'The common fields', *Past and Present* 29 (1964), pp. 3–25, and 'The origin of the common fields', *Past and Present* 33 (1966), pp. 142–7; and the powerful critique of her views by J. Z. Titow, 'Medieval England and the open field system', *Past and Present* 32 (1965), pp. 86–102.

usually a seigneurial monopoly. Altogether the lord's rights and demands could eat a long way into such profit as his tenants made from their holdings, while the demands of his own farming, for profit and for the supply of his household, always took priority over theirs in the communal business of cultivation. Once again, we see all the advantages of the system working in the landlord's favour.

Most lords did not farm the demesnes of all their manors directly. The greater ecclesiastical landlords tended to concentrate much effort on the direct exploitation of their estates with a degree of self sufficiency always in mind as an objective, but many of them and most lay magnates drew a considerable proportion of their income from rents, including leases of demesne. Edmund Earl of Cornwall in 1297–8 was for instance drawing most of his revenue from rents and the judicial profits of courts; Elizabeth de Burgh in 1329–30 was drawing about half the profits of her great honour of Clare from rents.[35] The leasing of demesnes encouraged the commutation of villein labour services for a money rent. This practice seems to be almost as old as the history of the manor itself; but its incidence was uneven, varying from period to period and on some estates from season to season, for a lord could always reimpose services instead of taking rent. Some lords commuted all their tenants' labour services, some only a part; if they were cultivating their own demesnes they almost always reserved at least some boon works at harvest.[36] No landlord was ever entirely dependent on labour services; wage labour was essential in addition and probably more efficient. Many kept a permanent staff of labourers on the manor, the *famuli*, paid in money or kind; on the Earl of Norfolk's manor at Forncett, for instance, there was a *domus famulorum* and a group of *famuli* that included eight or nine people, four ploughmen, a carter, a cowherd, a swineherd, a dairymaid and a maid hired to cook pottage for them all.[37]

[35] See G. A. Holmes, *The Estates of the Higher Nobility in Fourteenth Century England* (Cambridge, 1957), pp. 109, 112.

[36] The chronology of commutation is problematic and controversial. For an excellent summary see Kosminsky, *Studies in the Agrarian History of England in the Thirteenth Century*, ch. III, esp. pp. 172–8. See also E. Lipson, *The Economic History of England* (London, 1949 ed.), pp. 93–113.

[37] See F. G. Davenport, *The Economic Development of a Norfolk Manor 1066–1565* (Cambridge, 1906), p. 24. On the *famulus* see further M. M. Postan, *The Famulus, Econ. H. R. Supplements* No. 2 (1934).

For the profitable management of estates scattered over a wide area, often over many counties, the greater landlord depended largely on the conscientiousness of his local officials and a very strict system of accounting. Manors were grouped together in a given locality under a bailiff, responsible to the lord's steward. On the individual manor, the key figure was the reeve, usually a villein elected in the manor court and relieved of his labour dues for his term of office. At Michaelmas each year he had to appear before the lord's auditors; from their examination of his stewardship the manorial account was put together. This account furnished full details of all his receipts and disbursements, and of what he had paid into the lord's treasury; the grain and stock account was usually given on the back of the account roll. The auditors, going through the account, surcharged on his cash receipts if they thought sale prices too low, and disallowed disbursements that they regarded as unjustified, both of money and stock (allowances of oats for horses might be over-ample, for example). What was disallowed was debited to the reeve's account, and he was expected to find the extra cash. The auditors also set a target for the productivity of the farm, fixing in advance the ratio of grain to seed sown, the average weight of fleeces and the quantity of dairy produce per cow or ewe milked; if the yield fell short of the target, the reeve's account was again debited. If the reeve could not pay his debts, the community that had elected him – the tenants of the manor – was ultimately liable. This was an effective system for ensuring that, come wind or weather, fair times or foul, the lord's profit was assured. It was not very just and did not encourage honesty among reeves. It could also promote inefficient farming. Auditors tended to be complacent when conditions were favourable and a satisfactory sum was paid into the lord's treasury; and to meet the strains of hard times by tightening up the audit, passing the burden of unavoidable loss on to the reeve and the tenants whom he managed.[38] If the increased rents that some landlords managed to impose on new tenants immediately after the plague of 1348–9 are any guide, there must have been quite a bit of complacently inefficient farming in the years preceding.

[38] On estate administration generally see N. Denholm Young, *Seignorial Administration in England* (Oxford, 1937). On accounting J. S. Drew, 'Manorial accounts of St Swithun's Priory, Winchester', *E.H.R.* 62 (1947), pp. 20–41, is valuable, and I owe much to this paper in what I have said.

When the plague struck in 1348 the whole balance of social relations and economic pressures in the countryside was thrown out by its mortality. The effect on the position of the landlord was not clear absolutely immediately. Most landlords found that they had no major problem in filling vacant tenements; and there was a short-term profit to be taken in the way of *heriots* and entry fines as numerous holdings changed hands.[39] Time, however, made the real consequences of the mortality apparent; acute shortage of labour; a collapse of demand for tenant land; falling prices for arable produce as demand slackened. Gradually it began to infiltrate the seignorial consciousness that things had changed very much to the disadvantage of landlords as a class. The response was instinctively reactionary.

At the national level, the most important symptom of the seignorial reaction was the Statute of Labourers; and in the first decade of its operation it certainly seems to have done something to curb the rise of wages. There was also a determined effort on the part of most lords to retain their advantage over their tenants at the manorial level. Auditors tightened up on the reeves of manors, and became more vigorous in pursuit of arrears of rent and of debts. Some lords sought to economize on wages by reimposing labour services that had been commuted (but this was not as common as historians once used to believe). Some, like the Abbot of Evesham, charged substantial sums for permission to employ their villein tenants; others charged their villeins for leave to work for other masters. Generally, manorial lords sought to exploit all their legal advantages, especially in relation to their unfree customary tenants, insisting on their preferential right to their labour, strictly enforcing the rules which bound them to the soil of the manor, making the most that they could out of such dues as *merchet* and *leyrwite*.[40] For a period they seem to have been remarkably successful in minimizing by such means as these the disadvantageous economic consequences of the pestilence. Dr Holmes has calculated that, on the great lay estates, seignorial income in the 1370s was not

[39] See further, A. E. Levett, *The Black Death on the Estates of the See of Winchester*, pp. 76–86; and for comparable evidence Page, *The Estates of Crowland Abbey*, p. 123; J. A. Raftis, *The Estates of Ramsey Abbey* (Toronto, 1957), p. 252; *V.C.H. Berkshire* vol. II, pp. 186–7.

[40] On this seigneurial reaction see R. H. Hilton, *The Decline of Serfdom in Medieval England* (The Economic History Society, 1969) pp. 36–43. I owe much that I have said in this chapter to this admirable book.

on average quite 10 per cent lower than it had been in the 1340s.[41]

Seignorial efforts to stem the economic tide that had turned against the landlord inevitably generated friction. In the confusion of the years that followed the Black Death, order was not easy to enforce in the countryside. Justices of labourers were threatened; at Totenham in Middlesex in July 1351 they were driven from their judgement seat. Efforts to force tenants to perform labour dues and boon works broke against a rising tide of manorial strikes. In 1377 a petition of the commons in parliament complained that 'in many lordships and localities in this kingdom of England the villeins and those who hold in villeinage . . . are refusing the customs and services due to their lords . . . for by colour of certain exemplifications out of Domesday Book they claim that they are quit and utterly discharged of all manner of serfdom'.[42] Finally, in 1381, when tempers everywhere had been sharpened by the unjust incidence of the poll tax, resentment culminated in the Peasants' Revolt.

Significantly, given the pattern of seignorial reactions to the pressures of the post-plague period, the abolition of serfdom was in the forefront of all the demands made by the rebels in 1381. The men of Somerset concocted a charter freeing all men of their county from manorial bondage. Those of Essex were prepared to return home from London after Richard II, at Mile End, had promised them charters of manumission. Wat Tyler demanded that 'no man should be a serf, nor do homage or any manner of service to any lord, but should give fourpence rent for an acre of land, and that no one should work for any man but at his own will, and on terms of a regular covenant'.[43] Wherever they went the rebels made great bonfires of the records of manorial courts, and those who had helped to administer the Statute of Labourers were singled for special persecution. The revolt of course achieved nothing; and when it was over charters of freedom granted in the heat of the crisis were revoked and old obligations reimposed. Yet there was no repetition of the events of 1381. Already by that time many landlords were beginning to realize that the struggle to maintain old ways would never be won, and were taking steps that in the long run (quite unintentionally) reduced to insignificance the grievances which had led to the revolt.

[41] Holmes, *The Estates of the Higher Nobility*, pp. 114–15.
[42] *R.P.*, vol. III, p. 21.
[43] *Anonimalle Chronicle*, ed. V. H. Galbraith, pp. 144–5.

John Smyth, the historian of the Berkeley family, noted a great change during the time of Lord Thomas IV, in the mid 1380s:

> Then began the times to alter, and he with them . . . and then, instead of manureing his demesnes in each manor with his own servants, oxen, kine, sheep . . . under the oversight of the reeves of the manors . . . this lord began to joyst and tack in other men's cattle into his pasture grounds by the week, month, and quarter: and to sell his meadow grounds by the acre, and so between wind and water as it were continued part in tillage and part let out . . . for the rest of that king's reign: and after in the time of Henry the fourth let out by the year still more and more as he found chapmen and price to his liking. . . . But in the next age that succeeded his nephew and heir male lord James who succeeded in these manors . . . let out [all] the manor houses and demesne lands, sometimes at racked improved rents according to the estimate of the time and sometimes at smaller rents . . . which is the general course and husbandry for far the most part to this very day [1618].[44]

The development that John Smyth so splendidly describes was a general one. Everywhere, in the late fourteenth century and the fifteenth, we find that lords were leasing out their demesnes, and that leases, with the passage of time, were becoming longer. Prior Chillenden of Canterbury between 1391 and 1411 leased virtually all the demesnes of Christ Church, taking food rents on some of the Kentish manors to supply the monastery. Crowland abbey had let most of its demesnes by 1430; Leicester abbey did the same over the period from 1408 to 1477. The process was not always fast but it was sure; every decade, as Miss Harvey writes of the Westminster Abbey estates, saw more leasing of demesne.[45] The result was nothing less than a complete change in the predominant role of the landlord in agriculture, from farmer to *rentier*. There were also very important results for customary tenants and labourers. The commutation of labour services became virtually universal, and wage labour, always important, became the pivot of all cultivation on any scale larger than that of the single peasant's family

---

[44] J. Smyth, *The Lives of the Berkeleys*, ed. Sir J. Maclean (Gloucester, 1883), vol. II, pp. 5–6.

[45] See B. F. Harvey, 'The leasing of the Abbot of Westminster's demesnes in the later Middle Ages', *Econ.H.R.* 2nd ser., 22 (1969), pp. 17–27. See also R. A. L. Smith, *Canterbury Cathedral Priory* (Cambridge, 1943), pp. 192–4; Page, *The Estates of Crowland Abbey*, pp. 154–5; R. H. Hilton, *The Economic development of some Leicestershire Estates* (Oxford, 1947), pp. 88–94.

holding. Among the chief employers of labour was a figure
newly significant on the rural scene, the substantial tenant
farmer, of whom Bishop Latimer has left us an excellent por-
trait in his sketch of his father. The elder Latimer 'was a yeoman,
and held no land of his own: only he had a farm of three or four
pounds by the year, and hereupon he tilled so much as kept half
a dozen men. He had a walk for a hundred sheep and my mother
milked thirty kine, . . . he kept me to school . . . he married my
sisters with £5 a piece or twenty nobles: he kept hospitality for
his poor neighbours, and some alms he gave to the poor'.[46]
It was not only demesne land that was often up for lease in the
fifteenth century, and on which men like Latimer's father
throve. From the last decade of the fourteenth century on the
flight of customary tenants from the manor began, in many
places, to reach alarming proportions. Ever since the 1350s
internal migration had been increasing in England, and had
opened opportunities to those left behind on the manor to
consolidate their holdings into small farms. But now more land
was being deserted than could find new tenants. It was this that
made the early decades of the fifteenth century the gloomiest
period of all from the point of view of the agricultural landlord.
An inquisition *post mortem* of 1427 of the Beaumont estates in
Leicestershire gives a good picture of his problems; at Whitwick,
an important manor, twelve houses were vacant out of thirty-one,
and 289 acres had gone to waste; at Markfield twelve out of
twenty-nine houses were decayed; at Hugglescote ten messuages
were in the lord's hand for want of tenants.[47] In some places the
desertion was on such a scale as to empty whole villages, especially
where the land was poor, like the lost village of Dunsthorpe in
Lincolnshire which was ruined, so the rector declared in 1437,
'by the lack of parishioners, the fewness of the peasants, the
bareness of the lands, lack of cultivation, and the pestilences and
epidemics with which the Lord afflicts his people'.[48]
This process of desertion of manorial tenements was one of

[46] *Sermons by Hugh Latimer*, ed. G. E. Corrie (Parker Soc., 1844). On
this subject of the men who leased demesnes, see the important article
by F. R. H. Du Boulay, 'Who were farming the English demesnes at
the end of the Middle Ages', *Econ.H.R.* 2nd ser., 17 (1964–5), pp. 443–
455.
[47] W. G. Hoskins, *The Midland Peasant* (London, 1957), p. 85; and
compare J. A. Raftis, *Tenure and Mobility* (Toronto, 1964), pp. 190–7.
[48] Quoted from Beresford, *The Lost Villages of Medieval England*,
p. 171.

the factors which, in the course of the fifteenth century, began to encourage systematic enclosure for pasture farming. The early history of enclosure is elusive, but a good deal was going on, and we catch a glimpse of it here and there, as for instance at Compton Verney in Warwickshire. Here Professor Hilton has traced a steady tale of surrenders of holdings by customary tenants from the late fourteenth century on. By 1461 (for which year there survives a rental) six large fields had been enclosed and were let for pasture, at nearly 20 marks each; the remaining rents from customary and other tenures brought the lord no more than £4. Enclosure had changed the whole physical aspect of the village land and substantially increased the lord's profits.[49] Before the end of the fifteenth century the enclosure movement was widespread; peasants and tenants were engaged as well as landlords in the business of laying holding to holding and hedging fields. Landlords were not always scrupulous about the ways by which they persuaded tenants to abandon their holdings when these were convenient for enclosure, and concern was growing about the consequences. 'Where in some towns two hundred persons were occupied by their lawful labours', an act of 1489 declares, 'now be there occupied two or three herdsmen, and the residue fallen in idleness: the husbandry . . . is decayed, churches destroyed, the service of God withdrawn, the bodies there not prayed for; the patron and the curate wronged, the defence of this land against outward enemies enfeebled and impaired.'[50]

There can be little doubt that the changes in the agricultural world in the late Middle Ages were favourable to the peasant and the labourer, at least until the beginning of the enclosure move-

[49] R. H. Hilton, 'A study in the pre-history of English enclosure' in *Studi in onore di A. Sapori* (Milan, 1957), pp. 675ff. The most important and thorough study of the early history of enclosure is Beresford, *The Lost Villages of Medieval England*: the difficulties about estimating the extent of enclosure before 1485 are explained carefully in ch. IV (see esp. pp. 117–21).

[50] *Statutes*, 4 Henry VII, c. 19. Compare the lament of John Rous, the Warwickshire antiquary, writing before 1491, in *Historia Regum Anglie*, ed. T. Hearne (Oxford, 1745), pp. 113–18, and especially 'what shall be said of the modern destruction of villages which brings dearth to the commonwealth . . . if such destruction as that in Warwickshire took place in other parts of the country it would be a national danger' (quoted from the translation by Beresford, *The Lost Villages of Medieval England*, p. 81).

ment. We must not exaggerate the improvement in their lot; the labourer and the smallholder remained always the people nearest the mercy of chance – of poor harvests, cattle murrains, and scarcity of food. But working men were better paid and better fed in the period after the plague; Langland was frankly shocked by their ample diet:

> May no peny ale hem paye, ne a pece of bacon
> Bot hit be freesch flecsch other fysh fried other ybake
> And that chaud and plus chaud for chilling of here mawe
> Bot he be heylich yhyred eles wol he chide.[51]

Low rents opened opportunities for peasants to turn themselves into small farmers. Above all, the changed situation in the countryside rang the death knell of serfdom. It ceased to be practicable for lords to take advantage of the legal disabilities of villeins. To quote an example, a sum called a recognition had been paid traditionally by customary tenants on the Bishop of Worcester's estates when a new lord entered. In 1433, when the estates were in the king's hand in a vacancy it was reported that 'the customary tenants of the aforesaid manors were . . . in such great poverty that if these recognitions were levied from them they would leave the land, holdings, and tenures of the aforesaid lordships vacant, to the great prejudice of the lord king and the final destruction of the aforesaid manors'.[52] The bishop's tenants in fact never paid another recognition; they shook themselves free, too, of seignorial tallage and a host of minor dues and 'pleas and perquisites of court'. It was no good trying to bully tenants who would leave the land if they were pressed too hard; that would only reduce further the lord's already diminished customary rents. At the same time, as men of greater substance became involved more often in leasing customary holdings, and as anxiety began to rise about the depopulation of the countryside, the law at last began to offer greater protection to the manorial tenant. The council and chancery were upholding the customary terms of manorial tenures early in the fifteenth century, and in Edward IV's reign the common law began to entertain actions of trespass brought by customary tenants against their lords. Villein tenures were now more often spoken of as copyholds (by copy of court roll of the manor); villein status, though never

[51] *Piers Plowman*, C Text, ll. 333–6.
[52] Quoted from C. Dyer, 'A redistribution of incomes in fifteenth century England', *Past and Present* 39 (1968), pp. 11–33, a valuable article.

abolished, had ceased to be relevant in new conditions and slid into oblivion.

As far as can be made out, the circumstances that favoured labourers and tenants late in the Middle Ages did not affect the fortunes of great landlords quite as adversely as we might expect. These were difficult times, but there was no real crisis for the seignorial class. Some ecclesiastical landlords found themselves in serious trouble, but mismanagement, or misfortune (as on some Durham estates, which suffered heavily in the fighting between the Yorkists and Margaret of Anjou), seems usually to have been involved. Enterprising abbots found means to maintain, even sometimes to increase their revenue: John Whethamstede at St Albans added to his rent roll by the purchase of substantial properties, and the Prior of Canterbury, seeing that rents for grazing were profitable, spent money heavily but intelligently to reclaim land from Appledore Marsh and to make it fit to let as a sheep pasture.[53] The great secular landlords seem to have suffered even less than the religious. The tendency, among the greater nobility at least in the fifteenth century, was towards the concentration of ever greater acreage in fewer hands; what was lost in diminished rents was more than offset, for the successful, by a sheer increase of properties from which rents were drawn. For lay magnates there were, besides, many ways of offsetting a decline in agricultural profits. Many enriched themselves abroad in the war with France, winning ransoms, booty, and estates overseas. For their services, at home and abroad, lords expected and obtained rewards from the crown, new estates, offices of profit, annuities, wardships – and, of course, advantageous marriages for themselves and their heirs which would increase further the acreage of their inheritances. The one great secular landlord whose landed revenue did fall seriously and steadily was the crown itself. The trouble, however, was not the adverse economics of agriculture, but the over-generosity forced on it by the pressure of political circumstances.

Gains of war were of course unreliable windfalls, and the crown's resources from which to reward good service were not endless. There was much competition for court favour, which complicated the relations of magnates with the king and with each other. There was nothing new about this, however; competition for patronage was as old as the baronage, and was as

[53] See *Registrum J de Whethamstede* (R.S.) vol. I, pp. 187, 190, 357–60, 428–33 (I was kindly referred to this source by Miss B. F. Harvey); and Smith, *Canterbury Cathedral Priory*, p. 203.

much a factor in the civil disorders of Stephen's reign and John's and Henry III's as it was in the fifteenth century. It is very difficult to explain the Wars of the Roses in terms of a *crise seigneuriale*, of the cut throat competition for the profits of royal favour and service among a magnate class whose way of life was threatened by a dramatic depression in their landed revenues. When one looks at a figure like Richard of York, with some £6000 in rents from his lands in England and Wales, at the vast debts that the crown owed him and which he blithely allowed to accumulate (£38,000 were owing to him at the exchequer in 1446); when one sees Richard Beauchamp of Warwick in 1420 spending twice his princely annual income on building alone, yet remaining among the richest in the land – then it becomes difficult to think of the magnates as a class labouring under the threat of economic ruin. Politics, their hereditary preoccupation, were what endangered their fortunes in the fifteenth century, not vanishing rent rolls.[54]

What, we must ask in conclusion, of the men in between, who were neither peers nor peasants, the knights and county gentry? It is much harder to find evidence about the state of their fortunes than those of greater landlords, and it is sometimes suggested that for them particularly the times were difficult. But it is hard to reconcile this with the steady growth, in the period, of their political influence and independence; and if there were, as always, some declining gentry, there were clearly plenty of rising gentry too. For gentlemen of county family the same opportunities to augment declining rents were open as to the peerage, though on a different scale: annuities, fees, and offices obtained as the reward of service, and the gains of war. John Fastolf, as McFarlane has shown, was regularly sending home from France through the hands of his Paris banker, Jean Sac,

[54] On magnate revenues see C. D. Ross and T. B. Pugh, 'Materials for the study of baronial incomes in fifteenth century England', *Econ.H.R.* 2nd ser., 6 (1953–4), pp. 185–94; also their article, 'The English baronage and the income tax of 1436', *B.I.H.R.* 26 (1953), pp. 1–28 (which shows that H. L. Gray underestimated magnate wealth in 'Incomes from land in England in 1436', *E.H.R.* 49 (1934), pp. 607–39). York's estates have been studied in detail by J. Rosenthal, *The Estates and Finances of Richard Duke of York*, in *Studies in Medieval and Renaissance History* vol. II (Nebraska, 1965): he believes that Pugh and Ross have overstated Richard of York's wealth, but that it is clear that York's finances were too buoyant for their state to provide any key to his political action (p. 151).

moneys which his English agents invested in the purchase of lands and manors. He inherited lands worth £46 per annum from his father and he made a good marriage, worth £225 per annum to him; but in 1446 he had lands in England to the clear value of £1061 per annum. Besides that he had books and plate and jewels (including a diamond set in a rich collar worth 4000 marks that Richard of York gave him) and spent largely on building.[55] Fastolf, of course, was a spectacularly successful soldier. But other men who did not go to the wars and were not, like Fastolf, in the councils of princes of the blood also prospered. Judge Paston, the founder of his family's fortunes, was a successful lawyer who built up his estates by shrewd purchases and the good marriages he made for himself and his sons. He was not as big a man as Fastolf, but he was a bigger man than Bartholomew Bolney, who got a start in life when he went to Winchester College as 'founder's kin', and then took to law. He never rose beyond being steward to the Abbot of Battle, and serving on a great many local commissions in Sussex. Nevertheless he busied himself with purchase and exchange, and was able to leave behind the stout little book of his title deeds by which we know him: 'the record of a small estate, acquired piece by piece, by an up and coming member of the administrative middle class'.[56] The times do not seem to have been plagued by dearth of opportunity for the gentry at any level.

It is significant that Fastolf, Paston and Bolney alike all invested in land; so did London merchants like Sir Geoffrey Boleyn. Land remained the safest and most satisfactory investment for ambitious men to the end of the Middle Ages. It is also significant that we find, among those who were taking up leases of demesne in this period, a fair sprinkling of gentlemen;[57] farming (or improving land with a view to subletting) was clearly not so depressed as to discourage substantial men from going in with a view to making themselves a profit. The assumption still held, that the more land a man had at his disposal the better for him. The effects of the plague in the long term caused a social

---

[55] See K. B. McFarlane, 'The investment of Sir John Fastolf's profits of war', *T.R.H.S.* 5th ser., 7 (1957), pp. 91–116.

[56] M. A. Clough, intro. to her edition of *The Book of Bartholomew Bolney* vol. 63 (Sussex Record Soc., 1964), p. xxviii.

[57] See F. R. H. Du Boulay, 'Who were farming the English demesnes at the end of the Middle Ages', pp. 450–1; and B. F. Harvey, 'The leasing of the Abbot of Westminster's desmesnes in the later Middle Ages', p. 21.

revolution in the humbler strata of society, which brought to birth a new society of tenant farmers and labourers out of the debris of the manorial community. They did not, however, seriously alter the position of landownership as the basis of the political, social and economic authority of the dominant classes.

9

Church and state in the later
Middle Ages

The period from the end of the thirteenth to the end of the fifteenth century was a very important one in the history of the relations of church and state in England. It witnessed developments whose cumulative consequence was to establish, by gradual degrees, an effective royal supremacy in the English church long before that supremacy was legally enforced by Henry VIII. The spiritual authority of the pope and the general currency of Roman canon law in England were never challenged, it is true, except by the heretical Lollards, in whose persecution the state took its part. Lyndwood, when he put together his great collection of the provincial constitutions of the English church (completed in 1430) assumed as the basis of their authority their conformity with the general canons of the church. The great volume of correspondence in the *Calendars of Papal Letters Concerning England* shows that Roman authority permeated the day-to-day administration of the English church at every level. Nevertheless the popes found, and increasingly as our period went on, that the effective exercise of their authority depended almost entirely on the willingness or otherwise of the English monarchs to cooperate and acquiesce in it. As Martin V ruefully put it, 'it is not the pope but the king of England who governs the church in his dominions.'[1]

Just before the beginning of our period, in 1279, Edward I's Statute of Mortmain pointed the shape of things to come. It had often given rise to complaint, the statute's preamble declared, that when laymen alienated estates to the church, the lords from whom they held these estates lost the prospect of ever again enjoying such feudal incidents as reliefs, wardships

[1] Quoted by C. Davies, 'The Statute of Provisors of 1351', *History* 38 (1953), p. 133.

and marriages, because the church would never die or marry or leave an heir under age. Henceforward, therefore, no man was to alienate land to the church without the licence of the king. The church bitterly resented this intrusion into her relations with her patrons, but the statute stood. It had been carefully drafted. Edward I did not forbid men to endow collegiate churches with land; he merely brought endowment under royal supervision, and offenders against the statute were not prosecuted for giving land to pious uses, but for doing so without the king's permission.[2] This was the way things were to work in the future in many more areas beside that of endowment.

The relations of church and state are a broad subject. For the sake of simplicity we may concentrate our attention on three important matters: clerical taxation, papal provisions, and the problem of church endowments which Mortmain has already raised.

Before the end of the thirteenth century the question of clerical taxation culminated in a crisis which largely decided things for the future. During this century, the popes had on a number of occasions imposed taxation, on their own authority, on clerical incomes, usually for crusading purposes. For this purpose incomes were assessed in each rural deanery by juries, which included laymen as well as clergy; the assessment made for Pope Nicholas IV's tenth of 1291 became the standard valuation for the rest of the medieval period.[3] Henry III and Edward I acquiesced in this papal taxation, and were usually rewarded with a substantial share of the proceeds, which they employed for purposes of their own. The crown in consequence came to expect the church to make a contribution towards its extraordinary expenditure. When at the outbreak of war with France in 1294 Edward found himself in exceptional need, he expected exceptional assistance. The king summoned the bishops and clergy to Westminster in September, and gave them three days to make him an aid; their offer of two tenths was curtly rejected, and he

[2] On the Statute of Mortmain see T. F. T. Plucknett, *The Legislation of Edward I* (Oxford, 1949), pp. 94–102; and on its application K. L. Wood-Legh, *Church Life in England under Edward III* (Cambridge, 1934), ch. III, 'Alienations in Mortmain'.

[3] On this see further W. E. Lunt, *Financial Relations of the Papacy with England*, vol. I (Cambridge, Mass., 1939), pp. 346–65; and R. Graham, 'The taxation of Pope Nicholas IV' in her *English Ecclesiastical Studies* (London, 1929), pp. 271–301.

asked for a half of their revenues.[4] Those who demurred were warned that they would lose the royal protection if they did not pay, and the grant was made; something like £80,000 had been collected by September 1295. In November that year the representatives of the clergy were again summoned, this time to parliament along with the nobility, knights and burgesses; they granted a tenth and had to promise that they would give more if the need arose.

King Philip IV in France had at the same time been making heavy demands of his clergy, and complaints from disgruntled ecclesiastics in both lands reached Pope Boniface VIII. It was in response to these that he issued his famous bull *Clericis Laicos*. It was a trenchant restatement of the independent sovereignty of the pope over all that regarded the affairs of the clergy, and forbade ecclesiastics to contribute in any way to taxes imposed by the secular authorities, on pain of excommunication, unless the pope had given them leave to do so. It was issued in February 1296; when Edward in November again assembled the clergy at the parliament at Bury in order to obtain the further grant that they had promised, the new archbishop, Robert Winchelsey, had seen the bull. Edward wanted a fifth; he gave the archbishop and his clergy a delay till January to consider the matter, and when they then refused a subsidy, he put them outside the protection of his law. In face of this appalling threat to their security, the majority began to waver. Winchelsey for himself felt that he must stand firm and published the bull, but at the March convocation he agreed that others must be guided by their own consciences. Most clergy and religious houses were glad to come to terms with the king and buy his peace. Winchelsey stuck to his guns personally, but his position had been undermined. Edward, on his way to Flanders in August 1297, told the bishops, who assured him that they would seek the pope's leave to make a grant, that he would have his fifth right away, or a third of the clergy's temporalities if they preferred, and that he would permit no sentences of excommunication against those who paid.[5]

[4] On this grant, and on all those made voluntarily by the clergy in this period, see H. S. Deighton, 'Clerical taxation by consent 1279–1301', *E.H.R.* 68 (1953), pp. 161–92.

[5] The most illuminating discussion of the ecclesiastical side of the crisis of 1297 is that given by H. Rothwell, 'The confirmation of the charters', *E.H.R.* 60 (1945), pp. 16–35. I have endeavoured to follow his account in my outline, but space has made it impossible to do justice to some of the finer points, in particular concerning the bull

Before there were any further developments the face, and probably the fortunes, of Winchelsey and the other papal loyalists were saved by Boniface's new bull, *Etsi de Statu*. This explained that *Clericis Laicos* should not apply when, in the opinion of the prince and his advisers, a realm was faced with an emergency. The archbishop thankfully accepted that there was an emergency, and both the southern and the northern convocations made grants in the autumn of 1297. In return the crown ceased to collect the earlier levy (the fifth), and the threat of excommunications dropped out of the picture.

Edward I in 1297 won a major victory. He demonstrated effectively that, faced with the threat of outlawry, the English clergy would not and could not take a stand against him, even with assured papal backing. He gained, from the pope and his Archbishop of Canterbury, the all important admission that, in an emergency, he had the right to ask for an aid from his English clergy without seeking papal permission (he was successful here, it must be admitted, largely because he was able to cash in on the firm line that Philip of France took on the same issue). Viewed in the light of the ancient claims for clerical independence of the secular authority, upon which *Clericis Laicos* was based, this was a crucial concession.

Edward himself used his success with wise moderation. He never again asked the convocations for an aid. Boniface, with equal wisdom, was agreeable to himself authorizing the levy of a tenth for three years in 1301, and letting Edward take the lion's share. His successors Clement V and John XXII followed his example when they imposed taxes on the English clergy.[6] By the second half of the fourteenth century things had so far changed that, when Urban VI in 1388 sought to collect a twentieth in England, the response to his effort was a petition from the commons that anyone who levied such a tax without the assent of the *king* should be adjudged a traitor. The roles of king and pope were well on the way already to complete reversal; and the trend was to continue. In Winchelsey's day it

---

Etsi de Statu (and the earlier *Romana mater ecclesia*), whose reference was principally to the situation in France, not England.

[6] On papal taxation in Edward II's reign see W. E. Lunt, 'Clerical tenths levied in England by papal authority during the reign of Edward II' in *Haskins' Anniversary Essays*, ed. C. H. Taylor and J. L. La Monte (New York, 1929), pp. 157–82.

had been the pope who claimed that he was protecting the clergy from uncustomary royal taxation; Edward IV, in 1463, claimed when he persuaded Pius II not to levy a tax in England that he was protecting the clergy from an uncustomary imposition that his ancestors had never permitted. A number of popes did try to collect subsidies in England on their own authority, but they were never successful. Henry VI, Edward IV and Henry VII all permitted the collection of taxes or voluntary gifts from the clergy, but that was a different matter: their permission had been sought and given in advance.

Long before the fifteenth century, the pope's right to authorize clerical taxation had ceased to be a lively issue. The issue that did remain alive was the right of the clergy to tax themselves independently through the two convocations. They objected to being summoned to make their grants in parliament, as they had been in 1295. Archbishop Stratford in 1341 succeeded in establishing that they should not be asked to contribute to taxes levied by parliamentary consent,[7] but this did not protect the clergy from the threat of parliamentary authority in a more subtle form; namely from attempts by parliaments to make their grants conditional on the clergy also making a grant, of a stipulated size. In 1371 the bishops (who sat in parliament as well as in convocation) had to struggle to avoid their hands being tied. In 1385 the laity agreed to grant two fifteenths if the clergy would grant two tenths; but they met their match in the formidable Archbishop Courtenay, who was so incensed by the offence to clerical privilege as to insist that the request be erased from the roll.[8] In the troubled reign of the needy Henry IV parliament returned to the attack and the clergy found themselves under still more severe pressure. The commons had come to suspect that a good many clergy were altogether escaping from the net, since stipendiary chaplains were not assessed to the clerical tenths. In 1406 the convocation of Canterbury was twice visited by a deputation of knights from the commons, and in the end agreed to a levy of 6s. 8d. on all salaried clergy not assessed to the tenth.[9] We do not know what arguments were used on the occasion; we can only conclude that the clergy, who had resisted a similar

[7] R.P. vol. II, pp. 129 (No. 25) and 130 (No. 32).

[8] See further D. B. Weske, Convocation of the Clergy in the Thirteenth and Fourteenth Centuries (London, 1937), p. 170.

[9] See further E. F. Jacob, 'The Canterbury convocation of 1406' in Essays in Medieval History Presented to B. Wilkinson, pp. 345–53.

demand in 1404, had concluded that more important privileges would come under threat if they held out.

The clergy had much to gain from maintaining their privileged position with regard to taxation. It enabled them to make their own conditions with their grants, to ensure that their complaints were forwarded from convocation to parliament, and to apportion the inevitable fiscal burden in the way that they chose. But the knowledge that, if they did not give to the king, parliament would make them give with the laity undermined any capacity they might have had to resist royal demands. The English kings of the later Middle Ages sometimes hesitated to approach the intractable commons in parliament, but they looked to the convocations with a contrasting confidence. We are accustomed to think of Edward IV as a king who sought to 'live of his own', and as far as parliament was concerned he had much success after 1471. In these years when parliamentary grants had all but dried up, he could rely, however, on obtaining at least some grants from the convocations. He and others did not think this was inconsistent with living of his own. That of itself is a sign of how, in one respect at least, a royal supremacy had grown within the framework of the English church, still linked though it was to Rome by ties of constant communication.

The question of papal provisions was a more important issue in our period than clerical taxation. The controversies to which it gave rise were more complicated, and it took longer for the dust to settle. In the end, the honours were not quite so unevenly divided.

As the universal ordinary, the pope could claim in canon law the right to collate to all ecclesiastical benefices. In practice he only 'provided' to those that he had reserved to his own collation. From 1265 onward, when Clement IV reserved all benefices whose holders died at the papal court, the classes of reserved benefices were greatly extended, especially in the fourteenth century. Clement V reserved all benefices of cardinals, papal chaplains and *nuncios*, and benefices vacant by resignation, transfer or exchange at the papal court. John XXII added all benefices vacated as a result of provisions (when a great pluralist like William of Wykeham was promoted to the episcopate and had to resign his preferments these could be very numerous). Urban V in 1363 formally reserved the appointment to all archiepiscopal and episcopal churches (in practice in England all bishoprics were already before that normally filled by provision). The system was further extended by the frequent grants of bulls of expectation, assuring the grantee preferment in a particular church when a vacancy next occurred.[10]

Provision was of course valuable to the popes as a means of extending papal influence, but it was much more valuable to them for financial reasons. Provisions (usually to benefices without cure of souls) afforded the popes a means whereby they could maintain the staff of the *Curia*, from the cardinals down to minor clerks and officials. Besides, a system of papal taxation was, as it were, built into the system of provision. The revenues of any benefice that was filled by provision, both for the preceding period of vacancy and for the first year of occupation, were due to the apostolic see (bishops and higher clergy paid what were called 'common services' on confirmation or provision by the pope, which were calculated on a slightly different basis to this one).[11] These taxes, often lumped together under the general title of 'annates', were a rich source of income to the pope and were a considerable burden for those who paid. They went towards meeting the heavy expenses of the papal household and the households of the cardinals, and to paying for the defence and enlargement of the patrimony of Peter in Italy (which consumed more of the papal revenues in the fourteenth and fifteenth centuries than anything else did).

Explicitly the principal ground for the widespread objection of Englishmen to the system of provision was the way in which it interfered with the normal course of ecclesiastical patronage. Lay patrons were not much affected, since the pope did not as a rule provide to benefices that were in their gift. The king, however, could be, because he claimed among his *regalia*, when a bishopric was vacant and the temporalities were in his hand, the right to present to benefices to which the bishop ordinarily collated. This claim naturally brought his nominees into frequent

[10] On provisions and benefices, see G. Barraclough, *Papal Provisions* (Oxford, 1935), the most useful general study of the system. On its financial aspects, see W. E. Lunt, *Financial Relations of the Papacy with England* vol. II (Cambridge, Mass., 1962). There is useful discussion of the problems in both in E. Perroy, *L'Angleterre et le Grand Schisme d'Occident* (Paris, 1933), ch. I, §I and §II; and W. A. Pantin, *The English Church in the Fourteenth Century* (Cambridge, 1955), ch. IV.

[11] For definitions, see Lunt, *Financial Relations*, vol. II, pp. 170ff., 307. Lunt's discussion of annates and common services in this second volume of his book is the most authoritative study of the working of the system of provisions in late medieval England.

conflict with papal provisors; but the king had the whip hand, because in England it was an established custom that cases involving advowson (the right to present to benefices) were tried in the lay courts. The real sufferers from provisions were ecclesiastical patrons, and above all the bishops.

> On the ides of October [Bishop Grandison of Exeter wrote to Clement VI in 1342] I was present in the council of the province of Canterbury in London, where among other things, if I may say so by your leave, no small wonder arose at the burdensome and hitherto unknown multitude of apostolic provisions. For it was said that from now onwards prelates, both greater and lesser, . . . will never be able to provide for the well deserving or necessary servants of their churches or of themselves.[12]

The bishops were afraid that soon they would not retain sufficient patronage to provide for the administrators of their dioceses and the clients of their households. Perhaps most of all bishops resented grants of expectancies; these could accumulate to the point where an incoming diocesan had little hope of using any of his patronage for years to come.

Other and wider interests besides those of the ordinaries were disturbed by the papal inroads into ecclesiastical patronage. Archbishop Romeyn of York put the point well, writing in the 1290s to Nicholas IV, to protest against papal plans to annex a prebend in his cathedral to a Roman hospital.

> This was not the intention of the catholic kings of England of famous memory or of those other faithful in Christ who founded not only our churches but the whole church in England for the spreading of the faith, and endowed her amply with temporal goods . . . they were thus generous to the churches for the saving of souls and the forgiveness of sins, that divine worship should be increased, that hospitality should be served and alms given to the poor, and that the churches should be served by good ministers, who would take their stipends for the time from the yield of the said temporal goods.[13]

Papal provisions and annexations thwarted directly the pious intentions of the founders of churches, Romeyn argued. His view was echoed by the community of the land in the parliament of Carlisle in 1307, by parliamentary petition in 1343, and in the preamble to the Statute of Provisors in 1351.

[12] From Grandison's *Register*, quoted by Pantin, *The English Church in the Fourteenth Century*, p. 70.

[13] Quoted by A. Hamilton Thompson, *The English Clergy and their Organisation in the Later Middle Ages* (Oxford, 1947), p. 10, note 2.

The view that Romeyn put forward, with its emphasis on the respect due to the intentions of founders and the right of their heirs, had deep roots in the old idea of the proprietary church, of the ecclesiastical benefice as the feudal property of a lord and patron. It also appealed to the principle, at first sight beyond challenge, that the English church was endowed to serve the needs of Englishmen. This argument does not look quite so sound when we consider what was the alternative to provision by the pope. The continuator of the *Flores Historiarum* praised John XXII, because his reservations saved the English church in Edward II's reign from a plague of illiterate and unworthy royal clients.[14] The maintenance of learning at the universities depended on provision of benefices for scholars; Oxford and Cambridge in the later fourteenth century were regularly sending lists to the *Curia* of those whom they wished to see preferred.[15] Archbishop Romeyn's ideal vision of a church 'served in person by good ministers' was not the real alternative to provision that so many took it to be; that was rather a church in which the clients of the king and the aristocracy had a richer share of ecclesiastical plums. They would probably not have been at their posts any more often than the pope's clients. Romeyn's view nevertheless was the normal coin of criticism of papal provisions, and was held at large to enshrine a principle of self-evident validity.

Still stronger with people, but perhaps less heavily laboured in clerical correspondence with the *Curia*, were objections to the financial consequences of provision. When an alien resident at the pope's court was provided to an English benefice, its revenue was taken out of the country, an offence to the bullionist instinct of the late medieval commons. The collection of annates had the same effect, and everyone knew that whatever was done at the *Curia* cost gold, for there were fees to be paid for the writing, expedition and sealing of all bulls of provision. 'Thousands of pounds have been paid here to the Lombards for exchange [and transfer to Rome]', wrote Thomas Gascoigne in Henry VI's reign, 'to the impoverishment of the realm.'[16] In the Avignon period in particular there were suspicions that money from Eng-

[14] *Flores Historiarum* (R.S.) vol. III, pp. 175–6.
[15] On this see further E. F. Jacob, 'Petitions for benefices from English universities during the Great Schism', *T.R.H.S.* 4th ser., 27 (1945), pp. 41–59.
[16] T. Gascoigne, *Loci e Libro Veritatum*, ed. J. E. Thorold Rogers (Oxford, 1881), p. 52.

land was finding its way, by the medium of a francophile papacy, to the war chest of the French king. Opinion at large greatly exaggerated both the number of aliens provided to English benefices and the sums which were being carried out of England as a result of provisions.[17] From our point of view the exaggeration is not so significant as the fact that Englishmen believed it, and believed that 'among the *curiales* of the apostolic see it has become a proverb that the English are good asses, ready to carry all the intolerable burdens that are put upon them'.[18]

The first formal attack upon the system of provisions was made in the parliament of Carlisle in 1307. Parliament returned to the charge in 1309, and still more bitterly in 1343, when the number of provisions had sharply increased with the coming of Pope Clement VI. In response to the commons' agitation Edward III put an embargo on the entry of bulls prejudicial to the king and his people, and had the ports watched for them. When the mortality caused by the Black Death was followed by another wave of new provisions, the upshot of renewed parliamentary pressure was the Statute of Provisors of 1351.

The statute of 1351 ordained that henceforward elections to bishoprics and in collegiate churches should be free, and that clerical patrons should enjoy the free exercise of their rights of presentation. If any reservation or provision from the court of Rome interfered with these rights and processes the king would present to the office or benefice himself. If anyone presented by the king or by an ecclesiastical patron was disturbed by a papal provisor, the provisor and his agents should be arrested and imprisoned until he should renounce his provision. If the provisor could not be found he was to be outlawed. The effect of the statute was thus to impose the responsibility for defending the English church against provision on the king, by recognizing him as 'patron paramount' in his kingdom. Two years later the Statute of Praemunire tidied up the legal position by forbidding men to take abroad cases cognizable in the king's courts (as matters of ecclesiastical patronage certainly were).[19]

[17] Pantin quotes some useful figures to show the number of provisions and the proportion in favour of aliens, *The English Church in the Fourteenth Century*, pp. 60–3.

[18] *Chron A. Murimuth* (R.S.), p. 175.

[19] On these two statutes the following articles are particularly useful: A. Deeley, 'Papal provision and royal rights of patronage in the early fourteenth century', *E.H.R.* 43 (1928), pp. 497–527; C. Davies, 'The

The statutes of Provisors and Praemunire were not in practice the bulwarks against papal authority that they appeared to be on paper. The onus of implementing them fell to the king, and he in fact only enforced them when it was convenient for him to do so. Usually he found it more satisfactory to work with the pope rather than against him. In spite of the statutes the pope continued to provide English bishops to their sees and to translate them from see to see, taking annates when he did so. The men whom he provided were usually the crown's nominees. The king, lay patrons, and the universities continued to petition the popes for provision for their clients. But though the king did not enforce the statutes often, he found them a very useful weapon when the papacy proved either recalcitrant or demanding. In 1365, for instance, when Urban V renewed the demand for Peter's pence from England, which were long in arrears, the Statute of Provisors was reissued. There was a running battle between Edward III and the next pope, Gregory XI, which was not ended until 1375 when the king allowed the pope to resume provision, in return for a papal promise to confirm current royal nominees in their benefices and to moderate his provisions for the future. The Statute of Provisors was reissued yet again in 1390, after Urban VI had made difficulties about the translation (for political reasons) of a number of English bishops during the domestic crisis of 1388. Both sides, however, were by this time clearly playing for advantage, not victory. The same parliament that in 1393 approved a new and stiffer version of the Statute of Praemunire empowered Richard II to seek an accommodation over provision with Pope Boniface IX. And when, five years later, Richard and Boniface did agree to a formal *concordat*, which but for the revolution of 1399 might have become permanent, it effectively sold the pass on provisors, reserving the nomination to bishoprics to pope and king together, and allowing to the former the right to collate to one in every three important vacancies in cathedral and collegiate churches.[20]

The Great Schism, which lasted from 1378 until 1417, greatly

Statute of Provisors of 1351', *History* 38 (1953), pp. 116–33; E. B. Graves, 'The legal significance of the Statute of Praemunire of 1353' in *Haskins Anniversary Essays*, pp. 57–80: W. T. Waugh, 'The great Statute of Praemunire (1393)', *E.H.R.* 37 (1922), pp. 173–205.

[20] On Gregory XI's relations with Edward III see E. Perroy, *L'Angleterre et le Grand Schisme d'Occident*, ch. I, §III and §IV; and on Boniface IX's relations with Richard II and the abortive *concordat* of 1398, see ch. VIII of the same work.

strengthened the hand of the king in his dealings with the pope, and there was not much trouble over provisions in this period. After the end of the Schism, Pope Martin V made a last great effort to obtain the repeal of the offending English statutes. In 1421 his collector in England, Simon of Teramo, discoursed to the Convocation of Canterbury on the pope's need to have provision in England, and Martin believed that he had persuaded Henry V, before his death, to do away with the statutes. A series of *nuncios* were despatched to England in the next few years, to work on the king's council and the convocations, and in 1426 Martin formally forbade the bishops to collate to any benefices that were reserved to the apostolic see. Things reached a climax in the next year when Martin suspended Archbishop Chichele, whom he suspected of sympathy with the opponents of provision, from his status as legate, and refused to reinstate him unless he, with the bishops, would formally apply to parliament for the repeal of the statutes. Chichele went through the painful and embarrassing process as ordered, in the spring parliament of 1428. With the bishops, he addressed both the lords and the commons separately, warning them of the possibility of an interdict if they were refractory. He made no impression, and he probably did not expect to. Martin V had to admit failure; a few months later he reinstated Chichele as legate.[21] After this, for the remainder of our period, the vexed question of provisions remained quiescent.

The opposition to provisions secured, largely as a result of the weakness of the papacy in the period of the Great Schism, the virtual elimination, after 1400, of alien provisors from English benefices. This was of course very far from eliminating provision; Thomas Gascoigne half a century later was still fulminating against the 'disgraceful promotions of men in England who had licence . . . to sue out and accept provisions from the pope'.[22] That they still did so was largely owing to the connivance in the system of the kings of England. The crown was much less Erastian than the commons. The crown was also the real gainer both from cooperation with the papacy and from the anti-papal statutes; the two worked together to strengthen royal control over the episcopate and the composition of the higher clergy in general. Hamilton Thompson calls eloquent witness to this effect from the register of the Bishop of Hereford, Richard

---

[21] See further W. E. Lunt, *Financial Relations* vol. II, pp. 424–8; and E. F. Jacob, *Archbishop Henry Chichele* (London, 1967), pp. 47–52.

[22] T. Gascoigne, *Loci e Libro Veritatum*, p. 26.

Mayhew, who was appointed 'by apostolic authority and by the nomination of the aforesaid most illustrious prince [Henry VII]'. Mayhew's successor, Charles Booth, was like him provided to the see, but the register did not in his case even mention the apostolic authority: he was 'nominated by the said most illustrious prince [Henry VIII] to the church and bishropric of Hereford, vacant by the death of the lord Richard Mayhew of honest memory'.[23] We see here the royal supremacy in action and almost acknow-ledged, long before the calling of the Reformation Parliament.

The act of supremacy apart, the most revolutionary step in the sixteenth century reformation was the dissolution of the monas-teries. This too was foreshadowed, but much less clearly, in the late Middle Ages.

The impact, in the thirteenth century, of the order of St Francis with its claims for the special sanctity of holy poverty inevitably raised with new sharpness questions which had always been lurking about the justification for the endowments of the religious. The Statute of Mortmain, with its clear implication that no benefit to a church should justify injury to the legitimate interest of a lay overlord, was symptomatic of the altering out-look later in that century. Two events of the twenty years follow-ing its publication showed that the property of the religious was not so safe, nor held so sacred, as it had once been.

The more dramatic of these two events was the dissolution of the Order of the Templars. The charges that were brought against this rich and famous crusading order by Philip IV of France were largely unjustified, and, outside France at least, owed such confirmation as they obtained to confessions ex-tracted under torture. But Pope Clement V was too weak to make a stand against the French king, and in 1312 he dissolved the order on his apostolic authority and transferred its property to the Order of the Hospital. Though this dissolution was not in any sense to the direct profit of the secular power in England, the royal officials had to play a major part in the process by which it was achieved. The Templars' lands were in the king's hands all the time that the charges against them were being investigated, and some never found their way out of them.[24] More important than any material consequence of the dissolution was the im-pression that it made on people's minds. Langland, writing at the

[23] See Hamilton Thompson, *The English Clergy and their Organisa-tion*, pp. 36–7.
[24] See further Tout, *Chapters*, vol. II, pp. 316ff.

other end of the fourteenth century, had marked the lesson: he saw close at hand the time when others would go the same way as the Temple and for the same reason:

> Both rich and religious that rood they honour
> That on groats is engraven and on gold nobles.
> For covetousness of that cross men of Holy Church
> Shall turn as Templars did: the time approacheth fast.[25]

Langland did not expect the blow to other possessioners to come from the pope, but from the king and the lords. It is not at all surprising that he did so, especially in the light of the other event of the late thirteenth century to which we referred. In 1295, after the war had broken out between France and England, Edward I took the lands of the alien priories – those cells and priories in England that owed obedience to French monasteries, as Cluny and such Norman houses as Bec – into his own hands. The revenues were collected in each case by a royal official, who paid the proceeds into the exchequer and made the monks a bare allowance to sustain themselves. The lands were returned to their owners when the war ended, but the same thing happened again in 1324 when war with France broke out, and in 1337, and on the renewal of the Hundred Years War in 1369. As the war continued, what had begun as a temporary royal occupation began to wear an air of permanence.

The fate of the alien priories was decided in the fifteenth century. By that time many of the larger priories had solved their problem by purchasing from the crown letters of denization. Among the Cluniacs Lewes was the first to obtain this concession in 1351; Montacute was the last in 1407. Most of the non-Cluniac houses which were of sufficient size to be properly called conventual saved themselves in the same way. The case of the smaller cells, isolated properties where two or three or perhaps just one monk had resided to supervise the estates, was different. After 1369 most of them were farmed to the highest bidder, and some were sold; William of Wykeham thus obtained most of the lands of Tiron, which went to endow his colleges at Winchester and in Oxford. In 1408 the council agreed that the income from the farms of the remaining cells and priories should be earmarked toward the expenses of the royal household. Finally, by an act of 1414, the possession of all confiscated properties was taken into the king's hands, with a right of pre-emption to the existing farmers. Most of the estates in question were in the end trans-

[25] *Piers Plowman*, B Text, Passus XV, ll. 506–9.

ferred to religious and collegiate foundations; to Henry V's two
houses (for the Carthusians and Bridgettines) at Sheen and Syon;
to Henry VI's foundations at Eton and King's Cambridge; to
the charterhouse of Mount Grace and the chapel of St George
at Windsor.[26]

As Knowles and others have stressed, the suppression of the
alien priories did not directly anticipate the sixteenth-century dissolution. Most of their estates passed not into secular hands but
to religious foundations, as the wealth of the Templars had. This
was in line with the view that Archbishop Romeyn had voiced so
strongly in another context, that the endowments of the church
in England were for the sustention of religious life there, and for
no other purpose. The real hostility that the petitions of the
commons evinced with regard to the alien priories seems to have
been based rather on suspicion of aliens, who sent wealth out of
the land and probably betrayed the king's secrets to his enemies,
than on enthusiasm for dissolution. Nevertheless the treatment
of the priories showed what the lay power could do. As Professor
McKisack writes, 'in the dissolution of religious communities at
the bidding of the secular power, and not without profit to it,
the historian may discern, albeit faintly, the shape of things to
come'.[27]

Professor McKisack's words are reinforced when one looks at the
pressures for that greater measure of disendowment that Langland thought was already impending in the late fourteenth
century. The fiscal burdens of the Hundred Years War, and the
suspicion among the aristocracy and gentry that the church was
not pulling its weight in its financial contributions, brought the
subject into the open in the parliament of 1371. This parliament
witnessed a violent attack on the king's clerical ministers which
led to the dismissal of bishops Wykeham and Brantingham, the
chancellor and treasurer. Some of the lay lords apparently
wanted to go much further. It was to this end that two Austin
friars were brought into parliament, to expound and defend the
view that, in a national emergency, the prince who has given
property to churches may take it back, so as to use the revenues
for national purposes.[28] The friars argued their case with care and

[26] On the alien priories see further M. M. Morgan, 'The suppression
of the alien priories', *History* 26 (1941), pp. 204-12; and D. Knowles,
The Religious Orders in England, vol. II (Cambridge, 1955), ch. XI.

[27] M. McKisack, *The Fourteenth Century* (Oxford, 1959), p. 295.

[28] On this affair see A. Gwynn, *The English Austin Friars in the Time*

learning from the fathers of the church, but what it meant to the lords was something very radical: 'when war breaks out we must take from the endowed clergy a portion of their temporal possessions, as property that belongs to us and to the whole kingdom'.[29] This statement adds a new and startling dimension to the familiar view, rehearsed in the Statute of Provisors, that the wealth of the church endowed in England should stay where it belonged, in that kingdom.

Nothing came of the proposal of 1371, but the subject remained very much in the air for the next forty years. The events of 1371 sparked off a vigorous academic controversy, in which the Benedictines Ughtred Boldon and William Binham defended the sacrosanct nature of ecclesiastical property, while Wyclif came to the defence of the Austin friars and restated their case at greater length and with new ramifications. By 1381 these arguments were striking an echo at the popular level, as we see from the demand of the peasant rebels that 'the goods of Holy Church should not remain in the hands of the religious, nor of the parsons and vicars, and other churchmen; but those who are in possession should have their sustenance from the endowment and the remainder of their goods should be divided among the parishioners'.[30] It was only a few years before this that Langland had prophesied that possessioners would soon see 'Constantine's coffers' (as he called their endowments) broken open. Most alarming of all to churchmen (outside the crisis of 1381) was the extent to which talk of disendowment found sympathy among the higher ranks of the laity. Both in 1378 and in 1385 it was feared that proposals would again be aired in parliament; in the latter year laymen were already talking about what they should get for themselves, Walsingham says.[31] In 1410 a petition demanding a measure of disendowment was actually brought forward in parliament. We do not know precisely what was asked; but we do know that some of those concerned in presenting it had been looking at a Lollard tract whose proposals were very striking. 'Our lord the king may have of the temporalities by bishops, abbots and priors occupied and wasted proudly within

---

of *Wyclif* (Oxford, 1940), pp. 212–16. The articles put forward by the Friars are printed by V. H. Galbraith in *E.H.R.* 34 (1919), pp. 579–82.

[29] Wyclif, *De Civili Dominio* vol. II (Wyclif Soc., 1900), p. 7.

[30] *Anonimalle Chronicle*, ed. V. H. Galbraith (Manchester, 1927), p. 147.

[31] T. Walsingham, *Historia Anglicana* vol. II (R.S.), p. 140.

the realm, fifteen earls, 1500 knights, 6200 squires and 100 houses of alms more than he hath at this time.'[32] There would be enough besides, the Lollard author estimated, to endow five new universities!

One should of course be chary of paying too much attention to tracts written by Lollards, who at their strongest were a sectarian minority. The association of plans for disendowment with Lollardy in fact went far to discredit the whole idea, especially after Oldcastle's revolt in 1414 had shown that it was not clerical property holders only that it threatened. This was the main reason why so much less was heard of disendowment in the fifteenth century than in the fourteenth. It is hard to gauge how dangerous the threat to the possessioner really was before Oldcastle; probably the Benedictines exaggerated it. But they were not the only ones who did so; there were also the men like Langland who foresaw something very like a dissolution in the proximate future. Ideas that would be familiar in the sixteenth century were in the air for a time at least, and at a moment when the lay farmers of the property of alien priories were in a very good position to imagine what advantage to their class could accrue from a major measure of disendowment.

Again and again in this chapter we have come across the same phenomenon, the growing authority of the king in the English church. It was to the king that patrons looked to protect their rights against papal provisors, and to the king that the popes looked to moderate the effect of parliament's anti-papal legislation. The king licensed the denization of the alien priories that were conventual, and organized the distribution of the properties of those that were not. It was to the king that the clergy appealed to protect the property of the church from Lollards and the privileges of convocation from parliaments. This is what we meant when we said at the beginning of this chapter that the fourteenth and fifteenth centuries witnessed the growth, by gradual degrees, of an effective royal supremacy in the English church.

The king, however, could not have withstood papal claims, in the matters of taxation and provision, or have laid hands on the property of the priories, if he had not known that he could rely on the full backing of the lay lords and commons in parliament.

[32] See *The St Alban's Chronicle*, ed. V. H. Galbraith (Oxford, 1937), pp. 52–5; and H. B. Workman, *John Wyclif*, vol. II (Oxford, 1926), pp. 397–9 and Appendix Z.

The kings took advantage of the groundswell of popular feeling in the background, anti-alien, anti-papal, and anti-clerical; they did not create it. If the English church was becoming recognizably a national church in the centuries before the reformation, it was because the people at large (without much precision in their ideas) wished it to do so, rather than as a result of conscious and premeditated royal policy.

This raises an important question. If we accept that anti-clerical feeling was a crucial factor in the history of relations between church and state in this period, then we are bound to ask how far its prevalence was justified by genuinely unsatisfactory conditions of contemporary ecclesiastical life. That it was prevalent, sometimes seemingly almost universal, we can judge not just from parliamentary petitions, but from a great *corpus* of anti-clerical satire and invective, both Latin and vernacular. There is no doubt about the cloud of testimony: Chaucer, Langland, Wyclif and Gascoigne are only the most famous names in the army of critics. But do they tell more than the truth?

Let us start at the top level of the hierarchy, and look at the episcopate. No one can deny that the English bishops of the later Middle Ages were, taken by and large, an impressive body of men.[33] They were drawn from all walks of the clerical and the social world; from the professional administrators both of church and state, from the universities, from the religious orders; from among the cadets of noble houses and from the humble ranks of the middle and poorer classes. There was a steady rise, over our period, in the number of graduates among their number. Of these who owed their position to high birth or to the service of the crown, most showed themselves to be thoroughly fitted for their office both by their energy and their ability; one might instance Courtenay and Arundel among the aristocrats, and Wykeham, Chichele and Morton among the civil servants. Their registers reveal them as careful and conscientious ecclesiastical administrators. Many devoted their surplus revenue to enlarging and beautifying their cathedrals, to the support of poor scholars, and to the endowment of new foundations, some of which, like Wykeham's twin colleges of St Mary at Oxford and Winchester, were to have a long and important future.

[33] For what follows, and throughout the rest of this chapter, I have relied heavily on Hamilton Thompson. *The English Clergy and their Organisation*, a quite outstanding study. The bishops are discussed in ch. I and II.

Nevertheless there were things amiss. Too many bishops were absent from their sees for too long. They had duties elsewhere, attendance at parliaments and convocations; many were directly involved in royal administration. This did not, probably, much impair the day-to-day running of their dioceses. The diocesan administrative system in England was so developed that it could operate with complete efficiency in the bishop's absence. Suffragans, Irish bishops or mendicants with a see *in partibus infidelium*, could almost always be found to discharge such necessary episcopal functions as confirmations and ordinations. The bishop's vicar general in spirituals acted administratively and judicially as his deputy, with wide powers; he could take the oath of obedience to the bishop from incumbents, summon and hold diocesan synods, examine candidates for the priesthood. In the consistory court the bishop's official (often the same man as the vicar general) presided. The archdeacons in their jurisdictions carried out most of the routine administrative work and saw that sinners, when they were found, were fined. When, as often happened, the archdeacon was an absentee, his duties were usually discharged by one of the rural deans. The bishops' registers attest that most dioceses were run equally well by these people, whether the bishop was there or not.

What was too often lost by his absence was not efficiency but a sense of direction. As Langland put it:

> Every bishop that beareth the cross by that he is held
> Through his province to pass and to his people show him:
> Tell them and teach them on the Trinity to believe,
> And feed them with spiritual food and needy folk to help.[34]

Day-to-day business ran smoothly, most of the time, in the late medieval diocese, but the lack of spiritual leadership from the top was felt. It was reflected in very uneven standards among the diocesan clergy.

Chaucer was kinder to the parson, among the clergy of the prologue to the *Canterbury Tales*, than to any other. There were many incumbents who resided in their parishes and discharged their duties as this parson did, no doubt, but we cannot claim that they were the rule. Lack of diocesan supervision was only one reason for this, and probably not the most important. The prevailing attitude to benefices (the freehold of a church that carried with it the greater tithe) was not healthy; they were too often regarded as a kind of property. There were great pluralists,

[34] *Piers Plowman*, B Text, Passus XV, ll. 560–4.

like Bogo de Clare and William of Wykeham in his early days, who drew a princely income from a multitude of benefices, including too many with cure of souls. Some rectories were attached to prebendal stalls in cathedral and collegiate churches; a great many were appropriated to monastic houses. In other cases livings helped to support clerks in the king's household or that of some aristocrat, or scholars at the universities; these men seldom had trouble in obtaining licences for non-residence. In these circumstances the greater tithe, the main revenue of the parish church, went to support the prebend or the monastery, the clerk or the scholar or the pluralist; the parish duties were discharged by a vicar on an often exiguous stipend. In effect, the income of benefices was being widely, almost systematically, exploited for purposes other than those for which they had been intended. The consequence of this was a low standard of literacy and life among the clergy who actually served parishes, their insufficient remuneration and perennial discontent.

There was no ready remedy for this condition of things. For a number of reasons, in the late Middle Ages it seemed to be growing worse rather than better. There was a steady increase in the number of churches appropriated to monasteries, as these found their revenues from estates diminishing in unfavourable economic circumstances. Literacy and bureaucracy, spreading hand in hand, increased the demand for clerical talent in the royal and aristocratic administrative services. A new factor was the growing number of chantry priests, who for a small stipend sang masses at a separate altar in the parish church, or in a collegiate church, or in a private chapel. Their life was easier than that of a parish vicar, and often financially more secure. The vision, which the heretic Wyclif and the orthodox Gascoigne shared, of a highly trained, resident parish clergy who could offer the intelligent among the laity a sound exposition of doctrine, was an impossible dream in the conditions of the time. Life as a vicar was too hard to attract men of talent; and too many vested interests stood in the way of rerouting parochial revenues to their original and proper purposes.

For the monasteries, the later Middle Ages were a difficult time.[35] The rise of the mendicant orders offered a rival vocation to theirs,

[35] On the monasteries see further the authoritative study of D. Knowles, *The Religious Orders in England*, vols I and II (Cambridge, 1947, 1955), and Hamilton Thompson, *The English Clergy and their Organisation*, ch. VI.

and with the rise of grammar schools and universities they ceased to play an important role in education. The Great Schism severed the connexion of the Cistercian monasteries with the general chapter of Citeaux (which was in the Avignon obedience) and a decline of standards and discipline followed. The Black Monks also suffered from the effects of the Schism, but less seriously; their real trouble was that they were being swept out of the main stream of religious life. Chaucer's picture of the monk is of a man often away from his cloister, richly dressed, who loved to dine off a fat swan and whose passion was the chase, nearer a celibate squire than a professed religious.

The records of the visitations of monasteries confirm Chaucer's picture and sometimes heighten it. There was too much comfort. Monks often had their own servants and in some houses had their own rooms and did not even take their meals together. There was often a good deal of drinking after compline. When Bishop Alnwick visited Bardney in 1438 he found that Brother Thomas Barton was accused of adultery with a washerwoman; that Brother Richard Partney had goods of his own and played dice; and that Brother John Hole had excused himself from his course in the saying of mass. Most of the brethren had been haunting taverns in the town.[36] This was a bad case but it was not atypical. The canons of Dorchester in 1441, we are told, were wont to sit down after compline, call for good ale and settle down to chess.[37] At Peterborough 'religion was almost perishing', what with the incompetence of the abbot and the simplicity of the prior. A great many houses were in financial difficulties owing to mismanagement. As Hamilton Thompson wrote, 'the English monasteries in the fifteenth century needed spiritual quickening to justify their existence as a whole'.[38]

Not that the old vigour of the monasteries was entirely gone. In the late fourteenth century they contributed some notable leaders of the life of the church: scholars, like Ughtred Boldon; in Bishop Brunton of Rochester one of the greatest preachers of the age; in Thomas de la Mare, Abbot of St Albans, a leader of monks who was both an able administrator and an example of spiritual austerity. There was besides, we should note, a fairly steady rise in the number of monastic vocations from the time of

[36] See *Visitations of Religious Houses in the Diocese of Lincoln* vol. II, ed. A. Hamilton Thompson (Lincoln Record Soc., 1918), p. 11.

[37] See Knowles, *The Religious Orders in England* vol. II, p. 211.

[38] Hamilton Thompson, *The English Clergy and their Organisation*, p. 177.

the Black Death right through to the reign of Henry VII. One order, moreover, the austere and recluse Carthusians, flourished in this last medieval age more than it ever had before. There were seven new foundations between 1370 and 1420. The most famous were the London Charterhouse, of which Sir Walter Manny, courtier and Garter knight, was an early benefactor, and Henry V's magnificent royal foundation at Sheen. The de la Poles were the chief patrons of the Charterhouse at Hull; Thomas Holland, Richard II's nephew, of Mount Grace in the Cleveland Hills. There was still, it is clear, some confidence in the value of the professed religious life, and especially in the upper ranks of society.

Of the whole clerical body, the friars were undoubtedly the most sharply impugned by the critics. 'A good friar is as rare as the phoenix', Wyclif wrote. Chaucer's friar knew the taverns of the town and the houses of the genteel better than the hospitals, and could coax her last mite out of a widow. Langland scorned friars as fat with begging and for their easy confessions. Once, he admitted, he had seen Charity in a friar's coat, 'But that was far off in St Francis' time'.[39] Earlier Archbishop Fitzralph of Armagh the great Oxford scholar and Irish metropolitan, had treated the whole structure of mendicant religion to a terrible trouncing in his *De Pauperie Salvatoris*; Langland and Wyclif are full of echoes of his denunciation.

It was natural that the friars should attract hostile attention. Beggars and scroungers are seldom loved, especially when they prosper, as the friars did. Because their orders were not enclosed and they wandered at large in the world, their backslidings were seen at large. There were too many friars, too many vocations, almost certainly, that proved hollow. Their competition with the parish clergy for the hearing of confessions and for burial fees aroused resentment in one ecclesiastical quarter, their independence of diocesans in another (this was what specially roused the anger of Archbishop Fitzralph). To severe moralists it looked often as if their ministrations, which had to be gentle to catch a clientele, were unhinging Christian discipline rather than re-vivifying the faith.

[39] *Piers Plowman*, B Text, Passus XV, 1. 226. On the friars in this period see Knowles, *The Religious Orders in England*, vols. I and II; A. G. Little, *Studies in English Franciscan History* (Manchester, 1917); J. R. H. Moorman, *The Grey Friars in Cambridge*; Gwynn, *The English Austin Friars*.

The view of the friars' critics was not the whole truth, how-ever. They made a powerful contribution to the religious life of the fourteenth and fifteenth centuries. Duns Scotus and Ockham, the two greatest English scholastic philosophers of the whole Middle Ages, were Franciscans. It was the mendicants who took the lead in answering Wyclif's academic challenge to catholic orthodoxy. The friars were also the greatest preachers of the age, and the impact of their sermons is well attested by the popularity of such books as the *Summa Praedicantium* of the great Dominican, John Bromyard. Bromyard's homely anecdotes, drawn from everyday scenes of life to illustrate a profound moral teaching, had an impact that the exposition of sound doctrine, which learned seculars like Reginald Pecock and Thomas Gascoigne regarded as a first priority, could never have had.[40] The bequests to the mendicant orders from all sorts of people, which recur over and again in late medieval English wills, show how their words went home; and that their intercession was prized, often more highly than that of any other religious, in the very age when Chaucer and Langland were denouncing them.

Taking the lights and shades together, the picture that we are forming of the clerical life and standards in the late Middle Ages is certainly not a happy one; and the facts go a long way to explain the strong anti-clerical tenor of popular feeling. But we have not yet applied with any rigour the yardstick which is probably the most important measure of the value that men set on the life of their church: endowment. By this standard the fourteenth and fifteenth centuries did as well as most in the Middle Ages. True, apart from the Carthusians, the monasteries were not attracting patrons in the way that they once had. This, however, was because the foundation of collegiate churches, served by the secular clergy, and of chantries now took pride of place. Of the former an excellent example was the church at Higham Ferrers, founded in 1422 by Archbishop Chichele, for a community of eight chaplains, eight clerks and six choristers, who would pray daily for the lives and souls of King Henry V, Queen Catherine, the founder and all Christian people. There was annexed to the church a grammar school and a bede-house for old people.[41] Edward Duke of York's great college at Fother-

[40] On Bromyard's preaching technique see G. R. Owst, *Literature and Pulpit in Medieval England* (Cambridge, 1933), pp. 24ff.

[41] On Higham Ferrers see Jacob, *Archbishop Henry Chichele*, pp. 87–90.

inghay and Lord Cromwell's at Tattershall were on very similar lines. Tattershall, like Higham Ferrers, had a grammar school attached. This should remind us, as should also the history of the foundations of colleges in Oxford and Cambridge, that this was a key period in the history of education, and one in which the church played, as it had traditionally, the leading role.

Chantry endowments, which supported a chaplain to sing mass either at an altar in a church or in a separate chapel, were also multiplying throughout our period. In the parish church of Newark-on-Trent alone there were no less than fifteen perpetual chantries at the end of the fifteenth century, each with its own chaplain.[42] Most of these Newark chantries were endowed by gilds. Wealthy associations of townsmen, such as the gilds were, were great founders of chantries, but private benefactors were no less generous. Both gilds (as that of St Lawrence, at Ashburton in Devon) and individual patrons on occasion made provision for a chantry priest also to teach a grammar school. In social and spiritual service to the community, the church did not lag, and nor did its patrons.

No one, in fact, who knows the parish churches of England, and their buildings, wall paintings, tombs and glass which date from the last two medieval centuries, can doubt that the church remained at the very centre of communal life. The men who attacked the pope's right of provision, jeered at the friars, and questioned the monks' title to their lands, were proud of their English church and ready to dedicate their goods to its well being. The anger of Langland and the gentler satire of Chaucer are not symptoms of declining religious fervour; they are symptoms of the universal concern for religion, for the church, and for her standards.

[42] On the Newark charities see Hamilton Thompson, *The English Clergy and their Organisation,* p. 134 and note.

10

Mysticism and Lollardy

Lollardy, at the end of the fourteenth century, brought the English medieval church face to face with the problem of a popular heresy for the first time. The Lollards were, or were claimed to be, followers of the doctrines of the great Oxford philosopher, John Wyclif. If one is to understand his career, and the significance of the teaching that he fostered, one must know a little about two things: about the contemporary climate of popular religion, and about English scholastic learning.

The tone of religion in fourteenth-century England was, by comparison with that of the preceding age, anti-sacerdotal and private. As we have seen, it was not a happy period for the established religious orders. The most respected among them were the austere and withdrawn Carthusians, who cultivated the solitary life. We hear much in the period of individual hermits and anchorites, as the recluse at Westminster and the monk solitary of Farne. The construction of chapels by great laymen in their own houses, and the popularity of the privilege of employing one's own confessor remind us of a new emphasis among laymen upon private devotions. The growth of a conscious, articulate and puritanical moral fervour among the laity was another marked feature of the age. This was partly the fruit of the great preaching and pastoral efforts of the friars. It also owed much to the spread of literacy and the increasing use of the vernacular, which brought the laity into closer contact with gospel authority. The great body of religious literature in the vernacular is perhaps the most impressive evidence of English spirituality in the fourteenth century.

Two aspects of this literature deserve special emphasis. One is its mystical bent, which we shall examine presently; the other is the popularity of sermons, whose prevailing tone was moral and puritanical. The sins of the rich, the idle and the luxurious, lay and clerical alike, were castigated with an eloquence firmly founded in Holy Writ.[1] This was how the great Dominican preacher John Bromyard pictured the strong and wealthy of the world after they had passed from it:

> Their soul shall have instead of the palace and hall and chamber the deep lake of hell, with those that go down to the depth thereof. In place of scented baths the body shall have a narrow pit in the earth . . . instead of wives they shall have toads, instead of a great retinue and throng of followers, their bodies shall have a throng of worms and their souls a throng of demons. Instead of a large domain they shall have an eternal prison house, cramped for both body and soul.[2]

This sort of denunciation was typical. It was not of course the rich only that the preachers flayed with hot words; the terrors of hell were being prepared for all, high and low alike, who would not amend. Hence the parallel emphasis in the sermons on the things necessary for salvation, an understanding of the scriptures, of the Creed, and of God's commandments. To men eager for knowledge of the faith in which they walked the preachers pointed a hard way to salvation:

> As a child willing to be a clerk beginneth at the ground, that is A.B.C., so he who thus desires to speed the better beginneth at the ground of health, that is the Christian man's belief [i.e. the Creed] . . . for thus it behoves to climb up as it were by a ladder of divers rungs, from the ground of belief into the keeping of God's commandments, and so up from virtue to virtue, till he see the God of Sion reigning in everlasting bliss.[3]

'If I had gold enough I would give every day a noble to have every day a sermon, for Thy word is worth more to me than all the world,'[4] exclaimed Margery Kempe, the burgess's wife turned visionary from fifteenth-century Lynn. There can be no doubt about the way in which the sermons and the literature that they inspired reached right down among the people. The homilists' pictures of Bible scenes and of the day of doom were

---

[1] On homilectic literature see G. R. Owst's two important books: *Preaching in Medieval England* (Cambridge, 1926), and *Literature and Pulpit in Medieval England* (Cambridge, 1933).

[2] Quoted and translated by Owst, *Literature and Pulpit*, pp. 293–4.

[3] *Pore Caitiff*, quoted by W. A. Pantin *The English Church in the Fourteenth Century* (Cambridge, 1955), p. 249.

[4] *The Book of Margery Kempe*, ed. W. Butler Bowdon (London, 1936), p. 214.

the basic source for popular dramas such as the miracle and mystery plays. The propaganda letters which circulated at the time of the Peasants' Revolt were full of saws drawn from sermons. It is a striking, but not in the light of the sermons surprising, fact that it is in the fourteenth century that we first come across religious treatises written by laymen. The most famous is the *Livre des Seyntz Medicines* written by Henry Duke of Lancaster about 1354: an allegory treating of the wounds that sin inflicts upon the soul, composed by one whose sense of his own moral backsliding was clearly vivid. The honour of being the first layman to write a homily in English seems to belong to Sir John Clanvowe, a knight of Richard II's chamber and one who was, interestingly enough, rumoured to be a Lollard. It is a stern, austere tract about the quest for the narrow way, in walking which a man may free himself of the 'foul stinking muck of this false fleeting world'.[5] In new conditions of wider literacy and armed with the weapon of the vernacular, laymen showed that they could now assume the homilectic mantle of the clerk.

Of all the works on which the influence of the homilists has left its imprint, the greatest is the *Vision of Piers Plowman*. It was written by an obscure, probably unbeneficed priest of the western midlands, William Langland. Its very structure, the personification in familiar contemporary dress of virtues, vices, and the qualities of the soul, reveals its deep roots in the sermon literature of the age. Because of the wonderful series of vignettes of contemporary life that it affords, it has most often attracted the attentions of social historians. But Langland's social gospel was essentially simple and scriptural:

> Such work to work, while we been here
> That after our death day Do-well rehearse
> At the day of Doom we did as he highte [i.e. commanded].[6]

Langland's eye was on the next world rather than this; and his way to salvation led by the familiar steps of sustained moral endeavour, knowledge of the faith, and keeping of God's commandments – 'all that the Book bids'. There is no message here that the homilists had not laboured a thousand times. What sets

---

[5] V. J. Scattergood, 'The two ways – an unpublished religious treatise by Sir John Clanvowe', *English Philological Studies* 10 (1967), p. 45. Scattergood here prints the whole of this very interesting treatise with a brief introduction (pp. 33–56).

[6] *Piers Plowman*, B Text, Passus VII, ll. 198–200.

Langland apart is his instant sense of Christ's redeeming love, and his flashes of poetic religious insight:

> And if Grace grant thee to go in this wise,
> Thou shalt see in thyself Truth sit in thy heart:
> In a chain of charity as thou a child were,
> To suffer him and say naught against thy sire's will.[7]

The message of the mystics was not the same as that of the homilists, but they should not be set too far apart from one another. The mystical writers take as read the groundwork of knowledge of the faith and the commandments which are the sermons' recurrent themes. What they do is to add something more, and something which, as the circulation of their works among the clergy and devout lay people shows, had a profound impact on the religious life of the age.[8]

The teaching of the mystics can best be illustrated through the works of four people: Richard Rolle, the Yorkshire hermit (d. 1349); the anonymous author of the *Cloud of Unknowing* (c. 1350); Walter Hilton, an Augustinian canon of Thurgarton in Nottinghamshire; and Dame Julian of Norwich (1343–c. 1420). All four, in differing ways, were concerned with the same matter, the mystic's experience of union with God in contemplation. This is an experience which, by definition, man cannot reach by reason or works, or hope to understand: to pierce the 'cloud of unknowing' that separates God from man is God given, an ecstasy vouchsafed only to His chosen ones. But those who have known it can point the way, through prayer and meditation and forgetting of the world. Both the author of the *Cloud* and Hilton were steeped in the *Mystica Theologica* of Dionysius, a Syrian monk of the sixth century, which was the basis of most mystical teaching in the western Middle Ages; the author of the *Cloud* translated it into English as *Deonis Hid Divinitie*. Rolle and Dame Julian were independent of this tradition. The former found his own way through reading and meditation: 'In searching the scriptures I have found that the highest love of Christ consists in three things: fire, song, and sweetness.'[9] Dame Julian's experience came by direct revelation, when she was sick, as she

[7] ibid. Passus V, ll. 614–17.

[8] On the mystics see D. Knowles, *The English Mystical Tradition* (London, 1961). In what I have written here, I have relied very heavily on this inspiring book.

[9] *The Incendium Amoris of Richard Rolle of Hampole*, ed. M. Deanesly (Manchester, 1915), pp. 184–5.

thought, to death, and saw the crucifix that the priest held before her changed: 'I saw the blood trickling down under the crown of thorns hot and fresh and right plenteously . . . like to the drops of water that fall off the eaves of a house after a great shower of rain.'[10]

Common to all four writers is their concern with a direct experience. Rolle, the *Cloud* and Hilton all discuss exercises preparatory to this experience, and two aspects of their instruction are striking. One is the private and personal nature of the devotions that they describe. The author of the *Cloud* and Hilton in his *Scale of Perfection*, his most famous work, were both writing for individual disciples. There is no sense, of course, in which their works are anti-sacerdotal, but they are not concerned with priestly mediation, only with the direct approach of the individual soul to God. Secondly, one is struck by their anti-intellectual bias. This is important because it is a reminder that the road to mystical experience is one that all may tread, not a private path for the priest and the learned. The monk solitary of Farne was the contemplative who, perhaps, put this point most eloquently: 'Let the meek hear and rejoice, that there is a certain knowledge of Holy Scripture which is learnt from the Holy Ghost and manifested in good works, that the fisherman knows and not the rhetorician, that the old woman has learned and not the doctor of theology.'[11]

The mystical bent of fourteenth-century religion was evinced in many ways, but most clearly of all in a new emphasis on the humanity of Christ. Behind this we can discern a widespread desire to find room, in the everyday life of the Christian, for direct contact with God. We find this emphasis in Langland, in his glimpse of Jesus going to joust in Jerusalem in Piers Plowman's arms: 'In his helm and his hauberk *humana natura*'.[12] We find it in Henry of Lancaster, the soldier with the rough experience of war setting his mind on 'the precious flesh, which was bound by its nature to shiver and shrink from this hard passion', and on the body on the cross 'with the heart split open and the blood all warm'.[13] Margery Kemp, when on her pilgrimage to

[10] Juliana of Norwich, *Revelations of Divine Love*, ed. G. Warrack (London, 1901), pp. 8, 16 (quoted by D. Knowles, *The English Mystical Tradition*, p. 122).

[11] W. A. Pantin, 'The monk solitary of Farne, a fourteenth century English mystic', *E.H.R.* 59 (1944), p. 178.

[12] *Piers Plowman*, B Text, Passus XVIII, l. 23.

[13] Henry of Lancaster, *Le Livre de Seyntz Medicines*, ed. E. J.

Jerusalem she was shown the place where Jesus had suffered, 'wept and sobbed as plenteously as though she had seen Our Lord with her bodily eye. suffering his passion at that time. Before her in her soul she saw him verily in contemplation and that caused her to have compassion.'[14] In the round of the church's year this emphasis on Christ's humanity found expression in a new importance attached to the feast of Corpus Christi; in its rituals in the anxiety of the laity to see at the mass the elevated host, the true body of Christ under the likeness of bread.

There are reminders here of just how much Wyclif, the heretic who stepped out of the trodden way, was in religion the child of his age. He too longed to bring men face to face with the incarnate Christ, 'our true brother, a man with the rest of us'.[15] In another age, moreover, one less obsessed by the sacrament of the altar, he might not have found it so hard to dodge his conviction of the error of the church's eucharistic teaching, which was in the eyes of his opponents his central heresy.

John Wyclif was first and foremost a don, a figure of the schools in the Oxford that he loved. Oxford, when he came to her in the 1350s, was a university a hundred and fifty years old, an established and famous centre of European learning. Cambridge was a little younger. It was a great period for the endowment of colleges in both universities: at Oxford Queen's, Oriel, Exeter and New College were all founded in the fourteenth century, and at Cambridge Clare, Corpus and Pembroke. The colleges, with their endowed fellowships, were the home of a privileged *élite* among scholars. The majority of students (there were something like 1200 at Oxford at the beginning of the century) lived not in colleges but in private halls and inns under principals approved by the university, or in lodgings. The friars lived in their own convents, and the monks maintained halls of their own. Life was easier for the professed religious than for the secular clerks, who in order to maintain themselves had to find a patron – or a benefice. As a consequence of shortage of cash, most students proceeded no further than the degree in arts (compulsory as a prelude to higher studies for all except the friars, who read arts in their own *studia*, a privilege which others

Arnould (Oxford, 1940), pp. 163, 195. Both passages are translated by A. R. Myers in *English Historical Documents 1327–1485* (London, 1969), p. 813.

[14] *The Book of Margery Kempe*, p. 107.

[15] Wyclif, *De Benedicta Incarnacione* (Wyclif Soc., 1886), pp. 28, 85.

resented). Both universities were largely self-governing bodies: at Oxford the chancellor was elected from among the doctors of law and theology by the congregations of masters of arts, the ruling assembly of the university. The archbishops of Canterbury claimed a right of visitation, which was resented and at Oxford contested; but before the controversy over Wyclif's teaching arose it had not been used for a long time. To all intents the universities were independent administratively, and this independence was reflected in the freedom of academic speculation in their schools.[16]

The artists and theologians were the men principally concerned in the great scholastic debates of the fourteenth century. Earlier, both Aquinas and Scotus had endeavoured in their teaching to hold together the two disciplines of philosophy and theology, to show reason and faith, philosophy and religion, working in harmony. In the fourteenth century the teachers in their tradition were faced with the challenge of the philosophy of the Franciscan, William of Ockham. Human knowledge, as Ockham saw it, was limited to what the intellect could apprehend, in the last resort through experience. There could therefore be no knowledge of the reality, outside the mind, of universal concepts, no means by which men could, in the strict sense, *know* God's ways and will or the workings of his grace. His will, unlimited and unknowable, Ockham concluded, must be absolutely free, in a manner beyond human comprehension. For this reason Ockham as a theologian concentrated on the human will and act, viewed in a context almost completely independent of the operation of divine grace.[17] Ockham's supremacy as a logician won him a great following in the schools, both in Oxford and Paris. But teaching which set so far apart the worlds of faith and reason, and which seemed to imply that human action could condition grace, was bound to evoke a counter-challenge.

[16] On all that concerns the history and development of the English universities see H. Rashdall, *The Universities of Europe in the Middle Ages*, ed. F. M. Powicke and A. B. Emden (Oxford, 1936), vol. III.

[17] For an introduction to Ockham's logical work see P. Boehner's two works, *Ockham: Philosophical Writings* (selected passages, with an introduction, London 1957), and *Medieval Logic* (Manchester, 1952). For a short and illuminating account of Ockham's views on grace and human merit see G. Leff, *Bradwardine and the Pelagians* (Cambridge, 1957), pp. 188–210. See also on Ockham E. F. Jacob, 'Ockham as a political thinker, in his *Essays in the Conciliar Epoch* (3rd ed. Manchester, 1963), pp. 85–105.

In the long run it was the disciples of Scotus, the most 'subtle' of all the doctors who had emphasized the divine will as the cause of all things, who made the best attempt at an answer to Ockham. Scotus was very widely read in Oxford in the fifteenth century. Earlier opponents of the Ockhamites, in particular Thomas Bradwardine, had stressed not God's will but his knowledge which, embracing all things, past, present and future, determined them.[18] Bradwardine thus rescued the operation of grace from the semi-Pelagianism of Ockham; and he also reinstated the knowledge of the 'universal', because for him all knowledge was derivative from God's omniscient knowledge. The price of this new position was a rigid predestinarianism; God had to know, from before the beginning, who were the elect. The father of the church to whom Bradwardine owed most was Augustine, who was also a strong predestinarian. The most important thinker who was directly influenced by his *De Causa Dei* was John Wyclif.[19]

In his very early years at Oxford Wyclif was apparently attracted by the teaching of Ockham; later he became the leader of the out and out opponents of the Franciscan's teaching on both knowledge and free will. His thought, like Bradwardine's, had its roots in Augustine. His other great debt was to the famous English master of the thirteenth century, Robert Grosseteste. Grosseteste's was a principal influence on his ideas on cognition. God's knowledge was for Wyclif the very foundation of existence; universals exist, he taught, not in the mind of man, but in the mind of God. God is not beyond knowledge, he is the source of all knowledge. God's reason and his will are not therefore beyond human comprehension. Wyclif, in rejecting experience of the singular as the key to human knowledge, advanced a theory of cognition that was avowedly Platonist; he did not reject Aristotle, the master of the logic *par excellence* to the Middle Ages, but he

[18] On Bradwardine see G. Leff, *Bradwardine and the Pelagians*, note 17.

[19] Wyclif, both as a thinker and a would-be reformer, has attracted much attention from religious historians (especially protestant historians of the nineteenth century), and some estimates of him have been far from sound. The most important modern works on him seem to me to be H. B. Workman, *John Wyclif*, 2 vols (Oxford, 1926); K. B. McFarlane, *John Wycliffe and the Beginnings of English Nonconformity* (London, 1952) – perhaps a rather too unsympathetic assessment; J. A. Robson, *Wyclif and the Oxford Schools* (Cambridge, 1961). Perhaps the best rounded view is that given by G. Leff, *Heresy in the Later Middle Ages*, vol. II (Manchester, 1967), ch. VII and VIII.

regarded his 'logic' as inferior to that of Augustine, which was founded in Plato. His new Platonist 'logic' won him a tremendous *éclat* in the Oxford schools, and he was early acknowledged as among her most renowned masters in the arts faculty.

When Wyclif proceeded from arts to incept in theology in the early 1370s, he had two principal duties in his new faculty: to lecture on the *Sentences* of Peter Lombard (the textbook of the theologian) and on the Bible. From the first he was determined to apply his philosophical system to the exposition of Christian doctrine and of Scripture. Here the implications of his metaphysics were far reaching indeed. His rigid predestinarianism coloured his concept of the church, which he elaborated in his *De Ecclesia*: the true church was not the church of priests but the body of God's elect, and those who were not elect, the 'foreknown' to damnation, were not part of it. It also led him to question the priestly powers to absolve, to impose penances and to excommunicate; the relation of individual souls with God was for him direct, beyond the control of any human agent. Predestinarianism further gave a special slant to the ideas on lordship which he took over, almost bodily, from Archbishop Fitzralph of Armagh, and which he expounded in his *De Dominio Divino* and his *De Civili Dominio*. True lordship, Fitzralph had taught, is founded in grace: therefore, Wyclif concluded, only the elect (who by definition are alone in grace) can enjoy true lordship. Lordship among men he regarded as the product of accidents of secular history (his biblical studies had taught him a sound historical insight). The temporal power of the popes, founded on the Donation of Constantine, had therefore no religious significance. If the Khan of the Tartars were to become lord of the world and make the Bishop of Cambalek in Cathay his universal patriarch, his grant would have an exactly parallel validity with Constantine's.[20] Following this lead, Wyclif turned to the Bible: the word pope was not used therein, he pointed out. The pope was a man; he might not be one of the elect, but of those predestined to damnation. There was nothing sacred about his lordship, or about the temporal endowment of any church; their origins were human. Human lordship was quite different from the 'evangelical' lordship of the elect who live in conformity with scripture's commands, which was the only true lordship for Wyclif.[21] Wyclif did not make very clear what he meant by this

[20] Wyclif, *De Potestate Papae* (Wyclif Soc., 1908), pp. 215–16 (where he is following Fitzralph).

[21] Wyclif, *De Civili Dominio*, Lib. I, ch. III, XIV.

'evangelical' lordship; he seems, though, to intend the right of the just to the use, in common, of what God has provided for men in the way of goods in this world – something very different. from property in any ordinary sense. The implications of such teaching were radical indeed.

In the theology schools, Wyclif made Scripture his special mastery. He was the first English academic since Stephen Langton to comment in his lectures on the whole of the Bible.[22] Here his philosophical system led him to take a rather peculiar view. Scripture was the foundation of faith, the truths in it were God given: therefore, Wyclif argued, they must be truths pure and timeless, known to God eternally. The Bible was more to Wyclif than words upon parchment. It was eternal truth, the will and testament of God the Father, containing in it all that was necessary to salvation. This conclusion led Wyclif, by the time he wrote his *De Veritate Sacrae Scripturae* (*c.* 1378), virtually to reverse the original relation in his thought of Platonist metaphysic to Holy Writ. The Bible, mirror of eternal truth, became the very centre of his theory of cognition now, the source of all genuine human knowledge; the logic of Holy Scripture was the only and all sufficient logic, he claimed, the rest mere sophistry. It was because of their plain conformity to Scripture that the 'logic' of the Neoplatonist Augustine and of Plato himself was superior to all other philosophy.

All the ills of contemporary Christianity now stood clearly revealed to Wyclif as attributable to a failure to grasp this central truth. Mahomet had taken the Bible and overlaid it with a veneer of human interpretation, which served mainly his own carnal ends, especially his greed for human lordship. In Christendom 'western Mahomets', the popes with their decretals and Ockham's disciples with their confidence in the human intellect, had done the same. The only hope for the future was 'evangelical reform', a return to the way of the Holy Book in its simplicity, stripped of all accretion. This was why Wyclif was insistent that the Bible

[22] That Wyclif commented on the whole of the Bible was first demonstrated by B. Smalley, 'John Wyclif's Postilla super Totam Bibliam', *Bodleian Library Record* 4 (1953), pp. 186–205. Smalley's studies of Wyclif's views on Scripture seem to me to contain the most perceptive and illuminating discussion of this aspect of Wyclif's thought that is in print; see 'The Bible and eternity: John Wyclif's dilemma', *Journal of the Warburg and Courtauld Institutes* 27 (1964), pp. 73–89; and 'Wyclif's *Postilla* on the Old Testament and his Principium' in *Essays Presented to D. Callus* (Oxford, 1964), pp. 253–96.

must be translated into their mother tongue for laymen, and expounded to them in sermons by a learned priesthood. Since it had been the pope's church that sent the Bible along the path of the cross as a martyr by the promulgation of its 'carnal' decretals, it was to the lay power that he looked for the institution of evangelical reforms; it was the only power that he could look to. But Wyclif was more than another fourteenth-century apologist of the authority of the prince over the clergy in their secular lives. He was much more radical; in the long run the logic of his claims for the all sufficiency of the Bible as a law for men was not Erastian reform, but the holy democracy, anarchic in its practical implications, that was the ideal of the seventeenth-century sects.

The extremism of Wyclif's views naturally made him enemies. We know that, quite early in his career as a theologian, some of his critics were pointing out that there were difficulties about squaring his philosophical views with the teaching of the church about the eucharist. The matter was one that Wyclif could not leave on one side; to him as to his contemporaries, the eucharist was a central sacrament in the life of the church. Wyclif's critics were quite right; what he said would not square with the doctrine of transubstantiation. He himself found that he had common sense objections to it; he could not believe that what he saw in the priest's hand was no longer bread. There was also a philosophical difficulty. He could not accept the current Scotist interpretation, that after consecration the bread ceased to exist; according to his metaphysics, nothing that had existed could, in the Scotist sense, be 'annihilated'. Finally, Wyclif could find no authority in Scripture for the doctrine of transubstantiation. It was, it seemed, yet another human, carnal addition to the eternal truth, which was aimed to enhance the dignity of priesthood by a claim to semi-magical powers. Wyclif did not for a moment deny that Christ was really present at the mass, but his presence was, he said, sacramental, not the 'seven foot Christ'; and he was quite sure that the bread remained after consecration. Wyclif put forward his views on the eucharist publicly in the schools of Oxford in 1379. Next year they were condemned by a committee appointed by the chancellor, but he would not retract them. Soon after their condemnation he left Oxford for ever for his rectory at Lutterworth in Leicestershire.

From Lutterworth, a stream of angry works flowed from his pen. He restated his views on the eucharist. He furiously attacked the friars who presumptuously dared to follow an order which they called holier than that of the gospels, and who spread the new, idolatrous teaching on the eucharist (Wyclif believed that transubstantiation had only been the church's doctrine since the time of Innocent III). Harking back to the 'evangelical' conditions of the primitive church, he denounced the whole contemporary ecclesiastical hierarchy in resounding terms. His last work was his *Opus Evangelicum*. Its main theme was the sufficiency of the Bible both as a moral law and as a law for the church (in so far as it had a theme; anger at the end was diminishing his coherence). He never finished the work. As he was hearing mass on Holy Innocents' day, 1384, 'he fell down, smitten by a paralysis, especially in his tongue, so that neither then nor afterwards could he speak'.[23] Three days later he was dead.

Wyclif in religion was in many ways the child of his age. His concern for a clear understanding of true belief among the faithful and for a morality with a scriptural basis he shared with an army of eloquent homilists. But he turned their orthodox, if puritanical, pulpit oratory into a questioning of the whole structure of the contemporary church and its beliefs. His works do not reveal him as lovable: he was arrogant, wordy and censorious. Yet he remains impressive. He was consumed with a passion for the truth, and was intellectually undauntable. His readiness to thrust aside the pope, cardinals and all authority save that of Scripture was founded in a real religious conviction, which had drawn strength in long years of philosophical training and of exhaustive biblical study. The stern evangelical morality which was the positive side of his teaching brought him close to the doctrine of justification by faith. The three things necessary to salvation, he stated, were a belief in God, in his Holy Church, and a hope of glory.[24] Beyond that point the path must be that of Christ, who sent his disciples into the world to preach, not to build palaces and to keep the poor at the gate; who hated worldly pomp, and forbade his disciples to take to the sword; who came humbly to John to be baptized – not like the pope who calls men from the ends of the earth to his tribunal.[25] For all his limitations, Wyclif was a powerful intellect – he anticipated many of the fundamental positions of the sixteenth-century protestants – and he was a passionately religious man. That was what made him important and persuasive.

[23] See Workman, *John Wyclif* vol. II, p. 316.
[24] Wyclif, *De Veritate Sacrae Scripturae* vol. I, p. 243.
[25] Wyclif, *Polemical Works* vol. II (Wyclif Soc., 1883), pp. 680–92.

Wyclif's teachings were rapidly and widely disseminated by his disciples. In 1382 Archbishop Courtenay proceeded against their leaders in Oxford (though not against Wyclif at Lutterworth; it looks as if he may have been protected by his old patron, John of Gaunt), and forced them to abjure their master's views. But the most important among them at the time, Nicholas Hereford and John Aston, soon returned to their heresy, though not to Oxford. Over the next five years both men were active preachers of Lollardy – the name by which Wyclifite heresy came to be known – among the people at large. The dioceses of Worcester and Hereford and the marches of Wales were the chief scenes of their ministrations. Aston died a heretic (c. 1387), but Hereford was arrested, in 1387, and in the end abjured his heresy for good. John Purvey, who had been Wyclif's secretary at Lutterworth, was another active preacher, and was the founder of the long lived Lollard community at Bristol. Apart from these, the most famous of the early Lollards was William Swinderby. Swinderby's first religious allegiance had been not to Wyclif but to the little pious group whose leader was one William Smith, called William the Hermit, and whose activities centred round a deserted chapel of St John outside Leicester. He probably acquired his Wyclifite views from the Oxford master, Philip Repingdon, a canon of St Mary's Leicester, who was one of those academic Wyclifites who recanted in 1382 and did not relapse. Swinderby is a perfect example of the kind of devout, unlettered, but religiously self-confident person to whom Wyclif's teaching, with its emphasis on Scripture and on the direct relation of the individual Christian and his God, had a strong appeal. He was prohibited, along with Aston and Hereford, from preaching in the diocese of Worcester in 1387; later he was a source of much disquiet to Bishop Trefnant of Hereford. After the early 1390s he disappears from history, but he had left his mark.[26] Oldcastle, the later Lollard leader, whose patrimonial estates were at Almeley in Hereford, was almost certainly brought into contact with Lollardy through his evangelism.

The most remarkable evidence of the activity of the early Lollards is the very large body of heretical tracts in vernacular English that they have bequeathed to us. Though the modern printed versions of them cover hundreds of pages, they are not much read by historians and their sheer number is often forgotten.[27]

[26] On Swinderby see further McFarlane, *John Wycliffe and the Beginnings of English Nonconformity*, pp. 103–5, 121–36.

[27] The most important collections in print are T. Arnold, *Select*

The authorship of most of them is hard to establish; Aston and Hereford were among their authors, but Purvey was the most prolific, 'the Lollards Library' as an orthodox opponent called him. There is very little in English, if anything at all, that can be attributed to Wyclif himself, but some of the tracts are straightforward paraphrases of his Latin works; others, which are individual products of their authors, are permeated by his ideas. Two deserve special mention, because they are the most commonly mentioned in charges against suspected Lollards, and clearly enjoyed a very long vogue. They are the *Lantern of Light* and *Wyclif's Wicket* (both early fifteenth-century productions). The theme of the *Lantern* is the contrast between the fiend's church, whose head is the pope of Rome, a church of 'mumbling' of prayers and the 'vain din' of music, and the true church of the 'chosen number' that shall be saved, the church of the worship of the heart and of 'reading with mindful devotion'.[28] The *Wicket* is basically an English paraphrase of Wyclif's teaching on the sacrament, and as such reminds us that there was a direct connexion, through their manuals, between the later Lollards and the father of their sect.

The most important work of the Lollard authors is of course not a tract: it is the English translation of the Bible. Parts of the Bible had been translated before Wyclif's time; Richard Rolle's vernacular version of the Psalms was for instance popular. But the Lollards were the first to translate the whole of the Bible into English, and Wyclif's own emphasis on the need for a vernacular Bible was their first direct inspiration. The Lollards actually made two translations. The earlier was a literal version, following the word order of the Vulgate so carefully that it is often barely comprehensible. The later translation, completed before 1397, was in excellent readable English. Over two hundred manuscripts of this version survive, and it is clear that it reached a far wider circle of readers than just the Lollards.[29] Most of the manuscripts

---

English Works of Wyclif, 3 vols (Oxford, 1869–71), and F. D. Matthew, *The English Works of Wyclif Hitherto Unprinted* (E.E.T.S., 1880). None of the works in these collections can be safely attributed to Wyclif himself, in their vernacular versions.

[28] See the *Lantern of Light*, ed. L. M. Swinburn (E.E.T.S., 1917).

[29] The authoritative work on the Lollard translations remains M. Deanesly, *The Lollard Bible* (Cambridge, 1920). See besides S. L. Fristedt, *The Wycliffe Bible* (Stockholm, 1953; and part II, 1969); also his 'The authorship of the Lollard Bible', *Stockholm Studies in Modern Philology* 19 (1956), pp. 28–41.

are without the openly Lollard prologue with which the trans-lator (usually thought to have been John Purvey) prefaced the work. But for Archbishop Arundel's ban on the unlicensed reading of vernacular Bibles, the work would have been still more popular. There was a large literate public of lay people who knew no Latin but were anxious to discover Scripture for themselves.

Among the Lollards in the early days we may distinguish three groups. First there were the academic followers of Wyclif. Courtenay's synod at Blackfriars in 1382 condemned Wyclif's teachings, drove Aston and Hereford out of Oxford, and obtained the firm recantation of Philip Repingdon; and later in the year he carried out a formal visitation of the university to purge it of heresy. Things were quiet for a time after this, but it did not root out Lollardy thoroughly or permanently. In 1397 a group of petitioners from the university complained of the continued teaching of Wyclif's doctrines in the schools, and Archbishop Arundel complained in 1407 that the university 'now brings forth bitter grapes, and so it comes to pass that our province is infected with the unfruitful doctrines of the Lollards'.[30] There were some notable Lollards in Oxford in the early fifteenth century, as Peter Payne, the principal of St Edmund's Hall, and John Mybbe, the principal of Cuthbert Hall who was involved in Oldcastle's rising in 1414. Jerome of Prague at the turn of the century found plenty of *codices* of Wyclif's work at Oxford, which he and other Bohemian scholars copied and carried home with them. In these early days there was too a significant leavening of M.A.s among the Lollard preachers outside Oxford, as William Taylor (burned in 1423), William James (once of Merton College), and Ralph Mungyn (a pupil of Payne). Lollardy was only really eradicated in the university by Archbishop Arundel's visitation of 1411; from 1412 onwards all masters had to take an oath not to teach or uphold any of the 267 heresies and errors which a commission, appointed by Arundel in 1409, had identi-fied in Wyclif's works.

In this same period in which we continue to hear of Lollards in the university we come across a number of references in chronicles to Lollard knights. Walsingham and Knighton mention in particular a group of influential knights of Richard II's chamber; Sir Richard Stury, Sir Lewis Clifford, Sir John Neville, Sir John Clanvowe, Sir John Montagu. These were all

[30] See H. Rashdall, *The Universities of Europe* vol. III, p. 129; and Workman, *John Wyclif* vol II, p. 326.

rich and successful men, who had made careers for themselves in war and the royal service, and they had business interests in common.[31] They were also educated: Stury was a friend of Froissart and Clifford of Chaucer; Clanvowe was the first layman to write a homily in English. Not all of them can be proved to have been Lollards, but Clanvowe's homily has Lollard overtones, and Neville certainly befriended Hereford in his heretical days, as Montagu is also said to have done. Closely associated with this group were two other knights. One was Sir Thomas Latimer of Braybrook in Northamptonshire, an undoubted Lollard; his rector, Robert Hook, was a notorious heretic. The other was Sir John Cheyney, another chamber knight. The Buckinghamshire branch of the Cheyney family, with whom he was connected, was certainly in sympathy with Lollardy. Thomas Cheyney presented to the living of Drayton Beauchamp in Buckinghamshire Thomas Drayton, a Lollard and a friend of William Taylor, the university trained Lollard. It was owing to the influence of the Cheyneys that the Chilterns and Buckinghamshire long remained one of the most resilient centres of rural heresy.

The Cheyney family apart, we do not hear very much of Lollard knights by name after about 1400. The passage of the statute *de Heretico Comburendo* was no doubt a strong deterrent to the genteel. Only two knights, Sir Roger Acton from Worcestershire and Sir Thomas Talbot of Kent, were involved with Oldcastle in 1414. All the same it seems certain that the Lollard knights are very important in the history of the sect. Knightly patronage of Lollard rectors and preachers helped to establish the sect in the very early days, and to permit the dissemination of Lollard teachings to a wide audience. It is no accident that Buckinghamshire and Northamptonshire, where the Cheyneys and Latimer respectively had influence, were long infected with Lollardy. And it is interesting to note that Clanvowe had lands in Herefordshire where Swinderby was so active; they were close to Almeley, where John Oldcastle himself originated. Oldcastle was regarded by the chroniclers as the acknowledged leader of Lollardy in the early fifteenth century; knightly leadership gave the sect a certain definition that it lost in later days.

[31] The most important study of the Lollard knights that is in print is W. T. Waugh, 'The Lollard Knights', *S.H.R.* 11 (1913), pp. 55–92. K. B. McFarlane, however, in a work in press, *Lancastrian Kings and Lollard Knights* (Oxford, 1972), shows that the charges of heresy levelled at these knights had more foundation than Waugh supposed.

The third group among the Lollards were the humble adherents of heresy in the towns and the countryside, the only
group that survived beyond the early fifteenth century. These
are much the hardest Lollards to track down, for we only really
hear about them when there were proceedings against them.
Dr Thomson's exhaustive inquiries have shown that there were
quite vigorous Lollard communities in a number of towns, as
London, Bristol and Coventry, and that they survived into the
sixteenth century and maintained some degree of contact with
one another.[32] In the countryside Lollardy seems to have gained
its local vigour often (but not always) from the missionary
activities of individual priests, like William of Thaxted in Essex
and William White in East Anglia in the 1420s. It is virtually
impossible to make any estimate of the numbers that may have
been attached to the sect at any one time. The authorities in the
fifteenth century clearly thought that Lollards were numerous;
from the records that we have it would seem that their estimates
were unnecessarily alarmist.

It becomes difficult, in this later period, to be sure just how
much identity the Lollards had really retained as a sect, and to
what extent their beliefs preserved significant connexions with
the teaching of Wyclif and his first disciples. In the early days,
when Purvey and others who had known the master were still
alive, the links were often strong and conscious; William Thorpe
counted himself proudly, he told Archbishop Arundel, among
those who 'purpose to conform their living to this learning of
Wyclif'.[33] The case of Joan Boughton, an 'old cankered heretic'
of more than eighty years who was burned at Smithfield in 1494
and held Wyclif to be a saint,[34] shows that this attitude long
survived, but she may have been exceptional. The basis of
charges against many later Lollards is rather vague, often merely
the possession or study of English bibles. Bible reading and
Bible study seem to be the main link between Wyclif's ideas and
the proletarian heretics of the later period.

The best picture of Lollardy in its late, underground phase is
that given in the mid-fifteenth century by Bishop Pecock, who
by his own admission was well acquainted with 'the wittiest and
cunningest men of thilk said sort'.[35] There was a good deal of

[32] See J. A. F. Thomson, *The Later Lollards* (Oxford, 1965). I am
much indebted to this very thorough and illuminating study.

[33] See *The Acts and Monuments of John Foxe*, ed. J. Pratt (4th ed.
London, 1877), vol. III, p. 258.   [34] ibid. vol. IV, p. 7.

[35] R. Pecock, *The Book of Faith*, quoted by V. H. H. Green, *Bishop*

variety in their beliefs, as he recognized, but essentially they
were Bible men: their first and most general 'trowing' was that
'no governance is to be held the law of God save that which is
grounded in Holy Scripture'.[36] 'They ween themselves to ken at
full and substantially and pithily Holy Scripture,' he says, 'for
that they ken by heart the texts of Holy Scripture, and can lush
them out thick at feasts, and at ale drinking, and upon their high
benches sitting.'[37] Pecock's picture tallies with what the records
of proceedings against Lollards tell us, of groups of simple
people, not very dangerous and not very educated, meeting
surreptitiously at one another's houses to read the Bible. Their
naïve faith in their own knowledge of Scripture and their sense
of belonging to the little band of God's chosen ones are their
chief identifying features. There are echoes of Wyclif here, but
they are only echoes. It is not the schools of the fourteenth
century but the sects of the seventeenth that are recalled by these
'unlearned apostles and saints', as Jacob calls them, who were
not 'graduate men, but the Holy Ghost inspired them and made
them plenteous of heavenly lore'.[38]

As Courtenay's vigorous intervention at Oxford in 1382 shows,
the ecclesiastical hierarchy was quick to respond to the challenge
of Lollardy, once the publication of Wyclif's eucharistic opinions
had alerted authority to the measure of the danger. Outside the
lettered clerical world, it was not so easy to see how sharp the
distinction was between Wyclif and the general run of radical
anti-clericalism, and it was only gradually that the church
succeeded in enlisting adequate support against Lollardy from
the secular arm. As a result of pressure from Courtenay, a statute
of 1382 ordered the sheriffs, upon certification from their bishops,
to arrest unlicensed preachers and their abetters and to hold them
until they cleared themselves in the ecclesiastical courts.[39] This
was not a very effective measure. The statute *de Heretico Comburendo* of 1401 was sterner stuff, forbidding upon royal authority

---

Reginald Pecock (Cambridge, 1945), pp. 21–2. This is the most substantial modern study of Pecock and his work; see also E. F. Jacob,
'Reynold Pecock, Bishop of Chichester', *P.B.A.* 37 (1951), pp. 121–53.

[36] *Pecock's Repressor* (R.S.) vol. I, p. 5.

[37] ibid. p. 129.

[38] E. F. Jacob, *The Fifteenth Century* (Oxford, 1961), p. 283; and
Lantern of Light, ed. L. M. Swinburn, p. 5.

[39] See further H. G. Richardson, 'Heresy and the lay power under
Richard II', *E.H.R.* 51 (1936), pp. 1–28.

unlicensed preaching, the holding of conventicles, and the dissemination of unlicensed books, and commanding that obdurate heretics who refused to abjure in the church courts should be handed over to the secular arm and burned. In fact, only two heretics were burned between 1401 and 1414; and it is interesting to note that there were parliamentary protests against the measures of both 1382 and 1401. Much more effective was the statute of the Leicester parliament of 1414, passed after Oldcastle's revolt had sharply stiffened the attitude of secular authority. This empowered the justices of the peace and of assize to make search for Lollards and to deliver them to the bishops, and thus brought the ordinary machinery for the suppression of civil crimes to bear in the prosecution of Lollardy.[40]

John Oldcastle, the leader of the Lollard revolt of 1414, was a prominent man.[41] He had risen to distinction in the Welsh wars against Glendower; through Henry V's influence in the days when he was Prince of Wales he married Joan de la Pole, heiress of Lord Cobham, in whose right he came as a peer to parliament. He was also a recognized leader of the Lollards, and Archbishop Arundel knew from at least 1410 that his castle at Cooling in Kent was a resort of heretics. In 1413, soon after Henry V's accession, it was revealed in convocation that a search of a scrivener's shop in Paternoster Row had revealed a number of heretical books belonging to Oldcastle, and Arundel decided to act against him. His close associations with the new king made it necessary for the Archbishop to proceed carefully; they also made it particularly important that Oldcastle should be brought to book.

Oldcastle, if he had been less obdurate, could certainly have got off through royal influence. But his heresy was founded in a real religious conviction, and he would not take the easy way. He was arrested in the summer of 1413 and was brought before his ecclesiastical judges in October. Cross-questioned on his beliefs

[40] On procedures for the investigation and trial of Lollards subsequent to this statute see Thomson, *The Later Lollards*, ch. XI. Thomson here also explains the importance of the ecclesiastical legislation of the convocation of 1416, which was a vital complement to the secular measures of the Leicester parliament.

[41] On Oldcastle and his revolt see K. B. McFarlane, *John Wycliffe and the Beginnings of English Nonconformity*, ch. 6 (one of the most valuable chapters in an important book); see also W. T. Waugh, 'Sir John Oldcastle', *E.H.R.* 20 (1905), pp. 434–56, 637–58.

on the eucharist and confession, he denied the right of the pope, or of any other bishop, to define belief on these matters. Arundel provided him with a schedule in English setting forth the catholic teaching; he studied it and returned with still more uncompromising answers, denouncing his judges as traitors to God before all present. He was pronounced convicted, excommunicated, and was handed over to the secular arm. At Henry V's request, there was a stay of execution, to give the king himself a chance to reason his friend into abjuration.

On 19 October, during this delay, Oldcastle escaped from the Tower with the aid of outside supporters. By December, the court had wind of plans for a Lollard rising, and on Twelfth Night in the new year a number of London Lollards were arrested at the 'Sign of the Axe' in Bishopsgate. They revealed the details of the conspiracy, of a *coup* timed for the night of 7 January whose first object was to capture the king. Oldcastle must apparently have decided that it was too late to change his arrangements, for his followers were already converging on the capital from far afield. Their assembly point was in St Giles's Fields, and there in the darkness they stumbled into the strong professional forces that King Henry had ready. It is unclear how many Lollards had turned up: modern estimates have varied from a few hundreds to over a thousand. Some were killed, about eighty were taken prisoner, and the rest completely scattered. Oldcastle was one of those who escaped, but his rising was over. It was a complete fiasco.

Oldcastle's force was clearly not militarily impressive, an assorted throng of mostly very humble people, but they had come long distances. There were contingents from Buckinghamshire, Leicestershire, Warwick and Derby. Not all the known Lollard communities contributed; Bristol, so far as we know, sent no one. It would seem also that by no means all the rebels were Lollards; of those who were executed for their part in the affair, only a handful were convicted of heresy as well as treason. Apart from those taken at St Giles's Fields, few paid the penalty of their lives. By 14 March it was considered safe to issue a pardon, from which Oldcastle and a few other notorious Lollards were excepted. He remained at large for another three years, a bogey to the authorities but not very dangerous; he was finally run to earth in Herefordshire in 1417, and the sentence passed on him was duly, if tardily, executed.

Oldcastle's revolt was the end of Lollardy as a movement with any political significance. Ever since the 1380s, its ecclesiastical

opponents had been making determined efforts to discredit the
sect with the socially respectable among the laity, by labouring
the revolutionary implications for them of Wyclif's teaching.[42]
His view that all true lordship was founded in grace could, these
detractors pointed out, be turned against the secular prince and
the aristocracy quite as easily as against the endowed religious.
A rumour began to circulate that Wyclifite missionaries had
helped to stir up the peasants against their lords in 1381. The
revolt of 1414 seemed to demonstrate incontrovertibly that the
churchmen were absolutely right, that Lollardy was a socially
disruptive force that threatened lay lords and clerical ones equally.
It completely discredited heresy with the upper classes. There
were, it is true, plans for another rising in 1431, but no substantial people were involved; the only place where there was
actual violence was Abingdon where Jack Sharp was ready to
attack the abbey, but this did not pass the proportions of a riot.[43]
Though Lollardy survived right down to the sixteenth century
it did so only as a proletarian movement, underground and un-
organized, which was no longer a serious threat to the church
establishment.

Lollardy was long lived because, in the context of the religious
feeling and attitudes of the late Middle Ages, it had a genuine
appeal. In many respects this appeal had much in common with
that of the mystics. Both teachings touched the religious aspirations of the lay and simple at sensitive points, in their desire for
a closer contact with Scripture and with the life of Christ, for
assurance of personal salvation, and for moral regeneration. Both
had anti-clerical overtones. It is not so very remarkable that
Margery Kemp, on whom the real religious influences were
Hilton and Julian of Norwich, was more than once mistaken for
a Lollard. But in the end, of course, mysticism and Lollardy led
in opposite directions. At the popular level Lollardy was anti-
sacramental, contemptuous of pilgrimage, image worship and
spiritual direction. All the things that moved Margery Kemp to
ecstasies, the scene of our Lord's birth, the crucifix, the elevation
of the host at the mass, moved the Lollard who had lifted the
latch of Wyclif's wicket to anger at superstition.

[42] On this aspect of the campaign against Lollardy, see the important
article of M. E. Aston, 'Lollardy and sedition', *Past and Present* 17
(1960), pp. 1–44.

[43] On Sharp's rising see Thomson *The Later Lollards*, pp. 58–60,
146–7.

In fifteenth-century England, the influence of the mystics remained a stronger force than Lollardy ever was. The treatises of the fourteenth-century authors continued to enjoy an impressive vogue, and at the end of the century Caxton and Wynkyn de Worde early produced printed editions of them. Nicholas Love, the Carthusian prior of Mount Grace, rendered into English Bonaventura's meditative life of Our Lord, under the title *Mirrour of the Blessed Lyf of Jesus Christ*; it is a book to which we often find reference in wills of the period.[44] Bequests do not only tell us who possessed books of this kind; they also give us a picture of how they were treasured. This is the colophon of a manuscript of Hilton's *Eight Chapters Necessary for Men that give Themselves to Perfection*:

> This book was made of the goods of Robert Holland for a common profit. [And let] that person that hath this book of the person that hath power to commit it have the use thereof for the term of his life, praying for the soul of the same Robert. And that he that hath the foresaid use . . . when he occupieth it not, lend he it for a time to some other person. Also [let that] person to whom it was committed for the term of his life under the foresaid conditions deliver it to another person for the term of his life. And so be it delivered and committed from person to person, as long as the book endureth.[45]

Robert Holland was a citizen of London who died in 1441. The spirit of Hilton's readers, devout and generous, shines through his words to remind us that it was the tradition of the mystics, much more than that of Wyclif, that coloured the religious life of the fifteenth century. It also reminds us of the strength of an English catholicism, pre-Tridentine, insular and vernacular, which even the reformation never really succeeded in eradicating from English religion.

---

[44] On the mention of religious treatises in wills see further M. Deanesly, 'Vernacular books in England in the fourteenth and fifteenth centuries', *Modern Language Review* 15 (1920), pp. 349–58. The vogue of mystical works is also discussed perceptively by R. Lovatt, 'The *Imitation of Christ* in late medieval England', *T.R.H.S.* 5th ser., 18 (1968), pp. 97–121.

[45] Quoted by R. W. Chambers, 'The continuity of English prose', intro. to *Harpsfield's Life of More*, ed. E. V. Hitchcock and R. W. Chambers (E.E.T.S., 1932), p. cviii.

The uncertain years
1360–1415

11

Defeat abroad and unrest at home
1360–1381

For nearly nine years after the Treaty of Brétigny England and France were nominally at peace. In England these were carefree years, politically. Edward III, presiding over a magnificent court, felt that he had earned rest after his high deeds; 'I am growing old,' he told the king of Cyprus, who visited him to urge him to take the cross as a crusader, 'I shall leave it to my children.'[1] The Black Prince took his beautiful bride, Joan of Kent, to Aquitaine, which his father in 1362 granted to him as a principality, and at their court 'abode all nobleness, all joy and jollity, largesse, gentleness, and honour'.[2] Adventurous spirits meanwhile sought martial renown in wars overseas; on the crusade that the king of Cyprus led; in the Breton war of succession, which still continued; and in Spain. In their *insouciance*, the English seem hardly to have noticed the slow drift towards a new confrontation with France. When in 1369 the Hundred Years War reopened as a result of deliberate provocation on the French side, they were ill prepared. The pattern of events which followed this resumption of hostilities was, partly in consequence, in very marked contrast to that of the years which preceded the Treaty of Brétigny.

Peace did not much alter internal conditions in England in the 1360s. There was no great change in the approach of the king's advisers to problems of government. The general control over expenditure which Edington had established for the exchequer when he was treasurer in the 1350s was maintained. Peace did give the exchequer officials a chance, in 1363, to prepare something like a budget statement, a disappointing exercise which

[1] K. de L. vol. VI, p. 380.
[2] Chandos Herald, *The Black Prince*, ed. H. O. Coxe (Roxburghe Club, 1842), p. 126.

showed that even without the strains to which war exposed the royal revenues, they were hardly adequate to meet current expenditure. No special measures were taken, however, to improve the position: it was supposed that the ransoms of the kings of France and Scotland would make up for the deficit. The ransoms brought in some £268,000 in these years, but it was all quickly spent. When the war began again 'nothing was found in the king's treasury, but he was in such great poverty that he had to burden the clergy and commons with subsidies and loans'.[3] William of Wykeham, who had been the king's secretary, then the keeper of his privy seal, and finally became chancellor in 1367, was held by many to be chiefly responsible for the fact that, in the end, nothing was left of 'the great sums in gold' that the ransoms had brought in.

Abroad, in this period, England's most important involvement was in the affairs of the kingdom of Castile. The enlargement of the boundaries of English Aquitaine under the terms of Brétigny had made it more important than ever before for the English to take an interest in the affairs of the Spanish kingdoms. The Black Prince, who had just arrived with his wife in Bordeaux, was probably the chief architect of the treaty of alliance between England and King Pedro of Castile which was agreed in 1362. One of its stipulations was that the English would, if need arose, provide soldiers for service in Castile against Pedro's enemies. The threat of internal rebellion was what Pedro had in mind, and in particular the designs which his bastard brother, Henry, Count of Trastamara, entertained upon his throne. Henry at the time was in exile, and seeking aid at the French court in the furtherance of his plans. This was why the English alliance with Pedro, in due course, became a key factor in the chain of events which led to the reopening of war with France.[4]

In France, the Treaty of Brétigny had brought peace in name only. Great tracts of the countryside were still overrun by free companies of soldiers, who had nowhere else to go, and no means of living except as they were wont, by terrorizing the countryside and plundering merchants and travellers. Their activities presented the foremost of the formidable problems that Charles V

[3] *Anonimalle Chronicle*, ed. V. H. Galbraith (Manchester, 1927), p. 96. On finance in the 1360s see also T. F. Tout and D. M. Broome, 'A national balance sheet for 1362-3', *E.H.R.* 39 (1924), pp. 404-19.

[4] For the foregoing and for what follows, as for all that concerns Anglo-Spanish relations over the period 1362-90, see further P. E. Russell, *The English Intervention in Spain and Portugal* (Oxford, 1955).

had to face in 1364, when King John died in London (he had
returned there as a prisoner when the Duke of Anjou, a hostage
for his ransom, broke parole). Charles's position was eased in
that year by the end of the Breton war. When Knowles and John
de Montfort defeated and killed Charles of Blois at Auray,
Charles V accepted the *fait accompli* and allowed de Montfort to
do homage for the duchy. In 1365 the Franco-Navarrese war,
which had also broken out anew, was ended by the victory of
French forces at Cocherel over a largely English force led by the
Captal de Buch and John Jewel. Charles thus obtained a free
hand to deal with the problem of the free companies, and agreed
to advance money to Henry of Trastamara, to take as many of
them as he might into his pay and lead them out of the kingdom
to make war on Pedro in Castile.

In the autumn of 1365 a great host of mercenaries began to
assemble. Its chief captains were the Breton veteran, Bertand Du
Guesclin, and Arnold d'Audrehem, Marshal of France, and there
was a powerful Anglo-Gascon contingent under Sir Hugh
Calverley. In February 1366 their force was concentrated in
Aragon, whence they crossed into Castile; and on 29 March
Henry was crowned at Burgos. Pedro could muster no army
capable of facing these tried soldiers, and fled from Toledo to
Seville, thence to Portugal, and finally arrived in Gascony. He
had already made contact with the Black Prince, to request him
to implement the treaty of 1362 by providing forces which might
restore him to his throne.

The Black Prince and his father were willing to do this,
provided that Pedro would shoulder the expense. In the autumn
of 1366, of course, Pedro was in no position to pay anyone anything, and the Prince agreed to be responsible for the payment of
the army that was to be raised, upon promise of repayment from
the king of Castile, once he was restored to his throne. He then
began to assemble his army; the English and Gascons in the
service of Henry were recalled, and a great host marched into
Spain in 1367. At Najera this host routed the army of Henry, and
took prisoner his two chief French captains, Du Guesclin and the
Marshal d'Audrehem. It was the last of the victories that made
the Black Prince famous in the annals of chivalry, and ended an
age of martial success for the English.

Pedro was back on his throne after Najera, but it rapidly
became apparent that he would not for a long time yet be able to
raise funds to pay off the Black Prince's soldiers, who were
clamouring for pay. Relations between the two rapidly deterior-

ated, to the point where Edward even began to consider fore-
closing upon his creditor's realm, and making himself a king
there. This dream did nothing towards satisfying the immediate
problem of his unpaid army, however. The Prince seems to have
regarded the claims of these his chivalrous companions as paramount, and decided that there was no option but to look to his
subjects in Aquitaine for ready money. They had already borne
heavy taxation at his hands, and the grant of a new hearth tax,
which was agreed at Bordeaux in the autumn of 1367, raised
bitter complaint. Two of the most important southern lords, the
counts of Amagnac and Albret, refused to permit its levy in their
domains, and appealed to Charles, king of France, to support
them in their refusal. This gave the French king his chance to
exploit the non-fulfilment of the famous renunciation clauses of
his father's peace treaty with the English of 1360, and to reassert
the traditional French claim to sovereignty over the duchy of
Aquitaine.

Everyone knew that if Charles of France received the appeal
of the Gascon lords in his *Parlement*, it must mean the renewal
of the war. He moved circumspectly, consulting with his councillors and with experts in the law of nations and of treaties from
the universities. But the Gascon lords knew that he would receive
their appeal, and that hesitation was for form's sake. Charles had
always assumed that the war would reopen one day, and prospects
of concerting a Franco-Castilian offensive in Gascony had
prompted him in the first place towards alliance with Henry of
Trastamara. He believed the time for action was now ripe:
Gascony was in ferment, and England unprepared. So he declared
that he was bound to hear the appeal of the two lords, and
summoned the Black Prince to come and defend himself against
their complaints before the *Parlement* of Paris.[5]

The Black Prince told the men who brought the summons to
Bordeaux in January 1369 that he would come to Paris – at the
head of 60,000 men. In England King Edward followed the
advice of his parliament, that he might 'of right and in good
faith' reassume the title of King of France, which he had not
used since 1360. In the skirmishes that flared up all along the
frontiers of Aquitaine, the banners of St Denis and St George
were unfurled once more in engagement.

[5] See further R. Delachenal, *Histoire de Charles V* vol. IV (Paris,
1928), pp. 53–109; and P. Chaplais, 'Some documents regarding the
fulfilment of the Treaty of Bretigny', *Camden Miscellany*, vol. XIX
(1952).

Over the years 1369 to 1381 the course of military operations in
the war, which now began again in earnest, and the turns of
English domestic politics were intimately connected. The story
may be easier to understand if we follow first the course of the
war, and then turn to examine the public reactions in England
to the events that took place overseas.

The French, in this period of the war, were more fortunate
than the English in their diplomatic alliances. A new treaty
restored their old relations with the Scots in 1370. They were
lucky in Spain also: by 1369 the Black Prince had abandoned
Pedro, who was defeated and killed at Montiel, after Henry and
Du Guesclin (who had paid his ransom) reappeared with a new
French army. This meant that from the early 1370s, once Henry
had established himself, the French enjoyed the important
support in the Channel of the Castilian fleet. This enabled them,
at least intermittently, to control the narrow seas, to prey constantly on English shipping, and to mount several alarming raids
on the English coasts. Pedro's death had important consequences
for the English also. When he died, his two daughters were at
Bordeaux. In 1371, at Roquefort, Constanza, the elder of them,
was married to John of Gaunt, Duke of Lancaster in right of his
former wife Blanche, and the second of the surviving sons of
Edward III. Next year, with the assent of the English council,
Gaunt assumed the title of King of Castile. For the next sixteen
years his influence in English politics made sure that plans for a
Lancastrian intervention in Castile were always in the background of English military and diplomatic planning. This com-
plication was not an advantage to the English war effort.

In France, the main sphere of operations, things did not go
well for England after 1369. English councillors had no experience of the massive problems of maintaining a defensive war, and
did not fully understand what they involved. They put their
faith instinctively in the offensive methods which had paid off in
the 1350s, and were no longer appropriate. A series of costly
chevauchées were mounted, but achieved nothing. In 1370
Robert Knowles led an army through Picardy and past the gates
of Paris, but he had little to show for it when he reached Brittany.
Gaunt in 1373 led a more impressive host from Calais to the
borders of Burgundy; but he lost more than half his men afterwards, marching to Bordeaux across the *massif* of central France
in a freezing winter. In 1372, a year before, the Castilian fleet had
caught and destroyed another expensive force which the Earl of
Pembroke was shipping to Aquitaine, and destroyed it before it

ever set foot on land. In 1375 an expedition to Brittany, where John de Montfort had again broken with his sovereign, started more promisingly, but had to be abandoned when the English negotiators at Bruges, headed by Gaunt, agreed a general truce with the French for a year. On all sides the English record was one of abject and costly failure.[6]

The French had won notable successes in the years from 1369 to 1375, but by the end of them they were beginning to feel the strain. By 1372 they had recovered all Poitou, and, pressing further into the south west, had taken Pons, Taillebourg and St Jean d'Angely, confining the English effectively to the Bordeaux district. In 1373 Charles V's famous constable, Du Guesclin, and the Duke of Bourbon cleared most of Brittany of English troops. Du Guesclin's tactics, refusing to be drawn into engagement with the English on their long, destructive *chevauchées* and then massing troops to reduce the undermanned garrisons in English territory, were, however, expensive and only partly successful. The French never succeeded in clearing the central *massif* of the numerous free companies that operated in name for the English, and who were very hard to dislodge from their near impregnable hill forts in Auvergne and Limousin. There was little prospect in 1375 of administering a *coup de grace* either in Gascony or in Brittany, and that was why the French were glad of a truce.

The truce of 1375, initially agreed for a year, was later extended, to run until 24 June 1377. It represented the first concrete achievement of the papal mediators, who had been busy at the thankless task of peacemaking since 1369. During this two year interlude there was much discussion between the French, the English and the legates at Bruges about the terms of a possible final peace, but the mediators failed in the end to find any means towards a permanent accommodation. The French were willing to be generous in concessions of territory, but insisted that their king's sovereignty must be recognized through all Aquitaine. The English were prepared to listen to ideas for a partition of the

[6] On the military and diplomatic development of this period see further Delachenal, *Histoire de Charles V* vol. IV; J. W. Sherborne, 'English expeditions to France 1369-80', *E.H.R.* 79 (1964), pp. 718-46; C. C. Bayley, 'The campaign of 1375 and the Good Parliament', *E.H.R.* 55 (1940), pp. 370-83; E. Perroy, 'The Anglo-French negotiations at Bruges', *Camden Miscellany* vol. XIX (1952). On the activities of the Castilian fleet in the Channel, see Russell, *The English Intervention in Spain and Portugal*, ch. XI.

duchy which would reduce the area of their authority, but they would not hear of admitting French sovereignty in whatever part remained to them. The question of sovereignty defied resolution, as it was to continue now to do for the rest of the duration of the war. The experience of Brétigny had taught both the English and the French that it was the one thing that neither could abandon. The Cardinals had therefore to resign themselves to the recommencement of hostilities. When they left Bruges they could not know that theirs would prove to be the last effort at peacemaking by papal servants for many years. The Great Schism broke out in 1378, and peace ceased to be a priority with the warring popes of Rome and Avignon.

When the war reopened in the summer of 1377 Edward III had just died, after celebrating his jubilee. His government, during the truce, had had to face a serious domestic crisis and the English were no better prepared than they had been in 1369. The Duke of Anjou was soon threatening Bordeaux, and Burgundy moved up a force to besiege Calais. A Franco-Castilian fleet appeared in the Channel; Hastings, Rottingdean, Dartmouth and Plymouth all suffered, and Rye was burned. The late summer of 1377 was the darkest hour, however; stalemate was achieved much more rapidly between the two sides than it had been earlier, after 1369.

Charles V had in fact overreached himself in recommencing hostilities so soon. Riots in many cities and local revolts in the French provinces in 1378 showed that the strain of supporting the war was too severe. The king's attempt to annex Brittany, which his *Parlement* declared forfeit to the crown, was a major political blunder: too many Bretons saw it as a threat to provincial independence and rallied to de Montfort and England.[7] The Duke of Anjou's designs on Majorca also proved an embarrassment. They drove his Aragonese rivals towards an English alliance, which the Navarrese were ready to join. In consequence Cherbourg, Charles of Navarre's last stronghold in Normandy, was placed in English hands.

English fortunes in the field did not markedly improve, in spite of the difficulties of the French. John Neville, who came to Gascony as lieutenant in 1378, did manage in some degree to reactivate local resistance to the French. But the more ambitious expeditions which the government managed to organize and of

[7] See further Delachenal, *Histoire de Charles V* vol. V, pp. 235–83; and M. Jones, *Ducal Brittany 1364–99* (Oxford, 1970), pp. 85–92.

which much was hoped were uniformly unsuccessful. In 1378
Gaunt sailed with a force that was supposed to be destined for
Bordeaux; he stopped to besiege St Malo, without success, and
returned empty handed. In 1379 a substantial force was mustered
for a campaign in Brittany, under Sir John Arundel; it was caught
by a storm at sea, and most of the ships were wrecked off the
Irish coast. Sir John was drowned; the chroniclers saw in his fate
a judgement of God, because of the disorders that his men had
committed ashore while waiting for their transports. In 1380
Thomas of Woodstock, the youngest of Edward III's sons and
Earl of Buckingham, crossed to Calais with a powerful host,
which numbered many famous captains among its leaders, as
Sir Robert Knowles, Sir Hugh Calverley, Sir John Harleston.
Following the line of Knowles's march in 1370 they raided as far
as the borders of Burgundy, before turning west with Brittany as
their objective. While they were marching John de Montfort's
bitter enemy Charles V died in Paris, and when the English
arrived in his duchy he was already negotiating a peace with
Charles VI's councillors. In April 1381 Buckingham was told
that the French and the Bretons were no longer at war, and he
had no option but to return, indignant and unvictorious, to
England.

Despite these setbacks and failures, the English government in
1381 was less prepared to consider peace than the French were.
They believed, and with some reason, that new opportunities
might shortly open for them, and turn the tide of misfortune.
In 1378 the Great Schism in the church had broken out, when
the cardinals who in the spring had elected Urban VI in Rome
deserted him, and elected in his stead in September Robert of
Geneva, who became Clement VII, and made Avignon his seat.
Charles of France recognized Clement as the true pope, but the
English remained firmly loyal to Urban, as did also the Emperor
Wenceslas and, in France, the Flemings, who in 1379 had once
again rebelled against their count. In these circumstances the old
idea of a great continental coalition against the French was
resuscitated. It would have the standing now of a crusade, in
Urban's favour. It looked further as though Lancaster's Iberian
diplomacy, which had already achieved an alliance with Portugal
and an understanding with Aragon, might be tied in with the
scheme.[8] When the disappointed Buckingham got back to
England in 1381 Simon Burley, Richard II's tutor, was on the

[8] See E. Perroy, *L'Angleterre et le Grande Schism d'Occident* (Paris,
1933), pp. 51-62, 139ff.

point of leaving the realm to seek a bride for his master in Anne of Bohemia, the sister of Wenceslas; and Edmund Earl of Cambridge was assembling an army at Plymouth, destined for Portugal.

What Buckingham was in time to witness was not the successful foundation of an anti-French confederacy, however, but the Peasants' Revolt.

The Peasants' Revolt of 1381 was the climax of a crisis of confidence in government, which was largely generated by failures in the war. The effect of those failures was felt directly in England. The activities of the Franco-Castilian fleet and of French and Scottish privateers severely damaged English merchants and their commerce. The French carried out damaging raids on the Channel coasts in 1369, and again in 1377, 1378 and 1380. In 1377 Rye and Portsmouth were sacked; in 1378 Cornwall suffered severely; in 1380 Gravesend and Winchelsea were burned. The whole country had suffered as a result of the financial burden which the effort to fit out substantial and uniformly unsuccessful military and naval forces imposed. Taxation was heavier and more sustained than it had been at any time since the 1340s. In spite of this, the English had lost control of the narrow seas, together with most of what they had once held in the south-west of France and their footholds in Brittany and Normandy.

Past experience did not help people in England in the 1370s to understand this pattern of events. Remote from the scene of the great campaigns, they could not comprehend that the new strategy of Charles V and Du Guesclin had rendered their previous methods of waging war obsolete, or that these were inappropriate to essentially defensive military objectives. Victories such as Crecy and Poitiers could not be won if the French would not meet the English *chevauchées* in the field; and *chevauchées*, in themselves, did nothing to protect under-defended territory. Because the English did not understand this, but knew that they were paying heavily to no apparent purpose, they attributed their failures to disloyal leadership, profiteering by captains and dishonest financial administration at home. There was consequently continuous pressure, especially from the sectors of opinion represented in parliament, for more stringent control and audit of expenditure, for investigation into military and administrative incompetence and disloyalty, and for the displacement of discredited councillors (often in favour of inexperienced ones).

Concessions to demands of this sort, always partial, did little to alter things. This fact, in itself, served to increase public bewilderment and distrust.

This situation was aggravated by lack of royal leadership. Edward III by 1369 was ageing fast. Happy in the ceremonious life of the court and with his mistress, Alice Perrers, he was content to leave the direction of affairs to others. The health of the Black Prince, his heir, had been permanently damaged in the Spanish campaign; in 1370 he had to resign the command in Aquitaine and came back to England, where he died before his father, in 1376. Lionel of Clarence, his next brother, had died earlier, in 1369. John of Gaunt, the Duke of Lancaster, was the most active member of the royal family, a powerful influence in council, often presiding on the king's behalf in parliament. But he had neither the political experience nor the military record to inspire general confidence. When Edward III died no regent was appointed for Richard II, the Black Prince's son who succeeded at the age of ten, probably because there was no one who commanded sufficient respect to fill the office. Throughout the years 1369 to 1381 there was thus no natural leader to focus the efforts and rally the loyalties of a frustrated and bewildered people.

By 1371 popular discontent had become vocal in parliament. The commons complained to the king that 'the government of the realm has long been in the hands of men of Holy Church, who cannot in all matters be brought to justice', and prayed that he would henceforth choose laymen as his ministers.[9] William of Wykeham, the Bishop of Winchester, had in consequence to resign as chancellor, and Bishop Brantingham of Exeter as treasurer. There were other troubles too in this parliament. Anti-clericalism, to which distrust of clerical ministers gave a sharp edge, encouraged suspicion that the clergy as a whole were not pulling their weight in the national emergency. The commons and lay lords tried to make their grant (of £50,000, to be raised by a levy of 22s. 3d. on every parish) conditional on the clergy making a grant of the same sum, and the bishops had to fight to maintain the fiscal independence of their convocations. More alarming still in the eyes of most churchmen, two Austin friars were brought forward to argue the case for impounding church lands for the king's use. Wyclif later recalled that their scheme for partial disendowment was supported by 'a certain lord wise in

[9] *R.P.* vol. II, p. 304.

counsel'.[10] The monastic chroniclers believed that the leader of the anti-clericals was the Earl of Pembroke, and regarded the disaster which overtook his expedition at La Rochelle in 1372 as a judgement.

The rift between lay and clerical leaders of 1371 was not easily healed. The clergy were still touchy about taxation in 1373, when William Courtenay, the young Bishop of Hereford, protested sharply that the grievances of his clerics should be met before they paid any more to the king. The friars' scheme of disendowment had meanwhile stimulated a vigorous pamphlet warfare, in which Wyclif took a prominent part. It was this, probably, that first brought him to the attention of John of Gaunt. Meanwhile, the new secular leadership was discrediting itself. The parliament of 1373 was cooperative enough, but that was before it was known that Gaunt's great *chevauchée* of this same year would achieve nothing. When parliament next met, in 1376, the failure of that expedition and also of the expedition to Brittany in 1375 was exposed. The assembling of this parliament triggered off a furious outburst of public anger, which the government for the time being was quite unable to control.

The 'Good Parliament' of 1376 sat for longer than any previous parliament, and is exceptionally well recorded. Besides the official parliament roll, we have in the *Anonimalle Chronicle* what appears to be an eye witness account of the debates of the commons. The most striking point that this latter source reveals is the dominant part played by the commons in the proceedings that took place. No sooner had they returned to their own allotted 'chamber' in the chapter house at Westminster, after hearing the chancellor's speech which outlined the king's financial needs, than they took an oath to stand together as a single and united body to see through together all that should be proposed. Then, as they all sat round, a knight of the 'south country' came up to the lectern and spoke thus:

> My lords, you have heard the points put before this parliament, which are grievous matter, how the king demands a tenth and a fifteenth of clergy and commons . . . which to me seems a heavy burden, for the commons are enfeebled by the taxes and tallages

---

[10] Wyclif, *De Civili Dominio* vol. II, p. 7. On this affair see further V. H. Galbraith, 'Articles laid before the parliament of 1371', *E.H.R.* 34 (1919), pp. 579–82; and A. Gwynn, *The English Austin Friars in the Time of Wyclif* (Oxford, 1940), pp. 210–24.

of time past . . . and besides all we have given for the war for a long while we have lost, for it has been wasted and falsely spent . . . and as I have heard, there are certain persons who without the king's knowledge have got into their hands a great treasure in gold and silver to a great sum from him, and have concealed this wealth and gained extortionately for themselves by divers means, to the ill of the king and the kingdom.[11]

This was the opening round in a salvo of speeches attacking the administration of the last few years. Three days later, Sir Peter de la Mare, the steward of the Earl of March who had come as a knight for Herefordshire, was chosen to put the articles, which the commons as a united body wished to raise, to the lords and the king. Originally chosen simply for this occasion, he managed so well for the commons that he continued to act as their spokesman through the parliament, and became the first man to be recognized as a Speaker of the Commons.[12]

De la Mare's first demand, which was duly met, was the appointment of a committee of lords to aid and counsel the commons.[13] After this, he and his fellows made themselves very busy. They presented the longest list of petitions ever sent to the king by the commons in a medieval parliament. They conducted their own investigations into maladministration and examined witnesses in the chapter house. They demanded the appointment of a new council about the king, to be named in parliament, and got their desire. They had a series of meetings with the lords and with John of Gaunt, who was presiding in parliament on the king's behalf, and in their course made it plain that they would not proceed further in the matter of finance until the offences of the men whom they suspected of maladministration and peculation were investigated and punished.

The impeachment of these suspected individuals was the most important business of the Good Parliament. The people of whom they complained were, primarily, Lord Latimer, the king's chamberlain; Alice Perrers, his mistress; and a group of rich

[11] *Anonimalle Chronicle*, p. 81.

[12] See further J. S. Roskell, 'Sir Peter de la Mare', *Nottingham Medieval Studies* 2 (1958), pp. 24-37, and *The Commons and their Speakers in English Parliaments 1376-1523* (Manchester, 1965), pp. 10-22, 119-20.

[13] On the commons' activities, and especially on their inter-communication with the lords, see the masterly paper by J. G. Edwards, *The Commons in Medieval English Parliaments* (Creighton Lecture, 1957), esp. pp. 15-18.

merchant capitalists of London, Richard Lyons, John Pyall, John Pechey and Adam Bury. Latimer was charged with responsibility for the loss of the forts of St Sauveur and Becherel, of which he had been captain (it was alleged that money had changed hands for their surrender). Alice Perrers was accused of wasting the king's goods and of maintenance and bribery in the courts. The charges against the Londoners all concerned illegal profiteering. The most serious was that against Lyons, that he, in conjunction with Lord Latimer and abetted by him, had made loans to the king totalling £20,000, and had charged interest at the usurious rate of $33\frac{1}{3}$ per cent. As the details of the charges make clear, it was not, strictly speaking, the government as such that was under fire in the impeachments of 1376. The people that the commons accused were not the chancellor and the treasurer, but a soldier-courtier, the king's mistress, and a group of corrupt financiers, who had used court influence to secure illegal profits to themselves from 'deals' with the government. This amounted, however, to a serious indictment of the government which had allowed these people and their 'covyn' to batten on the crown.

1376 was the first occasion on which charges were preferred against individuals by the commons as a body, and were tried before the lords in parliament. This is the procedure which came to be known technically as impeachment, and much attention has focused on the question of its origin as a legal process.[14] The lords in parliament had acted before as judges in state trials, in the cases of Roger Mortimer in 1330 and of Archbishop Stratford in 1341; what was new in 1376 was the role of the commons. Professor Plucknett believes that the model for their action was the old common law procedure of conviction based on notoriety. Miss Clarke believed that the whole commons acted as a jury presenting an indictment. Previously the only method

[14] On impeachment see M. V. Clarke, 'The origin of impeachment' in her *Fourteenth Century Studies* (Oxford, 1937), pp. 242–71; T. F. T. Plucknett, 'The origin of impeachment', *T.R.H.S.* 4th ser. 24 (1942), pp. 47–71; B. Wilkinson, 'Latimer's impeachment and parliament in the fourteenth century' in his *Studies in the Constitutional History of the Thirteenth and Fourteenth Centuries* (Manchester, 1937), pp. 82–107; and J. G. Bellamy, 'Appeal and impeachment in the Good Parliament', *B.I.H.R.* 39 (1966), pp. 35–46. On the charges levelled against merchants in 1376 see R. Bird, *The Turbulent London of Richard II* (London, 1949), pp. 18–22; and K. B. McFarlane, 'Loans to the Lancastrian kings', *C.H.J.* 9 (1947), pp. 63–4.

they had found of proceeding against influential men was by petitioning for their removal from office and for their trial; by presenting an indictment the commons asserted their right to see justice done in the court of parliament. The arguments put forward by these two historians are technical ones, and it may be doubted whether 'in the heat of the moment' (as John of Gaunt put it) the commons themselves were very sure of the technical status of what they were doing. What is clear, however, is that the precedent which was set in 1376 was constitutionally and politically of the highest importance. In impeachment, the commons found a means whereby any person of authority or influence (except of course the king in person) could be held responsible to the nation at large. Be he courtier, or captain, or councillor, or simply the holder of a patent of monopoly, the man with the king's commission could no longer regard himself as answerable to the king alone.

The secret of the effectiveness of impeachment was, of course, the ability of the commons to withhold cooperation in the matter of supply until their charges were heard. This was why impeachment opened to the commons a way to achieve what previously magnates had so often achieved only by force of arms, or the threat of it, the punishment of royal servants and agents whose malpractices had made them odious. It thus made a great breach in the theoretical defences of the system of personal monarchical direction which in practice was the day-to-day basis of national government in medieval England. It also gave a quite new significance to the force of public indignation.

John of Gaunt, who had acted on behalf of the king throughout the Good Parliament, clearly regarded its proceedings as an affront to the royal dignity and an unwarranted interference with royal freedom of action. No sooner had it dispersed, than he began to labour to undo its work. He suspected that the commons had had influential men behind them in their protests, notably William of Wykeham, the ex-chancellor who had been driven from office in 1371, and the Earl of March, the lord and patron of Peter de la Mare. Wykeham was the chief target of his anger; it was probably to prepare the ground for his disgrace that Gaunt brought Wyclif up to London from Oxford to preach against the over wealthy clergy; and in a great council at the end of the year the bishop was formally charged with administrative offences committed when he was chancellor and was deprived of his temporalities. March, about the same time, was relieved of the office of Marshal of England, and Peter de la Mare was arrested and imprisoned. In the spring parliament of 1377 the sentences on those impeached in the Good Parliament were quashed, at the request of the commons through their speaker, John of Gaunt's own steward Sir Thomas Hungerford.

This 'curialist révanche', if it may be so called, was not very effective. Gaunt's patronage of Wyclif involved him in a clash with the bishop of London, William Courtenay, which led to a more serious rift between him and the citizens of London. Some of his followers were roughly handled by the mob, and his political stock fell to a very low ebb. After Edward III's death in the summer of 1377 Wykeham was restored to his temporalities, with no protest on Gaunt's part, and de la Mare was released. Things were back by then very much to where they had been on the eve of the Good Parliament; what had happened since had served only to make the kingdom's governors a little less confident, and sharpen tensions among them.

This condition of things altered little through the years from 1377 to 1381, while the pattern of military failure set in the early 1370s repeated itself. There were many symptoms of domestic unease. In the autumn parliament of 1377 de la Mare was again speaker: he demanded that the commons should know the names of the members of the king's continual council, who had authority in his tender age and spent his money; that steps should be taken to ensure that they did not use their position to advance their personal interests; and that there should be more rigorous control of expenditure on the king's household.[15] In 1378 parliament was summoned to Gloucester instead of Westminster, because it was feared that it would be disturbed if it met in London, where the arrest in Westminster Abbey of two soldiers who concealed a diplomatically important prisoner, the Count of Denia, had roused strong feelings. This incident, and rumours that plans for the dispropriation of church endowment would be mooted again, sharpened tensions between the secular and the ecclesiastical aristocracy. Relations were also tense between Gaunt and the court on the one hand and on the other the leading London merchants, who believed he was anxious

[15] *R.P.* vol. III, pp. 5–6; and see further J. F. Baldwin, *The King's Council* (Oxford, 1913), pp. 120–4; and N. B. Lewis, 'The continual council in the early years of Richard II', *E.H.R.* 41 (1926), pp. 246–51. Lewis's analyses of the party allegiances of council members during the minority can be questioned.

to curtail their civic privileges. The Londoners were deeply suspicious too of the loyalty of the aristocratic military leadership, and their consequent unreadiness to lend to the crown added to the government's financial worries.

Despite these alarming signs of general uneasiness, the parliaments of this period were generous with their money grants. The spring parliament of 1377 granted a poll tax of 4d. per head on the whole male population of the land between the ages of twelve and sixty. That of October in the same year granted a double subsidy, and in the spring of 1379 another poll tax was approved, with liability graded by rank, from 10 marks for the Duke of Lancaster down to 4d. for the labouring man. The commons showed much concern over the way in which their grants were spent. In 1377 they appointed war treasurers to supervise the expenditure of the double subsidy. In 1379 they asked for a full investigation of the state of the king's finances by a committee of lords. All was spent, however, and to little effect. In the spring of 1380 Richard Le Scrope, the chancellor, had to explain to the commons that the continual council had nothing in hand to pay for the force which was to be sent to Brittany under the Earl of Buckingham.

In the spring of 1380 the commons granted a subsidy, but on the ominous condition that the continual council be dismissed, since their services were to no purpose and the officers of state could run the administration on their own at less expense. When in the autumn parliament at Northampton they were again asked for money their first reaction was that this demand was 'outrageous and insupportable'. There followed some long and angry wrangles between the lords and the commons as to how sufficient money could be raised. For a long time the commons were not prepared to make a grant unless the clergy would undertake to raise a third of the total sum needed, but in the end a grant was made without any important strings attached.[16] It was to be a poll tax again, as in 1377, spread over the entire male population; but the rate was now a shilling a head, three times its previous level.

This grant was to have a fateful history. The attempt to collect it led directly to an outburst of popular anger far more alarming than that of 1376, the great Peasants' Revolt of 1381.

[16] *R.P.* vol. III, pp. 88–90, and see Edwards, *The Commons in Medieval English Parliaments*, pp. 20–2.

The poll tax fell most heavily on the poor, especially in those areas where there were no wealthy men resident to help them out with their contributions. Originally it was planned to levy the tax in two instalments, in January and June 1381. As soon as the first instalment began to come in, it became clear that there had been evasion on a massive scale. In consequence the government decided to collect the whole of the second instalment forthwith, and ordered inquiries into evasion and fraudulent collection in a number of counties, mostly in the south and east. When John Bampton arrived to collect cash at Fobbing in Essex on 30 May, the people of the township 'roundly gave him answer that they would have nothing to do with him nor give him one penny'.[17] He was driven away with force, and in consequence Robert Bealknap, Chief Justice of the Common Pleas, was sent down with a commission of *trailbaston* to punish the rioters. Meanwhile the men of Fobbing had called out their neighbours. When Bealknap came to Brentwood, his party was set upon, and expelled from the town with bloodshed. While he was hurrying back dismayed to London, the whole county was beginning to rise. The men of the Thames estuary villages were often in contact with their neighbours of the Kentish shore; and on 2 June, the same day that Bealknap was thrust out of Brentwood, Abel Ker of Erith and a party of rebels attacked the Kentish Abbey of Lesness.[18]

From this point the revolt spread in Kent and Essex with a rapidity that argues a measure of preparation and organization. In Kent the rebels attacked Dartford on 4 June, on 6 June they were at Rochester, and the next day at Maidstone, where they 'chose as chief Wat Tyler'. What Wat's antecedents were is not known; one story is that he was an old soldier, another that he was later recognized as 'the greatest robber of all Kent' (the two are not irreconcilable). He was clearly an able captain, capable

[17] *Anonimalle Chronicle*, p. 134.

[18] Among the many works devoted to the revolt of 1381 the following are important: A. Reville, *Le Soulèvement des Travailleurs d'Angleterre* (Paris, 1898) – a detailed narrative account based on record evidence with an invaluable appendix of documents; C. Petit-Dutaillis, *Studies and Notes Supplementary to Stubbs' Constitutional History* (English translation, Manchester, 1914) vol. II, pp. 252–304; C. Oman, *The Great Revolt of 1381* (new ed. Oxford, 1969, with introduction and notes by E. B. Fryde); E. Powell, *The Rising in East Anglia in 1381* (Cambridge, 1896); and R. B. Dobson, *The Peasants' Revolt of 1381* (London, 1970) – collected documents with introduction.

of instilling a sense of purpose and an impressive degree of discipline. The other important Kentish leader was John Ball, the revolutionary hedge-priest whose catchwords have gone down to history:

> When Adam delved and Eve span
> Who was then the gentleman?[19]

On 10 June, under Tyler's leadership, the rebel host entered Canterbury, where they sacked the Archbishop's palace. From there they set off for London. The Essex rebels meanwhile had taken Colchester and Manningtree. At Waltham they burned all the muniments of the Abbey of the Holy Cross. Then they too headed for the capital. On 12 June the main body of the Essex men was at Mile End; and the Kentishmen were at Blackheath, where John Ball preached to their assembled host.

The king was in London with his mother, Princess Joan, the chancellor (Archbishop Sudbury), the treasurer (Sir Robert Hales), the earls of Buckingham, Derby and Arundel, and other peers. It should have been easy to put the city in a state of defence, but no steps were taken, perhaps because the king's advisers feared that, in the event of an attack by the rebels, the mob would rise inside the walls. This fear was justified. On 13 June, with the help of friends within the city, the Kentishmen entered by London Bridge, and the Essex rebels by Aldgate. The king withdrew to the Tower, where there was a garrison. Once in the city, the first objective of the rebels was the Savoy, the great London palace of John of Gaunt. They threw the furniture out of the windows, tore down the curtains and rich hangings; the plate they broke and carried out to throw in the river Thames. Nothing was stolen; the rebels were insistent that they had come to punish and destroy, not to rob. A man who had stolen a silver goblet was lynched. Another group of insurgents made its way to the Temple, the headquarters of the legal profession, who were hated as the advocates of their oppressors, and there made a great bonfire of legal books. The hospital at Clerkenwell was also sacked, and the prisons at Newgate and the Fleet opened. As night fell discipline, which had been impressive at first, began to deteriorate, and there was much housebreaking and arson.[20]

[19] *Chronicon Anglie* (R.S.), p. 321.

[20] On the rebels in London and their supporters in the city (four aldermen were later charged with complicity in the revolt) see Bird, *The Turbulent London of Richard II*, pp. 52–62; and B. Wilkinson, 'The

It was probably late on 13 June that the king held a council at the Tower, at which it was decided that he should agree to a parley with the rebels at Mile End. The object was, if possible, to persuade at least some of the rebels to disband, and to give Sudbury and Hales, whose heads the rebels were demanding, a chance to escape. So, on the morning of 14 June the fourteen-year-old king rode out from the Tower at the head of a little band of councillors. At Mile End they found the rebels, mostly Essex men, assembled; their demands were for the abolition of serfdom, that all tenants should be free and rents limited to 4d. an acre – and for the heads of Chancellor Sudbury, Treasurer Hales and other 'traitors' about the king (John of Gaunt, whom they were certainly after, was fortunately for himself in the north). All that they asked was granted – except the last point: Richard refused to let anyone be punished before he was tried. Thirty clerks were set down at once to commence writing charters of liberty; and the Essex rebels, leaving representatives to collect these when they had been sealed, began to go home.

Half the king's plan thus succeeded; the other half did not. While Richard was at Mile End Tyler and his Kentishmen broke into the Tower, where the guards put up no resistance (presumably for fear of endangering the king) and found Sudbury and Hales in the chapel, preparing for death. They were dragged out and beheaded, together with John Legge, serjeant at law, and William Appleton, John of Gaunt's physician. This was the signal for a 'carnival of anarchy' in the city, in which a great many lost their lives. There was a terrible massacre of Flemings, whom the London artisans hated for taking employment from themselves. Richard, returning from Mile End, found pandemonium loose; he did not try to press on to the Tower, but took refuge for the night at the Great Wardrobe, near St Paul's.

The climax came on the next day, Saturday 15 June, when the king summoned the Kentish rebels to Smithfield, to try if the tactics of the day before would succeed a second time. When the royal party, who had stopped to hear mass at Westminster, reached Smithfield, they found the rebels drawn up in orderly battalions, and Tyler with a single companion rode out to meet them. His demands were very like those of the Essex men, for the abolition of serfdom, for limited rents, that there should be

---

Peasants' Revolt of 1381', *Speculum* 15 (1940), pp. 12–35, esp. pp. 20–4. Wilkinson's article is also important for its detailed reconciliation of the conflicting accounts of events in the capital: I have followed his reconstruction of their pattern, which appears to me entirely convincing.

no lordship save that of the king; to which was added a demand for the disendowment of the church's temporalities and their partition among the people (John Ball's inspiration, most probably, was at work here).[21] There was some heated argument; Tyler began to be abusive, and called for a drink. As he was remounting, after draining it at a draught, he touched his weapon; Mayor Walworth of London, seeing the king threatened, cut him down on the spot. As they saw Tyler fall his followers were beginning to fit arrows to their bows, when Richard, with incredible courage, rode forward: 'Sirs, will you shoot your king? I will be your chief and captain, you shall have from me what you seek. Only follow me into the fields without.'[22] As the king began to lead the rebels into the fields round St John's Clerkenwell, Mayor Walworth turned back into the city to raise a force for his rescue.

Loyalists must have had orders to muster earlier, for within the hour Walworth was back, with a strong force led by the veteran Sir Robert Knowles. These men now blocked their way home for the Kentishmen. The king wisely avoided an engagement; he simply gave the rebels leave to depart, under escort. By evening the main body of the dead Tyler's force had passed out of the city over London Bridge, where Tyler's head had already replaced that of Archbishop Sudbury.

After 15 June the king and his council were again in control in the capital and the climax of the revolt had passed, but it was by no means over. From London and the neighbouring counties it had spilled outwards. At St Albans the townsmen, led by one William Grindcobbe, had risen against their lord the abbot, and forced him to grant them a charter of liberties. In Suffolk John Wrawe, curate of Ringsfield, had put himself at the head of the country rebels, and the townsmen of Bury, long at odds with the abbey, called in his bands to pursue their vendetta. The prior, John of Cambridge, was executed; so was Sir John Cavendish, Chief Justice of the King's Bench, who was captured by Wrawe's men at Lakenheath. Wrawe made Bury his headquarters, and made a profitable business of pillaging the local gentry. From Suffolk the revolt spread into Norfolk, where it found a leader of Tyler's standing and ability in Geoffrey Lister, to whom Norwich opened its gates. There his followers crowned him 'King of the Commons'. Cambridge and Huntingdon were also affected by the revolt, and it seems clear that it might have spread

---

[21] *Anonimalle Chronicle*, p. 147.
[22] Oman, *The Great Revolt of 1381*, p. 76.

further, into counties which saw no trouble or only isolated outbreaks, if the news of Tyler's death in London had not stiffened
resistance. Geoffrey Lister and his men evacuated Norwich
when her warlike Bishop, Henry Despenser, appeared with
forces that he had personally raised. Lister attempted a stand at
North Walsham, but his men were dispersed by a charge and he
himself was killed. Wrawe surrendered without a fight to the
Earl of Suffolk, who had come at the head of 500 lances from
London. In Essex those rebels who remained under arms were
defeated on 28 June after stiff skirmishing at Billericay by troops
under the Earl of Buckingham and Sir Thomas Percy. In Kent
the local gentry combined together to restore order. By the
beginning of July the revolt had run all its course.

The suppression of the Peasants' Revolt was marked by clemency. Apart from those who fell at North Walsham and Billericay,
few died for their part in it. Wrawe, Grindcobbe and some others
were executed, but even among the leaders a good many were
spared. On 30 August the king ordered that all proceedings pending against rebels should be transferred into King's Bench, and
no new cases instituted. In December a pardon was published
from which only a few individuals and towns (notably Bury)
were excepted. Apart from the cessation of the poll tax, which
was never again levied, the rebellion achieved nothing. The
charters granted at Mile End were quashed, and the ancient
bondage of the peasant was enforced again at law as if the
charters never had been.

The causes which led men and communities to join in the movement of 1381 were multiplex. The grievances of the London
artisans were not the same as those of the men of Kent and Essex;
the townsmen of St Albans and Bury had particular quarrels
with the abbeys which had denied them the chartered freedoms
of other boroughs; at Cambridge, where the mayor led the rebels,
the revolt gave the town its chance to strike at university privilege. Deep seated and long-term factors, the consequences of
recurrent plague and the slow decay of the manorial system, lay
behind the demands of the rustic insurgents for the abolition of
serfdom, and for fair rents and wages. Their discontent had been
fanned by the insurrectionary preaching of friars and of poor
priests like John Ball, who had taught them to doubt that the
social order of the day could find any justification in the Gospels.[23]

[23] On this aspect of the revolt see further G. R. Owst, *Literature
and Pulpit in Medieval England* (Cambridge, 1933), pp. 287–307; and

These men were the revolutionary intellectuals of 1381. What united all, peasants, poor priests, artisans, and wealthy townsmen of Bury and Cambridge, was the common burden of the poll tax and a common surge of discontent with governors who had achieved nothing but the oppression of the people. The degree of organization of which the rebels showed themselves in the circumstances capable is impressive. In the countryside the basis of the rebellion was not the manor but a much larger unit, the shire; and around London, in Kent, Essex, and the capital the rebels managed to combine their efforts, for a time at least. This argues a greater degree of political awareness, and a greater capacity for corporate political action, than we might have expected from the fourteenth-century countryman.

From our immediate point of view, it is the political aspects of the revolt of 1381 that are most interesting. It was in political terms that many contemporaries explained it. Sir Richard Waldegrave, speaker in the commons in 1381, put the blame for what had happened on heavy taxation, the extravagance of the court, and illegal maintenance by lords and their retainers, 'in spite of which the common people have not been succoured against the enemies of the realm: for they and their homes have been pillaged and robbed and burned . . . for which no remedy has been or is yet provided'.[24] The rebels were, in fact, sharply conscious of the threat of French raids, ordering those in Kent who lived in coastal areas not to leave their homes in case there should be an attack. They were also clear about who, in their eyes, were responsible for the misgovernment of the kingdom, and were insistent in their demand for the heads of named traitors: Sudbury, Hales, John of Gaunt. Here their attitude was not very different from that of the commons in the Good Parliament, who had raised like them the cry of 'traitors about the king'. The rebellion is a remarkable demonstration of the way in which distrust of all concerned in government and administration had percolated right down to the grass roots social level.

Corruption in high places and among the powerful was the obsession of the peasant rebels, as it was of their betters:

> Truth is set under a lock
> And Falseness reigneth in every flock:

N. Cohn, *The Pursuit of the Millennium* (revised ed. London, 1970), pp. 198–204.

[24] *R.P.* vol. III, p. 100.

No man may come Truth to,
But he sing *dedero* [i.e. offer a bribe].[25]

This jingle, taken from one of a number of little letters which circulated among the rebels, couched in the obscure language of religious allegory, has direct echoes of Langland's *Piers Plowman*, in which Lady Meed, the personification of bribery, holds pride of place before the law, and has friends all about the royal court. Langland can have had no sympathy with the rebels, as the naïve and conservative social philosophy of his poem shows. Resentment of misrule and failure was no sectional feeling in the 1370s and after them, but a general one. Politically, the Peasants' Revolt comes in direct line after the parliamentary protests of 1371 and 1376: it was the flood tide of popular indignation.

Let us listen again to the words of Sir Richard Waldegrave, as the roll of the autumn parliament of 1381 records them: 'To speak the straight truth, the outrages and other things which the poor commons have suffered of late, and have suffered in common to a degree not before known ... was the cause that moved them to do the riot and mischief that they did.' If matters were not remedied, he declared, 'the whole kingdom will be lost and utterly destroyed for ever, and our lord the king and the lords and the commons along with it'.[26] These are the most doleful words that were ever uttered by a speaker of the medieval commons. It is no accident that they were spoken when they were. In 1381 ten years and more of heavy taxation, political instability at home and defeat abroad had combined with the effect of poor harvests and recurrent plague to foster a mood of desperation. The kingdom was a house divided, and seemed destined to fall. The fissures ran deeper than those that the rivalries of aristocratic houses so often engendered in late medieval England. The clergy believed they were threatened in their material interests by the lords and commons of parliament. The merchants of London thought their civic privileges and their mercantile monopolies were threatened by the lords and the country gentry. The common people felt themselves threatened on all sides, by economic oppression and legal corruption, and by lack of defence against the French. The cohesion of the body politic seemed threatened; mutual trust, the foundation of medieval government, had ceased to exist. Nothing so terrible as the events of the summer of 1381 ever occurred again, in fact, but long years of political instability and recurrent crisis lay ahead.

[25] *Chron H. Knighton* (R.S.) vol. II, p. 139.
[26] *R.P.* vol. III, p. 100.

12

The reign of Richard II

Richard II's minority ended effectively in 1380, when the last of the 'continual councils' which had been in charge since 1377 was dismissed.[1] There were nineteen more years left of his reign, after that, and it proved to be a stormy and unhappy one. It was also a crucial period in the history of England in the later Middle Ages. Events that it witnessed were to have a direct influence on English politics for the best part of a century after Richard was dead. The years of his personal rule may be divided for convenience into two periods. The first culminated in a crisis, which began with the impeachment of the chancellor, Michael de la Pole, in the autumn parliament of 1386, and ended with a purge of the royal court and the courtiers in the 'Merciless Parliament' of 1388. The second period also culminated in a crisis, which began in 1397 when Richard carried out a systematic purge of his enemies of 1388, and ended in 1399 when the most important of them to survive, Henry Bolingbroke, deposed him.

The early 1380s are, at first sight, a rather amorphous period in English politics. The attention of the chroniclers focuses largely on two matters, the alarms of the ecclesiastical authorities about the spread of Wyclifite heresy, and the stormy mayoralty in London of John of Northampton, a *protégé* of John of Gaunt whose efforts to break the control over city government of the oligarchy of great merchant capitalists ended in 1384 with his exile from the city.[2] The tensions among the ruling classes observable in the 1370s endured, it is clear. Among the king's advisers, much time and attention was taken up with plans for the

[1] *R.P.* vol. III, p. 73.

[2] On Northampton and the city see R. Bird, *The Turbulent London of Richard II* (London, 1949), esp. ch. I and V; on Wyclif see above, Chapter 10.

furtherance of the French war, but things did not go any more
smoothly than they had in the preceding decade; and in the aftermath of 1381 money was harder to raise. The London merchants
became more hesitant than ever over lending, especially during
Northampton's term as mayor.

English military and diplomatic hopes tended to centre on the
possibility of exploiting the Great Schism in the church to English
advantage. Much was looked for from the marriage of Richard
to Anne of Bohemia, sister of the Emperor Wenceslas who like
the English supported Urban VI against Clement of Avignon,
but he proved incapable of offering effective alliance. Gaunt was
anxious to further his own plans for an invasion of Castile, whose
throne he claimed, under the guise of an Urbanist crusade. This
plan was favoured by many among the peers, preferably in conjunction with a royal expedition, but money for that enterprise
was not forthcoming. The commons and the mercantile interest
preferred the idea of an expedition to Flanders, which had
declared for Urban, and where the men of Ghent were in revolt
against their count. After the defeat of Philip van Artevelde of
Ghent at Roosebek in 1382 the wool route from Calais to Ghent
was threatened and this decided the matter. There was insufficient cash for a royal expedition, and Bishop Henry Despenser
of Norwich was allowed to recruit a force for Flanders, on which
bulls from Rome conferred the status of a crusade. After some
initial success in the summer of 1383, the bishop's campaign
ended in ignominious defeat, and he and his captains were impeached in the autumn parliament. In the hurry of retreat they
had sold out the places that they had taken to the French for
cash down, though it is not quite certain that the bishop knew
what was going on. Englishmen felt that, once again, the advantage which should have been bought with the money that they
had laid out had been lost through treachery.[3]

In 1385 Richard at last did lead a royal host to war; not to
France, however, but to Scotland, where hostilities had been resumed after the arrival there of French troops under John of
Vienne. The army of 1385 was a large one, and before entering
Scotland Richard created his two uncles, Edmund and Thomas,
dukes of York and Gloucester respectively, and made his
chancellor, Michael de la Pole, Earl of Suffolk. He advanced as
far as Edinburgh, but failed to bring the Scots to an engagement.

[3] See further E. Perroy, *L'Angleterre et le Grand Schisme d'Occident
1378–1399* (Paris, 1933), ch. V; and M. Aston, 'The impeachment of
Bishop Despenser', *B.I.H.R.* 38 (1965), pp. 127–48.

The best news of the year for the English came in fact from Spain, where, with the aid of a small force of English archers, James of Aviz, the new king of Portugal, resoundingly defeated the Castilians at Aljubarotta. James was the champion of national, Urbanist and anti-Castilian feelings in Portugal, and his success suggested that the time was ripe for Gaunt to make his bid for the Castilian throne. In the spring of 1386, he made an agreement with Richard, whereby the king should pay for the transport of a Lancastrian army to Spain, and advance 20,000 marks to Gaunt for expenses, to be repaid when he had won his kingdom. On 8 July Gaunt sailed from Plymouth for Galicia. He was to remain abroad for the next four years.

John of Gaunt departed at an ill moment for England. In the summer of 1386 a great French host was gathered at Sluys, and an invasion seemed imminent. After it had disbanded, a wave of indignation against the government whose repeated failures abroad had exposed the kingdom to such risk was unleashed in the autumn parliament, where chancellor Pole was impeached. The first great crisis of the reign had commenced.

In order to understand this crisis, we must try to peer a little behind the façade of events in the period 1381-6. Parliamentary and popular reactions to the government's lack of success, especially abroad, were reminiscent of the previous decade. In 1381 and 1382 there were demands in parliament for the investigation of the expense of the king's household. The commons hedged their grants for Despenser's crusade with conditions. Distrust of leading men was apparent; in the spring parliament of 1384 Pole was openly accused of bribery by one John Cavendish, a London fishmonger, and in the autumn parliament allegations of maintenance were raised against the king's intimate Robert de Vere, Earl of Oxford. The parliament of 1385 asked for an annual review of the expenditure of the household, and to know the names of the king's councillors, who, says Walsingham, were publicly reputed to be 'knights of Venus rather than Bellona'. He and other chroniclers confirm the impression given by the parliament rolls, of widespread distrust of those in high places. A number of aristocrats seem to have associated themselves with the general dissatisfaction, notably the Earl of Arundel, and the king's youngest uncle, Thomas of Woodstock, who until 1386 was denied much influence in politics. Arundel and Woodstock were both men with military ambitions and inclinations, and shared the suspicions of the commons that the king's advisers were preparing a 'sell-out' abroad to the French.[4]

The reaction that criticism evoked from the government was strikingly different, in this period, from what it had been in the days of Edward III's wise pliancy. The men who charged Pole and de Vere in 1384 found themselves severely punished for defamation. The demand of the parliament of 1385 for an inquiry into household expenditure led to the drawing up of a new ordinance, but it was simply not implemented by the king and his advisers, and the names of the king's councillors were not made known.[5] It looks as if the king and his circle were determined to make as few concessions to popular pressure as they could, and to establish a tighter control over the direction of events. In 1383 the initiative in the impeachment of Despenser was taken out of the hands of the commons, and the chancellor conducted the prosecution *ex parte regis*. The increasing use of the king's personal seal, the signet, as a warrant to the chancery, and complaints at the extension of the jurisdiction of the court of the royal household, point in the same direction.

Signs of the emergence at court of a political group close to the young king are also significant. Two figures in particular were notable. One was Robert de Vere, a close intimate of Richard's from 1383 onwards, who was created Marquis of Dublin in 1385, a title which set him apart from all the rest of the peers, except the royal dukes. The other was Simon Burley, an experienced soldier who had been long in the service of the Black Prince, and subsequently was Richard's tutor. He was made under-chamberlain for life in 1383 and chief justice of South Wales, and later became Warden of the Cinque Ports. His influence helped to gather in the chamber a group of knights dedicated to the curialist interest, many of them like himself old servants of the Black Prince, with a leavening of younger men, as the trio Beauchamp, Berners and Salisbury whom chroniclers

---

[4] The early years of Richard II, especially those from 1381 to 1386, have been heavily studied. The most important secondary accounts are those in Tout, *Chapters* vol. III; and of A. Steel in *Richard II* (Cambridge, 1941), ch. IV. See also J. Armitage-Smith, *John of Gaunt* (London, 1904), and P. E. Russell, *The English Intervention in Spain and Portugal* (Oxford, 1955), for what concerns Lancaster, and Spain; and M. V. Clarke, 'The Lancastrian faction and the wonderful parliament' in her *Fourteenth Century Studies* (Oxford, 1937), pp. 36–52.

[5] On this ordinance see J. J. N. Palmer, 'The impeachment of Michael de la Pole in 1386', *B.I.H.R.* 42 (1969), pp. 96–101.

mention with particular resentment.[6] Two important additions to this court circle were Nicholas Brembre, the city merchant and financier who had replaced Northampton as mayor, whom Richard knighted; and Pole, the chancellor (whose original connexions had been Lancastrian). Pole's ancestry was mercantile; his promotion to the Earldom of Suffolk in 1385 was much resented by many among the older aristocracy.

Gaunt's departure from England in 1386 was important to this growing royal clique. With his immense wealth, his great following of retainers and his large experience of affairs, Gaunt's influence in politics was inevitably powerful, and the wilder among the young men close to Richard seem to have mistaken him for the chief brake upon their freedom of action. De Vere was almost certainly the moving spirit behind a plot to discredit Gaunt in 1384, when an Irish Carmelite produced a story that the duke was plotting against the king's life.[7] In the spring of 1385 the king himself is said to have been privy to a plot to get rid of Gaunt. In 1386 Richard was no doubt glad to make his uncle's departure for Spain easy. Gaunt in fact seems to have been entirely loyal; the king and the king's cronies were wrong in seeing him as their chief enemy. They were meanwhile making for themselves other foes, less scrupulous than he, who would be formidable when he was gone.

Gaunt's departure for Spain, instead of freeing the hands of Richard's associates, brought them face to face with crisis. When parliament assembled in the autumn of 1386, the first demand of the commons was for the dismissal of Pole, whom they wished to impeach, and of the treasurer, Bishop Fordham of Durham. Richard, who had left Westminster for Eltham, replied that he would not dismiss a scullion from his kitchen at their request.[8] In defiance of what he must have known was the popular feeling, he elevated Robert de Vere, from Eltham, to a new dignity, to be Duke of Ireland, with viceregal powers there. But when a delegation appeared from parliament, headed by Thomas of Wood-

[6] On Burley and the chamber see Tout, *Chapters* vol. III, p. 404; Steel, *Richard II*, pp. 114–16; N. B. Lewis, 'Simon Burley and Baldwin Raddington', *E.H.R.* 52 (1937), pp. 662–9; also C. D. Ross in 'Forfeiture for treason in the reign of Richard II', *E.H.R.* 71 (1956), pp. 564–5.

[7] On this incident see Tout, *Chapters* vol. III, pp. 391–3; and L. C. Hector, 'An alleged hysterical outburst of Richard II', *E.H.R.* 68 (1953), pp. 62–5.

[8] *Chron. H. Knighton* (R.S.) vol. II, p. 215.

stock and Thomas Arundel, bishop of Ely and the earl's brother, he found his position would be hard to maintain. When he declared that their attitude amounted to rebellion and threatened to seek the aid of the king of France, they reminded him that there was past precedent, if a king would not be governed by the laws of the realm 'with the common assent of the people, for deposing the king himself from the royal throne, and to elevate some near kinsman of the royal line'.[9] Before the threat of Edward II's fate, uttered by the king's own uncle and a bishop of high birth who came as spokesmen for the whole parliament, Richard had no alternative but to bow.

So parliament was able to go ahead with its work, and Pole was duly impeached. The most important charge against him was his failure to succour Ghent, which had held out against the French until 1385; it is an index of the general determination to see the last of him, that when he cleared himself on this score, the prosecution was pressed forward to convict him on technical charges of maladministration and peculation.[10] He was sentenced to forfeiture of a large part of his estates, and to imprisonment at 'the king's pleasure'. Worse offence to the royal dignity was to follow. A great and continual council was appointed, by statute, to govern for a year. It was given full control of all revenues and subsidies, and powers to survey the expenses of the household, inquire into all gifts of fees, land or office that the king had made, and to correct what had been done amiss. The composition of the council was not extremist; besides Woodstock, Arundel and his brother the bishop, there were men of more moderate leanings, the two archbishops, William of Wykeham and Bishop Brantingham of Exeter, Sir John Devereux and Sir Richard Scrope, who was a connexion of Pole himself. Richard's attitude was decided not by its personnel, however, but by the fact that it was appointed against his will, with offensive powers which effectively restored the situation of a minority. This was a weak point in the authority of the 'commission council'. Edward III, in 1341, had set a clear precedent for repealing, on his own initiative, statutes which in the king's view ran contrary to the royal prerogative and the law of the land. There was no clear reason why Richard should not do the same.

⁹ ibid. p. 219.
¹⁰ See N. B. Lewis, 'Article VII of the impeachment of Michael de la Pole', *E.H.R.* 42 (1927), pp. 402–7. Pole's failure to implement the reforming ordinance of 1385 was also a serious charge, as Palmer explains in his article, cited in note 5.

The council seems to have gone about its work conscientiously, but it had, from the outset, to contend with absolute non-cooperation from the king. Before parliament dispersed, Richard appeared in person before those assembled, 'and made public protest by his own mouth, that on account of any thing done in the said parliament, he was not willing that prejudice should be incurred by himself or his crown, and that his prerogative and the liberties of his said crown should be saved and guarded'.[11] Pole, whom parliament had condemned, had the fine imposed on him remitted by the king, and his 'imprisonment' took the form of house arrest at Windsor, where Burley was his gaoler. Then, early in February 1387, Richard quitted Westminster, where the commission council was sitting, taking with him Pole, de Vere, Burley, Sir John Beauchamp and a number of household men, and Sir Robert Tressilian, the Chief Justice of the King's Bench. These formed virtually a rival council to the one set up by parliament. Richard did not return to Westminster until the commission's year of authority was all but ended.

In the spring and summer of 1387 Richard was mostly in the midlands and the marches of Wales. There and in Cheshire the king retained archers and others in his service. On a visit to York he won over Archbishop Neville, who was a member of the commission, to his cause. He sounded out the sheriffs, about the forces that they could raise on his behalf, and about whether they could ensure that men favourable to the king's interest were sent to the next parliament. From them Richard got little change; all the commons, they declared, were favourable to the lords of the commission. He got more satisfactory responses from the city authorities of London, whom he consulted through the ex-mayor, Nicholas Brembre. But the most favourable response of all was from those 'old and trusted friends of the king', the judges of the common law who were Sir Robert Tressilian's colleagues.

At two great councils, at Shrewsbury on 21 August, and at Nottingham on 25 August, Richard and his advisers put a series of questions about the king's legal position to a group of judges who included (besides Tressilian) the Chief Justice of the Common Pleas, Robert Bealknap, with three of his colleagues, and the chief baron of the exchequer. The questions were subtle, the answers significant. It was first asked if the statute appointing the commission council 'derogated from the regality and prerogative of the lord king'. When this was answered affirmatively, two further questions and answers established that those who com-

[11] *R.P.* vol. III, p. 224.

pelled the king to assent to such a statute ought to be punished 'as traitors'. So, in the judges' view, ought all generally who hindered the king in the exercise of his regality. The next two answers established that the king could in law dissolve parliament whenever he wished, and further that the lords and commons had no legal right to put forward articles of their own and insist on their discussion before dealing with the king's business (i.e. they had no right to insist on redress before granting supply). This cleared the way to the answer to a following question, which defined it as unlawful to impeach a minister in parliament without the king's assent. The judges further made it clear that in their view those who had claimed for the deposition of Edward II the status of a lawful precedent acted treasonably, and that the sentence recently passed on Pole was erroneous.[12]

The judges' answers branded the action of those who had forced the commission council on the king as a crime 'like treason'. The plan clearly was to arraign such of Richard's enemies as he thought fit on charges based on the answers, as soon as the commission's year of office had expired. The judges' answers were also constitutionally of great significance. They constitute the most clear and reasoned statement of the role of royal prerogative in government that was ever made in England in the Middle Ages. They made it plain that it was the king's prerogative to choose his councillors; that they were responsible to him, not to parliament; that parliament was dependent on his will for summons and dismissal; that it had no right to initiate business or impeach without his assent. Legally, the most doubtful point in the answers was that, in defining attempts to thwart the prerogative as treasonable, they ran counter to the definition of treason given in Edward III's statute of 1352, which limited the scope of treason to such acts as aiding the king's enemies, and levying war against him in his realm. Nevertheless, though the judges later were to claim that they responded under duress, they seem actually to have given their answers freely and even enlarged on certain points. According to the received canons of legal learning of the time, they were right in law. Their answers formed a decisive challenge to the power and authority which parliament had been quietly establishing for itself in its dealings with the crown over half a century past, and to the multiplying

[12] The text of the questions to the judges is given by the Monk of Westminster, printed in Higden, *Polychronicon* (R.S.) vol. IX, pp. 99–101. The most illuminating discussion of them is S. B. Chrimes, 'Richard II's questions to the judges', *L.Q.R.* 72 (1956), pp. 365–90.

precedents for parliamentary insistence on redress preceding supply.

No such challenge could have been formulated at a less appropriate moment. Common opinion was generally behind the commission council. The prospect of a new definition of treason brought with it the threat of large-scale forfeitures, to embitter the family relations and party alignments of the aristocracy as they had done in the reign of Edward II. The news of what the judges had told the king, with its implied threat to security of property, solidified support behind the king's opponents, and their leaders began to prepare for a show of force. When Richard returned to London, Gloucester (Thomas of Woodstock), Arundel and the Earl of Warwick were gathering their retainers. When they appeared before the king at Westminster on 17 November, they were ready to carry the war into his camp by 'appealing' five of his intimates, de Vere, Pole, Tressilian, Brembre and Archbishop Neville, of treason. The foundation of their charge was that these five favourites, by the undue influence that they had exercised over the king, were 'accroaching royal power'. This was a charge quite outside the limits of the 1352 statute, and harked back to the bad old days of Edward II, when it had been used against both Gaveston and the Despensers.

At Westminster Richard promised that his five friends should be kept under arrest until the next parliament, which was summoned for 3 February 1388, when the appeal against them would be heard. This gained him time; but after the army, which de Vere was leading out of Cheshire to his support, was dispersed by the appellants (now joined by Gaunt's son, Henry Bolingbroke, and Mowbray of Nottingham) at Radcot Bridge in Oxfordshire, all that time gained was a chance for his friends to flee the country. After Radcot Bridge the Londoners were not prepared to make a stand on the king's behalf. When the victorious appellants arrived in the capital, Richard at the Tower was entirely at their mercy.[13]

On the day that the Merciless Parliament of 1388 assembled, the five appellant lords, Gloucester, Arundel, Warwick, Bolingbroke and Nottingham, entered the assembly together 'arm in arm,

[13] On the Radcot Bridge campaign see J. N. L. Myres, 'The campaign of Radcot Bridge in December 1387', *E.H.R.* 42 (1927), pp. 20–33. On the possibility that Richard may have been temporarily deposed, after the appellants' arrival in London, see Clarke, *Fourteenth Century Studies*, pp. 91–5.

dressed in cloth of gold'[14] to uphold their appeal. Of the five men accused, only Brembre was there to stand his trial; the others had all fled, and proceedings against them were in absence. At the beginning, the appellants were in some difficulty over their manner of proceeding. The common lawyers declared that the appeal would not hold by their law (the treasons alleged were not among those defined in 1352 by statute), and the civil lawyers that their law would not apply to the case, since England had never been subject to Roman civil law. The problem was solved by a solemn declaration that the 'law and course of parliament' took precedence over the law of any other court in the kingdom, and that the lords of parliament, as the judges of its law, could hear the appeal. There was some legal justification for this claim. The statute of 1352 had stated clearly that new treasons, over and above those which it defined, should not be judged in the common law courts, but in parliament. Appeal was a method of criminal accusation recognized at common law, and there was precedent (in spite of what some historians have claimed to the contrary) for hearing appeals in parliament.[15] Thus, in parliamentary appeal of treason, the appellants found a way of proceeding without overriding either the common law or the statute of 1352. They also provided a direct answer to the opinions which Richard's judges had expressed at Shrewsbury, by asserting the judicial supremacy of parliament over all other courts.[16]

There is no need to examine the details of the trials in the Merciless Parliament; their results were a foregone conclusion. All five of the king's friends were convicted of treason. Only Brembre and Tressilian, who was found in hiding after he had been sentenced, were executed; the others were safe overseas. Their lands, of course, were forfeited.[17] A number of Richard's other supporters were impeached: Simon Burley; the three chamber knights Beauchamp, Berners and Salisbury; and the

[14] T. Favent, *Historia Mirabilis Parliamenti*, ed. M. McKisack (*Camden Miscellany* vol. XIV), p. 14.

[15] See for an instance Sir J. Stephen, *A History of the Criminal Law* vol. I (London, 1883), p. 152; and on the process of appeal of treason see A. Rogers, 'Parliamentary appeals of treason in the reign of Richard II', *American Journal of Legal History* 8 (1964), pp. 95–124.

[16] On this see the invaluable note by H. M. Cam in Steel, *Richard II*, pp. 178–9.

[17] On these forfeitures see C. D. Ross, 'Forfeiture for treason in the reign of Richard II', *E.H.R.* 71 (1956), pp. 560–75, which corrects in important respects Clarke's 'Forfeitures and treason in 1388' in her *Fourteenth Century Studies*, pp. 115–45.

king's confessor Rushook. Burley and the three knights were executed. The judges who had subscribed to the famous opinions, and Blake, the serjeant at law who had framed the questions, were sent into exile in Ireland. It is significant that the appellants had considerable difficulty in securing the conviction of Brembre, the only appellee who was tried in person. A committee of peers declared that they found nothing in the charges against him worthy of death, but they were overborne by pressure from the commons. Some of the peers also wished to spare Burley; again, it was the commons' insistence, and the determination of 'the undivided Trinity', Gloucester, Warwick and Arundel, that ensured the death sentence. Opinion at large was behind the most extreme measures of the parliament. If it had not been, the king could never have been so ignominiously humbled through the execution of his friends.

Having purged the king's intimates and censured the opinions of his judges, the Merciless Parliament had achieved what the appellants desired of it. To ensure permanence for its measures, they were formally declared irrevocable, binding on all future parliaments (a contradiction in terms, as Steel has pointed out).[18] At the same time, in order that the processes of the parliament should not be used against their inventors, it was declared that its procedures and convictions did not constitute a precedent. The appellants, at the request of the commons, were awarded £20,000 'for their great expenses in procuring the salvation of the realm and the destruction of the traitors'.[19] This was as far as the Merciless Parliament's achievement went, which reminds us sharply of the limited aims of the group of lords who dominated its proceedings. They wished to secure themselves, to get rid of the men who had been close to the king, to have a taste for themselves of the fruits of power and office, not very much more.

On behalf of the king's friends, it may be said that they at least, in the crisis of 1386–8, showed themselves capable of thinking in broad terms, about policies which, if they had been able to put them into practice, would have brought about a real change of direction in constitutional development. The judges' opinions outlined, by a series of legal definitions, a system of government which would rescue royal policy (and the officials responsible for carrying it out) from the constant and frustrating necessity of adjustment to meet the demands of public opinion, as expressed in parliament. In the mood of the kingdom of 1387,

[18] Steel, *Richard II*, p. 153.
[19] *R.P.* vol. III, p. 245.

their plans were, however, simply unworkable. Nor were the royalists any more moderate than the appellants, in their human intentions. If fortune had gone their way, they certainly meant to purge their enemies, and would not have shown them more mercy, probably, than they were shown themselves.

The fact that the appellants had no new salve, apart from changes of governing personnel, was soon apparent. After initial success with a naval victory in the Channel in 1387, belligerence in foreign policy got nowhere. Before the end of 1388 negotiations with the French for a truce had been resumed, while in the north, English arms suffered a severe defeat at Otterburn at the hands of Douglas. When the autumn parliament of 1388 met at Cambridge, the commons were full of old and familiar complaints about the poor enforcement of the statute of labourers, misgovernment of the Calais staple, and the excesses committed by the liveried retainers of noblemen.[20] By May 1389, the initiative had passed to Richard again. At a great council at Westminster he appeared in person, and declared that he intended to assume the rule of the kingdom himself, with the aid of councillors of his own choice. Without protest, Bishop Arundel, the appellants' chancellor, and his colleagues Gilbert and Waltham, the treasurer and the keeper of the privy seal, surrendered their seals of office.

The main consequence of the crisis of 1386–8 was the venom that it instilled into the feuds of the aristocracy. Such feuds were bound to involve not the principals only, but also the whole train of friends, relatives and retainers that constituted the 'affinities' of great noblemen. The revival of the charge of treason as a political crime was a particularly ominous feature, evoking unhappy memories of the days of Edward II. It was probably because they were aware of the terrible consequences which could stem from executions and forfeitures among the great that so many peers were anxious to restrain the vindictive anger of the appellants and the commons in the Merciless Parliament. They failed, as we have seen, and when that parliament dispersed, a crop of vendettas that would not be easily forgotten had been baptized in blood.

[20] The roll of this important parliament does not survive. For a useful examination of its activities and the sources bearing on it see J.A. Tuck, 'The Cambridge parliament 1388', *E.H.R.* 84 (1969), pp. 225–43.

The men who in 1389 took over at the chancery and the exchequer were Wykeham and Brantingham; Master Edmund
Stafford became keeper of the privy seal. All three were experienced administrators, who had been uncommitted in the
recent troubles. Their appointment is one of the features that
have led some historians to label the early 1390s a period of
'appeasement'. Certainly the tenor of politics was very different
from that of preceding years. The parliaments of the period
1390–6 had none of the stormy quality of those of the 1370s
and 1380s; they did not sit so long, and were summoned less
frequently. There was a studied deference to parliamentary
opinion; in 1390 the chancellor, the treasurer and all the lords
of the council resigned their offices in parliament so that charges
might be brought against them, and when none were forthcoming, were reappointed and resworn, in parliament. The commons were regularly consulted on such matters as peace negotiations with France. There were numerous great councils, to which
the appellant lords were regularly invited. The council records
show that Gloucester, in particular, always received that respect
which was due to him as an uncle of the king. When Wykeham
and Brantingham, both ageing men, relinquished their posts,
the men who replaced them were none other than the appellants'
chancellor and treasurer, bishops Arundel and Gilbert. When
Archbishop Courtenay of Canterbury died in 1396, Arundel was
the man who succeeded him.

The return of John of Gaunt had much to do with the surface
harmony in exalted circles of the years 1390–6. In 1388 he had
come to terms with John of Trastamara the king of Castile, who
could not expel him from Galicia even after he had lost most of
his army through disease, and his daughter was betrothed to
John's heir.[21] In the autumn of 1389 he was back in England,
and though he was in 1390 made Duke of Guienne for life, he
did not spend much time there. In England he held a unique
position among the aristocracy. He was the most experienced
and easily the wealthiest of the peers, the father of one appellant,
Henry Bolingbroke, and the elder brother of another, Gloucester.
In the king's eyes he was uncontaminated by any association
with the events of 1388. His views on the dignity of the royal
office and prerogative were sympathetic to Richard's, as his conduct as lieutenant for his father long ago in the Good Parliament
of 1376 had shown. Unquestionably loyal to the king, respected

[21] On Gaunt's Castilian expedition see Russell, *The English Intervention in Spain and Portugal*, ch. XVII–XIX.

by most of his brother peers and feared by others, his influence was a powerful force to keep internal feuds in the background.

Bitterness, however, was very far from dead, notwithstanding Gaunt's influence and conciliatory policy, and there were plenty of signs of it. In 1392 Richard had to promise in council that 'he would do no harm to any lord or other his liege on account of things done in time past . . . nor would he seek to restore any of those who were condemned in full parliament in his kingdom'.[22] Richard never in fact tried to restore de Vere or Archbishop Neville (Pole had died abroad in 1389), but his old opponents were almost certainly right in thinking that he wished to do so. In 1393 there was a rising of the commons in Cheshire, and Richard had to deny publicly rumours that he was conniving at it for political ends of his own. Arundel thought the independence which Gaunt's intimacy gave Richard so dangerous that he even attempted to discredit the former by charging him with using undue influence on the king, in the parliament of 1394. The charge fell through, and he had to make a humiliating apology. In that same year Queen Anne died, and there was an ugly scene at her funeral when Richard struck Arundel across the face, because he was showing insufficient respect for the corpse. Arundel was so alarmed about his political position that he took the trouble to sue out for himself a formal pardon for all that he had been concerned with in 1387-8.

With the king wearing Gaunt's device in public, there was nothing that the ex-appellants could do to prevent him gathering about him a body of committed royal supporters far more for-midable than the little group of curialists of 1387. Prominent in this new 'royal party' were a number of younger noblemen: John and Thomas Holland (earls of Huntingdon and Kent, and the king's half-brothers), John Montagu Earl of Salisbury, York's son Edward Earl of Rutland, and Sir Thomas Percy, who was steward of the household and represented the northern magnate interest. A number of clerks who had personal associations with the king were preferred to high ecclesiastical office: Medford, Bishop of Salisbury, and Walden, Dean of York, had both acted as secretary to Richard; Tydeman Bishop of Worcester had been his physician and Burghill of Lichfield his confessor; Merke of Carlisle was said to have been his boon companion. The chamber knights, who discharged most of the routine administrative and judicial business of the council in these years, formed another

[22] *Prophet's Journal of the Council*, printed in J. F. Baldwin, *The King's Council* (Oxford, 1913), p. 495.

group of supporters, able and experienced as well as influential. Baldwin Raddington (a connexion of Burley's), Richard Stury, William Scrope and Edward Dalyngryg, men with a martial background, were among the most prominent. The famous trio, Bushy, Bagot and Green, contributed experience of a different order. All three had sat in more than one parliament, and Bushy served as speaker in 1394. He and Green had both been in Lancaster's retinue, and continued to take his fees when they took the king's also. Their influence in the royal service created a link between the court and the kind of opinion which was mirrored in parliament by the views of the shire knights.

Two important developments helped to alter the political situation of the 1390s. The first was Richard II's expedition to Ireland in 1394.[23] The situation of the Anglo-Irish administration, centred on Dublin Castle, had long been unsatisfactory, and the king's chief justice now barely maintained control in the coastal towns of the Pale. The native chiefs, especially Art Mac-Murrough in Leinster, were pressing the Anglo-Irish so hard that many were leaving the country. Richard's first plan was to send Gloucester over as lieutenant, but his commission was revoked in 1393 and a royal expedition organized. The army that Richard raised was a very large one, and he marched at its head from Waterford to Dublin; this demonstration in force cowed the native chiefs into submission. The success thus achieved (very temporarily as it proved) gave Richard some cachet as a military leader. More importantly, it gave him and his officials an immensely valuable experience of military administration. The largest contingent in the army was raised and paid through the household. The process of raising large numbers of 'yeomen and archers of the crown', especially in Cheshire and north Wales, who received a fee and swore to stand by for service, pointed the way for the recruitment of a standing reserve of royal retainers, the famous 'Cheshire guards'. The badge of the white hart, Richard's personal emblem, was given as an outward sign that a yeoman had taken the king's fee. Thus, as Tout put it, 'the forces of autocracy began to be clothed in military garb'.[24]

The other factor that dramatically altered the aspect of English politics in this period was the movement towards a *rapprochement* with France. A truce had been agreed in May 1389 for three

[23] On all matters concerned with this expedition, see E. Curtis, *Richard II in Ireland* (Oxford, 1927).

[24] See Tout, *Chapters* vol. III, pp. 487-9, and vol. IV, pp. 10, 199.

years, and this was subsequently renewed while negotiations for a final peace went forward. Gaunt was very prominent in this business: he led the English deputation, which in 1392 was magnificently received at Amiens by Charles VI in person, and in 1394 he and York were in charge of talks at Leulinghen with the dukes of Burgundy and Berry. Final terms agreeable to both sides proved, however, hard to find. The French coveted the return of Calais, which even the most pacific in Richard's circle hesitated to contemplate. The thorniest question of all was, of course, the sovereignty over Aquitaine; Gaunt seems to have hoped to get round it by the establishment of his own line there as hereditary dukes, holding from the crown of France, but this scheme broke down as a result of resistance from his putative subjects, the Gascons themselves.[25] Gloucester would have gone along with this arrangement, but he remained deeply suspicious of the French, unwilling to stretch points in conciliation.[26] The final result was, in consequence, short of a peace. It was a truce to last for twenty-eight years. This was a period long enough to relieve Richard of all concern about raising money for war overseas for the foreseeable future. To cement the truce, Richard took a new bride, Isabella, the eldest daughter of Charles VI. She was only six, but Richard was not yet thirty: there was a prospect of an heir in due course, and in the meantime the new queen brought a dowry of 800,000 francs.

In special instructions, given just before the arrangements for his marriage were completed, Richard told his negotiators that they might reduce the sum demanded by way of dowry, if the French king and his uncles would promise to support him, if the need arose 'against all manner of folk . . . and to sustain him with all their power against any of his own subjects'.[27] No such agreement, of course, appeared in the final text of the treaty, but there was almost certainly a tacit understanding. When, at the end of 1396, Richard returned from Calais with his new bride, he was certainly in an immeasurably stronger position vis-à-vis potential domestic enemies than he had been ten years earlier.

[25] See further J. J. N. Palmer's important article, 'The Anglo-French peace negotiations 1390–1396', T.R.H.S. 5th ser., 16 (1966), pp. 81–94.

[26] For Gloucester's attitude see Chronique de la Traison et Mort de Richard II, ed. B. Williams (English Historical Soc. 1846), pp. 2–3; J. G. Bellamy has some useful comments on him in his 'Northern rebellions in the later years of Richard II', B.J.R.L. 47 (1964–5), pp. 254–74.

[27] Foed. vol. VII, p. 811.

France was now an ally, not an enemy, and he was relieved of the dependence on parliament for war finance that had so long hampered the free rein of regality. He could afford to think again about putting into practice ideas about the way in which his kingdom ought to be governed that had been much in the minds of his intimates ten years earlier.

In the spring parliament of 1397 the commons presented the famous petition of Thomas Haxey: 'that the great and excessive charge of the king's household be amended and diminished'.[28] The subject of the petition was one that had sparked off Richard's anger before, and his reaction was the same as it had been in 1386. But his position was now different, far stronger; the consequence of the petition was Haxey's arraignment for treason. Not only was he convicted, but the lords in parliament declared further, on the king's behalf, 'that if anyone, of whatsoever estate or condition, shall move or excite the commons of parliament or any other person to make remedy of any matter which touches our person or our government or our regality, he shall be held a traitor'.[29] The echo of the judges' answers of 1387 is unmistakable.

Haxey's condemnation was the first warning of the gathering storm of the royalist *révanche*, which broke in the autumn parliament and swept away both the men of 1388 and their measures. Historians have been divided as to whether what happened was simply the fruition of the king's long laid plans, or whether it was triggered off by the discovery of a new plot by the old appellants, as Richard and his friends claimed in the summer when Gloucester, Warwick and Arundel were all arrested. Two facts strongly militate in favour of the first explanation. One is that in spite of the allegations that a new plot and been uncovered, the public charges which were brought against the three noblemen were, without exception, based on what they had done between 1386 and 1388. Secondly, Richard's actions were aimed just as much at the measures as at the men of 1388. This was not just a purge; it was an effort to force English government into conformity with doctrinaire principles of regality.

This intention was made plain at the opening of the parliament, when the chancellor, the Bishop of Exeter, preached upon the text from Ezekiel 'there shall be one king for all'. Kings, he explained, were sworn at their coronation to guard the regality and

[28] *R.P.* vol. III, p. 339.
[29] ibid. p. 408.

prerogatives of the crown, which were inalienable: 'Wherefore
the king has caused his estates of parliament to be assembled on
this occasion, to be informed if any rights of the crown are sub-
tracted or diminished: so that by their good advice and discretion
such remedy can be provided, as will make the king in his liberty
and power as his ancestors were before him . . . there shall be
one king for all and he shall govern all.'[30] The acts of the parliament were faithful to the spirit of the bishop's sermon. At an
early stage the question of the statute empowering the 'commission council' of 1386 was raised by the commons (Bushy was
their speaker), because 'it seemed prejudicial to the king and a
usurpation of his regality'.[31] Not only was it struck off the statute
roll, but it was declared that it would henceforward be high
treason for anyone to 'pursue or purchase' any such commission.
The finishing touches to this part of its programme were given
when the parliament reassembled at Shrewsbury in January 1398.
All the acts of the Merciless Parliament of 1388 were annulled.
All and any who were involved in opposing the king in 1387–8
had in consequence to sue for pardon.[32] The questions that had
been put to the judges in 1387 were rehearsed, and their answers
were formally pronounced good law with the assent of the whole
parliament. Finally, the king's financial independence was
strengthened by the grant for life of subsidies on wool and leather
exports.

Careful plans had been laid in advance to secure the conviction
of Warwick, Arundel and Gloucester, whose cases came before
the first session of the parliament. In a great council at Nottingham in the late summer a group of eight lords, the earls of Rutland, Huntingdon, Kent, Somerset, Nottingham and Salisbury,
with Lord Despenser and Sir William Scrope, formally appealed
the three ex-appellants of treasons committed ten years before.
In parliament, before the appeals were tried, the points of
treason were formally rehearsed in a wording slightly different
from the 1352 statute, to make sure that the charge would hold.
Then the charter of pardon which Arundel had taken out in
1394 was solemnly revoked, as granted 'under duress' (a singular
description of the so called period of appeasement). In order to
leave no doubt about the legality of the forthcoming conviction,
the spiritual lords, who would take no part in a judgement of

[30] ibid. p. 347.
[31] ibid. p. 350.
[32] See C. Barron, 'The tyranny of Richard II', *B.I.H.R.* 41 (1968),
pp. 1–18, esp. pp. 7–10.

blood, were forced to appoint a proctor, Sir Thomas Percy, the steward of the household, to act for them in the process. As a preliminary to the main trials, Archbishop Arundel was got out of the way; impeached by the commons, he was exiled, and a papal bull conveniently translated him to a see in the Avignon obedience. The appeals were then heard. Warwick broke down, confessed his guilt, and was exiled to the Isle of Man. Arundel took his stand on his pardon, but it was already revoked, and Gaunt, speaking as Steward of England for all the lords, sentenced him to execution. Gloucester did not stand his trial, because he had died in prison at Calais. It is virtually certain that he was murdered at Richard's orders with the connivance of Nottingham. Before he died he had written a confession, admitting his guilt in 1387 and that he had even withdrawn his homage from Richard, and he was condemned posthumously.[33] All the estates of the condemned men, including lands entailed as well as those held in fee simple, were forfeited.

Those who had helped in the undoing of the men of 1388 were amply rewarded. Henry Bolingbroke was created Duke of Hereford; Mowbray of Nottingham Duke of Norfolk; John and Thomas Holland dukes of Exeter and Surrey respectively; John Beaufort (eldest of Gaunt's sons by Catherine Swinford) became Marquis of Dorset; and Thomas Despenser, Thomas Percy, Ralph Neville and William Scrope became earls of Gloucester, Worcester, Westmoreland and Wiltshire. These men got the lions' shares of the forfeited estates of Gloucester, Warwick and Arundel. The work of revenge was not yet complete, however. The lesser men who had abetted and aided the appellants in 1387 remained unpunished. Besides, in 1387–8 there had been five appellants, and two remained still, Bolingbroke and Mowbray, though now both seemed to be in the king's camp. Both these matters received attention in the Shrewsbury parliament.

The commons at Shrewsbury asked for and received a general pardon for past offences. From it were excepted, however, all those who in 1387 had 'ridden in arms and risen forcibly against the king'.[34] This exception was interpreted so widely as, in fact, to include no less than seventeen counties. In order to obtain full pardon, the proctors of these counties had to buy the king's grace, at the rate of 1000 marks per shire, and to take, in the

[33] For the confession see *R.P.* vol. III, pp. 378–9. On the question of Gloucester's murder and Richard's complicity in it see Steel, *Richard II*, pp. 237–9, and the literature there cited.
[34] *R.P.* vol. III, p. 369.

name of their communities, a new oath of special allegiance to the king. Over and above this, they were forced to put their seals to blank charters, in effect pledging all the goods and persons of their communities to the king for loyal behaviour. One writer at least believed that the sealing of these charters, which put all seventeen counties at the legal mercy of the king, was 'the cause afterwards of the destruction of the king himself'.[35] Besides these pledges from the counties, Richard took a personal oath from each of the lords spiritual and temporal individually, and from the commons collectively, to support and uphold all the judgements and statutes of the 1397 parliament. These oaths and pledges suggest that, even now, Richard and his closest advisers had little confidence in either lords or commons. Dread of the terrific consequences of straying from the path of obedience was to be the foundation of the new autocratic dispensation, not mutual love and regard between king and people.

It was at Shrewsbury, on 30 January, that Henry Bolingbroke appeared before the king in parliament, with a schedule concerning treasonable advances which, he alleged, Mowbray had made to him before Christmas. The king's intention, Mowbray had said, was 'to do with them [both] as he had done with the others already', on account of 'what was done at Radcot Bridge'.[36] Bolingbroke had gone to his father, who advised him to go to the king. There was, of course, no ready proof that the words really had passed, and Richard, in a hurry to complete the work of the parliament, had no desire to see the matter thrashed out in public on the spot. A committee of eighteen persons was about to be appointed, to examine and answer the petitions which the parliament's more pressing work had left outstanding. The same persons were therefore empowered to investigate Bolingbroke's allegations.[37]

The committee met twice, at Bristol and at Windsor, in the spring of 1398. Since Bolingbroke's proofs were insufficient and Mowbray denied the charges, it was settled that the matter should be decided, as an issue touching the honour of noblemen,

[35] M. V. Clarke, *Fourteenth Century Studies*, pp. 107, 111. On the question of fines and blank charters more generally, see ibid. pp. 106–9; and C. Barron, 'The tyranny of Richard II' (the most important contribution to the study of Richard's tyranny since Clarke's work).

[36] *R.P.* vol. III, p. 382.

[37] On this committee, and all its activities, see J. G. Edwards, 'The parliamentary committee of 1398', *E.H.R.* 40 (1925), pp. 321–33.

by a judicial duel. The combatants met at Coventry on 16 September. As soon as they appeared in the lists ready for combat, the king threw down his baton, and ordered them to disarm. He had decided (very likely at Gaunt's insistence) to avoid the shedding of blood by taking the quarrel into his own hands. He then pronounced sentence of banishment on both lords, on Mowbray for life, on Henry for ten years. Ten years is a long time, and Richard no doubt reckoned that the ex-appellant, on his return, would be a stranger and a spent political force; if, that is, he ever intended to permit his return.

Before they left England, both Bolingbroke and Mowbray were given permission to appoint attornies to receive the revenues of their estates while they were in exile. Just over four months after the abortive duel at Coventry John of Gaunt died, on 3 February 1399, and the question arose directly as to whether Bolingbroke should now be permitted to add to his already substantial estate the vast inheritance of Lancaster. It is not surprising, given their past and bitter experience of the power of overmighty subjects and Bolingbroke's record as an appellant, that Richard and his advisers were determined not to let him do so. Their difficulty was how to stop him inheriting with some colour of legal authority, especially since the grant of letters of attorney seemed to recognize and guarantee his full enjoyment of his right as a lord of lands. The expedient that they hit on was to make some significant alterations to the parliament roll of 1398. Where the original terms of appointment of the committee of eighteen had been to 'examine and answer petitions still outstanding', the words were now added 'and to terminate all matters moved in the presence of the king'.[38] Armed with this pseudo-parliamentary authority, the committee met again. They revoked the grant of letters of attorney of October 1397 as 'inadvertent', extended Bolingbroke's sentence of banishment to one for life, and took the whole of his inheritance into the king's hand.

Just a fortnight after the meeting of the committee that authorized the sequestration of the Lancastrian estates, instructions went out to mobilize the yeomen of the crown for a royal expedition to Ireland. Ten months previously Art MacMurrough had surprised and killed the king's lieutenant, the Earl of March, near Carlow. If English authority in Ireland were to survive in anything but name, intervention in force was necessary, and it was with a substantial army that Richard sailed from Milford

[38] *E.H.R.* 40 (1925), pp. 323–4.

Haven in May. Most of his closest associates among the aristocracy were with him; York was left behind as keeper of England,
with Wiltshire, the treasurer, and the chamber knights Bushy,
Bagot and Green. Pressing as the situation in Ireland was, the
king's decision to leave the country was hardly wise. To many
who were already alarmed by the novel courses of Richard's
government, the seizure of the Lancastrian estates seemed the
last straw. No man or family appeared to be secure in his
property; the sacred right of inheritance was threatened. Lam-
poons and satires on the courtiers bore witness to a wave of
popular resentment, and wild rumours were beginning to circulate. Richard was planning to make Dublin his capital and to
tyrannize his English subjects from a distance; unheard of taxes
were to be imposed; noblemen were going to be murdered and
their estates farmed by Wiltshire for the king's profit. Richard's
departure made the moment ideal for an attempt by Henry
Bolingbroke to retrieve his fortunes.

The king no doubt trusted that he had rendered Henry harm-
less by the fears that his recent measures had inspired, and by the
favours by means of which he had bound round himself what
seemed a solid body of support. He had been careful, in 1398, to
make sure that plenty of men profited by the fall of the old
appellants, and he had been careful too to make sure that few
suffered by the sequestration of the Lancastrian estates, confirming the pensions that Henry and his father had granted. Since
the Shrewsbury parliament, he had continued to retain in his
service more men of rank in the counties, and to ensure that his
loyal supporters were prominent in local offices, as sheriffs and
on judicial commissions. For all the *furore* over the confiscation
of the Lancastrian inheritance, he might perhaps have been right
in calculating that he could safely leave the land, but for one
factor that he seems to have wholly ignored, the attitude of the
magnates of the north whom he left behind in England.

Their attitude, and in particular that of the Percys, had in
1399 a long history behind it.[39] The Anglo-Scottish wars of the
earlier fourteenth century were feuds between the great families
who held lands on either side of the uncertain border (as for
instance between the Percys and the Douglases), which were
pursued without much reference to the governments at either
Westminster or Edinburgh. The difficulty of imposing any

[39] For what follows, I have relied on R. L. Storey, 'The wardens of
the marches of England towards Scotland', *E.H.R.* 72 (1957), pp. 593–
614; see also J. A. Tuck, *Northern History* 3 (1968), p. 27 f.

measure of control was, on the English side, the result partly of
sheer distance, partly of the independence of northern society –
an independence precious to its leaders because their fortunes
and their standing so often depended on their freedom to prosecute vendettas against their private enemies. In these conditions
the royal government had no option but to rely, almost entirely,
on the local nobility for the safe-keeping of the land. When in
the 1380s the problem of the defence of the northern border
became acute again after the reopening of active war with
Scotland, new experiments were made in the administration of
the wardenships of the marches. They were made now the subject
of formal indentures, the wardens contracting to serve for a period
of years and to maintain forces for the defence of the border in
return for stipulated wages. The rates of remuneration were
princely (Henry Percy the younger in the East March in 1396 was
assured of £3000 per annum in time of peace, rising to £12,000 in
time of open war). This new system, which became permanent,
offered opportunities to the magnates of the north, who normally
controlled the wardenships, to consolidate their position locally
by retaining what rapidly became, in effect, subsidized private
armies. It also, naturally, accentuated their mutual competition
for local office and influence.

    Much the same period that witnessed the introduction of
these new arrangements witnessed also the rise of the Percy
family to new and spectacular prominence. The Percys had been
lords of Alnwick since early in the century; in 1370 they acquired
the Umfraville barony of Prudhoe, and a little later added to this
the lordship of Cockermouth which carried their power into the
West March. In 1377 Henry Percy was created Earl of Northumberland. In the late 1380s, when the new system of retaining
wardens by indenture came in, the government from Westminster
did its best to maintain a balance of power in the north, by
ringing the changes among the wardenships between Percys,
Nevilles and Cliffords, but between 1391 and 1395 the wardenships of both marches, East and West, were in Percy hands.
Then in 1396, John Holland Earl of Huntingdon became
Warden of the West March, and in 1398 he was succeeded by
Edward, Duke of Aumale; both were courtiers, and lacked any
family connexion with the border country. Northumberland, in
1381-2, had shown considerable resentment when Gaunt, also
a magnate without border connexion, was for a time the king's
lieutenant in the north, and his reaction now seems to have been
similar. To add to the anxieties of the Percys for their new found

dominance in their homeland, Ralph Neville in 1397 was created Earl of Westmorland. Royal favour, to which they owed their power, seemed bent on raising up rivals to them.

The Earl of Northumberland and his son Henry 'Hotspur' were both men of soaring ambition, and without much scruple when it came to maintaining the position of the family. Thanks to the crown's past generosity, in 1399 they disposed of military retinues of sufficient size to make their allegiance crucial in a political crisis. Richard believed that he had handled them with enough delicacy to keep them trustworthy (he had recently made Northumberland's brother Thomas, who was steward of his household and who had been very prominent in the proceedings against the old appellants in 1397, Earl of Worcester). But he was wrong in thinking so, as events proved all too soon after he had left for Ireland.

When Henry Bolingbroke landed at Ravenspur in early July he was accompanied by Thomas Arundel, the exiled archbishop, and a little band of his own faithful friends. Robert Waterton, John Leventhorpe, and others of his old officials and retainers were waiting to greet him. Near Doncaster he was joined by the Earl of Northumberland with his son Hotspur, by Ralph Earl of Westmorland, and other northern lords. On 2 August, by a commission under Henry's seal of the duchy of Lancaster, Northumberland was appointed warden of the West March, and thus both wardenships were again in Percy hands. As the price of their support, their restoration to an almost viceregal position in the north was well worth it to Henry; from this point forward the success of his intervention was assured by military power which Richard's lieutenants had no chance of challenging. Thus, in the hour of crisis, border polities proved decisive.

While Henry's host gathered strength York, as keeper of the realm, took no effective steps to meet the mounting threat. From St Albans he withdrew west with the royal councillors; Wiltshire and the three chamber knights made for Bristol, while York himself took refuge in Berkeley castle. Their assumption presumably was that Henry would make for London and so give them time to organize resistance, but he struck west instead. York joined him when he reached Berkeley, and the constable of Bristol surrendered Richard's friends into his hands. Wiltshire, Bushy and Green were executed there on 29 July, a few days before Richard had landed from Ireland at Haverfordwest. He ought, for his own sake, to have been back earlier, but Aumale, apparently, persuaded him to divide his forces, sending Salisbury ahead to raise more troops in Wales and himself following later. By the time Richard reached the Welsh coasts Salisbury's men were beginning to desert in panic. Aumale, whose original advice may have been intentionally treacherous, now deserted the king, as did Thomas Percy, Earl of Worcester. Richard, with only a tiny remnant left of his forces, marched along the Welsh coast and reached Conway, but by then Henry was already in control at Chester, which would have been his next objective and was the natural centre from which to organize royalist resistance.[40]

At Conway, on or about 10 August, Thomas Arundel and Henry Percy, Earl of Northumberland, arrived with messages from Henry. They assured Richard that his crown was not in jeopardy; all would be forgotten if he would agree to restore Henry to his inheritance, to summon a parliament, and to surrender five members of his council for trial therein. Richard, cornered without an army, accepted these demands after some deliberation, and agreed to go with Percy and Arundel to meet Henry at Chester. There is good reason to believe that Northumberland, though he was later to deny it, had already agreed to Richard's deposition, and that Henry should succeed him. Before they reached Flint the party had been 'ambushed'. When Richard reached Chester, whence writs went out in his name to summon parliament, he was already a prisoner. He was never free again. He resigned his throne on 29 September at the Tower of London, probably under some duress; on 30 September parliament assembled and the estates renounced their fealty to him.

Richard lost his throne partly through the weakness and treachery of men whom he had trusted, and largely through his own folly.

[40] In this paragraph and the next I have followed the reconstruction of events given by M. V. Clarke and V. H. Galbraith, 'The deposition of Richard II' in M. V. Clarke, *Fourteenth Century Studies*, pp. 53–89. They clearly demonstrate both that (a) the account of events given in Lancastrian sources (as Walsingham's *Annales*) and in the formal Lancastrian account of the deposition on the parliament roll are thoroughly unreliable; and (b) that in the light of the evidence of the chronicles of two Cheshire Abbeys – Dieulacres and Whalley – the accounts given by Creton (*French Metrical History of the Deposition of Richard II*, ed. J. Webb, London 1819) and in the *Chronique de la Traison et Mort de Richard II* appear to be substantially correct. On Northumberland's part, and especially on his conduct at Conway and after, see J. M. W. Bean, 'Henry IV and the Percies', *History*, 44 (1959), pp. 215–21.

We should, however, look circumspectly at the view that portrays him at the end of his reign at the brink of insanity. Richard did not and could not seek to impose autocracy on his own and unaided. His councillors were not, as his contemporary critics liked to suggest, a band of young and irresponsible upstarts. They were men of wealth and influence, and of wide and varied experience. Even on the notorious committee that licensed the sequestration of the Lancastrian estates the great secular magnates were well represented. Richard's advisers may have acquiesced in decisions that we can see to have been imprudent, but they were not the sort of men who could be browbeaten into submission to the will of a half-mad ruler. Nor was it just the desire for private gain that led them to cooperate in Richard's experiment in absolutism; it was a governmental policy that seemed to offer solider and more important advantages than that.

In the early 1390s there was widespread dissatisfaction with the way in which the country had been governed for more than twenty years. To seasoned councillors and administrators it must have looked as if there was much to be said for a retrenchment of the royal prerogative which would elevate the monarchy above partisan clamour. What they and Richard attempted was in many ways very like what Edward IV and the early Tudors were to achieve, the shaping of what historians have called a 'new monarchy'. Their methods anticipated those which were successful in these later reigns: the wider use of the prerogative courts; the effort to manœuvre committed royalists into key positions in local government; above all the effort to secure the king a more ample income, and so relieve conciliar government of the most embarrassing brand of parliamentary pressure. In this respect the grant of the wool subsidy for life in 1398 was important. It was a concession entirely without precedent, and one which greatly enhanced the crown's freedom of financial manœuvre; later it was taken as a sign of the culpable subservience of the commons at Shrewsbury, and of Richard's sinister determination to be free of all customary trammels on his regality. Henry VII and Henry VIII, moreover, would have had no difficulty in appreciating the motives of Richard's councillors for seeking, when an opportunity arose, to sequestrate a dangerous concentration of landed wealth in the hands of a single and not very trustworthy magnate. Richard's absolutism was perhaps a little more doctrinaire than that of later monarchs; some of his circle had almost certainly been influenced by the intellectual apologetic of French royal absolutism, especially that of the court circle of Charles V. But this did not much affect what they tried to do in practice.

The reason why Richard's experiment was a disastrous failure was that the basic principle of his absolutism was unsound. It was founded not on popular respect, but on fear. Richard and his familiars believed that they could make people obedient by frightening them. They bound men to take unfamiliar oaths, the breach of which would automatically be construed as treason. They excepted from the general pardon of 1398 all acts done in the 'eleventh year' of the reign (1387–8) with the deliberate object of making ex-opponents of the regime reveal themselves, and pledge themselves in the king's mercy for good behaviour. They really did frighten people thus; we know that some 600 people went to the length of sueing out individual pardons. Not only individuals but whole communities too felt their security threatened. London, which had seen its privileges seized into the king's hand once already in 1392 and had paid £10,000 to get them back, paid another 10,000 marks in 1398 for a surer reconfirmation. All these proceedings of Richard's were, when the time came, listed in the articles of deposition that were drawn up as evidence that he was a tyrant and unfit to rule.[41] Other sections of these articles, notably their account of his willing abdication, are barefaced tampering with the truth. In these particular matters, however, it is hard to quarrel either with the facts that they relay or with their conclusion.

The fines, blank charters, forced loans and conditional pardons through which Richard blackmailed his subjects into obedience proved self-defeating. In the fourteenth century the military, financial and bureaucratic resources of the monarchy were not sufficient to maintain royal authority without a basis of trust between sovereign and subject. Richard's methods undermined that trust and made his own weakness plain, for they revealed that he too was frightened. He did not sufficiently understand the need to woo his subjects, as did Edward IV and Henry VIII, and Henry VII too until avarice got the better of everything in his later years. Richard II was more like Richard III, who also relied on fear to secure his authority, and whose rule also crumbled in the face of an usurping invader.

There were flaws in Richard II's character, as well as his policies, that helped to bring about his fall. He could be arrogant, he could

[41] *R.P.* vol. III, pp. 417–22, and see C. Barron, 'The tyranny of Richard II'.

be wilful, and he showed himself on occasion both vengeful and treacherous. Yet he remains one of the most interesting of the kings of England of the later Middle Ages. His court was the most splendid and sophisticated that ever gathered about an English monarch in that period.[42] He was the patron of Chaucer, and it was for him that the Wilton diptych, the finest product of medieval court art that has survived in England, was executed. Cultivated foreigners with a knowledge of the courts and chivalrous society of Europe, like Froissart and Philip de Mezieres, were impressed by the magnificence of his entourage. He had a sharper sensitivity to the cult of kingship than any other medieval king of England (the Wilton diptych shows him kneeling, with John the Baptist and the two English royal saints, Edward the Confessor and St Edmund, beside him, before the Christ child in the arms of the Virgin, amid angels who wear the badge of the white hart). He was a lover of fine things (witness his clasp showing a damsel carrying a parrot, and his white satin doublet embroidered with golden orange trees), and of richly illuminated manuscripts. His fancy for the colour of royal magnificence may have had much to do with the attraction of some of the wilder projects in which he became involved more than half seriously – his expensive efforts to get himself elected king of the Romans, for instance. There is a genuinely tragic irony in the fate which decreed that his reign should end dismally with a deposition. Its chief legacies to England in the next generation were ones that worked not for the glorification of monarchy which was Richard's dream, but to weaken it: a profound popular distrust of royal autocracy, and a line of kings with a questionable title to the throne.

[42] On the court of Richard II see further G. Mathew, *The Court of Richard II* (London, 1968), esp. ch. V.

13

The reign of Henry IV

On 30 September 1399 an assembly met in Westminster Hall that was not officially a parliament, since the summons to parliament had been in the name of Richard II, and had lapsed on his renunciation of the crown the day before. The throne stood vacant, covered with cloth of gold. First, charges against Richard were read out, and a commission representing all the estates of the realm was appointed, to renounce homage and fealty to him on behalf of the whole realm. Then Henry of Lancaster stood up and in his mother tongue claimed: 'this realm of England, and the crown with all the members and appurtenances, as I am descended by right line of the blood coming from the good lord Henry the third; and through that right that God of his grace hath sent me, with the help of my kin and of my friends, to recover it; the which realm was in point to be undone for default of government and undoing of the good laws'.[1] The lords spiritual and temporal asked severally and together what they thought of this claim, gave their assent to it. For good measure it was reported to the assembly that Richard had approved that Henry should be his successor (which was probably not true). Archbishop Arundel of Canterbury preached a sermon on the text *vir dominabitur in populo*, and dwelt on the ills which must overtake a kingdom governed by a child (the alternative claimant to Henry was the infant Earl of March). Subsequently the parliament, now formally summoned in the name of Henry IV, tidied things up by recognizing his eldest son Henry as his heir.

It is never easy to explain in constitutional terms the deposition of a monarch, but the Lancastrian lawyers and churchmen who drew up the lengthy articles against Richard II which were read to the parliament of 1399 made a very reasonable job of it. The theme was that Richard, by actions and statements which were rehearsed, had broken the fundamental rules which he had sworn

[1] *R.P.* vol. III, pp. 422–3.

at his coronation to uphold, and that this perjury demonstrably unfitted him for kingship. As we have seen, many of their specific charges had considerable substance. It was much less easy to explain why Henry should succeed Richard. The young Earl of March, Edmund Mortimer, was hereditarily of a line senior to Henry's, being descended in the female line from Lionel of Clarence, the second son of Edward III (John of Gaunt, Henry's father, was the third son). March was also the son of the man who in 1397 had been recognized in parliament as Richard II's heir. The way in which Henry and his advisers got round this child's inconvenient claim could not be straightforward, which is why historians have long argued about the exact nature of his title to the throne.[2]

Henry himself would have liked to claim the throne by clear descent, on the ground that his ancestor, Edmund 'Crouchback' of Lancaster, had been older than Edward I, but was passed over because of his alleged physical deformity. The most diligent search of the chronicles failed, however, to unearth any evidence in favour of this Lancastrian fable. Henry's legal advisers were anxious that there should be some sort of recognition of his title by clergy and people, so that his royal right should not rest merely on successful conquest. The proceedings of 30 September combined all the possible lines of approach. Henry *viva voce* claimed the throne by blood and conquest, and the people assented; parliament ratified what had happened afterwards by recognizing Henry's heir as heir to the throne. The king's title was thus justified by descent, by conquest, by acclaim and by subsequent parliamentary recognition, without its being clear which, if any, of the ingredients was the crucial one.

Politically Henry's throne was not as secure as it looked at first sight. He had got the crown because he was the man of the moment; it was impossible to leave Richard on the throne, and a council of regency for the Earl of March could not have given the effective government that was needed. The Percies, whose

[2] The question, whether Henry IV's title can be described as 'parliamentary' has been the focus of dispute in a considerable literature; see S. B. Chrimes, *English Constitutional Ideas in the Fifteenth Century* (Cambridge, 1936), pp. 106–16; G. T. Lapsley, 'The parliamentary title of Henry IV', *E.H.R.* 49 (1934), pp. 423–49, 577–606, and 'Richard II's last parliament', *E.H.R.* 53 (1938), pp. 53–78; H. G. Richardson, 'Richard II's last parliament', *E.H.R.* 52 (1937), pp. 39–47; and B. Wilkinson, 'The deposition of Richard II and the accession of Henry IV', *E.H.R.* 54 (1939), pp. 215–39.

support had been so crucial after he landed at Ravenspur, had everything to gain from his succession; so had Archbishop Arundel, the companion of his exile. He had plenty of committed aristocratic supporters, not just in the north where he could count on both Nevilles and Percies but in the south too, as the Earl of Stafford and lords Willoughby, Fitzwalter and Burnell. But Richard's old intimates, the Holland brothers and Salisbury and Despenser, were also powerful and influential men, and Aumale, the most important of them all, was the son of the Duke of York, whom Henry could not possibly afford to alienate. These men were not popular, but they had their own followings. They lost their new titles as a result of Henry's usurpation. One chronicle hints that Henry would have liked to proceed further against them, but that the commons urged him not to. The same chronicle makes it clear that some thought it would have been better for the people to hear from Richard's own mouth that he renounced the crown.[3] The official record of the change of dynasty that we have is an edited one, designed to make the operation look smooth; it omits all mention of murmurings such as these, as also of the public protest which the courageous Bishop Merke of Carlisle made on behalf of the ex-king. Henry did not succeed because the opposition to him was negligible, but because he caught Richard and his friends hopelessly off their guard.

Henry had been king for barely four months, when he had to face his first revolt. It was organized by Richard's former friends, the two Hollands, Montagu of Salisbury, and Rutland (Aumale), and its object was his restoration. Thomas Merke, now deprived of his bishopric, and the Abbot of Westminster were also involved in the plot, and the plan was to seize Henry at Windsor, on the eve of the tournament arranged there for Epiphany, 1400. It failed, because Rutland revealed the scheme to his father, the Duke of York, who informed the king. Even so, Henry left Windsor in a hurry only twelve hours before the rebels arrived, and his son Henry was briefly their prisoner. The king at once began to gather forces in London and when the rebels decided to retreat their men began to melt away. Thomas Holland and

[3] *Giles' Chronicle*, p. 5; and see E. F. Jacob, *The Fifteenth Century* (Oxford, 1961), p. 24; see also M. V. Clarke and V. H. Galbraith, 'The deposition of Richard II' in M. V. Clarke, *Fourteenth Century Studies* (Oxford, 1937), pp. 53–89, on the more general question of the doctoring of the record of the deposition.

Salisbury surrendered at Cirencester, and were lynched by a mob, as was Lord Despenser at Bristol; John Holland was taken at Pleshy in Essex, and beheaded by his captors. Some other leading rebels were executed at Oxford by the king's order. Among the lay leaders, Rutland alone was pardoned, because of his father's influence and because it was his information that had given Henry warning.

Very soon after the rising Richard II was dead, probably before the end of January. It was claimed that he had refused to eat, and died of starvation; but the date of his death seems too convenient, and he was probably killed at Henry's order. To allay any doubt of his death, his body was brought from his prison at Pontefract to London, and lay in St Paul's, with the head showing outside the lead coffin. The lands of his supporters were declared forfeit. The reflections of the council, after the new regime had thus weathered its first storm, were not very comfortable, however. Its members did not think it would be politic to call a parliament, because there would be too much opposition to any request for taxation. They were alarmed about the possibility of war breaking out with France and Scotland, and of the fiscal problem that that would pose. They were frankly frightened by the way in which Richard's friends had died; at this rate the judges would not be able to enforce order 'for fear of the unruliness and pride of the commons who do not wish to be under any governance'.[4] They advised the king to retain men in the counties by fee to aid in the keeping of the peace – an ugly reminder that they understood very clearly the part that Richard's Cheshire archers had played in sustaining tyranny.

Henry IV had fought in many wars; he had commanded the appellant army at Radcot Bridge, and had been on crusade to Prussia. He had a reputation as a warrior, and was expected to redeem the unmartial record of his predecessor. At the begining of his reign his councillors felt, however, that to court war with France was too risky, and advised playing for peace by returning Isabella, Richard's queen, and her jewels. Scotland seemed a more promising quarter for aggression, partly, no doubt, because of the influence of the Percies in the council; and Henry's servants began looking into all the old records of the English kings' claim to the homage of Scotland. The flight from Scotland of George Dunbar, Earl of the March, helped to raise English hopes, and in August 1400 Henry, after summoning Robert III

4 *P.P.C.* vol. I, pp. 107-8.

to do him homage, led a large army over the border. He reached Edinburgh, but achieved nothing of moment, and added no lustre to his name.

Bad news met Henry on his way south. In mid-September 1400, a quarrel between Owen Glendower, Lord of Glyndyfrdwy in north Wales, and Lord Grey of Ruthin, who was a stout supporter of Lancaster and a councillor, had blown up into an armed Welsh revolt. On 16 September Owen was proclaimed Prince of Wales by a group of Welsh landowners, most of them his relations; they and their followers descended on Ruthin, burned it and ravaged the English through Flint and Denbigh. Further afield, in Anglesey, the Tudors, who were related to Glendower and had had associations with Richard II, were also in revolt.[5] Henry appeared from Scotland with his army at the end of September and carried out a punitive march through north Wales, which temporarily restored the situation. But none of the Welsh leaders were taken, and when he was gone the situation began to deteriorate again.

At the end of the first full year of Henry's reign, the situation looked shaky. Wales was in ferment. In the north the acquisition of George Dunbar as an ally was a double-edged benefit; the favours and influence that he achieved were not calculated to please the Percies, part of whose reward for 1399 had been an increased freedom of action in the marches. The Scottish expedition had proved costly both to the king and to the many peers who had made direct contributions in men and money, and after it, it was clear that parliament would soon have to be summoned and asked for a money grant. Henry at his accession had made much of his intention not to burden his people with taxes, but he could not fulfil his promises. Popular support for his regime at the outset had really been based on popular antipathy to the preceding one, and it was bound to wane once it became clear that the revolution of 1399 would not lead to greater stability in local government. The only men on whom Henry could count with complete confidence in 1400 were the tried servants and retainers of the duchy of Lancaster. The Lancastrian 'affinity' was the greatest private retinue in England, but in the circumstances of the day Henry needed support much more broadly based than that.

The events of the years 1401 and 1402 did not improve the

[5] On Glendower, and all that concerns him, see J. E. Lloyd, *Owen Glendower* (Oxford, 1931), and also G. Williams, *Owen Glendower* (London, 1966); on the Tudors see Jacob, *The Fifteenth Century*, p. 39.

situation. Parliament was critical of royal expenditure, of the royal council, and of the general lack of governance. In both years there were royal expeditions to Wales, neither of which achieved very much. The return of Isabella to the French court did not solve any problems; there was less now to hold the French back from war. In Gascony the situation of the English looked critical. The one ray of hope in 1402 was in the north, where in September Henry Percy (Hotspur) and his father the Earl of Northumberland overthrew the raiding Scottish host at Homildon Hill in Durham, and took prisoner the Douglas, Murdach of Fife, and the earls of Orkney, Angus and Moray. The lustre of the victory, however, went to the Percies, not to Henry. The king ordered that the magnate prisoners should not be ransomed, but put at his disposal. The earl handed over his prisoners in the autumn parliament, but Hotspur did not produce the Douglas. Relations between the king and the most powerful of all his late supporters were becoming uneasy.

'We hoped that at your wonderful entry into the realm of England you would have redeemed Israel', Philip Repingdon (the ex-Lollard, now a royal chaplain and a future Bishop of Lincoln) wrote to Henry IV in 1401, '. . . but now our joy is changed to sorrow, while all evils multiply, and the hope of healing has gone out from the hearts of men.'[6] It is not clear quite at what point general discontent began to foster rueful reflections about the justification of the revolution of 1399, but by 1402 they were beginning to be widespread. It was in this year that the Lady of the Isles produced the man whom some chose to regard as Richard II escaped from his prison: the 'Mommet' whose presence in Scotland was to be a long embarrassment to the house of Lancaster. Another rumour had it that Richard was alive in Wales. A number of Franciscans were involved in spreading pro-Ricardian propaganda, and convents as well scattered as Aylesbury, Northampton, Leicester, Nottingham and Stamford were affected. Friar Walton of Leicester, who turned informer, told the king's officers of plans to mobilize 500 men at Oxford, to go to join Richard II in Wales. The *Eulogium* gives a graphic account of the interview between Henry IV himself and Richard Frisby, chief of the conspirators whom Walton implicated. 'I do not say that Richard is alive,' Frisby told the king, 'but I say that if he is alive he is the true king of England.' He frankly did not believe the story of Richard's abdication: 'he would never have resigned had he been at liberty; a resignation

[6] *The Correspondence of Thomas Bekynton* (R.S.) vol. I, pp. 151–4.

made in prison is not a free resignation'.[7] The ugly truths about the manner in which Richard had been deprived of his throne, which the official record concealed, had somehow leaked out, and were being made public property through Franciscan sermons.

These signs of the impact of legitimist propaganda are significant, because they appear on the eve of very serious rebellions, in which Henry might easily have lost his throne. These rebellions involved a number of English magnates who had acquiesced in the revolution of 1399, with the Percies at the head of the list. Legitimism was not of course the reason for their rebellion, but aristocratic risings, in the later Middle Ages, had little prospect of success unless they could obtain a degree of popular support, and to this end needed the cloak at least of some general and readily understandable political objective. The rights of Richard, or if he was dead of the young Earl of March, provided just such a cover for the objects of ambitious men who had their own grievances against Henry IV, and thought it could be to their interest to overthrow him.

The first rebellion in point of time, that of Owen Glendower, cannot strictly be called a legitimist rising. Richard II, however, had always looked for support to Wales and Cheshire and certainly there was sympathy for his cause there; and as we shall see, Glendower's rising began to acquire in time a distinct colour of English legitimism. But in 1401 his appeal was to the Welsh nation, and the agents of rebellion were the bards, with their sagas of past independence and prophecies of a day when the Saxon yoke would be lifted. This was how the English saw the revolt too. In 1402 the commons petitioned that no Welshman should hold office in Wales, that gatherings to listen to the bards should be forbidden, and that Welshmen should not be allowed to be armed in public.

What was needed was not statutes, but money and reinforcements for Henry Prince of Wales and his council at Chester, who found their men constantly on the brink of mutiny or desertion for lack of pay. The situation was so serious that in 1401 both Hotspur and his father advised the king to offer Glendower terms, a pardon and the guarantee of his territorial rights, but they could not carry the council with them. In 1402 the Welsh leader felt himself sufficiently secure to suggest both to the Irish

[7] *Eulogium Historiarum* (R.S.) vol. III, p. 391; see also I. D. Thornley, 'Treason by words in the fifteenth century', *E.H.R.* 32 (1917), pp. 556–61.

chiefs and to Robert III of Scotland a grand Celtic alliance against England. Two other events of the same year opened new vistas for him. In April his forces took Lord Grey of Ruthin himself prisoner. He was ransomed for 10,000 marks, which put Glendower in funds of a new order. A few weeks later he captured a still more significant prisoner, Edmund Mortimer, the uncle of the Earl of March. This time Henry would not negotiate with the rebels for a ransom. He was probably glad to have the eldest male member of the dangerous house of Mortimer out of the way, but the decision was not a wise one. Edmund's sister was married to Hotspur, and the king's refusal to allow a ransom created new ground for discord between him and the Percies. Glendower soon found he could exploit the situation by persuading his captive, since he could not be ransomed, to throw in his lot with him. Mortimer then married Glendower's daughter. On 13 December he wrote to his friends among the gentry and commons of Radnor to tell them that he would henceforward be fighting to secure Owen his right in Wales and to put the Earl of March on the throne of England.[8]

In 1402 the Percies were probably already considering breaking with Henry IV. They had been the chief architects of his usurpation and so amply rewarded for their part in it that it is not easy to explain their *volte face*.[9] Northumberland had been made Constable of England and Warden of the West March; Hotspur Warden of the East March and justiciar of north Wales; Thomas, the Earl of Worcester, was made Admiral of England, and in 1401 steward of the household. A number of factors seem to have contributed to a steadily deteriorating pattern of relations between them and Henry. Affairs connected with the Scottish march were the most important: the new influence with the king of George Dunbar; the re-grant of the custody of Roxburgh castle (entrusted to them for ten years in 1399) to their bitter rival Neville, the Earl of Westmorland; their difficulties over obtaining full payment from the exchequer of monies owing to them as wardens. Henry's rejection of their offer to mediate between him and Glendower, his refusal to allow them to ransom the prisoners of Homildon, and his refusal to ransom Edmund Mortimer also must have played their part. Besides, the Percies did not trust Henry; their troubles over getting pay for their men, both in

---

[8] H. Ellis, *Original Letters*, 2nd ser. (London, 1827), vol. I, pp. 24–6.,
[9] On the Percy revolt and all that concerns it, see J. M. W. Bean, 'Henry IV and the Percies', *History* 44 (1959), pp. 212–27.

Scotland and in north Wales, convinced them that he would leave them in the lurch at his convenience. If Dr Rogers is right in his suggestion that the Percies were deeply involved in the political crisis of 1401, when Henry was forced to name his council, their lack of faith in him must have been apparent from an early stage.[10]

By 1403, at all events, the Percies had decided that they would try their hand a second time at king-making. The main charge against Henry in Hotspur's manifesto, which the chronicler Hardyng has preserved, was his unjust treatment of the house of March, whom he had cheated of the inheritance to the throne.[11] From a Percy this was pretty brazened, but Hotspur's claim was that in 1399 he and his father had supported Henry only in his claim to his duchy of Lancaster. He also charged the king with packing parliaments and levying taxes contrary to the promises of his accession. In May 1403, a month before the revolt, Henry already had wind of rumours that in the north men were preaching 'that the king had not kept his promises that he made at his advent into the realm'.[12] At the time Hotspur was already, almost certainly, in direct contact with Glendower. Nevertheless Henry was taken apparently by surprise on 12 July at Nottingham, on his way north with forces for the Scots border, by the news that Hotspur and Earl Thomas Percy were in revolt and had issued a manifesto at Chester, and that Northumberland was gathering men in the north to join them.

George Dunbar, according to the *Annales*, was the man who urged Henry to act swiftly, or all might be lost. It was sound advice. By 20 July Henry was at Shrewsbury, and Hotspur and his uncle withdrew from before the town, where they had hoped to capture the Prince of Wales before the king could help him. His speed brought him face to face with the main rebel army before there was any chance of either Northumberland or Glendower joining it. Before the battle there was a last minute attempt to negotiate, initiated by the king: the story ran after the battle that Hotspur would have accepted the terms offered, but that they were misrepresented by Thomas Percy, who actually spoke to the royal messengers. The battle was one of the hardest fought of the age; and little groups of combatants were still struggling on the field when darkness fell. But by that time Hotspur had fallen,

[10] See A. Rogers, 'The political crisis of 1401', *Nottingham Medieval Studies* 12 (1968), pp. 85–96.

[11] J. Hardyng, *Chronicle*, ed. H. Ellis (London, 1812), pp. 352–3.

[12] See Jacob, *The Fifteenth Century*, p. 51.

and both Worcester and Douglas were the king's prisoners; on the next day, the rebel army had disappeared and the king was the clear victor.

Thomas Percy and a number of other notable prisoners were tried and beheaded at Shrewsbury. Northumberland, when he heard that his brother and son were dead, was ready to come to terms with Henry. He made his submission at York, and was placed in custody for the time being. He lost the office of Constable and his wardenship of the West March, which went to his rival Neville. His key castles were taken into the king's hand. The lands of Hotspur and Worcester were forfeited for their treason; George Dunbar was one of those who were well rewarded out of the confiscations.

The Earl of Northumberland was set at liberty, after the lords in the spring parliament of 1404 had decided that his conduct did not amount to treason, but to trespass only. His first step on being freed was formally, before his peers in parliament, to clear Archbishop Arundel and the Duke of York (the erstwhile Rutland, who had succeeded his father in 1402) of complicity in his rebellion. At the same time he was reconciled, before parliament and the peers, to both Neville and Dunbar. There were fears, it would seem, both that the recent revolt had had wider ramifications than had come into the open, and that border rivalry might, with Northumberland at large again, lead to the reopening of civil war.

The latter fear was well founded. The first sign that trouble was brewing again was an attempt by Northumberland to surprise Neville of Westmorland at the house of one of his retainers, Ralph Viners. The revolt of 1405 was in fact to reproduce all the elements of that of 1403, and potentially was quite as dangerous. Glendower had strengthened his position in Wales over the two years. In 1404 he had taken Harlech and Aberystwyth; most of west Wales as well as the north was now in his power, and he was solemnly recognized as Prince of Wales in a parliament to which men were summoned from every *cantref* obedient to his authority. As Prince he sent his envoys to the French court and received a promise of assistance, which materialized in 1405 with an expeditionary force under John de Hangest. Edmund Mortimer was still his ally, and two Welsh bishops, Trevor of St Asaph and Byford of Bangor, had thrown in their lot with him. These two men were probably the intermediaries between him and Northumberland. Their mutual alliance, together with Edmund

Mortimer as a third party was sealed on 28 February in the famous 'tripartite indenture'. This proposed nothing less than a threefold division of the kingdom of England. Northumberland was to have all the north, as far into the midlands as Leicester and Northampton; Glendower a greater Wales, stretching into England as far as Worcester; Mortimer 'the whole of the rest of England'.[13] This was king-making with a vengeance.

One cannot be sure quite how seriously to take the tripartite indenture. One can be sure of the perilousness of the situation in 1405. Apart from the Welsh, the French and the Scots were ready to move, and the plans for revolt had strong backing in England. Thomas Mowbray the Earl Marshal, Lord Bardolf, and no less a man than Archbishop Scrope of York were all in the affair with Northumberland; Lord Clifford and Sir John Fauconberg were also apparently involved. Two manifestos survive which are connected with the revolt, and they make it clear that the tripartite indenture was not an agreed programme. One, to which Archbishop Scrope certainly gave his authority and which was 'posted in the ways and streets of York', complains of the lack of governance in the realm; of the taxes which weigh on clergy, secular men and merchants alike and undo them; and of the lack of defence of the realm against foes without (there had been a number of French raids on the Channel coasts). It also shows that Scrope had had contact with Glendower, directly or indirectly: 'if these matters be remedied', it declares, 'we have full information and promise from those now in revolt in Wales, that they will be content as they were in the days of King Edward and King Richard'.[14] The other manifesto is more extreme, charging Henry with usurpation, with the death of Richard II and the blood of his friends and the blood also of Hotspur, and of having brought nothing but misery and confusion to the land. It is not certain who framed this second manifesto; its tone is that of Ricardian 'Jacobitism' run wild.[15]

As events turned out, the only formidable military danger in 1405 came from Glendower, who with Hangest's Frenchmen

[13] For text see Ellis, *Original Letters*, 2nd ser., vol. I, pp. 27–8. Lloyd gives the date of the agreement as 28 February 1405 (*Owen Glendower*, pp. 93–5); both J. Wylie (*History of England under Henry IV* vol. II, pp. 378–81) and J. L. Kirby in his recent *Henry IV of England* (London, 1970, pp. 218–19) incline to believe that it belongs not to this year, but to 1406.

[14] *Annales Ricardi II et Henrici IV* (R.S.), pp. 403–5.

[15] *Anglia Sacra*, ed. H. Wharton, vol. II, pp. 362–8.

raided out of Wales up to the gates of Worcester. The northern revolt crumbled. A band of Percy retainers was defeated at Topcliffe; Scrope, who had drawn to his standard a substantial body of Yorkshire knights as well as clergy, was brought to parley by Neville of Westmorland, and tricked with a promise of support into dismissing his men. He, with Mowbray and his nephew Sir William Plumpton, were all then arrested. They were executed at York at the king's command, in spite of hot protest from Archbishop Arundel at the breach of Scrope's privilege of clergy. Northumberland and Bardolf, isolated in the far north, withdrew to Berwick, and thence into Scotland. The captains of Warkworth and of Berwick castle both attempted to hold out against the king for the earl; but Berwick could not stand the battering of the king's siege train, and William Clifford, captain of Warkworth, made terms and retired after his master into Scotland. A number of northern gentry were afterwards tried for their part in the rebellion, and put to death.

After 1405, Henry IV never again had to face a full-scale domestic rebellion. His troubles were not by any means over yet, for Glendower in Wales was still dangerous; Harlech and Aberystwyth were still in rebel hands three years later. It was not until 1409 that it was clear that the Welsh revolt was under control, and Glendower was still at large when Henry IV died. Henry had not finished with the Percies either. From Scotland Northumberland and Bardolf travelled into Wales in 1406; next year they were in France seeking aid for new moves from the Duke of Orleans; Adam of Usk met them at Bruges and was tempted to throw in his lot with them. Returning to Scotland, they made a last bid at invasion. Both died in battle, fighting the king's forces under the sheriff of Yorkshire at Bramham Moor in 1408. This was the last battle (outside Wales) to be fought on English soil in Henry IV's reign; but sentiment for the causes of Percy and Mortimer was not even now extinguished, and their names were still ones to conjure with.

The series of great rebellions in the first part of Henry IV's reign throws a very significant light on the revolution of 1399. They reveal how shaky the foundations of the Lancastrian succession were. It is a point too easily forgotten that the house of Lancaster, which was in the end displaced by the descendants of the March line, was very nearly extinguished in their favour in its infancy. The danger was not from northern and Welsh dissidents only. In 1404 the Lady Despenser was very nearly

successful in a plot to abduct the young Earl of March, in which
the Duke of York and Mowbray were both implicated. York had
been suspected earlier, in 1403, of complicity with the Percies,
and so had even Archbishop Arundel. According to the *Annales*,
in that year the question of Richard's rights and the rumour that
he was still alive were the talk even of the king's household.[16] We
have seen how, in the same period, the Franciscans acted as
agents of Ricardian and March propaganda. Two informers in
1405 accused a number of other religious orders of lending
clandestine support to Glendower, including the abbeys of
Ramsey, Crowland, Thorney and Woburn, all far away from
Wales and the scene of action.[17] It was impossible, in an age in
which so much revolved about questions of inheritance, for
people at large not to be troubled about what had happened in
1399. The usurpation injected into the political life of the kingdom a new and perilous force working in favour of disruption.

Legitimism was only one theme in the manifestos through which
Hotspur in 1403 and Archbishop Scrope in 1405 sought to rally
popular support. They both clearly believed that there was
general dissatisfaction with Henry IV's record in government,
and that it too could be exploited in their favour. It is time that
we made the attempt to see how serious that dissatisfaction was,
and what its roots were.

Finance was the foremost besetting problem for the councillors
of the first Lancastrian king. The average annual revenue of
Henry IV was lower than that of his predecessor (it has been
calculated at approximately £90,000, compared with about
£116,000 for Richard II), and there were more serious calls upon
it than there had been in Richard's later years.[18] Henry's treasurers were in a state of constant alarm. 'There is not enough in
your treasury at the moment to pay the messengers who are to
bear the letters which you have ordained to the lords and knights
who are to be of your council', wrote Lawrence Allerthorpe in

[16] *Annales*, p. 391.
[17] See R. Griffiths, 'Some secret supporters of Owen Glyn Dwr',
B.I.H.R. 37 (1964), pp. 77–100.
[18] On Henry's financial situation see further Jacob, *The Fifteenth
Century*, pp. 73–90; A Steel, *The Receipt of the Exchequer 1377–1485*
(Cambridge, 1954) ch. II and III; and Kirby, *Henry IV of England*, esp.
pp. 90–1 and 126–7. Kirby stresses in particular the difficulty which the
unforeseen fall in the yield of the customs presented in Henry's early
years.

1401; years later, in 1411, his successor was explaining to the council that the books still simply would not balance.[19] Something would have to go, he said; perhaps the budget for the defence of Aquitaine could be reduced. Councillors were frightened by the consequences of insolvency: Archbishop Arundel, speaking in 1406 on behalf of the lords named in parliament to be of the council, declared that they were ready to take up their duties 'if sufficiency of goods could be found to carry on government properly: otherwise not'.[20] The government found it a far from easy task to raise loans in anticipation of revenue. A letter from the council to the king in the early summer of 1405 gives a good picture of the kind of problem that Henry's advisers had to face. They have raised loans, they say, with great difficulty, which will cover the costs of Calais and of the fleet which is being fitted out under Prince Thomas, but they have nothing for Guienne at all. They have had to drive a hard bargain with the councillors of the Prince of Wales (who was defending the Welsh march against Glendower), who have only accepted an assignment on the subsidy due at mid-summer because there was nothing else to offer them.[21] This is a picture of a government which is simply not able to meet all the justified calls made on its pocket.

Parsimony, enforced by adverse circumstances, meant that Henry IV's government had to make demands on its aristocratic supporters which put a real strain on their sympathies. The Percies, before 1403, were constantly complaining that they had not been paid what was due to them for duties that they had performed. The same complaint that they made, that they were in constant danger of being deserted by their own men for lack of pay, and the same threat, that they would be forced to throw up their offices if there was no remedy, were echoed by many others, even on one occasion by the king's own son Prince Thomas. In 1405 Lord Grey of Codnor wrote that he was so embarrassed that even his harness was in pawn for wages to his own soldiers. The Duke of York in the same year obtained letters of privy seal to help him raise loans in the west country in order to pay his men at Carmarthen, but the men to whom they were addressed would lend nothing, because they had not yet been repaid earlier loans to the crown. His retainers had to be content

[19] M. D. Legge (ed.), *Anglo Norman Letters* (Oxford, 1941), quoted by Jacob, *The Fifteenth Century*, pp. 75-6, who corrects the date of Allerthorpe's letter; and *P.P.C.* vol. II, p. 8 (statement of 1411).

[20] *R.P.* vol. III, p. 573.

[21] *P.P.C.* vol. I, pp. 259-63.

with his personal promise 'as a true gentleman' that the revenues of his Yorkshire estates should be put into their hands from 1 August if no other way of paying them could be found.[22] Many lords were clearly advancing money of their own to pay their men in the king's service; this was quite normal, but repayment was so slow and inadequate that they were afraid of being faced with a choice between the alternatives of their own financial ruin, or of sacrificing the trust and respect of their own followers. The attitude of men thus placed could shade very easily from distrust and dissatisfaction with royal government into disloyalty.

In order to ease his financial difficulties, Henry had to look frequently to the commons in parliament for grants of taxes and subsidies. They usually gave him a good deal of trouble before they made their grants.[23] Though they were not niggardly, they were determined that the king should stretch his own resources as far as was humanly possible. They were outspokenly critical of all forms of waste, demanding in 1402 and again in 1410 that grants for life, when they fell in, should be kept to the king's use; in 1404 they passed a stiff act of resumption, asking for a stop for one year on all fees and annuities from the crown. They made strenuous efforts, too, to make certain that moneys were really spent on the purposes for which they were voted; in 1404 they made the appointment of treasurers of war to supervise expenditure a condition of their grant; in 1406 they imposed the same duty on the council and appointed auditors at the exchequer. This is a record of sustained action with a consistent objective, and one not flattering to the king's dignity.

The commons of Henry IV's reign were sharply conscious of the strength which their control over financial grants gave their influence. In 1401 they went so far as to suggest that their grants should not normally be finalized until all their petitions had been heard and answered; the king did not concede the principle, but in practice he had more or less to observe it. They used their influence to some purpose when dealing, for instance, with the matter of the king's household and its expenses, constantly seeking to fix the source of its revenues, so that these could not be a charge on the grants that they made. Clearly they did not regard

[22] See *P.P.C.* vol. I, pp. 150–3 (Percies' complaints), pp. 263–4 (Prince Thomas), p. 277 (Grey of Codnor), pp. 271–4 (York).

[23] For an important survey of Henry's difficulties in this respect, and of the commons' aims, see A. Rogers, 'Henry IV, the commons, and taxation', *Medieval Studies* 31 (1969), pp. 44–70.

Henry's household with any more favour than their predecessors had that of Richard II. Their attitude towards the king's council was also significant. In 1404 they insisted that they should know the names of the king's councillors, in 1406 and 1410 that they should not only be named but also sworn in parliament. The object of the commons appears not to have been to control the composition of the council themselves; they simply wanted to be sure that the king was being guided by a representative group of the most substantial and experienced men of the kingdom, and not by a clique of *familiares*.[24]

The best insight into the attitude of the commons towards the council is furnished by the lengthy series of articles which the commons in 1406 insisted that councillors should swear to observe. These stressed that all important decisions should be agreed by the whole council, not simply by those whom the king happened (or chose) to have about him. They also made it the duty of councillors to ensure that grants were not made under the great or privy seal unduly, out of favour; to make sure that persons about the king and queen did not use their position to maintain or further quarrels which could be decided at common law; to watch the expenditure of the household; to regularize the procedures for hearing petitioners for favour. It is unwise to read too much constitutional significance into these articles, which were only to remain in force until the next parliament. Their political significance is, however, important. They indicate a very considerable distrust of the king's personal intimates and *entourage*, strongly reminiscent of the attitude of past parliaments to the *entourage* of Richard II.

There was never, in the Middle Ages, so much plain speaking between king and commons as there was in Henry IV's reign. This was in spite of the fact that a number of their speakers were men high in the king's confidence, as Arnold Savage, Thomas Chaucer and John Tiptoft (the speaker of 1406). On occasion rather more than plain speaking was involved. In 1401 the commons asked the king not to listen to informers among their number, who to advance themselves might report debates in a manner which would 'grievously move the king against the said commons'.[25] In 1411 they referred to 'the great murmuring

---

[24] On Henry, the commons, and the council, see A. L. Brown, 'The commons and the council in the reign of Henry IV', *E.H.R.* 79 (1964), pp. 1–30; also J. L. Kirby, 'Councils and councillors of Henry IV', *T.R.H.S.* 5th ser., 14 (1964), pp. 35–65.

[25] *R.P.* vol. III, p. 456.

among your people, that your heart is heavy toward some of your lieges who have come at your summons to this your parliament, and to the last at Westminster', and asked for an assurance that there was no such ill will.[26] These remarks are entered on the parliament roll. A detailed account in a news letter of 1404 gives a stormy picture of the kind of wrangling that the roll must often conceal. Savage, the speaker, declared that the outrageous grants made by the king had brought the commons to the end of their patience. The advice of some of the king's councillors he pronounced frankly malicious. This letter also reveals, most significantly, that it was at the commons' petition that in this parliament Northumberland was allowed to appear to clear himself of the charge of treason, and that they even threatened to make no grant when the king tried to demur.[27] This was not the only occasion when the commons took an interest in high politics that was not pleasing to the king. The vote of thanks in 1411 to the Prince of Wales and other councillors who had just been dismissed (some of whom were rumoured to have suggested that the king should abdicate in favour of his eldest son) cannot have been much more welcome.[28]

There is no hint of direct sympathy with Ricardian or March legitimism in the records of any of Henry IV's parliaments. The attitude of the commons reflects rather an opposite feeling, anxiety that the succession should be unequivocally entailed on Henry's descendants. Their attitude seems to have been rather like that of the later Elizabethan commons, who constantly petitioned the queen to marry or recognize a successor. The motivation in both cases was the same: fear of the civil disorder that might follow a disputed succession. Disorder was a subject very much in the minds of the commons of Henry IV's reign, not surprisingly. It is interesting to note that their concern about lack of governance was not confined to the early part of the reign, the period of the rebellions. Nor were their complaints about other matters, as taxation, and the expenses of the household. Tensions between king and people underlay the comparative tranquillity of the later years of Henry IV, as they had the earlier years of open instability.

Despite the continued grumbling, there is a real contrast between the domestic peace of the years after 1406, and the civil confusion

[26] R.P. vol. III, p. 658.
[27] See C. M. Fraser, 'Some Durham documents relating to the Hilary parliament of 1404', B.I.H.R. 34 (1961), pp. 197–9.
[28] R.P. vol. III, p. 649.

that reigned before. This contrast between the earlier and later periods of Henry's reign is interestingly repeated in the pattern of England's relations with external powers.

At the outset of the reign, Henry's uncertain circumstances posed two objectives, to maintain the truce with France, and to achieve recognition for himself and his dynasty in Europe. The latter object was complicated by the Schism in the church, which divided Europe ecclesiastically into two 'obediences', and by the parallel schism in the Empire, where both Wenceslas of Bohemia and Rupert of the Palatinate claimed to be the elected king of the Romans. The French, although they confirmed the truce with England in 1400, cleverly avoided formally acknowledging Henry as king of England. Henry did succeed in forging a series of dynastic connexions for his house: his daughter Blanche was married in 1402 to Lewis of Bavaria, King Rupert's eldest son; and Philippa in 1406 to the king of Norway. He himself married a second time in 1403; his new bride was the Dowager Duchess of Brittany, Joan. None of these marriages brought any material benefit for the time being. Henry's efforts to secure French agreement to the marriage of Isabella, Richard's ex-queen, to one of his sons, a connexion which would have had great political potential, were wholly unsuccessful.

It is questionable how much the successive confirmations of the truce with France in the early years were worth. The French court was constantly disturbed by the rivalries of the dukes of the royal house, who quarrelled and intrigued in Paris around the mad King Charles VI, and agreements were not always effective in binding all parties. Louis of Orleans, the king's brother, consistently urged hostile action against the English, and in 1404 his son Charles was betrothed to Isabella. Count Waleran de St Pol had married Richard II's sister and could not obtain her dowry; there was bitter fighting in the *pas de Calais* between the English and his men. There was also fighting in Guienne, and a privateering war in the Channel between English seamen and both the Bretons and the Flemings. Relations deteriorated with the years. There were numerous French raids on the Channel coast and islands, and in 1404 the French formally allied with Glendower, Henry's enemy. A French force marched with Glendower's men on his great raid into England in 1405. In 1406 there were plans for two simultaneous offensives against the English in France, in the Calais march and in Guienne. They came to nothing, but the reason why they did was not the firmness of the English; it was the quarrels of the French princes.

There cannot be much doubt that in the early years of Henry IV the French could have ended English dominion on French soil fifty years earlier than they actually did. The reason why they did not was the rivalry of the dukes of Orleans and Burgundy. Relations between these two were already strained when Henry IV came to his throne. Both had ambitions outside France: Burgundy, who was also Count of Flanders, in the Low Countries, and Orleans, who was married to a Visconti princess, in Italy. Both wished to use control of diplomacy and finance at Paris to further their own ends. After the death of Philip of Burgundy in 1404 and the succession of his son John the Fearless, mutual hostility became less restrained. It ruined the campaign plans of 1406. In 1407 Louis of Orleans was assassinated in Paris by retainers of John the Fearless, and France was brought to the brink of civil war. From this point onwards England no longer had much to fear from France; it was the turning point in her external relations in Henry IV's reign.

Another event, which took place shortly before this, strengthened Henry's position with regard to the old ally of the French, Scotland. In 1406 James, the heir of Robert III, was taken at sea by the English, while on his way to France. Robert III died shortly after this, and the man who was named as 'governor' of Scotland was Albany. His son, Murdach of Fife, was Henry's prisoner, and Albany was more anxious to see Murdach back in Scotland than the young James. With a hold over the Scots governor, and with France clearly on the verge of civil war, Henry at last began to look more formidable as a European monarch. The English were able to play a very prominent part, in consequence, in the negotiations which led up to the summons of the Council of Pisa, the first major European effort to end the Schism in the church. This made a considerable impression, both abroad and at home.[29]

When in 1410 open war broke out in France between John of Burgundy and the princes who were allies of the young Charles of Orleans (the most formidable among them being his new father-in-law, Count Bernard of Armagnac), both parties were anxious for alliance with Henry IV. There seemed to be a real chance of securing from one or other at least the recognition of

[29] See E. F. Jacob, 'English conciliar activity 1395-1418' in his *Essays in the Conciliar Epoch* (Manchester, 1953), esp. pp. 70-84, and 'The conciliar movement in recent study', *B.J.R.L.* 41 (1958-9), pp. 33-8.

English sovereignty in the lands ceded to Edward III by the Treaty of Brétigny, an object which had dominated English diplomatic thinking ever since the 1370s. The question was, with which side should the English ally?

In 1411 Henry Prince of Wales was at the head of the council, and his choice was in favour of Burgundy. There was much to be said for this alternative. Because Burgundy's Flemish subjects were dependent on supplies of English wool, it looked as if it should be possible for the English to put effective pressure on him to steer any French government that he directed clear of intervention in Aquitaine. John was prepared besides to offer inviting terms: a marriage of one of his daughters to the prince, and to put certain important towns, Gravelines, Dunquerque, Sluys and Dixmude, into English hands. This satisfied Prince Henry, and in October an English force under the Earl of Arundel was despatched to Arras. They played a distinguished part in the campaign that followed, and entered Paris with Burgundy's army.

Before Arundel's force was back, the Armagnacs (the Orleanist party) had outbid Burgundy. Their negotiations commenced in the new year of 1412, and culminated in an agreement made at Bourges, by which the dukes of Orleans, Bourbon and Berry promised, in return for support against Burgundy, to restore to Henry IV the duchy of Aquitaine, and to do homage to him for their own lands in the duchy. As a first step towards implementing the English side of the bargain, a large host, under the command of Henry's second son, Thomas Duke of Clarence, was recruited. The Duke of York, Thomas Beaufort and Sir John Cornwall led important contingents. The muster was at Southampton, and Clarence landed at La Hogue in Normandy on 10 August 1412.

Clarence's expedition did not achieve the glory that was hoped for it, largely because the French parties had come to terms with each other, unknown to the English, when it landed. But it achieved enough to demonstrate forcefully the potential of English intervention in the disordered French kingdom. Clarence took St Rémy and Bellême, marched through Anjou, and crossed the Loire. The French had to buy him off, and showed their weakness by the sums that they agreed to pay: Clarence was to receive 120,000 crowns, York 36,000, and Sir John Cornwall 21,000. The Count of Angoulême was handed over as a hostage; and the treasures of Jean de Berry were ransacked for pledges for the sums due. Clarence passed into Gascony, and was at

Bordeaux before Christmas, where plans were mooted for a campaign in 1413. Before they could mature, Henry IV was dead, and the whole aspect of things in England had begun to change.

The sudden *volte face* in English diplomacy in 1411, from alliance with Burgundy to alliance with the Armagnacs, was almost certainly the direct consequence of the dismissal, in November 1411, of the council headed by the Prince of Wales. This was the climax of a long period of tension among the groups close to Henry IV's throne. From at least 1405 onwards, the king had been often sick, and his eldest son in consequence gradually assumed a dominating influence in the council. From 1409 he was virtually its president. Always close to him were his half-brothers, the Beauforts; and the council named in the spring of 1410 was dominated by their party. Henry Beaufort, Bishop of Winchester, was a prominent member; Sir Thomas Beaufort became chancellor in succession to Archbishop Arundel; Lord Scrope of Masham, the treasurer, with the Earl of Warwick and Henry Chichele, who were appointed at the end of the parliament, were also associates of the prince. Archbishop Arundel, Lord Roos, and the Lancastrian knights who had been prominent in earlier councils were dropped; and it is clear that there were soon tensions between the new council and Prince Thomas, Henry IV's second son. The group that in 1411 forced its way to the front, with a consequent redistribution of offices, was headed by Archbishop Arundel, probably in alliance with Thomas; Arundel became chancellor, and Sir John Pelham replaced Scrope at the treasury.

The party divisions that lay behind this change seem to have been of a quite serious order. It was said later that at the time Prince Henry's court was always 'more abundant than the King his father's'.[30] Just before the autumn parliament of 1411 there was apparently a suggestion from the Beauforts that the king ought to abdicate in the prince's favour. In June 1412 in an open letter written at Coventry Prince Henry complained of malicious rumours that he was seeking to seize the throne, and that he had tried to thwart the expedition to Aquitaine. The reason why he would not sail with the expedition, he explained, was not that he was plotting sedition, but because he had been told to bring so small a force that it would not suffice for his own safety. It was the king's own familiars, according to Walsingham, who were

[30] *The First English Life of King Henry V*, ed. C. L. Kingsford (Oxford, 1911), p. 11.

so busy sowing rumour against him. Clearly a dangerous political situation was developing.[31]

A sick king, divisions among councillors and princes of the blood, open manifestos from persons maligned at court; all these things anticipate the symptoms of disarray that were later patent in the years when Henry VI's government was losing control on the eve of the Wars of the Roses. So do the tales from the end of Henry IV's reign of the disorders committed in London by the retainers of Thomas of Clarence and his brother John, and of Prince Henry 'coming to the council with an huge people' of followers.[32] The situation when Henry IV died in March 1413 was, of course, infinitely less dangerous than that of, say, 1450; though the symptoms of disease in the body politic were similar, it had not yet taken hold as it was to later. Nevertheless we can see that Henry's victories over his opponents in the first part of his reign had failed to solve his problems. The shadow of civil discord was looming again in the last years, with party groupings among the nobility crystallizing into hostile factions.

Henry IV's record as a ruler should not be undervalued. In the days of his vigour he showed himself an able commander in the field. He managed his relations with the intractable commons in parliament with a skill that ensured that, for all their difficulties with one another, confrontation never reached the point where there was a real threat to royal government. The men whom he chose as counsellors and administrators showed marked ability, for the most part, and served him faithfully. Long before he died he had won over the greater magnates to acquiescence in his regime, in appearance at least. Yet no one regretted his days when they were over. The first request of the speaker in Henry V's first parliament was for 'more abundant government', which had been so often promised before; but 'how the promises were kept the king who now is knows well enough'.[33] Henry V did, in fact, provide better government than Henry IV had, but before the period of his great successes he had to deal with an ugly legacy of disaffection from his father's time.

The story of the Cambridge plot, hatched in 1415, is essentially

[31] *The St Albans Chronicle 1406–1420*, ed. V. H. Galbraith (Oxford, 1937), p. 65f. The prince was apparently also at this time accused of embezzling the pay of the Calais garrison, *P.P.C.* vol. II, pp. 34–5.

[32] See Sir J. H. Ramsay, *Lancaster and York* vol. I (Oxford, 1892), p. 139.

[33] *R.P.* vol. IV, p. 4.

an epilogue to the story of the reign of Henry IV. The leader
of the conspiracy was Richard Earl of Cambridge, the younger
brother of the Duke of York; his two chief associates were
Lord Scrope of Masham and Sir Thomas Grey of Heton.
The plan was to assassinate the king, while he was with the host
that was mustering at Southampton for the Agincourt campaign,
and to place the Earl of March on the throne. It is clear from the
conspirators' confessions that March knew about the plot; Grey
indeed said that he had been urging him for two years past to
take action to regain the throne that was rightly his. Lord Clifford
seems also to have been on the margin of the conspiracy, and
Sir Robert Umfraville. March, however, gave the business away
to the king, who wisely made no inquiries about any except the
principals. Cambridge, Scrope and Grey were tried by a court
of their peers, and executed for high treason.[34]

All the ramifications of this affair led back into Henry IV's
reign. Scrope was the nephew of the archbishop who had been
executed at York in 1405. Through Clifford, whose sister he had
married, he was connected to the Percies; Elizabeth Percy was
Clifford's wife. An important item in the conspirators' plan was
to seize Murdach of Fife, Albany's son and the king's prisoner,
and to exchange him for Hotspur's heir, who was still at the court
of Scotland. The return of a Percy to the north would mean much
to northerners like Clifford and Umfraville. The conspirators had
also made contact with the old adherents of Glendower in Wales.
Their whole plan was based on a network of connexions, which
reproduced, in a new generation, the patterns of disaffection of
1403 and 1405.

The Cambridge plot points back, once again, to the significance of 1399. Sixteen years later it had not been forgotten that
the Lancastrian title was better *de facto* than *de jure*. Henry IV
never won the full loyalty and respect of the people whose government he had seized, and new aristocratic attempts at king-
making never ceased to be a possibility while he was on the
throne. With its long tale of civil war, sedition and popular dissatisfaction with government his reign gave England an ugly
foretaste of the troubles of the time of his grandson, Henry VI,
who was ultimately deposed by the heir of the line of March,
Edward IV (who happened ironically also to be the grandson of
Richard of Cambridge). Henry IV was of course infinitely abler

[34] The only really detailed examination of the Cambridge plot is that
of J. H. Wylie in *The Reign of Henry V* vol. I (Cambridge, 1914), pp.
513-38.

than Henry VI, but there is not much to choose between the career as a king-maker of Henry IV's Earl of Northumberland, and the later and more famous king-maker, Richard of Warwick. What really made the difference between the two reigns was that Henry IV was lucky enough always to defeat his enemies in the field; his grandson was not.

14

Politics and society: parliament
and the council

In tracing the turbulent political history of the reigns of Richard II and Henry IV we have repeatedly found it necessary to view the attitudes and the shifting alliances of the great magnates in the context of opinion in the country at large. We shall find in due course that, later in the fifteenth century, the view of the political classes continued to be an important factor in politics. 'Public opinion' and 'the political classes' are good general terms, but ones whose connotations change with time. It will help us to understand our period better if we can explore a little more carefully what they mean with reference to the late fourteenth and fifteenth centuries.

In the *Prologue* to the *Canterbury Tales*, Chaucer has provided for us in a series of vignettes, drawn with poetic insight, a cross section of the society of his day. His best pictures, perhaps, are those of the clergy, whose calling laid them particularly open to his satire, but his lay figures are for our immediate purpose even more interesting. Here at one end of the social scale we meet the knight (almost certainly a banneret), who stands apart from all the rest), an aristocrat who has travelled far and wide in chivalry. At the other extreme there is the ploughman, a 'true swinker and a good'. Between these two in the social scale stand a group of people of middling rank, and one of the first things that must strike anyone who reads their descriptions is their prosperity. This is true even of those who do not stand high in the scale. The miller and the reeve are manorial figures, but the miller has a white coat and a blue hood, and a sword and buckler at his side; and the reeve is a trusted, experienced steward, 'rich astored privily', with a fair dwelling shadowed with trees. The manciple, bursar to a society of lawyers, is another experienced steward, who can run business better than his learned masters.

The weaver, the dyer and the carpenter, humble as their crafts are, are solid burgesses, with chattels enough to fit them for a seat on their guildhall dais. Even the ploughman, it would seem, is some way short of real poverty; he can afford to lend his neighbours a hand without hire, and his brother is a parson.

The most interesting figures, for us, are the merchants and the gentry. They are also the most notably prosperous. The wife of Bath, overdressed on Sunday, has laid three husbands at the church door, and substantial men they must have been, for in her business of cloth making 'she passed them of Ypres and Ghent'. The merchant himself is a man playing for high stakes, changing currency, lending money and lading ships between Middleburgh and Orwell. Three men, the shipman, the man of law and the franklin, though they are not knights, all belong to what historians often call the 'knightly class', or the 'gentry'. The shipman, who knows every harbour from Gotland to Finisterre, might almost be John Hawley of Dartmouth, who in Chaucer's own time made a fortune largely through piracy, and prospered to be a man of wealth and landed estate. He sat in the commons for Dartmouth, was employed from time to time on commissions, and even acted as deputy to the lord admiral.[1] The man of law is one of those successful barristers raised to the rank of serjeant-at-law, who were not only recognized as leading advocates in the central courts, but also often served as justices of assize, and from time to time attended the king's council to advise on points of law. Most interesting of all is the franklin. He is a 'great householder', a man of standing in his county, a justice of the peace, who has served as sheriff and represented the shire in parliament 'full oft'. Not a man of the knight's ancestry, he is a man of estate and authority, ambitious for the recognition of his kin as genteel. In him we recognize quite clearly the lineal ancestor of Shakespeare's Justice Shallow, Robert Shallow esquire, justice of the peace, a 'gentleman born', who 'writes himself *armigero* in any bill, warrant, quittance or obligation'[2] – of a rising gentleman, that is to say, of the Tudor age.

Chaucer, of course, does not tell us anything about the political influence of his characters, or in detail of their economic status; that was not germane to him. We can get some way towards viewing the wealth and influence of the kind of men that

[1] On Hawley and other west country seamen see C. L. Kingsford, 'West country piracy: the school of English seamen' in his *Prejudice and Promise in Fifteenth Century England* (Oxford, 1925), pp. 78–106.

[2] *Merry Wives of Windsor*, Act I, Scene 1.

he depicted in comparative terms, by looking at the instructions for the levy of the graduated poll tax of 1379.[3] In this very interesting social record we find the dukes of Lancaster and Brittany heading the list of those liable, in a class of their own, paying ten marks. Immediately after them come the earls, liable to £4. Barons, we shall find to our surprise, are not considered for the purpose of the tax as a class apart. They are lumped together with bannerets (knights of outstanding note, usually with a military background), and with knights bachelor who can 'afford the same style'. It is in this group, who pay 40s., that Chaucer's knight would belong. There are bigger surprises when we look for the equivalent of the man of law and the merchant. The justices of the bench are taxed at £5, a higher rate than even earls paid; and serjeants-at-law pay at the same rate as barons and bannerets. Turning to the mercantile figures the Mayor of London of 1379 has to pay 'as an earl', and his colleagues the aldermen at the same rate as barons (this is near where Chaucer's merchant would come into line). It is hard to be sure where the shipman, the franklin and the wife of Bath would be, but all most likely in the group immediately following the barons and bannerets, which paid £1 and included all those whose estates would support knighthood, as well as successful merchants, and apprentices-at-law (junior barristers). They might have just fallen short of it, and certainly would have had connexions among the host of less influential people assessed at a mark, half a mark, three and fourpence, or one or two shillings, all of whom stood clear of the peasants and labourers who paid a groat, fourpence a head. That is probably what the ploughman would have paid, but perhaps even he might just have rated a shilling.

The men who devised the gradations of the poll tax of 1379 were of course seeking to tax wealth, not political influence. The two, however, can never stand far apart. That is why it is so striking to find the Mayor of London rated as high as an earl, and rich knights and serjeants-at-law set on a footing with barons who sat apart in parliaments and dressed retainers in their own livery. A London alderman, a knight banneret or a serjeant might be a man who had started from very small beginnings. Political influence in the late fourteenth century, we are drawn to conclude, was not the monopoly of a narrow caste; it was shared by the great of ancient blood with a numerous body of substantial men of middle rank, and social barriers were far from inflexible.

[3] *R.P.* vol. III, pp. 57–8.

It is useful to compare the poll tax assessment of 1379 with another fiscal source which can throw light on the distribution of wealth in England in the later Middle Ages: the returns to the tax on income from land and annuities of 1436. H. L. Gray, who studied the returns in detail, found fifty-one lay peers with an average income of £768 per annum, 183 greater knights with an average of £208 per annum, 750 lesser knights with an average of £60, 1200 esquires with an average of £24, and a further 5000 men with incomes varying between £5 and £20.[4] A good many of these 5000 would have called themselves esquires, and some would certainly have done so who did not have so much. Gray's figures for the lords and knights tally well with the nearest available heraldic evidence, the Parliamentary Roll of Arms which was compiled in Edward II's reign; it lists over 940 armigerous lords and knights but is known not to be quite complete for its day[5] (it was only late in the fourteenth century that esquires began to be accepted as heraldically armigerous, and in the absence of reliable heraldic evidence comparable with the Parliamentary Roll we cannot estimate their number in this way). Denholm Young, calculating on the basis of the heraldic evidence and using Professor Russell's population figures, reckons that perhaps one family in twenty might aspire to call itself genteel.[6] This figure probably gives an exaggerated impression of the size of a prosperous class; we know that there were plenty of rural communities, none of whose members could by normal standards have been rated a gentleman (though the word is, of course, elusive of definition). Cornwall, writing on the early Tudor landed gentry, suggests a proportion of one in fifty or so.[7] The difference between one in fifty and one in twenty is large, but a broad conclusion still remains. Given the substantial variety and number of men who stood, in terms of wealth and status, between the poor squire and the really humble labourer, we get a picture of a remarkably wide distribution of wealth, with many gradations.

Our conclusion here is borne out by the explicit comment of a fifteenth-century observer. 'England is so thick spread with rich and landed men', wrote Sir John Fortescue, 'that there is scarce

[4] H. L. Gray, 'Incomes from land in 1436' *E.H.R.* 49 (1934), pp. 607–639.

[5] See N. Denholm Young, *History and Heraldry* (Oxford, 1965), p. 19.

[6] N. Denholm Young, *The Country Gentry in the Fourteenth Century* (Oxford, 1969), pp. 1–8.

[7] See J. Cornwall, 'The early Tudor gentry', *Econ.H.R.* 2nd ser., 17 (1964–5), pp. 456–75.

a small village in which you may not find a knight, an esquire, or some substantial householder called a franklin; all men of considerable estates. There are others who are called freeholders; and many yeomen of estates sufficient to make a substantial jury. There are several of those yeomen who are able to spend by the year a hundred pounds.'[8] These social conditions – the prosperity of solid men of middle rank – had, so Fortescue believed, a profound effect on the English national character. They were what enabled Englishmen to resist tyranny, and to enjoy an independence and equality before the law which contrasted with the state of other peoples and ought to be their envy.[9]

The picture that we are beginning to form of the middle ranks of lay society in late medieval England has so far been based on literary description and fiscal statistics. It may help to give more body to it, if we look at the careers of two or three historical individuals in rather closer detail. Sir Richard Stury, William and John Paston, and Richard Whittington all led lives that can help to give definition to the generalities in which we have so far been dealing.

Sir Richard Stury was probably the son of a Shropshire knight, William Stury, who had served in the royal household, but from whom he inherited, as far as we know, nothing. We first hear of him as a yeoman of the household of Edward III, about 1350. He served with distinction in France, and rose to be an esquire, then to be knighted and retained in the chamber. Service brought him wealth: he had annuities from the king, the Duke of Brittany, and Joan of Kent, and accumulated substantial estates. He married Alice, daughter of Sir John Blount and widow of Richard Stafford, Lord Stafford's son. Under Richard II he continued to prosper; he was made justice of Cardigan in 1387 and of south Wales in 1391. As a curialist, he was in trouble both in 1376 and in 1387-8, but he weathered all storms. In the 1390s he figures prominently in Prophet's journal of the council, where he was one of the most regular in attendance, drawing a salary of 10s. a day. Froissart, who knew him personally, was able to get from him details of what the council had decided about Gascon matters in 1395, and to obtain an audience with Richard II. Stury was by then a man of long and mingled experience,

---

[8] J. Fortescue, *De Laudibus Legum Anglie*, ed. S. B. Chrimes (Cambridge, 1942), p. 69. I have retained the English of the older translation of F. Gregor (London, 1775), less accurate but to my mind more vivid.

[9] ibid. pp. 86-8.

military, diplomatic and administrative, and also, we gather, of independent ideas, a suspected sympathizer with Lollards. He was an acquaintance of Chaucer, and possessed books of his own. He died in 1395, full of years, a man who had built for himself a career, estates and influence at the very centre of affairs by his own unaided talents and energy.[10]

John Paston, born in 1421 and from 1444 to 1466 head of the Norfolk family whose letters have made them famous, held a position in society not so very different from that of Stury, but his career was entirely so. His father William was the founder of the family fortunes. Clement Paston, John's grandfather, borrowed money to send William to school; afterwards he studied the law, at which he prospered, rising to be a serjeant in 1421 and in 1429 to be a justice of the common pleas. He made extensive purchases of land in Norfolk, and built a small inheritance into a substantial holding. His wife Agnes, heiress of Sir Edmund Berry, brought him lands in Hertfordshire and Suffolk too. John he sent first to Cambridge, then to London to study law, for his experience had taught him the value of a legal training to the county landowner: 'whosoever should dwell at Paston should have need to know how to defend himself'.[11] The old judge was right enough, for John, when he inherited, found himself plunged in disputes with neighbours who had the ear of Suffolk, Henry VI's chief councillor. Chief among them were Lord Moleyns and John Heydon, who contested his right to the manor of Gresham, one of William's important purchases. John's knowledge of the law stood him in even better stead in his dealings with his wife's relative, Sir John Fastolf, the great soldier who had invested in landed estate a fortune made in the wars in France, and who was building himself a castle at Caistor in Norfolk. John became Fastolf's lawyer and chief adviser; and by a will drawn up just before his death in 1459 became his principal heir, as well as the administrator of his will.

Fastolf's will was of course contested. There was a long suit at law, and after John's death the rivals of his family positively besieged Caistor; his son in the end had to make a compromise with the other claimants. Nevertheless the addition to the family fortunes was very considerable. John Paston was able to send

[10] For a review of Stury's career see W. T. Waugh, 'The Lollard knights', *S.H.R.* 11 (1913), pp. 64–8. Waugh missed some important points, and our picture of the man will be clearer when K. B. McFarlane's study appears in his *Lancastrian Kings and Lollard Knights*.

[11] *P.L.* No. 46.

his son to court and lived to see him knighted; and in 1460 he himself for the first time went to parliament as a knight of the shire for Norfolk. It was the only capacity in which he ever took a formal part in national affairs. But though, unlike Stury, he was never at the political hub of events and lacked patrons of the standing of those that his rivals found, he was always a formidable man in local affairs, and always had contacts and correspondents in London. Greater men than he set store by his influence in Norfolk. Long before the Fastolf inheritance came his way it was said of him 'as for Paston, he is a squire of worship, and of great livelihood, and I wot he will not spend all his goods at once . . . he may do his enemy a shrewd turn and never fare the worse in his household, nor have the less men about him'.[12] His career is a splendid example of the solid success that could be built on shrewd sense and sound understanding of the law and local politics, without the consistent patronage of any of the great men of the realm.

Richard Whittington, the great London merchant, sprang, interestingly enough, from the same social class as Stury and Paston.[13] Born in the 1350s, he was the youngest son of a not very prosperous landowner in Gloucestershire. He got no inheritance and went to London, where he made a good start in business as a mercer. Already in the 1380s he was doing well, supplying over £2000 worth of mercery to Richard II's favourite, Robert de Vere, and in the 1390s he began to supply large quantities of goods to the Great Wardrobe. His connexion with Richard II did him no harm, and he continued to supply the Great Wardrobe for Henry IV, who owed him £1000 in 1403. By that time he was already advancing large sums to the crown. He was also exporting wool on a considerable scale, and most of his loans were secured on the custom on wool exports. He had been elected an alderman of London in 1393; and in 1397 had been mayor for the first time (he was mayor again in 1406 and in 1419, and was also twice mayor of the staple at Calais). In November 1399, just after Henry IV's accession, he was appointed a member of the king's council. He was then a made man, with a great fortune, substantial properties in London, and con-

---

[12] *P.L.* No. 211.

[13] The most recent study of Whittington is C. Barron, 'Richard Whittington: the man behind the myth' in *Studies in London History Presented to P. E. Jones* (London, 1969), pp. 197–248. What I have written of him here is based on this very interesting and perceptive paper.

stantly employed about the king's business. For the next twenty years, until he died in 1423, he continued to prosper as one of the greatest merchants in the city who was always in the public eye.

Whittington was childless, and his wife Alice, daughter of a Dorset landowner, predeceased him. If he had had heirs, he might have founded a dynasty of landed gentry (Chaucer's father was a merchant, his son a councillor and married to John of Gaunt's stepdaughter; Michael de la Pole, son of a merchant prince, married a Scrope and rose to be an earl). Perhaps it was because he was childless that Whittington, unlike most of his contemporaries, invested little of his fortune in land. As he left no books in his will, we may conclude that he did not share their literary tastes either. He left behind instead solid memorials of his achievement. He founded an almshouse for thirteen poor men and women and a college for secular priests attached to the church of St Michael in Paternoster Row, where he was buried. He helped to build the library at Grey Friars in London, and left large charitable bequests which helped to repair St Bartholomew's hospital and to build the new Guildhall. His success and standing made him a legend in his lifetime: after his death the legend grew, and he was remembered as the 'lode star and chief chosen flower'[14] among the sons of merchandise.

Two points deserve special emphasis in the careers of the three men that we have been examining: their education, and their interest in national politics. Whittington, it is true, does not seem to have been much of a man for books, though he was a patron of libraries; but in this he was untypical of the London merchants as a class, many of whom possessed and prized books of their own. Stury, the acquaintance of Froissart and Chaucer, was a man of real culture, as were also some of his close associates among the chamber knights: one of them, Sir John Clanvowe, was the author of the poem the *Cuckoo and the Nightingale*, which in early days was sometimes ascribed to Chaucer, as well as of a religious treatise in English.[15] The court of Richard II was a centre of cosmopolitan culture where art and poesy were in

[14] See *The Libelle of Englyshe Polycye*, ed. Sir G. Warner (Oxford, 1926), p. 25.

[15] See W. W. Skeat, *Chaucerian and Other Pieces* (Oxford, 1897), pp. 346–58, for 'The Cuckoo and the Nightingale' (whose attribution to this John Clanvowe is uncertain); and for the homily see V. J. Scattergood, 'The two ways – an unpublished religious treatise by Sir John Clanvowe', *English Philological Studies* 10 (1967), pp. 33–56.

high esteem, as Chaucer's poems and the Wilton diptych remind us. But from the point of view of education, John Paston is the most interesting of all the three. He himself was educated at Cambridge and in the Inns of Court. Among his sons, John went to Cambridge, to Trinity Hall; Edmund was at Clifford's Inn; Walter went to Oxford and William to Eton. John Paston was essentially a county man, whose business and interests were firmly centred in Norfolk, but there was nothing local about the academies to which he sent his children to get their learning. They were brought up to find their station not just among the gentry of their own neighbourhood, but of England.

The letters of the Pastons, the Stonors, the Plumptons, and of other gentry families witness to the generally high standard of literacy of their class. William Paston the younger, we have seen, went to Eton. It was becoming commoner in the fifteenth century for gentry to send their sons to board at school, and to the universities, even if they did not intend them to follow a clerical career. But the most important centres of lay education were the lawyers' Inns. There was scarcely an eminent lawyer in the kingdom, Fortescue reckoned, who was not a gentleman by birth, and the Inns offered a training not in law only, but in 'accomplishments suitable to their quality' too. 'The knights, barons, and the greatest nobility of the kingdom often place their children in those Inns of Court', he wrote proudly, 'not so much to make the laws their study (having large patrimonies of their own) but to form their manners.'[16] No doubt many gentlemen whose sons were at the Inns were actuated by a combination of snobbery with a sense of the solid value of a legal training to a landowner. William of Worcester, John Paston's contemporary, complained that the changing pattern of genteel education was eroding the traditional chivalrous values of the knightly class and that knights' sons lacked training in arms.[17] But the change that he lamented was one that was teaching the gentry a more sophisticated approach to politics than the old fashioned upbringing in a lord's household could inculcate, and to take a more informed view on general questions, political, legal and religious.

The growth of a professionally educated gentility was a factor of profound importance in late medieval England. It left a powerful mark on the king's council and service, in which laymen began to assume a steadily increasing share of administrative

[16] J. Fortescue, *De Laudibus Legum Anglie*, p. 118.

[17] *The Boke of Noblesse*, ed. J. G. Nichols (Roxburghe Club, 1860), pp. 76-8.

duties. From the beginning of the fifteenth century the treasurer of England, hitherto usually a high ecclesiastic, was more often a lay peer. Knights and esquires like Stury, Edward Dalyngrygg, Thomas Erpingham and John Norbury were among the men most regularly discharging business in the council in the reigns of Richard II and Henry IV. Laymen like Thomas Vaughan and William Alyngton were, in the Yorkist period, key figures in the new system for the administration of crown lands which helped to put the royal finances on their feet after the long disorder of the Lancastrian period. This growing preponderance of laymen in the administration of the kingdom was one of the distinctive features of the fifteenth century, and reminds us that in many respects it had more in common with the so called 'early modern' period than with the central Middle Ages.

Given their education and their material interests, the lively concern of the genteel and merchant classes with national politics is not surprising. For men like Stury politics were a career. For the Pastons, with their law suits and the great Fastolf inheritance at stake, politics were something that they could not afford to neglect, because success at law was so often dependent on having friends who could bring pressure to bear in the right quarter. The bulletins of news from the capital with which their correspondence is rich reflect their constant and anxious endeavour to stand well with those whose fortunes were in the ascendant. It is clear, however, that they and their correspondents were interested in politics for more besides their effect on local and personal interests. They watched the collapse of the English regime in France with a sense of direct involvement in the national cause. To Friar Brackley, Paston's friend who was with him at the making of Fastolf's last will, politics were deeply absorbing. A passionate Yorkist, who looked forward eagerly to the day when he should see Warwick the king-maker a duke, he had watched ever since the parliament of 1447 to see Jeremiah's prophecy fulfilled in the downfall of Henry VI's courtiers, he told Paston. He had a text for every turn of events, and longed to air his views at St Paul's Cross.[18]

Whittington's attitude to politics is perhaps the most interesting of all among the men whose lives we have been examining. A London merchant of his standing could not be indifferent to domestic political developments, or to foreign relations which could have a direct relevance to his commercial affairs. But

[18] *P.L.* No. 355; see also No. 364.

Whittington's involvement went much further than this. Over a period of more than twenty years he was one of the most significant individual lenders to the crown. Though repayment was not easy to obtain, he seems to have preferred to keep a large part of his fortune liquid, so as to be able to make further loans. There is no evidence that he ever charged interest on his money, and he did not, as far as we can make out, use his readiness to lend in order to secure profitable grants of land or office. He seems to have acted from a straightforward desire to be involved in matters of 'high policy'. In short, as Mrs Barron puts it, 'it was Whittington's intention, in lending money to the crown, to buy the royal ear and the public eye'.[19] He was in the game for its own sake.

The concern of Englishmen at large with politics and political issues is clearly reflected in the literature of the age. There is much here that is very general, reflections on the nature of kingship, government, and social obligations, with the Bible taken as the basic textbook of political science. These sorts of matters were first concerns with, for instance, William Langland, the author of *Piers Plowman*, and John Gower, both social moralists in their poetry. But Langland showed himself a keen observer of day-to-day politics (his picture of the rats' parliament in the *Prologue* may be directly related to the events of 1376),[20] and the recensions of Gower's works show clearly how, as he watched developments, his initial optimism about the government of Richard II changed to a bitter and critical hostility. Still more significant of active political interest are works directly inspired by political events, such as *Mum and the Sothsegger*, a long allegorical treatment of the events and issues of 1399. Here we find a poet whose chief concern is with political personalities and institutions, the council and parliament, and who is anxious to discuss such matters as the justification of subsidies and the duties of members of the commons, who are

> . . . assembled for to show the sores of the royaulme,
> And spare no speech, though they spill [i.e. die] should![21]

Later, in the fifteenth century, we find the broadsheet political ballad beginning to be a significant instrument of propaganda,

[19] C. Barron, 'Richard Whittington: the man behind the myth', p. 204.
[20] *Piers Plowman*, B Text, Prologue, ll. 146–209.
[21] *Mum and the Sothsegger*, ed. M. Day and R. Steel (E.E.T.S., 1936), ll. 1120–1.

and writers like Fortescue and the author of the *Somnium Vigilantis*[22] seriously tackling, in vernacular tracts, the problems of English government and political obligation.

Fortescue has a good claim to be regarded as the first man to attempt an explanation of the principles of the English constitution. He regarded it as combining the merits of two well-known systems of government which he found described by St Thomas Aquinas and Giles of Rome: royal dominion, in which the king's decrees are the foundation of the laws, and political dominion, under which the people are governed by laws to which they themselves have assented.[23] The origins of England's mixed 'royal and political' government were, he believed, historical, dating back to the first 'incorporacion' of the people into a 'body politic', when they chose Brutus the Trojan to be their king and to minister to them laws of their own choice. From this institution all the powers of the English kings derived, and therefore they could not, without the assent of the people, change the laws.[24] This was what distinguished English kingship from purely royal government, which had its origins in conquest and which Fortescue saw exemplified in Biblical times in the kingship of Nimrod and Saul and in his own day in France. Conversely England's hereditary monarchy, which worked within the limits set by popular assent, distinguished her government from what he called the purely 'political' dominion of the ancient classical republics and of Israel in the time of the Judges.

Fortescue, a working lawyer who had risen to be Chief Justice of the King's Bench, felt a very particular regard for the English legal system, above all for the method of trial by jury. This, he considered, gave a better protection to the property and person of the subject than any other procedure. What made the jury system workable in England was the great body of substantial men in the country, who could easily be brought together to serve on juries, and whose regard for their own honour and

[22] Printed by J. P. Gilson in *E.H.R.* 26 (1911), pp. 513–25. Parts of this work are in French and Latin; the meat of it is in English.

[23] On Fortescue's use of these sources see S. B. Chrimes, *English Constitutional Ideas in the Fifteenth Century* (Cambridge, 1936), pp. 314–318. Fortescue's own views on dominion are most clearly expressed in his *De Natura Legis Nature* (in the collected *Works*, ed. Lord Clermont), Lib. I, ch. 16.

[24] See Fortescue, *De Laudibus Legum Anglie*, pp. 24, 30–2; and *The Governance of England*, ed. C. Plummer (Oxford, 1885), pp. 111–13.

reputation should restrain them from abusing their position as jurors. These social conditions he regarded as the 'fruit' of the system of government under which Englishmen lived, which fostered their spirit of sturdy independence. Fortescue's ideas here led him naturally to take pride in parliament as an institution, and particularly in the role of the commons in law making. 'The statutes of England are not enacted by the will of a prince, but with the concurrent consent of the whole kingdom, by their representatives in parliament, and they must needs be full of wisdom and prudence, since they are the result not of one man's wisdom only, nor of a hundred, but of such an assembly as the Roman Senate was of old, more than three hundred select persons.'[25] It seemed to him that it was because the king could not alter the laws or impose taxes by his own authority 'without the express consent of the whole kingdom in parliament'[26] that men in England were free to enjoy their own and prospered. Conscious pride in English institutions, and the direct association that he saw between the nature of these institutions and the political virtues of her people, are the most striking themes in Fortescue's major works. We see here the first, sometimes groping articulation of views about the English constitution and its special merits, to which Burke 300 years later was to give the classic expression.

The commons of parliament brought together in a single assembly drawn from all over the realm a representative cross section of those 'middle' classes of substantial men, whose importance both Chaucer and Fortescue in their different ways emphasize for us. It is therefore significant that the parliamentary history of the late fourteenth and fifteenth centuries bears out in many respects Fortescue's picture of their independence. The commons displayed remarkable vigour in their insistence that grants of taxation should be accompanied by measures which they thought (often wrongly) would lead to better government: in their efforts to force better economy on the king and the council, and in pressing the king to surround himself with 'sad and substantial councillors'. On one or two occasions, as we have seen, they even succeeded in impeaching councillors who, they believed, had betrayed the king's trust. This vigour so struck Stubbs that he believed it was deliberately fostered by the Lancastrian kings, and spoke of a

[25] *De Laudibus Legum Anglie*, p. 40.
[26] ibid. p. 86.

Lancastrian 'constitutional experiment'. But the initiative was not from the king, it came from the commons themselves.[27]

Much has been said elsewhere in this book about the activities of the commons during particular reigns which need not be repeated. Two matters do, however, need further examination: the development, in the fifteenth century, of the traditions and institutions of the commons' house, and the evidence of a quickening interest in elections to parliament. Both subjects have a bearing on the important question of how far the commons in parliament in this period were influenced in their activities by the connexions of individual members with patrons of superior wealth and status. This in turn bears on another significant issue, the independence or otherwise of the gentry, of whom we have heard so much.

The sense of corporate identity among the commons was developing fast in the late Middle Ages. In the fifteenth century we find the practice growing whereby private individuals and communities addressed their petitions to the commons, or to the commons and their speaker (as opposed to the king in parliament).[28] When in 1407 the lords reported to the king on their own initiative what they thought was necessary in the way of a finance grant, the commons hotly protested that this prejudiced the liberties of their estate; and they obtained a ruling that nothing concerning grants should be reported until lords and commons were agreed, and that then it should be reported by the commons' speaker.[29] The development of the office of

[27] There is a considerable literature on the commons and their activities in the later fourteenth and fifteenth centuries. The most important general studies seem to me to be J. S. Roskell's two works: *The Commons in the Parliament of 1422* (Manchester, 1954) and *The Commons and their Speakers in English Parliaments 1376–1523* (Manchester, 1965), an outstandingly useful work that is virtually a parliamentary history; H. L. Gray, *The Influence of the Commons on Early Legislation* (Cambridge, Mass., 1932); K. B. McFarlane, 'Parliament and bastard feudalism', *T.R.H.S.* 4th ser., 26 (1944), pp. 53–79; and J. G. Edwards, *The Commons in Medieval English Parliaments* (Creighton Lecture, London, 1957). J. Wedgwood (ed.), *History of Parliament: Biographies of the Members of the Commons House 1439–1509*, is an invaluable companion to any study of the subject.

[28] On petitions generally see A. R. Myers, 'Parliamentary petitions in the fifteenth century', *E.H.R.* 52 (1937), pp. 385–404, 590–613.

[29] *R.P.* vol. III, p. 611. On all questions concerned with the speaker's office and its development see Roskell, *The Commons in the Parliament of 1422*.

speaker was another feature of great significance. His original function was to speak in parliament for the commons as a whole, before the lords and the king. The first speaker so to act for the duration of a whole parliament was Peter de la Mare in 1376. From the early years of Richard II's reign the commons were regularly electing their speaker and presenting him to the king, usually on the second or third day of parliament, when he made his 'protestation'. This was to the effect that he would say nothing of his own initiative, only what was the express will of all the commons, and that they should have the right to correct him if he misrepresented them in any way. Through the speaker, the commons found a means to given regular expression to their views as a body, independent of the lords.

By the middle of the fifteenth century it is clear that the speaker was doing a good deal more than just report the opinions of his house. He was becoming responsible for steering the commons through the *agenda* set out in the king's charge to parliament, and had acquired considerable influence over the passage of bills that were sent forward as common petitions. Abbot Whethamstede in 1454 spoke of him as having the *regimen* of the lower house.[30] In 1483 Bishop Russell compared the speaker to the Roman tribune of the people: 'in the lower house, all is directed by the speaker, *quasi per tribunum*'.[31]

In the fifteenth century we begin to find among the speakers of the commons a predominance of men trained in the law, which was later to be still more marked. Such a training was obviously invaluable to a man who had much to do with the drafting of bills and with procedure. We also find that the speakers, who were always prominent men, usually had connexions with the government, or with some peer with major political interests. Thus in 1397 the chamber knight Sir John Bushy was speaker, and in Henry IV's reign a series of royal councillors, including Thomas Chaucer, Arnold Savage and John Tiptoft; in 1450 York's retainer William Oldhall was chosen; in 1453 Thomas Thorpe, who had close connexions with Somerset; and in 1461 James Strangeways, a Neville retainer. Is this a sign that the king and the great peers were using the office of the speaker to control the commons? Useful as the friendship of the speaker must often have been to the government (or on occasion to its opponents) it is hard to pursue this line of argument very far. The commons

[30] *Registrum J. de Whethamstede* (R.S.) vol. I, p. 136.
[31] Chrimes, *English Constitutional Ideas in the Fifteenth Century*, p. 174.

were quite prepared, if they thought themselves misrepresented, to disavow their speaker, and they took a real interest in his election, for which there was sometimes keen competition.[32] The choice of men acceptable to the king or to influential peers seems to have been inspired by the hope that this would help the commons to get their own business attended to, not that of the speakers' patrons. The speakers' connexions certainly do not seem to have hampered the free expression of the opinion of the commons as a whole. Very few speakers were ever as outspoken in their criticisms of the council, the king's household and the government's economy as Sir Arnold Savage was in 1404,[33] notwithstanding the fact that he was a royal councillor.

It is sometimes claimed that in the early days of parliaments, attendance among the commons was regarded as an onerous and unwelcome duty. This was certainly not the case in the fifteenth century. Though a good many of the smaller boroughs no longer sent resident burgesses to parliaments, they had little difficulty in finding instead gentlemen or lawyers who had property there and were more than willing to represent them, and as time went by they more and more often sent men who had no residence qualification at all but wished to go to parliament, and who can be broadly described as gentry rather than merchants.[34] We come across a good many men among the knights of the shire of the fifteenth century who had sat in previous parliaments for boroughs. These developments helped to give the commons a more homogeneous social character and indicate clearly the widespread interest in obtaining a seat in parliament, as does the willingness of many borough members to waive, in part at least, their right to claim their expenses from their constituents. A new interest in the qualifications both of electors and members points in the same direction. In 1406 it was laid down by statute (in response to a common petition) that the returns of elections in the shires

[32] See Roskell, *The Commons and their Speakers*, pp. 51–3, 63–4. The classic example of a contested election to the speakership was 1420, when Roger Hunt was elected by a majority of four votes.

[33] See Chapter 13; and see further J. S. Roskell, 'Sir Arnald Savage of Bobbing, speaker for the commons in 1401 and 1404', *Archaeologia Cantiana* 70 (1956).

[34] See further Roskell, *The Commons in the Parliament of 1422*, ch. VII; M. McKisack, *The Parliamentary Representation of the English Boroughs during the Middle Ages* (Oxford, 1932), pp. 106–18; and also K. N. Houghton, 'Borough elections to parliament during the later fifteenth century', *B.I.H.R.* 39 (1966), pp. 130–40.

should be attested by all the electors (though it is clear that usually not all did so – only the most important men who were present on the occasion).[35] In 1429 the county franchise was limited to forty shilling freeholders, because of the disturbances that had been caused at elections by crowds of lesser men claiming the right to vote (this was to remain the county franchise until 1832). In 1445 it was decreed that no one of yeoman or lesser status should be eligible for election to parliament.

A fifteenth century election could be a tumultuous affair. In 1450 in Huntingdon, for instance, a group of no less than 124 freeholders complained that some seventy commoners, supporters of Henry Gimber, who was not 'of gentle birth according to your writ', appeared 'by labour of divers gentlemen of other shires and of this your said shire of Huntingdon' and disturbed the under-sheriff in his duty of examining the qualifications of electors. In consequence the petitioners, who had abandoned the field for fear of a riot, feared that the choice that they and 300 other electors had made in 'full shire' would be set aside and Gimber returned.[36] There was often a good deal of jockeying for position at an earlier stage than this. Peers with influence would write to their supporters and tell them who they wished to see elected. Thus John Paston in 1450 was told who York's candidates were and asked to help them; and in 1472 his son Sir John was warned that he had better give up his hope of being returned, as the dukes of Norfolk and Suffolk were agreed in advance as to who the Norfolk members should be.[37] Influence, however, was by no means always able to get its way, for the leading gentry of the shires were not men easily overawed. 'I told my lord of Norfolk that I laboured divers men for Sir Roger Chamberlain and they said they would have him', John Jenny, who was working in the Norfolk interest in 1455, wrote to Paston, 'but not Howard, inasmuch as he has no livelihood in the shire.' 'It is an evil precedent for the shire that such a strange man should be chosen, and no worship to my lord of York nor to my lord of Norfolk to write for him', he wrote again later, 'for if the gentlemen of the shire will suffer such inconvenience, the shire shall not be called of such worship as it hath been.'[38] Sir John Howard

[35] *R.P.* vol. III, p. 601; and see Roskell, *The Commons in the Parliament of 1422*, pp. 5–12.

[36] Roskell, *The Commons in the Parliament of 1422*, p. 12.

[37] *P.L.* Nos. 119, 701.

[38] *P.L.* Nos. 249, 250; and see on these Norfolk elections K. B. McFarlane, 'Parliament and bastard feudalism'.

was in fact returned and Jenny proved wrong, but for this occasion only. One of the Mowbray candidates for Norfolk was defeated in 1450; and in 1461 John Paston himself secured one of the county's seats in a hotly contested election, in spite of the efforts of the Mowbray interest.

The county gentry of the fifteenth century could afford to be very independent in their choice of representatives. They included, in almost all counties, a fair sprinkling of men who were in terms of wealth the equals of many peers. The late K. B. McFarlane, looking at the returns for the tax on landed incomes in 1412, found that in Dorset, out of fourteen landowners whose incomes were assessed at more than £200 a year, eight were peers and six commoners; in Sussex there were two peers and two commoners of this standing. All of the eight rich commoners in question sat at one time or another for their shires in parliament, and most of them a number of times.[39] Men like Sir John Pelham (of Sussex) and Sir John Mautravers (of Dorset) were of a standing that made it quite as easy for them to influence peers as vice versa. The crown could of course always count on seeing a leavening of household men among the shire knights (eighteen counties had a 'householder' as one of their representatives in 1453, for instance), and every magnate hoped to see some of his retainers returned there (in 1422 Warwick 'topped the poll' with five clients among the county knights). Unless there was a very considerable degree of unanimity between king and lords, however, these connexions were nothing like sufficient to enable any single interest to control the commons. As a body, the lay lords were too irregular in their attendance in parliament to lead the lower house in any effective sense.[40] The collective wealth, education and parliamentary experience of the commons put them in a position in which they were entirely capable of working on their own and taking their own independent stand, as they showed by their plain speaking, both to the lords and to the king, on a whole series of occasions.

The key to the influence of the commons on government was their control over grants of taxation. They could use this to secure new legislation, which might be aimed to secure improved local

[39] K. B. McFarlane, 'Parliament and bastard feudalism', pp. 65–8. Compare Roskell, *The Commons in the Parliament of 1422*, pp. 79–82.

[40] On this topic see the important article by J. S. Roskell, 'The problem of the attendance of the Lords in medieval parliaments', *B.I.H.R.* 29 (1956), pp. 153–204, esp. pp. 199–200.

governance, or to regulate prices, wages or commerce; but it was
not easy to ensure that the resulting statutes were enforced. They
were normally consulted about the making of treaties, and were
in a position to influence foreign policy, but did not often do so.
What really decided the issue in these sorts of matters was the
activity, or lack of it, of the king's council. The most effective way
in which the commons could influence the day-to-day government of the realm was therefore by bringing pressure to bear on
the king in connexion with the personnel of the council and the
manner in which it discharged its functions. This they sought to
do on a number of occasions, notably in 1376 and 1386, in 1401,
1404 and 1406, and in 1422.

In dealing with the council, one must be careful to distinguish
between the great council and the continual council. Stubbs long
ago remarked that the great councils of the late Middle Ages may
be regarded as 'either extra parliamentary sessions of the house
of lords, or as enlarged meetings of the royal council'.[41] The
former was the view of the lords themselves, as they gave it in the
parliament of 1427. In a minority, they claimed, the king's
authority was vested in the lords assembled in parliament or
great council, and when these were not in session in the (continual) council.[42] Fortescue's description of the lords as *con-
siliarii nati* tallies with this opinion.[43] When the king was of age,
what happened in practice eludes sharp constitutional definition.
When he wanted weightier advice on matters of national importance, as issues of war or peace or relations with the pope, he
summoned peers to counsel him, and sometimes others too,
under privy seal letters, but he did not always summon all the
peers, and by no means all those summoned attended. But the
people who really mattered in everyday government were the
continual councillors, the men in constant attendance who
received the petitions of suitors, organized the raising of loans,
and authorized privy seal letters, to move the great seal to
authorize grants and appointments (this involved the council in
the disposition of much valuable and important crown patronage).
It was the composition of this body that agitated the commons.

This smaller council, in the later Middle Ages, was becoming
a steadily more professional body.[44] It had a clerk and possessed

[41] W. Stubbs, *Constitutional History of England* vol. III, p. 262.
[42] *P.P.C.* vol. III, p. 232.
[43] Fortescue, *The Governance of England*, p. 147.
[44] Much work has been done on the council since J. F. Baldwin's
pioneer study *The King's Council* (Oxford, 1913) appeared. The follow-

its own rudimentary records. The administration of a special councillor's oath and the payment of salaries to councillors were beginning to be regular practice. In the 1390s, when Prophet's journal affords us a particularly close insight into the workings of the council, we find that some of Richard II's knights, like Stury and Sir Edward Dalyngrygg, were so regular in their attendance as to class virtually as professional councillors.[45] The council had developed a jurisdiction of its own, dealing with the cases of petitioners who could not get redress at common law and with disturbances caused by great men and their followers (out of this jurisdiction the Court of Star Chamber later developed). This growth of professionalism helped to differentiate the administrators, who discharged conciliar business, from the court, the king's personal entourage. The personal influence of a strong king or a determined favourite might blur the distinction, but not wholly. In the period of Suffolk's ascendancy over Henry VI, for instance, most important political and diplomatic decisions were taken at court and the signet, the king's personal seal, was often used to move the great seal; but the court did not assume the jurisdiction of the council. The fact that some at least of the council's functions were specific and identifiable made it easier for the parliamentary commons to discuss its methods and composition.

The commons on a series of occasions insisted that the names of councillors should be declared in parliament. This might suggest that they were being used by interested parties among the lords, to help secure power in the hands of partisan groups. Analysis of the connexions of councillors who were named in parliament on such occasions as 1386, 1401 and 1406 does not support this view. The composition of these named councils tends to follow a pattern, including (besides the three officers of state who were regular members) the Archbishop of Canterbury,

---

ing articles are of importance: T. F. T. Plucknett, 'The place of the council in the fifteenth century', *T.R.H.S.* 4th ser., 1 (1918), pp. 157–89; A. L. Brown, 'The king's councillors in fifteenth century England', *T.R.H.S.* 5th ser., 19 (1969), pp. 95–118; R. Virgoe, 'The composition of the king's council 1437–61', *B.I.H.R.* 43 (1970), pp. 134–60; J. R. Lander, 'The Yorkist council and administration 1461–85', *E.H.R.* 73 (1958), pp. 27–46; and J. R. Lander, 'The council, administration and councillors 1461–85', *B.I.H.R.* 32 (1959), pp. 138–80.

[45] Prophet's Journal of the fifteenth and sixteenth years of Richard II is printed by Baldwin in *The King's Council*, Appendix II, pp. 489–507. On Stury and Dalyngrygg see ibid. pp. 132–3.

one or two of the greater lay peers, selected bishops and lay barons, and three or four distinguished knights – a kind of representative distillation of the estates represented in parliament. What the commons seem to have valued in this structure was that it brought together a council of really substantial men with the independence and experience to form their own views, whose standing was so secure that they would not need to use their position for self-advancement, and which would represent (and reconcile) the interests of the realm as well as of the king. They regarded with suspicion anything that looked like the dominance of a household clique, particularly if the greater magnates, lay and ecclesiastical, were ill-represented (as was the case with the group that gathered round Pole and de Vere under Richard II, and was replaced by a named council in 1386; or the little nucleus of devoted Lancastrians, men like Erpingham and Norbury and Leventhorpe, on whom Henry IV relied heavily in his early years). This was not just a prejudice of the parliamentary commons. Appeals to the king to take substantial men into his council could normally count on widespread support, as the manifestos of Cade, York and Warwick in the later fifteenth century remind us.[46]

The commons were not just interested in the composition of the council; they wanted to be sure that councillors did their job. Hence their efforts to ensure that there was always a quorum of officially appointed councillors in attendance (for example in 1401); to make those appointed take an oath in parliament (as in 1406 and 1410); and to regulate the manner in which the council dealt with bills presented to it. The most determined effort of the commons to overhaul the council's activities was made in 1406, and kept parliament in session for much of the time from March until Christmas.[47] Two series of articles, the second very long, were produced, which the councillors appointed in parliament had to swear to observe. They were to act together as a body, a number were always to attend the king, and days were to be set aside for hearing petitions. They were to consider and approve all matters, except routine ones, that would eventually pass under the great and privy seals. Elaborate regulations guarded against the abuse of influence by suitors from the royal household and by councillors themselves. But the overriding concern that the commons evinced in 1406 was about the council's supervision of

[46] See Chapters 18 and 19.

[47] On this see A. L. Brown, 'The commons and the council in the reign of Henry IV', *E.H.R.* 79 (1964), pp. 1–30, esp. pp. 20–4, 28.

government finance. It was to review all grants made by the crown, to set aside revenues for the expenses of the household, and generally to check the expenditure of the king's money. This was, in the eyes of the commons, the chief business of government, and to them good government meant government that was cheap to the subject.

It is interesting to compare what the commons wanted of the council in the Lancastrian period with Fortescue's ideal, set out in his *Governance of England*. Fortescue proposed that the council should be composed of four bishops and four peers, and twenty-four others, 'twelve spiritual men and twelve temporal men of the wisest and best disposed men that can be found in all the parts of this land'.[48] The numerical balance of this council is a little different from what usually satisfied the commons, but the basic assumption about its composition is the same, that it should represent the interests of the realm at large. All councillors should take an oath, and the twenty-four lesser councillors should be salaried. A book of regulations should be compiled, laying down hours of business and rules of procedure. The kind of affairs that Fortescue pictured his council weighing most carefully were 'how the going out of the money may be restrained, how bullion may be brought into the land, how also plate, jewels and money late borne out may be gotten again ... and also how the prices of merchandise grown in this land may be upheld and increased, and the prices of merchandise brought into this land abated'.[49] Above all, he wanted to see very strict regulations to limit grants made out of the crown's revenues and lands, over which even the council's control needed to be limited by parliament, in order to reduce the need for taxation. This seemed to him to be the straight road to securing the prosperity not just of the king, but of the whole realm: 'for every man of the land shall by this foundation be the merrier, the surer, fare the better in his body and all his goods ... this [land] shall be a college [i.e. a *real* community] in which shall sing and pray for evermore all the men of England, spiritual and temporal'.[50]

Fortescue's essay on governance ends with a fine flourish of national spirit. The common national interest which he extolled was what bound together the commons of England in and out of parliament, and was at the root of their political involvement. A

[48] Fortescue, *The Governance of England*, p. 146.
[49] ibid. p. 148.
[50] ibid. p. 153.

broad sector of the population had achieved sufficient wealth and education to think about this common interest in articulate and independent terms. The social force of a rising gentry and a *bourgeoisie* conscious of national identity was fast changing the role of the aristocracy in politics, from that of lords into that of leaders. Wealth and influence were too widely distributed for any one partisan group to rule the roost for long, unless its dominance seemed to secure the public advantage. Though men of middle rank still instinctively looked to their social superiors for the patronage that they called 'good lordship', they were not prepared to tolerate any faction that jeopardized what they saw as the interest of the country at large.

Because it is still from time to time claimed that the growth of English national self-consciousness was a feature of the Tudor rather than the late medieval period, we may close this chapter with two quotations that illustrate the pride of fifteenth-century Englishmen in their country as a national community. One comes from the speech of the English representatives at the Council of Constance in 1417, protesting against the French claim that England should not rank in the council as a nation: 'As regards all the requirements for being a nation . . . whether a nation be understood as a race, relationship, and habit of unity separate from others, or as a difference of language which by divine and human law is the greatest and most authentic mark of a nation and the essence of it . . . in all these respects the renowned nation of England or Britain is one of the four or five nations that compose the papal obedience.'[51] The other comes from a sermon, preached by an anonymous clerk in the reign of Henry V, who was rejoicing that the new king had restored to the land the prosperity and honour that she seemed, before his day, to be in danger of losing:

A great ship which sailed for many a day in the sea of prosperity is that plenteous realm, the realm of England. The forecastle of this ship is the clergy, prelates, religious, and priests; the hindcastle is the barony, the king with his nobles; the body of the ship is the commons, merchants, craftsmen and labourers . . . when our ship was full tackled, the three castles full apparelled with streamers and shields, it was a fair vessel to look upon, it was a fair ship! . . . The swift gallies of Spain, if they had sighted it upon the sea, would have wanted to take flight . . . the brave towered (vessels) of Scotland, as far as they might see her upon the sea, would have wanted to

---

[51] See Fillastres's diary of the Council of Constance, translated in L. R. Loomis, *The Council of Constance* (Columbia, 1961), p. 344.

strike sail and honour her. The whole of Christendom feared and honoured the English for their bravery, their good realm, and the good life they led.[52]

This is the sort of way in which the men of fifteenth-century England were accustomed to thinking of their homeland. The sixteenth century may have celebrated English nationality with more eloquence, but not with any sharper sense of England's separate identity, or any clearer sense of the priority of the national interest over issues of local and political affinity.

[52] G. R. Owst, *Literature and Pulpit in Medieval England* (Cambridge, 1933), pp. 72-3.

SECTION V

The rise and fall of the Lancastrian empire

15

The reign of Henry V

Henry V came to the throne determined, it would seem, that his reign should open a new chapter in the annals of his dynasty, and that the trouble of his father's time should be forgotten. One of his very first acts was to grant the Earl of March, the head of that house of Mortimer that had raised so much trouble for Henry IV, full livery of his lands. Just before Christmas in 1413 Richard II's body was brought by his order from Langley, where it had lain since death, and was buried with pomp at Westminster. The families that had suffered in the revolts against his father were progressively restored; in 1414 negotiations were opened that led to the restoration of Hotspur's son, the Percy heir, in 1416; Thomas Holland was restored in name and blood as the heir of his father John, who had been lynched at Pleshy in 1399; the process recorded on the 1399 parliament roll against the Duke of York (then Aumale) was quashed. The new king's intention to reconsolidate aristocratic loyalty around the throne and to have done with old feuds was patent.

The early years of the reign saw some significant creations of peerages with these same ends in view. York's youngest brother Richard was made Earl of Cambridge. Henry's own brother John was made Duke of Bedford, and Humphrey, the youngest son of Henry IV, was made Duke of Gloucester and Earl of Pembroke (Thomas, older than both of these, was already Duke of Clarence). In 1416 there was another important promotion when Thomas Beaufort, Earl of Dorset, was created Duke of Exeter. Later in the reign there were not many new English creations. This was no doubt wise, for the grants of land that usually went with such promotions had in the past been a sore point between king and commons. Besides, by that time many English lords were winning new titles and lands on French soil. Henry's policy towards the aristocracy paid the intended dividend. There were, it is true, occasions early in the reign when revolt threatened. But

John Oldcastle, Lord Cobham, was the only peer involved in the abortive Lollard rising of 1414. The Cambridge plot of 1415, which aimed to put the Earl of March on the throne, had by contrast wide ramifications among the peerage, but Henry chose wisely to proceed only against the principals, Cambridge, Lord Scrope of Masham, and Sir Thomas Grey. The affair had no sequel, and during the rest of the reign there was never a threat of aristocratic revolt.[1]

There was no important difference between the reigns of Henry IV and Henry V in the methods by which England was governed. The commons under Henry V played the same role in parliaments as they had in the past, without winning any new rights or privileges. The councils of the two kings tackled the same sort of tasks with the same sort of membership, except that, when Henry V was out of the realm along with many of his lay peers, the three officers of state had to transact most of the routine business on their own. Ecclesiastics were rather more prominent, perhaps, in Henry V's councils. Particularly influential were Henry Chichele, a trained lawyer and an experienced diplomat, who as Henry's personal choice succeeded Archbishop Arundel at Canterbury; Thomas Langley, Bishop of Durham, who had been chancellor to Henry IV and was chancellor again from 1418; Philip Morgan, doctor of laws and king's clerk, who rose to be chancellor of Normandy and Bishop of Worcester. Most important of all – until he began to entertain ambitions outside England in the European church – was Henry Beaufort of Winchester, Henry's uncle, his first chancellor, and the most generous source of loans to the crown through the reign.[2] The Lancastrian knights, who had been so prominent under Henry IV, played an equally significant role under Henry V. Thomas Chaucer, John Tiptoft and Walter Hungerford all had long experience from the time of the father, and were the intimate,

[1] On the Cambridge plot see Chapter 13; on Oldcastle see Chapter 10.
[2] There are useful biographies of Chichele and Langley: E. F. Jacob, *Archbishop Henry Chichele* (London, 1967), and R. L. Storey, *Thomas Langley and the Bishopric of Durham* (London, 1961). A good biography of Beaufort is much needed; the most useful studies are two articles by K. B. McFarlane: 'Henry V, Bishop Beaufort, and the red hat', *E.H.R.* 60 (1945), pp. 316–48, and 'At the deathbed of Cardinal Beaufort' in *Studies in Medieval History Presented to F. M. Powicke*, ed. R. W. Hunt, W. A. Pantin and R. W. Southern (Oxford, 1948), pp. 405–28; and G. L. Harriss, 'Cardinal Beaufort – patriot or usurer?', *T.R.H.S.* 5th ser., 20 (1970), pp. 129–48.

honoured and trusted servants of the son. His service, however, took most of his knights further afield, for longer periods, than that of Henry IV had ever done.

For it was in the field of foreign relations that the decisive change in the tempo and direction of English political history that came with the accession of Henry V was really apparent. The focus of concern shifted away early from the problem of domestic unrest to the chances of the Anglo-French war, in much the same way as it had in the fourteenth century after the accession of Edward III. The difference was that in this case the change was more abrupt, and that Henry achieved more than Edward III did, in a shorter time.

The accession of Henry V marked a clean break with the past in Anglo-French relations. The situation created by the civil war in France and the opportunities that it offered for the English were little different, it is true, from what they had been in 1411 and 1412, but the approach to them was new. English diplomatic thinking at the end of Henry IV's reign was dominated by the question of Gascony, as it had been ever since the 1370s, and by the hope of re-establishing something like the terms of the 'great peace' of Brétigny. Alliance with either of the French parties, Armagnacs or Burgundians, seemed to offer a prospect of achieving just this: the question was, with whom should the English ally? As Prince of Wales, Henry had favoured alliance with Burgundy; Arundel and Clarence preferred to treat with the Armagnacs. Henry V's initiative as king was much bolder. His diplomatic strategy was to negotiate with both sides simultaneously, an exercise that he developed in the course of the reign into a fine art. The object was to force them to raise their bids for English support (or neutrality); and besides, the negotiations helped to keep the two parties separate, so furnishing Henry with opportunities to improve his situation further by well-timed military interventions. In these circumstances, while keeping his claim to the crown of France always prominent in diplomatic exchanges, he was able to greatly extend the active discussion of those English territorial claims in France that were separable from that claim, to Gascony as a duchy, to Normandy, and to the one time empire of the Angevins.

Because the struggle between the French parties was the key to Henry's diplomatic and military strategy, it is necessary, if one is to understand English policy, to keep a constant eye on internal developments in France. When Henry came to the throne,

Armagnacs and Burgundians were nominally reconciled, following the pacification of Auxerre, which had dashed the high hopes
of the English for Clarence's expedition and the Anglo-Armagnac
alliance of 1412. In 1413 disturbances in Paris, originally fomented
by the supporters of John the Fearless, gave his rivals the
chance to stage a *coup* against him. In August Duke John left
Paris precipitately for his own dominions. With the return of the
partisan Armagnac leaders to the capital the civil war was
resumed, and the summer of 1414 saw hard campaigning in
Picardy and on the border of Flanders. This campaign was
ended by a new peace, agreed at Arras on 4 August. Duke John
was not, however, readmitted to Paris, and so remained excluded
from all direct influence on royal government.

These events in France dictated the pattern of English negotiations in the early years of Henry V. As was to be his wont, Henry
talked with both sides simultaneously. On paper, it looked as if
Burgundy had most to gain by alliance with the English, and
some very interesting ideas were mooted with the duke's representatives during the parliament held at Leicester in the summer
of 1414. The plans discussed included an offensive alliance, in
which each party should share the conquests in proportion to
their military contribution, and which would be cemented by a
marriage between Henry and a daughter of the duke (this in
spite of the fact that Henry had, in the previous January, promised
representatives of the French court at Paris that he would not,
for a year, consider marriage to anyone but Catherine, the
daughter of Charles VI of France). The English thought at this
stage that John would go further, and could even be persuaded to
renounce his homage to Charles VI, but the peace of Arras was
patched up between him and his French rivals before anything
came of their suggestions along these lines. At Arras John
promised that he would make no alliances with the English, but
in fact he remained in close contact with Henry. There was so
much duplicity on both sides that it is not easy to be dogmatic
about the significance of their exchanges. John's hope was, probably, that he could get Henry to do some of his work for him
without his having to commit himself irreparably to the English.
Henry's calculation, that John at the least would not intervene if
he made war on the other party, was in the event to prove surer.[3]

[3] On Anglo-Burgundian relations in 1414 see further J. Calmette and
E. Deprez, *La France et l'Angleterre en conflit* (G. Glotz, *Histoire du
Moyen Age* vol. VII, pt. 1), pp. 299–305; and R. Vaughan, *John the
Fearless* (London, 1966), pp. 205–7.

The negotiations between the English and the Paris government of the princes and the Armagnacs are easier to interpret. In
January 1414 a truce was agreed between them for a year, and
the English appeared genuinely interested in the proposal for a
marriage between Henry and Catherine of France. The Armagnacs were really anxious for a settlement with Henry; the
question that had to be thrashed out during the year's truce was
the price that they would have to pay for it. This was discussed at
length in the summer of 1414 and in Paris in the early days of
1415, in formal negotiations. The French showed themselves
prepared to offer something like the Brétigny terms with regard
to Gascony, and under pressure were ready to enlarge their
offers of territory in the south-west; they were also ready to offer
a dowry for Catherine of 600,000 crowns (raised, under pressure,
to 800,000). These were generous proposals, in any light except
that of the English demands. Henry's envoys wanted a dowry of a
million crowns. On the question of territory, they insisted that
their king would not waive his right to the crown of France for
less than the restoration, in full sovereignty, not just of Gascony
but of the whole of the old Norman-Angevin empire: Maine,
Anjou, Touraine, Normandy, with feudal superiority over
Brittany and Flanders. This was much more than the French
could contemplate ceding. In the spring of 1415 the English
allowed an impression to be given that there might be concessions on their side after they had consulted with their king, and
for this reason the truce, which ran out in February, was extended. This gave time for a last minute round of negotiations in
July at Winchester, where the Agincourt host was assembling.
The exchanges there were heated, and nothing was offered that
the French envoys could accept as a basis for negotiations. When
Archbishop Boisratier of Rheims and his colleagues returned to
Paris an English invasion of France was clearly imminent.[4]

It seems highly unlikely that the English meant these long
negotiations to be anything but abortive. The Armagnac leaders
had shown in 1412 that they were willing to offer what then
seemed generous terms, and nothing had happened since to make
the English think that they would concede as much more in the
way of territory as was demanded in 1414 and 1415. The English
were simply endeavouring, it would rather seem, to keep talks
going until Henry was ready for powerful military intervention.

[4] The English negotiations with the Paris government in 1414–15 are
minutely examined in J. H. Wylie, *The Reign of Henry V* vol. I (Cambridge, 1914), ch. 23 and 24.

Preparations for this began early. In the autumn parliament of 1414 the commons voted a double subsidy. By the beginning of the next year, 1415, the king was borrowing heavily on the expectation of what this grant would raise, pledging crown jewels and other valuables as security for repayment. At a great council at Westminster in April a large number of peers promised to serve at the king's wages with substantial contingents. Orders were given to impound ships, and envoys were despatched to the Low Countries to hire additional marine transport. The king was bent on raising a force of at least 10,000 men, and was putting himself heavily in debt to do so. Henry was not in earnest in his professed desire for a peaceful settlement; what he wanted was time to complete his preparations for massive military intervention.

Sedulous propaganda, both at home and abroad, paved the way for Henry's venture. There was much careful scrutiny of ancient records to establish to public satisfaction the legal basis of the English claims both to the crown of France and to a wide inheritance of territory there quite apart from that claim. At Winchester in July 1415 Henry, in the presence of the assembled English nobility, treated Archbishop Boisratier to a learned (but partisan) disquisition on these claims, and on the duplicity of the French who had tried at every turn to dodge the issues. While he was on his way to Southampton, so the author of the *Gesta Henrici Quinti* tells us, 'he caused to be transcribed all the pacts and conventions made in the past between the serene prince his father, Henry IV, and certain of the greater princes of France, over divine right and the conquest of Aquitaine . . . and he sent off these transcripts to the General Council, and to Sigismund the Emperor, and to other catholic princes, that all the world might know what wrongs the duplicity of the French had inflicted on him'.[5] This labouring of the justice of the English claims in France, based in a precise antiquarian legalism, was to be a recurrent theme throughout Henry's reign, both in English diplomacy and in royal appeals for support from the community for the king's war.

Henry sailed with his army from Southampton on 11 August 1415. On 14 August he disembarked on the Norman coast, and settled down to the investment of Harfleur. It took more than a

[5] *Gesta Henrici Quinti*, ed. B. Williams (English Historical Soc., 1850), p. 10.

month to reduce the town, which surrendered on 22 September. Henry treated his new conquest in the same way that Edward III had treated Calais. The well born of the garrison were treated as prisoners of war, and the main body of the townsfolk were deported wholesale. A strong English garrison under the Earl of Dorset was then placed in the town, pending the arrival of colonists from England.

After the fall of Harfleur it was clear that the season was too late for any attempt to press on towards Paris or Bordeaux (as had probably been the original plan). The army was depleted by the necessity to garrison Harfleur, and had lost a good many effectives when dysentery broke out during the siege. A large French force was gathering at Rouen to oppose any further move. Many thought that enough had now been achieved, but Henry was determined to see something more of the country that he called his own. On 6 October he set out to march the 150 miles through upper Normandy from Harfleur to Calais, where his prisoners, released on parole, were bidden to meet him at Martinmas.

The sequel to his decision is too well known to need recounting in detail. At Blanchetaque the English found the crossing of the Somme barred by the French, and though they managed to ford the river much further south, at Béthencourt, the French meanwhile had got ahead of them, and blocked the way to Calais at Agincourt with a vastly superior force. If the French had followed the advice of their experienced commanders, Marshal Boucicaut and the Constable d'Albret, who did not wish to force an action, the English king might have been lost. But the marshal and the constable were overruled by younger men who were eager for glory, and the French forced on the engagement in which, with tremendous losses, their whole force was overthrown. The carnage was terrible, with great mounds of dead men piled on each other in front of the English position.[6] The Constable of France, and the dukes of Bar, Brabant and Alençon were among those killed. Among the prisoners who survived (a number were slaughtered when the rumour went round that a fresh French army was in the offing) were the dukes of Orleans and Bourbon, and the counts of Vendosme, Eu and Richemont (this last being the younger brother of the Duke of Brittany). The English losses were not heavy. The Duke of York and Michael de la Pole, Earl

[6] For a good military account of the engagement, see A. H. Burne, *The Agincourt War* (London, 1956), ch. 5. J. H. Wylie, *The Reign of Henry V* vol. II, pp. 129–77, gives even more detail.

of Suffolk, were the only prominent men killed, among a total of perhaps 400 men.

Agincourt was fought on St Crispin's day, 25 October; the news of the victory reached London on 29 October. Six days later the parliament met at Westminster, and heard the chancellor, Bishop Beaufort, dilate on the trinity of divine judgements that now stood in the English favour in their king's quarrel with France – Sluys, Poitiers and Agincourt. The reaction of the commons is a telling tribute to the impression that the news made. They voted a new subsidy, and agreed to accelerate the collection of the second of the two subsidies granted a year before; and they granted the king a subsidy on wool for life. Such a life grant had been made before once only, to Richard II in 1398. Contemporaries regarded that grant as symptomatic of the helpless subservience of the Shrewsbury parliament. In Henry IV's reign the commons consistently refused to extend grants of a wool subsidy beyond the term of a few years. The grant of 1415 is therefore the clearest possible demonstration of the extent to which Henry V's great victory won him a new, full confidence from the people that he ruled.

After Agincourt, the question of the right of the Lancastrian dynasty to sit upon the English throne ceased to be an issue in English politics. The focus of interest henceforward, until 1420, was on the prospect of new offensives and further victories. The mood of the moment was well expressed by the chaplain who presented an address to the king just before the meeting of convocation, after his return to England in November 1415:

> The winter is gone, . . . flowers have appeared, the flowers of vigorous and warlike youth: and flourishing vines, whereby I understand that noble progeny of kings of England which formerly spread their branches throughout the world, have given forth odours of fame and worthiest probity. . . . And you, dread prince [he concluded], receive not the glory of God in vain, but in the prosecution of your right, casting away the lust of power, go forward manfully.[7]

This was what was now expected of Henry, to press forward until a just peace should be established, that would guarantee the ancient rights of the English royal house in France.

[7] *The Letters of Margaret of Anjou . . . and Others,* ed. C. Monro (Camden Soc., 1863), pp. 2–6.

Henry V's victory at Agincourt placed him in a very favourable bargaining position with regard to the parties in France. The Duke of Orleans, the nominal leader of the Armagnacs, was his prisoner; so were the Duke of Bourbon and Arthur de Richemont, the brother of the Duke of Brittany. John of Burgundy, who had taken no part in the Agincourt campaign, was still excluded from the government of Paris, and so Henry could entertain high hopes of making him a useful ally. He could also hope for generous offers from Paris to induce him not to ally with John.

These diplomatic advantages were complicated and to some extent compromised in 1416 by the intervention in Anglo-French politics of the Emperor Sigismund. Sigismund had been the prime mover in bringing together the general council of the church at Constance in order to end the Schism, and like many others at the council he believed that the duration of the Schism was being perpetuated by 'the discords among the kingdoms' of Europe. Late in 1415 he had succeeded at Narbonne in persuading the Iberian kingdoms to abandon Pope Benedict XIII and adhere to the council. From there he travelled to Paris, where he arrived in March 1416. The councillors of Charles VI, shaken by Agincourt and anxious about the possibility of an alliance between Henry of England and the Duke of Burgundy, were very ready to let him try his hand as a mediator between them and the English. Henry, as a Christian prince who had given his adherence to the council and who was represented there by a powerful English delegation, could hardly refuse to entertain the proposals of a mediator, whose prime avowed purpose was to restore unity to the church. On 1 May Sigismund landed at Dover, and was received with a lavishness of display fitting to his high position.

The visit of the emperor posed a problem for the king of England. Henry had already in 1415 drawn the attention of both Sigismund and the council to the English claims arising out of the Treaty of Brétigny, and to the recognition, by the Armagnac princes in the Treaty of Bourges of 1412, of the justice of the English claim to Gascony. After his victory at Agincourt, he was in a good position to insist that the Brétigny terms at least must be accepted as the minimum basis for a definitive settlement. As a mediator, Sigismund was likely to press him to waive higher claims. But Henry wanted more; and in order to get more without appearing to disadvantage at the international level he knew that he would have to proceed with great delicacy. No expense needed to be spared on the entertainment of his imperial guest. Hence the lavish ceremonial and heraldic welcome that was prepared for him; his admission to the order of the Garter at Windsor; the presentation to the emperor of the gold collar of SS, the Lancastrian emblem; his state visit to parliament, which had been kept in session specifically for the purpose.

During the first stage of the negotiations that were conducted under Sigismund's auspices, it began to be clear that the French would not raise their offers, nor the English lower their demands to a point which could be the foundation of an immediate peace. By mid June 1416 the hopes of Sigismund and the Count of Holland (who was the dauphin's father-in-law and also an imperial vassal and had been associated with the emperor as a mediator) had come to centre on proposals for a three year truce, and for a personal 'summit' meeting between Henry, Sigismund and Charles VI, probably on the Calais march. The French royal prisoners were enthusiastic for this scheme, and the envoys from Paris thought it should be acceptable; when they left England in late June it was to arrange a preliminary meeting to discuss the terms of the truce. They had been preceded to Paris by an embassy from Sigismund, commissioned to represent there the advantages of his plans. Unfortunately, the two embassies arrived to find the council in Paris divided. Though Anjou and a number of other leading men were in favour of the truce, there was also an influential 'war party', headed by Count Bernard of Armagnac. Recalled to Paris after Agincourt and granted the constable's sword, his first act had been to organize the investment of Harfleur. In March 1416 he had caught Dorset's garrison in the open on an extended sortie, near Valmont, and inflicted severe losses on them. He believed that the proposals for the truce were, on the English side, simply a device to save their new won town. In a crucial meeting on 15 July his views carried the day, and it was agreed to spin out dealings with the English until Harfleur should fall, with the prospect of being then able to negotiate from a new position of strength.[8]

Militarily, there was no doubt much to be said for Armagnac's views; diplomatically they were blundering. The count's martial policy was in itself a direct affront to the emperor's mediation, and the affront was aggravated by the undignified treatment and the evasive answers that the English envoys, who had been sent to discuss the details of the proposed truce, received from the

[8] See *Chronique du Religieux de St Denis*, ed. L. Bellaguet (Paris, 1852), vol. VI, pp. 24-6.

French at Beauvais in July. At this point the pressure on Harfleur was being increased. Henry could thus point out to Sigismund direct evidence of the duplicity of the French, and of the insincerity of their professed desire for a peace. Sigismund took the point. In consequence Henry was able to change the whole tenor of Anglo-Imperial relations, which had commenced in an effort at mediation, and to turn them into the foundation of a series of important diplomatic victories for the English cause at the expense of Valois France.

The first open sign of the new direction that events were taking was the treaty which was agreed between Henry and Sigismund at Canterbury on 15 August 1416. This completely altered the position of the emperor. In the preamble to the formal terms he gave an account of the course of his mediation, retailing his efforts to achieve a reasonable settlement and the way in which the French king had spurned them and, by doing so, had proved himself to be a promoter of discord in Christendom. It was time for the pride of the French to be punished, the emperor declared. He and Henry, 'his brother', had therefore made a treaty of perpetual friendship, binding themselves and their heirs (note here the recognition of the dynastic legitimacy of the house of Lancaster) each to support the other in the prosecution of his just rights in France. Detailed clauses of the treaty provided for free commercial exchange between England and the Empire; that neither sovereign should harbour or assist the enemies of the other; and it was clearly understood that the emperor would be prepared to give Henry direct military support in France.[9] On the same day that the treaty was sealed, an English fleet under the Duke of Bedford defeated the Franco-Genoese squadron that was blockading Harfleur from the sea, and revictualled the town. By this time feelers had already been put out with a view to bringing into the Anglo-Imperial alliance a third party, none other than John the Fearless of Burgundy himself. Armagnac's policy had rebounded with a vengeance.

As early as July, the Earl of Warwick had met Duke John at Lille, and had conveyed to him an invitation to be present at the conference between the English, the French and the emperor that it was planned to hold at Calais in October. After the sealing of the Canterbury treaty, the possibility of bringing John to the conference assumed greater importance for the English than any putative negotiations that there might be with the Paris government.

[9] For text see *Foed.* vol. IX, pp. 377–81.

The new plan of Henry and his ally Sigismund was for a majestic alliance of England, Burgundy and the Empire, which would overthrow the Valois and reunite strife-riven France under Henry's kingship. Under the aegis of Henry and Sigismund the council would then be brought to a triumphant conclusion, the Schism healed and the church reformed. Perhaps then they would join in a crusade against the Turk. The hard material advantages of this scheme were to the benefit of the English specifically, and their enthusiasm for it is written clear in the tremendous efforts that they were prepared to make to get Duke John to Calais. Henry was ready to shoulder the whole cost of the meeting. A plethora of carefully worded instruments were drawn up to guarantee the duke safe conduct to Calais with a vast retinue, and Henry's own brother, Humphrey of Gloucester, was placed in Burgundian hands as a hostage for his security.

Henry and Sigismund were waiting for Duke John when he reached Calais on 4 October. An embassy from Paris had just left, having concluded a truce until the following February. The duke remained in Calais until the 13 October, engaged in a continuous round of ceremonial meetings and secret negotiations, and departed on apparently affable terms with the king of England and the emperor. What precisely passed between the parties is not easy to tell. It is known that John at Calais did homage to Sigismund for the counties of Burgundy and Alost, and so formally reinforced his relations with one member of the Anglo-Imperial alliance, but what he said to the other is unclear. 'It passed not beyond the royal breast or the silence of the council', says the author of the Gesta.[10]

A text that purports to be an agreement with Henry in Duke John's name does indeed survive, and a very remarkable text it is. The gist of it is that the duke has come now to accept the justice of Henry's claim to the throne of France; he promises that he will do Henry homage as king, not directly, however, but as soon as 'he shall have conquered a notable part of the kingdom'; and he assures Henry that if, in the meantime, he appears still to recognize Charles VI as his sovereign this is but 'dissimulation for the sake of a greater good'. There is too an explicit, if undated, promise to help Henry with men and arms. The trouble with this text, which has often been accepted as the record of a formal agreement, is that no copy of it survives that is in John's hand or sealed with his seal (as it is supposed to be). The question whether its authenticity can be accepted therefore remains endlessly

[10] *Gesta Henrici Quinti*, p. 103.

debatable.[11] This does not mean that it is not a key document. If, as the sceptics suggest, it is only a draft of what the English hoped John would agree to, it still reveals what was under discussion at Calais. John, we should remember, had come to the town of his own free will to debate personally with two sworn enemies of his liege lord, the king of France. He compromised himself simply by going there; he did homage to Sigismund for his Imperial lands, and the fact that, two years later, the English still thought that he might decide in certain circumstances to do homage to Henry for his French fiefs[12] does not suggest that he excluded the possibility at all clearly. It seems safe to conclude, in short, that John said and did enough at Calais to satisfy Henry that, unless the French political situation altered radically, he would not oppose an English invasion, and that he might support it. John may of course have really promised all that the text of what the French have called the 'infernal pact' says that he did. This, however, is at present impossible to demonstrate, and will probably remain so.

John of Burgundy was not the only French prince with whom Henry was in contact at this stage. John of Brittany, the other great duke of northern France, had long had close connexions with England (he was the son of the queen dowager, Joan of Penthièvre, by her first marriage). There is some evidence that he may have actually visited England in April 1417, though no chronicler says anything about the matter or what the purpose of a visit would have been (not that there can be much doubt about that).[13] We are on surer ground about Henry's relations with the French princes who were his prisoners. For their prospects of freedom and future influence in France, the failure of Sigismund's mediation and the Anglo-Imperial alliance could bode no good; and Henry had hopes that he could gain much by playing on their anxieties. It was with the Duke of Bourbon that he had most success, as he confided in a letter written in January 1417, to

---

[11] For text see *Foed.* vol. IX, pp. 395–6. The authenticity of the treaty is accepted by, for example, Wylie and Waugh (*The Reign of Henry V* vol. III, pp. 28–9) and by J. Calmette and E. Deprez (*La France et l'Angleterre en conflit*, p. 337); but is questioned, on impressive grounds, by P. Bonenfant (*Du Meutre de Montereau au Traité de Troyes*, Brussels, 1958, pp. 9–10) and by R. Vaughan (*John the Fearless*, pp. 213–16).

[12] *P.P.C.* vol. II, p. 354.

[13] See G. A. Knowlson, *Jean V de Bretagne et l'Angleterre* (Rennes, 1964), pp. 100–1.

John Tiptoft his personal envoy to Sigismund, who after the Calais meeting had returned to Constance. Bourbon had agreed, the king wrote, that the English suggestions about what they would accept as the basis for peace terms were 'great and reasonable'; the duke had further agreed that if he were freed on parole to urge acceptance of these terms and the French refused them still, he would renounce his homage to Charles VI and acknowledge Henry as king of France. He had hinted that others among the prisoners might follow suit.[14] It was beginning to look as if the whole structure of loyalties on which the Valois monarchy depended might be pushed towards collapse.

Henry's letter to Tiptoft mentioned that Bourbon had insisted that he must be allowed to conceal his change of allegiance at least as long as he was on French soil (a condition parallel to that of the 'infernal pact' of Henry and John the Fearless). This remark shows that Henry understood that diplomacy alone could only undermine his rival's authority, not unseat him. The last words of his letter indicate how he intended to finish the job. 'But Tiptoft, . . . I will not leave my voyage for any treaty that they make.' The time was ripe for a second military intervention, with the prospect this time of support from the Empire and perhaps from Burgundy.

The last months of 1416 and the spring of 1417 witnessed, as had the spring of 1415, a great burst of administrative energy channelled into military preparations. The autumn parliament of 1416 granted a double subsidy, but there was soon an urgent need for ready money, and the spring saw the government indulging in much short-term borrowing. Commissioners were sent into the counties to raise loans; and some very large sums were advanced by individuals, notably by Bishop Beaufort. Parliament, in June 1417, ratified the agreement by which the customs of Southampton were pledged to him as security for the repayment of a great loan of 14,000 marks. Certain features of the proposed expedition involved more careful advance planning and heavier expenditure than two years earlier. Henry's plans in 1417 were for the conquest of territory, and it was therefore desirable that his army should not have to live off the country. This meant making arrangements to supply the army from England. The force which was in fact brought together numbered about 10,000 men, and carried a powerful siege train, so this was no mean task. A large fleet had also to be assembled to transport the army

[14] *Foed.* vol. IX, pp. 427–30.

across the Channel. Among the captains of the host were two dukes and eight earls; among the lay peers John of Bedford (who was named as lieutenant in the king's absence), the Duke of Exeter and the Earl of Westmorland were almost the only really prominent men who remained at home.[15]

Henry sailed from Southampton, and landed with his army at Touques, close to Harfleur in Normandy, on 1 August 1417. By the beginning of September the important town of Caen had been taken by assault, and Henry made it his headquarters for the time being. No field army appeared to oppose his siege, nor was there any attempt by the French to save Argentan, Verneuil or Alençon, which also fell during the autumn. Falaise was taken just before Christmas. After the fall of Alençon, which put the English in a position to threaten Maine, John of Brittany came to meet Henry at Caen, where in November he made a truce with him both for his own duchy and for the lands of his young son-in-law, Louis of Anjou. Henry was thus secure for the time being as far as the great French feudatories of the west were concerned, and could consolidate his hold on lower Normandy. In the spring of 1418 he was able to detach forces under Gloucester and Huntingdon to reduce the Cherbourg peninsula, and another task force under Warwick to besiege Domfront. Domfront fell early in July, Cherbourg not until September. By then Henry himself with the mainguard had pressed forward along the Caen–Paris route; they took Louviers on 20 June and Pont de L'Arche on 20 July, thus severing communications between Paris and Rouen, the ancient, prosperous and populous capital of Normandy lower down the Seine.

The English, when they began to settle down to the siege of Rouen in August 1418, were in effective control of the whole of lower Normandy. This conquest had taken them just a year, in the space of which the political situation in France had altered dramatically. Almost at the same moment that Henry landed at Touques in August 1417, John the Fearless led a host that he had been gathering at Arras out towards Paris. Early in September,

[15] On preparations for the 1417 expedition, financial and military, see Wylie and Waugh, *The Reign of Henry V* vol. III, pp. 31–48, 50–3; A. Steel, *The Receipt of the Exchequer 1377–1485* (Cambridge, 1954), pp. 154–8 (on Beaufort's loans Steel should be checked with Harriss, 'Cardinal Beaufort – patriot or usurer?'; and R. A. Newhall, *The English Conquest of Normandy* (Yale, 1924).

when he had taken Beaumont and Pontoise, he could threaten the capital directly; this was why the Armagnac government was unable to attempt to relieve Caen or any of the other towns that the English besieged in the autumn of 1417. Up to this point, the Burgundian intervention lived up to all the hopes which, after the Calais meeting of 1416, the English must have entertained. But in November near Tours, Burgundy 'captured' Isabella the queen of France, who had been banished from court since the preceding April. From Chartres, she issued a manifesto declaring that she now took upon herself the regency on behalf of her husband Charles, and that she would support the Duke of Burgundy in his efforts to 'save' the country. At Troyes she and the duke began to organize a new 'national' government in opposition to that of Paris. The hopes of Burgundian sympathizers in the capital began to revive, and in May 1418 the gates were opened to the Burgundian captain, the Lord of l'Isle Adam. A number of leading Armagnacs were taken prisoner; most of them, including the count himself, were later lynched by the city mob.

John the Fearless thus recovered what he had always sought, control of the government of France and its capital. There was only one drawback to his victory and the queen's: Tanneguy du Chastel, the Breton who had been Provost of Paris for the Armagnacs, succeeded in getting the heir to the throne, the dauphin Charles, safely out of Paris. The Armagnacs had strong military forces in the Loire valley, and behind their protective screen they were soon busy organizing a new government of their own around the dauphin at Poitiers. The Duke of Brittany, in September 1418, made an effort to bring the parties together, but the dauphin and his councillors repudiated his so-called Treaty of St Maur-les-Fossés, because it gave them no share in the control of affairs in Paris. Henry V, therefore, as his army settled down to besiege Rouen, was in an excellent position to play his old game of keeping the French parties at loggerheads by negotiating with both simultaneously, pushing ahead meanwhile with his own military operations.

To do John of Burgundy justice, he did try to bring together an army to relieve Rouen. It encamped at Beauvais and supplemented its inadequate wages by living off the country. South and west of Paris the Armagnacs remained formidable, and the duke's stock, which had stood high in the summer, began to fall in the hungry city. He knew that his rivals were meantime discussing at Alençon projects for alliance with the English against him. In the circumstances he did not feel it safe to leave the Paris area, and Henry was able to press forward the siege of Rouen without hindrance.

Henry called Rouen 'the most notable place in France save Paris'.[16] The high walls were more than 5 miles in circumference, with a deep ditch before them; and there were more than sixty towers at intervals between the five great forts at the city gates. From these the garrison's artillery and engines kept the besiegers under fire. The English lay before the town from August until January, and there was some fierce fighting in the course of the numerous sorties. But what really won the city for the English was not deeds of arms, but the commanding diplomatic position that Henry had achieved with regard to the parties in France, coupled with the security of his financial position. Henry's army was paid regularly, firmly disciplined, and victualled by fleets which plied between England and Harfleur; one single shipment in September conveyed from London thirty butts of wine, 1000 pipes of ale and 2500 cups 'for your host to drink of'.[17] He was therefore able at the same time to maintain his siege, and to make sure that Burgundy was too concerned about the possibility of an Anglo-Armagnac alliance to attempt to relieve Rouen.

By the new year of 1419, famine had done Henry's work for him in the city. It had been crowded with refugees from the countryside when the siege commenced, and at Christmas a crowd of poor men, driven out of the city to save rations, were fed by the English. A week later negotiations for a surrender opened. It was finally agreed that, if no relief came by 19 January at noon, the English should take possession; all who would take the oath of allegiance to their king should remain in enjoyment of their property and privileges, but the citizens must pay an indemnity of 300,000 crowns, for having kept the king out of a city that was his own inheritance. On that date, with cries of 'Welcome, Rouen, our King's own right', the English entered.

After the fall of Rouen, resistance in Normandy crumbled. By the end of January Longueville, Arques, Nesles and Torcy were in English hands; Mantes capitulated on 5 February and Dieppe on 8 February. Virtually the whole of the ancient duchy was in English control by the spring.

[16] J. Delpit, *Collection générale des documents français qui se trouvent en Angleterre* (Paris, 1847), p. 223.
[17] ibid. p. 225.

In Normandy, as elsewhere later, Henry took practical steps to make his rule acceptable to his new subjects. From a very early stage of the conquest he showed himself anxious to guarantee the freedom and privileges of all who would take the oath of allegiance to him. This meant maintaining a very strict discipline in his host, to restrain soldiers who were avid for plunder and ransoms. As the conquest proceeded, the basic structure of provincial administration was taken over unaltered: the old *baillages*, the administrative districts, were maintained, and so was the sovereignty of the exchequer at Rouen, the highest judicial authority in the duchy. Certain measures seem to have been aimed to enhance Norman pride in provincial individuality, as the reassembling of the Norman estates (which had not met since the 1390s), and the revival of the ancient Plantagenet office of seneschal of the duchy. Some high offices were naturally granted to Englishmen: in 1419 the seneschal, the president of the exchequer, all the *baillis*, and of course the captains of castles were all English. The president of the provincial *chambre des comptes*, whose headquarters were at Caen, was however a Frenchman, Louis Burgeys, and so were nearly all the *prévots*. Henry made no attempt to introduce Englishmen into high office in the church, moreover, and typically showed special anxiety that the pastoral clergy should not leave their posts and people – this in spite of the fact that the clergy generally were among those least willing to recognize the new regime.[18]

There was, however, another side to Henry's Norman policy. As at Harfleur in 1415, at Caen and at Cherbourg steps were taken to encourage English settlement. To those Frenchmen who left the country, and to towns that did not open their gates to him, the king became progressively sterner. Louviers and Rouen both had to pay substantial indemnities for excluding him. After the fall of Rouen, there was a very considerable enfeoffment to Englishmen of lordships that had been deserted by their Norman seigneurs: in the first five months of 1419 something like 250 fiefs were granted to Englishmen. Some of the peers and captains in Henry's service received very large estates. Clarence was

[18] On the administration of conquered Normandy see W. T. Waugh in Wylie and Waugh, *The Reign of Henry V* vol. III, pp. 235–64, and also Waugh's article 'The administration of Normandy' in *Essays in Medieval History presented to T. F. Tout*, pp. 349–59. On the discipline of Henry's armies see Newhall, *The Conquest of Normandy*, pp. 222–38; and B. J. H. Rowe, 'Discipline in the Norman garrisons under Bedford', *E.H.R.* 46 (1931), pp. 194–201.

granted the three *vicomtés* of Auge, Orbec and Ponteaudemer; Salisbury became Count of Perche, and Exeter (who had come over in 1418) Count of Harcourt; Lord Roos became the lord of Braqueville and Sir Walter Hungerford the lord of Homet. But the great majority of those enfeoffed were lesser men, who were not captains even of small contingents. 'From this we may infer', Professor Newhall writes, 'a policy seeking to create in Normandy an English petty nobility which would be chiefly interested in the duchy.' The fiefs that Henry granted carried, of course, an obligation to help in the defence of the duchy, but they also promised their new owners a considerable potential of profit as landowners.[19]

Here are the outlines of a remarkable attempt to provide a settlement of Norman affairs, which would preserve the duchy's ancient customs, its provincial identity, and its Frenchness, but would at the same time forge special ties with England, through a leavening of English settlers both in the commercial towns and among the landowning classes, and also in the higher ranks of the administration. Henry's policy guaranteed security and their traditional way of life to those Normans who would accept him, and also ensured a share in the benefits of the conquest to the Englishmen who carried it out. A constructive balance of firmness and conciliation was made the basis of an effort to engender, with the least possible friction, a new spirit and new conditions in the province. Henry did not quite succeed in achieving this ambitious object, it is true, but he laid strong foundations. Normandy remained in English hands for thirty years after the fall of Rouen.

After the fall of Rouen, the English were militarily in a position to threaten Paris directly. It therefore became clear that neither of the French parties could hope to master the other, without first reaching some sort of agreement with Henry. When the siege began, alliance with the dauphin had seemed to offer the most interesting possibilities, but the long exchanges between his representatives and the English at Alençon in November 1418

[19] On the English settlement see L. Puiseux, *L'émigration Normande et la colonisation Anglaise en Normandie au XVme siècle* (Caen, 1866); R. A. Newhall, 'Henry V's policy of conciliation in Normandy 1417–22' in *Haskins Anniversary Essays in Medieval History* (New York, 1929), pp. 205–29 (whence the above quotation); and C. T. Allmand, 'The Lancastrian land settlement in Normandy', *Econ.H.R.* 2nd ser., 21 (1968), pp. 461–79.

ended abortively, and in 1419 hopes refocused on an accommodation with Duke John of Burgundy. On 30 May he and Queen Isabella came to meet Henry face to face at Meulan, bringing with them the princess Catherine. Two days later Henry saw her for the first time, kissed her, and was instantly in love.[20]

These were very serious negotiations, and at their start there were men on both sides who thought that peace must come of them. The Meulan conference was also the last occasion on which Henry appeared to be willing to consider terms that fell short of promising him the crown of France. The English demands, given the military and diplomatic circumstances, were realistic: the hand of Catherine with a fitting dowry, together with the cession in full sovereignty of the duchy of Normandy and all the lands in the south-west that had been ceded by the Treaty of Brétigny. Yet the negotiations soon ran into difficulties, over the terms on which Henry would renounce his right to the French crown, and his right to the Angevin lands which he claimed separately therefrom. The real trouble seems to have been that Queen Isabella and John were afraid that, if they ceded so much to France's ancient adversary, their own followers would desert them. While the conferences with Henry continued, they therefore opened negotiations with the dauphinists on the side. On 3 July the French did not turn up for the talks that had been projected for that day with the English. On 11 July the queen and the duke were reconciled with the dauphin at Pouilly.

All that was arranged was a formal, personal reconciliation between the principals: detailed terms between the new allies had still to be arranged. This was why the English met with little resistance when they began to push toward Paris again, after the truce that had covered the conferences at Meulan ran out on 29 July. Negotiations were then going forward busily for a further meeting of the dauphin and the Duke of Burgundy. It took place at Montereau, on 10 September 1419. They met in an enclosure on the bridge over the Yonne. When the gates were closed on the duke's party, he was cut down by Charles's retainers. In consequence, as the prior of the Charterhouse at Dijon later put it, the English entered France 'through the hole in the Duke of Burgundy's skull'.[21]

[20] This reaction appears to have been quite genuine: see J. Waurin, *Chronique* (R.S.) vol. II, p. 286.

[21] See Wylie and Waugh, *The Reign of Henry V* vol. III, p. 187.

The prior spoke truly, for the murder left the French totally disorganized in face of the advancing English. There could now be no hope of reconciliation between the dauphin and the old Burgundian party, to whom fell as a dire debt of honour the task of avenging their dead leader. The Burgundians were, however, in confusion; John's heir, Philip, was in Flanders, without an army, out of contact with both the queen at Troyes and the Burgundian garrison in Paris. The dauphin, after the murder, had even less chance than before of re-entering Paris. There was only one man who could be master of the situation, and that was Henry of England.[22]

Henry knew that he was in charge as soon as he heard the news. To the Count of St Pol, who was captain of Paris and knew that the alternative to a truce with the English would be siege and starvation, he made it clear that the French could not hope to resume talks where they had broken off at Meulan; he was fighting for the crown, not for 'the duchies', though he would be prepared to allow Charles VI, old and mad, to keep the throne while he lived. This was in September; in the ensuing weeks he made it clear to Duke Philip, who was seeking time to gather an army and to concert a policy with his relatives and with the towns and nobility of northern France, that the Burgundians must accept his terms. Otherwise he would press on alone and seek alliance with the dauphin. By December the duke had come to the conclusion, in spite of serious misgivings, that he had no option but to meet Henry's demands, and to try to persuade the French court to follow suit. On Christmas Day, the English and the Burgundians became allies. At this stage, the queen at Troyes was still hoping to reconcile the court with the dauphin, but she had no forces and no money and in the new year she gave way. A proclamation in the name of Charles VI declared the dauphin guilty of treason for his part in the murder of Duke John, and Duke Philip was granted the powers that he needed to arrange things, on the king's behalf as well as his own, with Henry.

A formal draft of a treaty of peace between France and England was drawn up early in April; on 21 May it was ratified at Troyes in the presence of Henry V, Charles VI and Philip of Burgundy.

[22] The diplomatic manœuvres of the English, the Burgundians and the French court between September 1419 and April 1420, when a draft treaty was agreed, are highly complicated. Far the best account is that of P. Bonenfant, *Du Meurtre de Montereau au Traité de Troyes* (*Mémoires de l'Académie Royale de Belgique, Lettres, 2me série* 1958).

Its terms were substantially those that Henry had stood out for when he allied with Philip in December. Henry was to marry Catherine; Charles VI would keep the throne for his lifetime, but at his death it must pass to Henry, and to his heirs for ever. Between France and England there should be peace and perpetual alliance, but the two kingdoms would be kept entirely separate, to be ruled in accordance with their own ancient laws and customs. Henry promised that France should be ruled by Frenchmen, that her great lords and churches should be maintained in their estate, and likewise the *Parlement* and other offices. Normandy, it was stipulated, should remain under English government until Charles VI's death, when it should revert to the crown of France. The Duke of Burgundy gained by the treaty valuable territorial concessions, and Henry's promise of aid in avenging his father's murder. The treaty bound the parties to it to make war to reduce to the obedience of Charles VI (and so of Henry, who was to be regent for him) all those lands and towns held by the dauphin and his supporters. At the time this included Languedoc and most of the country south of the Loire, besides much of Champagne and a good many strong places both in Picardy and the Paris area itself.[23]

These military facts bring out one point which sharply differentiates the Treaty of Troyes from the other great settlement of the Hundred Years War, the Treaty of Brétigny of 1360. Its chief clauses enshrine a settlement about the succession to the throne of France and the government of that kingdom, and concern one nation only. The clauses about the dauphin, and the obligation to make war upon him and his followers, emphasize another respect in which the Troyes treaty differed from that of Brétigny; it was not in the same sense a treaty of peace. Other Frenchmen besides the dauphin were not parties to it. The position of such great feudatories as the Duke of Brittany and the Count of Foix was not clear: the decision, whether to take the oath to observe its terms, had to be left for them to sort out themselves. This meant that the success of the treaty, as a settlement, must depend in large part on the speed and effectiveness with which Henry and Duke Philip could deal with the dauphin Charles. The longer that fighting continued, the less likely such great men as Brittany and Foix would be to commit themselves to the Lancastrian succession. One of the great weaknesses of the treaty was that, while in name it established peace between

[23] For text see *Foed.* vol. IX, pp. 877–82 (preliminaries of April) and 895–904 (final treaty).

England and France, in reality it only established peace between the English and a party in France.

The fact that the Treaty of Troyes established a formal peace between the kingdoms of France and England was in one way very important, however. The English commons, in the parliament of 1420, petitioned for confirmation that in the future the crowns of England and France should be kept strictly separate.[24] They attached importance to the terms of the treaty in this matter for good reasons. The clear separation of the kingdoms meant that, now that the two countries were at peace, the subjects of the king of England had no obligation, as such, to aid Henry in the war that he was waging as regent and heir of France. The custom, clearly recognized, that the king had a right to demand subsidies from his parliaments to support his wars did not bind his subjects to contribute to a war in which he was not engaged as king of England. The commons in fact only once more made a grant of subsidy in Henry V's reign, in the second parliament of 1421, and that grant was significantly, in name, for the defence of the realm. After his death, they did not make any grant for the war for six years. By 1420 England, it is clear, was beginning to feel the strain of the war. We are reminded how formidable the task was with which Henry saddled himself at Troyes, and how desirable it was that serious fighting be brought speedily to a successful close.

Henry himself understood the need for speedy and determined action. It is hard for the historian to regard the last two years of his reign as anything but an epilogue, but for him they were probably the most active years of all. He gave himself no respite. The Treaty of Troyes was finalized on 21 May; on 2 June Henry was married to Catherine in the cathedral there; two days later she was following her husband to the siege of Sens. By the end of the month that town and Montereau were both taken and Henry was pressing on to invest the formidable dauphinist stronghold at Melun. That siege occupied him until mid November. In December he was in Paris for the meeting of the Estates General which ratified the Treaty of Troyes. He was able to find time to supervise measures for raising new taxes and for strengthening the coinage before he left, a bare two days after Christmas, on what was to be his last visit to England, pausing on his way to be present at the meeting of the Norman estates at Rouen in January.

[24] *R.P.* vol. IV, p. 127.

Henry landed at Dover on 1 February 1421, and gave himself no more rest in England than he had in France. On 23 February Catherine was crowned queen in Westminster Abbey. Immediately afterwards the royal couple set out on a lightning tour of the kingdom, which took them to Bristol, Shrewsbury, Coventry and Leicester before Easter; then on to Nottingham, York, Beverley, Lincoln and Norwich. A tour of holy places, Walsingham called it, but there was sterner business to the fore all the way; wherever he went the king was busy pressing men to promise loans for the war, or service in arms. He did not want to mar the impression that he had made in his homeland by his triumphs by asking parliament for a subsidy, but he was determined to find men and money. He was back in London for the opening of parliament on 2 May. By June he had collected large sums (Beaufort, admittedly under pressure, lent no less than £17,666) and reinforcements for his host to the number of some 4000 soldiers. It was at their head that he landed at Calais on 11 June.

It was time for him to be back. On the Saturday before Easter, his brother the Duke of Clarence had been defeated and killed in a bloody engagement at Baugé in Maine by a combined force of Scots and Armagnacs. Militarily Baugé had no decisive consequence, for Salisbury with the main English field army eluded the victors' pursuit. Politically, however, it was a significant setback for the English. Within a few weeks the Duke of Brittany negotiated a formal truce with the dauphin,[25] and there was a temporary panic in Paris when the news of Clarence's death came through. Henry's return steadied the situation, but the task ahead of him had become more formidable. The dauphin's forces fell back from Chartres, which they were besieging, at his approach, and the English followed them to the Loire; but there was no battle. With the coming of winter, Henry and his tired army settled down to invest Meaux on the Marne, the most formidable dauphinist stronghold now left in the country south of Paris. They were seven months at the siege, for the fortified market of Meaux did not surrender until 10 May 1422. By then dysentery had thinned their ranks terribly, and the king's own health was broken.

Meaux was the last of Henry's conquests. He started out in July for the siege of Cosne-sur-Loire, but he was so sick that he had to be carried in a litter. After a few days he could go no

[25] On the complicated background of Anglo-Breton relations in this period, see Knowlson, *Jean V de Bretagne et l'Angleterre*, pp. 112–14.

further, so they brought him back as far as Bois de Vincennes, and there, in the small hours of 31 August 1422, he died. So he was never king of France after all. Charles VI did not die until nearly two months later, on 21 October. It was not Henry V, but the infant son whom Catherine had borne him in England on 6 December 1421, who inherited the two crowns of France and England, and the war in France to which his father had pledged him.

Henry V's reign is the record of a tremendous English achievement. There can be no need to labour the victories in the field, which speak for themselves; but the work and the sacrifices, at home and in the background, that made victories possible do deserve particular emphasis. Before this reign, no English royal host had ever been kept in continuous service, in the pay of the crown, for anything like the period that the army of 1417 was. This army was, further, largely supplied from England, at least until 1420. To finance campaigning on such a grand scale and for so long was a major fiscal and administrative triumph. In order to meet Henry's needs taxation had to be heavier than it ever was before or afterwards.[26] Yet Henry did not have to listen to plain speech from the commons about lack of governance or the mismanagement of royal expenditure, as his predecessor had so often been compelled to. There were of course complaints. Before Henry's return from France in 1421 the commons were becoming patently fretful about the inconveniences arising from his prolonged absence. On the whole, however, there seems to have been agreement that in spite of all the strains, the country was better governed than it had been, or would be, for many a long year.

More was needed to make Henry's campaigns financially feasible than the complaisance of the commons. His government also found it necessary to raise large sums by borrowing, to tide over delays while subsidies were still unpaid. The business of raising loans and seeing to their repayment, as well as the business of overseeing the collection of subsidies and of recording the indentures that the king sealed with his captains, fell on the council and the exchequer – the same exchequer whose processes have often been described as too slow and cumbersome to meet

[26] On war finance see the masterly article of R. A. Newhall, 'The war finances of Henry V and the Duke of Bedford', *E.H.R.* 36 (1921), pp. 172–98; see also Wylie and Waugh, *The Reign of Henry V*, esp. vol. III, pp. 259–60, 390–2, 399–401.

the needs of government in the fifteenth century. The council also had much to do with raising the reinforcements that were constantly needed for Henry's army. It could be just as strenuous to raise men as it always was to raise taxes. Both men and money were, however, consistently and successfully levied, and that without the load of crown debts getting out of hand. The whole achievement triumphantly demonstrated that the English administrative machine was up to any task that could be imposed on it.

What made the difference between the reign of Henry V and those of other medieval English kings before and after him was the directing mind of the ruler, and his personality.[27] Henry possessed in a remarkable degree those qualities that contemporaries looked for in a monarch: piety, chivalrous courage and devotion to justice. His religious conviction was personal to a degree that reached beyond ordinary conventions. He was ready to try his own hand at wrestling with the unregenerate Lollards, Oldcastle and Badby. He directed himself the quest abroad for religious staff for his foundations for the Carthusians at Syon and the Bridgettines at Sheen. In 1421 he summoned the chapter of the English Benedictines to meet in his presence, so as personally to impress on them the need to put their houses in order. His courage and chivalry were the theme of many stories told of him, as of his sleeping in his armour on the night before Agincourt, and of his sparing the life of the seigneur de Barbasan, because they had fought hand to hand in a mine under the walls of Melun. Above all, men were impressed by the quality of his justice, stern and impartial. 'He was the prince of justice,' Chastellain wrote, 'he gave support to none out of favour, nor did he suffer wrong to go unpunished out of regard for affinity.'[28] This quality won him appreciation not only from English and Burgundian writers, but also from otherwise hostile dauphinists, like Perceval de Cagny and Juvenel des Ursins.

Henry displayed other, more individual qualities as a ruler besides these traditional ones. He gave himself so fully to the business of government and warfare, attentive to every detail, as to leave little time for relaxation; he may even have lost the taste

[27] My estimate of Henry V owes much to a lecture which I was kindly allowed to see by Mr G. L. Harriss, the librarian of Magdalen College, Oxford: K. B. McFarlane's ch. 7, pt 1, of *Lancastrian Kings and Lollard Knights* (in press).

[28] G. Chestellain, *Chronique*, ed. K. de Lettenhove (Brussels, 1863), vol. I, p. 334.

for it. The records of his diplomacy are evidence not only of his skill and knowledge, but also of a ruthless and single minded determination to have what he was convinced was his own. His letters, many of them written in English (the preference for the native tongue was his own) give more personal glimpses of an imperious will: 'but Tiptoft, know that I will not leave my voyage for any treaty that they make'. With his reserve, his enormous ambition, and his conviction of his right to have things his own way, his is not a character that can command wide sympathy with the present generation. It is therefore the more important to remember how deeply he was admired, even venerated, by contemporaries who knew and served him. He was certainly the most successful king of England of the later Middle Ages, and probably the ablest.

The unity of purpose and the unprecedented effort that Henry was able to evoke in England make it possible to argue that, had he lived, he might have completed the conquest that he began. The tragedy was that no one else could, and yet that no one could afford, when he was gone, to retreat from the labour that he left unfinished. His victories convinced not only the king himself that God was on the side of his right, but also his subjects. No one could understand, when he died, that the will that had sustained success had died with him. Much later Lancastrian history is only explicable in terms of the bewilderment of people who felt sure that Henry's conquest could and ought to be maintained, but could see the edifice of his achievement crumbling before their eyes.

16

Henry VI and France
1422–1453

Henry V's death left his successor with a very intractable problem in the relationship of the two Lancastrian kingdoms, of England and France. English interests and aspirations were at once tightly associated with his French conquests, and insufficiently so. Up to 1419 it had always seemed likely that Henry would be content with Normandy and with the re-establishment of the boundaries of 1360 in Gascony. Englishmen, who were well aware of the advantage of such conquests to their commerce, shipping and defence, were prepared to pay for them. The advantage to them of the conquest of the whole of France was not so obvious, and they were not keen to shoulder the fiscal burden that it might involve. But Henry, through the terms of the Troyes settlement of 1420, had (probably deliberately) made it difficult to separate the two objectives. The Treaty of Troyes accepted that Normandy was part of France and should revert to the French crown at Charles VI's death. This made it difficult to distinguish between limited English objectives in northern France and Henry's own objective of complete conquest.

Henry's success in the war up to the time he died had besides complicated matters, by introducing a new element into the material interests of the English overseas. A number of English lords and knights had been rewarded with conquered land, and now held extensive estates on both sides of the Channel. Englishmen had been settled deliberately in some Norman towns, as Cherbourg, Caen and Harfleur, and had acquired property in many others. Normandy and the conquered lands in France had become for them a country of opportunity, and, as the records show, considerable numbers crossed the sea in quest of fortune there, the soldiers apart. To consolidate the English element, which promised to constitute a nucleus of Lancastrian loyalism in Normandy at least, it was laid down that Englishmen must pass on their properties, if they disposed of them, to Englishmen. Thus an English 'presence' in France was created which was more than just military, the preservation of which had to rank as a national commitment.[1] Yet Englishmen in England were no less anxious than they had been before to be relieved of war taxation. The commons in parliament had insisted that, as in the Troyes terms, the two kingdoms of England and France should remain clearly separated, so that there should be no doubt that the obligation to pay for the reduction of the dauphin's supporters should fall on the French. When Henry V died and the will that had driven men forward was still, the English parliament ceased to contribute to the war. No subsidy was granted for nearly seven years.

Parliament only resumed its contribution to the war when the conquests of Henry V seemed to be threatened. The result was that in the interim, though the house of Lancaster retained its commitment to making its kingship a reality in all France, Bedford (Henry's brother who directed the government there) was unable to pursue more than limited military objectives. The Norman estates made generous grants towards the war,[2] and he was able to keep the garrisons there and in conquered France up to strength, and by withdrawing men from them to put armies in the field. But he could not contemplate ambitious schemes for further conquests without straining his limited resources dangerously. He did not get adequate support from England until the moment of opportunity was passed.

The arrangements that were made for the government of the two Lancastrian kingdoms when Henry V and Charles VI were both dead aggravated the problem that the uncertainty of English war aims created. In France Bedford became regent. In England Humphrey of Gloucester, Henry V's younger surviving brother, was made protector and chairman of a regency council.[3] The only proviso in these arrangements which could

---

[1] On the Lancastrian settlement in Normandy see C. T. Allmand's interesting articles 'The Collection of Dom. Lenoir and the English occupation of Normandy', *Archives* 6 (1963-4), pp. 202–10; 'The Lancastrian land settlement in Normandy 1417–1450', *Econ. H.R.* 2nd ser., 21 (1968), pp. 461–79; and 'La Normandie devant l'opinion Anglaise', *B.E.C.* 128 (1970), pp. 345–68.

[2] On this see B. J. H. Rowe, 'The estates of Normandy under the Duke of Bedford', *E.H.R.* 46 (1931), pp. 551–78.

[3] See further Chapter 17.

help to coordinate policy in the two realms was the stipulation that Bedford, when in England, should take over as protector; but he could not do this without leaving his charge in France. There was thus no longer a single personal direction behind both governments, and the separation of the Lancastrian realms on which the Troyes terms had insisted was sharpened. It became possible, in these circumstances, for Henry VI's two governments to pursue policies that were not just separate but conflicting.

This in fact was to happen at an early stage, and with serious consequences. The trouble arose out of the continental ambitions of the protector of England, Humphrey of Gloucester. Henry V, in 1421, had given asylum to Jacqueline, countess in her own right of Hainault and Holland, who was estranged from her husband, John of Brabant. The couple were childless, and John's heir was Duke Philip of Burgundy, whose hope was to absorb the inheritance of both parties into his own dominions. Some time early in 1423, however, Gloucester, having obtained from the schismatic Pope Benedict XIII a dissolution of Jacqueline's former marriage, married her. The parliament of 1423 naturalized her as an Englishwoman, and in the next year he was able to set about raising money and an army in England to reconquer his wife's inheritance, apparently without any protest from the council. Burgundy at once prepared to aid John of Brabant. Gloucester's campaign, fortunately, proved a complete fiasco, and Burgundian forces did not actually have to engage the English. Bedford succeeded in smoothing over the anger of Duke Philip, for whom the quarrel with Gloucester had acquired an acutely personal edge, but not before Philip had begun to entertain overtures from the adversary of England, the dauphin Charles. Though he remained formally the ally of Lancaster, from this point forward he never lost contact with the other side. The Burgundian alliance, which had been the cornerstone of the settlement of 1420, was thus unduly strained very early in Henry VI's reign.

The dauphin, at the beginning of Bedford's regency, was not an adversary to be despised. He had settled his capital at Bourges, and his administrators, if lethargic, were highly competent. All south of the Loire, except Gascony, was his, and his financial resources were more ample than those of the regent. After the arrival of substantial forces from Scotland, under the command of the Earl of Buchan, he had a formidable field army at his disposal.

In spite of the dauphin's apparent strength and Bedford's difficulties, the English were remarkably successful in the field in the early years. In 1423 the Franco-Scottish forces took the offensive, in an attempt to cut across Burgundian held territory to join forces with the pockets of dauphinist resistance in Champagne. At Cravant the Earl of Salisbury, hurrying by Auxerre with an Anglo-Burgundian force, threw his men across the Yonne in sight of the enemy and defeated them. The next year saw an even more important victory. Bedford, having assembled a field army at Rouen, was preparing to invade Maine; at about the same time Buchan, whose army had been reinforced both from Scotland and with Italian mercenaries, began to advance from Le Mans. The two hosts met at Verneuil on the borders of Normandy, on 17 August. The battle was hard fought, but at the end of it the English and Burgundians had won a victory almost as decisive as Agincourt. The Scots, caught in a pincer between the corps of Bedford and Salisbury, were virtually eliminated. Buchan and his lieutenant Douglas were both killed; so were the counts of Aumale, Narbonne and Ventadour. The Duke of Alençon and Marshal Lafayette were taken prisoner. The dauphin's field army had been completely destroyed.[4]

In the aftermath of Verneuil, Bedford was able to settle down to consolidate the English position north of the Loire. In 1425 Salisbury, after 'tidying up' in Champagne and capturing Rambouillet and Étampes, took command in the west and captured Le Mans; by the end of the year all Maine was in English hands. Sir Thomas Rampston was despatched to the Breton border, after the duke had in 1424 allied with the dauphin, and more than held his own there. Things looked bright for the English when in 1428 Salisbury, who had gone home to raise men, arrived in France with much needed troops. The plan at first agreed was to use these forces for the reduction of Angers, but the earl had more ambitious ideas. His objective was to seize a bridgehead on the Loire much nearer Bourges, at Orleans, preparatory to carrying the war into the heart of the dauphin's 'kingdom'.

Between 1422 and 1428 Bedford had concentrated consistently on consolidating the English position north of the Loire, by the

---

[4] On this important battle see further A. H. Burne, *The Agincourt War* (London, 1956), pp. 196-215.

steady reduction of land and strongholds. He followed here the example that Henry V had set in Normandy, but it is questionable whether this was sound strategy. A bold offensive after Verneuil might have achieved more. Bedford's method was inevitably a slow one, and time was not on the side of the English. Salisbury's decision of 1428 was the right one, but it was taken too late.

With every year that the dauphin retained control south of the Loire and outside Gascony, the great French feudatories became more unwilling to commit themselves to one side or the other, and more anxious to keep the game in their own hands. Brittany hovered between Lancaster and Valois; in 1423 at Amiens he entered into a personal alliance with Burgundy and Bedford; in 1424, when Burgundy's relations with England were becoming strained as a result of Gloucester's activities, he allied with the dauphin; in 1427 he came back to the English side as a militarily non-effective ally. The Count of Foix was out for what he could get. Before Henry V died, he had virtually settled with England on terms which would give him the lieutenancy in Languedoc and the direction of the offensive against the dauphin in the south-west. When he learned that Henry was dead he held his hand, spinning out negotiations, and early in 1424 (before Verneuil) he allied with the dauphin on terms which gave him the lieutenancy but did not commit him to hazardous and expensive military operations.[5] These two reactions, self-interested and noncommittal, were typical.

Still more important, delay in pressing forward the English advance laid bare the artificial nature of the Anglo-Burgundian alliance. Forced on Duke Philip in the intractable political circumstances of 1419 when the duty of avenging his father seemed paramount, it offered few enduring advantages to Burgundy. It did not give Philip the control in Paris that his father had so long sought, and his part in the war cost money which he could only raise with difficulty from his own dominions. It exposed them to much incidental devastation, while the strain of their defence interfered with his pursuit of more interesting ambitions in the imperial Low Countries and the Rhineland. Gloucester's ill-judged bid for the inheritance of Hainault and Holland hurt him here, and reminded him sharply that his family's natural and traditional connexions were with the French and the Rhenish nobility, not the English.

[5] On the Count of Foix's position see further M. G. A. Vale, *English Gascony 1399–1453* (Oxford, 1970), pp. 82–3, 87–96.

Yolande of Aragon, Dowager Countess of Anjou, the dauphin's mother-in-law and a dominant personality at the court of Bourges, was able to turn the strains which were becoming apparent in the Anglo-Burgundian alliance to Charles's advantage. In 1423 the alliance of Bedford, Burgundy and Brittany had been cemented by the marriages of Anne (a sister of Duke Philip) to Bedford, and of Margaret (another of Philip's sisters) to Arthur of Richemont, John of Brittany's brother, who had accepted the Treaty of Troyes. In 1424, when before Verneuil things looked difficult for the English, Yolande succeeded in winning the Duke of Brittany round to her side. Then after Verneuil, she persuaded Arthur of Richemont to desert the English too, and to accept the constable's sword of France, which Buchan had held. Burgundy, significantly, was agreeable to his taking the office. Henceforward one of the marriages that had been intended to forge a family league on the Lancastrian side was therefore a bond working the other way – through Margaret of Burgundy, Richemont's wife, Yolande could hope to put pressure on Duke Philip. Another marriage reinforced this connexion between the dauphin's court and Burgundy – that of Charles of Clermont, Bourbon's heir, to Philip's third sister Agnes. The first effect of this new series of alliances, coupled with Gloucester's intervention in Hainault, was that Philip of Burgundy in 1424 agreed to make a truce with the dauphin.

Thanks to Yolande's efforts, the French at the end of 1424 were diplomatically very nearly in a position to turn the tables on the English. Two things made it impossible for them to exploit their advantage further. One was the destruction of Buchan's field army at Verneuil. All that the dauphin could count on thereafter were the unreliable companies, commanded by old Armagnac freebooters, like La Hire and Poton de Xaintrailles; these were ill paid and conducted themselves not much better than brigands. They were no match for Bedford's English soldiers, regularly paid and mustered, well disciplined and accustomed to coordinated operations.[6] The other difficulty that beset the dauphin's party was the atmosphere of intrigue and instability at the court of Bourges. Some of Charles's advisers were able men, but their greed outran their talents. With the rise to favour of the ex-Burgundian Georges de la

---

[6] On English military organization see R. A. Newhall, *Muster and Review* (Cambridge, Mass., 1940); and B. J. H. Rowe, 'Discipline in the Norman garrisons under the Duke of Bedford', *E.H.R.* 46 (1931), pp. 194-208.

Trémoille the old Armagnac counsellors, Louvet and Tanneguy du Chastel, were at last eclipsed; but confusion became worse than ever when a furious quarrel broke out between the new favourite and Richemont. The constable was driven from the court, and a private war broke out between his partisans and those of La Trémoille, with the dauphin taking the favourite's part. This internecine strife cost the dauphin all the advantage that Yolande's diplomacy had promised.

In 1428, when Salisbury settled down to invest Orleans, the English had lost the initiative in the diplomatic field. The English in 1428 still had the military initiative, however, and it is just possible that, if Salisbury had lived, he would have taken the city and carried the war successfully into the kingdom of Bourges. But a stray cannon ball carried away the victor of Cravant, and Suffolk who succeeded him in command was not taking any risks, seeing that the garrison was quite as large as his own force. The English were still before the city on 28 April 1429, when a relieving host appeared, with Joan of Arc at its head.

> At the which time, after the adventure fallen to the person of my cousin of Salisbury, whom God assoil, there fell, by the hand of God as it seemeth, a great stroke upon your people that was assembled there in great number, caused in great part as I trow of lack of sad belief and unfaithful doubt that they had of a disciple and limb of the fiend, called the Pucelle [i.e. the maid], that used false enchantments and sorcery: the which great stroke and discomfiture not only lessened in great part the number of your people there, but as well withdrew the courage of the remnant in marvellous wise, and couraged your adverse party and enemies to assemble them forthwith in great number.[7]

That is how Bedford later described the advent of Joan of Arc. He may have exaggerated the impact of her appearance on the English, but there is no doubt about its effect on the French. The peasant girl of Domrémy, who arrived at Chinon early in 1429 with the story of her 'voices' which had told her of her mission to deliver the dauphin and his kingdom from the English, had caught the imagination of the soldiers of France. She succeeded where no one else had since Verneuil, in welding

[7] *P.P.C.* vol. IV, p. 223. For English reactions to Joan of Arc, see further W. T. Waugh, 'Joan of Arc in English sources of the fifteenth century' in *Historical Essays in honour of James Tait*, ed. J. G. Edwards, V. H. Galbraith and E. F. Jacob (Manchester, 1933), pp. 387ff.

the scattered forces that passed for the dauphin's army into an effective field force, and in firing the troops with confidence. At Orleans the English had for the first time to face an army that was superior to theirs not only in numbers, but in determination and morale as well.[8]

Joan's army entered Orleans on 3 May 1429; by 8 May she had driven Suffolk from his lines before the city. On 12 June at Jargeau she defeated Suffolk's own corps, and took him prisoner. On 18 June her troops, now joined by Richemont with a Breton contingent, met Lord Talbot and Sir John Fastolf with the mainguard of the Orleans army at Patay and completely overwhelmed them. This left no substantial English force between her and Paris, and she might have pressed on to the capital. Bedford, regarding his forward position as untenable, withdrew into Normandy and made Rouen his headquarters.

But Joan's plan was different. Instead of advancing on Paris, her army swept north-east in a wide arc, and into Champagne. The towns on the route opened their gates to her with monotonous regularity. On 17 July, only a month after Patay, the dauphin was solemnly crowned, with Joan looking on, at Rheims, the ecclesiastical capital of France and the traditional place of coronation, by the Archbishop Regnault of Chartres. This was no empty ceremony. A crowned and anointed king's title was something very different from the claim of a dauphin. Moreover, though he did not come himself, the coronation was witnessed by representatives of the Duke of Burgundy. In a European context, the position of Charles VII had been immeasurably strengthened.

The remainder of the campaign of 1429 continued gloriously. Laon, Soissons, Senlis, Château Thierry and Compiègne all fell to the French. None of this achievement was followed up in 1430. The fighting in 1429 had emptied Charles's treasury, and La Trémoille, jealous of Joan's success, was determined to keep her as inactive as he could. Burgundy, with the generous

---

[8] There is naturally an immense literature on Joan of Arc. For a useful introduction to the subject see A. Buchan, *Joan of Arc and the Recovery of France* (London, 1948). R. Pernoud, *Joan of Arc* (English translation by E. Hyams, London, 1964) is a biography composed around the original sources, and enthralling. The most important evidences concerning her mission are printed in J. Quicherat, *Procés de condamnation et de réhabilitation de Jeanne d'Arc* (Paris, 1841-49); there are more modern editions of the condemnation edited by P. Champion (1920-1) and by P. Tisset (1960).

addition of Champagne to his apanage, re-entered the war as an active party on the English side. It was in Champagne, at Compiègne, whither she had marched to raise the Burgundian siege, that Joan of Arc was taken prisoner by the troops of Jean de Luxembourg.

Joan was bought by the English for 10,000 crowns, and was tried for heresy at Rouen in 1431. For them, it appeared to be a political necessity to discredit her. There was not much savour of justice about the proceedings against her: conviction was what the presiding judge, Pierre Cauchon, Bishop of Beauvais, was aiming for. The reports of the case were doctored at his orders. L'Oiseleur, the priest who heard Joan's confessions, played the part of a stool pigeon. In the end, worn out by the hardhip and loneliness of captivity, she gave way and abjured her 'voices' as lying impostures. Her sentence was imprisonment for life. Joan, before she 'confessed', had been led to suppose that she would be transferred to an ecclesiastical prison; when nothing was done to change her gaol she reassumed men's clothes (wearing male attire had been a principal charge against her) and withdrew her confession. As a relapsed heretic she was brought before her judges again and handed over by them to the secular arm. On 30 May 1431 she was burned as a witch and a heretic in the market place of Rouen.

By the time that Joan was burned her existence had ceased to matter in the world of high politics. No effort was made to save her by the court of Bourges, where La Trémoille was still supreme. Burgundy had got his hands full with a new concern, the struggle for the succession of Lorraine between his vassal Anthoine de Vaudemont and René of Anjou. To the English, in 1431, what mattered was not to ruin the maid but to undo the effect of her victories. Substantial forces were raised at home, and, at last, English money to pay them. There was hard fighting in 1431 and 1432, but not much to show for it, and in 1433 Bedford went home to raise more men and report on the ominous military situation. In 1434 the record was brighter, in spite of risings in Normandy against the English; Arundel restored some losses in Maine and Talbot campaigned successfully in the valley of the Oise. Given a little more time, the situation might have been restored to the *status quo ante* of 1428, but the English were not going to be given time.

In 1433 Richemont returned to Charles's court and at last toppled La Trémoille. With his return, there was a return to the diplomacy of Yolande's day, with its object of wooing Burgundy out of the English alliance. This diplomacy was furthered by the efforts of the papal mediators, who under the leadership of Cardinal Nicholas Albergati were working to bring all the parties in the war to the conference table. It was their efforts and Richemont's that persuaded Philip of Burgundy at Nevers, early in 1435, to agree to the calling of a peace conference, and to agree also with Richemont that if peace could not be made and if he could do so without dishonour, he would leave the English alliance.

The great peace conference which was held in the abbey of St Waast at Arras in August and September 1435 was a turning point in the diplomatic history of the war.[9] Cardinal Beaufort was the nominal leader of the Lancastrian embassy (for there were representatives of both Henry VI's kingdoms), but the real work was done by John Kemp, the Archbishop of York, and Pierre Cauchon. The leaders of the French embassy were the Archbishop of Rheims, the Duke of Bourbon, and the Constable Richemont. Burgundy was treated as an independent third party and his chief negotiator was his chancellor, Nicolas Rolin. The presidents of the congress were two cardinals, Albergati the papal legate, and Hugh de Lusignan, cardinal of Cyprus and legate of the Council of Basle. Since the English and French never met face to face but relayed their offers and counter offers for a settlement through the mediators, the cardinals were key figures. They were also key men because only the church, which had jurisdiction over oaths and perjury, could decide whether Philip of Burgundy was bound for all time to the English by the oath that he had undoubtedly taken in 1420 to uphold the Treaty of Troyes.

The exchanges between the English and French at Arras show clearly how the English commitment to the claim to the French throne, coupled with their inability to put into the field forces that could do more than hold their own against the French, had put the Lancastrians in a false position. The English would not recognize Charles's kingship; they would not even countenance a formal peace, insisting that nothing could be settled finally while their king was under age. They were prepared to offer a truce for twenty or even fifty years, and to go with it suggested a marriage alliance between Henry's line and Charles's; that the

[9] On all that concerns this congress, see the authoritative work of J. G. Dickinson, *The Congress of Arras* (Oxford, 1955), on which I have largely relied.

Duke of Orleans who had been a prisoner since Agincourt should be released; and that they would 'leave a part of the King's realm in France to his adversary'.[10] Charles equally would not recognize his rival's kingship. He was prepared to offer him all Normandy, Guienne, and perhaps more land west of the Seine, but insisted that Henry must renounce his title of King of France, and must hold any lands ceded to him as a vassal of the French crown. The French were prepared, it is true, to let him postpone his homage until he came of age, or for seven years. This was as far as they would go, and Cardinal Albergati declared that it must be regarded as a sufficient offer. From the point of view of the English it was hard to agree with him. They still held Paris and land south of it, much more of France than the French were even offering them as an apanage. The military balance in the war was very undecided. Not surprisingly, the maximum French offer was rejected by the English envoys on the spot and by their government when it was later reported to them. The English therefore left Arras, *re infecta*, on 6 September.

Up to the last moment the English would not let themselves believe that Burgundy would desert them. But they were no sooner gone than he and the French began to move towards their *rapprochement*. Philip and Richemont were closeted together nightly; and the final ceremony took place in St Waast's abbey on 21 September. The cardinals absolved Philip from the oath that he had taken at Troyes on the ground that it was legally invalid, endangering his soul by committing him to war and bloodshed, and founded on an illegal transaction, since Charles VI had no power to alienate his succession. Philip in return for this absolution remitted his rancour against his father's murderers, and recognized Charles VII as his king. He thus extricated himself from the English alliance publicly, and with his honour intact, which was what he had intended all along to achieve through the conference.

Since Burgundy did not immediately commit himself to fight the English but only to make further efforts to bring them into a peace, the gain to the French from Arras, great as it was, fell short of being decisive. For the English the outcome was a complete disaster. Without the Burgundian alliance, the Lancastrian dual monarchy ceased to be viable. There could no longer be any prospect of conquering new territories from Charles, and with Burgundy now a liegeman of the adversary, the line of communication to Paris was endangered. It could

[10] J. G. Dickinson, *The Congress of Arras*, p. 149.

only be a matter of time now before they would have to retreat into Normandy. To fill the cup of England's sorrows, the Duke of Bedford died on 15 September 1435. His first wife Anne, Philip of Burgundy's sister, who in her lifetime had done much to keep the alliance with her brother in being, had predeceased him by two years. With him the English lost the only leader who, after Henry V's death, had succeeded in achieving a measure of true respect among the French of the conquered lands.

The English reactions to their declining fortunes in the war over the period 1429 to 1436 are very interesting. The need to redress the balance after the victories of Joan of Arc evoked a determined response. The niggardly finance of the preceding period was abandoned, and parliament voted a double subsidy in 1430, followed by single subsidies in 1432 and 1433 and by a subsidy coupled with an income tax in 1436. In 1430 Henry VI himself was taken to France with substantial reinforcements. Bedford raised more men and money when he came over to England in 1433. The English were in consequence of these efforts able to reconsolidate their military position and to restore the headquarters of their government to Paris after its temporary withdrawal to Rouen. But after this they could do no more than hold their own, and there was no question of further increasing the effort. Financial *insouciance* in the 1420s had allowed the government to accumulate a serious backlog of debt. The result was that what was achieved in 1430 and 1433 increased the backlog of bad debt, in spite of parliament's generosity. The difficulty of the situation was clearly revealed in 1434 when Gloucester declared that he would restore the situation in France, if he could be granted £48,000 to fit out a new army. In terms of military logistics, he was right about the scale of forces that he would need to regain the initiative, but as the treasurer made plain, it would not be possible, given the current load of debt, to make available half the sum.[11]

Another English reaction to the success of Joan of Arc was of a different order. 'If the king might with God's grace obtain his crown within the obeisance that he hath in his city of Paris, it were a great confirmation of obeisance of all his subjects there.'[12] So the English lords concluded after they had heard of Charles VII's coronation at Rheims. In 1430 Henry VI, a boy of eight, was taken over to France, and he was crowned the next year

[11] *P.P.C.* vol. IV, p. 214.
[12] ibid. p. 92.

with due pomp in Paris. The decision to crown Henry in France was a very natural one, aimed to show his kingship as no less divinely sanctioned than his rival's. Nevertheless, it was not in all respects a very judicious step. A coronation at Paris inevitably lacked in French eyes the lustre of a ceremony at Rheims. Henry's coronation was not, in consequence, a full answer to that of Charles, but at the same time it committed him, and Englishmen, more seriously than before to sustaining his French kingship. An uncrowned Henry might, eight or ten or fifteen years after 1431, have been able to accept terms comparable to those that the uncrowned Edward III had accepted in 1360, when he promised to renounce the style of King of France. For a crowned and anointed king to abandon a God-given charge was much harder. The reaction of the Lancastrian government to mounting military problems was here incautious, committing the king more seriously than ever to a claim that was becoming all the time harder to uphold.

The reaction of the English to the Burgundian *volte face* of 1435 was in the same spirit as their coronation of Henry. In the heat of the moment, anger at betrayal drowned all thoughts of peace. Unless the king was to be asked to strip himself of the 'name, style, title and honour of King of France', the English must throw themselves into the war effort with renewed vigour, the chancellor told parliament;[13] and the commons responded with the grant not only of a subsidy, but also of a graduated tax on incomes from land and office. Envoys were despatched to the Empire, to Gueldres, Liège and Cologne, in the hope of forming an alliance against Burgundy. The mood of belligerence was well summed up by Sir John Fastolf, in a minute of advice to the king's council in France:

> Therefore it seemeth, under the noble correction aforesaid, that the king with all his might and power should sustain that right and title that he hath in France, of which he standeth this day possessed, not taking regard for the clamour of people, nor for wasting of the country, for better is a country wasted for a time than lost: and he should not depart from his right by any treaty and wilfully disinherit himself, his heirs and all his successors, but rather should abide the adventure that God should like to send him in the defence and pursuing of his right.

As to practical steps to achieve his end, Fastolf's recipe was a powerful raid, with a scorched earth policy of deliberate destruction, into Artois and Burgundy, which would frighten the

[13] *R.P.* vol. IV, p. 481.

duke and cost little, as the men would live off the land. 'And it may be thought', he concluded, 'that the king may and ought to make all this cruel war without incurring a charge of tyranny, seeing the terms he as a good prince has offered his adversary, the which are utterly refused.'[14]

Once again, as the threat of defeat became more apparent, the Lancastrian reaction was not strategic withdrawal, but to retrench the English commitment to the war. Their reaction to the Burgundian *volte face* was a deadlier struggle on more fronts. Betrayal only made them the more determined to go it alone.

There were of course those in England who saw the necessity of seeking some sort of compromise with the adversary. Parliament, in 1431, was agreeable to the opening of negotiations with Charles; and Hugh de Lannoy, a Burgundian ambassador to England, wrote in 1433 that 'from what we can perceive they know very well that the affairs of France cannot long continue in the state in which they are now'.[15] Lannoy visited the Duke of Orleans, who was much excited about the prospect of peace, and the Earl of Suffolk, Orleans's guardian, who appeared to be pacifically inclined. Suffolk was probably already converted to the idea of a settlement, as he most certainly was after Arras. The most important man who was of the same mind was Cardinal Beaufort. It was natural that he should be alive to the advantages of a peace, since as a prince of the church he was expected by the pope to employ his influence in the church's quest for an accommodation. With his long diplomatic experience and his Flemish contacts, Beaufort had also a clearer understanding than most English councillors of the vital role of the Burgundian alliance and the likely consequences of the end of it.

Beaufort and Suffolk were men with their own political followings, and their influence was destined, in the years following Arras, to become dominant in the councils of Henry VI. Unfortunately their views, founded in real diplomatic understanding and a sense of the limits of English resources, were not the predominant ones among Englishmen. In the council they had to face the uncompromising opposition of Humphrey of Gloucester, the king's uncle, his heir apparent and the old enemy of Burgundy, who made himself the champion of war to the utterance. Gloucester was trusted and respected among the

[14] *L. and P.* vol. II, pt II, pp. [577], [579] – [581]. I have paraphrased the original at points.
[15] ibid., pt I, p. 239.

people to a greater degree than either Beaufort or Suffolk, both of whom spoiled their reputations by their too open quest for self-advancement. Gloucester, besides, was not the only peer who had no time for peace-makers; others, like York and Huntingdon, tended to see the same way. As Fastolf's memorandum clearly witnesses, the English captains and men at arms in France were whole heartedly on the side of belligerence, and they were not men whose views were to be lightly disregarded.

Because the diplomatic realism of Beaufort, Suffolk and their friends had to contend both with the opposition of powerful rivals in council and of popular nationalistic chauvinism, it proved of no advantage to England. In the years after Arras her war efforts and her diplomatic quests for settlement were bedevilled by divided and uncertain counsels. The bitter personal rivalry between the leaders of contending groups in the council, especially of Beaufort and Gloucester, introduced an element of unreason into their disagreements over policy. As the leading men of the realm became more concerned to worst one another than to save the fast deteriorating situation in France, the auguries looked always darker.

From 1435 onward, Charles VII was becoming steadily more formidable as an adversary, even though Burgundy did little to help the French war effort. He had put aside now the lethargy of the days of his sorry dauphinate. His ordinance of 1439, organizing a standing military force and the regular channelling of taxation to the war exchequer, put his army on a newly effective footing.[16] Richemont's fidelity and Burgundy's refusal to risk a confrontation with his new liege lord led to the collapse of the aristocratic rebellion of 1440 known as the *Praguerie*. Militarily, the French kept the initiative in the war for most of the time. Early in 1436 Richemont's men retook Paris. In 1438 the French were able to resume the offensive in the south-west. In 1442 Charles himself appeared in Gascony at the head of an army and Bordeaux seemed directly threatened. It was only the hardness of the winter which put an end to the campaign and saved the English there.

In the north, which was the chief theatre of the war, the English nevertheless put up a startling resistance. In 1436, when Burgundy made his one effort on the French side by moving up a Flemish army to besiege Calais, Gloucester relieved the town and

[16] On Charles VII's military reforms see G. Du Fresne de Beaucourt, *Histoire de Charles VII* vol. III (Paris, 1885), pp. 384–416.

led a glorious raid unopposed into Artois. In the same year Talbot and Lord Scales routed La Hire at Ry; in 1437 the former took Pontoise from the French and threatened Paris; in 1440 he defeated Richemont at Avranches. But the most glorious moment of all was 1441, when York took command in Normandy for the second time since Arras. He and Talbot in a brilliant campaign crossed the Oise, broke up the French siege of Pontoise, and drove Charles and Richemont helter skelter before them in their anxiety to avoid a pitched battle. Had York had more men there is no knowing what he and Talbot would have done. But their army was not half the size of the French, and when their exhausted men got back to Rouen, there were no reserves to go to succour Pontoise, and the French came back and took it.[17]

1441 showed what the English could still do; shortage of money was what held up the despatch of reinforcements which were necessary if they were to do more. In 1442 and early in 1443 the council was feverishly trying to raise it; both in Gascony and Normandy the need for troops was becoming desperate. But the crown's credit was no longer good; money was not readily forthcoming; and by March 1443 the logic of looming insolvency was all too clear: 'it is unfeasible to make two armies'.[18] There was just enough to put together one force, and its command was entrusted to John Beaufort, newly created Duke of Somerset, and the leading member of his family after the cardinal. Originally intended for Gascony, its destination was changed at a late stage, and it was decided to reinforce York in Normandy.

The fate of this expedition was the saddest fiasco for the English in this period of the war. The plan for it, which Garter King of Arms was sent to explain to York, was not unsound: Somerset should work on York's western flank, in Maine, and lure the French away from Normandy. With luck and good cooperation, the two commanders might force them to engage in adverse circumstances.[19] There was, however, a sting in the tail of Garter's message: York had asked for £20,000 for arrears of pay, but he was told he must wait, since all that was available had gone to fit out Somerset's force. Somerset had in fact not only secured priority for his army in the matter of pay, he had also obtained a commission as the king's lieutenant which made him independent of York. York had always stood closer to Gloucester than to Cardinal Beaufort; John Beaufort had used his influence

---

[17] On the 1441 campaign see Burne, *The Agincourt War*, pp. 293–302.
[18] *P.P.C.* vol. V, p. 229.
[19] ibid. pp. 259–63.

with the faction now dominant in the English council to secure
for himself the status of an independent commander. This might
not have mattered if, once in France, he had been ready to treat
York as a colleague rather than a rival. But after he had crossed
to Cherbourg he never made contact with the Norman lieutenant.
He went off on a raid of his own into Brittany (nominally at
peace with England), and afterwards wandered for four months
aimlessly in Maine. His captains pressed him to reveal his plans,
but he would not, he said, divulge his 'secret'.[20] It remained a
secret when his force disbanded and he came back to England.
York in Normandy, meanwhile, managed to hold his own, more
or less, but with no margin for counter attacks like that of 1441.

Negotiations with a view to peace were going on continuously
from the moment that the English recovered from the initial
shock of the Burgundian change of allegiance. The first notable
effort in this direction was a second major conference, on the
lines of Arras (though the manner of proceeding was different),
held near Calais in the summer of 1439.[21] The English by this
time were much more ready to make substantial concessions
than they had been in 1435. In the way of territory they would
accept the lands which the English could claim separately from
the crown of France – in effect, what they still held. Beaufort and
Kemp, who led the English negotiators, were personally prepared, it seems, to concede Henry's title of King of France, but
Gloucester's influence in the council prevented them from doing
so. So they suggested that both Henry and Charles should be
called king, referring to Carolingian precedent: 'so hath been
seen before this time that such have been kings of France or part
thereof, that have each called themselves Kings of France'.[22]
The French were not interested. As at Arras, so at Calais they
were not prepared for any settlement unless the king of England
agreed to renounce his claim to their crown, and to hold what he
should have in France as their king's liegeman.

After it had become clear that acceptable terms for a peace
were not likely to be forthcoming, the Duchess of Burgundy who
was representing the French as a mediator put forward a suggestion which, it seemed at first, might prove acceptable and which

[20] T. Basin, *Histoire de Charles VII*, ed. J. Quicherat (Paris, 1855),
vol. I, p. 150.

[21] On this conference, see C. T. Allmand, 'The Anglo-French negotiations, 1439', *B.I.H.R.* 40 (1967), pp. 1–33.

[22] *P.P.C.* vol. V, p. 361.

Beaufort was initially ready to consider. There should be a long truce, perhaps for thirty years; without prejudice Henry should cease to use the title of King of France, and Charles, without prejudice, should raise no claim to sovereignty in the lands that the English held. All those who had been put out of their property by one side or the other should be reinstated. The English studied this proposal carefully, and sent home for new powers, but in the end rejected it. They could not get round the question of face; even if Henry only dropped his title for the truce's duration 'it would discolour and put in great suspicion and doubt his title and claim . . . and all the wars and labour done in and for the said title'.[23] They were also worried about the practical implications of the restitution of French owners. It would mean putting out the king's loyal subjects, and this could not be considered unless compensation was paid, and the French king would have to pay this, or at the least the greater part of it. It was beginning to be clear that the English settlement in France was an even more serious stumbling block in the way of peace than the claim to the throne. It was not a matter which diplomatic equivocation could hope to get round.

The question of the release of the Duke of Orleans was much discussed at Calais. After the conference there had proved abortive, this seemed to Beaufort and the peace-makers on the English side to be the only further step open to them which might produce concrete results. In the council the suggestion that he should be freed was bitterly opposed by Gloucester; he refused point blank to be a party to it, and put out a broadsheet giving his reasons and denouncing the diplomatic conduct of Beaufort and Kemp in 1439. Nevertheless the arrangements went forward in the spring of 1440. It was made a formal condition of the duke's release that he was to devote all his influence to bring about a peace. Diplomatically, this promise was something of a forlorn hope. It was long odds against Orleans, after his long captivity a stranger to France and to French politics, persuading his countrymen to alter their adamant stance of 1435 and 1439. The duke, to do him justice, did his best to prosecute a pacification. He soon found his personal influence would not be enough, but he hoped he might prevail with the backing of other peers of France, and this drew him into the edge of a renewal of the *Praguerie* in 1442. Armagnac was toying with the same plan of

[23] ibid. p. 392.

rebellion, and Orleans suggested that the possibility of a marriage between Henry VI and one of the count's daughters might be explored. The proposal, which the English and Gloucester in particular were ready to take seriously, unhappily coincided with Charles's appearance in the south-west with an army in 1442 and the count, who knew how unwelcome the match would be to his king, was in no position to commit himself. Nothing definite had come of the English discussions with him, when in 1443 Orleans came up with another suggestion for a bride for King Henry that seemed more attractive in the eyes of Suffolk, Gloucester's opponent and now the dominant influence at the English court.[24]

The bride suggested this time was Margaret, the daughter of René of Anjou and Charles VII's niece by marriage. The match seemed to offer the prospect of very much more cordial relations between the French and English courts, but, as Suffolk fully realized, that was not a feature that would recommend it highly to many Englishmen. He was at first positively unwilling to lead the negotiations in the matter, fearing to be charged with being a francophile who was ready to sell out English interests to the dishonour of king and country. Nevertheless, when pressed in council he agreed to do so, knowing, no doubt, that his relations with a future queen might in due course have an important bearing on his continuing dominance at court.

What Suffolk accomplished amply justified the suspicion of those who 'sowed rumour' on him for being too francophile. Henry was affianced to Margaret, but on terms that were not satisfactory. The French remained adamant that the sovereignty over all the English possessions in France must be reserved to their king. This Suffolk could not possibly concede, and all that he gained with Margaret in May 1444 was a truce for two years, with the armies halted at the points that they had reached on the day that it was sealed. Two years of truce were not enough. Given the indebtedness of the English crown and the impoverishment of war-weary Normandy, such a brief interval could only work in the interests of Charles VII, to whom it offered a welcome opportunity to consolidate his domestic authority in France. Suffolk in fact had committed himself to a position in which he had no option but to try to make Henry's marriage the founda-

[24] For the sources of the foregoing, see L. and P. vol. II, pt II, pp. 440–51 (Gloucester's protest over Orleans's release); Foed. vol. X, pp, 782–6 (the agreement for Orleans's release); Beckynton's Correspondence (R.S.) vol. II, pp. 177–248 (account of the embassy to the Count of Armagnac).

tion of a peace, but in which it was harder than ever before to insist on honourable terms.

From 1444 until the end of the war, English policy abroad was inextricably entangled with domestic politics. This was because Suffolk's position at home depended upon the Truce of Tours opening a way to a lasting settlement with France.[25] It was with such a settlement in view that an impressive French embassy, led by the Archbishop of Rheims and Louis de Bourbon, arrived in England in the summer of 1445. Their negotiations bore no fruit, however, because as in the previous year the French were not prepared to offer terms that the English could accept. The furthest that the negotiators got was a general agreement that it was desirable to arrange a meeting of the two kings, on French soil, in the next year. How this prospect was regarded at large in England was clearly seen when, with the meeting (which never took place) in view, Henry sought from the spring parliament of 1446 a release from the obligation which his father had entered into, not to make any terms with Charles without the assent of parliament. The release was granted, but the chancellor, on behalf of all the lords, made a formal declaration that they regarded the whole summit meeting plan as Henry's private affair: 'which said motions and stirrings, only our Lord has been pleased to arouse and instigate in you, as He knows; you have not been aroused or instigated by any of the lords or any other subjects of this your realm'.[26] The lords could hardly have made it plainer that they suspected that the meeting would be a prelude to concessions of which they did not approve and for which they would not be held responsible.

What the English lords did not know in the spring of 1446 was that Henry had already agreed to one tremendous concession to the French, the surrender of Maine. In 1445 the French had several times indicated that they would regard this as an excellent

[25] For a much more favourable view than the one given here of Suffolk's actions at this stage and later, see C. L. Kingsford, 'The policy and fall of Suffolk' in his *Prejudice and Promise in fifteenth century England* (Oxford, 1925), pp. 146–76. Kingsford's extimate of Suffolk has not, on the whole, been accepted by more recent scholarship; see Storey, *H. of L.*, pp. 43–60; and R. Virgoe's two articles, 'The composition of the king's council 1437–1461', *B.I.H.R.* 43 (1970), pp. 134–60, and 'The death of William de la Pole', *B.J.R.L.* 47 (1964–5), pp. 489–502.

[26] *R.P.* vol. V, p. 102.

first step towards a settlement, and they must always have reckoned
that once Henry was married to Margaret of Anjou, he could be persuaded to return Maine to her father, its ancestral count. Margaret,
from the moment of her arrival, had been pressing Henry hard,
and on 22 December 1445, in a personal letter to Charles VII
which quoted no authority but his own, he undertook to deliver
Maine and all the towns and castles there to Charles and René,
'in good faith and on our kingly word'.[27] It is impossible to be
sure how far this letter represents an entirely personal move on
the king's part. It seems, however, very difficult to believe that
Suffolk, the 'priviest' of the king's advisers, did not at least
know what was happening. That he was anxious to be as little
involved as might be is understandable; but he seems to have
preferred to acquiesce, rather than risk his influence with the
new queen by opposing a plan that she held dear.

The decision to cede Maine was not one that could be long
kept secret. The bitter anger with which it was greeted when it
became public, both in England and among the English in
France, posed a problem for Henry's advisers. Suffolk was so
alarmed by the 'slanders that were put on him in this regard'
that he got the king to make a formal declaration in council
exonerating him from any guilt (but not from any part) in the
affair.[28] In Maine itself, the commissioners appointed to hand
over the castles, Matthew Gough and Fulk Eyton, connived with
the garrison commanders to postpone for as long as possible
fulfilment of the king's promise. To old campaigners like these it
was almost impossible to reconcile themselves to the loss, without
a blow, of lands which English arms had conquered and defended.
They stuck vainly out to the end in demanding compensation for
the departing English, of which Henry's letter unhappily had
made no mention. Le Mans was in fact only surrendered by them
in March 1448, when Charles had made it clear that he would not
renew the truce unless it was given up, and had moved up an
army to besiege the town. The English who marched out mostly
laid their humiliation at Suffolk's door.

At home, Suffolk felt it necessary to obtain other guarantees of
his security besides the king's declaration in council. The man
from whom he believed he had most to fear was Gloucester, the
old apologist of vigorous war. The spring parliament of 1447
was summoned to Bury, safely remote from the capital where the

[27] *L. and P.* vol. II, pt II, pp. [639] – [641].
[28] *Foed.* vol. XI, pp. 172-4.

duke had always been popular. Humphrey arrived late, on 18 February; he had just taken dinner in his lodgings when a deputation arrived, consisting of Buckingham, Dorset, Salisbury and Viscount Beaumont, who placed him under arrest. A charge of treason, of having planned a rising that would coincide with the parliament, had been prepared, but it was not needed. Within a week, Humphrey had died in confinement, probably of a heart attack brought on by the shock of arrest.[29] Popular surmise naturally concluded that he had been murdered. There seems no reason to doubt that Suffolk was behind the move against Gloucester, prompted by fear of the advantage that the duke might take of dismay at the cession of Maine. At all events, it was he and his clique who were popularly blamed for Humphrey's death.

At about the same time as Gloucester's arrest, steps were also taken to isolate another potentially dangerous opponent of the regime, York. York himself believed that he too had run the risk of facing criminal charges, and that Adam Moleyns, keeper of the privy seal, had bribed his soldiers to accuse him of embezzling their wages. He was recalled from Normandy in 1446 and relieved of his lieutenancy. The man who replaced him was Dorset, a Beaufort who was well in with the court (he was the brother and successor of John, Duke of Somerset, whose lieutenancy in France in 1443 had been a slight to York). York was appointed to the lieutenancy of Ireland instead, for the unusually long term of ten years. Though he did not in fact leave England until 1449, the object was clearly to get him out of the way. From Suffolk's point of view he was the most dangerous potential opponent among the peers, once Gloucester, with whom he had past associations, was dead.

It might have been expected that Suffolk, having neutralized his chief opponents, would try to make the cession of Maine the stepping stone to a final peace with France. What he did was the complete opposite. It is not easy to understand why he embarked on the reckless course that he now chose. The most reasonable explanation seems to be that he was hoping to restore his reputation with those who thought that he, with Margaret of Anjou, had sold out England and Henry VI totally to the French.

Brittany was the pivot of the new plans hatching in the mind

[29] See further K. H. Vickers, *Humphrey of Gloucester* (London, 1907), pp. 292ff.

of Henry VI's chief councillor.[30] The duchy was one with which the English had traditionally friendly relations. Though Duke Francis was a French liegeman, his youngest brother Giles had been brought up at the English court and was the king's pensioner; he was also, in the right of his fiancée, Françoise de Dinan, heir to the richest inheritance in the duchy after the duke's. Unfortunately, he was on bad terms with both Charles VII and his brother, at whose orders he was arrested and imprisoned in 1446. His imprisonment was much resented among Englishmen, especially the captains in France, and Suffolk must have known that if he could obtain his release it might do much to restore his waning prestige. He may even have dreamt of substituting Giles for his brother on the ducal throne, and of so securing a *quid pro quo* for Maine in Brittany.

The trouble was that Giles was in prison, and that any attempt to rescue him must involve armed invasion of the dominions of a French liegeman, Duke Francis, which would endanger the truce with France. Nevertheless Suffolk was not deterred. When the English evacuated Maine, the troops from the garrison were redeployed in forts on the Breton border. When the truce was renewed in 1448, Suffolk took a daring step: in the text which was handed to the French, in other respects exactly similar to that of the previous truces, the Duke of Brittany was quietly listed among the allies of England, instead of France. The French failed to notice the alteration, verbally slight but diplomatically crucial. On paper this altered by a stroke of the pen the whole legal situation. With the duke listed as an English liegeman, Charles VII had no longer any right to intervene in his relations with Henry VI, which became a domestic issue between sovereign and subject.[31] The English insisted on the point in negotiations later in 1448: 'in the said truces Brittany is included as being of the English obedience'.[32] Finally, on 24 March 1449, François de Surienne, a famous routier in the English service and a knight of the Garter, was unleashed on the duchy and took the rich town of Fougères by escalade.

The immediate reaction of Duke Francis was to demand reparations – or the disavowal of de Surienne. When both

[30] On the events described in this and the following paragraphs, see A. Bossuat, *Perrinet Gressart et François de Surienne: agents de l'Angleterre* (Paris, 1936), ch. X–XIII.

[31] See A. Bossuat, *Perrinet Gressart et François de Surienne*, p. 310, and *Foed.* vol. XI, p. 207.

[32] See A. Bossuat, *Perrinet Gressart et François de Surienne*, p. 327.

demands were ignored, he appealed for aid to his liege lord, Charles VII. There seems no doubt that Suffolk and Somerset (Dorset had now been promoted Duke of Somerset) were involved up to the hilt in François's adventure, though this was never admitted;[33] and they paid no more attention to Charles than they had to Francis, sticking doggedly to the line that Brittany was in the English obedience. In consequence, on 31 July, when three months of negotiations had got the Franco-Breton demands for indemnity nowhere, Charles VII declared himself formally discharged from the truce, and his forces began to enter Normandy.

Suffolk's diplomacy, wildly rash on the most charitable view, now rebounded with a vengeance on his country and himself. The English were quite unprepared for the French offensive. Somerset, the lieutenant in Normandy, was caught in a position in which, if he withdrew garrison troops to form a field army, he must lose more towns than he could afford to. The French were in superior numbers, operating on exterior lines, and were abundantly supplied with artillery; no town, once besieged, stood much chance of relief. First Evreux and Louviers, then Coutances and Alençon and Argentan all fell. By 16 October Charles and Dunois had appeared before Rouen, where Somerset had assembled a substantial army. He might have made a serious show of resistance if the inhabitants had not risen and opened the gates to the French. Somerset had to parley from the citadel, and agreed to withdraw his men to Caen, but Charles would only allow him to do so on condition that Arques and Caudebec were also surrendered, and that Talbot, Somerset's ablest commander, was handed over as a hostage for good faith.

The critical situation was well understood in England. What was needed was a 'great puissance'; 40,000 men would be enough,

---

[33] The connivance of Suffolk and of English councillors in the affair of Fougères seems to be clearly established by the evidence given at the inquiry into it conducted by Guillaume Juvenel des Ursins at Rouen in October 1449 (printed by J. Quicherat in T. Basin, *Histoire de Charles VII et Louis XI* vol. IV, pp. 290–347), together with that of de Surienne's own deposition, which is independent (*L. and P.* vol. I, pp. 278–98); also by a note in an account of a debate of the English council in May 1449 (A. R. Myers, 'A parliamentary debate of the fifteenth century', *B.J.R.L.* 22 (1938), p. 404). The letter from de Surienne mentioned in this debate is presumably that referred to by him, as written to Suffolk (*L. and P.* vol. I, p. 289).

John Fastolf thought (his attitude had not changed much since 1435).[34] That 'puissance' ought to have been in Normandy six months earlier, however; and when an army was at last equipped, it was not of 40,000, but of some 3000, under Sir Thomas Kyriel. Kyriel landed at Cherbourg in March 1450, and after retaking Valognes began to march to join Somerset's mainguard at Caen. When he advanced there was only the inferior force of the Count of Clermont across his path, but he moved too slowly and was caught at Formigny between the corps of Clermont and the Constable de Richemont. His army was annihilated in the one pitched battle of the whole campaign, on 15 April – all save the troop of Matthew Gough, who cut his way out and got safely to Bayeux.

This was really the end. In June the French columns closed in on Somerset at Caen. After three weeks of bombardment he came to terms again; he would quit if he was not succoured by 1 July. There was not the slightest prospect of succour coming, and the condition only served to save face. The last town remaining to the English fell less than two months after Somerset had fulfilled these terms; on 19 August John Paston's agent wrote to him from London 'this morning it was told that Cherbourg is gone, and we have now not a foot of land in Normandy'.[35]

In the next year, 1451, it was Gascony's turn. There were virtually no English forces in the duchy. In England there were plans to make an army of the men who had come back with Somerset, but in the domestic crisis that followed the Norman collapse arrangements once again proceeded too slowly. Lord Rivers (who was to command) and his men were still in England when Bordeaux surrendered to the great French armies that were closing in upon the town.

In the south-west of France there was an epilogue. An English army did arrive, in 1452, in answer to the appeals of the Bordeaux townsmen and those Gascon leaders who did not much care for their new French lords. It was some 3000 strong and was led by Talbot. On 20 October he fell on Bordeaux; the inhabitants rose in support and it was quickly his. Libourne, Castillon, Cadillac and other towns followed suit, and early in 1453 Talbot was reinforced. Even so, he had not much more than 6000 men with which to face Charles's great army. Following the strategy that had won the day in 1450 and 1451 the French advanced in separate columns, and Talbot's only hope was to divide them and

[34] L. and P. vol. II, pt. II, pp. [598ff.], [723]–[725].
[35] P.L. No. 103.

defeat them in detail. But he seems to have misunderstood the nature of Jean Bureau's position when he attacked him at Castillon; his army was destroyed and he himself left dead on the field. After Castillon, there were neither men nor a captain to oppose the French when they appeared a second time before Bordeaux. The great war of the French and the English had drawn at last to its close.

The impact of the final disaster that overtook the English cause in France between 1449 and 1453 needs to be stressed. It is often understated by British historians. Material interests as well as the royal and national reputation were at stake in the maintenance of the overseas possessions of the house of Lancaster. 'Control of Normandy', as Richmond writes, 'gave the coastal shires of England about thirty years of security: no one wanted a repetition of the enemy raids of the 1370s. It was a wise strategy that kept the war as deep into France as possible.'[36] Control of the sea, we should note also, was almost certainly one important factor in the development, on the very eve of the final collapse, of English designs on Brittany. One warmonger in 1449 was even talking of forcing the Bretons (by a victory on land) to use English ships for all their carrying trade.[37] It is true, of course, that the author of the *Libel of English Policy* (c. 1437) did attach more importance to the navy and to the defence of Calais than to the retention of Normandy, but this was not a typical view.[38] It was certainly not that of Gloucester, for whose patronage of his policies the author hoped. The more general view was that the retention of the French provinces was a vital interest, the key to the safety of the Channel coasts and of English shipping in the Channel. Thirty years of occupation had taught Englishmen to set a high value on their control of the Northern French littoral.

The most important single factor that is neglected by those who underemphasize the importance of the loss of the French provinces is the nature of the English presence there in the fifteenth century. It has been alleged that, after Henry V's reign,

[36] C. F. Richmond, in his perceptive article, 'The keeping of the seas during the Hundred Years War 1422-1440', *History* 49 (1964), pp. 283-98.

[37] *L. and P.* vol. II, pt. II, p. [724].

[38] On this poem see G. A. Holmes, 'The Libel of English policy', *E.H.R.* 76 (1961), pp. 193-216. I cannot agree that the *Libel* reflects Gloucester's attitude, as that was expressed both in 1434 (*P.P.C.* vol. IV, p. 213) and in 1439-40 (*L. and P.* vol. II, pt II, pp. 440-51).

the English governing classes were losing interest in the war and were not as ready to serve abroad as they had been.[39] There is some evidence to support the latter point, but if fewer men who held important local offices or represented their shires in parliament served in this period than before, there is a ready explanation. The English involvement in France in this period was different from what it had been in the days of Edward III, or even at the time of Agincourt; the forces that fought abroad in Henry VI's time were not, for the most part, expeditionary armies, but a standing garrison. The Englishmen whose names are so familiar in the annals of the war – men like John Fastolf, William Oldhall, William Glasdale and Matthew Gough – made their careers in France, and not in England, for the time being at least. Permanent service, as part of a standing garrison, was not the kind of service that it was either easy or appropriate for noblemen or the heads of county families to discharge in person. Significantly, however, in the 1430s and 1440s the aristocracy continued to monopolize the prestigious and potentially rewarding high commands (there was even rivalry over them, as York's relations with the two Beauforts, John and Edmund of Somerset, remind us). There was not so much a loss of interest in the maintenance of the war in this period, but modification and alteration of the interests involved in its maintenance.

Soldiers apart, there were a considerable number of Englishmen who had settled in Lancastrian France, and had acquired property there, or trading interests, or administrative office. Together with the soldiers, these people constituted what was virtually a colonial presence. Twenty years after the English defeat (in 1472) the memory of the opportunities which the occupation of Normandy had offered to the enterprising was still green: 'many gentlemen, as well younger brothers as others, might there be worshipfully rewarded, and inhabit that land for the sure guard of the same'.[40] In the late 1440s the interests and opportunities of the war in Normandy and of Englishmen there were not a memory; they were a living concern, which their kinsmen at home could not ignore. Besides, these Englishmen in Normandy were men engaged in the defence of interests which those kinsmen at home regarded as important.

There was a great deal of anxiety about the men in France at

[39] The most trenchant statement of this case in recent years has been that of M. R. Powicke, 'Lancastrian captains' in *Essays in Medieval History presented to B. Wilkinson*, pp. 371–82.

[40] *Lit. Cant.* (R.S.) vol. III, p. 282.

the very end of the war. 'Consider', says a memoir of the year 1449, 'what inhumanity it would be, what lack of charity to one's neighbour, to desert now those gentlemen, and common people too, who for these thirty two years have borne such burdens in the king's cause.'[41] And think too, its author adds, of the problem that they may pose if they come back to England, where there is no occupation for them. This was no idle aside: 'and then', Bale wrote in his chronicle under the year 1450, 'were all the Englishmen driven and sent out from France, Normandy, Anjou, and came into this land in great misery and poverty by many companies and fellowships, and went into [the] several places of the land to be inherited with and live upon the alms of the people. But many of them drew to theft and misrule, and noyed sore the commonalty of this land spiritual and temporal, and many of them afterward hanged.'[42] The distress of the returning soldiery was visible proof of the damage that defeat abroad had inflicted on Englishmen; it was also an ugly reminder that England's enemies were now just across the Channel, that she was destitute of allies, that the harbours of Normandy, and, still more important from a commercial point of view, of Gascony, were not safe for her ships and merchants any longer; and finally, that the nation had been humiliated.

The psychological effect of the collapse overseas was naturally very great. For more than 100 years Englishmen had been fed sedulously with propaganda about their kings' rights in France; now all the blood and treasure that had been spent in pursuit of those rights was revealed to have been wasted. The fact that, at the last, all was over so quickly heightened the sense of shock, anger and bewilderment among the people, as they woke to the fact that a tremendous defeat had dishonoured the crown and the whole land. When Cade's rebels marched on London in the summer of 1450, they were demanding the blood of the traitors, by whom 'the realm of France was lost, Normandy, Gascony, Guienne and Anjou, and our true lords, knights and esquires, and many a good yeoman . . . lost and sold ere they went'.[43] Suffolk had then already been impeached by the commons, and murdered on his way abroad into exile. His friend Adam Moleyns had been lynched by mutinous soldiers at Portsmouth. The confusion had begun, which a few years later would plunge

[41] *L. and P.* vol. II, pt II, p. [726].
[42] *Six Town Chronicles*, ed. R. Flenley (Oxford, 1911), p. 128.
[43] *Three Fifteenth Century Chronicles*, ed. J. Gairdner (Camden Soc., 1880), p. 97.

the country into civil war. The issues that were at stake in the Wars of the Roses were, it is true, embedded in the domestic history of England in Henry VI's reign, which we must presently examine, and had only indirect connexions with the events of the French war. If, however, Henry VI's councillors (and above all, Suffolk and Somerset) had not totally discredited the king's government by their mismanagement of his affairs in France, the domestic strains, which culminated in civil war, might never have become so acute that only arms could resolve them.

17

Henry VI and England
1422–1450

The opening of the long minority of Henry VI in England was not very auspicious. At the very outset there was disagreement as to how the country should be governed. The Duke of Gloucester, who had been acting as guardian of the realm in Henry V's absence, claimed the office of protector of the realm as of right, on grounds of kinship with the late king, and of a clearly worded codicil in Henry V's last will (which unfortunately does not survive). His elder brother John, the Duke of Bedford, also claimed the office on the ground that 'by the laws and ancient custom of the realm', it fell to him as the next in line to the throne after Henry VI.[1] The magnates in England who met in council on 28 September took a different view: that whatever arrangements were made should be approved in parliament, to summon which writs were accordingly sent out in the name of king and council. Gloucester received a summons to this parliament (he had never had one when he was guardian for Henry V), and at a council meeting on 5 November, four days before it met, he was commissioned to open, conduct and dissolve parliament 'with the assent of the council'.[2] He objected that this commission was in prejudice of his status as the late king's will defined it, and claimed that he should not be fettered by the assent of the lords of the council. The commission passed the great seal nevertheless, on 6 November.

When parliament met on 9 November the commons asked 'who should have the governance of the realm under our sovereign lord the king by his high authority?'[3] The question took

[1] J. Delpit, *Documents Français qui se trouvent en Angleterre* (Paris, 1847) vol. I, p. 233.

[2] *Foed.* vol. X, pp. 257–8.

[3] S. B. Chrimes, 'The pretensions of the Duke of Gloucester in 1422', *E.H.R.* 45 (1930), p. 102.

time to settle; though Bedford was out of the country, shoulder-
ing his new burden as regent of France and could not press his
claim to the protectorship, Gloucester could and did. The lords
of the council stood firm, however. With the advice of the
crown's lawyers behind them, they rejected the codicil of
Henry V's will; the dead king could not, by will or otherwise
'without the assent of the three estates commit or grant to any
person the rule or governance of this land longer than he lived'.[4]
They upheld the precedent of 1377, when Richard II's minority
began, as showing that at the accession of a minor authority
must rest with the peers as councillors until new arrangements
were made in parliament. Gloucester had to give way, and on
5 December it was decided by the assent of both lords and
commons that Bedford should be protector whenever he was in
the kingdom, and that when he was overseas Gloucester should
be.[5] On 9 December the council over which the protector should
preside was named in parliament. One of the conditions on which
this council took office was that wardships, marriages, escheats
and such great patronage should be in its disposal, as also the
appointment of sheriffs, justices of the peace, escheators and
customs officials. Thus only the lesser patronage of the crown
was left in the free disposal of the protector.[6]

These arrangements had some unsatisfactory features. Of one
something has been said already, that there was absolutely no
formal provision for liaison between the English council and the
regent of France. The provision that when Bedford was in

[4] *R.P.* vol. IV, p. 326.

[5] *R.P.* vol. IV, pp. 174–5. The main sources for the debate over the
protectorship in 1422 are (i) Gloucester's statement, put forward in the
parliament of that year, printed by S. B. Chrimes, 'The pretensions of
the Duke of Gloucester in 1422', pp. 101–3; and (ii) the statement of the
Lords, giving their version of what had happened in 1422 in reply to
Gloucester's request for definition of his powers in 1428, *R.P.* vol. IV,
pp. 326–7. The matter is examined authoritatively by J. S. Roskell,
'The office and dignity of Protector of England, with special reference
to its origins', *E.H.R.* 68 (1953), pp. 193–233.

[6] *R.P.* vol. IV, pp. 175–6. On this council and its appointment see
J. S. Roskell, *The Commons in the Parliament of 1422* (Manchester, 1954),
pp. 105–9. The membership comprised the officers of state, the dukes of
Gloucester and Exeter, five prelates (Canterbury, London, Winchester,
Norwich, Worcester); five earls (March, Warwick, Marshal, Northum-
berland, Westmorland); and five barons and knights (FitzHugh,
Cromwell, Sir Walter Hungerford, Sir John Tiptoft, Sir Walter
Beauchamp).

England Gloucester must automatically give way to him was not calculated to promote harmony between the brothers. The fact that, at the very beginning of the minority, the peers of the council and the man who as protector was to preside over them had already found themselves at loggerheads boded ill for the future. A schedule of provisions concerning the council approved in parliament in 1423 suggests that further difficulties were appearing early. The first of them declared that 'neither my lord of Gloucester, nor no other man of the council, in no suit that shall be made to them, shall no favour grant, neither in bills [petitioning] for right, or office, or benefice, [whose decision] belongs to the council; but shall only answer that the bill shall be seen by all the council, and the party suing so have answer'. Still more disturbing was the sixth provision: 'forasmuch as it is too great a shame that unto strange countries our sovereign lord shall write his letters by the advice of his council . . . and singular persons of the council to write the contrary: that it be ordained that no man of the council presume to do it, on pain of shame and reproof'.[7] What precisely was in the mind of those who drew up this provision is not explicit, but almost certainly they were moved by Gloucester's determination to pursue his wife Jacqueline's rights in Hainault. This he could not do without straining the Anglo-Burgundian alliance, and we know that this danger was brought to the attention of the English council.[8]

One of the men who probably drew the council's attention to the dangers implicit in Gloucester's continental ambitions was Henry Beaufort. According to Hardyng, he was also prominent among those who in 1422 resisted Gloucester's claim to a virtual regency.[9] Between these two men a feud was developing which would shortly come out into the open, and which rumbled on, distracting and sometimes dominating the conciliar government of the kingdom, through the remainder of Henry's minority and beyond it. In order to appreciate the significance of the great quarrel, a brief examination of the careers and influence of the two protagonists becomes necessary.

Duke Humphrey is deservedly remembered by posterity as the great patron of scholars and writers, both Italian and English, whose influence did much to introduce Englishmen to the

[7] *R.P.* vol. IV, p. 201.

[8] *L. and P.* vol. II, pt. II, pp. 386–7: see also K. H. Vickers, *Humphrey of Gloucester* (London, 1907), pp. 130–1.

[9] J. Hardyng, *Chronicle*, ed. H. Ellis (London, 1812), p. 391.

thought and scholarship of the early Renaissance. But it was not until the 1430s that Humphrey began to make his mark as a patron and collector of manuscripts; in the early 1420s his experience was largely military. He had been created Duke of Gloucester and Earl of Pembroke in 1414, when he was twenty-three. At Agincourt he distinguished himself and was wounded; and when the expedition returned to England he was rewarded with grants from the forfeited estates of the Earl of Cambridge and with the office of Warden of the Cinque Ports. He served in France from 1417 to 1419, again with distinction, and commanded at the siege of Cherbourg. From the last day of 1419 until Henry's return to England in 1421, and again from May 1422 until his brother's death, he was 'keeper' or 'guardian' of England. His government was as far as we know entirely creditable, and established a firm place for him in the affections of the citizens of London, an important sector of opinion. After Henry's death, though, as we have seen, he had to accept unwelcome limits on his powers as protector, his opportunities for pursuing independent and personal policies were greatly extended. He was powerful enough to engineer the quasi-banishment of the Earl of March, one of his most significant potential opponents, to Ireland. When March died in 1425, leaving as his heir a minor, the young Duke of York, he obtained the wardship of his estates, which further strengthened his territorial influence. Early in 1423 he married Jacqueline Countess of Hainault, although she was not formally divorced from John of Brabant (she and Gloucester held that this first marriage was invalid). The parliament of 1423 recognized them as wed, and Gloucester was able, with his large resources, to raise an army in England for a bid to recover for her from John of Brabant the government of her county, with himself as consort. He sailed from England on 16 October 1424.

When Gloucester left England leadership in the council fell naturally to Henry Beaufort, Bishop of Winchester and chancellor of the realm. The second of John of Gaunt's sons by Catherine Swynford and the great uncle of the king, Henry had a long career in the church and in politics behind him. He had been chancellor of Oxford University in 1397; in 1398 he was consecrated Bishop of Lincoln, and in 1404 was translated to Winchester. The great estates of this rich diocese secured him a princely income, and his exports of wool brought him into contact with the merchant aristocracy. He was prominent in the council over which Henry V, when Prince of Wales, presided between 1409 and 1411, and with his accession as king he became chancellor. He was then already a quite substantial government creditor, and in the course of Henry V's reign he was to lend the crown over £35,000. The loan that he made in June 1417, of £14,000, was much his largest to date, however, and was made in rather special circumstances. Beaufort was at the point of resigning the chancellorship to embark on a pilgrimage to Jerusalem, which took him by Constance at just the crucial moment when the fathers of the Council were about to elect a new pope. It looks as if he had bought the freedom to play a hand for himself in the international politics of the church. At Constance he was able to be instrumental in bringing about the smooth and undisputed election of Martin V, and his reward was a red hat and a legatine commission to England. This commission was obtained in breach of praemunire and, as Archbishop Chichele pointed out, of the customs of the English church. Henry V made it clear to Beaufort that if he tried to implement his bulls it would mean the loss of the temporalities of his see and the forfeiture of his goods. It took the bishop two years to make up his mind to settle definitely for his English wealth in preference to an international ecclesiastical career; and the latter ambition was, as events proved, only postponed.[10] The price of his restoration to royal favour was another enormous loan to the crown (£17,666), and a postponement of repayment of his previous one. These loans were secured on the customs; after Henry V's death Beaufort foreclosed, and was permitted to appoint one collector in every port in the country. He had established what McFarlane called 'the beginnings of a stranglehold over the royal finances'.[11]

Both Gloucester and Beaufort sought to put their dominant position in England when Henry VI's minority began to the service of their private ambitions. Their rivalry was not only personal, moreover. When Martin V made Beaufort a cardinal he

[10] See further K. B. McFarlane, 'Henry V, Bishop Beaufort, and the red hat', *E.H.R.* 60 (1945), pp. 316–48.

[11] See K. B. McFarlane, 'At the deathbed of Cardinal Beaufort' in *Studies in Medieval History presented to F. M. Powicke*, ed. R. W. Hunt, W. A. Pantin and R. W. Southern (Oxford, 1948), pp. 405–28. In this article, and in his 'Loans to the Lancastrian kings', *C.H.J.* 9 (1947), pp. 51–68, McFarlane argued that Beaufort charged concealed interest on his loans. G. L. Harriss has recently shown that this is most unlikely: see his 'Cardinal Beaufort – patriot or usurer?', *T.R.H.S.* 5th ser., 20 (1970), pp. 129–48.

was hoping that he would be the means of restoring 'the pristine liberty of the church' in England through the repeal of the offensive Statutes of Provisors and Praemunire. With his Flemish mercantile contacts, Beaufort also understood better than most how vital the Anglo-Burgundian alliance was to maintaining the settlement that Henry V had achieved at Troyes. Gloucester's ambitions in Hainault cut clean across that alliance, since Duke Philip of Burgundy claimed that John of Brabant and Jacqueline were lawfully married and that he was their heir. Gloucester also, probably quite genuinely, sympathized with the English protectionist instinct which was behind the reduction, approved in 1422, of the customs for native merchants, aliens still paying at the higher rate; this was contrary to the interests of Beaufort's Flemish friends and favourable to Gloucester's London contacts. As protector, Gloucester was inevitably involved in the enforcement of the anti-papal statutes, which many saw as the bulwark of English ecclesiastical liberties and interests, and he soon learned to pose as their champion. Though Gloucester's political sympathies were less coherent and more insular than Beaufort's, they were at once more popular in England and quite incompatible with the bishop's.

Duke Humphrey cannot have been sorry to witness an outbreak of anti-Flemish agitation in London in 1424, just before he sailed for Hainault. Bills against the Flemings were circulated: 'some were set upon the Bishop's gate of Winchester, and some on other bishops' gates', and Beaufort, so he claimed afterwards, began to fear a serious insurrection 'in destruction of divers estates of England'.[12] Once Gloucester was fully occupied abroad, he placed Richard Woodeville in charge of the Tower with a strong company and instructions not to admit anyone without orders from the council. He also had a number of London citizens arrested. After Gloucester's return in the spring of 1425 the citizens naturally turned to him as their protector; people began to get excited and Woodeville apparently refused Humphrey admission to the Tower, acting on Beaufort's orders as chancellor. Through the summer matters rose towards a climax, which came at the end of September. Beaufort had assembled a force of retainers from as far afield as Lancashire and Cheshire at Southwark, and prepared for a surprise *coup* in the city, intending further, Gloucester alleged, to seize the

[12] *Great Chronicle of London*, ed. A. H. Thomas and I. D. Thornley (London, 1938), p. 136.

young king at Eltham. The *coup* failed, because the mayor raised the city in the protector's interest. There was an ugly skirmish at London Bridge on 30 October before a truce was arranged by Archbishop Chichele of Canterbury. Next day Beaufort decided that Bedford must be called in if a showdown was to be avoided. 'As you desire the welfare of the king our sovereign lord and of his realms of England and France, and your own weal and ours also, haste you hither', he wrote, 'for by my troth if you tarry we shall put this land in adventure with a battlefield. Such a brother as you have here!'[13]

It was high time that someone took charge of events. There had been other ominous signs in 1425 besides the skirmish at London Bridge; there had been 'much altercation' between lords and commons over tonnage and poundage in the summer parliament, which witnessed also a fierce dispute over precedence between the Earl Marshal and the Earl of Warwick: 'there was much trouble and heavyness in the land'.[14] When Bedford arrived his efforts to reconcile his brother and Beaufort at first met with little success; Gloucester was not prepared to make any move towards peace before parliament met, hoping no doubt that his cause would find favour with the commons. The estates were summoned to Leicester, so as to be out of range of London violence, and after a good deal of argument Beaufort and Gloucester were persuaded to accept arbitration. A committee of peers decreed that they should shake hands and admit each other to peace according to a prescribed form of words, promising to show good lordship and favour to one another's men. Beaufort's set speech was longer than Gloucester's, virtually a public explanation of his conduct. He had the worst of it and resigned the great seal on 13 March 1426 in favour of Bishop Kemp of London, preparatory to going abroad.

As long as Bedford remained in the country there was no further threat to the tranquillity of the government, and when he left he took Beaufort with him. They parted at Calais in the spring of 1427, and Beaufort, having received at last his cardinal's hat at the duke's own hands, proceeded for Bohemia as legate of the Roman *Curia*. Before Bedford left England, the lords of the council had taken the precaution of obtaining from him a confirmation that he accepted their interpretation of the proper relations of the protector and the council. They had clearly come

[13] ibid. p. 137.
[14] See J. S. Roskell, *The Commons and their Speakers in English Parliaments, 1376–1523* (Manchester, 1965), p. 186.

to regard Gloucester with some distrust. A loan was made to him for a further expedition to Hainault, but it never sailed, because pressure from Bedford prevented it. Soon Gloucester began to lose interest in the affair; he accepted Martin V's decision upholding the marriage of Jacqueline and John of Brabant, and left his ex-wife abroad friendless. He meanwhile regularized his relations with her former lady-in-waiting, Eleanor Cobham. This cost him popularity with the commons; his attempt to obtain a redefinition of his powers as protector in the spring parliament of 1428 was successfully resisted by the lords.

There was trouble again later in 1428, when Beaufort returned once more to England, armed now with a legatine commission to preach the crusade against the Hussites. Initially Gloucester had conciliar support in protesting against Beaufort's using a legatine commission in England without royal licence, and in questioning whether, now that he was a cardinal, custom could permit him to continue as Bishop of Winchester. But in 1429 the military situation began to look very ugly after the relief of Orleans, and Beaufort was recalled to the council. He and the men whom he had in the end been allowed to recruit for his crusade had to be diverted to serve in France.

In 1431 Gloucester returned to the attack. Henry VI had been taken to France to be crowned and he was now in the king's absence regent, not protector (which office had lapsed in 1429 after the English coronation). In November, under his instructions, the law officers presented a petition demanding that Beaufort be deprived of the see of Winchester on the ground that it was legally incompatible with his cardinalate. The petition was heard before the great council, and writs under the Statute of Praemunire were subsequently made out against the bishop. At the same council Gloucester's salary as chief councillor was increased to 5000 marks per annum, in spite of sharp opposition from Chancellor Kemp.

Affairs were once again moving towards crisis. The charges against Beaufort were postponed until he should be in England to answer them (in the event until the May parliament of 1432), but as soon as he landed from France certain jewels and plate that the bishop was holding as security for his loans were seized, probably on Gloucester's orders. About the same time a number of changes were made in the personnel of the court and the council. Kemp and Lord Hungerford left the chancery and treasury respectively and were replaced by Bishop Stafford and

Lord Scrope; Lords Cromwell and Tiptoft were replaced as chamberlain and steward of the household by Sir William Phelip and Sir Robert Babthorpe. Cromwell was later to complain that his dismissal was improper. It looks suspiciously as if Gloucester was trying to get awkward individuals out of office in preparation for a showdown with his rival.

When parliament did meet Beaufort took the initiative by declaring his readiness to answer the charges of treason, which he had heard, so he said, that men were making against him. No one charged him with treason, and the commons petitioned that, in view of 'the many great and notable services that he had done', he should be free of any charge under the anti-papal statutes.[15] He was in consequence formally authorized at last to hold his English preferment notwithstanding the cardinalate, but he had to pay for the privilege. He agreed to postpone repayment of 13,000 marks of old loans, to lend £6000, and to deposit a further £6000, which would be treated as a loan if on inquiry it proved that the jewels that had been seized from him earlier really were held as securities. Once again he had bought himself out of a difficult situation.

In the year 1433 Bedford was again in England. On his return Lord Cromwell returned to influence and replaced Scrope as treasurer, and Suffolk replaced Babthorpe as steward of the household. It would probably be wrong to read much partisan significance into these changes. What is significant is the evidence of real anxiety about the effect on government of factious rivalry among the great, and the attitude of the commons towards Bedford who in their eyes stood above the party strife. In the second session of the parliament of 1433 the speaker came forward with a petition to the duke personally. 'The said commons consider', he declared, 'that the presence and being of my said Lord of Bedford in this land, since his coming into it, hath been full fruitful, and that the restful rule and governance of this land hath greatly increased and grown thereby.'[16] In consequence the commons prayed that the duke would not go back to France but would remain with them. Bedford, in reply, made it clear that he could not consent unless he was given, as chief councillor, a really free discretion in government, such as none had enjoyed since 1422, especially in the matter of patronage. All that he asked was granted, without cavil. This shows how deep distrust

[15] *R.P.* vol. IV, p. 392.
[16] ibid. p. 423.

of divided counsels had bitten, for it was the abandonment of a
ten year effort to keep limits upon the influence of Henry VI's
uncles, Bedford as well as Gloucester.

As events turned out, Bedford was not able to stay in England
after all. Affairs in France were in too parlous a state. On 14
June 1434 he told the council that he must leave, and made some
suggestions for raising finance to strengthen his forces as far as
was feasible: 'For God is my witness, how great a pity it were ...
to lose that noble realm for the getting and keeping of which my
lord that was your father, to whose soul God do mercy, and other
many noble princes, lords, knights and squires and other persons in full great number have paid their lives.'[17] On 1 July he
left England for the last time; just over a year later, in September 1435, he was dead. At the time the great congress at Arras,
which proved a decisive turning point in English fortunes overseas, was about to close. A year after that, Henry's long minority
came to an end, so that there was something of a turning point
in domestic history too. Before we follow further the course of
political events, it will be useful to look back over conditions in
England in the minority; to see what substance there was behind
the alarm at deteriorating order at home which led the commons
to press Bedford to stay, and to examine the financial situation
which by 1435 was beginning to look critical.

The cost of maintaining the war in France in the 1430s was not in
principle beyond the resources of the crown and the taxpayers,
for the time being at least. Henry V's reign had shown that it
was possible to maintain military expenditure at a considerably
higher level than that of this period, without the crown's debts
getting out of hand. The difficulty of doing so had, however,
since then become greater than it ought to have been, on account
of the financial insouciance of the early years of Henry VI's
minority. Besides, since the commons did not have the same
confidence in the government of the 1430s as they had had in
Henry V, they were not prepared to respond to its demands with
the same generosity.

Englishmen had always assumed that, once a notable part of
France was conquered, their king's French subjects ought to
shoulder the fiscal burden of the war. There was in consequence
no grant of extraordinary taxation after Henry V's death until
1428. In the autumn parliament of 1422 the customs were reduced for English exporters. King Henry's death also gave the

[17] *P.P.C.* vol. IV, p. 225.

high born and influential among the crown's creditors their chance to insist on payment of long standing debts, and to gain other financial advantages too. Thus we find that Sir John Cornwall made sure of the compensation due to him for his prisoner the Count of Vendosme, taken at Agincourt, whom he had surrendered to the crown; that the Earl of Huntingdon was promised payment of arrears of wages of war and obtained a grant towards his ransom (he had been taken by the French at Baugé); that Bishop Beaufort secured his hold on the customs, so that by 1425 virtually all his loans to date had been repaid. Gloucester was able to make sure of a princely salary of 8000 marks as protector. Nearly all the new councillors in fact used their position to their own benefit in one way or another (some petitions for favour were endorsed by the very men who presented them).[18] The overall consequence was that through the early years of the reign, when there were no subsidies granted in parliament and no unduly heavy expenses to meet, the issues of the exchequer nevertheless regularly exceeded its net receipts. The failure to balance the account was not dramatic, averaging out at about £1600 a year; but the book-keeping totals are deceptive, concealing the true situation. By 1430, when it became clear that there would again have to be major expenditure on maintaining the war abroad, the exchequer was already carrying an uncomfortable load of accumulated debt; by 1433 the debts for which provision needed to be made had reached the frightening total of £164,815.[19]

In the new military situation after Joan's relief of Orleans the commons were in the first instance generous. The parliament of 1429 granted a double subsidy, that of 1430 a subsidy and a third, together with a graduated land tax on all estates of a whole knight's fee or more, or worth upwards of £20 per annum. But the parliament of 1432 granted only one half subsidy, and quashed the land tax (which, as the commons rightly complained, was too complicated). In 1433 the commons granted a whole subsidy but reduced the total assessment by £4000 'to the release and discharge of the poor towns, cities and boroughs, desolate, wasted or destroyed, or else to the said tax greatly overcharged'.[20] This

[18] See J. F. Baldwin, *The King's Council* (Oxford, 1913), p. 179.

[19] I have relied here on J. L. Kirby's careful and very detailed study 'The issues of the Lancastrian exchequer and Lord Cromwell's estimates of 1433', *B.I.H.R.* 24 (1951), pp. 121–51; but I am by no means sure that I have understood all his complicated calculations correctly.

[20] *R.P.* vol. IV, p. 425.

reduction became a regular feature of subsequent grants. The result of this growing niggardliness might not have been so very serious if, in 1429, the exchequer had not been carrying an accumulated deficit. But that was what it was doing, and there now arose heavy expenses quite apart from military expenditure, in connexion with the king's two coronations and with renewed diplomatic activity.

When he was appointed treasurer in 1433, Lord Cromwell decided on a full-scale investigation of the financial situation. The picture that he had to paint in the parliament of October was a gloomy one. His figures showed a deficit of £21,000 for the current year; over and above this there was a total of £164,800 of bad debt outstanding at the exchequer which had to be paid off in instalments, term by term. One major trouble, clearly, was that the king's ordinary revenues were overburdened with fees and annuities: 'now daily many warrants come to me of payments, as well for lords as for other divers persons, of much more than all your revenues would come to . . . the which warrants if I should pay them, your household, chamber and wardrobe, and your works should be unserved and unpaid: and if I pay them not, I run in great indignation of my lords, and great slander, noise and spite of all your people that bring me any warrants'.[21] Cromwell, a treasurer making a new start, wanted to be free of blame for past extravagance, and may have exaggerated a little. The real trouble was not the annual account, but the backlog of debt; until that had been cleared, even when war expenditure was discounted, something like an annual subsidy was needed if the government was to pay its way. This meant that even if the commons were to be as generous as they had been in the middle years of Henry V's reign, the council could not consider expenditure on the war on a scale approaching that of, say, 1417 and 1418. In fact, the commons were not inclined to be anything like as generous.

The last sentence in the terms of the commons grant of 1429 reveals one of the major reasons for this lack of confidence in Henry VI's minority government. 'We trust fully', they declared, 'that through such comfort as we have conceived by our lords on your behalf, that we shall have knowledge of good and sad government in every part of this your said realm, ere you dissolve this your present parliament.'[22] Ever since Henry V's

[21] ibid. p. 439: and see further Kirby, 'The issues of the Lancastrian exchequer'.

[22] R.P. vol. IV, p. 337.

death order had been deteriorating; now lack of governance was undermining confidence between governors and governed, in just the same way as it had in the reign of Henry IV. In this same parliament there was a strong plea from the commons for the better enforcement of the statute against liveries. In new articles governing the conduct of conciliar business, a special commitment was imposed on councillors to refrain from maintenance at law, 'by word, by message, or by writing to officer, judge, jury or party, or by gift of clothing or livery'. In 1433 the commons asked that this article should be read again, and an oath taken to observe it not only by the dukes of Bedford and Gloucester, and the other lords of the council, but by all the prelates, peers and magnates present individually.[23] The commons' request to Bedford to remain in England, because his presence was 'the greatest surety that could be thought' of the 'restful government' of the land, was made in the same session, and shows how serious was the loss of confidence in the continual council and its capacity to govern.

The complaints of the commons were amply justified. We have seen earlier how the quarrel of Beaufort and Gloucester brought the country to a point where civil war seemed to threaten in 1425; it reached another climax in 1432, when violence again seemed likely. The example of the two leading councillors was inevitably infectious. In 1428, a dispute between the Duke of Norfolk and the Earl of Huntingdon caused serious rioting in East Anglia, and very nearly developed into a private war. They were at loggerheads again in 1430, and now the Earl of Warwick had become involved as well. Norfolk and Huntingdon significantly were among a group of peers who were warned not to bring more than their normal retinues when they attended the parliament of 1432, along with Salisbury, Stafford and the disgruntled Cromwell. It was naturally difficult for the council to control these quarrels among the great; their protagonists were its members. This was what made them so dangerous. From the households of the great, moreover, disorder naturally radiated outwards. The consequence was that disturbances quite unrelated to the quarrels of the magnates, such as the abortive Lollard rising of 1431, caused more alarm than was really justified: people saw in them further signs of the inability of the council to maintain order, and feared for the whole social fabric.

At this point it is very important to stress that we are talking about fears rather than facts, about a decline in public confidence

[23] *P.P.C.* vol. IV, p. 64, and *R.P.* vol. IV, pp. 421-2.

and not a breakdown of government. There are heavy charges that stand out against the council that sought to govern England in Henry VI's minority, of insouciance, of self-seeking, of the inability of the members to obey the rules that they prescribed for themselves. It was with the council of this period in mind that Fortescue was later to write:

> The king's council was wont to be chosen of the great princes, and of the greatest lords of the land, both spiritual and temporal . . . which lords and officers had near hand as many matters of their own to be treated in council as had the king. Wherethrough, when they came together they were so occupied with their own matters that they attended but little, and other whiles nothing, to the king's matters. . . . Then could no matter treated in the council be kept privy. For the lords oftentimes told their own counsellors and servants, that had sued to them for those matters, how they had sped in them and who was against them.[24]

Fortescue's words have been widely remembered. It is therefore the more important to remind ourselves that the record of the minority council was by no means wholly discreditable. In the early years its members no doubt did spend too much time on private business. But when things became harder, from 1429 on, the records show them devoting themselves commendably to effort in the national cause, investigating the crown's finances and seeking remedies for their inadequacy, raising loans and reinforcements for the field in France, planning diplomatic overtures and looking for avenues towards an honourable settlement with the enemy. In the deteriorating military situation most of the great showed themselves ready to make personal sacrifices; Beaufort to stretch his resources to make further loans, Bedford and Gloucester to accept substantial cuts in the chief councillors' salary. The council did not solve any problems, it is true, but it was not for lack of trying.

What perhaps stands most of all to the credit of the councillors of the minority is that in spite of all their difficulties they managed to continue to work together. They refused to acknowledge Gloucester's right to a regency in 1422, but they cooperated with him first as protector and then as chief councillor. They would not let the pope or Beaufort browbeat the Archbishop of Canterbury; equally, they would not tolerate Beaufort's permanent exclusion from the council. Bedford and the council imposed peace between Gloucester and Beaufort; Gloucester and the

[24] J. Fortescue, *The Governance of England*, ed. C. Plummer (Oxford, 1885), p. 145.

council imposed peace between Norfolk and Huntingdon. There were times when it looked as if control was on the point of breaking down, but it never did; and the credit must go to the sense of responsibility, collective and individual, of council and councillors.

After 1435 there was a gradual quickening of the tempo of English domestic politics. Party strife among the great became sharper, the signs clearer of declining order in the country and of declining trust in the king's government. The change was partly related to the alteration in the English position abroad after the collapse of the Anglo-Burgundian alliance. It was also partly consequent on the king's coming of age. A third factor was the death of Bedford, the man who had been most successful in keeping the rivals of the council table at arm's length from one another, and the rise to prominence in politics of new figures, notably William de la Pole, the Earl of Suffolk.

The failure of the Arras peace congress had important domestic consequences, because it sharpened divisions of policy within the council over the conduct of the war. The need to achieve some sort of settlement with the French was now apparent to a number of councillors, notably Beaufort and Suffolk. Gloucester, on the other hand, had never appreciated the importance of the Anglo-Burgundian alliance, and stood forward as the champion of vigorous military action. He was now easily the most prominent aristocrat among those who had fought in the campaigns of Henry V, in which he had distinguished himself more often than either of his brothers, Bedford or Clarence. He was the natural person for the survivors of those great days to look to, in their disappointment at recent setbacks and their confidence that reinforcements and vigorous campaigning could still restore the situation. A political alignment began thus to develop between Gloucester and the young Duke Richard of York, who was lieutenant in Normandy from 1436 to 1438 and again from 1440 on, and whose personal retinue was attracting a number of veteran and successful soldiers, as John Popham, Andrew Ogard, Nicholas Molyneux and William Oldhall.

When parliament met early in 1437 the commons went out of their way to commend the noble service that Gloucester had performed at the relief of Calais the year before. Later in the year, when the king appointed a council to advise him in his majority, Gloucester's was the first name on the list, with a salary of 2000 marks per annum. In 1439 the peace conference at Calais brought him to the fore in the council. By his own account it was largely owing to his intervention that the English were adamant in refusing to waive the title of King of France: 'I answered and said I would never agree me thereto, and that I would rather die.'[25] After Calais, the next move of the peace-makers was to arrange the release of the Duke of Orleans. This brought about a showdown over policy between Gloucester and the king's other advisers.

When Humphrey found that he could not successfully hold out in council against the duke's release, he made his position clear publicly in two documents. One was a formal protest which at his request was enrolled as a record. This was in form a sober and quite accurate critique of the policy decision, which, Gloucester argued, would be interpreted abroad as a symptom of English weakness.[26] The other document was of a very different order: a political manifesto which publicly demanded the dismissal from the council of Beaufort and Kemp (who had also received a cardinal's hat and kept his English see), and denounced to the people both their policy and their political honesty.[27]

Beaufort, naturally, was the chief target. The whole story of his offences against the provisors legislation was rehearsed again, together with all the objections to the introduction of a red hat into the kingdom. His loans, Gloucester alleged, had always been to his own profit, and to the king's ultimate loss; he had established a stranglehold on the customs; he had foreclosed fraudulently to secure crown jewels that he held in pledge; and was now beginning to force the sale of crown lands, to the impoverishment of the king's heirs to all time. Particularly interesting are Gloucester's remarks about Beaufort and the council; he had achieved, he said, such mastery of the king 'as no true liegeman ought to usurp' and was calling the council to meet at his own house and on his own authority. Thus he had cut off and estranged 'me your sole uncle, together with my cousin of York, my cousin of Huntingdon, and many other lords of your kin from having knowledge of any great matters that might touch your high estate and realm'.[28] Government had fallen into the hands of a dishonest clique, who would defraud the king of his wealth and abandon his titles in France, this was the theme of the manifesto; the excuse for its publication was that this clique had

[25] *L. and P.* vol. II, pt. II, p. 446.
[26] *Foed.* vol. X, pp. 764–7.
[27] *L. and P.* vol. II, pt. II, pp. 440–51.
[28] ibid. p. 442.

established such a hold over the government that a loyal councillor had now no option but to appeal beyond the council, to
the king and to the king's true lieges.

Henry VI's advisers considered Gloucester's manifesto sufficiently damaging to call for a reply, a counter-manifesto to
quiet the 'noise and grouching' that it had stirred among the
people.[29] That the king's council should feel so vulnerable as to
need to justify their policy by public broadsheet is an ominous
sign, indicative of real instability. Their manifesto was ably
drafted, but in difficult times it is always easier to criticize than to
defend official policy, and it lacked the bite of Gloucester's
attack. The next step of the king's intimates seems to be a recognition of the political weakness of their position, and the im-
possibility of securing it against popular anger by mere argument.

Their new answer to Gloucester's intransigence was an effort
to discredit him by public scandal. In the summer of 1441
two clerks, Roger Bolingbroke and Thomas Southwell, were
arrested on the charge of practising against the king's life by
sorcery. Roger abjured his black arts publicly on 16 July at
St Paul's; a few days later it was noised abroad that he had
admitted, under examination, that he had been instigated to his
acts of sorcery by none other than Eleanor Cobham, Gloucester's
second duchess. She was arrested, and was tried in October before the bishops of London, Lincoln and Norwich. Suffolk himself had had a hand in the trial of her accomplices, and the man
who now conducted her prosecution was Adam Moleyns, the
clerk of the council, who was intimately connected with the clique
which, under Suffolk's leadership, was dominant about the king.
Eleanor admitted her traffic in sorcery and with sorcerers and
submitted herself to the correction of the bishops; but the charge
of plotting to destroy the king by magic she flatly denied. Her
sentence was to perform full and public penance, going on foot
through London with a taper in her hand to offer at the altars
of St Paul's, of Christchurch in Aldgate, and of St Michael's
Cornhill, on the three next market days in the city. After that,
she was committed to prison for life.[30] Of her accomplices,
Southwell died in prison and Bolingbroke was hanged; and
Margery Jourdemain, the witch of Eye who, it was said, pre-

[29] ibid. pp. 451–60.

[30] On Eleanor and her trial see further K. H. Vickers, *Humphrey of
Gloucester*, pp. 270–80; and R. A. Griffiths, 'The trial of Eleanor
Cobham: an episode in the fall of Humphrey Duke of Gloucester',
B.J.R.L. 51 (1969), pp. 381–99.

pared the potion that ensnared for Eleanor Humphrey's love, was burned at Smithfield.

Eleanor was undoubtedly guilty of dabbling in witchcraft; that the main object of her trial was political is suggested strongly by the composition of the court, the publicity of her penance and the public fate of her accomplices. Gloucester himself was not involved, and the affair did not completely destroy his influence, but for the time being it discredited him sufficiently for his rivals' purpose. It was not the first time that English politicians of this period had employed this rather unattractive type of manœuvre. The whole episode is strongly reminiscent of the deliberate English effort to discredit Joan of Arc at her trial as a sorcerer and a heretic. Beaufort, however, had never employed this sort of means in domestic political infighting, and the business smacks more of the methods of the Earl of Suffolk, who had been steward of the household since 1433 and was now beginning to emerge as a dominant figure at court. His rise seems to have been a consequence of the achievement of his majority by Henry VI, and of subsequent changes in the role of the council in government.

Henry came of age in 1437. When he did so there was no sudden change; the council that he appointed in November was virtually identical in composition with that of the preceding years. There were of course some changes in its powers; the king now reserved to himself control over collation to benefices in his gift, appointment to office, and the grant of charters of pardon. The new council was, however, intended to play a meaningful part in government (the regulations for the council of 1406 were reissued for its guidance), and in the first instance it certainly did so. But attendance began to decline early, and from 1438 on the warrants drafted by the council's clerk show a small group of persons constantly in attendance, Bishop Stafford the chancellor, Bishop Ayscough and the Earl of Suffolk being the most regular, with, of course, the clerk, Adam Moleyns. [31] These men had the king's ear; that was what Gloucester had in mind when he com-

[31] Much work has been published on the council in the period after 1437 since Baldwin wrote of it in his seminal book, *The King's Council*. For what follows I have relied mainly on T. F. T. Plucknett, 'The place of the council in the fifteenth century', *T.R.H.S.* 4th ser., 1 (1918), pp. 157–89, esp. pp. 181–4; R. Virgoe, 'The composition of the king's council 1437–61', *B.I.H.R.* 43 (1970), pp. 134–60; and on Storey, *H. of L.*, pp. 37–42.

plained that lords who were the king's kinsmen no longer got
knowledge of great matters. He also complained about the king's
intimates meeting at Beaufort's house; the cardinal was always in
the background and the emergent court party adopted his diplomatic attitudes, which were anathema to Humphrey. John
Beaufort, Earl of Somerset, and his brother Dorset were both
associated with Suffolk and the new men, and John, as we have
seen, used his influence with them in 1443 to obtain the lieutenancy in France, independent of York, that he used to such little
purpose. Gradually, the intimacy of the ruling clique with the
king rendered the old council otiose, and in due course its
members ceased to attend meetings with any regularity. By 1444
the old rule, that all major grants should be scrutinized by the
council, was a dead letter. Moleyns's endorsement of a bill was
accepted as adequate warrant by the privy seal, which moved
the great seal; and a new ordinance that the privy seal should
accept all warrants with the king's sign manual or under the
signet (which Moleyns kept) merely regularized the position.

The king's new friends did very well out of their position of
influence. Suffolk's promotions are the most dramatic witness to
this: in 1437 he became high steward of the duchy of Lancaster,
north of Trent, and in 1438 chief justice of south Wales; in
1442 he was granted the reversion of the Earldom of Pembroke
if Gloucester should die childless; in 1444 he was created a
marquis. Later he was to get still more; in 1447 he was appointed
Lord Great Chamberlain of England, Constable of Dover and
Warden of the Cinque Ports, and in 1448 he became a duke.
Ordinary people were naturally soon aware of the way that influence was going, and came to know that their petitions for
favour were most likely to be met if they were sponsored by one
of the curialist group. This had the effect of strengthening the
hold of Suffolk and his associates on government; it also, more
importantly, drove powerful men who had lost influence in
consequence of his rise into opposition to the government.
Gloucester as early as 1440 reckoned that he had more to gain
from opposing those in power than from cooperating with them,
and that York was probably in much the same position as himself.

Gloucester's opposition, even York's as well, might not have
mattered very much if Suffolk and his friends had pursued
policies calculated to endear the king whom they served to his
subjects. But they did not, and they did not succeed in doing
anything either about public order or public finance, two matters

on which popular disquiet had already been focused before Henry VI's minority had ended.

Lack of governance was no new complaint, and it is no surprise to find after 1437 more evidence of the kind of aristocratic misdemeanor that had troubled the minority. The earls of Salisbury and Westmorland came near to blows over a disputed inheritance in Yorkshire; the followers of the Earl of Devon and Sir William Bonville were involved in armed clashes in the west; in Gloucestershire a running fight of long standing between the heir male and the heirs general for the Berkeley inheritance continued to disturb the peace. But there was alarming evidence now of more general disorder. From the march of Wales came stories that in Hereford outlaws and evil-doers were coming openly into the market towns, no officer preventing them, so that 'they do not fear to kill and burn and rob in the said county'. The counties of the south coast complained of 'murders, mayhems, and batteries' and of the despoiling of goods by soldiers passing on their way to France.[32] In 1439 the commons in parliament took the remarkable step of petitioning for the penalty of total forfeiture against certain notorious criminals, if they could not be brought to book. One of these was the colourful Piers Venables, gentleman, of Derbyshire, who gathered a band about him, and 'in manner of insurrection, went into the woods in that county, like as it had been Robin Hood and his meiny'.[33] His band had ridden raiding into Cheshire, where another band from Shropshire under Philip Egerton had also gone raiding. The demand for extraordinary penalties for this sort of banditry shows that people felt things were getting out of hand. There was no longer any real confidence in the county officers; and the commons believed that they were as often as not in league with criminals. They denounced bitterly the misdemeanours of sheriffs and under-sheriffs, which threatened 'importable hurt, open disinheritance, supportation of manslaughter and great oppression to many of the liege people of our sovereign lord'.[34]

Government finance over the period 1436 to 1445 is a parallel story of the steady deterioration of an initially unsatisfactory situation. Late in 1435 the commons, nettled by what they regarded as the Burgundian betrayal of England, were generous, granting a whole subsidy and a graduated tax on all incomes from

[32] *R.P.* vol. V, p. 61 (south coast shires), p. 106 (march of Wales).

[33] ibid. p. 16, and see further J. G. Bellamy, *The Law of Treason in England in the Later Middle Ages* (Cambridge, 1970), pp. 189ff.

[34] *R.P.* vol. V, p. 108.

land and annuities of over £5 per annum. But afterwards they only granted in 1437 a subsidy, in 1439 a subsidy and a half, and in 1442 again a subsidy – all to be paid by instalments, and all subject to the now regular deductions. The king's advisers were very busy in these years in their efforts to raise new forces for the defence of Normandy and Gascony, and these grants did not meet the full cost of the troops that they needed to equip. The exchequer therefore found it harder than ever to meet its commitments, and the burden of accumulated debt grew more and more alarming. Even Beaufort found difficulty in obtaining adequate security for new loans, and satisfactory terms for the repayment of old ones. It is not surprising to find that the circle of those ready to lend to the crown was a dwindling one, and that arrears of pay owing to magnates and others in the king's service were accumulating.[35] At the same time purveyance for the household began once more to attract uncomfortable attention, always a sign that the king was short of cash. Certain revenues of the duchy of Lancaster were in consequence of complaint earmarked for the expenses of the household, but this did not solve the problem; in 1442 the commons asked the king to appoint a committee of lords to ensure that 'good and sad rule be had in your said household'.[36] This was the same familiar request that had been heard so often in the days of Henry IV, and, now as then, was a symptom of growing strain between the governors and the governed.

The difficulty of finding a solution to the growing financial problem was greatly complicated by the heavy load of fees and annuities that were assigned on the crown's regular revenues. In Henry IV's day this too had been a pressing problem, but then at least there was some attempt to curtail expenditure: there had even been a stop on annuities in 1404. In the 1440s there was not much serious attempt at parsimony. Henry VI from the time that he attained his majority was very free with grants of land, office and fee. Apart from his two great foundations at Eton and King's College Cambridge, those who gained most from his largesse were his intimate advisers and their clients. It was a case of the governors conniving at the impoverishment of the government, and did not enhance the reputation of Henry's friends.

[35] The sources of loans to the crown are examined in detail by A. Steel in his *The Receipt of the Exchequer 1377–1485* (Cambridge, 1954).
[36] *R.P.* vol. V, p. 63.

The difficulties with which Suffolk, the closest counsellor of the king, and his associates found themselves faced were inevitably connected with the conduct of the war. Unless some sort of settlement could be reached with the French there was not much chance of finding a solution to the problem of mounting royal insolvency. But it was difficult in practice to find an avenue towards settlement, because of the domestic political danger involved in conceding enough to the adversary to bring him to terms. Gloucester had made all too public in 1440 his suspicion that the king's advisers were intending to betray the national interest and all the achievement of the past by signing away the king's crown and title in France. He had made it clear too that in his opinion, if the king would take other advisers they would press his war abroad more successfully. The success that York and Talbot did achieve in Normandy with slender support from England lent colour to this suggestion, and it was in any case what most people wanted to believe. If Suffolk was to survive politically he had got to achieve not just peace, but peace with honour; otherwise his opponents would take advantage of public indignation to drive him and his friends from power. The decline of local order must have reminded him of the instability of his control, and he must have known, too, that the advantages that he was gaining from the king's favour were making him many powerful enemies. In 1443–4 Suffolk's hopes were centred, as we have seen earlier, on the Angevin marriage as a step on the way to an Anglo-French settlement, but his hopes were not well founded. Margaret of Anjou's influence as queen could indeed serve to buttress his authority at court, but, since the marriage agreement which he personally negotiated only carried with it a truce for two years, it did not really bring the prospect of a final peace much nearer. Though the truce was welcome in the short run as affording a respite to the hard pressed Norman garrisons and from taxation for war purposes, in the longer run the marriage merely aggravated rumours that a sell out to the French was in the offing.

For a little more than five years after the Truce of Tours was sealed, until the beginning of 1450, Suffolk strove not very competently to ward off the crises that were threatening. The underlying pattern of domestic history in this period was not sharply different from that of the preceding years. Nothing was done that offered any promise of better governance at the local level. Nothing was achieved that made any substantial difference to the deteriorating state of the crown's finances. The constitution of a new household for Queen Margaret added to a type of expenditure that was always regarded critically. Disillusion and distrust spread at home in consequence of this absence of achievement. Rumours began to circulate that the king was 'not so steadfast in his wits as other kings have been before'.[37] Numerous popular ballads circulated which inveighed against the clique with influence at court in a style ominously reminiscent of the adverse satires directed against Richard II and his household supporters in the last years of his reign.[38] The most constant refrain of this literature, as in that earlier time, was the evil of livery and maintenance, particularly of maintenance by members of the royal court and household. The ballads reflect a widespread suspicion that the whole administration of the kingdom was being controlled by a small group of individuals and their clients, for purposes of personal advantage and regardless of the common weal.

Such suspicions had ample foundations. The careers of men such as the household knight John Say or the civil servant Thomas Thorpe, both objects of the poets' scorn, fully justify the suggestion that men in favour were doing well for themselves in spite of the crown's poverty. Accusations of maintenance against the courtiers and their protégés were equally well founded. Margaret Paston in 1448 declared that in Norfolk none dared be so hardy as to say or do anything against Suffolk and his clients.[39] Indictments presented after Suffolk's fall bore her out all too clearly. Three men closely associated with the earl, Sir Thomas Tuddenham, John Heydon and John Ulveston, had been rigging the legal administration of the county for years. The sheriff had been a tool in their hands; juries were packed with their men: 'there can no man indict him, for Sir Thomas Tuddenham maintaineth him' had been a typical record.[40] In Kent, the associates of James Fiennes, Lord Say and Sele, chamberlain of the household from 1447 and a political client of Suffolk's, conducted themselves in much the same way as Tuddenham and Heydon in Norfolk. The activities of men such as these built up dislike of the favourites of Henry VI toward a climax of resentful bitterness. But for the time being nothing could be done, because they

[37] See Storey, *H. of L.*, pp. 34–5.
[38] See further C. L. Kingsford, *English History in Contemporary Poetry*, No. II, 1399–1485 (London, 1913), pp. 32–6.
[39] *P.L.* No. 56.
[40] *P.L.* No. 144.

had the ear of the king from whom all authority stemmed, and protest seemed hopeless.

The principal political events of the years 1444 to 1450 were nearly all in one way or another bound up with the problems of Anglo-French diplomacy, and have been discussed in an earlier chapter. There is no need to go over the ground again in detail. Suffolk's efforts to avoid or deflect the wave of public anger that followed the decision to cede Maine to the French were not very happy. Gloucester's death in confinement after his arrest at Bury in February 1447 labelled him in the public eye as the murderer of the 'good duke' Humphrey. Moleyns's attempt to discredit York by charging him with embezzlement of soldiers' wages and his quasi-banishment to Ireland alienated the only peer whose support might have done something to shore up the government's eroded reputation. Finally, the folly of the attack on Fougères in Brittany – in which both Suffolk and Somerset, the Beaufort who had replaced York as lieutenant in Normandy – were implicated, plunged the kingdom back into the war with France unprepared. Suffolk's miscalculations finally culminated in the military debacle of 1449–50 in which Normandy was lost for good, and from the consequences of this neither the king's favour nor anything else could save him.

On 7 February 1450 the commons in parliament impeached Suffolk who, as they put it, had been for so long 'priviest and best trusted' with Henry VI. Two sets of charges were brought against him, the first mainly concerned with his mismanagement of the war and of diplomacy, the second with frauds, peculations and maintenance committed at home in England.[41] He was accused of being responsible for the release of the Duke of Orleans, the surrender of Maine, the inadequate safeguard of Normandy and the alienation of England's old allies, as Brittany and Armagnac. He was also charged with using his influence to secure for himself rich grants from the crown (as the wardship of Margaret Beaufort and the reversion of the earldom of Pembroke); of embezzling the proceeds of subsidies; of making sheriffs of his own choice 'so that they that would not be of his affinity in their counties were overset'; of being privy to a murderous attack on Lord Cromwell and sheltering his assailant, Suffolk's own retainer William Tailboys. There were some very wild allegations besides, even that Suffolk had plotted with Dunois and other

[41] R.P. vol. V, pp. 177–9, 179–82.

Frenchmen to invade England, and depose Henry VI in his own favour.

This remarkable medley of indictments demonstrates very clearly how closely men associated Suffolk's mismanagement of affairs abroad and his misgovernment at home. Hurriedly put together, the charges were in no sense exhaustive, but they were enough to secure his dismissal. They were never fully tried, because Henry intervened personally to save his favourite from a worse fate by banishing him from the realm for five years, on his own authority. This did not in fact save Suffolk; the ship on which he was embarked for France was run down in the Channel by a vessel called the *Nicholas of the Tower*, and by order of its captain Suffolk's head was struck off. The sailors who executed him claimed that they were acting on behalf of the 'community of the realm'. He had made himself so hated in England that to put him to death appeared to them to be a patriotic service.[42]

No one knows who the captain of the *Nicholas of the Tower* was, or whether he had any special animus against Suffolk. The incident was just one of a series of clear indications that control was slipping from the hands of the government in England. When Suffolk died one of his recent associates had already met a violent end, Bishop Adam Moleyns, who had been lynched by a mob of malcontent soldiers at Portsmouth. This was an ominous beginning; much worse was to follow before the summer of 1450 was out.

In the early spring there had been a number of serious riots in Kent, which grew in May into a full-scale rebellion, the revolt of Jack Cade. The rising spread to Essex, which sent a contingent to join Cade before London, and areas further afield were affected too. Superficially, this revolt of the 'commons of Kent' bore a resemblance to the movement of 1381; but it was really very different.[43] It was not a peasants' revolt. A good many artisans of the Kentish towns were involved, but it also found support among men of higher status. Over seventy persons who described themselves as gentlemen were involved, and Cade's lieutenant, Robert Poynings, came of lordly blood. Cade himself claimed that his name was Mortimer and that he had connexions with the Duke of York (who he really was we do not know). The objects of his

[42] See R. L. Virgoe, 'The death of William de la Pole', *B.J.R.L.* 47 (1964–5), pp. 489–502.

[43] On Cade's revolt see Storey, *H. of L.*, pp. 61–8. A. H. Kriehn, *The English Rising in 1450* (Strasbourg, 1892), is now somewhat dated.

rebellion, as revealed by his manifestos, were quite as much political as social. They complained, it is true, of the statute of labourers, of maintenance by local officials in Kent, and of purveyance. But their chief demands were for the punishment of the traitors who were about the king, 'the false progeny and affinity of the Duke of Suffolk', in consequence of whose counsel the good Duke Humphrey was done to death, and 'the realm of France was lost, the duchy of Normandy, Gascony, Guienne, and Anjou'. The rebels demanded that the king should 'take about his noble person men of his true blood from his royal realm', to wit the Duke of York, and the dukes of Exeter, Buckingham and Norfolk. 'We say that our sovereign lord may understand this,' Cade's men concluded: 'His false council has lost his law: his merchandise is lost: his common people are destroyed: France is lost. The king himself is so placed that he may not pay for his meat and drink.'[44]

Cade's rebels were in control of London on 4 July. While they ruled there, another of Suffolk's late friends, Lord Say, was taken from the Tower and executed, along with his retainer William Cromer who had been sheriff of Kent. A third member of the recent governing clique, Bishop Ayscough, had been assassinated at Salisbury a few days before. The rebels were only dislodged from the city when Lord Scales brought up professional troops, and after a fierce fight which raged all the night of 5 July on London Bridge. A free pardon in the end dispersed them, though Cade himself and some others remained in arms; he died soon after, mortally wounded in an attack on Queenborough castle. The government did not even then feel strong enough to take repressive steps, and despatched instead a judicial commission into Kent to hear the grievances of the county. The momentum of rebellion died down only gradually: the threat of large-scale disturbance rumbled on in Kent for five years.[45]

Cade's revolt, and the deaths of Suffolk, Moleyns, Ayscough and Lord Say demonstrate clearly the degree to which, in the year 1450, the governing council had lost control of the kingdom. In the years preceding, Suffolk had maintained himself only by his personal influence with the king and queen, and by total unscrupulousness when it came to eliminating such potential opponents as Humphrey of Gloucester. In fairness to him, it must be admitted that he came to influence at a time when pub-

---

[44] See *Three Fifteenth Century Chronicles*, ed. J. Gairdner (Camden Soc., 1880), pp. 96–7.
[45] See Storey, *H. of L.*, p. 68.

lic confidence in government, shaken by aristocratic rivalry and financial mismanagement during the king's minority, had long been declining, and that he inherited a well nigh impossible diplomatic situation. But he succeeded only in making confusion worse. The misdoings of his long period of ascendancy, at home and abroad, built up popular resentment to flashpoint. When Englishmen suddenly saw what was left to them of Henry V's famous conquests in the process of being engulfed, the structure of central authority proved too fragile to stand the shock. The collapse of government that ensued brought old discords that were latent to the surface of English politics, and sowed the seeds of new ones. These together gave rise to the struggles which we call the Wars of the Roses.

18

The Wars of the Roses
1450–1461

The aristocracy and gentry of the fifteenth century were always inclined to use force when they could have gone to law: after Cade's revolt they had less hesitation than ever about putting their private quarrels to the issue of arms. The early 1450s witnessed recourse to violence in a whole host of disputes. Summonses of the offenders before the council, which was usually the only effective authority when the great were involved, now simply went unheeded. Lord Cobham's men clashed with those of Lord Wiltshire, those of Lord Cromwell with the men of the Duke of Exeter. In the west September 1451 saw the Earl of Devon formally besieging his old enemy Lord Bonville in Taunton castle. The worst troubles were in the north, where the long-standing feud of Nevilles and Percies threatened to achieve the stature of a full-scale private war. The Percies viewed with understandable dismay the rising fortune of their rivals. Richard Neville had married the heiress of Salisbury and had acquired important estates in Yorkshire and elsewhere from his sister, Joan Beaufort; his son Richard had married Anne Beauchamp, and in 1449 succeeded in her right to the earldom of Warwick and its magnificent inheritance. The younger Percies, in particular the Earl of Northumberland's tempestuous third son, Baron Egremont, saw no means of checking an influence which threatened to swamp their power in their traditional homeland, short of force. Many historians have regarded the battle at Heworth in 1453 between the followers of Nevilles and Percies as the first battle of the Wars of the Roses, 'the beginning of the sorrows of England'.[1]

[1] *L. and P.* vol. II, pt. II, p. [770]. On the quarrels of aristocratic families in the early 1450s, see Storey, *H. of L.*, which is certainly the most important book on the Wars of the Roses to have appeared recently, and my debt to it is enormous.

The most important of all the aristocratic quarrels that threatened the peace in these times was that of the dukes of York and Somerset. It was different from the others. Theirs was not just a quarrel over lands, or inheritance, or local influence; it was a political feud, which had close connexions with the earlier feud between Cardinal Beaufort and, latterly, Suffolk on the one side and Humphrey of Gloucester on the other. In order to understand the quarrel between these two men, which in the end drew into its orbit all the other vendettas of the aristocracy, it is necessary to remind oneself of the salient facts in their careers up to about the year 1450.

Edmund Beaufort succeeded his brother John Duke of Somerset, who died in 1444, leaving no male heir. The Beauforts were descended from John of Gaunt, by his third wife Catherine Swinford, so Somerset was the senior male member of the house of Lancaster after the king. But for the statute that barred the Beauforts from the line of succession, he would have been Henry VI's male heir in 1450 (Margaret, the daughter of his brother John, was in fact the mother of Henry VII). Edmund had always been a courtier, and although his wealth was negligible by comparison with York's in terms of land, he had done well for himself in the way of title and office. He had been created first Earl, later Marquis of Dorset; and in 1446 it was he who was appointed to succeed York as lieutenant in Normandy. As lieutenant he had been intimately concerned in the cession of Maine and knew of the moves that led up to the capture of Fougères; and he was the commander immediately responsible for the disasters of 1449 and 1450. But though he was, after Suffolk, the man most obviously to blame, he was not called to account when he came back to England with his bedraggled army after the fall of Caen. Instead he was called to the council table and promoted constable of England; he was soon to become also captain of Calais, the most important remaining military command overseas. He assumed the mantle of Suffolk, and it was to him now that the queen turned, as did householders like John Say and John Trevilian, who had been Suffolk's associates and felt the need now for a new protector.

Richard of York's career had been entirely different. After the king, he was the greatest landowner in the realm, with property in many English counties and in Wales, as well as vast estates in Ireland. The most important concentration of his properties was

in central Wales and in the English border counties.[2] He was of
the blood royal: his father was that Richard of Cambridge who
was executed for treason at Southampton in 1415, and who was
the younger son of Edmund of Langley, Edward III's fourth
son. Richard became the heir of York when his uncle was killed
at Agincourt. His mother was Anne Mortimer, and when the last
Earl of March died in 1425 he was his heir also. In the legitimate
line of succession he was closest to Henry VI's throne in 1450;
and through the Mortimers his line went back to Lionel of
Clarence, who was the second son of Edward III and older than
Gaunt; and so he inherited the Mortimer claim to the throne
which, if dormant, was technically senior in blood to that of the
house of Lancaster. He had never been close to the court and its
circle. He had twice been lieutenant in Normandy; and in his
second term there had been slighted first by the grant to John
Beaufort in 1443 of a lieutenancy independent of his, and secondly
when Edmund Beaufort superseded him in 1446. As lieutenant
he had incurred heavy expenses which the exchequer had been
slow to meet; in 1450 he was still owed more than £38,000. His
appointment to the lieutenancy of Ireland in 1447 had all the
appearance of a political exile. In France, where he had been
comparatively successful, he had attracted to his circle a number
of distinguished military figures such as John Popham and
William Oldhall, men of a class to whose pride and interests the
collapse of the English cause abroad was particularly painful.
He thus had numerous grounds for resentment against the
government in general and Somerset in particular. He had
suspicions, in 1450, that Somerset might use his influence with
Henry VI to quash the act barring the Beauforts from the
succession, so disappointing York and his heirs of their hopes
of a throne.[3]

The propaganda of Cade's revolt with its demand that Henry
take York into his council, showed that Duke Richard was in
1450 one of the few magnates who still enjoyed an untarnished
popular reputation. The confusion following the revolt and the
English collapse abroad gave him a clear opportunity to inter-

[2] On York's estates see J. T. Rosenthal, *The Estates and Finances of
Richard Duke of York, 1411–1460* (in *Studies in Medieval and Renaissance
History*, ed. W. M. Bowsky, vol. II, Nebraska, 1965).

[3] *P.L.* Intro., p. lxi. York's complaint was that 'certain persons
laboured instantly to have me indicted of treason, for to the intent to
have undone me and mine issue, and corrupted my blood'. Somerset
seems clearly to be the principal person indicated; see ibid. p. lxxiii.

vene in England, and secure a commanding position for himself.
At the beginning of September he came across from Ireland and
landed in Wales. The government very foolishly revealed its
hostility by attempting to arrest him. He nevertheless reached
London safely, with a retinue, to demand his place in the council
and the trial of those popularly accused of treason – to wit,
chiefly, Somerset. The stage was set for the confrontation from
which the Wars of the Roses directly sprang.

The years from 1450 to 1461 witnessed a dislocation of government which was often total, the outbreak of a ferocious civil war,
and the ultimate supplanting of the Lancastrian dynasty by that
of York, in the person of Duke Richard's son Edward IV. The
political events of the period are confused and complicated, and
historians are still disagreed about the factors that conditioned
their troubled pattern. For the sake of simplicity it seems easiest
to recount first what happened, as briefly as may be consonant
with coherence, before attempting to analyse the underlying
reasons for disorder.

York's protest to the king, on his arrival in England in 1450,
had no very visible effect. He was soon busy, 'labouring' to
ensure the election of men sympathetic with his views to the
parliament which was summoned for November 1450. He had
some success at least, and the man whom the commons elected
as their speaker when they assembled was William Oldhall, a
veteran of the French wars and a key figure in York's council.[4]
The popular mood was very bitter against Somerset, who was
threatened by the London mob during the parliament; there
seems besides to have been an attempt to have him put under
arrest, and the commons petitioned the king to dismiss him from
his court together with a number of other courtiers associated
with the late Duke of Suffolk, including Lord Hoo, John Say,
John Trevilian, and Alice, Suffolk's duchess. The commons also
made demands for reforming measures, which resulted in a new
and stringent act of resumption, and in an act to ensure that all
future royal grants should be scrutinized by a committee of the
council. On personal issues, however, the government would not
be stampeded. The king agreed to ask those courtiers whom the
commons had named and who were *not peers* to withdraw, but
that was as far as he would go, and the crown would not entertain

[4] On Oldhall see J. S. Roskell, 'Sir William Oldhall, speaker in the
parliament of 1450-1', *Nottingham Medieval Studies* 5 (1961), pp. 87-112:
also C. E. Johnston, 'Sir William Oldhall', *E.H.R.* 25 (1910), pp. 715-22.

a posthumous act of attainder against Suffolk. In the second session of the parliament the court was confident enough to take the initiative, and when Thomas Yonge, the member for Bristol, petitioned that York be recognized as heir apparent the parliament was dissolved, and Yonge was sent to the Tower. A little before this Somerset had been appointed captain of Calais, and Abbot Bowlers of Gloucester, whose dismissal from court the commons had requested, was named for provision to the see of Hereford.

York's attempt to shake the government through parliament thus failed. His next effort was based on a show of force. It was well prepared in advance. In the autumn of 1451 letters in his name were circulating, soliciting armed aid; Oldhall and others were busy organizing popular support. Further letters to various towns, such as Canterbury, Colchester and Oxford, inciting them to support an armed movement for the common weal, were sent out early in 1452.[5] On 3 February, at Shrewsbury, York in a great manifesto denounced the misdeeds at home and abroad of Somerset, 'who ever prevails and rules about the king's person, by which means the land is likely to be destroyed'.[6] Marching southward with his retainers, he was joined by allies from the west, the Earl of Devon and Lord Cobham with their followers. His hope probably was that this show of armed force, coinciding with a series of civic risings over southern England, would, without a battle, cause such panic among his opponents that he would be able to dictate terms to the king. Once again, however, these opponents acted more firmly than he expected. The king and Somerset mustered an army, and though York slipped past them into Kent, he found himself at Dartford facing a superior force, whose captains included most of the greater peers.

There could have been a pitched battle, but there was not; both sides agreed to negotiate. York seems to have had friends in Henry's camp; the bishops of Ely and Winchester and the two Neville earls of Warwick and Salisbury, who acted for the king, were ready to agree that, if York would dismiss his troops, Somerset should be placed under arrest, until he had answered

[5] On these activities see Storey, *H. of L.*, pp. 94ff., and J. S. Roskell, 'Sir William Oldhall', p. 104. For reference to letters sent out early in 1452 see *P.P.C.* vol. VI, pp. 90–2; the date here given is 1450, but Storey reassigns to 1452 with authoritative arguments (*H. of L.*, pp. 98, 249).

[6] *P.L.* Intro., p. lxxiii.

charges against him concerning his conduct in Normandy. (York it should be remembered, was married to Cicely Neville, Salisbury's sister.) York agreed: 'but when he came to the king's tent, the Duke of Somerset was still in attendance on the king, and the chief person in his company; and the Duke of York was made to ride before the king through London like a prisoner'.[7] Once again Somerset had turned the tables on York, not very honestly. York was in danger of facing a trial, but was in the end released, on the council's advice, on promising that he would never again proceed against any subject of the king by force, or raise forces without the king's licence. After that, on 7 April, a general pardon was issued for all who had been concerned in the late disturbances.

Somerset in the next few months consolidated his position. He seemed at last to be doing something to restore the court's tarnished reputation, and there was much activity to set on foot the force which in the autumn sailed under Talbot for Bordeaux. There, as we know, it won initially dramatic success. The parliament that assembled at Reading in March 1453 proved almost as sympathetic to the court as its predecessor had been hostile. Its speaker was Thomas Thorpe, a baron of the exchequer, who had associations with men who had been close both to Suffolk and to Somerset.[8] With the war in Gascony in mind, the commons voted generous subsidies, and granted the king the wool subsidy for life. It further made a grant to enlist 20,000 archers for service in 'defence of the realm', in effect as a reservist bodyguard for the king, reminiscent of the White Hart retainers of Richard II. Besides this, the commons demanded that all grants to persons 'who were assembled in the field at Dartford' be revoked, and attainted William Oldhall of treason.[9] The triumph of the court seemed complete when parliament went into recess for the summer, but before it reassembled the situation had changed out of recognition.

Violent disorders had broken out again in the north in the summer of 1453, and Nevilles and Percies had called out their men. Somerset had managed to embroil himself with the power-

[7] *Great Chronicle of London*, ed. A. H. Thomas and I. D. Thornley (London, 1938), p. 186.
[8] On Thorpe see J. S. Roskell, 'Thomas Thorpe, speaker in the parliament of 1453-4', *Nottingham Medieval Studies* 7 (1963), pp. 79-105.
[9] *R.P.* vol. V, pp. 230 (archers), 265-6 (attainders).

ful Neville Earl of Warwick by an attempt to poach off him the
wardship of his relative George Neville's share of the Beauchamp
inheritance in Wales.[10] Talbot's army in Gascony had been
annihilated at Castillon. Worst of all, in August, King Henry VI
lost his senses and memory. This was the first attack of a mental
disease whose periodic bouts would prostrate him at intervals
through the rest of his life. Its onset saved York from the threat
of complete political isolation. In blood and wealth he was the
greatest of the peers, and in this new crisis his colleagues could
not do without him. They insisted on his summons to the council.

When York returned to the centre of affairs, he was no longer
next heir in blood to Henry VI. On 14 October 1453, after eight
years of barren wedlock, Margaret had borne the king a son,
Edward. It was soon clear that she would claim, in his name and
her husband's, the regency, and this may be the reason why a
number of influential peers began to draw closer to York, for
Margaret had never been liked. York's old ally Devon was back
now at the council, and the Nevilles, having been threatened by
Somerset's influence, were friendlier than in 1452. In December
Somerset was put under arrest in the Tower. But when the
commons, prorogued in November and again in February,
finally reassembled in March, the question as to whether Margaret should be regent, or York protector, was still unsettled.
It might have been referred to arms, if the death of the chancellor,
Archbishop Kemp, had not precipitated matters. Someone had
to have authority to appoint a successor to the office which was
the lynchpin of royal administration. On 27 March York was
named protector and chief of the council, on terms almost
precisely similar to those on which Humphrey of Gloucester had
held the office in Henry VI's minority.

York's first protectorate on the whole does his reputation
credit. He of course took certain steps to secure his position. His
brother-in-law Richard Neville, Earl of Salisbury, became
chancellor. He himself replaced Somerset as captain of Calais,
whose garrison was the most important standing military force
in the crown's service.[11] In these appointments he acted with
the assent of a powerful and not notably partisan council of
peers, and, significantly, no extreme steps were taken against

[10] See further Storey, *H. of L.*, Appendix VI, pp. 239–41.

[11] On the importance of Calais, and the struggle of the rival Yorkist
and courtier parties to gain control there, see G. L. Harriss, 'The
struggle for Calais: an aspect of the rivalry between Lancaster and
York', *E.H.R.* 75 (1960), pp. 30–53.

Somerset. York's main claim to credit rests on measures taken to ensure better government. He made a genuine effort to get a better attendance of peers at the council. Moneys were earmarked for the keeping of the seas, for the expenses of the king's household, and for the cost of Calais, in an effort to ensure better accounting and economy of resources. In the summer of 1454 York personally headed a judicial commission to the north, in an endeavour to allay the disorders which the quarrels of Nevilles and Percies were causing. His coming frightened Lord Egremont and the Duke of Exeter into disbanding their men in Lancashire (and thus strengthened the friendship between himself and the Nevilles), but did not achieve much more; no one ever did achieve much in this county.[12] Perhaps York would have got further than others if he had been given time, but he was not. At Christmas in 1454 Henry VI recovered his senses, and after that York's commission as protector lapsed.

Somerset's release from the Tower followed Henry's recovery, and he once again replaced York as captain of Calais; the Duke of Exeter, who had been imprisoned for the violent part that he had taken against the Nevilles in the north in 1454, was also released. Salisbury and Worcester, the chancellor and treasurer, gave way to Thomas Bourchier, Kemp's successor at Canterbury, and the Earl of Wiltshire. York and his friends read these changes as a sure sign that, if they did not act, Somerset would again turn the tables on them, as he had done in 1452. In May 1455 a great council was called to Leicester, to 'provide for the King's safety',[13] and from all shires knights favourable to the court were summoned to attend. York and the Nevilles had already concluded that Somerset and Exeter were bent on their undoing. So they mustered their men, and began to march towards London.

The courtiers prevented the king from seeing the letters which York and his allies sent, through the Archbishop of Canterbury, explaining their purpose and demanding an audience. At St

[12] On these troubles and on the significance of York's intervention in the north for the formation of the 'Yorkist' party, see R. A. Griffiths, 'Local rivalries and national politics – the Percies, the Nevilles and the Duke of Exeter 1452-5', *Speculum* 43 (1968), pp. 589-632: see also Storey, *H. of L.*, pp. 142-9, 159-61.

[13] *R.P.* vol. V, p. 280. Storey, *H. of L.*, p. 161, discusses the summonses to the Leicester council.

Albans they found Henry, with Somerset and a hastily mustered army across their way.[14] They had come, they told the king's herald, 'to have the traitors that were about him punished, and in case he [York] could not have them with good will and fair consent, he would have them by force'.[15] The Duke of Buckingham, to whom Henry had entrusted command on his side, at first attempted to gain time by parleying, but it was soon clear that, since neither he nor the king would sacrifice Somerset, the chief 'traitor', the issue would be decided by arms. In the engagement that followed (22 May 1455), the Yorkists carried the day and captured the king. Very few lost their lives, but among them were Somerset, the Earl of Nothumberland and Lord Clifford. A new and terrible element thus entered into the quarrels of the great in England, the blood feud. 'By God's blood,' Lord Clifford was to cry to York's son at Wakefield in 1460, 'thy father slew mine, and so will I do thee and all thy kin.'[16]

The Yorkist lords who had shown so little moderation in rebelling, showed wise moderation in their victory. The letters that they had sent to the king before the battle at St Albans, proclaiming their intentions, were read in parliament, and all responsibility for the engagement was laid at the door of Somerset, Thomas Thorpe and William Joseph, of whom the first was conveniently dead and the other two unimportant. The archbishop carried on as chancellor, and his brother Viscount Bourchier became treasurer; Warwick now became captain of Calais. In the parliament's second session, in November, York at the request of the commons again became protector.[17] He remained so until 26 February 1456, when Henry came into parliament in person and relieved him of the office. From a partisan point of view York's brief second protectorate secured for his party one tremendous political advantage, the control of Calais and its garrison; Warwick was able to remain unshaken in command there for the four crucial years following, and it was

[14] The complicated course of events leading up to and surrounding the first battle of St Albans are examined in detail in a long and authoritative article by C. A. J. Armstrong, 'Politics and the battle of St Albans', *B.I.H.R.* 33 (1960), pp. 1–72.

[15] ibid. p. 63.

[16] E. Hall, *Chronicle*, ed. H. Ellis (London, 1809), p. 251.

[17] On the circumstances leading up to this appointment see J. R. Lander, 'Henry VI and the Duke of York's second protectorate 1455–6', *B.J.R.L.* 43 (1960–1), pp. 46–69.

from Calais that, in 1460, the Yorkist *révanche* after the rout of Ludford was organized. In other respects the second protectorate was less remarkable. York showed the same anxiety for better government as in his first, and he was still high in esteem with many sectors of the people at the end of it, but he did not have time to achieve anything of note. His dismissal did not mark a complete eclipse from power, for he remained a member of the council. It did, however, demonstrate that all power was still insecure. The death of Somerset at St Albans had solved nothing; political rivalry was as sharp as ever, and embittered now by bloodshed; and no secure administration had evolved which could steer the country away from further violence.

Moderate men, like the Bourchiers and the Duke of Buckingham, who was head of the great house of Stafford, seem to have hoped at the end of York's second protectorate for a political compromise, whereby the court and the Yorkist group should work together in council. The party that was centred on the queen's household and the heirs of the men who had died at St Albans was bent not on compromise with the Yorkists, but on their elimination. It was this party that steadily gained ground. The outbreak of private war in the Welsh marches between York's followers, led by Sir William Herbert, and Edmund Tudor, Earl of Richmond, must have strengthened their argument that compromise was not possible;[18] and the removal of the two Bourchiers from the offices of chancellor and treasurer late in 1456 was a sign of their growing dominance. Bishop Waynflete of Winchester became chancellor, and the treasurer was the Earl of Shrewsbury, now becoming an important figure in the court party; the queen's chancellor, Laurence Booth, became keeper of the privy seal about the same time. The last major effort towards compromise was made by the king in person in March 1458. York, Warwick and Salisbury agreed to pay for the foundation of a chantry at St Albans, in which prayers should be said for the souls of all who had fallen in the battle there, and to make compensation to their families.[19] There followed a formal reconciliation of the parties. The vast retinues that these brought to the meeting (Northumberland is said to have brought 1500 men south with him) suggested that

[18] On events in Wales see Storey, *H. of L.*, pp. 178–82. His account is much clearer than that given by H. T. Evans, *Wales and the Wars of the Roses* (Cambridge, 1915), ch. V.

[19] As Storey points out (*H. of L.*, p. 185) it was a cheap settlement for York and the Nevilles – who paid with debts owed them by the crown.

reconciliation was a form of words only, in which no one had much faith. So it proved to be.

Queen Margaret was now taking steps to strengthen her hold on the administration, and preparing for war. In the summer of 1459 she began to raise men in Cheshire and elsewhere, and the Yorkist army also mustered. Salisbury, marching to join York at Ludlow, defeated a Lancastrian force at Blore Heath; but when Henry VI in person arrived at Ludford Bridge with his army the Yorkist forces began to break up as soon as battle was joined. Too many were unwilling to fight their sovereign in person. The Yorkist leaders had to flee from the rout of their forces: York to Ireland, Salisbury and Warwick, with York's heir, Edward Earl of March, to Calais.

The parliament, which met at Coventry in November 1459, was packed with the court's supporters. The mood of Margaret's allies is well summarized in the curious tract called the *Somnium Vigilantis*, put out by one of their clerical supporters.[20] Mercy and pardon to their foes would now be only folly; their actions have condemned them, 'they been incurable'. A wholesale act of attainder convicted York, the Nevilles and their supporters of treason, and legalized the seizure of their lands. The distribution of the major part of the forfeitures to Margaret's loyal supporters eliminated for the future any room that may have remained for compromise or conciliation between the parties. The Yorkists had now to return to the fight or lose all. If the *Somnium* is any guide there were those who thought this was going too far,[21] but their voices were not much heeded in the 'parliament of Devils' at Coventry.

Those courtiers who received grants from the forfeited estates of the Yorkist leaders did not enjoy them for long, for in the summer of 1460 the wheel of fortune turned again. At the end of June Warwick and Salisbury, with March, slipped across from Calais. London opened its gates to them, and marching north they met and defeated the royal host at Northampton. The Duke of Buckingham, the Earl of Shrewsbury, Lords Beaumont and Egremont all fell in the battle, and the king was taken. York was still in Ireland when it was fought, and he did not cross to England until the eve of the parliament that opened on 7 October. Three days later he arrived with his host in London.

[20] Printed by J. B. Gilson, 'A defence of the proscription of the Yorkists in 1459', *E.H.R.* 26 (1911), pp. 512–25.

[21] ibid. pp. 514–15.

On 16 October his counsel came into parliament, and submitted on York's behalf a claim to the crown of England.

Up to 1460 York and his followers had always stuck to the claim that their sole aim was to secure the dismissal and punishment of those who had advised King Henry VI traitorously, and so to ensure the better government of his realm. Even now, after the parliament of Coventry, neither the Nevilles, nor the peers, nor the people at large as far as one can tell, were anxious to hear about the royal rights of the house of March. This is very understandable. York's claim was based, quite simply, on the assertion that he was the heir of a line senior by descent in blood from Edward III to all the kings of the house of Lancaster.[22] To admit his claim would therefore mean, for the great men at least, admitting that they and their ancestors had for sixty years lived under usurpers, conniving at the exclusion from the throne of the rightful heirs. It would also mean war *à l'outrance* against those of their fellow peers who remained loyal to the house of Lancaster, for everyone knew that Queen Margaret would never abandon the fight for her son's rights while he lived. It is not surprising therefore that the lords did not want to answer York's counsel, that they tried to pass the question over to the judges of the common law, or that the judges passed it back, declaring that such matters were beyond their science, being governed not by the common law but by the law of God and of nature. In such a matter, they averred, the lords of the blood and the peerage of the realm must be the judges.

This evident desire not to open up the question of the Lancastrian royal title makes it the more remarkable that the peers found such difficulty as they did in answering York's submission. Of all the arguments that they advanced against it, based on prescription, on the statutes, on York's own long acquiescence in Henry's rule, the only one in which they seem to have placed real confidence was the unquestionable fact that they themselves had all sworn personally to be Henry's true and faithful liegemen. A stand on this point was inevitably only a partial answer to York; it clarified the situation as regards Henry VI, but not for the future. In all other respects York's arguments seem to have carried a measure at least of conviction, and the peers decided

[22] *R.P.* vol. V, pp. 375–80, sets out York's claim and gives the record of the discussion and the final settlement. For a perceptive examination of the points raised see S. B. Chrimes, *English Constitutional Ideas in the Fifteenth Century* (Cambridge, 1936), pp. 26–31.

to take the same way out of the dilemma as the French had in the Treaty of Troyes, to recognize the reigning king for his lifetime and to entail the succession upon the claimant – York – and his heirs. Like the French lords who were parties to the Treaty of Troyes, the peers took oaths individually to uphold the new settlement. Thus the lords admitted that, however unwilling they might be to go back on their allegiance to Henry VI, they had no real answer to Richard of York's proud claim, based on seniority in blood, that 'though right for a time rest and be put to silence, yet it rotteth not nor shall not perish'.[23]

Before the year 1460 was out, Queen Margaret, with the Duke of Somerset, the Earl of Devon and the Earl of Northumberland, had gathered a new army in the north. On the last day of the year, this army overthrew York's at Wakefield. Duke Richard died fighting, and his ally the Earl of Salisbury, who was taken prisoner, was beheaded on the field. Later, both their heads were displayed on the walls of York, the duke's crowned with a paper cap. When Margaret advanced south in February she had promises of aid from both France and Scotland. On 17 February she defeated Warwick's forces at St Albans. King Henry, whom the Earl had brought to the battle, was freed to join his wife, but even with him at her side, the Londoners would not open their gates to Margaret. She withdrew north, and Warwick was able to join York's son Edward, Earl of March, who had just defeated the Earl of Wiltshire's Lancastrian army in the borders of Wales at Mortimer's Cross.

After Mortimer's Cross, as after St Albans, prisoners of distinction taken in the field were executed. Gregory's macabre description of the death of Owen Tudor brings home vividly the way in which such summary processes were introducing a new and demoralizing vindictiveness into English political strife:

And in that journey was Owen Tudor taken and brought unto Haverfordwest, and he was beheaded at the market place, and his head set upon the highest grice of the market cross, and a mad woman combed his hair and washed away the blood of his face, and she got candles and set about him burning more than a hundred. This Owen Tudor was father unto the earl of Pembroke, and had wedded Queen Katherine, King Harry the VI's mother, weening and trusting all alway that he should not be headed till he saw the axe and the block; and when that he was in his doublet he trusted on

---

[23] *R.P.* vol. V, p. 377.

pardon and grace till the collar of his red velvet doublet was ripped off. Then he said 'That head shall lie on the stock that was wont to lie on Queen Katherine's lap' . . . and full meekly took his death.[24]

At St Albans the Yorkist–Neville alliance had lost the advantage that had been crucial to them in 1460, their possession of the king. They now in consequence really had no option but to accept the logic of events, and to make a new king of their own. Acclaimed by the citizens of London, Edward of March was installed as king (but not as yet formally crowned, of course) in Westminster Abbey on 4 March, before he set out to follow Margaret's troops. He found them on the 29 March at Towton in Yorkshire, and won an overwhelming victory. Though Margaret, Henry and their son escaped in the rout, Edward was left king of England for the time being; a new reign had begun and a new dynasty had been founded.

There has been a great deal of debate among historians as to how we should try to explain the civil disorders, in the course of which the house of Lancaster was ultimately displaced. Traditionally the Wars of the Roses have been regarded, as they were by Shakespeare, as a straightforward struggle for the throne, a more or less direct consequence of the usurpation of 1399. Some have sought to connect the civil wars with the earlier struggles of Gloucester and Beaufort, the old apologists respectively of warlike and pacific policies abroad, and would make the English collapse in France the key to their commencement. Others would explain the outbreak of war as the consequence of the individual unfitness to rule of a single under-mighty king, Henry VI, who was too weak and too mad to restrain over-ambitious subjects. More recently, Dr R. L. Storey has argued very cogently a view which explains the outbreak of the civil wars almost entirely in terms of aristocratic rivalries, and of the social disorder to which maintenance, the chief abuse of aristocratic patronage, gave rise.

There can be no doubt that Henry VI's personal inadequacy as a monarch was a crucial factor in English politics in the 1440s and 1450s. It is not easy to find traces of any political decisions that were indubitably his own, and those that have been claimed for him, as the decision to cede Maine to the French in 1446, do not enhance respect for his judgement. Normally, the evidence suggests, he was ruled by other men and by his wife – and their

[24] *Gregory's Chronicle*, p. 211; quoted by J. R. Lander, *The Wars of the Roses* (London, 1965), p. 119.

unscrupulous *coterie* of clients. The long minority had destroyed the coherence of the body of faithful Lancastrian retainers and servants, on whom Henry IV and Henry V had depended so much. This was not Henry's fault, but he failed signally, after he came of age, to reconstitute a body of loyal supporters committed to him personally among the nobles and gentility, which was essential to maintain kingship in the fifteenth century. Those who were about his court owed their influence and position, for the most part, to others. The authority of royal command ceased to be respected, because men did not believe that it was Henry who gave the orders. So in the end war broke out, McFarlane argued, 'because the nobility were unable to rescue the kingdom from Henry's inanity by any other means'. Arms had to be the solution, because inevitably only a section of the nobility was ready to act; the king's incompetence had divided the aristocracy, setting those who profited by it fatally at odds with those who did not, and nothing short of force would remove the former.[25]

Storey's explanation of the outbreak of war is different from McFarlane's (though the difference is not really quite as sharp as Storey himself suggests). If Henry's patent unfitness to rule was the key factor, how comes it, he asks, that York could only muster a minority and partisan group among the peers in his bid to rescue the kingdom? For him, maintenance and lack of governance were what brought conflict to a head, not the undermightiness of the king. The Wars of the Roses were, he writes, 'the consequence of an escalation of private feuds. Gentry, with understandable lack of confidence in the processes of law, attached themselves to lords who could give them protection against their personal enemies, and in return supported their patrons in private wars with their peers. These baronial hostilities similarly resulted in the contestants aligning themselves with the major political rivals, and thus drawing their retainers into the conflict.'[26] Storey has backed his thesis with an impressive body of evidence, drawn from an intensive study of the local and family rivalries of both the gentry and the peerage in the 1450s. He has shown, firstly, how the disorderly conditions of the age made it imperative for the gentry to find powerful patrons and how those who were successful used the influence that they so acquired to further private ends, as Tuddenham and Heydon,

[25] See K. B. McFarlane, 'The Wars of the Roses', *P.B.A.* 50 (1964), pp. 87–119; a magisterial article which probably tells more, in a shorter space, about the civil wars than any other work so far published.
[26] Storey, *H. of L.*, p. 27.

for instance, did in Norfolk. He has shown, secondly, how the influence of the peers who were patrons depended on their standing with the court and the king, which could secure for peers themselves lucrative offices, grants of crown land and the prospect of advantageous marriage, and for their clients control of local offices, as those of sheriff and justice of the peace, which were the key to county influence. He has shown, thirdly, how the allegiance and the switches of allegiance of aristocratic families were conditioned by their own standing at court and that of their chief rivals. The key moment, according to Storey's thesis, came when the old family feud of Nevilles and Percies became aligned with the rivalry of York and Somerset, the protagonists on both sides being from then on too powerful to resign themselves to eclipse without an armed struggle.

A large part of the truth clearly lies with this thesis. Nevertheless, it is not quite a total explanation. The webs of influence that bound together the fortunes of peers and their retainers were not a relatively new feature in the 1450s, but a constant of the late medieval social and political scene (a point which McFarlane, whose work, more than that of any other, first brought home their importance in the disorders of Henry VI's reign, emphasized particularly). The ramifications of private feuds may explain a great deal about the Wars of the Roses, but not why they happened when they did. It does not explain why, in southern England at least, the Yorkists enjoyed a general popular sympathy which their opponents did not. Perhaps still more important, contemporaries, though they were aware that the civil wars were closely bound up with struggles for private influence among the great, believed that other and more serious issues were at stake as well. It is unlikely that contemporaries were entirely wrong.

Perhaps the most illuminating way in which to approach the problem posed by the outbreak of the English civil wars may be to compare them with the great civil war which disrupted the kingdom of France earlier in the fifteenth century, the war of the Burgundians and the Armagnacs. The similarities between the two struggles are in fact rather striking. The civil wars, in France as in England, developed out of competition for dominance at the court of a king who was periodically insane. The principals in the Armagnac–Burgundian struggle fought one another, as did the English peers, at the head of private armies raised by themselves and by their clients and supporters; and both sides, as in England up to 1460, claimed that they fought for the weal of the king and the kingdom. Bloodshed brought the same terrible element of feud into both struggles. In France the Armagnacs, like the Lancastrians in England, relied ultimately on their dominance at court and their control of the king's person and household, and on their consequent ability to keep key offices in the hands of loyal supporters. The Duke of Burgundy, on the other hand, built his position not only on the support of partisans, but also on cleverly directed popular propaganda. He claimed that he was fighting to purge the king's court of evil councillors who preyed on the crown's finances and pillaged and oppressed the people. He sent his manifestos abroad among the cities of northern France, posing as champion of the public weal, and won thereby an esteem which his actions, when he gained power, could never quite justify. York in England similarly appealed for popular, especially urban, support, pledging himself similarly to the purging of court and council, and to the cause of better government, and like John of Burgundy, when he obtained power he found it very difficult to combine the fulfilment of his promises with the satisfaction of his clients.

The dependence on court influence of the party which came to be called Lancastrian is beyond dispute. Both Suffolk and Somerset relied heavily on their friendship with Queen Margaret, who had all the political determination that her husband lacked, and who became the acknowledged leader of their one time associates when they were both dead. A close relationship between the two royal households, of the king and queen, and the administration both at national and local level was forged during the long period of Suffolk's ascendancy. As Storey has very expertly explained, the local influence of courtier peers, household knights and officers and their clients created a widespread web of support for the Lancastrians, which was bound too closely to the material interests of those involved to be easily shaken. As the division between the Yorkists and the courtiers sharpened, the household assumed even greater importance for the latter. After 1456, the court was not often long at Westminster (which was too close for comfort to hostile London), and contact with the exchequer and chancery posed a problem. By 1458, if not earlier, the treasurer of the household, Sir Thomas Tuddenham, was getting round his problems by drawing directly on the sheriffs (at least sixteen of whom, that year, had pensions in the household).[27] The treasurer was the Earl of Wiltshire, another entrenched Lancastrian, who was quite willing to acquiesce in this bypassing of the exchequer. The direct

[27] See E. F. Jacob, *The Fifteenth Century* (Oxford, 1961), pp. 513-14.

association of the household with the county administration proved invaluable again next year, when the household sheriffs got their instructions as to who they were to send to the parliament at Coventry. In the last years of Margaret's dominance the administration seems to have been developing into a household tyranny strongly reminiscent of that of Richard II's last years; it had indeed hit on some expedients which Richard II's courtiers did not think of.

York's answer to his rivals' control through court and household was to appeal for popular support, as John of Burgundy had done in France in similar circumstances. He did not try, we should note, to act the constitutionalist in the sense that old-fashioned English historians understood, and play on parliament's representative capacity; his appeal was directly to the people at large. Proclamations, manifestos and open letters were the instruments of his propaganda, and they were skilfully worded to show his devotion to the public good. It was the 'great complaining and rumour that is universal throughout this realm', he explained in 1450, that prompted his return from Ireland to take a hand in affairs.[28] Everything that he proposed to do, he assured men at Shrewsbury in 1452, would promote 'the ease, peace, tranquility, and safeguarding of the realm'.[29] In 1455 his letters declared that it was for the 'restful, politic rule' of the land that he was labouring.[30] His last great manifesto, put out in 1460, ranged over the whole history of a decade and more to charge the courtiers with all that had gone amiss: with the death of Humphrey of Gloucester; with responsibility for the loss of Normandy and Gascony; with embezzlement of subsidies and unscrupulous private profiteering on all sides; with the determination to make away with their rivals and have their lands. The queen's friends were openly aiming, he declared, at a tyranny, so that 'the king's subjects and their heirs and successors will be in such bondage as their ancestors never were'.[31]

York's propaganda was successful because the grievances that it aired were genuine popular grievances, and because a great many people supposed York to be entirely honest in his pro-

[28] *P.L.* No. 114.
[29] *P.L.* Intro., p. lxxiii.
[30] *R.P.* vol. V, p. 280.
[31] *English Chronicle*, ed. J. S. Davies (Camden Soc., 1856), p. 87. The bogy of tyranny was very much to the fore all through the period 1450-60; see for example Cade's proclamation in *Three Fifteenth Century Chronicles*, ed. J. Gairdner (Camden Soc., 1880), p. 94.

fessed desire to remedy them. 'The common people of the land hated Duke Edmund (of Somerset) and loved the Duke of York, because York loved the commons and preserved the profit of the land.'[32] Even the author of the Lancastrian *Somnium Vigilantis* had to admit that popular sympathy was with the other side.[33] This went a very long way to make up for York's exclusion from the council through long periods, and for the comparative weakness of his following among the peers, which was perhaps his most serious disadvantage. His place in popular esteem frightened his enemies, to the point where in the end they felt it prudent to keep the court that they controlled away from London, where popular feelings could be violently expressed. These facts have an important bearing on the dynamics of politics in mid-fifteenth-century England. The course of the great Burgundian–Armagnac struggle showed, in the end, that in France no party could hope to maintain power, if it pursued policies which clashed openly with what a general consensus identified as the national interest. Control of the court was not and could not be the sole key to successful dominance. The factious struggles of the 1450s point the same moral for England; control of the court, of royal patronage, even with local support woven round household connexions in the counties behind it, was not enough to ensure victory for the Lancastrians.

This should remind us forcibly of the relevance of the disasters of the English in France to the outcome of the civil wars in England. The loss of the English provinces was a tremendous blow to national pride. For the thirty-five years before 1450 their conquest and defence had been consuming blood and treasure, and the shock was traumatic. 'Hey alas we dolorous persons', wrote William of Worcester in his *Boke of Noblesse*, 'suffering intolerable persecutions and misery, as well in honour lost as in our livelihood unrecompensed, what shall we do or say? God forbid that such great wrongs should go unpunished, so great a loss unrepaired.'[34] The damage, moreover, was not merely psychological, as we have seen. The loss of the French provinces

[32] *English Chronicle*, p. 71.

[33] *E.H.R.* 26 (1911), p. 521: 'As for the favour of the people, there is no sure ground of argument [in that] . . . it is a shrewd consequence: the people favoureth them, *ergo* they be good.'

[34] *The Boke of Noblesse*, ed. J. G. Nichols (Roxburghe Club, 1860), p. 49. I have slightly paraphrased the original.

harmed trade. The Channel became less safe than ever to English shipping, and the long cherished English dream of controlling all commerce that passed through the narrow seas stood revealed as an empty wish. Mercantile interests were by no means the only ones to suffer. Soldiers apart, there were a good many Englishmen who had a direct stake in the retention of the overseas territories, because they held lands or houses or offices of profit there. The records show clearly that Englishmen were still interested in acquiring property in Normandy and Maine, even in the 1440s. The attitude of these sorts of people is well expressed in a petition of 1452, asking for compensation: 'here follows the sorrowful lamentation for the loss of Normandy of your most true, humble and loyal subjects, of late dwelling in the towns and county of Maine ... which is your right and proper inheritance belonging to you since the time of King Henry II after the conquest'. If they did not get some indemnity, these men declared, they would be forced to 'spend their lives in a different manner from what true Christians and loyal subjects ought to do'.[35] And we must not forget fighting men like Oliver of Kattersby, who had commanded at Domfront in 1450: 'and the said Oliver remained a prisoner, and afterward he returned out of the enemies' prison into England, and for want of comfort and relief he died of grief of heart at Westminster in very great poverty, in the year 1457'.[36] In the 1450s the individual ruin of those who had made the war in France their honourable livelihood was visible, and visible misfortune has a way of making those who see it angry.

It is not surprising, therefore, that the culpable loss of Normandy and Guienne was a recurrent theme of Yorkist propaganda. York knew that what he said on this subject would strike home, for he could read clearly between the lines of Suffolk's impeachment and Cade's proclamations. So in his Shrewsbury manifesto he called on men to consider 'first the worship, honour and manhood asserted of all nations to the people of England, whilst the kingdom's sovereign lord stood possessed of his lordship in the realm of France', and then to compare with this the 'derogation, loss of merchandise, lesion of honour, and villainy, reported generally for the loss of the same, namely unto the Duke of Somerset, when he had command and charge thereof'.[37] His ally Mowbray, when he charged Somerset with treason in the

[35] *L. and P.* vol. II, pt. II, p. [598].
[36] *L. and P.* vol. II, p. [633].
[37] *P.L.* Intro., pp. lxxii–lxxiii.

council in 1453, took up the same theme of 'the overgreat dis-
honours and losses that be come to this full noble realm of
England'.[38] In 1460 York's manifestos were still labouring the
point, charging the courtiers who had suffered 'all the old
possessions which the king had in France and Normandy . . .
to be shamefully lost and sold'.[39] By then York's one time success
as lieutenant in Normandy was passing into the mythology of his
party. 'Regent he was and governor of France', an anonymous
supporter wrote: 'Normandy he guarded from danger. He passed
over the river at Pontoise and drove away the King [Charles VII]
and his Dauphin in flight.'[40] This sort of half accurate memory
of better days past inevitably had a powerful emotive force amid
the calamities of the late 1450s.

Because it can be shown that by no means all those who had
fought in France were Yorkists, and because only a limited
number of Englishmen were directly affected by the loss of the
English provinces, the defeat of the English is usually neglected
in explanations of the English civil wars of the 1450s. This is a
misunderstanding of the contemporary dynamics of English
politics. The defeat was an important factor in the struggles. It
did more than anything else to discredit the court party, and
made it effectively impossible for them to build support on
genuine popular trust, as opposed to mere interest. It gave York,
who understood that public opinion was too strong and independent a force to permit interest and personal associations to be
a satisfactory basis for government on their own, his opportunity.
The sense that the country's interests had been damaged and its
honour outraged, and that the men who were responsible ought
to be punished, was genuine and widespread, and there were
plenty of people among the gentry and the merchant classes
whose connexions with patrons were not so tight as to govern
their political attitudes. In the circumstances, it was not un-
justifiable, according to contemporary standards and precedents,
for a great lord of the blood to take it on himself to right the
wrongs of king and country by force, when law could not prevail.
To some it seemed a loyal duty. To York himself, no doubt, the
opportunity and the duty were not unwelcome, but he did not
make either. Without the defeat abroad, without the sense that
it was not just a partial interest but the common weal of the
kingdom that had been damaged by the misgovernment of the

[38] *P.L.* No. 191.
[39] *English Chronicle*, p. 87.
[40] *Political Poems and Songs* (R.S.) vol. II, p. 257.

king's friends, his armed interventions would have been very hard to justify and very unlikely to succeed.

A final word must be said about the question of the succession. It is fashionable nowadays to regard this issue as something that only really became important after 1460. It is true, certainly, that up to 1460 York made no mention of his right to Henry VI's throne, but was, on the contrary, careful to stress that he was actuated by loyalty to his sovereign, seeking to save the crown from false councillors. The reaction of the peers to York's claim in 1460 shows how wise he had been to avoid this dangerous topic in earlier years. This does not, however, mean that in earlier years it was not important. The question of the succession had been much in men's minds from the beginning. York was thinking about it in 1450, when he complained that Somerset was seeking to 'corrupt' his blood and to 'undo' him and his issue – that is, to secure to the Beaufort family the succession which, since Henry was childless, looked likely to pass to York or his heirs.[41] Yonge was sent in the Tower in 1451 for demanding that York be recognized as heir apparent. Somerset and the court party moreover gave the succession issue deliberate prominence in the hope of thereby discrediting York as a traitor. Their packed juries in East Anglia in 1452 charged William Oldhall, York's councillor, and others with 'proposing to depose the king and put the Duke of York on the throne'.[42] York's claim to the throne was too much talked about to be kept out of sight at any time in the 1450s. As political events polarized the rivalries of the great amid the collapse of government, it became virtually certain that it would one day be advanced. Abbot Whethamstede, discussing the motives for the rebellion of the Yorkist lords in 1459, said that some thought they had risen because they were excluded from the council; others, that it was in order to rid the kingdom of the familiars of the king: 'a third group said that they had risen chiefly for this reason, that the lord Duke of York might sit on the throne of the lord king ... and that this should be confirmed and strengthened in him and his heirs by hereditary succession, from now on and for ever'.[43] Eighteen months later Edward IV was king, but he would not have been if a Yorkist succession had not seemed on the cards for a long time before.

[41] See note 5 above.
[42] See Lander, *The Wars of the Roses*, p. 63.
[43] *Registrum J. Whethamstede* (R.S.) vol. I, p. 337.

SECTION VI

The Yorkists

19

Edward IV and Richard III

Between 1461 and 1485 four kings sat upon the throne of England: Henry VI, Edward IV, Edward V and Richard III. All four were driven from the throne by force, one (Henry VI) twice, one (Edward IV) only temporarily. Edward IV was the only one of them who did not meet a violent end. As these dismal statistics witness, the political history of the twenty-five years of Yorkist rule was confused by kaleidoscopic changes of fortune, in which little else was at stake besides the power and influence of individual men. Their history is for us confused further by the fact that events in England were always closely connected with the turns of fortune in another power struggle which was going on simultaneously across the Channel, between the kings of France and their great vassals, the dukes of Burgundy.

In England, throughout the struggles of this quarter of a century, two issues remained principally at stake. One was the question of the right of succession to the crown, the other that of the direction of English alliances on the continent. These two issues were connected, but unfortunately for purposes of clarity, not in any entirely consistent way. It will be wise to say something about both, by way of introduction to the history that revolves around them.

The contending parties in England were already more or less inextricably entangled in continental power politics when Edward IV became king in 1461. This was inevitable. Henry VI's queen, Margaret, was a French princess, the kinswoman of King Charles VII and the daughter of Duke René of Anjou. The Yorkists had therefore natural ties with those who were the enemies of her family. Warwick, when in the late 1450s he was captain of Calais, established friendly contact with the dauphin Louis, who was at odds with King Charles and in exile from his court. In 1460 he and York made fruitful use of the friendliness of the papal legate, Francesco Coppini, who was also the agent of the Sforza of Milan; the Milanese were anxious to prevent

Charles VII from helping René to press his claim to be king of Naples, and hoped a Yorkist government would keep Charles occupied by an attempt to invade France and recover the lost English provinces there. This past history apart, at just about the time when Edward IV became king certain events abroad helped to make the entanglement of the English succession struggle with continental politics more important.

It had always been clear that the kings of France could not indefinitely tolerate the position of near independence which Philip Duke of Burgundy had been able to establish in his French territories as a result of his sovereign's preoccupation with the war with the English. In 1461 Charles VII of France died, and his son Louis, Warwick's one time friend, succeeded. There was a change of tempo, with a new king determined to assert himself, and a confrontation of France with the Duke of Burgundy, and perhaps with the Duke of Brittany also, became likely. It seemed certain that, in the event of such a confrontation, English support for one side or the other would decide the outcome – provided of course that whoever was king of England was capable of remaining so.

The question of the English succession was therefore of great significance to others besides Englishmen, including powers who at times might be interested in keeping the issue uncertain. Among the English themselves it was debated hotly, not only on the field of battle but on paper also as a question of law and right. Lancastrians and Yorkists concurred in making heredity central to the debate. John Fortescue, in the long years of exile to which his loyalty to the Lancastrians condemned him, defended Henry VI's title at length. His chief argument against the Yorkist claim was that, by 'the laws of God and of nature', no woman could succeed to the throne or pass on a title to it. He also sought to prove that Philippa, the daughter of Lionel of Clarence from whom the Yorkist title derived, was illegitimate.[1] There were apparently other tracts besides Fortescue's put out by the exiled Lancastrians in the 1460s, perhaps many more than have survived. Yorkist broadsheet propaganda engendered a whole historical mythology of its own. The troubles that had smitten England in Henry VI's time were God's punishment upon the people who in 1399 deserted their true born king, Richard II, in

[1] See J. Fortescue, *Of the Title of the House of York* and *Defensio Juris Domus Lancastriae* in his *Works*, ed. Lord Clermont (1869), vol. I, pp. 497–502, 505–10; and his *Governance of England*, ed. C. Plummer (Oxford, 1885), p. 75.

favour of a race of usurpers. The Lord had shown his wrath first when he struck Henry IV with leprosy, afterwards through the misfortunes that had dogged all Henry's progeny.[2] The justice of the claim of the true blood of York, the right heirs of Richard II, was attested by the victories that God had given them over their adversaries in the field. Yorkist kingship thus sought a martial, chivalrous glamour, such as that of Henry V and Edward III had enjoyed, which associated its claims with past prosperity and victories (an uncomfortable proportion of them fought, it must be admitted, on English soil), and with popular hopes for the recovery of the English cause abroad.

Caution is required in assessing the significance of the apparent preoccupation of the English parties with the question of hereditary royal right. Was it laboured in their propaganda because they knew that men felt the matter to be important, or because they wished to give the colour of a great legal issue to what was, in reality, not much more than a struggle for personal power and influence? The latter, it would seem, is probably nearer the truth, though a dispute over succession could never seem a light matter in an age when most individual and family fortunes stood or fell on issues of inheritance. Much noble blood was shed in the field in the Yorkist period; many men of fame and family were executed, and others whom the axe could not reach were attainted in parliament and lost lands and title. For all this the wars were not fought out in a spirit of implacable vendetta. A few families, bound by interest or loyalty to the house of Lancaster, proved irreconcilable to a Yorkist regime: the heirs of Somerset, the earls of Oxford, the Tudors. But even among the peers the majority could usually be counted upon to rally to the king *de facto*, if he could hold his own, without too much regard to his title *de jure*. A great many attainders were never enforced, and in the 1470s there were more restorations than new attainders.[3] These facts seem to make clear what was the true significance of the concentration of propagandists or hereditary right; it drew a thin veil over the fact that what was in dispute in the English civil wars was no longer the manner of government of the country, but more simply, what persons should govern it.

It will be wise here, before we embark on the confusing history of the wars themselves, to say a word about the chief protagonists

[2] *Political Poems and Songs* (R.S.) vol. II, pp. 256ff., 267ff., 271ff.

[3] See J. R. Lander, 'Attainder and forfeiture 1453–1509', *H.J.* 4 (1961), pp. 119–51.

in them. These were Queen Margaret of Anjou, Richard of York's old enemy; Richard Neville, Earl of Warwick, who had been York's most important supporter; and York's three surviving sons, Edward IV, George Duke of Clarence, and Richard Duke of Gloucester, who later became Richard III.

In 1461 the issues that had originally made Queen Margaret hated – her association with the Duke of Suffolk and his clique and their joint responsibility for the loss of Maine – were only memories. Most of the men who had once been her closest associates were dead: Suffolk, Somerset, and the earls of Wiltshire, Shrewsbury and Northumberland. She now had to look for support mainly in the north of England and in Wales. In Northumberland her supporters held the Percy castles of Alnwick and Bamburgh (Berwick had been surrendered to the Scots early in 1461); they included Henry, the new Duke of Somerset, Lord Roos and Sir Ralph Percy. In Wales the one time followers of the Beauforts (Somerset) and the Talbots (Shrewsbury) provided the nucleus of a Lancastrian group, now headed by the Earl of Pembroke, Jasper Tudor. Outside England, Margaret looked for support to James III of Scotland and to her relative Louis XI, the new king of France. It was into Scotland that she retreated in 1461 after Towton, with her husband Henry and her son Edward, and from there she renewed contact with the French court. Neither James nor Louis was to be much relied on, now that Margaret was no longer a queen regnant, for Edward IV could make himself dangerous to both. She, however, was indomitable, ready to meet any and every hardship and adventure to which exile, flight or poverty might condemn her, and determined to fight on for as long as her son remained alive and capable of inheritance.

Richard Neville, Earl of Warwick and called the king-maker, was in 1461 undoubtedly the man of the moment. His support and his father's had been vital to Richard of York, and after Edward IV's succession Warwick was easily the most powerful territorial subject of the new king. His grandfather, Earl Ralph of Westmorland, had acquired wide lands by his second marriage, to Joan Beaufort; and though the earldom went to Ralph's eldest son by the first wife, a great part of the family inheritance went to Joan's eldest son, Richard, the king-maker's father. He married Alice Montagu, heiress of Salisbury, and their son, the king-maker himself, married Anne Beauchamp, who became the heiress of Warwick and Despenser. Joan Beaufort's other children had been well married too: William to the heiress of Fauconberg and Cicely to none other than Richard Duke of York himself. Warwick could therefore, in consequence of his family's connexions, fairly call himself a lord of the blood royal, and he held land in more than half the counties of England.[4] He was besides chamberlain of England, Warden of the Cinque Ports and captain of Calais. The style of his living accorded with his rank and wealth, and earned him popularity. 'The earl was always held in great favour by the commons of the land, because of the exceedingly great household which he kept daily in every region wherever he stayed or passed the night. When he came to London he held such a household that six oxen were eaten at breakfast, and every tavern was full of his meat.'[5]

Warwick was not a wholly attractive character. His temper was short, and when thwarted he was sullenly unforgiving. His ambition knew no bounds: 'his insatiable mind could not be content . . . there was none in England who was before him or who owned half the possessions that he did . . . yet he desired more'.[6] His position, moreover, was one of great difficulty, especially after Edward IV's accession. Earlier, when he and Richard of York still professed to be loyal to Henry VI, he knew he could get what he wanted from York because his support was vital. Besides, if he could not get it, he could always abandon York, who was only a fellow peer. He could not hope to part so easily with Edward IV, because he himself had made him king. Yet he was bound to have difficulties with him. As a Milanese observer shrewdly remarked, it must be questionable how long Edward would endure Warwick's tutelage. Once Edward began to have a will of his own, in policy and about his court, Warwick would no longer be 'everything in the kingdom'.[7] It is never easy for an ambitious man who has been successful to relinquish power; Warwick's temperament made it, for him, virtually impossible.

Edward IV, who came to the throne in 1461 very much as Warwick's protégé, was the eldest of three surviving sons of Richard of York. Of the other two it is not necessary to say much

[4] On the Neville inheritance see J. R. Lander, 'Marriage and politics in the fifteenth century: the Nevilles and the Wydevilles', *B.I.H.R.* 36 (1963), pp. 120–3; on Warwick's Beauchamp inheritance see Storey, *H. of L.*, Appendix VI.

[5] *Great Chronicle of London*, ed A. H. Thomas and I. D. Thornley (London, 1938), p. 207.

[6] *A Remarkable Fragment of an Old English Chronicle*, ed. T. Hearne in *T. Sprotti Chronica* (Oxford, 1719), p. 299.

[7] *C.S.P. Milan* vol. I, pp. 76, 100.

now; events will bring their characters into perspective. George, the elder, who was created Duke of Clarence after his brother's coronation, was to entertain high ambitions, but lacked political skill; untrustworthy, his career fully justified Shakespeare's epithets 'false, fleeting, perjured'. Richard, who became Duke of Gloucester in 1461, was to be an able soldier and administrator; but there were flaws in his character which came out very clearly when his brother Edward was dead. Edward IV, the eldest, was probably also the ablest, all round. Handsome, affable (especially towards ladies), he was not quite twenty in 1461, a largely un-proven youth. Time was to reveal him a great soldier and a successful ruler. From his father he inherited lands and the service of loyal and able counsellors, the most notable of whom was William Hastings, created Lord Hastings in 1461.[8] At the beginning of the reign, however, the new king stood necessarily in the shadow of his great follower Warwick. He was not yet married, and it was clear that his marriage, and those of his brothers, must have in due course significant relevance to the policy and connexions of the new regime.

The natural match for Edward would have been a foreign noblewoman, probably a French princess (as Warwick would have wished) or a Burgundian lady (as others would probably have preferred). Edward decided to make his own choice, and a very surprising one it proved to be. On 1 May 1464 the king, while on his way to the north, rode to Grafton Regis and there secretly married the Lady Elizabeth Woodeville, the eldest daughter of Lord Rivers and the widow of Sir John Grey, who had been killed fighting for Henry VI at the second battle of St Albans. The secret was revealed a few months later, at a great council at Reading, and the match created a new territorial interest in English aristocratic politics. Elizabeth's advancement brought fortune to her family on a dramatic scale. Her brother John married the ageing Duchess of Norfolk, and her son by her first marriage the heiress of the Holland duchy of Exeter; her sisters married into the families of Buckingham, Arundel and Herbert.[9]

[8] W. H. Dunham, *Lord Hastings' Indentured Retainers* (Newhaven, Conn., 1955) offers a brief review of his career and a careful study of his affinity.
[9] On the Woodevilles and their new fortunes see Lander, 'Marriage and politics in the fifteenth century', pp. 134–43. On Edward's marriage see also C. Fahy, 'The marriage of Edward IV and Elizabeth Woode-ville – a new Italian source', *E.H.R.* 76 (1961), pp. 660–72.

Politically Edward's marriage was a serious mistake, straining relations dangerously between the king and the Nevilles, and sowing seeds of jealous discord among his other followers. We should beware, however, of exaggerating its folly. It is often said of Elizabeth Woodeville that she was a *parvenue*, that marriage to her demeaned the king in the eyes of his great subjects, and that the advancement of her relatives alienated them from Edward. The first of these assertions is certainly not correct. The new queen's father had only been created Lord Rivers in 1449, but her mother was Jacquetta of Luxembourg, a daughter of the great Burgundian Count of St Pol, and had been the second wife of the Duke of Bedford. Her brother Anthony had married the Scales heiress and assumed the title. Lack of reliable contemporary records makes it impossible to assess precisely the reaction of Edward's councillors at Reading to the news of the match, but it cannot have been quite the traumatic shock to the social exclusiveness of the peerage that it is usually said to have been.[10] Some may have resented the fortune that the marriage brought to the Woodeville family, but Edward was careful not to lavish on his new relations grants of office under the crown, and so their political influence was limited. The Woodevilles never quite became the focus of a dominating clique, like that which Suffolk and Margaret of Anjou had gathered about Henry VI; to the end they remained only one interest among a number that jostled one another for influence around the Yorkist throne. To Warwick, admittedly, the marriage of Anne Holland to a Woodeville must have been specifically galling, for she had been earlier pledged to his nephew George. The king was careful, however, to placate the Nevilles, promoting Warwick's brother George to the vacant archbishopric of York, and his other brother John to the earldom of Northumberland, in the same year as his own marriage. If the marriage of the king put a period to his friendly association with Warwick – and it did – this was not, it would seem, because of its domestic repercussions, but because it was a direct challenge to Warwick's continental diplomacy. Of this more must be said in due course.

We are beginning in fact to anticipate. It becomes necessary now to give some sketch of the events of the years before Edward IV's marriage in 1464, which led up to an open breach between the king and Warwick, and so to the first crisis of his reign.

[10] See further Lander, 'Marriage and politics in the fifteenth century', pp. 133 (esp. notes 2 and 3) and 134.

When Edward IV was crowned in June 1461, the Lancastrians were still formidable in the north, and it was not until November that he was able to meet his first parliament. By then most men were rallying to the rising star of York, and there was a gratifying attendance of peers; the commons, with James Strangeways, a Neville retainer, for their speaker, were very amenable. Edward's title to the throne was solemnly rehearsed and recognized, and all the acts of the Coventry parliament of 1459, which had attainted so many Yorkists, were reversed. A new crop of attainders disinherited the outstanding Lancastrian supporters. In a spirit of doctrinaire legitimism, the process against the Earl of Cambridge, the king's 'noble predecessor' who had been condemned to death in 1415 for his plot to unseat Henry V, was quashed.[11] Parliament thus set a seal of formal legality on what Warwick and Edward, in the course of the year, had already achieved by force. No formal action, it is interesting to notice, was taken against Henry VI. Yorkist legitimism did not demand a formal deposition, like that of 1399; it was enough that the old blood royal had returned at last to its right.

Through the first three years of Edward IV's reign the military activity of the Lancastrians in the north and west and the threat of Queen Margaret's diplomacy kept the king and Warwick together. The fighting was at times severe. In 1462 Warwick seemed to have triumphed in the north; he forced the lords in Bamburgh (Somerset and Sir Ralph Percy) to surrender into Edward's allegiance, on condition that their lands were restored. Margaret herself had by this time already left Scotland. But in 1463 she was back again; Percy let her French captain, Pierre de Brézé, into Bamburgh, which Henry VI made his capital. Though Warwick succeeded in checking the Scots allies of the Lancastrians at Norham, and Margaret left again for the continent, things were still uncertain in the north at the end of the summer. In the winter Somerset went back to the Lancastrian side, and Jasper Tudor raised their standard in Wales. His rebellion was contained by Lord Herbert, and the most serious fighting was in the north. There the Lancastrians were defeated in two engagements in the spring of 1464, at Hedgeley Moor and Hexham, by Warwick's brother Lord Montagu; at the latter field Somerset, Roos, Hungerford and a number of gentlemen were taken and summarily executed as traitors. After this Alnwick and Dunstanborough surrendered without resistance,

[11] *R.P.* vol. V, p. 484; for 'noble predecessor' see *Warkworth's Chronicle*, ed. J. O. Halliwell (Camden Soc., 1839), notes p. 39.

Bamburgh after a short siege. When, a year after this, the unhappy Henry VI was finally taken prisoner in Lancashire near a ford across the Ribble, the Yorkist victory was complete.

Edward IV might have found the task of holding the throne that he had seized in 1461 much harder if Margaret had been luckier in her quest for allies abroad. In 1462 it looked as if she would succeed in making a firm agreement with Louis XI, in return for the promise in her name and Henry's that Calais and its march would be ceded to France when they were back on their thrones.[12] A direct move against Calais was difficult to stage at this point, however, because it lay close to the dominions of the Duke of Burgundy, with whom Louis was simultaneously negotiating for the return of the Somme towns, and with whose court Warwick was in close touch. Warwick was in the circumstances able to insinuate skilfully that the French king might find alliance with the house of York more profitable than the support of its enemies. In October 1463 their communications bore fruit in a convention at Hesdin, where, with the Duke of Burgundy acting as mediator, a truce was agreed between Louis and Yorkist England, and Louis promised to give no further aid to Henry VI, Margaret, Prince Edward her son, 'or any other enemies of the King of England'.[13]

It was unfortunate for Warwick that he allowed his personal interest and national diplomacy to become very closely entangled at this important stage. The seigneur de Lannoy, who was in England as the special envoy of Louis in the spring of 1464 succeeded quite remarkably in charming the earl into a belief that between him and Louis there could be a special, personal relationship. Well before the truce was agreed, the suggestion had been mooted that the new Anglo-French *entente* might be cemented by a marriage between Edward and Bona of Savoy, the sister of the French queen, and Lannoy had sounded Warwick about the possibility of a secret alliance of France and England against Burgundy. Hints had been dropped that all this might pave the way towards a territorial title and apanage for Warwick himself in France.[14] Thus already, in 1464, prospects for an English royal marriage to a French princess, for an Anglo-French

[12] See further J. Calmette and G. Perinelle, *Louis XI et l'Angleterre 1461–83* (Paris, 1930), pp. 19–21.

[13] *Foed.* vol. XI, pp. 508–9.

[14] See further P. M. Kendall, *Warwick the Kingmaker* (London, 1957), pp. 142–4.

combination against Burgundy, and for a European role for the house of Neville had all become associated in negotiations in which Warwick personally was heavily involved. In the summer of this same year the earl was looking forward to a personal meeting with Louis XI at Calais, scheduled for October, where he hoped to push these plans a stage nearer fruition. The news that Edward was already married, revealed to the council at Reading in September, was for him a thunderbolt, therefore. It dashed the hopes that his soaring ambition had fostered. From now on he knew that his ascendancy over Edward and in England was insecure at best, and that the prospect of gains for himself and his house from an Anglo-French *entente* had become suddenly tenuous.[15]

At the time when the secret of Edward's marriage was made public, relations between France and Burgundy were openly deteriorating. Louis in fact knew during the summer of 1464 that Edward IV was in contact both with Charles Count of Charolais, the ageing Duke of Burgundy's heir, and with the Duke of Brittany, who were soon to be the main leaders of rebellion against Louis in the 'War of the Public Weal'. The king of England, independent of Warwick and in opposition to his diplomacy, was veering towards the traditional English ally, Burgundy, whose friendship offered the surest protection for England's commercial ties with Flanders and Brabant, and could pave the way towards a bid for the reconquest of Normandy and Guienne.[16] If Warwick had now been prepared to acquiesce in Edward's personal assumption of control over diplomatic initiative, the course of both French and English history might have been altered. To Louis XI's delight he was not. For the next four years he instead continued to pursue with Louis's encouragement what was in effect a private diplomacy of his own, independent and opposed to that of the king. An open breach between him and Edward was inevitably drawing nearer.

In 1466, the English council debated, hotly and at length, the arguments for and against two important diplomatic marriages,

[15] The degree to which Edward's marriage directly affronted Warwick has been somewhat exaggerated in the past, because it was believed that he had played an important *personal* role in negotiations with France in the summer of 1464, which was not in fact the case: see A. L. Brown and B. Webster, 'The movements of the Earl of Warwick in the summer of 1464 – a correction', *E.H.R.* 81 (1966), pp. 80–2.

[16] On Edward's relations with Brittany and Burgundy at this stage see Calmette and Perinelle, *Louis XI et l'Angleterre*, pp. 55–9.

both aimed to cement Anglo-Burgundian friendship. One was projected between Charles of Charolais (who became Duke of Burgundy next year) and Margaret of York, Edward's sister; the other between Clarence and Mary, Charles's daughter. In spite of Warwick's opposition, Edward seemed determined to push ahead with both arrangements. Margaret's marriage came off, but the other did not. There was a difficulty, it proved, over Clarence's matrimonial future, and one that brought a showdown between Edward and the Nevilles another step nearer. In 1467, Edward discovered that Warwick's brother George, Archbishop of York, was working to secure a dispensation from the pope to enable Clarence to marry Isabel Neville, Warwick's daughter, instead of the Burgundian lady. He reacted strongly. On 8 June George was relieved of his post as chancellor, and the great seal was entrusted instead to Robert Stillington, Bishop of Bath and Wells (about a year earlier Lord Rivers, the queen's father, had replaced Walter Blount as treasurer, apparently to Warwick's considerable chagrin, and had been made an earl).

Edward thus took the initiative a second time, but he was soon running into difficulties. Encouraged by the prospect of alliance with Burgundy to revive English continental ambitions, he had obtained a double subsidy from parliament for an expedition to France, but the project did not seem likely to materialize. People were beginning to murmur that none of the promises of prosperity and good government that the Yorkists had made in the past had been fulfilled. Warwick had acquired meanwhile an influence over Clarence, whose ambitions for political influence were so far unsatisfied. Louis XI, all the time, was encouraging the earl towards sedition, holding out glamorous prospects of a pension and a great lordship in the Low Countries, to be carved out of territories that would be conquered from the Duke of Burgundy.[17]

The crisis came in the summer of 1469. In the spring there was a serious rising in the north, led by one Robin of Redesdale. Robin's manifesto, behind which the hand of Warwick was clearly apparent, adapted all the old Yorkists' complaints against Henry VI to the damage of his Yorkist successor. The king, it was alleged, had estranged the lords of the blood (Warwick and Clarence) from his council; he had taken about him a 'meiny' of evil counsellors (the Woodevilles, William Herbert Earl of Pem-

[17] See ibid. pp. 83–7; and P. M. Kendall, *Warwick the Kingmaker*, pp. 203–4.

broke, Sir John Fogge) who had plundered his estate and 'would
not suffer the king's laws to be executed upon whom they showed
favour to';[18] he had oppressed and grieved the poor commons
with taxes and purveyances. Edward prepared to move north
against the rebels in July, but found that their forces were more
formidable than he had expected. Meanwhile, on 11 July, at
Calais, in Warwick's presence, Archbishop George Neville joined
Warwick's daughter Isabel in marriage to George Duke of
Clarence. After this, their party crossed to England and marched
on London, which opened its gates to them. Edward had not the
time to gather an adequate force. William Herbert, marching to
join him, was defeated at Edgecote near Banbury, and was beheaded by the rebels on the field as a traitor. After this the king
decided, wisely, to make no resistance, and allowed himself, with
Richard of Gloucester and Lord Hastings, to be taken prisoner
at Olney in Buckinghamshire. Lord Rivers and his son John, the
queen's father and brother, were captured at Bristol and executed.

Warwick was to learn, and very soon, that to capture a king and
kill his friends was only half a victory. All that he had really
achieved was to recreate the turmoil and insecurity of the last
miserable years of Henry VI's reign. In the wake of his *coup*, a
wave of disorder spread through the counties, as men who
anticipated a return to the bad old days took the law into their
own hands. A parliament was summoned to meet at York, but it
had to be countermanded because of 'the great troubles in this
our land not yet appeased'.[19] Warwick's original intention had
almost certainly been to use this parliament's authority to put
George of Clarence on Edward's throne, but he could not risk
going that far in the condition of spreading confusion that he
now faced. He found that he could not, after all, do without the
support of Edward's recognized authority. He could only get it
by releasing Edward from custody, and, once Edward was free,
men, even great men, began to rally to him. The authority of a
crowned king was preferable, in the eyes of all except committed
rebels and Lancastrian irreconcilables, to the uncertainty which
was all that Warwick had to promise.

Warwick had brought back the bad old days, to his own cost,
with a vengeance. With Edward at liberty again and in the saddle,
what could the king-maker and Clarence do but spin fresh plots
against the inevitable reconfrontation? The confusion that they

[18] See manifesto in *Warkworth's Chronicle*, pp. 46–51.

[19] See C. L. Scofield, *The Life and Reign of Edward IV* vol. I (London,
1923), p. 502.

had unleashed anew proved their undoing when, in the spring of 1470, Lord Welles, who was embroiled in a local quarrel in Lincolnshire, released a manifesto in their names.[20] Edward was on the alert; Clarence and Warwick could not muster men with sufficient speed, and took to the sea. Calais closed its gates to them, and in the end they dropped anchor off Honfleur. They had no one now to fall back on, except Louis XI, and had lost their independence even in their dealing with him.

From this point forward, effective direction of the English situation more or less passed out of the hands of native English leaders for a period, into those of their respective continental allies. Just as Warwick had found himself unable to consolidate a partial victory, so Edward was to prove unable to consolidate a partial recovery. Everything had been thrown out of joint. Warwick was out of England, but he still had important potential allies there, notably his brother John Neville. John had not moved against Edward in 1469, but the king, when he was free again, felt bound to try what conciliation could do in the north; Redesdale had demanded the restoration of the Percy heir, and restored he was in March 1470 to the earldom of Northumberland. John Neville, who had been created earl in Percy's place in 1464, after his victory at Hexham, was compensated for the loss of this title with a new Marquisate of Montagu, but it did not compensate for the loss of the Percy lands. Edward's move was not very astute. He gained the nominal allegiance of an ex-Lancastrian on whom he could not count in a crisis, and turned John Neville from an unreliable ally into an enemy, who was soon to serve him a particularly ill turn.

So Edward found himself in 1470 in possession, for the time being, of a restive kingdom. Warwick's position was worse, for he could not hope now to be more than a pawn in the schemes of Louis of France. Ever since 1467, or perhaps even earlier, Louis had hoped that he might somehow be able to yoke Warwick with Margaret of Anjou, in a bid to restore Henry VI. The alliance would be an unnatural one, for Warwick had upon his hands the blood of Somerset, Northumberland, Clifford, Roos and half a score of other late supporters of Margaret; and it would almost certainly break down in some new confrontation, but Louis did not care for that. He would only offer the earl support in a new

[20] *Chronicle of the Rebellion in Lincolnshire* in *Camden Miscellany* vol. I (1847), p. 6: see also S. Bentley, *Excerpta Historica* (London, 1831), pp. 282–4.

adventure in England on condition of his reconciliation with
Margaret, and on the promise of English support, once Warwick
and Margaret were in control, in his own war against Burgundy.
Warwick was prepared to put himself in this false position, and
Margaret was brought round to it for her son's sake. The two
strange allies of the future were reconciled at Angers, and Louis
thereon undertook to find money to pay the forces which Warwick and Clarence were gathering in Normandy. When a storm
broke up the English fleet which was watching the coast, Warwick embarked at La Hogue, and on 13 September 1470 he
landed in company with Clarence, the Earl of Oxford, and Jasper
Tudor at Dartmouth.

Edward was caught off his guard, as Warwick himself had
been earlier in the year. Marching south from York, he had
reached Doncaster when he learned that John Neville had gone
over to his enemies, and was only a few miles away, coming to
take him with a far larger force than his own. He had to move
quickly. Crossing the Wash with great difficulty, he reached
King's Lynn, and there, with a few followers, notably his brother
Gloucester and Lord Hastings, he embarked for the Low Countries. So Edward was thrown back on Charles of Burgundy, as
Warwick had been on Louis XI, and the autumn of 1470 became
formally the thirty-ninth year of the reign of Henry VI.

The 'readeption' of Henry VI was a sorry and short lived
affair. There does not even survive a roll recording the acts of its
single parliament, though we know that it did not vote any
subsidy for the war against Burgundy which Warwick, bound
to Louis XI, had to embark upon.[21] The king-maker's power
had been shaky a year before when he had tried to seize the reins
of government; now it was much less secure. Neville retainers
apart, there was no one upon whom he could rely, or who
wanted to rely on him. Clarence, whose hopes of a throne had
been dashed by Henry's restoration, was discontented, and was
soon in touch with his brother abroad. Margaret did not trust
Warwick sufficiently to come from France, or let her son cross
to England. The most faithful Lancastrians, those who had
endured exile, posed a further and dangerous problem for the
king-maker; what was to be done, for instance, about the young
Henry Tudor, whose earldom of Richmond had been conferred

[21] See A. R. Myers, 'The outbreak of war between England and
Burgundy in February 1471', *B.I.H.R.* 33 (1960), pp. 114–15. As
Myers shows, Warwick's fulfilment of his obligation to Louis was
decisive in committing Charles the Bold to Edward.

on Clarence, who was outwardly loyal to the new regime? Henry was too young as yet to cause serious trouble, but the heirs of Somerset and Holland were old enough, when they arrived home from exile. They had no love for Warwick and meant to do him harm if they could.

The deep division between Warwick and the true Lancastrians was the ruin of both when Edward reappeared. He arrived at the Humber with a fleet and 2000 men, equipped at Flushing in the dominions of Charles of Burgundy, on 14 March 1471. The Percies made no move against him, and when he got to York the city opened its gates. As his army began to swell, the story which he put about on his first arrival, that he had come only to claim his duchy of York, was forgotten. He reached London ahead of Warwick. At Barnet, on 14 April, Edward and the king-maker finally met in battle; the earl's host was defeated, and both he and his brother the marquis fell on the field. On the same 14 April, Margaret and her son Edward at last landed in England, too late. Edward caught the army that she and Somerset gathered in the west at Tewkesbury on 4 May, before they could join Jasper Tudor in Wales, and overthrew them. Prince Edward was killed, and Somerset was taken and executed. Margaret was captured a few days later at Little Malvern Priory.

Soon after Edward IV returned victorious from Tewkesbury to London, Henry VI was dead, murdered in the Tower of London. With Warwick dead also, Margaret a prisoner, and Edward on his throne again, the allies of Charles of Burgundy had carried the day everywhere in England against those of Louis XI.

The pattern of English involvement in continental politics, which had been set in the years between Edward's marriage and his recovery of his throne in 1471, remained unaltered for another four years. For Louis XI, the triumph of Edward was a major setback. Barnet and Tewkesbury cost him the control of English affairs which before he had all but achieved, and his only hopes of regaining influence now were either to persuade Edward to alter his alliances, or to stir up Clarence once more against his elder brother. Neither alternative was promising. Clarence was hardly in a position to try his hand again, and Edward's clear purpose was to turn his alliance with Charles of Burgundy from the dependence of exile into the opportunity for an English come-back in France, at Louis's cost.

Edward now badly needed to be able to point to some tangible success, which would endow his regime with the lustre of achievement in his subjects' eyes. The events of the last two years had shown that he had failed, in the first years of his reign, to engage their loyalty fully, and had nearly cost him the throne for ever. The prospect of intervention abroad, with a fair chance of success, was therefore most attractive to him. As a speaker on the king's behalf pointed out to the commons in parliament in 1472, ever since the Norman Conquest England had been most secure and prosperous in the times when her kings made 'outward war' on their enemies. Even Henry VI had 'stood ever in glory and honour while the war was continued beyond', so the speaker said.[22] Why should not massive intervention in France do the same thing for the Yorkists as it had done for the Lancastrians in the reign of Henry V – when likewise the quarrels of a Duke of Burgundy with a French king's councillors had given England her opportunity?

The responsibility of Henry VI's ministers for the loss of the English territories in France had been a traditional theme of Yorkist propaganda, and Edward had long ago been toying with the possibility of attempting their reconquest. Through 1472 and 1473 we find him, therefore, busily negotiating with all Louis XI's enemies with this object in mind, with Francis of Brittany and with John of Aragon, as well as with Charles of Burgundy. Surprisingly, it was with the last that he had most difficulties, for Charles was preoccupied with ambitions in the Empire, and was already showing signs of that defective judgement in politics which was to be his ruin. In 1474, however, a firm agreement was at last concluded. In a treaty sealed in London on 25 July Edward promised to invade France with an army of 10,000 men. Charles undertook, in return for this aid and the promise of the future cession of a vast bloc of territories in eastern France (including Rheims in Champagne, the traditional site of the French royal coronation), to recognize Edward as the rightful King of France.[23]

The army that Edward assembled in order to fulfil his part of the London treaty was, says Commynes, the largest and the best armed that any English king had ever led into France. It numbered perhaps 11,000 men, with a magnificent artillery, and among its captains were a great many of the highest nobility of the land.[24] The campaign of martial propaganda that preceded

[22] *Lit. Cant.* (R.S.) vol. III, p. 282.   [23] *Foed.* vol. XI, pp. 804–14.
[24] See F. P. Barnard, *Edward IV's French Expedition of 1475: The Leaders and their Badges* (Oxford, 1925).

the expedition met with an enthusiastic response: 'all applauded
the king's intentions and bestowed the highest praises on his
proposed plans.'[25] Parliament was persuaded to approve the
collection of substantial subsidies. A great deal of money was also
raised by way of benevolences, and commissioners were sent
busily about the counties to persuade men to make 'gifts': 'The
king goeth so near to us in this county, both poor and rich, that
I wot not how we shall live, but if the world amend', Margaret
Paston wrote from Norfolk.[26] Edward himself backed the efforts
of his servants by personal application to wealthy donors,
bringing the rich and unwilling 'by fair words up to the mark'.[27]
The efforts of the government to make adequate military and
financial preparation were of the same scale of seriousness as they
had been in the old days of Henry V, and seemed to portend a
similarly determined military venture.

Edward IV crossed to Calais with his host on 4 July 1475.
Thither Charles of Burgundy came to meet him, but he did not
bring his army; indeed, until just before Edward's crossing he
had refused himself to quit the unsuccessful siege that he had
laid to Neuss, and he left his men behind there, in Lorraine.
From Calais Edward advanced, with Charles in his company, to
St Quentin, which the duke told him would be surrendered, but
it was not. When the two princes parted in August, Louis had
already gathered a powerful army to oppose any further English
advance. Now totally disillusioned about the prospects of effective support from either Burgundy or Brittany, Edward, in mid-
campaign, decided to reverse his policy completely, and to enter
into negotiations with Louis. On 29 August the two monarchs
met, at Picquigny on the Somme. The treaty that they sealed
there established a truce for seven years between their kingdoms.
Their respective claims to the crown of France were referred to
a court of four arbitrators (which in fact never sat). Edward
abandoned his alliance with Charles, and agreed to evacuate his
army in return for 75,000 crowns in cash down, and – most important of all – on the promise of a French pension of 25,000 gold
crowns annually.[28]

The Treaty of Picquigny was a dramatic *volte face* in late
medieval English diplomacy. It had its disadvantages, of course.

[25] Continuation of the *Croyland Chronicle*, in W. Fulman, *Rerum
Anglicarum Scriptorum Veterum* (Oxford, 1684), vol. I, p. 558.
[26] *P.L.* No. 758.
[27] *C.S.P. Milan* vol. I, p. 194.
[28] *Foed.* vol. XII, pp. 14–21.

By retreating without striking any serious blow in France, the
king clearly ran the risk of losing face in the eyes of his soldiers
and his subjects. The expenses that the expedition had involved
were bound to seem more grievous when it proved empty of
achievement; and the excesses of the disappointed and disbanded
soldiery in England were to add to the public dissatisfaction.
Nevertheless most of the councillors who were with Edward
abroad were in favour of the treaty (Richard of Gloucester was
one of the very few significant exceptions). The main advantage
of the agreement, from the English point of view, was that it
offered a respite from continental entanglements, which was
much needed in the interest of organizing more secure government at home. Together with this it guaranteed a more than
welcome subvention to the crown's financial resources. It is an
index of the confidence of the Yorkist councillors in their ability
to contain the domestic situation, now that the threat of 'outward
war' and its pressures were removed for the time being, that they
were willing shortly after Picquigny to agree to release Margaret
of Anjou, in return for a ransom, and to let her go free into
France.

The diplomatic turnabout of Picquigny proved, in the event,
more important and more decisive in English history than anyone
at the time can have expected. Edward, when he made the treaty,
by no means abandoned his dreams of continental conquest; he
merely postponed them. Yet when he died in 1483 the serious
chances of restoring an English presence on the continent had
become infinitely remote, and the traditional Anglo-French
rivalry, which had dominated north European politics for more
than a hundred years, had ceased to matter. This was because, in
the interval, events had developed far more rapidly than could
be foreseen in 1475.
    Two years after the Treaty of Picquigny was sealed, Charles
the Bold of Burgundy was killed at Nancy, fighting the Swiss and
Austrians who were supported by subsidies from Louis XI. His
heiress Mary, and his wife Margaret of York were left virtually
at the mercy of the French king. Margaret's first and natural
hope was to save herself by an English alliance, to be cemented
by the marriage of Mary to Clarence (whose first wife had died),
but Edward, determined to preserve his French pension, would
not hear of this. Louis, in consequence, was soon in control of
ducal Burgundy, and seemed likely to succeed in absorbing the
whole Burgundian inheritance by marrying Mary to the dauphin.

Unfortunately for him, he tried to move too fast when he attempted to take over the direct government of Flanders; Flemish distrust of the French hardened into hostility, and Mary was married instead to Maximilian of Austria, the son of the Emperor Frederic III. Maximilian claimed all the lands that Mary should have inherited, and he and Louis were soon at war.

Maximilian's hopes of success were continually centred on alliance with England, while Louis XI's object was to keep Edward out of the war. Edward did not alter the policy he had adopted in 1475, and continued to play for time. He listened politely to Louis's proposals for an increase in his pension as a condition of closer alliance, for a marriage for one of his daughters with the dauphin, and for a combined offensive against Maximilian which would gain for England crucial trading privileges in the Low Countries. He listened also, more than politely, to Maximilian's proposals for joint action which would recover for himself Burgundy, and for England her lost French provinces, perhaps even the French crown. But though by 1480 Edward IV was veering towards Maximilian, he would not commit himself fully. He kept just sufficiently clear of involvement to draw annually his pension from Louis XI, which he was finding infinitely useful.[29]

Edward's delays permitted Louis in the end to outmanœuvre him. In 1479 English relations with the Scots were deteriorating, and the French king made the most of his chances to foster ill-feeling. In 1481 full-scale war broke out. In this year and again in 1482 Richard of Gloucester, acting as lieutenant for the king in the north, led armies across the border; and though he did not succeed, as Edward hoped he would, in displacing James III in favour of his brother Albany, he took Berwick and wasted the country as far as Edinburgh. While Edward was fighting this war with some success on a shoestring (for he deliberately avoided asking parliament for a subsidy until 1483), he was naturally unwilling to engage in any major commitment on the continent, and eager to keep his French pension. Louis was in consequence able to undermine the confidence of Maximilian's hopes for help from England, by judiciously informing him about the rival negotiations which he, Louis, had been conducting with Edward, behind Maximilian's back. The latter, already hard pressed, in consequence decided in 1482 to agree to terms with the French.

[29] On the complicated course of diplomatic negotiations in the period 1477–1482 see Calmette and Perinelle, *Louis XI et l'Angleterre*, ch. XII; and Scofield, *The Life and Reign of Edward IV*, vol. II, bk V.

The Treaty of Arras, sealed on 23 December, ended their war, and provided for a future marriage between Maximilian's daughter and the dauphin. England was wholly excluded from their arrangements, and the pension of 1475 ceased to be paid. All present hopes of a profitable English intervention abroad were dashed; and it looked as if English influence in the councils of Europe could for the time being be discounted.

Thus, just over seven years after Picquigny, Edward found that he had missed the last opportunities that an English king would be offered of intervening in France with any real hope of re-establishing the English presence there. The memory of past triumphs was so potent, it is true, that many did not realize this for a long time. Henry VIII could still dream of reconquering part, at least, of what had once been the Lancastrian empire. But it was an empty dream; between the years 1477 and 1482, with the collapse of the great power that Burgundy had once been, the traditional English ambitions had ceased to be realistic.

Edward, when he made peace with Louis XI in 1475, played for time, in order to consolidate himself at home. He needed the respite, for the years following his return in 1471 had not been easy. Though his conciliatory policy after Tewkesbury (there were no attainders) had paid dividends, bringing into his service such able ex-Lancastrians as Sir John Fortescue and Morton, there were still some irreconcilable Lancastrians at large (notably the Earl of Oxford and Jasper Tudor) who might prove troublesome, especially if they could obtain French military assistance. Oxford actually attempted a descent on Cornwall in 1473, and seized St Michael's Mount where he held out successfully for a considerable time. Even more dangerous were the divisions in the king's own family. Clarence, in the right of his wife Isabel Neville, had a claim on the vast inheritance of Warwick the king-maker. But Richard of Gloucester had his eye on the same lands, and secured a claim by his marriage, in 1472, to Warwick's younger daughter, Anne Neville. Though Clarence did rather the better in the final settlement, he remained on poor terms with Gloucester, and was generally dissatisfied.[30] He had once aspired to Edward's throne; in 1470, when Henry VI was restored, the succession had been entailed on his heirs if

[30] On Clarence, Gloucester and the Neville inheritance see Lander, 'Attainder and forfeiture 1453–1509', pp. 129–30.

Henry's line failed;[31] and he had not forgotten these things. He had his own contacts with Louis XI. There was plenty, in fact, to make Edward uncomfortable about his domestic position up to 1475, especially if Louis XI tried to fish in troubled waters. After 1475 he could feel easier, on that score at least.

In 1477 Edward took a chance, when it was offered, to deal with Clarence. Their relations had deteriorated after Edward refused to entertain his sister Margaret's plan for a marriage of Clarence to Mary of Burgundy (a refusal understandable enough in the light of Clarence's past conduct). In the summer Clarence seems to have been privy to a minor rising in Cambridgeshire, and Edward heard of it. Things came to a head before the end of the summer, as a result of a curious intrigue whose details remain obscure. John Stacey, an Oxford clerk, had been accused of attempting to compass the king's death by necromancy, and implicated as his accomplice Thomas Burdett, a member of Clarence's household. The two men were executed. On the day following their execution Clarence appeared unheralded at Westminster, to protest their innocence over the king's head before the council. Edward had had enough, and a few weeks later riposted by placing Clarence in custody. In 1478 parliament, at the royal instigation, proceeded against Clarence by bill of attainder. He was not heard in his own defence; and the Duke of Buckingham, as seneschal of England, passed sentence on him as a traitor. The commons pressed for execution, and he was put to death in the Tower of London – by what means it is not quite clear – on 18 February.[32]

The death of Clarence cleared from Edward's way the one figure who might still threaten him in England. Clarence's heir was a minor. With every year that Edward reigned, the significance of the surviving Lancastrian exiles dwindled. The best pretender that they could now raise was the obscure Beaufort claimant to the earldom of Richmond, Henry Tudor, who was in Brittany; and the Beauforts were statutorily debarred from the succession anyway. Edward's own surviving brother, Richard of Gloucester, did not seem dangerous; he had an impressive record of loyalty, and was the king's most trusted councillor,

---

[31] J. R. Lander, however, suggests that this entail was forged (either by Clarence, or by Edward in 1478 to ensure Clarence's conviction in parliament): 'The treason and death of the Duke of Clarence: a reinterpretation', *Canadian Journal of History* 2, pt. II (1967), pp. 1–28.

[32] Lander, 'The treason and death of the Duke of Clarence', is the most careful recent examination of the circumstances of Clarence's fall.

directing affairs for him in the north. Edward rewarded Richard
amply for his victories in 1481-2, with grants which directly
associated his interests with further conquest in the north.
Gloucester and his heirs were granted the wardenship of the west
march in perpetuity, together with the castle of Carlisle, and permitted to hold and exercise palatine rights in all lands they might
acquire in Lidderdale, Annandale and Clydesdale in Scotland.
These lands, if conquered, would give Richard an apanage fit
even for a king's brother.

So when at the end of 1482 Edward's continental diplomacy
collapsed and he found himself no longer allied to either Louis or
Maximilian, there was no need for undue fear that either would
now be able to disturb the domestic political situation in England.
There was no one left on whose disloyalty to the regime either
could hope to play. Edward seemed to have secured himself and
his dynasty; he was only forty, and his son Edward was growing
fast in his thirteenth year. Time, however, was once more not on
Edward's side. In April 1483, he died suddenly, after a short
illness. The country in consequence had to face all the tremendous problems which, in the political conditions of the age, inevitably attended a minority. England was probably lucky that
Louis XI died only a few months after Edward, also leaving an
heir under age; otherwise that inveterate intriguer would almost
certainly have seen to it that her troubles were even worse than
they proved to be.

In Edward's personal circle, there had always been tensions
between his old councillors and the queen's relatives, notably
between William Lord Hastings, the chamberlain, and the Marquis of Dorset, Queen Elizabeth's son.[33] While he was alive,
Edward had been able to keep their mutual hostility under
control; now that he was dead it was sure to come into the open,
as a political feud. The Woodevilles were, in April 1483, in a
strong position. The new king, Edward V, was at Ludlow, in the
charge of the queen's brother, Lord Rivers. In London, another
of her brothers, the Admiral Edward Woodeville, had command
of the fleet, and her son Dorset was in charge at the Tower. The
Woodevilles, however, were not on good terms with the late
king's brother Richard, who was the senior member of the royal

[33] On the position of the Woodevilles and their relations with other
prominent figures at this stage see E. W. Ives, 'Andrew Dymmock and
the papers of Anthony Earl Rivers', *B.I.H.R.* 41 (1968), pp. 216-29.

family. To him their rivals looked naturally for support, and his attitude became in consequence politically crucial.

Edward IV, like Henry V before him, left a will, in which he named his brother to be protector of the realm.[34] It was clear from the first, as it had been in the case of Henry V, that this will could cause difficulty. The majority of the peers who gathered in London (where, as we have seen, the Woodeville influence was strong) rejected the will, as their predecessors had done in 1422, preferring that a council should be named, with Gloucester as its president. In order to silence arguments on Gloucester's behalf, they were anxious to crown the new king, Edward V, as soon as possible, for the precedents of Henry VI's minority were clear. Then Humphrey of Gloucester's protectorship had ended at the king's coronation, and he had afterwards only been chief councillor. They therefore wrote to Rivers to bring the king to London as quickly as he might, with a good force of men. It would seem, however, that the council was more divided than it had been in 1422, and that Hastings wrote on behalf of the dissentients to Richard of Gloucester, urging him to come to London too, and to act to protect his right under the will. Gloucester was also promised support by Henry Stafford, the Duke of Buckingham, the richest territorial magnate in the kingdom after himself, and who also was absent from London when the council met.[35]

Unfortunately for Rivers and his charge, a very conciliatory letter from Gloucester put the queen's party off their guard.

[34] On this (lost) will see C. A. J. Armstrong in his new edition of D. Mancini, *The Usurpation of Richard III* (Oxford, 1969), pp. 60-1 and note 7.

[35] The course of events leading up to Richard III's usurpation is very complicated. The most important contemporary sources are the account of the Italian Mancini (*The Usurpation of Richard III*, which contains copious notes and an invaluable introduction by Armstrong), and the continuation of the *Croyland Chronicle*, on which see J. G. Edwards, 'The second continuation of the Croyland Chronicle – was it written in ten days?', *B.I.H.R.* 39 (1966), pp. 117-29. Polydore Vergil in his *Anglica Historia* and Sir Thomas More in his *History of Richard III* (ed. J. R. Lumby, Cambridge, 1883) both give further information, which is not all of it reliable and suffers in parts from their Tudor bias. On the sources in general see C. A. J. Armstrong, in Mancini, *The Usurpation of Richard III*, intro., pp. xvii-xx. The fullest recent reconstruction of events is that of P. M. Kendall in *Richard III* (London, 1955). I have followed, for the most part, the account given by E. F. Jacob in *The Fifteenth Century* (Oxford, 1961), pp. 610-23.

They dropped their emphasis to Rivers on the haste with which he should make for London with the king, and on the force that he should bring. When he and the young Edward reached Stony Stratford on 29 April, they found that Gloucester and Buckingham were at Northampton only a few miles away, with a stronger following. At dawn next day, the two dukes placed Lord Rivers under arrest. Sir Thomas Vaughan and Sir Richard Grey were arrested a little later in the king's own company, and Gloucester took control of his person and movements. Grey and Rivers were subsequently beheaded, though they had done nothing that formally deserved death. Gloucester and Buckingham marched on to London, and soon the capital as well as the king was in their hands. There was no force sufficient to resist them there, and the queen, with Dorset and her brother Lionel, Bishop of Salisbury, took refuge in Westminster sanctuary. The king was lodged in the Tower.

Events from this point moved rapidly. All went relatively peaceably at first. The council confirmed Gloucester in the office of protector, and gave him the *tutela* of the king's person, which granted to him the technical legal power to use the royal authority as if it were his own. There were some changes of office; Bishop Russell of Lincoln became chancellor, and Sir John Woode, an associate of Gloucester's, became treasurer. Buckingham was made chief justice of north and south Wales, with control of the principal royal castles there and the authority to array men in the western counties of England. Given the daily increasing military strength that Richard and Buckingham disposed in the capital,[36] it is not surprising that there was no protest from the retiring chancellor, nor from Archbishop Bourchier of Canterbury, the leading ecclesiastical peer. But the old servants of Edward IV were not happy; and early in June Richard heard that Lord Hastings, feeling he had gone too far in the first instance, had made contact with the Woodevilles in the Westminster sanctuary. Having used force to capture the king and to gain control of London, there seemed now no option but to use it again. In a council meeting on 13 June,[36A] Gloucester personally charged Hastings, Morton and Lord Stanley with conspiring against the government. Hastings was led out and beheaded, and Morton was taken to the Tower. Stanley, curiously, was soon freed.

A situation of political emergency had now clearly developed.

[36] For contemporary comment on these forces see *Croyland Chronicle*, p. 566, and Bentley, *Excerpta Historica*, p. 17. [36A] See note on p. 489.

We cannot tell what scruples, if any, Gloucester may have had about taking the logical step of seizing the throne for himself. He had very little time for hesitation, since, when Hastings was beheaded, the coronation was scheduled for little more than a week ahead. Some time between 13 and 22 June Buckingham went down to the Guildhall to address the mayor and citizens of London. Edward V, his brother, and all Edward IV's children were born out of wedlock, he told them, since, when King Edward married Elizabeth Woodeville, he was already under contract of marriage to Lady Eleanor Butler (a story which, as far as it can be checked, seems to be without foundation).[37] Clarence's heir was excluded from the succession, on the ground of his father's attainder. The crown must therefore pass to Richard of Gloucester, the sole representative of the old and true blood royal. On Sunday 22 June, the day that should have seen the coronation, the same story was taken up in the pulpits of the city by well briefed public preachers. On 25 June parliament met, and on the very grounds that Buckingham and the preachers had outlined petitioned Richard to take the crown that was his by right. Richard had plenty of troops in London, and the petition was probably not spontaneous. He accepted the request that it contained, and dated the beginning of his reign from 26 June.

Edward V and his brother Richard Duke of York, who was with him in the Tower, were last seen for certain during the mayoralty of Edmund Sha, which ended in October 1483. Everyone soon believed that they were dead – indeed the Italian Mancini thought they were as good as dead before he left England at the end of June.[38] There is no absolutely firm evidence that Richard III was responsible for their ends, but there is no good reason to doubt that he was. Their lives could not be anything but a direct threat to his throne. Though he was crowned in great pomp, and though he had organized successfully for himself a claim in blood and as the elected choice of the three

[37] See further M. Levine 'Richard III – usurper or lawful king?', *Speculum* 34 (1959), pp. 391–401.

[38] See *Great Chronicle of London*, p. 234, and Mancini, *The Usurpation of Richard III*, p. 93. On the fate of the princes, see C. A. J. Armstrong's introduction to Mancini, pp. 20–3, and note 91 (which furnishes a further bibliography). The most important single contribution to the controversy as to who killed them seems to me to be L. E. Tanner and W. Wright, 'Recent investigations regarding the fate of the princes in the Tower', *Archaeologia* 84 (1934), pp. 1–26.

estates,[39] what had really made him king was his military control of the capital in the crucial weeks of May–June 1483 – and the support of Buckingham. His subjects' acceptance of him was skin deep. If either of the princes had lived, he must inevitably, sooner or later, have become the focus of conspiracies to unseat Richard.

In a century in the course of which four kings (or five if one includes Richard II) lost the throne of England in consequence of rebellions, the usurpation of 1483 managed to be particularly shocking. Never, even in recent years, had so many powerful men been hurried out of the world with so little reason, or so little ceremony. Rivers, a pious, upright, apolitical peer, who wore a hair shirt and dreamed of going on crusade, had committed no crime with which he could be charged, and no more had Grey or Vaughan. The charges levelled by Richard against Hastings were unproven when he was beheaded without trial. Edward V had patently never been in a position to do anything to deserve to lose his throne. The reaction of Richard's subjects was what might have been expected. It was not respect which his actions inculcated, but fear, insecurity and distrust. Resentment and bewildered impotence are the dominant emotions in most contemporary accounts of events in London in the crucial days of June 1483: 'I have seen many men burst forth into tears and lamentation when mention was made of him [Edward V] after his removal from men's sight', wrote Mancini.[40] No one had said anything quite like that when Richard II or Henry VI lost their thrones, because the men who rose against them were actuated in part at least by resentment at genuine misgovernment. The usurpation of 1483 bore no such justification.

Richard of course did his best to discredit his brother's government. He told people about the laxness and luxury of Edward IV's court, and laboured the oppressive nature of his 'benevolences', but his propaganda failed to convince, because it

[39] On Richard's claim to the throne see S. B. Chrimes, *English Constitutional Ideas in the Fifteenth Century* (Cambridge, 1936), pp. 32, 123–6; and B. Wilkinson *Constitutional History of England in the Fifteenth Century* (London, 1964) pp. 161–3. I suspect that the latter overemphasizes the importance of election by the estates, and underestimates the importance of Richard's blood royal, in the explicit contemporary statements about his right, especially that in *R.P.* vol. VI, pp. 240–2.

[40] Mancini, *The Usurpation of Richard III*, p. 93.

touched no genuine sense of public grievance. Richard was perhaps rather more diligent in the discharge of business than his brother had been in late years, but there was really no difference in their methods of government, and he lacked Edward's intuitive understanding of the way in which men's hearts (and women's) were to be won. Richard might claim that Edward had been governed by a corrupt *coterie*, dominated by the Woodevilles, but more people were resentful of Richard's own friends. They felt rather with Thomas Collingbourne, gentleman of Wiltshire, whose famous rhyme earned him the gallows:

> The Cat, the Rat, and Lovel our dog
> Rule all England under the Hog.[41]

The Cat was William Catesby, Richard III's esquire of the body; the Rat Sir Richard Ratcliffe, perhaps the king's most intimate retainer; Lord Lovel was the chamberlain who succeeded the dead Hastings. The hog, of course, was Richard himself, whose badge was the white boar.

The reign of Richard III was short and unhappy. Once on the throne he had to learn the lesson that Warwick the king-maker had learned before him, that to seize power breeds insecurity, and insecurity sedition.

Richard was challenged first when he had been on the throne a matter of weeks. During August of 1483 a movement was forming in the home counties to rescue the children of Edward IV before it was too late. Some time in September, probably, Richard's late accomplice Buckingham was drawn into the affair. He was influenced in part, evidently, by Bishop Morton, who was in prison under his care at Brecon, and who was in touch with Henry Tudor in Brittany. Morton was one of those who had been loyal to Henry VI right up to 1471. The usurpation had revivified the lingering sympathies of all those who had once been attached to the Lancastrian cause, and given their affections a new point and purpose.

Buckingham's rising was a failure. By the time that he marched out of Wales the rebels of Kent and the home counties had been checked by the forces of the Duke of Norfolk, and Buckingham's men began to disperse when they heard the news. Morton escaped to the continent, but the duke himself was taken in

---

[41] C. L. Kingsford, *English Historical Literature in the Fifteenth Century* (Oxford, 1913), p. 249.

Shropshire, and executed after a summary trial. Henry Tudor appeared too late off the Devon coast, and never landed. Although it was contained, the rebellion had very disturbing features from the government's point of view. Particularly ominous were the number of independent gentlefolk who had been involved, men like Sir William Stonor and Sir William Berkeley, and the Surrey leaders Sir John and Sir Richard Guildford, and the way in which the yeomen of the home counties had rallied to them.[42] Their initiative in the revolt (for they were in arms before their ducal leader) showed how deeply Richard had alienated the sympathies of ordinary, decent folk, by his unashamed bid for personal power. Though the revolt was put down with politic lenience, this moderation demonstrably failed to solidify acquiescence in the regime. Henry Tudor remained in all too constant communication with prospective supporters. Lord Stanley, who had been spared when Hastings was beheaded and whose wife had been pardoned for her knowledge of Buckingham's movement, was one of the chief addressees of his letters. There was besides a steady trickle of defections to the pretender. James Blount, the keeper of Hammes castle, not only let his prisoner, the Earl of Oxford, escape, but went with him to Brittany to join the Tudor. Even when Richard had been a year and more king of England, it was clear that he was still failing to engage the loyalty of his subjects.

This was the decisive factor when the final act in the drama came, after Henry Tudor's landing at Milford Haven on 7 August 1485. Rhys ap Thomas and Sir John Savage, two of the principal men on whom Richard had relied for the defence of west Wales, went over to Henry, and so did Sir Walter Herbert. Their followers swelled the little army, which Oxford and the Tudor led, into a sizeable force. It met King Richard and his host at Bosworth in Leicestershire on 22 August. In the battle that followed there were more changes of side than at any other field in the civil wars of the century. The issue was decided when Lord Stanley, who had arrived with his followers uncommitted threw in his lot for Henry. Northumberland, who had been detailed by Richard to watch Stanley, was never engaged. Richard was killed in the *mêlée*, leading his household troops in an attack on his rival's centre. At the end of the day Stanley

[42] On the Kentish participants in the rebellion see A. E. Conway's useful study 'The Maidstone sector of Buckingham's rebellion', *Archaeologia Cantiana* 37 (1925), pp. 97–120.

placed the crown, which had been knocked from Richard's helmet, on Henry VII's head.

Richard III had abilities, and had it not been for the manner in which he seized the throne, he might have been a successful king. His success in the north in his brother's reign, both as a soldier and as an administrator, earned him genuine popular affection there. On the throne he showed an aptitude for business and a clearheaded insight into the problems confronting contemporary government. But there were no signs of originality in his approach; his methods as a ruler were not in any respect radically different from those of either Edward IV or Henry VII. Hence, if there is a tragic side to his story, the tragedy is purely personal. The only point at stake at Bosworth was whether England should be ruled by a Plantagenet or a Tudor. The death of the last of the Yorkists had no long-term significance.

NOTE

Alison Hanham's important article, 'Richard III, Lord Hastings, and the historians' (*E.H.R.* 87, pp. 233–48), appeared too recently for me to be able to take any note of its content in my text. She argues most cogently that Hastings was not in fact executed on 13 June 1483 (the date traditionally accepted by historians) but on 20 June. This is the date given in a letter written by Simon Stallworth to Sir William Stonor on the 21st. The re-dating is confirmed by evidence from the records of the Mercers' Company showing that Morton, who was arrested at the same time as Hastings, was at liberty and still regarded as an influential councillor on 15 June. Her conclusion is that Hastings, Morton and others were not arrested until after Richard had in his power not only the young king but also his brother York (fetched from Westminster sanctuary on 16 June so as to be able to attend the impending coronation), and had begun to 'sound out some of the magnates to see how much support he might obtain for a claim to the throne'. The firm loyalty of Hastings and Morton to Edward V, which now became apparent, made it necessary to get them out of the way. This was achieved at a council at the Tower on 20 June, when they were arrested on the charge of plotting against the Protector—at a point when, with the coronation imminent, it still looked to people at large as if his intentions towards Edward V could not be anything but honourable. The effect of this suggested chronology is thus to re-emphasize the shrewdness and the calculation of Richard's moves.

20

England under the Yorkists

The Yorkist kings have been often acclaimed as the authors of new ways in government, who laid the foundations upon which the despotism of the Tudors was built. It is doubtful whether their practices were in fact startlingly original, and nowadays it is questioned whether there ever was a Tudor despotism. It is none the less true that Edward IV was more successful in governing England than any king had been for a hundred years, except for Henry V. It is also true that there were striking similarities between the governmental practices of his reign and his brother's and those of Henry VII. The Yorkists did solve problems where the Lancastrians had failed lamentably to cope, and in ways that set important precedents.

There was nothing obscure about what was wrong with the government of Edward IV's Lancastrian predecessor in its last days. Sir John Fortescue, Henry VI's famous chief justice, made a clear and penetrating diagnosis of its shortcomings in his *Governance of England*. Two evils stood out for him: the insolvency of the crown, and the disordinate influence of great men and their retainers. He attributed the insolvency of Henry VI to inadequate control of expenditure, on the household and on fees and pensions granted with too free a hand; and to overlavish patronage which had substantially reduced the crown demesnes. This had driven the crown to borrow, and to borrow again to meet its creditors, in consequence of which they 'alway grouch for lack of their payment and defame his highness of misgovernment'.[1] The overgreat riches and ambition of the greater nobility had been in itself dangerous: 'there may no greater peril grow to a prince than to have a subject equipollent to himself'.[2] The private interest of the lords had made them bad counsellors. They had

[1] J. Fortescue, *The Governance of England*, ed. C. Plummer (Oxford, 1885), p. 118.
[2] ibid. p. 130.

used their influence to obtain the appointment of their retainers to key offices in local government, to the end that they might 'be more mighty in their countries to do what they list; and the king in less might and [to] have the fewer officers to repress them when they do amiss'.[3] To this analysis of the causes of Henry VI's difficulties, we would only wish to add one item: the discredit that military failure abroad brought upon the king himself and his advisers.

Fortescue had his own ideas about how the ills that he diagnosed should be remedied. There were those in his day, he tells us, who looked for a solution in a wholly different style of government, more like that of absolutist France, but for himself he had no desire to see the king's rule over England brought closer to despotism.[4] It was his special pride that in his native land the king ruled according to laws chosen by his people (statutes made in parliament) and could take taxes only with their assent.[5] This mixed constitution in which authority was shared between the king and his subjects (what Fortescue called *dominium politicum et regale*) was made workable by the prosperous independence of the commons of England, which was the glory of the land and made it strong.[6] Fortescue believed that constitutional change in an absolutist direction could only weaken the kingdom, and looked therefore for a solution to her troubles in practical administrative improvements, which would strengthen the monarchy, and yet preserve intact the virtue of the political laws. Measures should be taken to increase the king's revenue by acts of resumption, with parliament's assent; by a careful calculation of his needs and the provision of a regular revenue to meet his recurrent charges;[7] by careful scrutiny of grants of pensions and an embargo on the grant of demesne lands in fee without parliamentary consent.[8] He wished to see the wealth of the magnates kept within limits by a sharper insistence on the king's right to control their marriages and to vet all alienations of their estates, which ought not to be demised without a royal licence.[9] He also wished to see a very close

---

[3] ibid. p. 152.   [4] ibid. pp. 137–40.

[5] J. Fortescue, *De Laudibus Legum Anglie*, ed. S. B. Chrimes (Cambridge, 1942), pp. 40, 86.

[6] *Governance*, ch. I and II; see also *De Natura Legis Nature* (in the collected *Works*, ed. Lord Clermont), Lib. I, ch. XVI.

[7] *Governance*, ch. VI and XIV.

[8] ibid. ch. XIX, p. 154.

[9] ibid. p. 134.

scrutiny by the king's council of all petitions for office, and a limit set on the number of offices under the crown which any one man might hold; and to make all office holders swear that they would take no fee or livery from any man but the king for the term of the offices to which they were appointed.[10]

The most original of Fortescue's suggestions for better government was for a new kind of council.[11] In the past great lords had abused their position as councillors to further their own interests and those of their kinsmen, servants and tenants, and had neglected the king's business. He proposed the appointment of a council of twenty-four persons, twelve clerks and twelve laymen, wise and discreet men of middling means who should be salaried, and should swear to take no fee or livery of any but the king. These men would act together with eight of the great lords (four bishops and four secular magnates) whom the king would name annually to serve along with them. By this means Fortescue believed that private interest and corruption could be effectively eliminated from its heart and centre in the king's council.

To judge by their acts, the Yorkist kings saw eye to eye with Fortescue in his diagnosis of what was amiss in the government of England. Their remedies were not always the same as his, but they were often very reminiscent of what he wrote. This does not mean that he influenced them, simply that the lines of approach that he suggested were those which common sense and past experience suggested as most likely to restore things to a better frame.

The Yorkists, needless to say, did not adopt anything like Fortescue's plans for the reform of the council; these were too tidy to be practical. But their councils were very different from the continual councils of Henry VI's early years. Their composition was fluid, the personnel depending on the king's choice (though in the 1460s, of course, there was always a group of Neville supporters). We know of a great many men who were called councillors (124 names have been traced).[12] A large proportion were men of middle standing, including professional administrators and lawyers, such as Sir William Alyngton

[10] ibid. pp. 143–4, 153.

[11] ibid. ch. XV.

[12] The best study of the council in the period is J. R. Lander, 'Council, administration and councillors 1461–85', *B.I.H.R.* 32 (1959), pp. 138–180, on which I have relied heavily in this section.

(speaker in parliament in 1477), Sir Thomas Vaughan (treasurer of the chamber), Sir John Fogge and Richard Fowler (king's solicitor and later chancellor of the duchy of Lancaster); and under Richard III William Catesby (speaker in 1484), Sir Richard Ratcliffe (knight of the body) and Thomas Lynom (the king's solicitor). A number of clerics did good service too, the most notable of all, after 1471, being the ex-Lancastrian exile and future cardinal, John Morton. There was a close association between the council and the royal household, especially through those knights and esquires of the body who were also councillors. This meant that the council always had a leavening of men directly dependent on the king, who had fees and robes from him and had made their way in his service.

This does not mean that the Yorkists sought in any way to eliminate the aristocracy from their councils. There were always some peers present at its meetings; and under Edward IV William Lord Hastings, the chamberlain, was a dominant figure among the crown's advisers. John Tiptoft Earl of Worcester was twice treasurer of England in the first part of the reign, and as such was normally present at council meetings. Lord Audley, Lord Stanley and, in the reign of Richard III, Lord Lovel also gave much advice. The reason why the very great among the magnates, the men like Warwick and Clarence and Gloucester, were often absent when only routine business was in question was that they had plenty of affairs of their own – and indeed of the king's – to attend to, far from the court and Westminster. They and other peers were always summoned when major political decisions were to be taken. Great councils, at which a substantial body of peers were present, were summoned frequently enough by the Yorkists. It was to a great council at Reading in 1464 that Edward announced that he was married; to a great council that he expounded his plans for his sister Margaret's marriage in 1468. When the news of Charles the Bold's death reached England in 1477, a great council was immediately summoned to review the diplomatic implications of the new and unforeseen situation.

Though the Yorkist councils were very different from the continual councils of the 1420s and 1430s, there was nothing new about them. The lack of definition of the personnel of the small council in the Yorkist period, its close connexions with the household, and indeed its activities, were all reminiscent of the councils of Henry VI in the period of Suffolk's dominance, and later of that of Queen Margaret; and also, for that matter, of the council of Richard II's later years. With a king on the throne who was able bodied and of sound mind, the composition of the council always tended to reflect in large degree royal eclecticism; and the same factors also tended to make the trained royal servants prominent among its members.

What was most notable about the Yorkist council was its assiduous attention to business. The fact that there are few surviving enrolments in the chancery which quote conciliar authority for the issue of letters under the great seal does not mark a decline in its influence. It is clear that, in the case of a good many warrants under the signet and the king's sign manual, the council had in fact been consulted.[13] And it was not just the traditional routine business that kept councillors occupied. They were continuously busy coordinating the work of officials charged with, for instance, the management of royal estates, which was an important new side to their activity. Appointments to office were brought under closer scrutiny than in the past: 'As for the labour for the baileyships and farms', Godfrey Green wrote in 1475 to his patron Sir William Plumpton, 'your worship understands what labour it is to sue therefore: first to have a bill enclosed of the king, then to certain lords of the council (for there is an act made that nothing shall pass from the king until such time as they have seen it), and so to the privy seal and chancellor.'[14] Here is an 'act' that would have warmed Fortescue's heart. Calais was another matter which, in the early 1460s, took up a good deal of time, and it was to the credit of the councillors that at length measures were taken which both secured the regular payment of the garrison and offered the staplers the prospect of seeing their loans to the crown more rapidly repaid. The councillors were hard at work, day in, day out; when the king was away from his capital some went with him and some stayed at Westminster to dispatch business there. Their energy and activity was one major reason why the kingdom was better governed under the Yorkists than it had been for many years.

In Fortescue's advice on the governance of England, measures to improve the crown's financial position took pride of place. Indebtedness had been the bugbear of the Lancastrians, and had much to do with both Henry VI's military failures in France

[13] See J. R. Lander, 'The Yorkist council and administration 1461–1485', *E.H.R.* 73 (1958), pp. 27–46.

[14] *Plumpton Correspondence*, ed. T. Stapleton (Camden Soc., 1839), p. 33.

and his political misfortunes in England. In this sphere the efforts of the Yorkists to set things to rights were impressive.

The great breakthrough of the Yorkist period was the enlargement of the crown's revenue from land. The accession of Edward IV considerably increased the royal estates, adding to the old crown lands and those of the duchy of Lancaster his two great private inheritances of March and York. Edward IV also made better use of his right of wardship than his predecessor had, and held some very important inheritances in hand in this way at times, including those of Buckingham and Shrewsbury. Between 1461 and 1473 there were too a number of acts of resumption, though it must be admitted that the effect of these, as of previous Lancastrian acts,[15] was substantially reduced by the very large number of exemptions from them (besides, Edward was himself generous, sometimes beyond the point of policy). Attainders added further to his properties. Though many of these were ultimately reversed the additional revenue that they brought in meantime was considerable, and the Clarence estates, which included much of the great Warwick inheritance, were a really golden prize when they came in in 1478. This was the most important gain of the whole period; before it Edward had never come quite up to Fortescue's ideal of a king who had no subject near 'equipollent' with himself, [16] but afterwards he undoubtedly did.

The crown profited not only because it had more estates than before, but also as a result of their more efficient administration. The Yorkists extended to a much larger proportion of the crown lands than their predecessors had what have been called 'the normal methods of contemporary large scale estate management'.[17] The great private landowner employed professionals to oversee his estates – usually a surveyor, a receiver and an auditor to look after manors that were grouped regionally. Among the crown lands, until Edward IV's time, only the duchy of Lancaster lands had been administered in this way, most others being farmed out through the exchequer. Starting in 1461, the first year of his reign, Edward regrouped a series of complexes of estates, and put them under the management of professionals

[15] On Lancastrian acts of resumption see B. P. Wolffe, 'Acts of resumption in Lancastrian parliaments', *E.H.R.* 73 (1958), pp. 583–613.

[16] Fortescue, *Governance*, p. 130.

[17] The quotation is from B. P. Wolffe's masterly article 'The management of English royal estates under the Yorkist kings', *E.H.R.* 71 (1956), pp. 1–27. My discussion of the Yorkists' landed revenues is based on this important study.

in the royal service. John Milewater was appointed receiver for a group of estates in the Welsh border counties, some belonging to the earldom of March, some to the duchy of Lancaster, and some to the Stafford inheritance which was in wardship; his accounts were audited at Hereford by John Luthington. Other groups of estates in other areas were treated similarly, and when Clarence was attainted the system was further extended. Peter Beaupie, clerk of the greencloth, took initial control of the forfeited estates (an enormous accretion to the crown's landed wealth) which were divided into a series of local receiverships: thus the Clarence estates in the western midlands were entrusted to the management of John Harcourt, those in the central midlands to John Luthington, and those in the west country to John Hayes. A general supervision over all these officials was exercised by Sir Thomas Vaughan, the treasurer of the chamber, with a commission working under him. Richard III followed his brother's example in management when he seized the throne; John Fitzherbert was made responsible as receiver for most of the lands of Queen Elizabeth Woodeville, and Edmund Chadderton for those of the Earl of Buckingham when they were forfeited after his revolt.

The headquarters of this system of estate management was the chamber. The treasurer of the chamber (from 1465 Sir Thomas Vaughan) received a good proportion of the issues of the estates in cash; some was paid out in accordance with warrants under the signet, the king's private seal. Vaughan, with others of the council's professionals, usually audited the accounts before they were passed on to the exchequer, before which the receivers were not answerable. The exchequer was thus largely bypassed as far as accounting was concerned, and entirely as regarded the handling of the issues of the estates. As long as the household men to whom estate management was entrusted were faithful in discharging their duties, this made for much speedier and more efficient collection of revenue. Most important of all, it relieved the revenue of the crown estates in question from the burden of assignments made at the exchequer, with which the issues of crown lands had always been heavily loaded in the Lancastrian period. This did not really diminish the importance of the exchequer as a financial department; it continued to supervise the collection of subsidies, the customs, and some farms, and to meet major national expenses. It did mean that the king gained an independence in the control of a valuable proportion of his revenues which his predecessors had never enjoyed.

Edward IV took some other measures to improve the crown's income from estates and rights over landed property. In 1462 the exchequer was ordered to omit from the Pipe Roll accounts farms and fee farms of 40s. and above in annual value, and officials were appointed in eight regions to collect the issues and pay them over to the treasurer of the household. This does not seem to have resulted in a substantial increase in revenue. But the case was different with the commission appointed in ten counties in 1474 to inquire into feudal tenures and the king's rights arising therefrom; some of the fines imposed for evasion of incidents were very heavy.[18] These measures are interesting because they help to illustrate how the whole Yorkist system of management anticipated, often in detail, that of the early Tudors. The task of the commissioners of 1474 was essentially the same as that which the hated Dudley and Empson discharged for Henry VII. By 1485 the idea of something very like a court of general surveyors was already envisaged. We learn this from a memorandum on royal estate management attributed to Richard III's reign (but which may belong to the first year of Henry VII): 'all auditors, each year, between Candlemas and Palm Sunday, should make declaration of all the livelihood in their charge, before certain persons assigned to receive them'.[19] These declarations were what the general surveyors were to be concerned with, but their records do not begin until 1503-4.

Edward IV, like Henry VII, acquired in the end a reputation for avarice. Perhaps it was deserved. But it needed constant economy and careful accounting for his measures to have any effect at all. We can see this anxiety for economy written very clear in, for instance, the famous Ordinance of 1478 for the household (whose expenditure had been a constant source of complaint for a century) which made sharp restrictions on allowable expenses. Many of its regulations are directly related to passages in the *Black Book of the Household*, compiled a little earlier, and whose chief object was to ensure careful account of all moneys that the household spent.[20] Edward IV's household in fact cost less to

[18] On this commission see J. R. Lander, 'Edward IV: the modern legend: and a revision', *History* 41 (1956), pp. 48-9.
[19] *Letters and Papers Illustrative of the Reigns of Richard III and Henry VII* (R.S.) vol. I, pp. 83-4.
[20] The text of the ordinance is given by A. R. Myers, *The Household of Edward IV* (Manchester, 1959), pp. 211-28; for the relation between it and the *Black Book* see his introduction, pp. 39-44.

run than that of either Henry VI or Henry VII, though he
certainly lived with more magnificence than the former.

By the 1470s the effects of overall economy – of better management, better accounting, and cuts in unnecessary expenditure in
all areas of crown finance – were such that the king was able to
start paying off old debts. Between 1471 and 1476 debts owed
to Gerard Caniziani, the agent of the Medici, were reduced from
£14,390 to £3000. In 1478 the king was able to assign revenues
to pay off the whole of his debt of over £12,000 to the city of
London. In 1466 he had owed nearly £33,000 in Calais, mostly
to the staplers; by 1483 this was reduced to a mere £2000.[21]
Edward died solvent, which none of his Lancastrian predecessors
had done. He had broken the vicious spiral of mounting insolvency which in their day, as Fortescue noted, had brought the
king's name into disrepute and estranged his subjects from him.

The issues of crown lands and the profit of feudal rights were not
the only sources of revenue that made Edward IV a newly
wealthy king. The pension that Louis XI agreed to pay him at
Picquigny in 1475 was a very important subvention, and so
determined was Edward to keep it that he was prepared, as we
have seen, to sacrifice the coherence of English diplomacy to this
single end. Two other sources of revenue which were significant
demand special attention.

During the fifteenth century revenue from the customs fell,
largely because of the decline of the trade in wool on which the
duty was heaviest. Rather than raise the rate on other exports,
Edward preferred himself to engage in commerce: 'like a private
person who lived by trade, he exchanged through his agents
merchandise for merchandise with both Italians and Greeks'.[22] As
early as 1463 his agents shipped more than 300 sacks of wool, to be
sold for the king's profit. In 1464 James de Sanderico took charge
as his factor of the shipment of 8000 cloths, from Southampton. In
1466 Alan de Monteferrato was commissioned to ship 6000 sacks
of wool, 20,000 cloths, 16,000 blocks of tin and 10,000 'barrels'
of vessels of pewter via the straits of Gibraltar to Italy.[23] Ventures

[21] For figures and further discussion see J. R. Lander, 'Edward IV:
the modern legend', pp. 46–7.

[22] *Croyland Chronicle*, in W. Fulman, *Rerum Anglicarum Scriptorum
Veterum* (Oxford, 1684), p. 559.

[23] See E. F. Jacob, *The Fifteenth Century* (Oxford, 1961), pp. 591–2;
and C. L. Scofield, *The Life and Reign of Edward IV* vol. II (London,
1923), pp. 404–26.

such as these brought a handsome profit. Edward's mercantile enterprises besides brought him into much contact with foreign merchants (the larger part of his exports were shipped in foreign vessels) and he was able to borrow more money more often from alien merchants than any king since Edward III. Caniziani, the Medici agent, was particularly serviceable in this regard; he became a trusted intimate, and on occasion acted for the king in diplomatic business.

Benevolences were the other source of finance that Edward exploited with particular success. Notionally a benevolence meant a free gift, usually in lieu of obligatory military service, and it was not strictly a new source of revenue, for Richard II and the Lancastrians had from time to time obtained similar 'gifts' from their subjects.[24] But Edward was more systematic, especially with the benevolences that were raised to pay for the Picquigny expedition and for the Scottish war at the end of the reign. The benevolence of 1475 was solicited throughout the kingdom and the king took a personal hand in raising the money: 'he handled the people so graciously that he got more money than he would have got by two fifteenths', says the chronicle of London (this is an exaggeration).[25] The cash was collected by receivers appointed for the purpose and paid not to the exchequer but into the household. In effect, it was a national tax on incomes over £10 and movables of the value of £40 and upwards, and it certainly tapped fortunes (especially some commercial fortunes) which subsidies did not.[26] Its incidence indeed was probably more equitable than a subsidy's. Edward's benevolences raised a great deal of money. Though Richard III in 1484 tried to make political capital out of condemning them, it would seem that they were not in general very sharply resented.

An important point about benevolences was that, as 'free' gifts, they were not subject to parliamentary assent. This was true also of all the other sources of revenue that we have been examining in this chapter, and it is no accident. These are the words that Edward addressed to the speaker and the commons of parliament in June 1467: 'the reason why I have called and

[24] On benevolences and their nature see G. L. Harriss, 'Aids, loans and benevolences', *H.J.* 6 (1963), pp. 8–13.
[25] *Great Chronicle of London*, ed. A. H. Thomas and I. D. Thornley (London, 1938), p. 223.
[26] See H. L. Gray, 'The first benevolence' in *Facts and Factors in Economic History (Articles by Former Students of E. F. Gay)*, ed. A. H. Cole (Cambridge, Mass. 1932), pp. 90–113.

summoned this my parliament is that I intend to live on my own, and not to charge my subjects except for great and urgent causes, which concern rather their own welfare, and the defence of this my kingdom, than my own pleasure'.[27] Edward was quite determined to live as far as he could without parliamentary grants, and after 1475 he was remarkably successful in doing so. In the last years of the reign, in spite of the war with Scotland, he did not summon parliament and ask for a subsidy; and he only did so in the spring of 1483 when, after he had been outmanœuvred in continental diplomacy by Louis XI, there was a clear possibility of war with France. This does not mean that Edward IV wanted to rule without parliament in some sort of despotic manner. He knew well the value of the support of the commons in parliament, and exploited it skilfully; as his speech of 1467 makes plain, his object was to woo his subjects, not to overawe them. But he knew too that the independence of the commons could make parliamentary meetings awkward, especially at any moment of tension. The fact was one which all intelligent political managers of the age understood; the Lancastrian courtiers, preparing to move against York in 1455, thought it wiser to summon named knights from the counties to a council, rather than a parliament, and Warwick in 1469 cancelled the parliament that he summoned (probably to witness the deposition of Edward in favour of Clarence) because he was not sure that he could control it. By summoning parliament less frequently, and above all by not requesting grants that could be hedged with politically embarrassing conditions, Edward secured an important freedom of royal initiative in government.

The other great problem, besides finance, which Yorkist government had to face was that of public order. Fortescue outlined the difficulties aptly. The great nobles of the realm disposed of so much wealth and influence that men were as willing to put their trust in their favour as in the king's law. They were able to use their influence to infiltrate supporters who had taken their fees and liveries into key positions in local government, as sheriffs and on the commissions of the peace; even the king's judges might be their feed men. In consequence the common law ceased to offer the protection that it should; its officers were venal, its juries packed or easily intimidated. Maintenance had so distorted the effect of the law that force or the favour of a lord who had force at his beck offered a better protection than it did. This

[27] *R.P.* vol. V, p. 572.

state of affairs imposed two priorities: the restriction of the influence of the magnates, a task which a king could only tackle through the activity of the central courts and the council, and the establishment of tighter control over local government.

Edward IV had a threefold problem in his dealings with the aristocracy. He had not only to restrain their misdemeanours; he had also to make sure that loyal friends were well rewarded; and he had further, since he had taken the throne by force, to secure the allegiance of men who might doubt that he was the rightful king. Towards the last end his policy was a judicious mixture of terror and conciliation. Great men who were taken in arms in the field against him were tried summarily as traitors under martial law, and executed;[28] his constable, Tiptoft, who presided over many such trials, earned himself the ugly nickname of 'the Butcher of England'. Those whom the king could not touch, because they escaped his power, were attainted. Edward IV, however, made it clear early that he was willing to reverse attainders in favour of Lancastrians who would reverse their allegiance, and that he had no wish to see heirs of good family lose their inheritances. In 1462 he was prepared to take even Somerset back into favour, and in 1469 he positively created danger for himself by restoring the Percy heir. In the 1470s there were more reversals of old attainders than there were new ones. This policy paid off, and in his later years he was well served by ex-Lancastrians, including even Sir John Fortescue himself, who had spent ten years in exile for Henry VI.

To those who served him well and loyally Edward was not less generous than his royal predecessors. He built his brother Richard of Gloucester into a subject powerful enough to prove over-mighty, which after Edward's death he did. Wisely, he did not grant many offices to his wife's relatives, the Woodevilles, but they did spectacularly well in other ways, especially through advantageous marriages.[29] To others he was very generous with

---

[28] See M. H. Keen, 'Treason trials under the law of arms', *T.R.H.S.* 5th ser., 12 (1962). As J. G. Bellamy points out, I have failed to make it clear that in the Yorkist period the constable's jurisdiction over treason cases was extended beyond its normal, martial scope – probably because its procedures obviated the necessity of empanelling a jury; this was almost certainly the reason for Tiptoft's extreme unpopularity ('Justice under the Yorkist kings', *American Journal of Legal History* 9 (1965), pp. 135–55).

[29] See J. R. Lander, 'Marriage and politics in the fifteenth century: the Nevilles and the Wydevilles', *B.I.H.R.* 36 (1963), p. 143.

grants of profitable posts, and his chamberlain, William Lord
Hastings, did as well in this way as any courtier of Lancastrian
times. Hastings had started out on his career as a knightly
retainer of Edward's father, Richard Duke of York, and he was
only one of a substantial group of men promoted to the peerage
for their good service in the Yorkist cause. Among such were
Walter Devereux, Lord Ferrers, who had been with Duke
Richard at Ludford; Robert Ogle, Lord Ogle, a veteran of the
border struggles who had fought for him at St Albans, and who
was appointed in 1462 constable of the Percy castles of Alnwick
and Warkworth; Walter Blount, Lord Mountjoy, who had been
York's treasurer of Calais in 1460 and became treasurer of
England in 1464; John Lord Wenlock, once a Lancastrian but
attainted as a Yorkist in the Coventry parliament of 1459, who
was killed at Tewkesbury; Thomas Lord Lumley; John Lord
Dinham; Humphrey Lord Stafford. Two men rose much further
than these through their services, to glamorous dignity: William
Herbert who in 1468 was created Earl of Pembroke, and John
Howard, one time knight of the shire for Norfolk who became
Duke of Norfolk in 1483 and died fighting for Richard III on
Bosworth field. The Yorkist peerage was very much an aristocracy of service (as the Lancastrian peerage had also been in later
days when families like the Hungerfords and Tiptofts, descendants of old retainers, arrived in the lords). Edward's promotions
cost money, because peers had to be rewarded in a manner
fitting their rank, but the loyal support that he engaged by them
made it worthwhile.

Edward's efforts to place limitations on the aristocratic abuse
of livery and maintenance were to some extent compromised by
his lavish new creations and his need to count on the support of
retainers dependent on loyal peers. His statutes on this subject
did not go much further than those of Richard II. As the substantial collection of retaining indentures made with knights and
squires by his intimate Lord Hastings shows, he did not seek any
more than Richard had done to prevent peers from retaining men
for lawful purposes. His inhibition, in the statute of 1468, on the
granting of liveries and badges by peers (or anyone else) to men
who were not their household servants was not observed, and no
peer was prosecuted under the statute for giving liveries, so far
as is known (though three peers, the Earl of Shrewsbury, Lord
Grey and Lord Mountjoy, were prosecuted for giving liveries,
probably to yeomen, shortly before the statute was passed).
Edward was pleased, rather than the reverse, to see the retainers

of loyal men like Hastings well entrenched in local office and influence, and did not mind much whether they showed their badges or no.[30]

Nevertheless, Edward was determined that his justice should restrain aristocratic violence and maintenance better than his predecessor's had. The ordinary common law courts, which enforced statutes, were not up to this task; speedier and more arbitrary procedures were needed. In Henry VI's reign the Statute of Riots of 1453 had looked to action by the council to solve the problem, and had laid down dire penalties for peers who failed to answer summonses under the privy seal to appear before it.[31] This was the right answer, and anticipated the practice of the Tudor Court of Star Chamber; the trouble in the 1450s was that the summonses were ignored and the penalties not imposed. Yorkist action on the same lines seems to have been more successful, though it has not been very adequately studied. Edward's remark when John Paston failed to answer a summons suggests determination: 'we will send him another, and by God's mercy if he come not then he shall die for it. We will make other men beware by him how they shall disobey our writing'.[32] Paston, who was in fact flung into gaol, was of course not a peer, only a very substantial landowner. But Lord Grey was a peer, and in 1471 he found himself before the council in the Star Chamber, to be ordered by the king personally not to molest the mayor of Nottingham, and to refrain, under heavy penalties, from retaining a party in the town by giving men his livery.[33] In the 1470s there is evidence of very heavy fines being imposed on a number of noblemen who were not considered trustworthy.[34] Edward was making his authority effectively felt by the great men of the realm, and he was doing so by the very same means that Henry VII was to adopt later.

[30] See further W. H. Dunham, *Lord Hastings' Indentured Retainers* (New Haven, Conn. 1955), pp. 74–8. Bellamy, 'Justice under the Yorkist kings', p. 152, discusses the case of the three peers prosecuted before the 1468 statute was passed. He suggests that Edward did make a serious attempt to prohibit the granting of *liveries* (especially casual grants to men of yeoman status) though not, of course, to prohibit *retaining* in the traditionally lawful manner.

[31] *Statutes*, 31 Henry VI, c. 2.

[32] *P.L.* No. 417.

[33] See B. Wilkinson, *Constitutional History of England in the Fifteenth Century*, p. 363.

[34] See J. R. Lander, 'Attainder and forfeiture 1453–1509', *H.J.* 4 (1961), p. 129.

In one area, the north of England, where there was a particularly dire history of aristocratic unruliness, the Yorkists made a
very important experiment in the extension of conciliar jurisdiction. In the Lancastrian period the kings had relied largely on
the local magnates, in particular on the Nevilles and Percys, for
the keeping of the peace there. These families usually controlled
the wardenships of the marches, and they were also granted
special commissions of the peace, to hear and determine cases
that arose in the north with the assistance of lawyers and knights
of their own households. Their rivalries had, however, often
made their powers as much a menace as a benefit. Richard III,
who in his brother's reign had had supreme military command
in the north and had acquired great estates there, attempted a
new solution to the problem by setting up a council in the north.
At its head he placed the Earl of Lincoln, whose headquarters
were at Sheriff Hutton in Yorkshire, and its personnel included
both noblemen and professionals. It was formally the king's
council in the north; it could exercise the same equitable
jurisdiction outside the common law that the king's council in
London did in the south, and had complete authority in all
matters of rebellion and riot. Richard here went a step beyond
past reliance on the support of loyal magnates and their household men in a remote area; he brought direct royal authority
into the troubled north and set it on a permanent footing.[35]

Against men of lesser status than the nobility and the very great
gentry, Edward took steps to make the common law prevail. If
no peers were prosecuted under the 1468 statute against livery
and maintenance, this was not true of others; the King's Bench
rolls show that a great many lesser men were prosecuted.[36] We
should remember here that some of the worst symptoms of lack
of governance in the 1450s were the consequence of the gang-
sterism of lesser men and their followers, like Charles Nowell
and Robert Ledham of whom the Paston letters complain; and
that, in the eyes of Edward IV and his councillors at least, the
granting of liveries casually to men of yeoman status was probably the one genuinely anti-social aspect of the customary
practice of retaining. Early in his reign, in 1462, Edward himself

[35] On the council in the north see further R. R. Reid, *The King's
Council in the North* (London, 1921). F. W. Brooks, *The Council of the
North* (Historical Association pamphlet, 1966), is more recent and very
useful.

[36] See Dunham, *Lord Hastings' Indentured Retainers*, pp. 82–3.

sat in King's Bench for three consecutive days, 'in order to understand how his laws were prosecuted'. In 1476, when a wave of disorders had followed the disbanding of the Picquigny army, he himself went on tour in the counties with his justices; 'and he spared none, even of his own household . . . and by the execution of this stern justice everywhere, highway robbery soon ceased'.[37] Highway robbery of course did not cease for many years, but Edward's comparative success stands in sharp contrast to the failure, in the Lancastrian period, of the special commissions of justice sent into the counties (for example after Cade's revolt) to achieve anything of note.

The use that the Yorkists made of these same special commissions of justices of *oyer* and *terminer* was in fact a notable feature of their government. Here, once more, they were not original, but used tried methods to new effect. Their commissions were often large, with perhaps as many as a score of names; since two justices constituted a quorum to hold pleas, this made it possible to conduct a number of investigations simultaneously. The scope of the commissions was wide too, sometimes covering several shires at a time. A nobleman of high standing was usually in overall charge (Clarence, Gloucester, Hastings and, earlier, Warwick all served in this way on a number of occasions), and at least one justice of one of the benches was always included; the remaining members would be noblemen and gentry who were considered reliable by the regime. As Professor Bellamy writes, 'in any matter of vital importance, the special commission must have looked very much like the royal council in another guise'. The difference of guise was significant, however, as he points out, since these justices judged cases by common law and could give judgement of life and limb, which the council normally did not. They were probably the most important instrument that the Yorkists used for disciplining lawlessness at the local level, which, as everyone recognized, had got out of hand in the 1450s.[38]

In ordinary conditions, of course, the key men in the system for the enforcement of local order were the justices of the peace.[39]

[37] *Croyland Chronicle*, p. 559.
[38] On this topic see Bellamy, 'Justice under the Yorkist kings', an important contribution to the understanding of Yorkists' approach to the problem of 'lack of governance'.
[39] The best guide to the work of the J.P.s in the late Middle Ages is B. H. Putnam's introduction to *Proceedings before the Justices of the Peace in the Fourteenth and Fifteenth Centuries: Edward III to Richard III* (ed. B. H. Putnam, with a commentary by T. F. T. Plucknett,

Their responsibilities had been growing steadily since the mid fourteenth century, as the additions to the commissions of the peace testify. They were responsible now for enforcing not only the peace, but also the statutes of labourers; the statutes of livery and maintenance (upon lesser men and in the first instance); the statute against the Lollards; and the statutes against clipping and counterfeiting coin. They could hear and determine cases of felony and trespass, armed conventicles, maintenance, and labour offences. They could take surety from those who threatened bodily harm, and could inquire by sworn inquest into felonies and trespass, breaches of the assize of weights and measures, and the negligence of officials in enforcing statutes. They fixed maximum wages, and vetted gild regulations. Two statutes, of 1388 and 1390, made provision for their payment out of the penalties that they imposed, and for the payment of the clerk who kept their records. They were thus by the beginning of the Yorkist period well-established officials with very wide powers to supervise criminal justice and economic regulations, and this period saw still further additions to their powers. An act of 1461 transferred to them the petty criminal jurisdiction previously exercised by the sheriffs in their tourns, and an act of 1483 empowered them to admit to bail prisoners arrested by the sheriffs on suspicion of felony.[40] These two acts were among the latest steps in the long history of the decline of the sheriff, once the key figure in local justice. Though he was still responsible for empanelling the juries whose verdict as to fact decided most of the cases heard before the justices of the peace at their quarterly sessions, the justices had become the all important men.

The problem of making these justices effective in the local enforcement of the common criminal law was directly related to the problem of livery and maintenance. The justices of the peace were recruited largely from the gentry of the shires (with a leavening of lawyers and the occasional magnate), and the gentry were the class which, as the clientele of noble patrons, was most deeply involved in disorder, maintenance, and the packing of juries and commissions in the localities in the Lancastrian period. The Yorkist kings, as a result of their

---

Ames Foundation, 1938). See also B. H. Putnam, *Early Treatises on the Practice of the Justices of the Peace in the Fifteenth and Sixteenth centuries* (Oxford, 1924); and C. A. Beard, *The Office of Justice of the Peace in England* (New York, 1904), ch. I–III.

[40] *Statutes*, I Edward IV, c. 2; 1 Richard III, c. 3.

success in making the crown a greater landowner than it had ever been before and in bringing its estate managers closer to the countryside, were able to some considerable extent to counter the forces of maintenance with their own weapons. The council took a close interest in appointments to the commissions of the peace; and the links between the royal household (that is to say, in effect, the private retinue of the crown) and local government were systematically developed. Thus in Kent Sir John Fogge and Sir John Scott, squires of the body, were both often on the commission of the peace, and both served as sheriff; in Somerset Sir Giles Daubeny, squire and afterwards knight of the body, was sheriff in 1474–5, sat for the shire in parliament in 1478, and was a justice of the peace from 1475 to 1483; Avery Cornburgh, yeoman of the chamber, was sheriff of Cornwall and later of Essex and justice of the peace in Essex.[41] These are a few examples out of very many. The Yorkists of course remained far short of ever hoping to reach the position that Fortescue wished to see, where none held office who had clothing and fee of any but the crown, but they made a start towards his goal. In doing so, they began to forge that close connexion between the crown and the gentry of the localities, which was a marked feature of the Tudor period.

It should be stressed that there was nothing very new about this policy (Richard II and Henry IV had been keenly aware of the importance to the monarchy of committed support in the counties); and, once again, that Yorkist reliance on gentlemen was in no sense inimical to aristocratic interest, and was not intended to be. It was inimical only to the abuse of aristocratic power. The line of division between the peerage and the greater gentry was not a sharp one. Most of the peers promoted by the Yorkists were drawn from the gentry class, and many had performed locally the same sort of function that the knights and squires of the household were so useful in discharging. Lord Dinham had been sheriff of Devon when he was a knight; Lord Wenlock had represented Bedfordshire in six parliaments under Henry VI; John Howard, Duke of Norfolk, had been sheriff there and John Jenny had intrigued with the Pastons to keep him out of parliament in the days when he was plain Sir John. The secret of Yorkist success in government was not restraint of the aristocracy by means of a new alliance of the crown and the middle class, a notion far too modern for them to comprehend;

[41] These examples are among those given by Jacob, *The Fifteenth Century*, p. 599.

. it was the harnessing of all the forces of patronage, private
interest and good lordship – of 'bastard feudalism' – to the
support of the monarchy. This meant relying on peers as well as
gentry, and on others too, citizens and yeomanry; on all and any
whose trust could be personally engaged.

In order to foster that loyalty and pride of service which gave
psychological strength to 'bastard feudal' relationships, the
Yorkists took pains to make their kingship prestigious in their
subjects' eyes. They nursed carefully the mythology of Yorkist
legitimism. The attainders of the Earl of Cambridge and his
fellow conspirators, who had plotted to unseat Henry V and
crown Edward IV's 'noble predecessor' of March in 1415, were
solemnly reversed in 1461. Pamphlets and ballads laboured the
theme that the misfortunes of the house of Lancaster were a
judgement of God upon the race of Henry IV, who had seized
the throne of an anointed king. This emphasis on hereditary
right and legitimate succession subtly magnified the dignity of
kingship, whose inheritance was governed by the laws of God
and nature, laws beyond and above the common law and even
parliament. This was why there was no parliamentary deposition
of Henry VI; that would have demeaned the dignity both of
kingship and of legitimacy. This theme culminated in Richard of
Gloucester's claim in 1483 that he should be king because he
alone represented the old and true blood royal, sacred and
unadulterated.

   In spite of their attention to economy, the Yorkists were careful to make their state magnificent. Henry VI's too obvious
poverty had lost him respect; when he appeared in London in
1470 it was 'more like a play than a showing of a prince to win
men's hearts', an observer wrote, 'for by this means he lost many
and won none or right few, and ever he was showed in a long blue
gown of velvet, as if he had no more to change with'.[42] Edward
in contrast was the height of fashion, 'frequently appearing in a
great variety of most costly garments, of a quite different cut to
those which had usually been seen in our kingdom'.[43] A king
ought to be magnificent, wrote the author of the *Black Book of the
Household*, 'which means superabundant liberality'.[44] Edward
sought advice from the Burgundian court as to how to organize
his own with duly opulent ceremony. He showed what he could

[42] *Great Chronicle of London*, p. 215.
[43] *Croyland Chronicle*, p. 563.
[44] Myers, *The Household of Edward IV*, p. 86.

do on such occasions as that when he welcomed to England the Seigneur de la Gruthyse, who had been his host in exile in 1470. Gruthyse was presented, on his arrival at Windsor, with a gold cup set with precious stones and 'a great piece of an unicorn's horn'. He was lodged in chambers 'hung with white silk and linen cloth and all the floors covered with carpets', and undressed by the lord chamberlain. He was feasted, slept in a bed of state, and had a kind of pavilion erected over his bath.[45] To a modern ear this sort of reception can sound like excess blending into absurdity. In the fifteenth century respect for dignity and authority was not to be had without display and the Yorkists, wisely, did not spare expense to this end.

Edward IV sought to woo his people by address as well as magnificence. He was handsome, and could make himself familiar, especially with the ladies. The *Great Chronicle of London* tells a pleasant story of how, in 1475, as 'he passed through a town of Suffolk, he summoned a rich widow before him, amongst others, and asked her what her goodwill would be towards his great expenses. She liberally granted him £10. He liberally thanked her, and then drew her to him and kissed her. Which kiss pleased her so much, that for his great bounty and kind deed he should have had £20 for his £10.'[46] The shrewd Milanese ambassador noted his skill in dealing with people: 'I have frequently seen our neighbours here who were summoned before the king, and when they went they looked as if they were going to the gallows. But when they returned they were joyful, saying they had spoken to the king and he had spoken to them so benignly that they did not regret the money they had paid.'[47] The Londoners were Edward's special favourites. In 1481 he entertained the mayor and aldermen at a great hunting party in Waltham forest, and sent some of the game to their wives. Nothing, says Thomas More, had for many a day 'got him more hearts or more hearty favour among the common people, which oftentimes more esteem and take for greater kindness a little courtesy than a great benefit'.[48] Edward was adept at winning men, especially common men. The Yorkist cause in its old days of opposition had always drawn its greatest strength from

[45] *The Record of Bluemantle Pursuivant*, in C. L. Kingsford, *Historical Literature in the Fifteenth Century* (Oxford, 1913), pp. 386-7.
[46] *Great Chronicle of London*, p. 223.
[47] *C.S.P. Milan* vol. I, p. 193.
[48] Thomas More, *History of King Richard III*, ed. J. R. Lumby (Cambridge, 1883), p. 3.

popular support; he as king made this one of the props of his monarchy.

The conscious effort to make royal rule popular was a very important aspect of Yorkist kingship. In so far as Yorkist policies were in any way systematic, they were not very original. The clearest precedents for their methods, however, were not those of periods of successful government, but those of the least successful reigns of the later middle ages in England, Richard II's and Henry VI's. Edward IV succeeded in applying solutions to governmental problems formulated by these unpopular monarchs and their advisers without thereby alienating opinion at large, and it was the secret of his success.

Almost all the expedients of Yorkist government had been tried before. Richard II had seen, quite as clearly as Edward IV, how desirable it was to reduce the crown's dependence on parliamentary subsidies. He and his councillors had worked to create connexions between the court and the local ministers of government, by recruiting men with county influence to the household and by advancing householders to shrieval office. Suffolk, in the period of his dominance, had done the same, and so had Queen Margaret and her associates in the late 1450s; the Yorkists merely followed their example. The Lancastrian statute of riots of 1453 aimed to control aristocratic misdemeanour by the same conciliar jurisdiction that the Yorkists employed more effectively. Richard II had sought to enlarge the crown's regular revenues, including those from land (which was one important object of the confiscation of the Lancastrian estates). In the late 1450s, when Margaret's supporters the Earl of Wiltshire and Sir Thomas Tuddenham were treasurer and treasurer of the household respectively, an attempt had been made to route royal landed revenues direct to the household, bypassing the exchequer, with the connivance of householders among the shrievalty. Wiltshire and Tuddenham were no less aware of the value to the crown of funds outside exchequer control than the Yorkists and their chamber officials, though they would have made the wardrobe rather than the chamber the headquarters of private royal finance.[49]

There were of course many differences in detail between Yorkist practice and these earlier efforts to solve the same sort of problems by the same sort of means. The most important difference, however, was a very simple one. The servants of

[49] See Jacob, *The Fifteenth Century*, pp. 513–14.

Richard II and Henry VI were hated and they knew it. They were frightened of the people and kept away from their capital in times of trouble. In dealing with the commons in parliament they thought to pack and overawe, neither of which they were able to do effectively, instead of wooing them with fair words as Edward IV did. As Fortescue's book on *Governance* shows, it did not take any very startling originality to propound administrative proposals for strengthening the authority of the crown, which in the fifteenth century was clearly recognized as needful for the better government of the kingdom. But administrative solutions had no real chance of succeeding unless they could be made acceptable to opinion at large. Richard II and the advisers of Henry VI failed totally in this respect; the Yorkists, determined to engage their subjects' support for their government, were much more successful. The combination of popular address, of which Edward III and Henry V had in the past shown themselves masters, with the administrative expedients of kings who had been labelled 'tyrants', made their monarchy look 'new' (though it is worth remarking that, in 1469, Warwick and Clarence charged Edward IV with having estranged the lords of the blood from his council and of governing through a corrupt courtier clique, the very sins of which Richard II and Henry VI had been considered guilty). Edward IV, at an early stage, grasped what the right priorities were, but he also made political blunders; he was lucky to survive to give his regime the air of greatly increased solidity that it wore in the 1470s.

We should remember, in conclusion, one important respect in which the Yorkists were advantaged by luck rather than skill. Their governmental policies could never have succeeded, indeed could not have been followed at all systematically, if their kingdom had not been freed, before Edward IV's time, of the financial and military strain of the war with France. They did not understand this; Edward long hoped to base the appeal of his kingship on success in 'outward war' with France, and when he sealed the Treaty of Picquigny he only abandoned the idea for the time being. Events which he failed to control, and not he, made the decision a permanent one. The long-term consequences of his treaty and his subsequent mismanagement of diplomacy were to condemn England to a fringe position in European politics for a long time. But they also saved the English monarchy, albeit unintentionally, from the kind of difficulties that a major war entailed, dependence on parliamentary subsidies and on aristocratic military support, and a burden of indebtedness that reforms of estate management could barely have dented. The new monarchy of the Yorkists and early Tudors, which brought a better peace and order at home, was built on disengagement from the glorious risks of foreign war, which the Yorkists achieved, but largely by mistake.

Epilogue

The year 1485 marks no break in constitutional, social, economic, nor yet in religious history. In political history, however, it remains a useful dividing line. The government of the first Tudor was not, it is true, very different in its methods or its objects from that of the Yorkists. If, however, we look at things from the point of view not of the ruler but of the subject, then a change is apparent, and an important one. The political side of the human experience of an individual who lived through his adult life under Henry VII was different in quality from that of a man who reached maturity in 1450 or 1460. The humiliation of the English defeat in France, which up to 1460 and beyond was kept vivid by Yorkist propaganda and Yorkist continental ambitions, was for most of Henry VII's subjects only something in the memory of their fathers and grandfathers. Henry VII's reign, moreover, saw only the last flickerings of the civil Wars of the Roses. In 1500 it could not be said, as it was in 1472, 'every man of this land that is of reasonable age hath known what trouble this realm hath suffered, and it is to be supposed that none hath escaped but at one time or another his part has been therein'.[1]

The collapse of the English cause in France and the civil strife of the 1450s and 1460s were experiences that left marked scars. Those which the civil wars left were visible in the sixteenth century, often literally, on the face of the land.

> The Lord Roos took King Henry VI's part against King Edward [John Leland wrote, as he listed the hands through which Belvoir castle in Leicestershire had passed], whereupon the Lord Roos's lands stood as confiscate . . . and Belvoir Castle was put in keeping to the Lord Hastings, the which coming thither upon a time to peruse the ground . . . was suddenly repelled by Mr Harington, a man of power thereabout and friend to the Lord Roos. Whereupon

---

[1] *Lit. Cant* (R.S.) vol. III, p. 275.

the Lord Hastings came thither upon another time with a strong power, and upon a raging will spoiled the castle, defacing the rooves and taking the lead off them. . . . Then fell all the castle to ruin, and the timber of the rooves uncovered rotted away, and the soil between the walls at last grew full of elders, and no habitation was there until of late days the Earl of Rutland hath made it fairer than ever it was.[2]

Wherever he went, the Tudor antiquary heard stories similar to this one, of the ways in which the wars had shaken the fortunes of families that had lived in this manor or that castle. Leland wrote in the 1530s; in some places memories of the troubled past were green for much longer, as at Nibley in Gloucestershire where, in the confusion of the year 1469, the last skirmish was fought in the feud between William Lord Berkeley and Thomas Lord Lisle. It must have been late in Elizabeth's reign that John Smyth here heard old country people

relate the reports of their parents, kinsmen and neighbours present at this skirmish, some with the one lord and others with the other; and of such as carried victuals and weapons to some of those companies, as this lord's party lay hidden in the outskirts of Michael-wood Chase, out of which this Lord Berkeley broke when he first beheld Lord Lisle with his fellowship descending the hill from Nibley Church; and afterwards climbed up into the trees (being then boys of twelve and sixteen years) to see the battle.[3]

One important reason why the Tudor age was less disturbed than its predecessor by scenes such as this battle of Nibley Green was the accident of genetics which decided that the Tudors should never father any race of viceregal dukes of York or Gloucester, as the Plantagenets had done. But even more important was the fact that, by 1485, men were tired of the troubles and terrors of civil war, and disillusioned about the objectives which rebellious lords of the blood royal claimed to have in view in them. This is the extraordinary advice which, in the testament that he caused to be written within only a few weeks of the battle of Bosworth, John Lord Mountjoy gave to his sons: 'to live righteously, and never to take the state of baron upon them if they may lay it from them, nor to desire to be great about princes, for it is dangerous'.[4] John Blount had good reason to

[2] J. Leland, *Itinerary*, ed. L. Toulmin Smith, vol. I, pp. 97–8.

[3] J. Smyth, *The Lives of the Berkeleys*, ed. Sir J. Maclean (Gloucester, 1883), vol. II, p. 114.

[4] Quoted by K. B. McFarlane in 'The Wars of the Roses', *P.B.A.* 50 (1964), p. 119.

know how dangerous prominence could be. His father, the first baron, had risen with the rising fortunes of the house of York, but had been too close for comfort to Warwick in the 1460s. He himself had been allied by indenture with Lord Hastings, who lost his head at Richard III's command in 1483. His elder brother William had been killed at Barnet, fighting for the Yorkists. His stepmother, Anne, had lost her first husband, Humphrey Duke of Buckingham, at the battle of Northampton in 1460, and her eldest son at St Albans; both fell fighting for Lancaster. It is not much wonder, given experiences such as these, that the great families of the earlier Tudor period 'preferred almost anything to another civil war'.[5]

The loss of the English provinces in France left a mark that was at least as deep as that left by the civil wars. It is perhaps most clearly visible in the sense of England's isolation and her vulnerability to foreign invasion, which troubled Englishmen a good deal in the late fifteenth century, and after. 'Be it well considered', a speaker declared in parliament in 1473, 'how the next adversaries of this land, the Scots, be allied, and with whom, not only by an old league with the Frenchmen which be the greatest and ancient adversaries of this realm, but also now of late with the Danes; and what courage they have had to enter and trouble this land heretofore, the chronicles and histories be open.'[6] The day was drawing close, this speaker warned, when England, 'environed of mighty adversaries, destitute of old friends, should stand in greater doubt and peril than ever it did before'. Another fear expressed by this same speaker was that, if stern justice were meted out to all who disturbed the internal peace of the kingdom, there would be too few men left to defend it. A similar fear was among those uppermost in the minds of a growing host of critics of enclosure in the late fifteenth century. 'Where once the lord king had strong men for his warlike affairs, now instead of men nothing alive is found in some places but horses and mares and in other places sheep and oxen and cows.'[7] So wrote John Rous of Warwickshire. The sense of England's isolation, and of the necessity to provide for defence against outward enemies, was not just a feeling of Rous's generation, who lived through the times of trouble into the reign of Henry VII. It was a strong and lasting force in the sixteenth century.

The problem of the defence of the realm loomed large for

[5] ibid.
[6] *Lit. Cant.* (R.S.) vol. III, pp. 276–7.
[7] J. Rous, *Historia Regum Anglie*, ed. T. Hearne, p. 121.

another sector of opinion too at the end of the Middle Ages, for
those who like Caxton and William of Worcester lamented the
decline of chivalry among the well-born class. 'Now of late',
Worcester complained, 'many who are descended of noble blood
and are born to arms set themselves to singular practice . . . to
learn the practise of law or custom of land . . . and waste greatly
their time in such needless business as to hold courts and to keep
and bear out a proud countenance at the holding of sessions and
shires.'[8] How was it to be hoped that such men would uphold
the martial reputation of England? Caxton was even more
eloquently urgent.

> O ye knights of England [he cried in the epilogue to his *Book of the
> Order of Chivalry*], where is the custom and usage of chivalry that
> was used in those [past] days? What do ye now but go to the baths
> and play at dice? And some use not honest and good living against
> all order of knighthood. Leave this, leave it! And read the volumes
> of the Holy Grail, of Lancelot, of Galahad . . . of Gawain. . . .
> There shall you see manhood, courtesy and gentleness. And look in
> the latter days at the noble acts since the conquest; as in the days of
> King Richard Coeur de Lion; of Edward I and III, and of his
> noble sons; of Sir Robert Knowles, Sir John Hawkwood, Sir John
> Chandos. . . . Read Froissart! And also behold the victorious and
> noble King Henry V and the captains under him; his noble
> brethren, Montagu the Earl of Salisbury, and many others whose
> names shine gloriously by their virtuous and noble acts.[9]

Praise of a golden age in the past is a recurring theme in medieval
literature, but there is more to this lament than romantic sentiment. Caxton made this clear when he rounded it off with an
appeal to Richard III, king of England and France, to impose
on the justices of the peace the duty of seeing that all knights in
the kingdom had horse and harness in their possession 'so as to
be always ready to serve their prince when he shall call them or
have need'.

Caxton thought that something had been lost to English life
that had been there in the days of the Black Prince and Chandos,
and later too, in those of Henry V, and that the loss was real and
dangerous. If we look back to what Philip de Mézières, the
ex-councillor of Charles V of France, wrote, addressing the
English just 100 years before Caxton's time, it begins to be plain
that the latter was not in error.

[8] *The Boke of Noblesse*, ed. J. G. Nichols (Roxburghe Club, 1860),
p. 77.

[9] Caxton, *The Book of the Ordre of Chyvalry*, ed. A. T. P. Byles
(E.E.T.S., 1926), pp. 122–3.

Listen, you who have sown such terrible shedding of man's blood [Philip wrote]. By your evil war, raised by pride and by lust for what is after all but a little land, the whole of Christendom has for fifty years been turned upside down ... and, what is worse, what you have been empowered by God's permission to achieve for the chastisement of the sins of the Scots and French, you and your fathers have attributed solely to your own valour and chivalry, drunk as you are with pride and stirred up by stories of Lancelot and Gawain and their worldly valour.[10]

No French councillor would have dreamt of writing thus about the English in Caxton's time, and he and his like felt not only poorer in consequence, but less secure. Fear for the safety of the kingdom loomed uncomfortably behind the thought that, if a 'dire search' were now made as to how many knights there were in England that had the 'use and exercise of knighthood', there 'would be found many that lack'.[11]

Caxton's appeal for the revival of chivalry was one that went out too late. When he wrote the age of English territorial conquests in Europe was over, and so was the mood that had made them possible. A generation that had known only the humiliation of defeat in war overseas and the bitterness of internal strife was to be grateful to Henry Tudor for cultivating peace. There were deeper reasons, too, for lack of response to the chivalrous chauvinism that in Caxton and Worcester combined with fears for the safety of England. The 'bastard feudalism' of the late fifteenth century and of the Tudor age was fast losing touch with the martial ethos that had been its foundation in the days when indentures commonly recorded the retainer's duty to attend his lord, clothed in his livery, in the chivalrous mock-war of the tournament. Men were no longer looking to their aristocratic patrons for lordship in the old sense, for food in his hall, martial leadership, and justice in their quarrels with fellow retainers, but rather for patronage in a more modern sense, which would open avenues to advancement, and afford some kind of insurance amid the hazards of local and family litigation. That is why Worcester found himself complaining that men who knew the law were 'more esteemed among all estates than he who has spent thirty or forty years of his days in great jeopardy in your ancestor's conquests and wars'.[12] Though Worcester and his contem-

[10] P. de Mézières, *Le Songe du Vieil Pélérin*, ed. G. W. Coopland (Cambridge, 1969), vol. I, pp. 396–7.
[11] Caxton, *The Book of the Ordre of Chyvalry*, p. 124.
[12] *The Boke of Noblesse*, pp. 77–8.

poraries could not see it, in a world in which esteem was thus bestowed, things could never be the same as they had once been. The future now lay not with noblemen for whom service in the king's wars was an ancestral duty, nor with the captains of men at arms, but more and more with the gentry. Worcester was paying a tribute to forces which already in his own day had gone far towards shifting the balance of political power in England and altering its nature out of recognition.

Bibliography

The footnotes to the text of this book have been written with the object of providing detailed bibliographical references. The aim of this further bibliography is to list secondary works that may be useful to the student, under broad subject headings. Some works inevitably appear in more than one section. I have mentioned a number of works that are not quoted in my footnotes, and some that have appeared since the manuscript of my book was placed in the publisher's hands and whose point of view is not discussed in my text. The lists are not intended to be exhaustive, but simply to introduce the student to further material: they naturally reflect the compiler's eclecticism and the *lacunae* of his reading.

I General surveys of the period

V. H. H. GREEN, *The Later Plantagenets* (London, 1955).

G. A. HOLMES, *The Later Middle Ages 1272–1485* (Edinburgh, 1962).

E. F. JACOB, *The Fifteenth Century* (Oxford, 1961).

M. MCKISACK, *The Fourteenth Century* (Oxford, 1959).

A. R. MYERS, *A History of England in the Late Middle Ages* (Pelican History of England, 1952).

—— *English Historical Documents 1327–1485* (London, 1969) – a collection of documents which is a splendid companion to the study of the whole period.

A. L. POOLE (ed.), *Medieval England*, 2 vols (Oxford, 1958).

F. M. POWICKE, *The Thirteenth Century* (Oxford, 1953).

Two older works deserve special mention because of their seminal nature:

W. STUBBS, *The Constitutional History of England*, vols II and III (Oxford, numerous editions).

T. F. TOUT, *Chapters in the Administrative History of Medieval England*, 6 vols (Manchester, 1920–33).

Two other seminal works which should be mentioned on account of their influence are:

C. L. KINGSFORD, *Prejudice and Promise in Fifteenth Century England* (Oxford, 1925).

K. B. MCFARLANE, *The English Nobility 1290–1521* (Ford Lectures of 1953, to be published by the Oxford University Press in 1972) – perhaps the most influential lectures on late medieval history delivered in this century.

II Politics and political biography

The Hundred Years War and questions of Anglo-French relations are dealt with separately in section III below, and administrative and constitutional topics in section IV. Biographies of important ecclesiastical figures are mostly listed at the end of section VI.

(*a*) EDWARD I, II AND III (1290–1377)

E. M. BARRON, *The Scottish War of Independence* (Inverness, 1914).

G. W. S. BARROW, *Robert Bruce* (London, 1965).

J. C. DAVIES, *The Baronial Opposition to Edward II* (Cambridge, 1918).

K. FOWLER, *The King's Lieutenant: Henry of Grosmont* (London, 1969).

D. HUGHES, *A Study of Social and Constitutional Tendencies in the Early Years of Edward III* (London, 1915).

J. R. MADDICOTT, *Thomas of Lancaster* (Oxford, 1970).

M. MCKISACK, *The Fourteenth Century* (Oxford, 1959).

J. E. MORRIS, *The Welsh Wars of Edward I* (Oxford, 1901).

R. NICHOLSON, *Edward III and the Scots* (Oxford, 1965).

J. R. S. PHILLIPS, *Aymer de Valence, Earl of Pembroke 1307–1324* (Oxford, in press).

M. C. PRESTWICH, *War, Politics and Finance under Edward I* (London, in press).

T. F. TOUT, *The Place of Edward II in English History* (Manchester, 1914).

Articles

J. C. DAVIES, 'The Despenser war in Glamorgan', *T.R.H.S.* 3rd ser., vol. 9 (1915).

J. G. EDWARDS, 'The negotiating of the Treaty of Leake 1318', *Essays in History Presented to R. L. Poole* (Oxford, 1927).

—— 'The baronial grievances of 1297', *E.H.R.* vol. 58 (1943).

E. B. FRYDE, 'The deposits of Hugh Despenser the Younger with Italian bankers', *Econ.H.R.* 2nd ser., vol. 3 (1951).

—— 'Parliament and the French war 1336-40', *Essays in Medieval History Presented to B. Wilkinson* (Toronto, 1969) .

G. L. HARRISS, 'The commons petitions of 1340', *E.H.R.* vol. 78 (1963).

B. C. KEENEY, 'The medieval idea of the state: the great cause of 1291-2', *Univ. of Toronto Law Journal* vol. 8 (1949).

G. LAPSLEY, 'Archbishop Stratford and the parliamentary crisis of 1341', *E.H.R.* vol. 30 (1915).

H. ROTHWELL, 'The confirmation of the charters and baronial grievances in 1297', *E.H.R.* vol. 60 (1945).

T. F. TOUT, 'The captivity and death of Edward of Caernarvon', *Collected Papers* vol. III (Manchester, 1934).

B. WILKINSON, 'The ordinances of 1311', *Studies in the Constitutional History of the 13th and 14th Centuries* (Manchester, 1937).

—— 'The negotiations preceding the Treaty of Leake', *Studies in Medieval History Presented to F. M. Powicke* (Oxford, 1948).

—— 'The Sherburn indenture and the attack on the Despensers', *E.H.R.* vol. 63 (1948).

(b) RICHARD II (1377-1399)

J. ARMITAGE-SMITH, *John of Gaunt* (London, 1904).

R. BIRD, *The Turbulent London of Richard II* (London, 1949).

M. V. CLARKE, *Fourteenth Century Studies* (Oxford, 1937).

E. CURTIS, *Richard II in Ireland* (Oxford, 1927).

F. R. H. DU BOULAY and C. M. BARRON (eds.), *The Reign of Richard II: Essays in Honour of May McKisack* (London, 1971).

H. GOODMAN, *The Loyal Conspiracy* (London, 1972).

R. H. JONES, *The Royal Policy of Richard II: Absolutism in the Later Middle Ages* (Oxford, 1968).

A. STEEL, *Richard II* (Cambridge, 1941).

Articles

M. E. ASTON, 'The impeachment of Bishop Despenser', *B.I.H.R.* vol. 38 (1965).

C. BARRON, 'The tyranny of Richard II', *B.I.H.R.* vol. 41 (1968).

S. B. CHRIMES, 'Richard II's questions to the judges', *L.Q.R.* vol. 72 (1956).

J. G. EDWARDS, 'The parliamentary committee of 1398', *E.H.R.* vol. 40 (1925).

N. B. LEWIS, 'Simon Burley and Baldwin of Raddington', *E.H.R.* vol. 52 (1937).

J. N. L. MYRES, 'The campaign of Radcot Bridge in December 1387', *E.H.R.* vol. 42 (1927).

J. J. N. PALMER, 'The impeachment of Michael de la Pole in 1386', *B.I.H.R.* vol. 42 (1969).

C. D. ROSS, 'Forfeiture for treason in the reign of Richard II', *E.H.R.* vol. 71 (1956).

J. A. TUCK, 'The Cambridge parliament of 1388', *E.H.R.* vol. 84 (1969).

B. WILKINSON, 'The deposition of Richard II and the accession of Henry IV', *E.H.R.* vol. 54 (1939).

(c) THE LANCASTRIAN KINGS (1399 – c. 1450)

E. F. JACOB, *Henry V and the Invasion of France* (London, 1947).

C. L. KINGSFORD, *Henry V*, 2nd ed. (London, 1923).

J. L. KIRBY, *Henry IV of England* (London, 1970).

J. E. LLOYD, *Owen Glendower* (Oxford, 1931).

K. B. MCFARLANE, *Lancastrian Kings and Lollard Knights* (Oxford, 1972).

K. H. VICKERS, *Humphrey of Gloucester* (London, 1907).

J. H. WYLIE, *History of England under Henry IV*, 4 vols (London, 1884–98).

J. H. WYLIE and W. T. WAUGH, *The Reign of Henry V*, 3 vols (Cambridge, 1914–29).

Articles

J. M. W. BEAN, 'Henry IV and the Percies', *History* vol. 44 (1959).

A. L. BROWN, 'The commons and the council in the reign of Henry IV', *E.H.R.* vol. 79 (1964).

S. B. CHRIMES, 'The pretensions of the Duke of Gloucester in 1422', *E.H.R.* vol. 45 (1930).

R. A. GRIFFITHS, 'The trial of Eleanor Cobham: an episode in the fall of Humphrey Duke of Gloucester', *B.J.R.L.* vol. 51 (1969).

G. L. HARRISS, 'Cardinal Beaufort: patriot or usurer?', *T.R.H.S.* 5th ser., vol. 20 (1970).

C. L. KINGSFORD, 'The policy and fall of Suffolk', *Prejudice and Promise in Fifteenth Century England* (Oxford, 1925).

G. T. LAPSLEY, 'The parliamentary title of Henry IV', *E.H.R.* vol. 49 (1934).

K. B. MCFARLANE, 'England: the Lancastrian Kings', *Cambridge Medieval History* vol. VIII, chap. XI.

—— 'Henry V, Bishop Beaufort and the Red Hat', *E.H.R.* vol. 60 (1945).

—— 'At the deathbed of Cardinal Beaufort', *Studies in Medieval History Presented to F. M. Powicke* (Oxford, 1948).

A. ROGERS, 'The political crisis of 1401', *Nottingham Medieval Studies* vol. 12 (1968).

—— 'Henry IV, the commons and taxation', *Medieval Studies* vol. 31 (1969).

J. S. ROSKELL, 'The office and dignity of Protector of England, with special reference to its origins', *E.H.R.* vol. 68 (1953).

I. D. THORNLEY, 'Treason by words in the fifteenth century', *E.H.R.* vol. 32 (1917).

R. VIRGOE, 'The death of William de la Pole', *B.J.R.L.* vol. 47 (1964–5).

—— 'The composition of the king's council 1437–61', *B.I.H.R.* vol. 43 (1970).

(*d*) THE WARS OF THE ROSES (*c.* 1450 – *c.* 1461)

J. R. LANDER, *The Wars of the Roses* (London, 1965).

R. L. STOREY, *The End of the House of Lancaster* (London, 1966).

Articles

C. A. J. ARMSTRONG, 'Politics and the battle of St Albans', *B.I.H.R.* vol. 33 (1960).

J. P. GILSON, 'A defence of the proscription of the Yorkists in 1459', *E.H.R.* vol. 26 (1911).

R. A. GRIFFITHS, 'Local rivalries and national politics – the Percies, the Nevilles and the Duke of Exeter', *Speculum* vol. 43 (1968).

G. L. HARRISS, 'The struggle for Calais – an aspect of the rivalry between Lancaster and York', *E.H.R.* vol. 75 (1960).

J. R. LANDER, 'Henry VI and the Duke of York's second protectorate', *B.J.R.L.* vol. 43 (1960–1).

K. B. MCFARLANE, 'The Wars of the Roses', *P.B.A.* vol. 50 (1964).

(*e*) THE YORKISTS (1461–1485)

C. A. J. ARMSTRONG, *The Usurpation of Richard III* (Oxford, 1969).

J. CALMETTE and G. PERINELLE, *Louis XI et l'Angleterre 1461–83* (Paris, 1930).

W. H. DUNHAM, *Lord Hastings's Indentured Retainers* (New Haven, Conn., 1955).

J. R. GAIRDNER, *The Life and Reign of Richard III* (London, 1879).

P. M. KENDALL, *Richard III* (London, 1955).

—— *Warwick the Kingmaker* (London, 1957).

A. R. MYERS, *The Household of Edward IV* (Manchester, 1959).

C. L. SCOFIELD, *The Life and Reign of Edward IV* (London, 1923).

Articles

J. G. BELLAMY, 'Justice under the Yorkist kings', *Amer. J. of Legal History* vol. 9 (1965).

J. G. EDWARDS, 'The second continuation of the Croyland Chronicle – was it written in ten days?', *B.I.H.R.* vol. 39 (1966).

H. L. GRAY, 'The first benevolence', *Facts and Factors in Economic History*, ed. A. H. Cole (Cambridge, Mass., 1932).

E. W. IVES, 'Andrew Dymmok and the papers of Anthony Earl Rivers', *B.I.H.R.* vol. 41 (1968).

J. R. LANDER, 'Edward IV: the modern legend: and a revision', *History* vol. 41 (1956).

—— 'The Yorkist council and administration', *E.H.R.* vol. 73 (1958).

—— 'Council administration and councillors 1461–85', *B.I.H.R.* vol. 32 (1959).

—— 'Attainder and forfeiture: 1453–1509', *Historical Journal* vol. 4 (1961).

—— 'Marriage and politics in the fifteenth century: the Nevilles and the Wydevilles', *B.I.H.R.* vol. 36 (1963).

—— 'The treason and death of the Duke of Clarence: a reinterpretation', *Canadian Journal of History* vol. 2 (1967).

M. LEVINE, 'Richard III – usurper or lawful king?', *Speculum* vol. 34 (1959).

B. P. WOLFFE, 'The management of English royal estates under the Yorkist kings', *E.H.R.* vol. 71 (1956).

III England, France and the Hundred Years War

(*a*) GENERAL SURVEYS

P. CONTAMINE, *La Guerre de Cent Ans* (Paris, 1968).

K. FOWLER (ed.), *The Hundred Years War* (London, 1971).

E. PERROY, *The Hundred Years War* (English trans., London, 1951).

(*b*) THE WARS OF EDWARD I AND II, THE BEGINNING OF THE HUNDRED YEARS WAR

P. CHAPLAIS, *The War of St Sardos* (Camden Society, 1954).

G. P. CUTTINO, *English Diplomatic Administration 1259–1339* (Oxford, 1940).

E. DÉPREZ, *Les Preliminaires de la Guerre de Cent Ans* (Paris, 1902).

H. S. LUCAS, *The Low Countries and the Hundred Years War* (Ann Arbor, 1929).

J. DE STURLER, *Les relations politiques et les échanges commerciaux entre le duché de Brabant et l'Angleterre au Moyen Age* (Paris, 1936).

Articles

J. CAMPBELL, 'England, Scotland and the Hundred Years War', *Europe in the Late Middle Ages*, ed. B. Smalley, J. Hale and J. R. L. Highfield (London, 1965).

P. CHAPLAIS, 'English arguments concerning the feudal status of Aquitaine', *B.I.H.R.* vol. 21 (1948).

—— 'Le Traité de Paris de 1259 et l'inféodation de la Gascogne allodiale', *Moyen Age* vol. 61 (1955).

G. P. CUTTINO, 'The process of Agen', *Speculum* vol. 19 (1944).

H. S. OFFLER, 'England and Germany at the beginning of the 100 Years War', *E.H.R.* vol. 54 (1939).

H. ROTHWELL, 'Edward I's case against Philip the Fair', *E.H.R.* vol. 42 (1927).

G. TEMPLEMAN, 'Edward III and the beginnings of the Hundred Years War', *T.R.H.S.* 5th ser., vol. 2 (1952).

J. VIARD, 'Philippe VI de Valois – la succession au trône', *Moyen Age* vol. 32 (1921).

(*c*) THE HUNDRED YEARS WAR, FOURTEENTH CENTURY

A. H. BURNE, *The Crecy Wear* (London, 1955).

R. CAZELLES, *La Société politique et la crise de la Royauté sous Philippe de Valois* (Paris, 1958).

R. DELACHENAL, *Histoire de Charles V*, 5 vols (Paris 1909–31).

K. FOWLER, *The King's Lieutenant: Henry of Grosmont* (London, 1969).

H. J. HEWITT, *The Black Prince's Expedition of 1355–7* (Manchester, 1958).

—— *The Organisation of War under Edward III* (Manchester, 1966).

J. J. N. PALMER, *England, France and Christendom* (London, 1972).

P. E. RUSSELL, *The English Intervention in Spain and Portugal* (Oxford, 1955).

Articles

C. C. BAYLEY, 'The campaign of 1375 and the Good Parliament', *E.H.R.* vol. 55 (1940).

F. BOCK, 'Some new documents illustrating the early years of the 100 Years War', *B.J.R.L.* vol. 15 (1931).

E. DEPREZ, 'La Conférence d'Avignon (1344)', *Essays in Medieval History Presented to T. F. Tout* (Manchester, 1925).

E. B. FRYDE, 'Parliament and the French war 1336–40', *Essays in Medieval History Presented to B. Wilkinson* (Toronto, 1969).

D. GREAVES, 'Calais under Edward III', *Finance and Trade under Edward III*, ed. G. Unwin (Manchester, 1918).

J. LE PATOUREL, 'Edward III and the kingdom of France', *History* vol. 43 (1958).

—— 'The Treaty of Brétigny', *T.R.H.S.* 5th ser., vol. 10 (1960).

J. J. N. PALMER, 'The Anglo-French peace negotiations 1390–96', *T.R.H.S.* 5th ser., vol. 16 (1966).

E. PERROY, 'The Anglo-French negotiations at Bruges', *Camden Miscellany* vol. 19 (1952).

J. W. SHERBORNE, 'English expeditions to France 1369–80', *E.H.R.* vol. 79 (1964).

J. VIARD, 'Le siège de Calais', *Moyen Age* vol. 39 (1929)

(*d*) THE FIFTEENTH CENTURY

P. BONENFANT, *Du Meutre de Montercau au Traité de Troyes* (Brussels, 1958).

A. BOSSUAT, *Perrinet Gressart et François de Surienne: agents de l'Angleterre* (Paris, 1936).

A. BUCHAN, *Joan of Arc and the Recovery of France* (London, 1948).

A. H. BURNE, *The Agincourt War* (London, 1956).

J. CALMETTE and G. PERINELLE, *Louis XI et l'Angleterre 1461–83* (Paris, 1930).

J. G. DICKINSON, *The Congress of Arras* (Oxford, 1955).

G. DUFRESNE DE BEAUCOURT, *Histoire de Charles VII*, 6 vols (Paris, 1881–91).

E. F. JACOB, *Henry V and the Invasion of France* (London, 1947).

G. A. KNOWLSON, *Jean V de Bretagne et l'Angleterre* (Rennes, 1964).

R. A. NEWHALL, *The Conquest of Normandy* (Yale, 1924).

R. PERNOUD, *Joan of Arc* (English trans., London, 1964).

M. G. A. VALE, *English Gascony 1399–1453* (Oxford, 1970).

R. VAUGHAN, *John the Fearless* (London, 1966).

—— *Philip the Good* (London, 1970).

Articles

C. T. ALLMAND, 'The collection of Dom Lenoir and the English occupation of Normandy', *Archives* vol. 6 (1963–4).

—— 'The Anglo-French negotiations 1439', *B.I.H.R.* vol. 40 (1967).

—— 'The Lancastrian land settlement in Normandy, 1417–1450', *Econ.H.R.* 2nd ser., vol. 21 (1968).

—— 'La Normandie devant l'opinion Anglaise', *B.E.C.* vol. 138 (1970).

R. A. NEWHALL, 'The war finances of Henry V and the Duke of Bedford', *E.H.R.* vol. 36 (1921).

—— 'Henry V's policy of conciliation in Normandy 1417–1422', *Haskins Anniversary Essays* (New York, 1929).

M. R. POWICKE, 'Lancastrian captains', *Essays in Medieval History Presented to B. Wilkinson* (Toronto, 1969).

C. F. RICHMOND, 'The keeping of the seas during the Hundred Years War 1422–40', *History* vol. 49 (1964).

B. J. H. ROWE, 'The estates of Normandy under the Duke of Bedford', *E.H.R.* vol. 46 (1931).

—— 'Discipline in the Norman garrison under the Duke of Bedford', *E.H.R.* vol. 46 (1931).

W. T. WAUGH, 'Joan of Arc in English sources of the fifteenth century', *Historical Essays in Honour of James Tait* (Manchester, 1933).

—— 'The administration of Normandy', *Essays in Medieval History Presented to T. F. Tout* (Manchester, 1925).

(e) THE ORGANIZATION OF WAR AND THE SOCIAL CONSEQUENCES

R. BOUTRUCHE, *La crise d'une société: seigneurs et paysans du Bordelais pendant la guerre de cent ans* (Paris, 1963).

H. DENIFLE, *La désolation des églises, monastéres et hôpitaux en France pendant la guerre de cent ans*, 2 vols (Paris, 1899).

H. J. HEWITT, *The Organisation of War under Edward III* (Manchester, 1966).

M. H. KEEN, *The Laws of War in the Late Middle Ages* (London, 1965).

R. A. NEWHALL, *Muster and Review* (Cambridge, Mass., 1940).

M. R. POWICKE, *Military Obligation in Medieval England* (Oxford, 1962).

Articles

C. T. ALLMAND, see important articles listed in section (*d*) above.

E. B. FRYDE, 'Edward III's wool monopoly of 1337', *History* vol. 37 (1952).

D. HAY, 'The division of the spoils of war in fourteenth century England', *T.R.H.S.* 5th ser., vol. 4 (1954).

G. A. HOLMES, 'The libel of English policy', *E.H.R.* vol. 76 (1961).

N. B. LEWIS, 'The recruitment and organisation of a contract army, 1337', *B.I.H.R.* vol. 37 (1964).

K. B. MCFARLANE, 'The investment of Sir John Fastolf's profits of war', *T.R.H.S.* 5th ser., vol. 7 (1957).

—— 'War, the economy and social change', *Past and Present* No. 22 (1962).

—— 'A business partnership in war and administration, 1421–45', *E.H.R.* vol. 78 (1963).

J. W. MCKENNA, 'Henry VI of England and the dual monarchy: aspects of royal political propaganda 1422–1432', *Journal of the Courtauld and Warburg Institutes* vol. 28 (1965).

R. A. NEWHALL, see important articles listed in section (*d*) above.

M. M. POSTAN, 'Some social consequences of the Hundred Years War', *Econ.H.R.* 1st ser., vol. 12 (1942).

—— 'The costs of the Hundred Years War', *Past and Present* No. 27 (1964).

A. E. PRINCE, 'The indenture system under Edward III', *Historical Essays in Honour of James Tait* (Manchester, 1933).

—— 'The payment of army wages in Edward III's reign', *Speculum* vol. 19 (1944).

B. J. H. ROWE, 'Discipline in the Norman garrisons under the Duke of Bedford', *E.H.R.* vol. 46 (1931).

J. W. SHERBORNE, 'Indentured retinues and English expeditions to France 1369–80', *E.H.R.* vol. 79 (1964).

IV The government of England and her constitution

Works on military administration and organization are mostly listed in section III(*d*) above. On topics where church and state interests overlap, see section VI below.

(*a*) THE KING, THE CROWN AND THE CORONATION

S. B. CHRIMES, *English Constitutional Ideas in the Fifteenth Century* (Cambridge, 1936).

P. E. SCHRAMM, *A History of the English Coronation* (Oxford, 1937).

Articles

C. A. J. ARMSTRONG, 'The inauguration ceremonies of the Yorkist kings and their title to the throne', *T.R.H.S.* 4th ser., vol. 30 (1948).

S. B. CHRIMES, 'Richard II's questions to the judges', *L.Q.R.* vol. 72 (1956).

F. GILBERT, 'Sir John Fortescue's *Dominium Regale et Politicum*', *Medievalia et Humanistica* vol. 2 (1944).

R. S. HOYT, 'The coronation oath of 1308', *E.H.R.* vol. 71 (1956).

J. W. MCKENNA, 'The coronation oath of the Yorkist kings', *E.H.R.* vol. 82 (1967).

H. G. RICHARDSON, 'The English coronation oath', *T.R.H.S.* 4th ser., vol. 23 (1941).

—— 'The English coronation oath', *Speculum* vol. 24 (1949).

B. WILKINSON, 'The coronation oath of Edward II', *Historical Essays in Honour of James Tait* (Manchester, 1933).

—— 'The coronation oath of Edward II and the Statute of York', *Speculum* vol. 19 (1944).

—— 'Notes on the coronation records of the fourteenth century', *E.H.R.* vol. 70 (1955).

(*b*) ADMINISTRATION, LAW AND JUSTICE

Works on such topics as the Statute of York, impeachment and trials in parliament are listed in section (*c*) below.

J. M. W. BEAN, *The Decline of English Feudalism* (Manchester, 1968).

C. A. BEARD, *The Office of Justice of the Peace in England* (New York, 1904).

J. G. BELLAMY, *The Law of Treason in England in the Later Middle Ages* (Cambridge, 1970).

W. C. BOLLAND, *The General Eyre* (Cambridge, 1922).

S. B. CHRIMES, *English Constitutional Ideas in the Fifteenth Century* (Cambridge, 1936).

M. HASTINGS, *The Court of Common Pleas in Fifteenth Century England* (New York, 1947).

W. S. HOLDSWORTH, *History of English Law*, vols 1–3 (London, 1923).

W. A. MORRIS, *The Medieval English Sheriff to 1300* (Manchester, 1927).

A. R. MYERS, *The Household of Edward IV* (Manchester, 1959).

A. J. OTWAY RUTHVEN, *The King's Secretary and the Signet Office in the Fifteenth Century* (Cambridge, 1939).

T. F. T. PLUCKNETT, *The Legislation of Edward I* (Oxford, 1949).

M. R. POWICKE, *Military Obligation in Medieval England* (Oxford, 1962).

B. H. PUTNAM, *The Enforcement of the Statute of Labourers* (Columbia, 1908).

—— *Proceedings before the Justices of the Peace, Edward III – Richard III* (Ames Foundation, 1938).

T. F. TOUT, *Chapters in the Administrative History of Medieval England*, 6 vols (Manchester, 1920–33).

L. W. VERNON HARCOURT, *His Grace the Steward and Trial of Peers* (London, 1907).

B. WILKINSON, *The Chancery under Edward III* (Manchester, 1929).

—— *The Constitutional History of Medieval England*, 3 vols (London, 1948–58).

J. F. WILLARD and W. A. MORRIS (eds.), *The English Government at Work, 1327–1336*, 3 vols (Cambridge, Mass., 1940–50).

Articles

C. BARRON, 'The tyranny of Richard II', *B.I.H.R.* vol. 41 (1968).

J. G. BELLAMY, 'Justice under the Yorkist kings', *Amer. J. of Legal History* vol. 9 (1965).

S. B. CHRIMES, 'Richard II's questions to the judges', *L.Q.R.* vol. 72 (1956).

B. H. PUTNAM, 'The transformation of the keepers of the peace into the justices of the peace, 1327–80', *T.R.H.S.* 4th ser., vol. 12 (1929).

H. G. RICHARDSON and G. O. SAYLES, 'The early statutes', *L.Q.R.* vol. 50 (1934).

J. S. ROSKELL, 'The office and dignity of Protector of England with special reference to its origins', *E.H.R.* vol. 68 (1953).

R. L. STOREY, 'The wardens of the marches of England towards Scotland', *E.H.R.* vol. 72 (1957).

(*c*) PARLIAMENT AND THE COUNCIL

J. F. BALDWIN, *The King's Council* (Oxford, 1913).

M. V. CLARKE, *Medieval Representation and Consent* (London, 1936).

—— *Fourteenth Century Studies* (Oxford, 1937).

H. L. GRAY, *The Influence of the Commons on Early Legislation* (Cambridge, Mass., 1932).

F. W. MAITLAND, *Memoranda de Parliamento*, introduction (R.S., 1893).

C. H. MCILWAIN, *The High Court of Parliament* (Yale, 1910).

M. MCKISACK, *The Parliamentary Representation of the English Boroughs during the Middle Ages* (Oxford, 1932).

D. PASQUET, *Essay on the Origins of the House of Commons* (Cambridge, 1925).

H. G. RICHARDSON and G. O. SAYLES, *Parliaments and Great Councils in Medieval England* (London, 1961).

J. S. ROSKELL, *The Commons in the Parliament of 1422* (Manchester, 1954).

—— *The Commons and Their Speakers in English Parliaments 1376–1523* (Manchester, 1965).

J. WEDGWOOD (ed.), *History of Parliament 1439–1509*, 2 vols (London, 1936–8).

Articles

(i) Parliament

C. C. BAYLEY, 'The campaign of 1375 and the Good Parliament', *E.H.R.* vol. 55 (1940).

G. P. CUTTINO, 'A reconsideration of the *Modus Tenendi Parliamentum*', *The Forward Movement in the Fourteenth Century*, ed. F. L. Utley (Ohio, 1961).

J. G. EDWARDS, 'The *Plena Potestas* of English parliamentary representatives', *Oxford Essays in Medieval History Presented to H. E.
Salter* (Oxford, 1934).

—— 'Justice in early English parliaments', *B.I.H.R.* vol. 27 (1954).

—— 'The commons in medieval English parliaments', *Creighton
Lecture*, 1957.

E. B. FRYDE, 'Parliament and the French war 1336-40', *Essays in
Medieval History Presented to B. Wilkinson* (Toronto, 1969).

V. H. GALBRAITH, 'The *Modus Tenendi Parliamentum*', *Journal of the
Courtauld and Warburg Institutes* vol. 16 (1953).

G. L. HARRISS, 'The commons' petitions of 1340', *E.H.R.* vol. 78
(1963).

G. L. HASKINS, 'The petitions of representatives in the parliaments
of Edward I', *E.H.R.* vol. 53 (1938).

K. N. HOUGHTON, 'Borough elections to parliament during the later
fifteenth century', *B.I.H.R.* vol. 39 (1966).

G. LAPSLEY, 'Archbishop Stratford and the parliamentary crisis of
1341', *E.H.R.* vol. 30 (1915).

—— 'The interpretation of the Statute of York', *E.H.R.* vol. 56
(1941).

K. B. MCFARLANE, 'Parliament and bastard feudalism', *T.R.HS.*.
4th ser., vol. 26 (1944).

E. MILLER, 'The origins of parliament' (Historical Association, 1960).

A. R. MYERS, 'Parliamentary petitions in the fifteenth century',
E.H.R. vol. 52 (1937).

J. J. N. PALMER, 'The impeachment of Michael de la Pole in 1386',
B.I.H.R. vol. 42 (1969).

T. F. T. PLUCKNETT, 'The origin of impeachment', *T.R.H.S.* 4th
ser., vol. 24 (1942).

—— 'Parliament', *The English Government at Work*, vol. I, ed. J. F.
Willard and W. A. Morris (Cambridge, Mass., 1940).

D. RAYNER, 'The forms and machinery of the *Commune Petition* in
the fourteenth century', *E.H.R.* vol. 56 (1941).

H. G. RICHARDSON and G. O. SAYLES, 'The early records of the
English parliaments', *B.I.H.R.* vol. 5 (1928), vol. 6 (1929), vol. 8
(1930-1), vol. 9 (1931-2).

—— 'The king's ministers in parliament', *E.H.R.* vol. 46 and 47
(1931-2).

A. ROGERS, 'Henry IV, the commons and taxation', *Medieval Studies*
vol. 31 (1969).

J. S. ROSKELL, 'The problem of the attendance of the lords in medieval parliaments', *B.I.H.R.* vol. 29 (1956).

—— 'Certain aspects and problems of the English *Modus Tenendi Parliamentum*', *B.J.R.L.* vol. 50 (1967–8).

J. R. STRAYER, 'The Statute of York and the community of the realm', *A.H.R.* vol. 47 (1941).

J. A. TUCK, 'The Cambridge parliament 1388', *E.H.R.* vol. 84 (1969).

(ii) The council

A. L. BROWN, 'The commons and the council in the reign of Henry IV', *E.H.R.* vol. 79 (1964).

—— 'The king's councillors in the fifteenth century', *T.R.H.S.* 5th ser., vol. 19 (1969).

J. L. KIRBY, 'Councils and councillors of Henry IV', *T.R.H.S.* 5th ser., vol. 14 (1964).

J. R. LANDER, 'The Yorkist council and administration, 1461–85', *E.H.R.* vol. 73 (1958).

—— 'Council, administration and councillors, 1461–85', *B.I.H.R.* vol. 32 (1959).

N. B. LEWIS, 'The continual council in the early years of Richard II', *E.H.R.* vol. 41 (1926).

T. F. T. PLUCKNETT, 'The place of the council in the fifteenth century', *T.R.H.S.* 4th ser., vol. 1 (1918).

R. VIRGOE, 'The composition of the king's council 1437–61', *B.I.H.R.* vol. 43 (1970).

(*d*) ROYAL FINANCE

Works on taxation in the context of parliamentary representation and consent are listed in the preceding section.

N. S. B. GRAS, *The Early English Customs System* (Cambridge, Mass., 1918).

W. E. LUNT, *Financial Relations of the Papacy with England*, 2 vols (Cambridge, Mass., 1939, 1962).

J. H. RAMSAY, *A History of the Revenues of the Kings of England* (Oxford, 1925).

A. STEEL, *The Receipt of the Exchequer* (Cambridge, 1954).

J. F. WILLARD, *Parliamentary Taxes on Personal Property 1290–1334* (Cambridge, Mass., 1934).

Articles

E. B. FRYDE, 'Edward III's wool monopoly of 1337', *History* vol. 37 (1952).

G. L. HARRISS, 'Fictitious loans', *Econ.H.R.* 2nd ser., vol. 8 (1955).

—— 'Aids, loans and benevolences', *H.J.* vol. 6 (1963).

—— 'Cardinal Beaufort – patriot or usurer?', *T.R.H.S.* 5th ser., vol. 20 (1970).

J. L. KIRBY, 'The issues of the Lancastrian exchequer and Lord Cromwell's estimates of 1433', *B.I.H.R.* vol. 24 (1951).

K. B. MCFARLANE, 'Loans to the Lancastrian kings: the problem of inducement', *C.H.J.* vol. 9 (1947).

R. A. NEWHALL, 'The war finances of Henry V and the Duke of Bedford', *E.H.R.* vol. 36 (1921).

W. E. RHODES, 'The Italian bankers and their loans to Edward I and Edward II', *Historical Essays by Members of Owen's College* (Manchester, 1902).

J. F. WILLARD, 'The taxes upon moveables of the reign of Edward I', *E.H.R.* vol. 28 (1913).

B. P. WOLFFE, 'The management of English royal estates under the Yorkist kings', *E.H.R.* vol. 71 (1956).

—— 'Acts of resumption in the Lancastrian parliaments, 1399–1456', *E.H.R.* vol. 73 (1958).

V Social and economic affairs

(*a*) AGRICULTURE AND THE LIFE OF THE COUNTRYSIDE

M. BERESFORD, *The Lost Villages of Medieval England* (London, 1954).

F. G. DAVENPORT, *The Economic Development of a Norfolk Manor, 1086–1565* (Cambridge, 1906).

R. H. HILTON, *The Economic Development of some Leicestershire Estates* (Oxford, 1947).

—— *A Medieval Society: The West Midlands at the end of the Thirteenth Century* (London, 1966).

—— *The Decline of Serfdom in Medieval England* (Economic History Society, 1969).

G. C. HOMANS, *English Villagers of the Thirteenth Century* (Cambridge, Mass., 1942).

W. G. HOSKINS, *The Midland Peasant* (London, 1957).

E. A. KOSMINSKY, *Studies in English Agrarian History in the Thirteenth Century* (Oxford, 1956).

A. E. LEVETT, *Studies in Manorial History* (Oxford, 1938).

C. S. and C. S. ORWIN, *The Open Fields*, 3rd ed. (Oxford, 1967).

F. M. PAGE, *The Estates of Crowland Abbey* (Cambridge, 1934).

B. H. PUTNAM, *The Enforcement of the Statute of Labourers* (Columbia, 1908).

J. A. RAFTIS, *The Estates of Ramsey Abbey* (Toronto, 1957).

—— *Tenure and Mobility* (Toronto, 1964).

J. E. THOROLD ROGERS, *A History of Agriculture and Prices in England*, 4 vols (Oxford, 1866–82).

—— *Six Centuries of Work and Wages* (Oxford, 1909).

J. Z. TITOW, *English Rural Society 1200–1350* (London, 1969).

Articles

W. BEVERIDGE, 'Wages in the Winchester manors', *Econ.H.R.* 1st ser., vol. 7 (1936–7).

J. S. DREW, 'Manorial accounts of St Swithun's Priory, Winchester', *E.H.R.* vol. 62 (1947).

F. R. H. DU BOULAY, 'A *rentier* economy in the later Middle Ages', *Econ.H.R.* 2nd ser., vol. 16 (1964).

—— 'Who were farming the English demesnes at the end of the Middle Ages?', *Econ.H.R.* 2nd ser., vol. 17 (1965).

C. DYER, 'A redistribution of incomes in fifteenth century England', *Past and Present* No. 39 (1968).

B. F. HARVEY, 'The leasing of the Abbot of Westminster's demesnes in the later Middle Ages', *Econ.H.R.* 2nd ser., vol. 22 (1969).

R. H. HILTON, 'A study in the prehistory of English enclosure', *Studi in onore di A. Sapori* (Milan, 1957).

E. A. KOSMINSKY, 'Feudal rent in England', *Past and Present* No. 7 (1955).

M. M. POSTAN, 'The chronology of labour services', *T.R.H.S.* 4th ser., vol. 20 (1937).

—— 'The *Famulus*: the estate labourer in the twelfth and thirteenth centuries', *Econ.H.R.* suppl. No. 2 (1954).

(*b*) THE TOWNS

M. BERESFORD, *New Towns of the Middle Ages* (London, 1967).

R. BIRD, *The Turbulent London of Richard II* (London, 1949).

A. R. BRIDBURY, *Economic Growth: England in the Later Middle Ages* (London, 1962).

C. GROSS, *The Gild Merchant*, 2 vols (Oxford, 1890).

J. W. F. HILL, *Medieval Lincoln* (Cambridge, 1948).

J. TAIT, *The Medieval English Borough* (Manchester, 1936).

S. L. THRUPP, *The Merchant Class of Medieval London* (Chicago, 1948).

G. UNWIN, *The Guilds and Companies of London* (London, 1908).

G. A. WILLIAMS, *Medieval London: from Commune to Capital* (London, 1963).

(c) TRADE AND INDUSTRY

A. R. BRIDBURY, *England and the Salt Trade in the Later Middle Ages* (Oxford, 1955).

—— *Economic Growth: England in the Later Middle Ages* (London, 1962).

E. M. CARUS-WILSON, *Medieval Merchant Venturers* (London, 1954).

E. M. CARUS-WILSON and O. COLEMAN, *England's Export Trade 1275-1547* (Oxford, 1963).

W. CUNNINGHAM, *The Growth of English Industry and Commerce*, vol. 1 (Cambridge, 1905).

H. HEATON, *The Yorkshire Woollen and Worsted Industries* (Oxford, 1920).

G. R. LEWIS, *The Stannaries* (Cambridge, 1907).

E. POWER, *The Wool Trade in English Medieval History* (Oxford, 1941).

E. POWER and M. M. POSTAN (eds.), *Studies in English Trade in the Fifteenth Century* (London, 1933).

A. RUDDOCK, *Italian Merchants and Shipping in Southampton* (Southampton Record Series, 1951).

G. UNWIN, *Finance and Trade under Edward III* (Manchester, 1918).

Articles

E. M. CARUS-WILSON, 'Evidences of industrial growth on some fifteenth century manors', *Econ.H.R.* 2nd ser., vol. 12 (1959-60).

H. L. GRAY, 'The production and exportation of English woollens in the fourteenth century', *E.H.R.* vol. 39 (1924).

G. A. HOLMES, 'The libel of English policy', *E.H.R.* vol. 76 (1961).

E. MILLER, 'The fortunes of the English textile industry in the thirteenth century', *Econ.H.R.* 2nd ser., vol. 18 (1965).

Y. RENOUARD, 'Le grand commerce des vins de Gascogne au moyen âge', *Revue Historique* vol. 221 (1959).

(*d*) PLAGUE, POPULATION AND POPULAR UNREST

R. B. DOBSON, *The Peasants' Revolt of 1381* (London, 1970).

R. H. HILTON, *The Decline of Serfdom in England* (Economic History Society, 1969).

A. E. LEVETT, *The Black Death on the Estates of the See of Winchester* (Oxford, 1916).

C. OMAN, *The Great Revolt of 1381*, new ed. (Oxford, 1969).

C. PETIT DUTAILLIS, *Studies and Notes Supplementary to Stubbs' Constitutional History*, vol. II (Manchester, 1914).

E. POWELL, *The Rising in East Anglia in 1381* (Cambridge, 1896).

B. H. PUTNAM, *The Enforcement of the Statute of Labourers* (New York, 1908).

A. RÉVILLE, *Le Soulèvement des Travailleurs d'Angleterre* (Paris, 1898).

J. C. RUSSELL, *British Medieval Population* (Albuquerque, 1948).

J. F. D. SHREWSBURY, *A History of Bubonic Plague in the British Isles* (Cambridge, 1970).

P. ZIEGLER, *The Black Death* (London, 1969).

Articles

J. M. W. BEAN, 'Plague, population and economic decline in England in the later Middle Ages', *Econ.H.R.* 2nd ser., vol. 15 (1962–3).

C. M. FRASER, 'Some thirteenth century censuses', *Econ.H.R.* 2nd ser., vol. 10 (1957–8).

H. E. HALLAM, 'Population density in medieval fenland', *Econ.H.R.* 2nd ser., vol. 14 (1961).

B. F. HARVEY, 'The population trend in England between 1300 and 1348', *T.R.H.S.* 5th ser., vol. 16 (1966).

R. H. HILTON, 'Peasant movements in England before 1381', *Econ.H.R.* 2nd ser., vol. 2 (1949).

M. M. POSTAN, 'Some economic evidence of declining population in the later Middle Ages', *Econ.H.R.* 2nd ser., vol. 2 (1950).

B. WILKINSON, 'The Peasants' Revolt of 1381', *Speculum* vol. 15 (1940).

(*e*) THE NOBILITY AND GENTRY

J. M. W. BEAN, *The Decline of English Feudalism 1215–1540* (Manchester, 1968).

H. S. BENNETT, *The Pastons and their England* (Cambridge, 1932).

N. DENHOLM YOUNG, *Seignorial Administration in England* (Oxford, 1937).

—— *History and Heraldry* (Oxford, 1965).

W. H. DUNHAM, *Lord Hastings's Indentured Retainers* (New Haven, Conn., 1955).

A. B. FERGUSON, *The Indian Summer of English Chivalry* (Durham, N.C., 1960).

G. A. HOLMES, *The Estates of the Higher Nobility in Fourteenth Century England* (Cambridge, 1957).

K. B. MCFARLANE, *The English Nobility 1290–1521* (Oxford, in press).

J. T. ROSENTHAL, *The Estates and Finances of Richard Duke of York (1411–1460)* (Nebraska, 1965).

R. SOMERVILLE, *History of the Duchy of Lancaster* (London, 1953).

A. R. WAGNER, *English Genealogy* (London, 1960).

Articles

J. CORNWALL, 'The early Tudor gentry', *Econ.H.R.* 2nd ser., vol. 17 (1964–5).

H. L. GRAY, 'Incomes from land in England in 1436', *E.H.R.* vol. 49 (1934).

W. I. HAWARD, 'Economic aspects of the Wars of the Roses in East Anglia', *E.H.R.* vol. 41 (1926).

N. B. LEWIS, 'The organisation of indentured retinues in fourteenth century England', *T.R.H.S.* 4th ser., vol. 27 (1945).

K. B. MCFARLANE, 'Bastard feudalism', *B.I.H.R.* vol. 20 (1945).

—— 'The English nobility in the later Middle Ages', *XIIme Congrès international des sciences historiques* (1965).

T. B. PUGH and C. D. ROSS, 'The English baronage and the income tax of 1436', *B.I.H.R.* vol. 26 (1953).

——'Some materials for the study of baronial incomes in the fifteenth century', *Econ.H.R.* 2nd ser., vol. 6 (1953).

VI The church

(*a*) ECCLESIASTICAL ORGANIZATION AND RELATIONS WITH KING AND POPE

For works dealing with the church's estates and their exploitation, see section V(*a*).

G. BARRACLOUGH, *Papal Provisions* (Oxford, 1935).

I. J. CHURCHILL, *Canterbury Administration*, 2 vols (London, 1933).

E. L. CUTTS, *Parish Priests and their People in the Middle Ages in England* (London, 1898).

K. EDWARDS, *The English Secular Cathedrals in the Middle Ages* (Manchester, 1949).

L. C. GABEL, *Benefit of Clergy in England in the Later Middle Ages* (Northampton, Mass., 1929).

R. GRAHAM, *English Ecclesiastical Studies* (London, 1929).

A. HAMILTON THOMPSON, *The English Clergy and their Organization in the Later Middle Ages* (Oxford, 1947).

E. F. JACOB, *Essays in the Conciliar Epoch*, 3rd ed. (Manchester, 1963).

—— *Essays in Later Medieval History* (Manchester, 1968).

D. KNOWLES, *The Religious Orders in England*, 3 vols (Cambridge, 1947–59).

C. H. LAWRENCE (ed.), *The English Church and the Papacy in the Middle Ages* (London, 1965).

A. G. LITTLE, *Studies in English Franciscan History* (Manchester, 1917).

W. E. LUNT, *Financial Relations of the Papacy with England*, 2 vols (Cambridge, Mass., 1939–62).

W. A. PANTIN, *The English Church in the Fourteenth Century* (Cambridge, 1955).

E. PERROY, *L'Angleterre et le Grand Schisme d'Occident* (Paris, 1933).

D. B. WESKE, *The Convocation of the Clergy in the Thirteenth and Fourteenth Centuries* (London, 1937).

K. L. WOOD-LEGH, *Church Life in England under Edward III* (Cambridge, 1934).

—— *Perpetual Chantries in Britain* (Cambridge, 1965).

Articles

L. R. BETCHERMAN, 'The making of bishops in the Lancastrian period', *Speculum* vol. 41 (1966).

C. DAVIES, 'The Statute of Provisors of 1351', *History* vol. 38 (1953).

A. DEELEY, 'Papal provision and royal rights of patronage in the early fourteenth century', *E.H.R.* vol. 43 (1928).

H. S. DEIGHTON, 'Clerical taxation by consent, 1279–1301', *E.H.R.* vol. 68 (1953).

E. B. GRAVES, 'The legal significance of the Statute of Praemunire of 1353', *Haskins Anniversary Essays* (New York, 1929).

J. R. L. HIGHFIELD, 'The English hierarchy in the reign of Edward III', *T.R.H.S.* 5th ser., vol. 6 (1956).

E. F. JACOB, 'Petitions for benefices from English universities during the Great Schism', *T.R.H.S.* 4th ser., vol. 27 (1945).

K. B. MCFARLANE, 'Henry V, Cardinal Beaufort and the Red Hat', *E.H.R.* vol. 60 (1945).

M. M. MORGAN, 'The suppression of the alien priories', *History* vol. 26 (1941).

W. T. WAUGH, 'The great Statute of Praemunire', *E.H.R.* vol. 27 (1922).

(b) RELIGIOUS LIFE AND THOUGHT: LOLLARDY AND MYSTICISM

P. BOEHNER, *Ockham: Philosophical Writings* (London, 1957).

H. CRAIG, *English Religious Drama of the Middle Ages* (Oxford, 1955).

M. DEANESLY, *The Lollard Bible* (Cambridge, 1920).

V. H. H. GREEN, *Bishop Reginald Pecock* (Cambridge, 1945).

A. GWYNN, *English Austin Friars in the Time of Wyclif* (Oxford, 1940).

D. KNOWLES, *The English Mystical Tradition* (London, 1961).

G. LEFF, *Bradwardine and the Pelagians* (Cambridge, 1957).

—— *Richard Fitzralph* (Manchester, 1963).

—— *Heresy in the Later Middle Ages*, 2 vols (Manchester, 1967).

K. B. MCFARLANE, *John Wycliffe and the beginnings of English Nonconformity* (London, 1952).

—— *Lancastrian Kings and Lollard Knights* (Oxford, 1972).

B. L. MANNING, *The People's Faith in the Time of Wyclif* (Cambridge, 1919).

G. R. OWST, *Preaching in Medieval England* (Cambridge, 1926).

—— *Literature and Pulpit in Medieval England* (Cambridge, 1933).

J. A. ROBSON, *Wyclif and the Oxford Schools* (Cambridge, 1961).

J. A. F. THOMSON, *The Later Lollards* (Oxford, 1965).

H. B. WORKMAN, *John Wyclif*, 2 vols (Oxford, 1926).

Articles

M. E. ASTON, 'Lollardy and sedition', *Past and Present* No. 17 (1960).

M. DEANESLY, 'Vernacular books in England in the fourteenth and fifteenth centuries', *Modern Language Review* vol. 15 (1920).

S. L. FRISTEDT, 'The authorship of the Lollard Bible', *Stockholm Studies in Modern Philology* vol. 19 (1956).

R. LOVATT, 'The *Imitation of Christ* in late medieval England', *T.R.H.S.* 5th ser., vol. 18 (1968).

W. A. PANTIN, 'The monk solitary of Farne, a fourteenth century English mystic', *E.H.R.* vol. 59 (1944).

H. G. RICHARDSON, 'Heresy and the lay power under Richard II', *E.H.R.* vol. 51 (1936).

V. J. SCATTERGOOD, 'The two ways – an unpublished religious treatise by Sir John Clanvowe', *English Philological Studies* vol. 10 (1967).

B. SMALLEY, 'John Wyclif's *Postilla super totam bibliam*', *Bodleian Library Record* vol. 4 (1953).

—— 'The Bible and eternity: John Wyclif's dilemma', *Journal of the Courtauld and Warburg Institutes* vol. 27 (1964).

—— 'Wyclif's *Postilla* on the Old Testament and his *Principium*', *Essays Presented to D. Callus* (Oxford, 1964).

W. T. WAUGH, 'Sir John Oldcastle', *E.H.R.* vol. 20 (1905).

—— 'The Lollard knights', *S.H.R.* vol. 11 (1913).

(*c*) EDUCATION

A. F. LEACH, *The Schools of Medieval England* (London, 1916).

A. W. PARRY, *Education in England in the Middle Ages* (London, 1920).

H. RASHDALL, *The Universities of Europe in the Middle Ages*, vol. III, ed. F. M. Powicke and A. B. Emden (Oxford, 1936).

H. E. SALTER, *Medieval Oxford* (Oxford, 1936).

R. WEISS, *Humanism in England during the Fifteenth Century* (Oxford, 1957).

(*d*) ECCLESIASTICAL BIOGRAPHIES

M. E. ASTON, *Thomas Arundel* (Oxford, 1967).

J. H. DAHMUS, *William Courtenay, Archbishop of Canterbury 1381–96* (Pennsylvania, 1966).

C. M. FRASER, *History of Anthony Bek, Bishop of Durham 1283–1311* (Oxford, 1957).

V. H. H. GREEN, *Bishop Reginald Pecock* (Cambridge, 1945).

E. F. JACOB, *Archbishop Henry Chichele* (London, 1967).

R. J. MITCHELL, *John Free* (London, 1955).

542   BIBLIOGRAPHY

G. H. MOBERLY, *William of Wykeham* (London, 1893).

R. L. STOREY, *Thomas Langley and the Bishopric of Durham* (London, 1961).

H. B. WORKMAN, *John Wyclif*, 2 vols (Oxford, 1926).

VII Scotland and Ireland

(*a*) SCOTLAND

E. W. M. BALFOUR-MELVILLE, *James I, King of Scots* (London, 1936).

E. M. BARRON, *The Scottish War of Independence* (Inverness, 1934).

G. W. S. BARROW, *Robert Bruce* (London, 1965).

W. C. DICKINSON, *Scotland From the Earliest Times to 1603* (London, 1961).

J. DOWDEN, *The Medieval Church in Scotland* (Glasgow, 1910).

P. HUME-BROWN, *A History of Scotland*, 3 vols (Cambridge, 1911).

A. LANG, *History of Scotland*, vol. 1 (Edinburgh, 1900).

R. NICHOLSON, *Edward III and the Scots* (Oxford, 1965).

R. S. RAIT, *The Parliaments of Scotland* (Glasgow, 1924).

(*b*) IRELAND

O. ARMSTRONG, *Edward Bruce's Invasion of Ireland* (London, 1923).

E. CURTIS, *Richard II in Ireland* (Oxford, 1927).

—— *History of Medieval Ireland 1086–1513* (London, 1938).

G. ORPEN, *Ireland under the Normans*, 4 vols (Oxford, 1911–20).

A. J. OTWAY-RUTHVEN, *A History of Medieval Ireland* (London, 1968).

W. A. PHILLIPS (ed.), *History of the Church of Ireland*, vol. 2 (London, 1934).

H. G. RICHARDSON and G. O. SAYLES, *The Irish Parliament in the Middle Ages* (Philadelphia, 1952).

Appendix

A note on the political history of Scotland and Ireland

Scotland and Ireland in the later Middle Ages had histories separate from that of England. The claims of the English kings to be overlords of the kings of Scots and lords of Ireland provide only a very loose link between three disparate stories. Because of the connexion it may be useful to provide, as an appendix, a brief outline of events in these other British lands; to attempt more would be presumptuous for an English historian with no pretension to the Celtic scholarship which is prerequisite to any professional assessment of the late medieval history of Scotland and Ireland.

The history of Scotland in the late thirteenth and early fourteenth centuries was dominated by her struggle, under the leadership of Robert Bruce, for independence from England. The mood of the Scots in the war was well summed up in the letter of the Scottish communities to Pope John XXII, the famous Declaration of Arbroath of 1320: 'for so long as but one hundred of us remain alive, we will never subject ourselves to the dominion of the English'. Bruce's consistent success, from Bannockburn (1314) on (see Chapters 2 and 3), forced the English in the end to renounce formally their claim to superior lordship over Scotland, by the terms of the Treaty of Northampton (1328). This newly won independence was buttressed by the Scots alliance with France, reaffirmed in 1326 by the Treaty of Corbeil.

Robert I died in 1329 and was succeeded by his five-year-old son David. David II's was to be an ill-starred reign, and in its early years the whole of Robert's achievement was very nearly undone when Edward Balliol, with English backing (in breach of the Treaty of Northampton), made his bid for the throne of Scotland (see Chapter 5). After the outbreak of the Hundred Years War David's cause began, it is true, to recover, and by 1341 the guardians of the realm

thought it safe to bring him back from France, where he had been
sent to refuge in 1334. All southern Scotland was once more in his
power when in 1346 he took the war across the border – and was
defeated and made prisoner at Neville's Cross near Durham. It was
not till 1357 that he was released, against a ransom of 100,000 marks.
The strain of raising this sum in a poor kingdom was one reason why,
by 1363, the childless David was negotiating with Edward III towards
an agreement by which, in return for the cancellation of the ransom
arrears, the king of England or one of his sons should succeed him.
This faced David with a serious revolt, led by the heir apparent,
Robert Stewart, in alliance with the earls of Douglas and March; and
though he put down this rising the Scottish estates, when they were
consulted, would hear nothing of an English succession. So, when
David died in 1371, Robert, son of Walter the Steward and Marjorie
Bruce, succeeded.

The victory over the English at Otterburn (1388) was the one
glorious achievement of the reign of the first Stewart, and it was the
Douglases who won the day there, not the king. Generally, the reigns
of Robert II (1371–90) and Robert III (1390–1406) witnessed a
decline of internal order in the kingdom, and alliances ('bands')
among the greater barons posed a mounting challenge to royal
authority. Prominent among the trouble-makers were the Douglases
(whose power was founded on the generous grants of Robert I and
David II), and the earls of March; after Robert II's death the earls
of Strathearn presented a special danger because they were his descendants by his second marriage, and, if his older but doubtfully
legitimate sons by Elizabeth Mure could be excluded, could claim
the throne. The most dangerous man of all was Robert Duke of Albany,
Robert II's second son by Elizabeth Mure, who was regent for his
father from 1388 to 1390, and acted as governor for his brother Robert
III in 1390–3 and in 1402–6. He had designs on the throne and was
almost certainly behind the mysterious death of the king's son David
in 1402. This was probably why Robert III thought to send his only
surviving son, James, to France; but he was captured by the English
on his way there, in March 1406, a few weeks before his father died.
This meant a long extension of Albany's authority to misgovern;
since he was not anxious to see James back in Scotland, it also meant
a long lull in active hostilities between England and Scotland, which
had reopened with vigour in 1399. This did not prevent a good many
Scotsmen from taking service with the French against the English
and distinguishing themselves in war abroad.

It was not until 1424 that James I returned to his kingdom. The
treaty that set him free imposed a ransom, a truce and a marriage to

an English noblewoman – Jane Beaufort, the Duke of Somerset's daughter. His reign saw a determined effort to restore order and royal authority in Scotland, to which the parliament gave full backing. A number of measures were enacted to strengthen the royal finances and improve the administration of justice. Steps were taken too to curb the nobility. Murdach of Albany, Duke Robert's successor, together with his two sons and his father in law, Duncan Earl of Lennox, were all executed for treason. The Earl of Strathearn was deprived of his dignity and sent into England, and even Douglas was at one point arrested. In 1428 James made a demonstration in strength in the Highlands. By 1436 he was ready to take the offensive against the English again; but the enmities that his stern government had engendered caught up with him too soon. On the night of 20 February 1437 he was murdered at Perth by Sir Robert Graham, whom he had outlawed. His son, James II, was a boy of six, and his good work was undone by the feuds that dogged a long minority.

By the early 1450s James II was asserting himself. In 1452 the Earl of Douglas, whose power the minority had strengthened, refused in the king's presence to break his 'band' with the Earl of Crawford: James stabbed him to death. Crawford was defeated soon after at Brechin, and the Douglases, after a brief reconciliation, were finally overthrown in 1455 and their lands forfeited to the crown. If he had lived James II might have made much of the opportunities that the internal troubles of England were at this point beginning to offer. He intervened in the civil wars when the chance arose and was besieging Roxburgh in alliance with the Lancastrians when he was killed by the explosion of one of his cannons. So Scotland had to face yet another minority which was the prelude to a troubled and unsuccessful reign. James III contained threats from his brother Albany (who was in alliance with the English from 1482 and was recognized as king by Edward IV) and from the Douglases (also in alliance with England) who made a last bid to regain their lost position in 1484, but he was finally overthrown and killed in a rising led nominally by his own son, James IV to be, in 1488. This James IV was the king in whose reign Henryson and Dunbar wrote, who did much to introduce the new learning into Scotland, and who died at Flodden.

The reign of Edward I saw the Anglo-Norman colony in Ireland at the peak of its fortunes. Its government was presided over by the justiciar whom the king named (later more often called the lieutenant), and who itinerated with him; he was aided by a council, a chancellor and a treasurer, and from time to time there were meetings of parliament. Representatives of the shires, liberties and boroughs were already coming occasionally to these gatherings in Edward's time, and in the course of the fourteenth century their attendance and that of the lower clergy became regular. At the end of the thirteenth century the royal revenue in Ireland usually showed a surplus which could be put at the king's disposal for use elsewhere. The whole government of the colony was subject to England; English statutes and the common law ran in Ireland as in England, and cases from Ireland could be brought before King's Bench on writs of *certiorari*. The native Irish, however, were not admitted to English law, and lived by their own customs; those that were subject to Anglo-Norman lords could only sue before the king's courts through their lords.

Even in Edward I's time Ireland was a much disordered land. The chiefs and kings of the native Irish had no part in the royal government, and would not willingly admit that their powers were in any way dependent on the English crown's permission for their exercise. Disunited, they fought the king's governors and the Anglo-Norman lords, and feuded among themselves; and the Anglo-Norman lords, in their quarrels with the Irish and with one another, sought allies wherever they could find them. In the course of the fourteenth century a number of factors enhanced these tendencies towards endemic disorder in Ireland. Most of the great Anglo-Norman barons had lands in England, and in Edward II's reign the dissensions of the English nobility were reflected in the sister island. In 1315 Edward Bruce, brother of Robert of Scotland, landed in Ireland and defeated Richard de Burgh, the Earl of Ulster, near Connor; the O'Neill of Tyrone came out in support, and for three years, until he was defeated and killed by John de Bermingham at Dundalk, the whole land was troubled by the raids of Bruce's soldiers. The consequences of these troubles of Edward II's time were hard to undo. Besides, in the period between 1300 and 1350 more of the Anglo-Norman lords became absentees (the murder of the last de Burgh Earl of Ulster in 1333 and the grant of the two great fiefs of Leix and Trim to Roger Mortimer were here important). The creation of the palatine earldoms of Ormond, Desmond and Kildare strengthened the independence of the leaders among those who remained. The Black Death thinned the numbers of the Anglo-Irish colonists, and the financial demands of Edward I and Edward III for aid in their foreign wars helped to alienate the settlers from England.

All these factors contributed to a considerable renascence of the power of the native Irish in the fourteenth century, which the king's government was unable to stem. It began now to be pressed for money, and it became usual to assign the whole of the royal revenues to the

lieutenant; but that was still not enough to fight the endlessly recurrent wars. Little or no vestige of English authority remained, after
the middle of the century, in Ulster or Connaught; the colony was
driven back on the coastal lands of the east, and began to come under
threat in Leinster. Great lords like Desmond gathered bands of armed
men about them and levied 'coign' to support them – and they often
proved as much a danger to royal authority as the native Irish. It was
against this background that Lionel of Clarence, Edward III's second
son who had married the de Burgh heiress, was sent over as lieutenant
in 1361. Though a great deal of English money was spent on his
lieutenancy, and a little later on that of the vigorous William of
Windsor (husband of Edward's mistress, Alice Perrers), not much
was achieved. The most memorable event of Clarence's lieutenancy
was the passing of the Statute of Kilkenny, largely re-enactive of
former legislation and intended to buttress the solidarity of the
settlers. English was made compulsory as a language in English-held
districts; marriages between English and native Irish were banned;
Irishmen were barred from admission to cathedral and collegiate
chapters, and their minstrels were ordered not to be received among
the English. The statute was not very original and did not achieve
very much. No more did the money spent on Clarence and his successors. William of Windsor's efforts to raise more money in Ireland
to fight the natives only increased the lack of sympathy between the
Anglo-Irish and the English government, and consolidated parliamentary resistance to taxation.

Richard II was the only English king of the later Middle Ages to
visit Ireland, and his expedition came near to being a notable success.
He came in October 1394 with a major royal host, and by the spring
of the next year, after some hard fighting, most of the Irish chiefs
were ready to come into his obedience, among them the powerful Art
MacMurrough of Leinster, Neill O'Neill of Ulster, Teig MacCarthy
and, generally, 'our rebels who call themselves kings and captains of
Munster and Connaught'. In return for their homage and the promise
to surrender the lands that they had unlawfully occupied, Richard
confirmed the Irish chiefs in their hereditary possessions. The trouble
with this settlement was that it left Richard's new and by nature
unruly leigemen with no room left for expansion, and that when he
had gone they had no confidence that his lieutenant – the Earl of
March, one of the greatest landowners of Ireland – or the English
generally would interpret it justly. MacMurrough was soon in arms
again, and in July 1398 March was surprised and killed near Carlow.
Richard had by then already announced his intention of coming again
to Ireland, but his second expedition came to nothing; the events that

led to his deposition called him back to England and broke up his army less than two months after he had landed.

The Lancastrian kings had little time to think about Ireland's problems. John Talbot, appointed lieutenant in 1414, was a vigorous governor, but this vigour and his exactions, like those of Windsor earlier, stirred up opposition. His family (led after his departure by his brother, Archbishop Richard of Dublin) became involved in a long and bitter feud between the Talbots and the Geraldines of Desmond on the one side and the Ormonds on the other. Richard Duke of York, when he came to Ireland as lieutenant in 1449, achieved a little success during his first brief stay there. After his defeat in England at Ludford in 1459 he returned, and the support of Kildare and Desmond gave him a solid footing in the country (the Butlers of Ormond alone among the three great comital families of Ireland were committed Lancastrians). A foundation was laid of Irish loyalty to the Yorkist cause, which a quarter of a century later was to permit the coronation in Dublin of the pretender Lambert Simnel as Edward VI of England and Ireland.

After the accession of York's son, Edward IV, the king's brother Clarence was appointed lieutenant, and Desmond became his deputy in 1463. But when in 1468 Tiptoft replaced Desmond both he and Kildare were arrested and their lands seized; for a brief moment the deputy had not only their estates but also those of the Lancastrian Butlers in his hand. Desmond was executed, but Kildare survived, to become deputy briefly in 1470, when Tiptoft perished in the short-lived Lancastrian revival in England. The Kildares, in spite of Tiptoft, were loyal to the Yorkists, and in 1479 this Kildare's son, the eighth earl, became deputy to Richard Duke of York. He held the office through the rest of the Yorkist period and beyond. The dominance of his family in Ireland was to last in fact much longer, well into the Tudor age, in spite of their involvement with the pretenders to Henry VII's throne. But that is a story that is too long to follow here; it takes us right past Poynings' parliament of 1495 and the act which placed Irish government in new and rigorous subjection to that of England, and which, as Professor Otway-Ruthven writes, marked a 'clear watershed between medieval Ireland and the Tudor period'.

Genealogical tables

1 THE FRENCH SUCCESSION IN 1328 AND AFTER

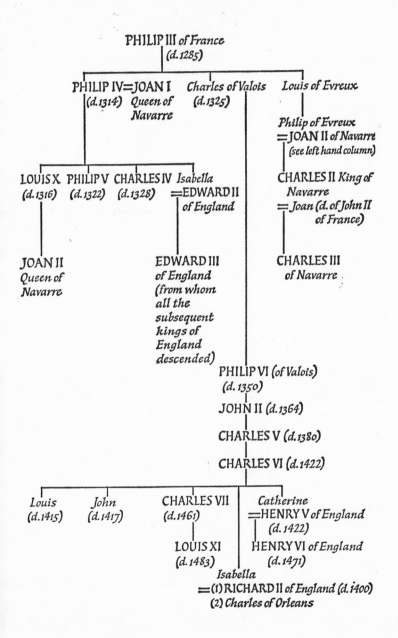

2 THE HOUSE OF PLANTAGENET AND ITS BRANCHES

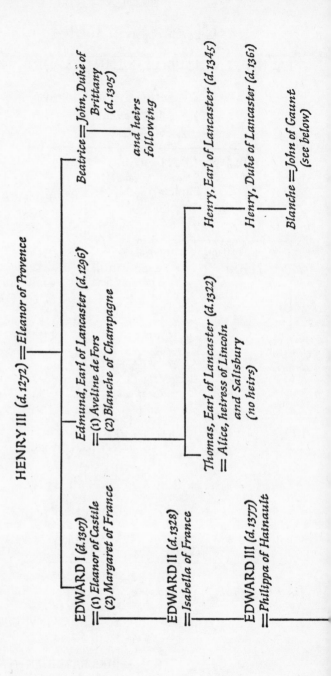

HENRY III (d.1272) ═ Eleanor of Provence

EDWARD I (d.1307)
═ (1) Eleanor of Castile
  (2) Margaret of France

Edmund, Earl of Lancaster (d.1296)
═ (1) Aveline de Fors
  (2) Blanche of Champagne

Beatrice ═ John, Duke of Brittany (d.1305)

and heirs following

EDWARD II (d.1328)
═ Isabella of France

Thomas, Earl of Lancaster (d.1322)
═ Alice, heiress of Lincoln and Salisbury
(no heirs)

Henry, Earl of Lancaster (d.1345)

Henry, Duke of Lancaster (d.1361)

EDWARD III (d.1377)
═ Phillippa of Hainault

Blanche ═ John of Gaunt
(see below)

Edward the Black Prince (d.1376) = Joan of Kent

Lionel, Duke of Clarence (d.1368) = (1) Elizabeth de Burgh (2) Violante Visconti

John of Gaunt, Duke of Lancaster (d.1399) = (1) Blanche of Lancaster (2) Constanza of Castile (3) Katherine Swynford (from whom descend the Beauforts and, via them, the TUDORS)

Edmund of Langley, Duke of York (d.1402) = (1) Isabel of Castile (2) Joan Holland

Thomas of Woodstock, Duke of Gloucester (d.1397) = Eleanor Bohun

RICHARD II (d.1400) = (1) Anne of Bohemia (2) Isabella of France (no heirs)

Philippa = Edmund Mortimer, Earl of March (d.1381)

HENRY IV (d.1413) = (1) Mary Bohun (2) Joan, Dowager Duchess of Brittany

Edward, Duke of York (d.1415) (no heirs)

Richard, Earl of Cambridge (d.1415) = Anne Mortimer (see left-hand column below)

Anne = (1) Thomas, Earl of Stafford (2) Edmund, Earl of Stafford (3) William Bourchier

Roger Mortimer, Earl of March (d.1398)

HENRY V (d.1422) = Catherine of France

Thomas, Duke of Clarence (d.1421) (no heirs)

John, Duke of Bedford (d.1435) = (1) Anne of Burgundy (2) Jacquetta of Luxembourg (no heirs)

Humphrey, Duke of Gloucester (d.1447) = (1) Jacqueline of Hainault (2) Eleanor Cobham (no heirs)

Edmund Mortimer, Earl of March (d.1425) (no heirs)

Anne = Richard, Earl of Cambridge

HENRY VI (d.1471) = Margaret of Anjou

Richard, Duke of York (d.1460) = Cicely Neville

Edward, Prince of Wales (d.1471)

EDWARD IV   George, Duke of Clarence   RICHARD III

3 THE HOUSES OF YORK AND MARCH

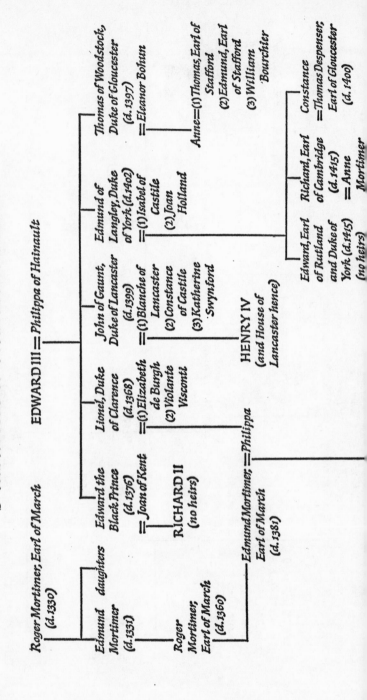

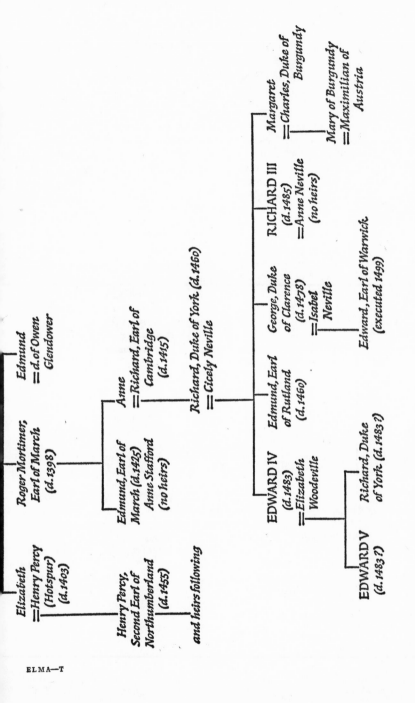

Elizabeth
=Henry Percy
(Hotspur)
(d.1403)

Henry Percy,
Second Earl of
Northumberland
(d.1455)

and heirs following

Roger Mortimer,
Earl of March
(d.1398)

Edmund
= d. of Owen
Glendower

Anne
=Richard, Earl of
Cambridge
(d.1415)

Edmund, Earl of
March (d.1425)
=Anne Stafford
(no heirs)

Richard, Duke of York (d.1460)
=Cicely Neville

EDWARD IV
(d.1483)
=Elizabeth
Woodeville

Edmund, Earl
of Rutland
(d.1460)

George, Duke
of Clarence
(d.1478)
=Isabel
Neville

RICHARD III
(d.1485)
=Anne Neville
(no heirs)

Margaret
=Charles, Duke of
Burgundy

Mary of Burgundy
=Maximilian of
Austria

Edward, Earl of Warwick
(executed 1499)

EDWARD V
(d.1483?)

Richard, Duke
of York (d.1483?)

ELMA—T

4 THE HOUSE OF BEAUFORT

John of Gaunt, Duke of Lancaster (d. 1399)
=(3) his mistress, Katherine Swynford

| John Beaufort, Earl of Somerset (d. 1410) = Margaret Holland | Henry Beaufort, Bishop of Winchester and Cardinal (d. 1447) | Thomas Beaufort, Earl of Dorset and Duke of Exeter (d. 1426) (no heirs) | Joan Beaufort = Ralph, Earl of Westmoreland (see Neville genealogy table 5) |

| John Beaufort, Earl and then Duke of Somerset (d. 1444) = Margaret, d. of Sir John Beauchamp | Jane = James I, King of Scots (d. 1437) and hence the Kings of Scots succeeding | Edmund Beaufort, Marquis of Dorset, Earl and then Duke of Somerset (d. 1455) = Margaret Beauchamp, d. of Richard Beauchamp, Earl of Warwick | Margaret = Thomas Courtenay |

| Margaret Beaufort = (1) Edmund Tudor, Earl of Richmond (2) Sir Henry Stafford (3) Lord Stanley | Henry, Duke of Somerset (d. 1464) | Edmund of Somerset (d. 1471) | John Beaufort (d. 1471) | Eleanor = James Butler, Earl of Wiltshire and Ormond |

HENRY VII

5 THE HOUSE OF NEVILLE

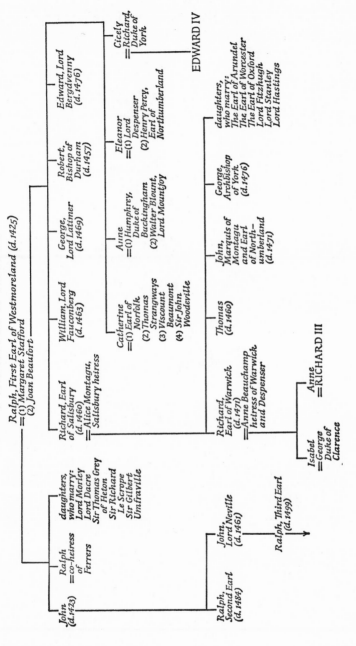

Map 1 France after the Treaty of Brétigny, 1360

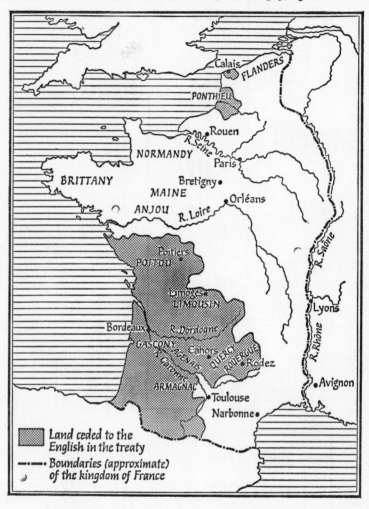

Calais
FLANDERS
PONTHIEU
Rouen
R. Seine
NORMANDY
Paris
BRITTANY
Bretigny
MAINE
ANJOU
Orléans
R. Loire
Poitiers
POITOU
Limoges
LIMOUSIN
R. Saône
Lyons
Bordeaux
R. Dordogne
GASCONY
Cahors
AGENAIS
QUERCY
R. Garonne
ROUERGUE
Rodez
R. Rhône
ARMAGNAC
Toulouse
Avignon
Narbonne

Land ceded to the
English in the treaty
Boundaries (approximate)
of the kingdom of France

Map 2 France at the time of the siege of Orleans, 1429

HOLLAND

Calais

FLANDERS
Ghent
ARTOIS
BRABANT
Agincourt
HAINAULT
PICARDY

Cherbourg

Harfleur
Rouen
Compiègne
Rheims

Formigny
Caen
NORMANDY
Paris
R. Marne

DUCHY
OF
BRITTANY
Fougères
Verneuil
Troyes

MAINE
Orleans

R. Loire
DUCHY
OF
BURGUNDY

Chinon
R. Saône
COUNTY OF
BURGUNDY

Bourges

Poitiers

FRANCE

THE EMPIRE

R. Meuse

Lyons

DAUPHINÉ

Bordeaux
R. Dordogne

R. Rhône

GUIENNE
R. Garonne
Avignon
PROVENCE

Bayonne
Toulouse

Anglo-Burgundian
France

Lands of the house of Burgundy

Boundaries of the kingdom of France

Index